STAGE LIVES

Recent Titles in
Bibliographies and Indexes in the Performing Arts

Memorable Film Characters: An Index to Roles and Performers, 1915-1983
Compiled by Susan Lieberman and Frances Cable

STAGE LIVES

A Bibliography and Index to Theatrical Biographies in English

Compiled by

GEORGE B. BRYAN

Bibliographies and Indexes in the Performing Arts, Number 2

GREENWOOD PRESS
Westport, Connecticut • London England

Library of Congress Cataloging in Publication Data
Main entry under title:

State lives.

   (Bibliographies and indexes in the performing
arts, ISSN 0742-6933 ; no. 2)
   Includes index.
   1. Theatre—Biography—Bibliography.   I. Bryan,
George B.   II. Series.
Z5781.S78   1985   [PN2205] 016.792 '092 '2 [B]   84-19833
ISBN 0-313-24577-0 (lib. bdg.)

Library of Congress Catalog Card Number: 84-19833
ISBN: 0-313-24577-0
ISSN: 0742-6933

First published in 1985

Greenwood Press
A division of Congressional Information Service, Inc.
88 Post Road West, Westport, Connecticut 06881

Printed in the United States of America

10 9 8 7 6 5 4 3 2 1

For

HUBERT C. HEFFNER

Distinguished Service Professor Emeritus of Theatre and Drama
of Indiana University,

whose erudition molded me and many who,

in Robert Browning's words,

"followed him, honoured him,

Lived in his mild and magnificent eye,

Learned his great language, caught his clear accents,

Made him our pattern...."

About the Author

GEORGE B. BRYAN is Associate Professor of Theatre at the University of Vermont. He is the author of *An Ibsen Companion* (Greenwood Press, 1984) and *Ethelwold and Medieval Music-Drama at Winchester* and has contributed to many theatre publications including *American Theatrical Companies: A Historical Encyclopedia* (forthcoming from Greenwood Press).

Contents

Acknowledgments

Numerous friends and colleagues have been supportive of this project, but its completion would have been impossible without the enthusiastic and efficient assistance of Sandra Gavett and Elizabeth Hoose of the Interlibrary Loan Department and Frank Gavett of the Reference Department of the Bailey-Howe Library of the University of Vermont. My heartfelt appreciation must also be expressed for the valuable and painstaking efforts of Andrew S. Ward, who verified hundreds of bibliographical citations and searched newspaper obituaries for biographical data.

Introduction

Fortunate are the children of Thespis whose names are recorded in this
and similar books, for their brief hours in the service of the stage
have brought them a sort of immortality that has eluded thousands of
their forgotten contemporaries. Because they had the foresight to in-
dite their autobiographies, or because others took sufficient notice
of their efforts to write about them, these lucky few are not entirely
lost to memory. It has been said that show business is a business of
names; to a marked extent the history of the theatre is a history of
its people. Editors and publishers have recognized this fact, and as a
consequence, the market boasts such useful, recent guides to theatrical biography as:

> American and British Theatrical Biography: A Directory. Com-
> piled by J. P. Wearing. Metuchen, N. J.: Scarecrow Press,
> 1979.
>
> Performing Arts Biography Master Index, 2d ed. Ed. Barbara
> McNeil and Miranda C. Herbert. Detroit, Mich.: Gale Re-
> search Company, 1979.
>
> Theatre, Film and Television Biographies Master Index. Ed.
> Dennis La Beau. Detroit, Mich.: Gale Research Company,
> 1979.

These volumes are almost indispensable to a study of Anglo-American theatre, yet they are limited in two important respects: (1) all these are indices of basic materials, are greatly repetitive, and ignore all but the most obvious sources; (2) none gives references to book-length biographies and autobiographies.

To this list of biographical indices must be added two specialized volumes:

> American Actors, 1861-1910: An Annotated Bibliography of Books Published in the United States in English from 1861 through 1976. Compiled by Ronald L. Moyer. Troy, N. Y.: Whitston Publishing Company, 1979.

> Nineteenth Century Theatrical Memoirs. Compiled by Claudia D. Johnson and Vernon E. Johnson. Westport, Conn.: Greenwood Press, 1982.

The titles of these books indicate their limitations, although each is eminently useful, especially in terms of lengthy annotations.

Stage Lives: A Bibliography and Index to Theatrical Biographies in English is intended as a supplement and extension of these five research tools, not as a substitute for them. With only a few exceptions, the works cited in the three general indices are not treated in this book. The items discussed by Moyer and by Johnson and Johnson naturally appear in Stage Lives, but there the similarity ends. The scope of this book ranges from 534 B. C., the first recorded date in theatre history, to the present. Its focus extends from the Anglo-American stages to those of Europe, South America, Australia, and Asia.

The principles that guided my selection of materials should be noted. Only works written in English are cited: that is the basic criterion. Beyond that, any person whose life is or was connected with the living, non-mechanical theatre in any way is an appropriate biographical subject. For too long, playwrights have been within the purview of strictly literary reference works; in this book they take their rightful place beside other artists of the theatre. Yet with dramatists such as James Joyce, D. H. Lawrence, and John Steinbeck, whose work in the theatre was minimal, I have made no effort to list every available biography.

Such a book as this can never be complete because the selection process is necessarily subjective. I have made choices that may seem arbitrary but which nevertheless impart my own theatrical leanings to Stage Lives. For example, the names of film stars John Wayne and Gary Cooper do not appear in this work; yet those of Barbara Stanwyck and Humphrey Bogart do. The difference is simply that, to my knowledge, the former pair were not associated with the living theatre, while the latter had brief stage careers. This principle is applied equally to workers in television.

Other choices had to be made. In the nineteenth century, for example, there was often a closer relationship among opera, musicals, and vaudeville than presently exists; for that reason, the names of early operatic personnel appear in this book while more recent ones do not. On the other hand, I have included the lives of circus people because plays were sometimes presented by circus managers, and circus performers sometimes worked in variety and vaudeville. Although I have avoided the inclusion of volumes of criticism, they have been cited when actual biographies do not exist. I have done so in the belief that biographical details often are given in books of literary criticism.

Stage Lives is comprised of two major parts, a bibliography and an index. Three types of book are cited in the bibliography: collective theatrical biographies, collective non-theatrical biographies, and individual biographies and autobiographies, including dissertations. Of the first type, I have listed and indexed every suitable volume I could discover, although some works are conspicuously absent because their formats do not facilitate indexing. The second group is a random selection of works that include theatrical lives among those of other professions; many of these biographical sketches, perhaps, have not been utilized by theatre students because of their less-than-obvious locations. The third and largest section is that of book-length biographies of people in every area of theatrical endeavor.

The index, however, is the heart of Stage Lives because it lists each of the biographical subjects in all three bibliographies and directs the reader to all references to a specific person. A particularly useful feature is that page-number references to the collective biographies enable the reader to go directly to the book without consulting another index, to judge the relative length of a write-up, and to request through Interlibrary Loan services certain photocopied pages rather than order a sometimes-expensive entire book.

The citations in the index give, whenever possible, the stage names, the actual names, the married names, the life dates, the nationalities, and the areas of specialization of the subjects. Such information is not always accurate, as theatrical people often embroider the truth for the sake of dramatic effect. Dates of birth are particularly susceptible of fantasy, but I have attempted to verify these dates whenever possible. Death dates of nineteenth and twentieth century individuals can sometimes be checked rather easily, so, when feasible, I have supported death dates with obituary notices. In some cases it was necessary to correct information found in other works. Yet, despite all efforts, vital statistics of some of the subjects are lacking.

An appendix entitled "Necrological Annals" completes the book. As an aid to viewing the synchronicity of theatrical lives, I have schematized the death dates of the biographees. There are separate headings for Classical and Medieval, 16th Century, and 17th Century. For each year between 1700 and 1984, however, there is a separate list of subjects who died in that year. Birthdates are given in parentheses.

How to Use This Book

Let us assume that the reader is interested in Al Jolson, about whom the index reads, in part:

JOLSON, Al [born Asa Yoelson] (1886-1950)

Russian-American singing actor: A13, p. 81;

...; B15, pp. 160-61;˙ ...; C921....

The initial name in the index is the individual's stage name: Al Jolson. His real name, Asa Yoelson, is bracketed. His life dates follow: 1886-1950. Jolson's nationality is given as Russian-American, and his type of theatrical work is cited as "singing actor." There are several references to Jolson in the bibliography. The code "A13" refers to a collective theatrical biography, Great Stars of the American Stage, by Daniel Blum. The entire bibliographical citation and an annotation appear in Part IA. The index shows that a life of Jolson is written on page 81 of Blum's book. "B15" refers to a collective non-theatrical biography listed in Part IB: Paul Gallico's The Revealing Eye, of which pages 160-61 are devoted to Jolson. "C921" directs the reader to

Part IC, where Michael Freedland's _Jolson_ is listed. By consulting the index, then, the reader can discover every brief and long biography of Al Jolson.

A few additional explanations are required. Some collective works are unpaginated, so the abbreviation "n. p." is employed in the index to indicate that no page numbers are given. I have, moreover, assumed that iconography is the handmaiden of biography. Since some of the books contain only pictures of theatrical personalities, I have used the abbreviation "por." to show that _only_ a picture appears. A citation in the index that reads "A9, p. 15, por." means that a picture of the subject is given on page 15, but there is no biographical commentary. Several biographical works are multi-volumed, which I have shown by the use of Roman numerals. "A81, II, 15-9" means that the entry appears on pages 15-19 of the second volume of that work.

STAGE LIVES

Part I:
Bibliography of Biographies

A. Collective Theatrical Biographies

A1.　The American Stage. Chicago: H. Sellschopp, 1894.

This handsome collection of eighty illustrations of famous players of the last quarter of the nineteenth century contains no biographical commentary.

A2.　The American Stage: Schiller Theatre Souvenir. Chicago: American Stage Publishing Company, 1895.

This souvenir program features illustrations and brief biographical sketches of sixty-one stars of the dramatic and musical stages.

A3.　The American Stage of To-Day: Biographies and Photographs of 100 Leading Actors and Actresses. Intro. by William Winter. New York: P. F. Collier and Son, 1910.

Impressively illustrated, this large volume contains biographical sketches of one hundred performers. The introduction by William Winter (1836-1917) is a generalized description of the current state of theatrical art.

A4.　Armstrong, Cecil Ferard. A Century of Great Actors, 1750-1850. London: Mills and Boon, 1912.

The title of Cecil F. Armstrong's book is self-explanatory. He details the lives of British players including David Garrick, Spranger Barry, John Henderson, George Frederick Cooke, John Philip Kemble, Edmund Kean, William Charles Macready, Charles Kean, William H. W. Betty, Joseph Munden, Joseph Grimaldi, Charles James Mathews, and Frederick Robson.

A5.　Ayres, Alfred [Thomas E. Osmun]. Acting and Actors, Elocution and Elocutionists: A Book about Theater Folk and Theater Art. New York: D. Appleton, 1894.

Alfred Ayres (1834-1902) was an elocutionist, so his biographical comments chiefly concern the way actors delivered their lines and respected the language. His book includes articles and letters as well as observations on the lives of Edwin

Booth, Clara Morris, Charlotte Cushman, Frederick B. Warde, Elizabeth Bowers, Edwin Forrest, and Ada Rehan.

A6.   Baker, Henry Barton. English Actors from Shakespeare to Macready. New York: Henry Holt, 1879.

Henry B. Baker (b. 1845) presents a compendious history of British actors, the roster of which includes Frances Abingdon, Robert Baddeley, John Bannister, Elizabeth Barry, Spranger Barry, George Anne Bellamy, Thomas Betterton, William H. W. Betty, Barton Booth, Anne Bracegirdle, Louisa Brunton, Richard Burbage, Colley Cibber, Susannah Maria Cibber, Theophilus Cibber, Catherine Clive, George Frederick Cooke, Anne Crawford, James W. Dodd, Thomas Doggett, John Edwin I, Robert W. Elliston, John Emery, Richard Estcourt, Elizabeth Farren, Maria Foote, Samuel Foote, David Garrick, Julia Glover, Eleanor Gwynn, Joseph Haines, John Hemings, John Henderson, Hildebrand Horden, Dorothy Jordan, Edmund Kean, Charles Kemble, Fanny Kemble, John Philip Kemble, Stephen Kemble, Will Kemp, Thomas King, Edward Kynaston, William Lewis, John Liston, Charles Macklin, William Charles Macready, Charles Mathews, Harriot Mellon, Henry Mossop, Susannah Mountfort, William Mountfort, J. S. Munden, James Nokes, Anne Oldfield, Eliza O'Neill, John Palmer, William Parsons, Mary Ann Porter, Hannah Pritchard, John Quick, James Quin, Mary Robinson, Samuel Sandford, Edward Shuter, Sarah Siddons, William Smith, Richard Suett, Richard Tarlton, Cave Underhill, Lucia Eliza Vestris, Thomas Weston, Tate Wilkinson, Robert Wilks, Margaret Woffington, Richard Yates, and Charles Mayne Young.

A7.   _____. Our Old Actors, 2 vols. London: Richard Bentley, 1878.

This volume is substantially the same as English Actors from Shakespeare to Macready except that the former contains entries on Mary Davis, Anthony Leigh, William O'Brien, Jane Pope, Samuel Reddish, David Ross, Henry Woodward, and Mary Ann Yates. The latter includes sections on Louisa Brunton, Richard Burbage, John Edwin I, Elizabeth Farren, John Hemings, William Lewis, Harriot Mellon, Richard Suett, Richard Tarlton, and Lucia Eliza Vestris that do not appear in the former.

A8.   Bassham, Ben L. The Theatrical Photographs of Napoleon Sarony. Kent, Ohio: Kent State University Press, 1978.

Forty-four theatrical portraits taken by Napoleon Sarony (1821-96) are the chief feature of this book, but Ben L. Bassham provides an excellent introductory description of the American theatre during the last thirty years of the nineteenth century.

A9.   Bax, Clifford, ed. All the World's a Stage: Theatrical Portraits. London: Frederick Muller, 1946.

Playwright Clifford Bax (1886-1962) writes biographical commentary to accompany photographs of the players who dominated

the British stage in mid-twentieth century: Henry Ainley, Mur-
iel Aked, Peggy Ashcroft, Robert Atkins, Angela Baddeley, Tal-
lulah Bankhead, Leslie Banks, Lilian Braithwaite, Clive Brook,
Roy Byford, O. B. Clarence, Fay Compton, Laura Cowie, Robert
Donat, Edith Evans, Barbara Everest, William G. Fay, Jean
Forbes-Robertson, Charles V. France, John Gielgud, Louise
Hampton, Nicholas Hannen, Baliol Holloway, Ursula Howells,
Martita Hunt, Isabel Jeans, Catherine Lacey, John Laurie, Bea-
trix Lehmann, Leon M. Lion, Miles Malleson, John Mills, Robert
Morley, Marie Ney, Laurence Olivier, Nancy Price, Leon Quar-
termaine, Margaret Rawlings, Michael Redgrave, Ralph Richard-
son, Flora Robson, Margaretta Scott, Athene Seyler, Glen Byam
Shaw, Alastair Sim, Abraham Sofaer, Robert Speaight, Godfrey
Tearle, Ernest Thesiger, Ann Todd, Irene Vanbrugh, Violet Van-
brugh, Wilfrid Walter, Alan Wheatley, and Emlyn Williams.

A10.   Benjamin, Lewis S. More Stage Favourites of the Eighteenth
          Century. London: Hutchinson, 1929.

        Sixteen illustrations accompany Lewis S. Benjamin's (1874-
        1932) study of the lives of actresses Frances Abingdon, Sarah
        Siddons, Mary Robinson, and Dorothy Jordan.

A11.   _____. Stage Favourites of the Eighteenth Century.
          London: Hutchinson, 1928.

        In this volume Benjamin delves into the lives of Anne Old-
        field, Lavinia Fenton, Catherine Clive, Hannah Pritchard,
        Charlotte Charke, Margaret Woffington, Susannah Maria Cibber,
        and George Anne Bellamy. The text is augmented by seventeen
        illustrations.

A12.   The Biography of the British Stage.... London: Sherwood,
          Jones, 1824.

        This anonymously assembled book is valuable because it takes
        notice of numerous minor players on the British stage. Al-
        though it lacks completeness and precision, the work is valu-
        able nonetheless. Its subjects are William Abbott, George
        Bartley, Sarah Bartley, George J. Bennett, William Blanch-
        ard, Sarah Booth, John Braham, William Broadhurst, James
        Browne, Margaret Bunn, Louisa Chatterley, Eliza Chester,
        Charles Connor, Thomas P. Cooke, Thomas S. Cooke, Mary Ann
        Davenport, Maria Davison, William Dowton, John Duruset, Miss
        Edmiston, Daniel Egerton, Sarah Egerton, Charles Farley, Wil-
        liam Farren, Helen Faucit, John Fawcett, Edward Fitzwilliam,
        Fanny Fitzwilliam, Maria Foote, Henry Gattie, Mary Gibbs, Jul-
        ia Glover, Joseph Grimaldi, John Harley, Sarah Harlowe,
        Charles E. Horne, J. C. Hughes, Francis Huntley, Mr. Isaacs,
        Richard Jones, Edmund Kean, Robert Keeley, Frances H. Kelly,
        Frances M. Kelly, Lydia Kelly, Charles Kemble, Henry Kemble,
        Edward Knight, John Liston, Mrs. John Liston, Emma Love, Wil-
        liam Charles Macready, Clara Fisher Maeder, Charles Mathews,
        Drinkwater Meadows, Joseph S. Munden, Mary Ann Orger, William
        Oxberry, Mary Ann Paton, William Penley, Tyrone Power I, James
        F. Pyne, L. B. Rayner, John Reeve, Ralph Sherwin, John Sin-

clair, George Smith, Harriet Smithson, Kitty Stephens, Daniel
Terry, Maria Tree, Lucia Eliza Vestris, Frederick Vining, Mrs.
Frederick Vining, James W. Wallack, Harriet Waylett, W. West,
Mrs. W. West, Tate Wilkinson, Benjamin Wrench, Frederick H.
Yates, and Charles Mayne Young.

A13.   Blum, Daniel. Great Stars of the American Stage. New York:
        Grosset and Dunlap, 1954.

        Daniel Blum (1899-1965) presents the lives of 150 performers
        through biographical sketches and numerous photographs. His
        subjects range from stars at the turn of the twentieth century
        to newcomers (such as Marlon Brando) who Blum thinks will dom-
        inate the American stage of the future. The pictures are more
        useful than the commentaries.

A14.   Bodeen, De Witt. Ladies of the Footlights. Pasadena, Cal.:
        Pasadena Playhouse Association, 1937.

        De Witt Bodeen (1908--) devotes this volume to players who
        performed on the West Coast of the United States. His sub-
        jects include Lola Montez, Lillie Langtry, Sarah Bernhardt,
        Eleonora Duse, Adelaide Neilson, Ellen Terry, Mary Anderson,
        Charlotte Crabtree, Pauline Cushman, Fanny Davenport, Julia
        Dean Hayne, Matilda Heron, Laura Keene, Julia Marlowe, Adah
        Isaacs Menken, Helena Modjeska, Clara Morris, Ada Rehan, Lil-
        lian Russell, and Catherine Sinclair.

A15.   Brazier, Marion H. Stage and Screen. Boston: M. H. Brazier,
        1920.

        By the time Marion H. Brazier (1850-1925?) wrote this book,
        she had served as society editor for two newspapers in Boston.
        In the course of her work, Brazier met numerous theatre art-
        ists, some of whom she writes about in this book. There are
        entire chapters on Charlotte Cushman, William Seymour, and
        Mary Anderson. References to many other actors are scattered
        throughout.

A16.   Briscoe, Johnson. Actors' Birthday Book, 3 ser. New York:
        Moffat, Yard and Company, 1907-9.

        In each of these volumes Johnson Briscoe (1883?-1969) provides
        a biographical sketch of an actor whose birthday falls on each
        day of the year, insofar as that scheme was practicable. The
        first volume contains 345 biographies; the second, 363; and
        the third (with some repetitions from previous volumes), over
        400.

A17.   Brook, Donald. A Pageant of English Actors. London: Rock-
        liff, 1950.

        The actors whose lives are described by Donald Brook range
        from Elizabethan to contemporary and include Richard Burbage,
        Richard Tarlton, Will Kemp, Edward Alleyn, Thomas Betterton,
        David Garrick, John Philip Kemble, Edmund Kean, William

Charles Macready, Samuel Phelps, Henry Irving, Johnston Forbes-Robertson, Herbert Beerbohm Tree, John Gielgud, and Laurence Olivier.

A18.   Burton, Hal, ed. Acting in the Sixties. London: British Broadcasting Corporation, 1970.

The biographical materials in Hal Burton's (1908--) book were gleaned from interviews conducted by the BBC. Handsome photographs augment transcripts of conversations with Richard Burton, Harry H. Corbett, Albert Finney, John Neville, Eric Porter, Vanessa Redgrave, Maggie Smith, Robert Stephens, and Dorothy Tutin.

A19.   _____. Great Acting. New York: Hill and Wang, 1967.

Burton edited this series of interviews conducted by various people under the auspices of the BBC. The accompanying photographs are diverse and informative, but the players themselves provide the greatest interest: Laurence Olivier, Sybil Thorndike, Ralph Richardson, Peggy Ashcroft, Michael Redgrave, Edith Evans, John Gielgud, and Noël Coward.

A20.   Cantor, Eddie. As I Remember Them. New York: Duell, Sloan, and Pearce, 1963.

The salient feature of these reminiscences of singing actor Eddie Cantor (1893-1964) is that he writes about people with whom he worked. This book, then, is primary source material on the lives and careers of Gus Edwards, Florenz Ziegfeld, Jr., W. C. Fields, Fanny Brice, Al Jolson, Bert Williams, George M. Cohan, Perry Como, Ted Lewis, Enrico Caruso, James Cagney, Greta Garbo, Jack Benny, Groucho Marx, Jimmy Durante, Milton Berle, Red Skelton, Danny Thomas, Danny Kaye, Beatrice Lillie, Judy Garland, and Will Rogers.

A21.   Carroll, David. The Matinee Idols. New York: Arbor House, 1972.

David Carroll's (1942--) book is advertised as a "behind-the-scenes story of the magnificent stars...who held America's women in thrall...." In addition to 183 photographs, Carroll narrates the more sensational events in the lives of Edmund Kean, John Wilkes Booth, Harry Montague, Kyrle Bellew, Charles Fechter, Frank Mayo, Maurice Barrymore, Chauncey Alcott, Henry Dixey, Wilton Lackaye, James J. Corbett, Robert Mantell, John Drew II, James K. Hackett, Henry Miller, and William Faversham. There is a short section on "The Matinee Ladies," and the second part of the book concerns film actors.

A22.   Chetwood, William Rufus. The British Theatre, Containing the Lives of the English Dramatic Poets, with an Account of All Their Plays Together with the Lives of Most of the Principal Actors, as Well as Poets.... Dublin: Peter Wilson, 1750.

W. R. Chetwood (d. 1766) provides one of the earliest and most

useful of theatrical biographies. His list of British playwrights is extensive, and his treatment of their lives, though
brief and necessitating emendation, is a good starting place
for the student. His work is also frustrating because in several instances, Chetwood does not provide enough information
on his subjects to render them distinct from others who bore
the same or similar names.

A23.   Clapp, John B. and Edwin F. Edgett. Players of the Present, 3
        vols. in 1. New York: Dunlap Society, 1899-1901.

John B. Clapp and Edwin F. Edgett (1867-1946) hoped "to issue
a book which will include all the names which have been prominent on the American stage." Perhaps they did not attain
their goal, but their book is a useful collection of biographical sketches.

A24.   Clark, Barret H. Intimate Portraits. New York: Dramatists
        Play Service, 1951.

American critic Barrett H. Clark (1890-1953) penned these
astute evaluations of the careers of Maxim Gorky, John Galsworthy, Edward Sheldon, George Moore, Carl B. Clinton, and
Sidney Howard.

A25.   Cohen, Alfred J. Familiar Chats with the Queens of the Stage.
        New York: G. W. Dillingham, 1890.

Alfred J. Cohen (1861-1928) is better known as drama critic
Alan Dale, and the twenty-nine biographies that comprise this
book appeared in the New York Evening World. The subjects of
these anecdotal, illustrated pages include Mary Anderson,
Georgie Drew Barrymore, Louise Beaudet, Agnes Booth, Elizabeth
Bowers, Georgia Cayvan, Rose Coghlan, Charlotte Crabtree,
Fanny Davenport, Effie Ellsler, Pauline Hall, Gertie Homan,
Marie Jansen, Lillie Langtry, Nellie McHenry, Marion Manola,
Sadie Martinot, Helena Modjeska, Clara Morris, Minnie Palmer,
Lillie Post, Cora Urquhart Potter, Ada Rehan, Lillian Russell,
Ellen Terry, Isabelle Urquhart, Rosina Vokes, and Marie Wain-
wright.

A26.   Coleman, John. Plays and Playwrights I Have Known: A Review of
        the English Stage from 1840 to 1880, 2 vols. Philadelphia:
        Gebbie, 1890.

John Coleman (d. 1904) was an actor/manager who worked exten-
sively in the British provinces but came to know and associate
with the leading lights of the stage. This work is the result
of that association. Coleman mentions scores of theatrical
folk, but he is most useful when writing of Charles and Ellen
Kean, William Charles Macready, Charles J. Matthews, Charles
Reade, Thomas W. Robertson, and Charles Fechter. There are
fifty illustrations.

A27.   Collier, John Payne. Memoirs of the Principal Actors in the
        Plays of Shakespeare. London: Shakespeare Society, 1846.

Journalist and critic John Payne Collier (1789-1883) set himself a nearly impossible task when he tried to reconstruct the lives of Elizabethan actors using only the resources available to him at the time. Although some of his conclusions have been altered, Collier's basic work remains extremely valuable.   Collier's biographical sketches range from important actors such as Richard Burbage to the relatively obscure George Bryan.

A28.   Cook, Edward Dutton. Hours with the Players, 2 vols. London: Chatto and Windus, 1881.

By the time Dutton Cook (1829-83) assembled this book, he had served as dramatic critic for the Pall Mall Gazette (1867-75) and The World (1875-83). Much of the material in these volumes appeared in the pages of those journals. Cook's subjects are Frances Abingdon, Robert Baddeley, Sophia Baddeley, Junius Brutus Booth I, James W. Dodd, William Farren, Charles Fechter, Julia Glover, Charles Kean, Thomas King, Charles J. Mathews, William Mountfort, Susan O'Brien, William O'Brien, John Palmer, William Parsons, Elizabeth Pope, Rachel, Mary Robinson, William Smith, Harriet Smithson, Margaret Woffington, and Richard Yates.

A29.   Curtis, Anthony, ed. The Rise and Fall of the Matinee Idol: Past Deities of the Stage and Screen, Their Roles, Their Magic and Their Worshippers. New York: St. Martin's Press, 1974.

Various contributers provide their recollections of performers of the past. Anthony Curtis weaves them into a rich tapestry of narrative and photographs that gives something of the appeal of Lily Elsie, Charles Wyndham, George Alexander, Gerald du Maurier, Gladys Cooper, Gertrude Lawrence, Jack Buchanan, Ivor Novello, Noël Coward, Lillian Gish, and others.

A30.   Dale, Alan [Alfred J. Cohen]. Queens of the Stage. New York: G. W. Dillingham, 1896.

Alan Dale (1861-1928) was dramatic critic of the New York Evening World from 1887 to 1895, and much of the material in this book appeared in the pages of that newspaper. The content is substantially the same as that of Familiar Chats with the Queens of the Stage.

A31.   Darbyshire, Alfred. The Art of the Victorian Stage. New York: Benjamin Blom, 1969 [1907].

Although a trained architect, Alfred Darbyshire (1839-1908) associated himself with most departments of theatrical endeavor. He was chiefly interested in production problems, but his pages provide interesting biographical information about Charles Kean, Samuel Phelps, Henry Irving, and Charles Calvert.

A32.   Davies, Stan G. Chichester 10: Portrait of a Decade. Drawings by Zsuzsi Roboz. London: Davis-Poynter, 1975.

This book by Stan G. Davies (1943--) is a celebration of the
tenth anniversary of the Festival Theatre at Chichester.
Davies provides biographical commentary on Michael Aldridge,
Eileen Atkins, Sarah Badel, Keith Baxter, Jeremy Brett, Anna
Calder-Marshall, Richard Chamberlain, John Clements, Fay Comp-
ton, Tom Courtenay, Roy Dotrice, Fenella Fielding, Frank Fin-
lay, Albert Finney, John Gielgud, Alec Guinness, Doris Hare,
Laurence Harvey, Anthony Hopkins, Celia Johnson, Beatrix Leh-
mann, Margaret Leighton, Millicent Martin, Geraldine McEwan,
Keith Michell, Sarah Miles, John Neville, Laurence Olivier,
Nigel Patrick, Joan Plowright, Michael Redgrave, Heather
Sears, Alastair Sim, A. T. Smith, Maggie Smith, John Standing,
Robert Stephens, Haym Topol, Peter Ustinov, Simon Ward, Billie
Whitelaw, and Irene Worth. Handsome portraits augment the
text.

A33.   Donaldson, Frances. The Actor Managers. Chicago: Henry Regnery, 1970.

Lady Donaldson (1907--) is a daughter of dramatist Frederick
Lonsdale and so grew up in the theatre; for a brief time she
was an actress. In this book she examines the careers of
Squire and Marie Bancroft, Henry Irving, George Alexander,
Johnston Forbes-Robertson, Herbert Beerbohm Tree, and Gerald
du Maurier.

A34.   Donohue, Joseph W., Jr., ed. The Theatrical Manager in England and America, Player of a Perilous Game. Princeton,
N. J.: Princeton University Press, 1971.

A collection of lectures delivered at Princeton University in
1969-70 by various authors, this book focuses on the careers
of Philip Henslowe, Tate Wilkinson, Stephen Price, Edwin
Booth, and Charles Wyndham.

A35.   Earley, Mary D. Stars of the '20's. Photographs by James E.
Abbe. New York: Viking Press, 1975.

Mary D. Early contributed the brief biographical commentary
that amplifies a handsome array of theatrical portraits photo-
graphed by James E. Abbe (1883-1973).

A36.   Eaton, Walter P. The Actor's Heritage: Scenes from the Theatre
of Yesterday and the Day Before. Boston: Atlantic Monthly
Press, 1924.

Walter P. Eaton's (1878-1957) book is not a biographical volume, but most of its chapters are devoted to the careers of
stage folk. He focuses on Thomas Holcroft, Charles Macklin,
William Charles Macready, Rachel, Colley Cibber, Weber and
Fields, David Douglass, and Olive Logan.

A37.   Edwards, H. Sutherland. Idols of the French Stage, 2 vols.
London: Remington, 1889.

H. Sutherland Edwards (1828-1906) at some length describes the careers of Sophie Arnould, Armande Béjart, Sarah Bernhardt, Marie-Anne Camargo, Hippolyte Clairon, Louise Contat, Louise-Rosalie Dugazon, Justine Favart, Madeleine Guimard, Adrienne Lecouvreur, Rachel, Françoise Raucourt, and Anne Saint-Huberty.

A38.   Famous Players of Today. New York: G. A. Melbourne, 1904.

This book is useful as a pictorial record of some of the principal actors and actresses at the turn of the twentieth century. The biographical commentary is brief and not particularly informative.

A39.   Findlater, Richard. The Player Kings. New York: Stein and
        Day, 1971.

Richard Findlater is the nom de plume of Kenneth Bruce Findlater Bain (1921--), the author of several books of theatrical biography. This volume deals principally with Shakespearean actors and includes chapters on David Garrick, John Philip Kemble, Edmund Kean, William Charles Macready, Henry Irving, Johnston Forbes-Robertson, John Gielgud, Laurence Olivier, and Michael Redgrave.

A40.   _____. The Player Queens. New York: Taplinger,
        1977.

This book is a companion piece to Richard Findlater's The Player Kings. Although his discussion ranges from the introduction of actresses onto the English stage, he stresses the lives of Sarah Siddons, Ellen Terry, Sybil Thorndike, Edith Evans, Peggy Ashcroft, and several other contemporary players.

A41.   Fitzgerald, Percy. The Romance of the English Stage. Philadel-
        phia: J. B. Lippincott, 1875.

Irish author Percy Fitzgerald (1834-1925), the author of several theatrical biographies, states that their "chief attraction is...[their] air of personal confession." That factor permeates his sketches of Tate Wilkinson, George Anne Bellamy, David Garrick, Sarah Siddons, Edmund Kean, Henry Mossop, Mary Robinson, George Frederick Cooke, Robert W. Elliston, Gerald Griffin, and William H. W. Betty.

A42.   Fyvie, John. Comedy Queens of the Georgian Era. New York:
        E. P. Dutton: 1907.

John Fyvie provides excellent brief biographies of the stalwart actresses of the English stage of the eighteenth century. After describing stage conditions and the social position of actors during this period, Fyvie turns to the lives of Lavinia Fenton, Charlotte Charke, Catherine Clive, Margaret Woffington, George Anne Bellamy, Frances Abingdon, Sophia Baddeley, Elizabeth Farren, Mary Robinson, Mary Sumbel, Dorothy Jordan, and Harriot Mellon. Eight illustrations accompany the text.

A43.   _____. Tragedy Queens of the Georgian Era.   London:
         Methuen, 1908.

         In this volume Fyvie examines the careers of Elizabeth Barry,
         Susannah Maria Cibber, Anne Crawford, Julia Glover, Elizabeth
         Inchbald, Anne Oldfield, Eliza O'Neill, Elizabeth Pope, Mary
         Ann Porter, Hannah Pritchard, Sarah Siddons, and Mary Ann
         Yates.

A44.   Gallery of [Plays and] Players from the Illustrated American,
         Nos. 1-12. New York: Illustrated American Publishing Com-
         pany, 1894-5.

         Actors and actresses on the American stage near the end of the
         nineteenth century are herein handsomely photographed. The bi-
         ographical comments are brief and rather uninformative.

A45.   Galt, John. The Lives of the Players, 2 vols. London: Henry
         Colburn and Richard Bentley, 1831.

         Scottish novelist John Galt (1779-1839) brings considerable
         narrative skill to his lives of important performers on the
         British stage. Like Chetwood before him, Galt produced a sem-
         inal work, albeit one that requires the correction of modern
         scholarship. The anecdotal quality of the book helps to limn
         the players' personalities but gives little insight into their
         craft.

A46.   Gard, Robert E. and David Semmes.   America's Players. New
         York: Seabury Press, 1967.

         Robert E. Gard (1910--) and David Semmes' audience is young
         people. They colorfully introduce their readers to important
         actors on the American stage, ranging from Lewis Hallam to
         P. T. Barnum to Edwin Booth.

A47.   Gielgud, John. Distinguished Company. Garden City, N. Y.: Dou-
         bleday and Company, 1973.

         Distinguished actor John Gielgud (1904--) amusingly and some-
         times poignantly remembers his own theatrical relatives (the
         Terrys) and other members of the profession. The book is not a
         collective biography but rather a record of Gielgud's own
         "theatrical enthusiasms." He writes of Fred, Marion, and Ellen
         Terry; Edward and Edith Gordon Craig; Mrs. Patrick Campbell,
         Maud Tree, Lilian Braithwaite, Pauline Lord, John Barrymore,
         Jane Cowl, Leslie Howard, Vivien Leigh, Charles Hawtrey, Allan
         Aynesworth, Gerald du Maurier, Ronald Squire, A. E. Matthews,
         Ada King, Haidée Wright, Esmé Percy, Ernest Thesiger, Robert
         Farquharson, Marie Tempest, Yvonne Arnaud, Leslie Faber, Ced-
         ric Hardwicke, Charles Laughton, Gertrude Lawrence, Robert
         Loraine, Claude Rains, and various music hall performers.

A48.   Goddard, Arthur.   Players of the Period, 2 vols. London:
         Dean, 1891.

Among others, Arthur Goddard (b. 1853) writes of Squire Bancroft, Rutland Barrington, Lionel Brough, Arthur Cecil, George Grossmith, Sr., John Hare, Henry Irving, William H. Kendal, Henry Neville, William Terriss, Edward Terry, Thomas Thorne, John L. Toole, Herbert Beerbohm Tree, Charles Warner, E. S. Willard, and Charles Wyndham.

A49.   Grau, Robert. The Business Man in the Amusement World: A Volume of Progress in the Field of the Theatre. New York: Broadway Publishing Company, 1910.

As a theatrical manager himself, Robert Grau (1858-1916) writes from experience of the business man in the theatre. Not primarily a biographical volume, this book contains brief sketches of the lives of managers F. F. Proctor, Alfred G. Rogers, Henry Dazian, Charles L. Wagner, Ambrose J. Small, J. J. Murdock, Michael Shea, J. H. Moore, Martin Beck, and others.

A50.   Grebanier, Bernard D. Then Came Each Actor: Shakespearean Actors Great and Otherwise. New York: David McKay, 1975.

Bernard D. Grebanier's (1903--) volume is a rich mine of biographical materials. It is, however, presented in a narrative form that does not allow ease of indexing or annotating. The title of the book is its best description, and its subjects range from Will Kemp to John Gielgud and Laurence Olivier.

A51.   Hallowell, John. The Truth Game. New York: Simon and Schuster, 1969.

John Hallowell's book is about theatrical press agentry. His most interesting discussions center on Rosemary Harris, Angela Lansbury, and Barbra Streisand.

A52.   Hamm, Margherita A. Eminent Actors in Their Homes: Personal Descriptions and Interviews. New York: James Pott, 1902.

Canadian journalist Margherita A. Hamm (1871-1907) is particularly interested in portraying theatrical performers as ordinary people in the environment of their own homes. The illustrations are chosen to provide a glimpse of the offstage settings of the subjects' lives: Viola Allen, Mary Anderson, Marie Bates, Amelia Bingham, Beatrice Cameron, William H. Crane, Elsie de Wolfe, Robert Edeson, Maxine Elliott, Minnie Maddern Fiske, Nat C. Goodwin, James K. Hackett, Virginia Harned, Edward Harrigan, Joseph Jefferson III, Burr McIntosh, Mary Mannering, Richard Mansfield, Julia Marlowe, Chauncey Olcott, Annie O'Neill, May Robson, Annie Russell, Otis Skinner, E. H. Sothern, Annie Ward Tiffany, David Warfield, and Francis Wilson.

A53.   Horton, William Ellis. About Stage Folk. Detroit: Free Press Printing Company, 1902.

William E. Horton (d. 1938) is not primarily a biographer, yet scattered throughout this impressionistic book about the theatre are vital statistics about famous and relatively unknown thespians.

A54.   Iles, George, ed. <u>Actors</u>. Little Masterpieces of Autobiography, Vol. 4.   Garden City: N. Y.: Doubleday, Page, and Company.

The autobiographical statements that appear in this book are merely excerpts from longer accounts. Iles adds brief introductions to the cuttings from the lives of Joseph Jefferson III, Edwin Booth, Henry Irving, Ellen Terry, Richard Mansfield, Tommaso Salvini, and Adelaide Ristori.

A55.   <u>The Illustrated American Stage: A Pictorial Review of the Most Notable Recent Theatrical Successes, Together with Many Drawings and Portraits of Celebrated Players</u>. New York: R. H. Russell, 1889-1901.

Biographical data are incidental to this work, which is mainly focused on productions, specifically <u>L'Aiglon, Janice Meredith, Brother Officers, Richard Carvell, A Royal Family, The Little Minister, Sherlock Holmes</u>, and <u>When Knighthood Was in Flower</u>.

A56.   Izard, Forrest. <u>Heroines of the Modern Stage</u>. New York: Sturgis and Walton, 1915.

Believing that existing biographies of actresses of his own day are "insufficient or inaccessible," Forrest Izard sets out to describe without adulation the lives and careers of contemporary actresses. The result is admirable. Izard writes of Sarah Bernhardt, Helena Modjeska, Ellen Terry, Gabrielle Réjane, Eleonora Duse, Ada Rehan, Mary Anderson, Minnie Maddern Fiske, Julia Marlowe, Maude Adams, and others.

A57.   Johns, Eric. <u>Dames of the Theatre</u>. New Rochelle, N. Y.: Arlington House, 1974.

As editor of <u>The Stage</u> from 1952 through 1972, Eric Johns (1907--) is eminently qualified to describe the careers of Great Britain's theatrical dames: May Whitty, Genevieve Ward, Ellen Terry, Madge Kendal, Sybil Thorndike, Marie Tempest, Irene Vanbrugh, Lilian Braithwaite, Edith Evans, Peggy Ashcroft, Flora Robson, Judith Anderson, Margaret Rutherford, Gladys Cooper, Anna Neagle, and Cicely Courtneidge.

A58.   Keegan, Marcia. <u>We Can Still Hear Them Clapping</u>. New York: Avon Books, 1975.

When Marcia Keegan (1943--) was asked to do a photographic essay on hotels in New York's Times Square district that were to be demolished, she discovered that numerous aged but intrepid vaudevillians inhabited them. Their energy and optimism prompted her to assemble biographical chapters and pictures of Rae Davis, Lillian Ashton, Florence Ashton, Sally Demay, Fred

Estelle, Nona Otero, Katherine Murray, Harriet Waldron, Elea-
nor Cody, Phil Foote, Al Greiner, Edna Thayer, Emma Hyman,
Harry Kadison, Teddy Leslie, Cleo Lewis, Joe Madden, Morris
Lloyd, Helen McArdell, Elaine Stiller, Strawberry, Clarice
Withers, Johnny Guerre, Al and Harriet Felder, Mighty Andy,
and Vesta E. Wallace.

A59.   Keese, William L. A Group of Comedians. New York: Dunlap Society, 1901.

Author and business manager William L. Keese (1835-1904) con-
centrates on the pre-Civil War careers of Henry Placide, William Rufus Blake, John Brougham, George Holland, and Charles
Fisher. There are six illustrations.

A60.   Knepler, Henry W. The Gilded Stage: The Years of the Great
International Actresses. New York: William Morrow, 1968.

Henry W. Knepler's (1922--) subject is the first and last of
the international actresses who performed throughout the world
regardless of language barriers: Rachel, Sarah Bernhardt,
Eleonora Duse, and Adelaide Ristori.

A61.   Kobbé, Gustav. The American Stage and Those Who Have Made It
Famous. New York: Gebbie, 1901.

Dramatic critic and editor Gustav Kobbé (1857-1918) writes of
numerous players on the American stage. His biographical
sketches are brief and anecdotal, but he succeeds in humaniz-
ing his subjects, which include Maude Adams, Viola Allen, Margaret Anglin, Julia Arthur, Ethel Barrymore, Mrs. Leslie Carter, Ida Conquest, William H. Crane, Elsie de Wolf, John Drew
II, William Faversham, Lew M. Fields, Minnie Maddern Fiske,
Anne H. Gilbert, William Gilette, Nat C. Goodwin, James K.
Hackett, Virginia Harned, Anna Held, James A. Herne, E. M.
Holland, Henry Irving, Isabel Irving, May Irwin, Joseph Jef-
ferson III, Herbert Kelcey, Madge Kendal, W. H. Kendal, Sarah
C. Le Moyne, Mary Mannering, Richard Mansfield, Julia Marlowe,
Edna May, Henry Miller, Jessie Millward, Edward J. Morgan, Ol-
ga Nethersole, Alice Nielsen, James O'Neill, Ada Rehan,
Charles Richman, May W. Robson, Stuart Robson, Gus and Max
Roberts, Annie Russell, Lillian Russell, Sol Smith Russell,
Effie Shannon, Otis Skinner, E. H. Sothern, Hilda Spong, Ellen
Terry, Blanche Walsh, Joe M. Weber, and Francis Wilson.

A62.   _____. Famous Actors and Their Homes. Boston: Little,
Brown and Company, 1905.

This book is distilled from Kobbé's Famous Actors and Actresses in Their Homes. He interviewed John Drew II, William Gillette, Richard Mansfield, E. H. Sothern, and Francis Wilson in
their homes and presents them to his readers as humans rather
than other-worldly luminaries.

A63.   _____. Famous Actresses and Their Homes. Toronto,
Ont.: Musson, 1905.

Marie Bancroft, Lawrence Barrett, Edwin Booth, Dion Boucicault and Agnes Robertson, John S. Clarke, the W. J. Florences, Henry Irving, Joseph Jefferson III, Madge and W. H.
Kendal, Helena Modjeska, Clara Morris, John T. Raymond, Ellen
Terry, John L. Toole, and Lester Wallack.

A72.   _____. Kean and Booth and
Their Contemporaries. Actors and Actresses of Great Britain
and the United States, Vol. III. Boston: L. C. Page, 1900.

Fifteen engravings illustrate the biographies of George Frederick Cooke, Thomas A. Cooper, Robert W. Elliston, Dorothy
Jordan, Charles Kemble, John Philip Kemble, John Liston,
Charles Mathews, Joseph S. Munden, Eliza O'Neill, Sarah Siddons, and Charles Mayne Young.

A73.   _____. The Kembles and Their
Contemporaries. Actors and Actresses of Great Britain and
the United States, Vol. II. Boston: L. C. Page, 1900.

Matthews and Hutton describe the lives of Junius Brutus Booth
I, John Brougham, John B. Buckstone, William E. Burton, Mary
Ann Duff, James H. Hackett, Edmund Kean, Fanny Kemble, Clara
Maeder (Fisher), Charles J. Mathews, John Howard Payne, Henry
Placide, Lucia Eliza Vestris, James W. Wallack, and Benjamin
N. Webster. There are sixteen engravings of the subjects.

A74.   _____. Macready and Forrest
and Their Contemporaries. Actors and Actresses of Great
Britain and the United States, Vol. IV. Boston: L. C. Page,
1900.

Among the subjects of this book are Charlotte Cushman, E. L.
Davenport, Charles Fechter, Edwin Forrest, Matilda Heron, and
E. A. Sothern. There are also fifteen illustrations.

A75.   _____. The Present Time. Ac-
tors and Actresses of Great Britain and the United States.
New York: Cassell and Company, 1886.

This volume inspired the entire series and is identical to
Edwin Booth and His Contemporaries.

A76.   McCall, Margaret, ed. My Drama School. London: Robson Books,
1978.

American Margaret McCall studied theatre in England and became
a producer for the BBC. She asked several actors and actresses
to reminisce about their theatrical training; the ensuing es-
says are in their own words. The subjects are Flora Robson,
Robert Morley, Lilli Palmer, Dulcie Gray, Patrick Macnee,
Yvonne Mitchell, Mai Zetterling, Ann Jellicoe, Peter Sallis,
Lee Montague, Paul Bailey, Hugh Whitmore, and Anna Calder-
Marshall.

A77.   McKay, Frederic Edward and Clarles E. L. Wingate, eds. Famous

American Actors of To-Day, 2 vols. New York: Thomas Y. Crowell and Company, 1896.

Frederic E. McKay (1872-1944), editor of Theatrical Tidings, conceived of the idea of this book and then enlisted the aid of editor and dramatic critic Charles E. L. Wingate (1861-1944). Although both editors were inveterate theatre-goers, they knew that the book would be more worthwhile if the biographies were written by people who had worked with the subjects. Vol. I contains essays on Joseph Jefferson III, Fanny Janauschek, Edwin Booth, Mary Anderson, Lawrence Barrett, Helena Modjeska, Dion Boucicault, Clara Morris, the W. J. Florences, Fanny Davenport, Lester Wallack, Mrs. John Drew, Richard Mansfield, Ada Rehan, John Drew II, Julia Marlowe, John Gilbert, William Warren II, Mary Ann Vincent, and Charles Fisher. Vol. II includes Charles R. Thorne, Jr., Agnes Booth, James H. Stoddart, Maurice Barrymore, Rose Coghlan, William J. Le Moyne, E. M. Holland, Georgia Cayvan, E. H. Sothern, Alexander Salvini, James O'Neill, Maggie Mitchell, Charlotte Crabtree, Minnie Maddern Fiske, W. H. Crane, Stuart Robson, John T. Raymond, Sol Smith Russell, Nat C. Goodwin, Denman Thompson, and Edward Harrigan.

A78.   Moses, Montrose J. Famous Actor-Families in America. New York: Thomas Y. Crowell and Company, 1906.

When dramatic critic Montrose J. Moses (1878-1934) wrote this volume, he was dramatic editor of The Reader Magazine. His approach to theatrical biography is rather unusual in that he writes of acting families and their continuing traditions. Moses studies the lives of the Booths, Jeffersons, Sotherns, Boucicaults, Hacketts, Drews, Barrymores, Wallacks, Davenports, Hollands, and Powerses.

A79.   National Portrait Gallery. Portraits of the American Stage 1771-1971. Washington, D. C.: Smithsonian Institution, 1971.

This volume is the program of an exhibition of theatrical paintings that was assembled by the National Portrait Gallery for the opening of the Kennedy Center for the Performing Arts. The ninety-odd portraits range from Nancy Hallam to Barbra Streisand. Biographical commentary amplifies the pictures.

A80.   Ormsbee, Helen. Backstage with the Actors: From the Time of Shakespeare to the Present Day. New York: Thomas Y. Crowell and Company, 1938.

Helen Ormsbee (d. 1957) set out to investigate whether the actor's creative process is the same now as it was in the past. She interviewed contemporary players backstage and dead ones through their writings, criticisms, and biographies. Ormsbee discusses David Garrick, Sarah Siddons, George Frederick Cooke, Edmund Kean, Junius Brutus Booth I, Matilda Heron, Edwin Booth, Joseph Jefferson III, James A. Herne, Richard Mansfield, Henry Irving, Ellen Terry, Minnie Maddern Fiske,

Maude Adams, Arnold Daly, and others.

A81.   Paul, Howard and George Gebbie, eds. The Stage and Its Stars,
        Past and Present, 2 vols. Philadelphia: George Gebbie,
        1887-9.

The large format, slick paper, and abundance of illustrations
make this one of the most attractive theatrical biographies.
Howard Paul (1835-1905) and publisher George Gebbie devote the
first volume to British actors; the second, to American. Hundreds of lives are presented, and each volume contains fifty-
six illustrations.

A82.   Pearson, Hesketh. The Last Actor-Managers. London: Methuen,
        1950.

This book is based on a series of radio talks given by writer/
playwright/actor Hesketh Pearson (1887-1964). He personally
met all his subjects and saw them in their greatest roles:
Johnston Forbes-Robertson, Herbert Beerbohm Tree, George Alexander, Frank R. Benson, Lewis Waller, John Martin-Harvey,
H. B. Irving, Laurence Irving, Oscar Asche, and Harley Granville Barker.

A83.   _____. Modern Men and Mummers. New York: Harcourt,
        Brace and Company, 1922.

Herein Pearson writes of George Bernard Shaw, George Alexand-
er, Frank R. Benson, Edmund Gosse, Arthur Bourchier, Hall
Caine, Lewis Waller, Mrs. Patrick Campbell, Irene Vanbrugh,
Genevieve Ward, and the Irvings, H. B. and Laurence.

A84.   Phillips, Julien L. Stars of the Ziegfeld Follies. Minnea-
        polis: Lerner, 1972.

Julien L. Phillips (1945--) writes for the young reader. His
book is, therefore, of slight interest to the serious scholar.
He includes a number of illustrations with his biographical
sketches of Eugene Sandow, Anna Held, Bert Williams, W. C.
Fields, Marilyn Miller, Will Rogers, Eddie Cantor, and Florenz
Ziegfeld, Jr.

A85.   Pitzer, F. P. Comical Confessions of Clever Comedians. Ed. De
        Wolf Hopper. New York: Street and Smith, 1904.

This small book by F. P. Pitzer is mainly recollections of em-
barrassing moments in the lives of American comedians; most of
the material is excerpted from other works. Its contributers
are Digby Bell, Sam Bernard, Charles A. Bigelow, William Collier, Peter F. Dailey, Frank Daniels, Jefferson De Angelis,
Lew Dockstader, De Wolf Hopper, Walter Jones, Ezra F. Kendall,
James T. Powers, David Warfield, Joe M. Weber, and Francis
Wilson.

A86.   Players of the Day: A Series of Portraits in Colour of Thea-
        trical Celebrities of the Present Time. London: Newnes,

c. 1900.

There is no biographical commentary in this volume that portrays George Alexander, Lena Ashwell, Jessie Bateman, Sarah Bernhardt, Arthur Bourchier, Miriam Clements, C. Hayden Coffin, Constance Collier, Florence Collingbourne, B. C. Coquelin, Connie Ediss, Willie Edouin, Winifred Emery, Vane Featherstone, Johnston Forbes-Robertson, Louie Freear, William Gillette, Charlotte Granville, Evie Green, Weedon Grossmith, Charles Groves, Jane Hading, Charles Hawtry, Seymour Hicks, H. B. Irving, Ellis Jeffreys, Maud Jeffries, Cyril Maude, Mrs. Maesmore Morris, Walter Passmore, Edmund Payne, Cora Urquhart Potter, Isabel Raleigh, Ada Reeve, Réjane, Kate Sarjeantson, Kate Seymour, Marie Studholme, Ellaline Terriss, Edward Terry, Fred Terry, Herbert Beerbohm Tree, Irene Vanbrugh, Lewis Waller, Herbert Waring, E. S. Willard, and Huntley Wright.

A87.   Pond, James Burton. Eccentricities of Genius: Memories of Famous Men and Women of the Platform and Stage. New York: G. W. Dillingham Company, 1900.

In 1874 Maj. J. B. Pond (1838-1903) bought the Redpath Lyceum Bureau, then situated in Boston, and entered upon a career of managing the appearances of various types of celebrities on the lecture circuit. His book registers his experiences with orators, preachers, singers, writers, humorists, explorers, war correspondents, politicians, entrepreneurs, and, of course, theatre folk: Joseph Jefferson III, William Winter, Henry Irving, Charlotte Cushman, and Ellen Terry. Pond also discusses the lives of dramatists Hall Caine, Anthony Hope, and Joaquin Miller.

A88.   Robins, Edward. Twelve Great Actors. New York: G. P. Putnam's Sons, 1900.

In the preface of this volume, writer Edward Robins (1862-1943) speaks of the growing importance of the theatre to civilized pursuits. His choice of subjects is intended to demonstrate the actor's progress from the status of rogue to that of respected member of society. Among the British and American players of whom Robins writes are David Garrick, John Philip Kemble, Edmund Kean, Junius Brutus Booth I, Edwin Forrest, William Charles Macready, Charles J. Mathews, Edwin Booth, Charles Fechter, William E. Burton, Edward A. Sothern, and Lester Wallack.

A89.   _____. Twelve Great Actresses. New York: G. P. Putnam's Sons, 1900.

Asserting that the contribution of women to the theatre has been no less vital than that of men, Robins delineates the careers of British, American, French, and Italian actresses: Anne Bracegirdle, Anne Oldfield, Margaret Woffington, Frances Abingdon, Sarah Siddons, Dorothy Jordan, Mary Robinson, Fanny Kemble, Rachel, Charlotte Cushman, Adelaide Neilson, and Adelaide Ristori.

A90.   Rollins, Charlemae H.   <u>Famous Negro Entertainers of Stage,</u>
        <u>Screen, and TV</u>. New York: Dodd, Mead and Company, 1967.

        Charlemae H. Rollins intended this work for juvenile readers.
        A modest photographic section augments brief biographies of
        black entertainers, including Ira Aldridge, Josephine Baker,
        Sidney Poitier, Paul Robeson, Bill Robinson, and Bert Willi-
        ams.

A91.   Rowlands, Walter.   <u>Among the Great Masters of the Drama</u>:
        <u>Scenes in the Lives of Famous Actors</u>.   Boston: Dana Estes
        and Company, 1903.

        Walter Rowlands (b. 1855) ranges extensively throughout his-
        tory and geography in choices of subjects, which include Wil-
        liam Shakespeare, Molière, Voltaire, Adrienne Lecouvreur, Dav-
        id Garrick, Margaret Woffington, Frances Abingdon, Sarah Sid-
        dons, John Philip Kemble, Dorothy Jordan, Talma, John Liston,
        Mlle. Mars, Edmund Kean, William Charles Macready, Pauline Dé-
        jazet, Edwin Forrest, William Warren II, Charlotte Cushman,
        Rachel, and Adelaide Ristori. Since Rowland describes so many
        lives, his chapters are accordingly brief.

A92.   Russell, William Clark.   <u>Representative Actors: A Collection</u>
        <u>of Criticisms, Anecdotes...Referring to Many Celebrated</u>
        <u>British Actors</u>.... London: Frederick Warne, 1888.

        W. Clark Russell (1844-1911) aptly entitles his work, for he
        amassed a wealth of critical excerpts, juicy anecdotes, and
        pithy reminiscences of scores of British actors from the six-
        teenth century to his own day. Although the entries are some-
        times useful in themselves, the chief merit of the book is its
        bibliographical content.

A93.   Scott, Walter Sidney.   <u>The Georgian Theatre</u>.   London: West-
        house, 1946.

        Walter S. Scott (1900--) decided to "give a general view of
        the period, amplified by sketches of various persons and e-
        vents of importance to the theatrical history of the time." In
        this he admirably succeeded. The book is illustrated by con-
        temporary engravings, some of them tinted. Scott's subjects
        include Catherine Clive, Henry Woodward, David Garrick,
        Spranger Barry, Margaret Woffington, John Moody, Thomas King,
        William Parsons, Frances Abingdon, J. W. Dodd, Sophia Badde-
        ley, John Palmer, Priscilla Hopkins, Elizabeth Younge, James
        Aickin, Robert Bensley, Richard Wroughton, Sarah Siddons,
        George Frederick Cooke, Joseph Munden, and Edmund Kean.

A94.   Shaw, Dale.   <u>Titans of the American Stage: Edwin Forrest, the</u>
        <u>Booths, the O'Neills</u>. Philadelphia: Westminster Press, 1971.

        Author Dale Shaw (1927--) illustrates his slight biographies
        of Edwin Forrest, Junius Brutus Booth I, Edwin Booth, John
        Wilkes Booth, James O'Neill, and Eugene O'Neill with twenty-
        four photographs.

A95.   Shipman, Louis E. Group of Theatrical Caricatures: Being Twelve
        Plates by W. J. Gladding. New York: Dunlap Society, 1897.

        Editor, author, and playwright Louis E. Shipman (1869-1933) pro-
        vides brief biographical comments on W. J. Gladding's carica-
        tures of Dan Bryant, Charles T. White, Tony Pastor, Edwin Booth,
        John Brougham, Frank S. Chanfrau, William J. Florence, Edwin
        Forrest, George L. Fox, John E. Owens, Lester Wallack, and Wil-
        liam Wheatley--all of which were drawn in 1868.

A96.   Sherman, Robert L. Actors and Authors with Composers and Man-
        agers Who Helped Make Them Famous. Chicago: privately print-
        ed, 1951.

        Robert L. Sherman (1867-1952) provides a most frustrating volume
        of theatrical biographies. On the one hand, its coverage is
        vast, extending to stars and journeymen theatrical artists. On
        the other hand, some of the entries suggest that Sherman depend-
        ed on his memory alone: names are misspelled, dates patently in-
        correct, and facts obviously wrong. Yet some of his subjects
        are mentioned nowhere else, so that Sherman's notice of them be-
        comes important. This book is to be used with caution.

A97.   Simpson, Harold and Mrs. Charles Braun. A Century of Famous Ac-
        tresses 1750-1850. London: Mills and Boon, 1913.

        Simpson and Braun id not intend to present exhaustive biograph-
        ies of their subjects; they were content with providing charact-
        er sketches. Many actresses appear in these pages, but the
        principal ones are Susannah Maria Cibber, George Anne Bellamy,
        Margaret Woffington, Catherine Clive, Hannah Pritchard, Mary Ann
        Yates, Anne Barry, Frances Abingdon, Elizabeth Farren, Dorothy
        Jordan, Eliza O'Neill, Helen Faucit, and Ellen Kean.

A98.   Six Years of Drama at the Castle Square Theatre, with Portraits
        of the Members of the Company and Complete Programs of All
        Plays Produced, 1897-1903. Boston: Charles E. French, 1903.

        This illustrated book is a celebration of six years of continu-
        ous performances at Boston's Castle Square Theatre. In addition
        to providing a history of the theatre and complete playbills,
        the anonymous author gives biographical sketches of the company
        and crew. That number includes James R. Pitman, Lillian Law-
        rence, Jane Irving, Mary Sanders, Leonora Bradley, Izetta Jew-
        ell, Alexia Durant, John Craig, John M. Sainpolis, John T. Crav-
        en, James L. Seeley, Thomas MacLarnie, George E. Mack, Edward
        Wade, Lindsay Morison, Louis Thiel, William J. Hasson, John J.
        Geary, Mary Hall, Lavinia Shannon, Eva Taylor, Grace Atwell,
        Maye Louise Aigen, Maude Odell, Corona Riccardo, Nina Morris,
        Adelaide Cushman, Katherine Clinton, Mary Young, Mary Young,
        Marian Chapman, Fanny Addison Pitt, Lizzie Morgan, Leonora
        Gnito, Jennie Kendrick, Cordelia Macdonald, Rose Morison, J. H.
        Gilmour, William Courtleigh, Franklyn Ritchie, Frank Sheridan,
        Hallett Thompson, Robert Elliot, William Humphrey, Ned H. Fowl-
        er, Edmund Breese, Charles D. Mackay, James O. Barrows, Horace
        Lewis, Giles Shine, Tony Cummings, James A. Keane, Stanley Kent,

William Charles Masson, William Paul, Alban W. Purcell, Leon
Fairbrother, Max Hendle, and C. G. Alexander.

A99.   Skinner, Otis. Mad Folk of the Theatre: Ten Studies in Tempera-
ment. Indianapolis: Bobbs-Merrill, 1928.

Actor Otis Skinner (1858-1942) amusingly presents aspects of the
personalities and lives of George Anne Bellamy, Thomas Betterton, Junius Brutus Booth I, George Frederick Cooke, Eleanor
Gwynn, Dorothy Jordan, Edmund Kean, James Quin, and Tate Wilkinson. A final chapter is devoted to "Will-of-Avon."

A100.   Smith, Bill. The Vaudevillians. New York: Macmillan Company,
1976.

Bill Smith, an editor and critic, introduces the subject of
vaudeville and gives a brief history of the form. Afterwards,
performers such as Will Ahern, Edgar Bergen, Sammy Berk, Milton
Berle, Block and Sully, John Bubbles, George Burns, Jean Car-
roll, Alan Corelli, Jean Dalrymple, Jack Durant, Sylvia Froos,
Billy Glason, Janette Hackett, Jack Haley, Lou Holtz, Buddy
Howe, George Jessel, Mack Lathrop, Sammy Lewis, Rose Marie,
Charles Mosconi, Ken Murray, Percy Oakes, Harry Ritz, Benny
Rubin, Rae Samuels, Joe Smith, Arthur Tracy, and Rudy Vallee
tell their own stories.

A101.   Stephens, Robert N.   Queens of the Drama. Etched portraits by
F . L . Kirkpatric k an d Clarenc e A. Worrall. Troy, N. Y.:
Nims and Knight, 1889.

Robert N. Stephens (1867-1906), drama editor of the Philadelphia
Press, wrote the brief biographical material that accompanies
the handsome etched portraits of the actresses who dominated the
American stage late in the nineteenth century. Among the many
subjects are Fanny Davenport, Jane Hading, Lillie Langtry, and
Adelaide Neilson.

A102.   Stevens, Ashton. Actorviews: Intimate Portraits. Drawings by
Gene Markey. Chicago: Covivi-McGee Company, 1923.

As theatre critic of the Herald and Examiner (Chicago), Ashton
Stevens (1872-1951) conducted over five hundred interviews with
stage personalities, forty-eight of which appear in this book.
Stevens' subjects include John Drew II, Blythe Daly, Leo Ditrichstein, Elsie Ferguson, A. H. Woods, Maire O'Neill and Arthur Sinclair, Mildred Walker, Herbert Beerbohm Tree, Ina
Claire, John Barrymore, Frank Craven, Elsie Janis, William Col-
lier, Ethel Barrymore, Ike Bloom, Mrs. Leslie Carter, Bert Sa-
voy, Laurette Taylor, Louis Wolheim, Georgie O'Ramey, Ruchard
Bennett, Sophie Tucker, Arnold Daly, Clara Moores, David Warfield, Dale Winter, George Arliss, Marie Vernon, Al Jolson, Lynn
Fontanne, Raymond Hitchcock, Fay Marbe, E. H. Sothern and Julia
Marlowe, Fanny Brice, Bert Williams, Justine Johnstone, Morris
Gest, Helen Hayes, Nora Bayes, Lynne Overman, Pauline Lord,
Brownie Curtin and Bunny Butler, Patricia Collinge, Irene Bor-
doni, Frank Bacon, Jane Cowl, and Minnie Maddern Fiske.

A103.   Storms, A. D., ed. The Players' Blue Book. Worcester, Mass.:
         Sutherland and Storms, 1901.

         A. D. Storms claims that in assembling this book, "accuracy has
         been sought above all else." The book is comprised of 149 one-
         page biographies and photographs of contemporary players.

A104.   Strang, Lewis C. Celebrated Comedians of Light Opera and Musi-
             cal Comedy in America. Boston: L. C. Page and Company, 1900.

         When Lewis C. Strang (1869-1935) published this book, he had al-
         ready served two years as critic and drama editor of the Boston
         Journal. In that capacity Strang frequented the theatre and
         talked with its artists. He claims that his theatrical biograph-
         ies have been shorn of "the imaginings of press agents." He
         devotes chapters to Henry Clay Barnabee, Digby Bell, Richard
         Carle, Peter F. Dailey, Dan Daly, Frank Daniels, Jefferson De
         Angelis, Henry E. Dixey, Richard Golden, Otis Harlan, De Wolf
         Hopper, Walter Jones, James T. Powers, Thomas Q. Seabrooke, Jer-
         ome Sykes, and Francis Wilson.

A105.   _____. Famous Actors of the Day. Boston: L. C. Page
             and Company, 1899.

         The subjects of this volume are Joseph Jefferson III, James A.
         Herne, Richard Mansfield, E. M. Holland, Edward H. Sothern, John
         Drew II, William Faversham, John B. Mason, Nat C. Goodwin, James
         O'Neill, William H. Crane, Wilton Lackaye, William Gillette,
         Henry Miller, James K. Hackett, Henry Jewett, Stuart Robson,
         Melboourne MacDowell, Sol Smith Russell, Otis Skinner, J. E.
         Dodson, Robert B. Mantell, Roland Reed, Joseph Haworth, and Her-
         bert Kelcy.

A106.   _____. Famous Actresses of the Day in America. Bos-
             ton: L. C. Page and Company, 1899.

         In this book Strang features Maude Adams, Viola Allen, Margaret
         Anglin, Julia Arthur, Blanche Bates, Marie Burroughs, Mrs. Les-
         lie Carter, Rose Coghlan, Ida Conquest, Elsie De Wolf, Maxine
         Elliott, Minnie Maddern Fiske, Virginia Harned, Isabel Irving,
         May Irwin, Kathryn Kidder, Lillian Lawrence, Sarah C. Le Moyne,
         Mary Mannering, Julia Marlowe, Helena Modjeska, Ada Rehan, Cor-
         ona Riccardo, May Robson, Annie Russell, Effie Shannon, Mary
         Shaw, Odette Tyler, and Blanche Walsh. A 1901 edition of this
         work includes Valerie Bergère, Amelia Bingham, Henrietta Cros-
         man, Phoebe Davies, Grace George, Anna Held, Mary Sanders, and
         Elizabeth Tyree.

A107.   _____. Prima Donnas and Soubrettes of Light Opera and
             Musical Comedy in America. Boston: L. C. Page and Company,
             1900.

         Strang provides biographies of Minnie Ashley, Marie Celeste,
         Hilda Clark, Jessie Bartlett Davis, Marie Dressler, Virginia
         Earle, Paula Edwardes, Della Fox, Mabelle Gilman, Lulu Glaser,
         Josephine Hall, Pauline Hall, Edna Wallace Hopper, Madge Les-

sing, Christie MacDonald, Edna May, Alice Nielsen, Maude Raymond, Lillian Russell, Marie Tempest, and Fay Templeton.

A108.   Townsend, Margaret. Theatrical Sketches: Here and There with Prominent Actors. New York: Merriam, 1894.

Playwright Margaret Townsend writes of late nineteenth-century theatre and the people with whom she worked. Much of the book describes Townsend's association with Kyrle Bellew, Louis James, Cora Urquhart Potter, and Lester Wallack.

A109.   Trease, Geoffrey. Seven Stages. New York: Vanguard Press, 1965.

Geoffrey Trease (1909--) presents seven stages in the development of western theatre. As epitomes of the sixteenth through the nineteenth centuries respectively, he delineates the lives of Christopher Marlowe, Molière, Sarah Siddons, and Henry Irving.

A110.   Trumble, Alfred. Footlight Favorites: A Collection of Popular American and European Actresses in Various Roles in Which They Have Become Famous. New York: Richard K. Fox, 1881.

As a journalist for the National Police Gazette, Alfred Trumble interviewed numerous players; his books largely are collections of those conversations. The twenty-five biographies that comprise this book are illustrated by engraved portraits. Among Trumble's subjects are Jennie Yeamans, Minnie Palmer, Pauline Markham, Adelaide Neilson, and Sarah Bernhardt.

A111.   _____. Great Artists of the American Stage: A Portrait Gallery of the Leading Actors and Actresses of America. New York: Richard K. Fox, 1882.

Biographies and engravings of thirty actors constitute this work. Trumble's subjects include Frank S. Chanfrau, Kate Claxton, Henry Crisp, and John McCullough.

A112.   Vance, Marguerite. Hear the Distant Applause: Six Great Ladies of the American Theatre. New York: E. P. Dutton, 1963.

The lives of Maude Adams, Mary Anderson, Charlotte Cushman, Minnie Maddern Fiske, Julia Marlowe, and Ada Rehan, are presented to young readers by Marguerite Vance (1889-1965).

A113.   Wagenknecht, Edward C. Merely Players. Norman, Okla.: University of Oklahoma Press, 1966.

Calling his biographical excursions "psychographs," Edward C. Wagenknecht (1900--) examines the lives and careers of David Garrick, Edmund Kean, William Charles Macready, Henry Irving, Edwin Forrest, Edwin Booth, Joseph Jefferson III, and Richard Mansfield.

A114.   _____. Seven Daughters of the Theatre. Norman, Okla.: University of Oklahoma Press, 1964.

Wagenknecht's focus in this volume is on female performers, including Jenny Lind, Sarah Bernhardt, Ellen Terry, Julia Marlowe,
Isadora Duncan, Mary Garden, and Marilyn Monroe.

A115. Wagner, Frederick and Barbara Brady. Famous American Actors and
       Actresses. New York: Dodd, Mead and Company, 1961.

       Writing for juvenile readers, Frederick Wagner (1928--) and Bar-
       bara Brady discuss the lives of Maude Adams, Edwin Booth, George
       M. Cohan, Katharine Cornell, Lynn Fontanne, Edwin Forrest, Julie
       Harris, Helen Hayes, Joseph Jefferson III, Alfred Lunt, Julia
       Marlowe, and E. H. Sothern.

A116. Weintraub, Stanley, ed. Modern British Dramatists 1900-1945, 2
       vols. Dictionary of Literary Biography, Vol. X. Detroit: Gale
       Research Company, 1982.

       Various writers contributed biographical/critical essays on
       British playwrights to this volume edited by Stanley Weintraub
       (1929---). The entries vary in length and complexity but com-
       prise perhaps the best of current views of the dramatists. The
       subjects are William Archer, W. H. Auden, Harley Granville
       Barker, James M. Barrie, Clifford Bax, Arnold Bennett, Gordon
       Bottomley, James Bridie, Harold Brighouse, Gilbert Cannon, Paul
       Vincent Carroll, Charles Haddon Chambers, G. K. Chesterton,
       Austin Clarke, Joseph Conrad, Noël Coward, Louis D'Alton, Clem-
       ence Dane, Gordon Daviott, John Drinkwater, Ashley Dukes, Lord
       Dunsany, T. S. Eliot, St. John Ervine, James Elroy Flecker, John
       Galsworthy, Walter Greenwood, Lady Gregory, Cicely Hamilton,
       Patrick Hamilton, St. John Hankin, Alan Patrick Herbert, Stanley
       Houghton, Laurence Housman, N. C. Hunter, Jerome K. Jerome, Den-
       is Johnston, Henry Arthur Jones, James Joyce, Edward Knoblock,
       D. H. Lawrence, Frederick Lonsdale, Brinsley MacNamara, Louis
       MacNeice, Edward Martyn, John Masefield, W. Somerset Maugham,
       A. A. Milne, Allan Monkhouse, George Moore, Gilbert Murray, Sean
       O'Casey, Stephen Phillips, Eden Phillpotts, Arthur W. Pinero,
       J. B. Priestley, Lennox Robinson, Dorothy L. Sayers, Mordaunt
       Shairp, George Bernard Shaw, R. C. Sherriff, George Shiels,
       Dodie Smith, Alfred Sutro, John Millington Synge, Ben Travers,
       John van Druten, Sutton Vane, Oscar Wilde, William Butler Yeats,
       and Israel Zangwill.

A117. Whitton, Joseph. Wags of the Stage. Philadelphia: George H.
       Rigby, 1902.

       Fifty years of playgoing prepared Joseph Whitton to write this
       book in which he chronicles the waggery (merriment) of a small
       group of British and American theatrical personalities. Heading
       Whitton's list is Junius Brutus Booth I, who is followed by John
       Brougham, Peter Richings, William Rufus Blake, Edwin Forrest,
       William E. Burton, John Drew II, William J. Florence, H. L.
       Bateman, Sam Hemple, P. T. Barnum, Charles M. Barras, Edward A.
       Sothern, James Quin, Samuel Foote, and William Wheatley.

A118. Williams, Hugh N. Queens of the French Stage. New York: Charles
       Scribner, 1905.

Hugh N. Williams (b. 1870) writes of the lives of Armande Béjart, Marie-Ann Camargo, Marie de Champmeslé, Hippolyte Clairon, Justine Favart, and Adrienne Lecouvreur.

A119.   Wilson, John Harold. All the King's Ladies: Actresses of the Restoration. Chicago: University of Chicago Press, 1958.

John H. Wilson (1900--) seeks to correct a serious oversight in Restoration scholarship: the almost total neglect of actresses of the period. In the body of the book, Wilson discusses the nature of the seventeenth-century stage and the emergence of the actress. Actual biographies, anecdotal and readable, comprise a long appendix. The lives of scores of actresses are described insofar as rather meager documentation allows.

A120.   Winter, William. Other Days: Being Chronicles and Memories of the Stage. New York: Moffat, Yard and Company, 1908.

William Winter (1836-1917) was dramatic editor and critic of the New York Tribune from 1865 through 1909. As "dean of American theatre critics," Winter championed the best of Romantic theatre and was enthusiastically disinterested in the emergence of theatrical Realism. That bias is evident in all his biographies. Drawing from his letters and newspaper columns, Winter writes of Mary Anderson, Lawrence Barrett, Dion Boucicault, John Brougham, Charlotte Cushman, Joseph Jefferson III, John McCullough, Edward A. Sothern, and others.

A121.   _____. Shadows of the Stage, 3 vols. New York: Macmillan and Company, 1892-5.

Winter's subjects in this volume are Mary Anderson, Lawrence Barrett, Edwin Booth, Charlotte Cushman, Charles Fisher, William J. FLorence, Anne H. Gilbert, Joseph Jefferson III, James Lewis, John McCullough, Richard Mansfield, Ada Rehan, Genevieve Ward, John Brougham, John Gilbert, James H. Hackett, George W. Jamieson, Jean Davenport Lander, Helena Modjeska, Clara Morris, John E. Owens, and William Wheatley.

A122.   _____. Vagrant Memories: Being Further Recollections of Other Days. New York: George H. Doran Company, 1915.

In this his last book Winter tells of William Warren II, Laura Keene, Matilda Heron, Lester Wallack, James W. Wallack II, Mark Smith, Edwin Adams, Henry J. Montague, Edwin Booth, Augustin Daly, Henry Irving, Johnston Forbes-Robertson, Edward H. Sothern, and Julia Marlowe.

A123.   _____. The Wallet of Time: Containing Personal, Biographical, and Critical Reminiscences of the American Theatre, 2 vols. New York: Moffat, Yard and Company, 1913.

Vol. I deals with Lawrence Barrett, John Brougham, Charles Coghlan, Charlotte Cushman, Charles Fechter, Edwin Forrest, Anne H. Gilbert, George Holland, James Lewis, John McCullough, Helena Modjeska, Clara Morris, John E. Owens, and John T. Raymond.

Vol. II includes Maude Adams, Blanche Bates, Mrs. Leslie Carter, Minnie Maddern Fiske, Julia Marlowe, Ada Rehan, Edward A. Sothern, David Warfield, and Frank Worthing.

A124.   Woollcott, Alexander M. Enchanted Aisles.   New York: G. P. Putnam, 1924.

Journalist and humorist Alexander Woollcott (1887-1943) salutes the theatre in this volume of reminiscences of his days as dramatic critic of the New York Times and the New York Herald. He writes of many players, but his treatment of Irving Berlin, Sarah Bernhardt, Eleonora Duse, Minnie Maddern Fiske, Elsie Janis, Pauline Lord, Maurice Maeterlinck, and Booth Tarkington is particularly interesting.

A125.   Young, William C. Famous Actors and Actresses on the American Stage, 2 vols.   New York: R. R. Bowker, 1977.

William C. Young (1928--) provides what is perhaps the best contemporary book of theatrical biographies. He writes of scores of players ranging from the eighteenth century to the twentieth in a thoughtful, useful manner.

A126.   Zolotow, Maurice.   No People Like Show People. New York: Random House, 1951.

Journalist Maurice Zolotow (1913--) interviewed the subjects of this book and augmented his research by talking with their associates. Zolotow attempts in each biography to analyze the psychological nature of his subject. The book includes chapters on Tallulah Bankhead, Jimmy Durante, Oscar Levant, Jack Benny, Frank Fay, Jed Harris, Fred Allen, and Ethel Merman.

B. Other Collective Biographies

B1.   Abbott, Lyman. <u>Silhouettes of My Contemporaries</u>. Garden City:
      N. Y.: Doubleday, Page and Company, 1922.

      Noted American minister and author Lyman Abbott (1835-1922) re-
      calls his acquaintance with entrepreneur P. T. Barnum, tragedian
      Edwin Booth, and temperance lecturer John B. Gough.

B2.   Barry, Philip B. <u>Sinners down the Centuries.....</u> London: Jar-
      rolds, 1929.

      Philip B. Barry's theme is notorious behavior throughout the
      ages. His theatrical "sinners" are Aphra Behn and Edmund Kean.

B3.   Bleackley, Horace. <u>Ladies Fair and Frail: Sketches of the Demi-
      monde during the Eighteenth Century</u>. New York: Dodd, Mead and
      Company, 1926.

      Horace Bleackley (1868-1931) deals primarily with courtesans of
      the eighteenth century. One of them, Gertrude Mahan, also had a
      theatrical career.

B4.   Boyd, Ernest A. <u>Portraits Real and Imaginary: Being Memories
      and Impressions of Friends and Contemporaries....</u> New York:
      George H. Doran, 1924.

      Critic and journalist Ernest A. Boyd (1887-1946) focuses on the
      lives of numerous men who lived by their pens; all were his
      friends or acquaintances. His subjects include Eugene O'Neill,
      George Bernard Shaw, G. K. Chesterton, George Jean Nathan,
      George Moore, and William Butler Yeats.

B5.   Bradford, Gamaliel. <u>American Portraits 1875-1900</u>.   Boston:
      Houghton Mifflin Company, 1922.

      Gamaliel Bradford (1863-1932) seeks to write psychological por-
      traits of his subjects. This volume is devoted to writers and
      politicians, in the company of whom Joseph Jefferson III ap-
      pears.

B6.   _____. <u>As God Made Them: Portraits of Some Nine-</u>

teenth Century Americans. Boston: Houghton Mifflin Company, 1929.

Politicians, journalists, scholars, and scientists are the subjects of this volume. One man of the theatre—Edwin Booth—is also included. Much of the information on Booth comes from the private collection of Robert Gould Shaw.

B7.   _____. Bare Souls. New York: Harper and Brothers, 1924.

Bradford explores the writer's craft in this volume. Voltaire is the only dramatist included.

B8.   _____. Biography and the Human Heart. Boston: Houghton Mifflin Company, 1932.

Charlotte Cushman is the subject of one of Bradford's essays, most of which deal with writers.

B9.   _____. Damaged Souls. Boston: Houghton Mifflin Company, 1931.

P. T. Barnum is part of Bradford's collection of politicians and patriots with a vein of unscrupulousness in their souls.

B10.   _____. Daughters of Eve. Boston: Houghton Mifflin Company, 1930.

Bradford's essay on Sarah Bernhardt is an interesting part of his treatment of French women (and Catherine the Great).

B11.   _____. Portraits and Personalities. Ed. Mabel A. Bessey.   Freeport, N. Y.: Books for Libraries Press, 1968 [1933].

Among the politicians and authors included in this book are William Shakespeare and Joseph Jefferson III.

B12.   Carr, Joseph W. Comyns. Cruising Bohemia. London: The Macmillan Company, 1914.

Sometime critic and playwright Joseph W. Comyns Carr (1849-1916) was a fixture of Victorian and Edwardian artistic life and was thus able to observe the public and private lives of the people about whom he wrote. A numer of the chapters of this book appeared in the (London) Daily Telegraph. Allusions to the theatre are scattered throughout, but there are separate chapters on Henry Irving and Arthur Sullivan.

B13.   Croft-Cooke, Rupert. Feeding with Panthers: A New Consideration of Some Late Victorian Writers. London: W. H. Allen, 1967.

Rupert Croft-Cooke examines the effects of their homosexuality on the lives and works of Algernon Charles Swinburne, John Addington Symonds, and Oscar Wilde.

B14.   Cumberland, Gerald [Charles F. Kenyon].   Set Down in Malice: A
        Book of Reminiscences. London: Grant Richards, 1919.

        Writer Richard Cumberland (1879-1926) moved in the Bohemian
        world of Victorian and Edwardian London where he encountered
        numerous artists of the theatre. Some of those noticed by Cum-
        berland are Janet Achurch, Hall Caine, Edward Gordon Craig,
        Annie E. F. Horniman, Stanley Houghton, Henry Arthur Jones, and
        Herbert Beerbohm Tree.

B15.   Gallico, Paul. The Revealing Eye: Personalities of the 1920's.
        Photographs by Nickolas Muray. New York: Atheneum, 1967.

        Writer Paul Gallico (1897-1976) and photographer Nickolas Muray
        (1892-1965) endeavor to describe the 1920s in America through
        the people who created the essence of those years. Of the 150
        subjects, the theatre artists are George Abbott, Zoë Akins, John
        Murray Anderson, Judith Anderson, Fred and Adele Astaire, Tallu-
        lah Bankhead, Ethel Barrymore, Richard Barthelmess, Nora Bayes,
        David Belasco, Humphrey Bogart, Irene Bordoni, Alice Brady, Jack
        Buchanan, Billie Burke, Hall Caine, Irene Castle, Charles S.
        Chaplin, Ina Claire, Jean Cocteau, Claudette Colbert, Katharine
        Cornell, Noël Coward, Jane Cowl, Ruth Draper, Jeanne Eagels,
        Lynn Fontanne, John Galsworthy, George Gershwin, Yvette Guil-
        bert, Walter Hampden, Jed Harris, Lorenz Hart, Helen Hayes,
        Theresa Helburn, Hedda Hopper, Langston Hughes, Al Jolson, Law-
        rence Langner, Gertrude Lawrence, Eva Le Gallienne, Cissie Loft-
        us, Anita Loos, Alfred Lunt, Charles MacArthur, Cyril Maude,
        Thomas Meighan, Philip Merivale, Jo Mielziner, Marilyn Miller,
        Philip Moeller, Ferenc Molnar, Helen Morgan, Alla Nazimova,
        Eugene O'Neill, Rosamond Pinchot, Cole Porter, Florence Reed,
        Elmer Rice, Paul Robeson, Edward G. Robinson, Richard Rodgers,
        George Bernard Shaw, Lee Simonson, Otis Skinner, Clifton Webb,
        Helen Westley, Louis Wolheim, and Blanche Yurka.

B16.   Garland, Hamlin. Roadside Meetings. New York: Macmillan, 1930.

        In this autobiographical volume, novelist Hamlin Garland (1860-
        1940) writes of his encounters with interesting people. Garland
        writes at length of Edwin Booth, James A. Herne, James M. Bar-
        rie, and George Bernard Shaw. A number of other theatre artists
        are mentioned.

B17.   Gray, William Forbes. The Poets Laureate of England: Their His-
        tory and Their Odes. New York: E. P. Dutton, 1915.

        William Forbes Gray (1874-1915) bases his book on the premise
        that the English laureateship, despite its venerability, has
        seldom been in the hands of a competent poet. Dramatists and men
        of the theatre who have been poets laureate include Ben Jonson,
        William D'Avenant, John Dryden, Thomas Shadwell, Nahum Tate,
        Nicholas Rowe, and Colley Cibber. Poet Alfred Tennyson, another
        laureate, also wrote dramas that were produced by Henry Irving.

B18.   Griswold, Hattie E. Personal Sketches of Recent Authors. Chica-
        go: A. C. McClurg, 1899.

Hattie E. Griswold (1840-1909) remembers writers known to her as she pursued a literary career. The only dramatist she discusses is James M. Barrie.

B19.   Ketchum, Richard M. Faces from the Past.   New York: American Heritage, 1970.

Author Richard M. Ketchum (1922--) provides biographical material for a collection of evocative historical prints and photographs. Among the well-known faces are those of the theatrical Booth family and Evelyn Nesbit ("The Girl in the Red Velvet Swing").

B20.   Kunitz, Stanley J. and Howard Haycraft. Twentieth-Century Authors: A Biographical Dictionary of Modern Literature. New York: H. W. Wilson, 1942.

Stanley J. Kunitz (1905--) and Howard Haycraft wished to present the lives of current authors to readers of English; foreign writers whose works were not disseminated in English were not included in this book, much of the research for which was conducted by letter. The 1,850 authors represented include dramatists George Ade, James Agate, Zoë Akins, Enid Bagnold, George Pierce Baker, James M. Barrie, Paul Vincent Carroll, John Drinkwater, St. John Ervine, Martin Flaven, Jean Giraudoux, Cosmo Hamilton, Georg Kaiser, Lawrence Langner, George Middleton, Beverley Nichols, Lynn Riggs, Arthur Schnitzler, Augustus Thomas, Lula Vollmer, and Frank Wedekind.

B21.   MacCarthy, Desmond. Portraits,I.   New York: Macmillan, 1932.

Critic Desmond MacCarthy (1878-1952) ranges throughout human history in his choice of biographical subjects, most of them drawn from literature and politics. Of particular interest are the chapters on Horace, Voltaire, Johann Wolfgang von Goethe, Hall Caine, Mrs. Patrick Campbell, and August Strindberg.

B22.   McCarthy, Justin. Portraits of the Sixties.   New York: Harper and Brothers, 1903.

Irish politician and journalist Justin McCarthy (1830-1912) provides his own recollections of important British figures of the 1860s as an accompaniment to Fisher Unwin's photographs. In an attempt to describe people whose lives colored the decade, McCarthy writes about novelists, politicians, philanthropists, and an array of others, including Edward H. Sothern, Charles Fechter, Robert Keeley, Frederick Robson, Benjamin Webster, Squire and Marie Bancroft, Lydia Thompson, Adah Isaacs Menken, and Nellie Farren.

B23.   Nash, Jay Robert. Zanies: The World's Greatest Eccentrics. Piscataway, N. J.: New Century Publishers, 1982.

Jay Robert Nash selected for inclusion in his book over 200 people whose lives showed consistently eccentric behavior. Such a collection must have representatives of the stage: Mary Astor,

P. T. Barnum, John Barrymore, Sarah Bernhardt, Junius Brutus Booth I, Charles S. Chaplin, Robert Coates, Sergei Diaghilev, Isadora Duncan, W. C. Fields, William Frawley, Texas Guinan, William Henry Ireland, Al Jolson, Charles MacArthur, the Marx Brothers, W. Somerset Maugham, Wilson Mizner, Hesketh Pearson, Mary Roberts Rinehart, George Bernard Shaw, Richard Brinsley Sheridan, Tristan Tzara, Mae West, Walter Winchell, and Alexander Woollcott.

B24.   Pearson, Hesketh.   Extraordinary People. New York: Harper and Row, 1965.

The author of several theatrical biographies, Hesketh Pearson (1887-1964) was intimately acquainted with numerous figures of the English stage. In this book he sets out to describe a number of individuals who merited the epithet "extraordinary." Pearson's list includes novelists, ecclesiastics, politicians, and Wilkie Collins, Johnston Forbes-Robertson, and George Bernard Shaw.

B25.   Pickett, La Salle C.   Across My Path: Memories of People I Have Known.   New York: Brentano's, 1916.

La Salle C. Pickett (1848-1931), a poet and historical writer, conducted something like a literary salon and therefore associated with many of the creative artists of her day. This book is a collection of her memories of them. Actresses Charlotte Cushman, Laura Keene, Helena Modjeska, Adelaide Ristori, and Adelaide Neilson appear in these pages.

B26.   Pleasants, Henry. The Great American Popular Singers.   New York: Simon and Schuster, 1974.

Henry Pleasants (1910--) studies the lives of American musical performers. Those who are directly related to the theatre are Al Jolson, Ethel Waters, Ethel Merman, and Barbra Streisand.

B27.   Seitz, Don C. Uncommon Americans.   Indianapolis: Bobbs-Merrill, 1925.

Newspaperman Don C. Seitz (1862-1935) examines the lives of Americans who failed at critical points in their lives, thus becoming uncommon representatives of the American dream. The rivalry between Edwin Forrest and William Charles Macready, resulting in the Astor Place Riots, is one of Seitz's examples.

B28.   Untermeyer, Louis. Makers of the Modern World.   New York: Simon and Schuster, 1955.

Louis Untermeyer (1885-1977) says that his purpose is to examine the lives of those who have "formed the pattern of our century." His theatrical subjects are Richard Wagner, Henrik Ibsen, Émile Zola, George Bernard Shaw, Anton Chekhov, Isadora Duncan, T. S. Eliot, Eugene O'Neill, Charles S. Chaplin, George Gershwin, Jean-Paul Sartre, and W. H. Auden.

C. Individual Biographies and Autobiographies

C1. Abbott, George. "Mister Abbott." New York: Random House, 1963.

C2. Abdullah, Achmed. The Cat Had Nine Lives: Adventures and Reminiscences. New York: Farrar and Rinehart, 1933.

C3. A'Beckett, Arthur W. The A'Becketts of "Punch": Memories of Father and Son. Westminster: A. Constable, 1903.

C4. _____. Green Room Recollections. Bristol: J. W. Arrowsmith, 1896.

C5. _____. Recollections of a Humourist, Grave and Gay. London: Pitman, 1896.

C6. An Account of the Life of That Celebrated Actress, Mrs. Susannah Maria Cibber. London: n. p., 1887.

C7. An Account of the Life of That Celebrated Tragedian, Mr. Thomas Betterton. London: J. Robinson, 1749.

C8. Ackerman, Forrest J. Boris Karloff: The Frankinscience Monster. New York: Ace Publishing Company, 1969.

C9. Adam, Ronald. Overture and Beginners. London: Victor Gollancz, 1938.

C10. Adams, Allen J. "Peter McCourt, Jr., and the Silver Theatrical Circuit, 1889-1910: A Historical and Biographical Study." Unpublished doctoral dissertation, University of Utah, 1969.

C11. Adams, Cindy. Lee Strasberg: The Imperfect Genius of the Actors. Garden City, N. Y.: Doubleday and Company, 1980.

C12. Adams, Hazard. Lady Gregory. Lewisburg, Penn.: Bucknell University Press, 1973.

C13. Adams, Joey. On the Road for Uncle Sam. New York: Bernard Geis, 1963.

C14. _____. From Gags to Riches. New York: Frederick Fell,

1946.

C15.   _____ . Cindy and I. New York: Crown Publishers, 1957.

C16.   Adams, Joseph Quincy. A Life of William Shakespeare. Boston: Houghton Mifflin Company, 1923.

C17.   Adams, Samuel H. Alexander Woollcott: His Life and His World. New York: Reynal and Hitchcock, 1945.

C18.   Adeler, Edwin and Con West. Remember Fred Karno? London: John Long, 1939.

C19.   Adlard, Eleanor, ed. "Edy": Tributory Essays by Old Companions and Colleagues. London: Muller, 1949. [Edith Craig]

C20.   Adler, Irene. I Remember Jimmy [Durante]. Westport, Conn.: Arlington House, 1980.

C21.   Adolphus, John. Memoirs of John Bannister, Comedian, 2 vols. London: Richard Bentley, 1839.

C22.   Agate, James. Ego: The Autobiography of James Agate. London: Hamish Hamilton, 1935.

C23.   _____ . Ego 2: Being More of the Autobiography of James Agate. London: Victor Gollancz, 1936.

C24.   _____ . Ego 3: Being Still More of the Autobiography of James Agate. London: G. G. Harrap, 1940.

C25.   _____ . Ego 4: Yet More of the Autobiography of James Agate. London: G. G. Harrap, 1940.

C26.   _____ . Ego 5: Again More of the Autobiography of James Agate. London: G. G. Harrap, 1942.

C27.   _____ . Ego 6: Continuing the Autobiography of James Agate. London: G. G. Harrap, 1944.

C28.   _____ . Ego 7: Continuing the Autobiography of James Agate. London: G. G. Harrap, 1945.

C29.   _____ . Ego 8: Continuing the Autobiography of James Agate. London: G. G. Harrap, 1947.

C30.   _____ . Ego 9: Concluding the Autobiography of James Agate. London: G. G. Harrap, 1948.

C31.   _____ . Rachel. London: Gerald Howe, 1928.

C32.   Agate, May. Madame Sarah [Bernhardt]. London: Home and Van Thal, 1946.

C33.   Aherne, Brian. A Proper Job. Boston: Houghton Mifflin Company, 1969.

C34.   Aitken, George A. The Life and Works of John Arbuthnot, M. D,
        F. R. C. P. London: Oxford University Press, 1892.

C35.   _____. Life of Richard Steele, 2 vols. London: W.
        Isbister, 1889.

C36.   Akerby, George. The Life of Mr. James Spiller, the Late Famous
        Comedian. London: J. Purser, 1729.

C37.   Albanesi, Effie M. Meggie Albanesi. London: Hodder and Stough-
        ton, 1928.

C38.   Albani, Emma. Forty Years of Song. London: Mills and Boon,
        1911.

C39.   Albery, Wyndham, ed. The Dramatic Works of James Albery, Togeth-
        er with a Sketch of His Career, Correspondence Bearing There-,
        on, Press Notices, Casts, etc. London: P. Davies, 1939.

C40.   Aldrich, Richard S. Gertrude Lawrence as Mrs. A. New York: Grey-
        stone Press, 1954.

C41.   Alexander, Peter. Shakespeare's Life and Art. New York: New
        York University Press, 1961.

C42.   Alfieri, Vittorio. Life of Vittorio Alfieri. Trans. Henry McAn-
        ally. Lawrence: University of Kansas Press, 1953.

C43.   Alger, William R. Life of Edwin Forrest, the American Tragedi-
        an, 2 vols. Philadelphia: J. B. Lippincott, 1877.

C44.   Alkofer, Daniel W. "The Theatrical Career of James Quin." Unpub-
        lished doctoral dissertation, Indiana University, 1971.

C45.   Allan, Maud. My Life and Dancing. New York: P. R. Reynolds,
        1908.

C46.   Allen, Fred. Letters. Ed. Joe McCarthy. Garden City, N. Y.:
        Doubleday and Company, 1965.

C47.   _____. Much Ado about Me. Boston: Little, Brown and Com-
        pany, 1956.

C48.   _____. Treadmill to Oblivion. Boston: Little, Brown, and
        Company, 1954.

C49.   Allen, Percy. The Stage Life of Mrs. [Fanny] Stirling. London:
        Fisher Unwin, 1922.

C50.   Alltree, George W. Footlight Memories: Recollections of Music
        Hall and Stage Life. London: S. Low, Marston, 1932.

C51.   Alpert, Hollis. The Barrymores. New York: Dial Press, 1965.

C52.   Altemus, Jameson T. Helena Modjeska. New York: J. S. Ogilvie,
        1883.

C53.   Ambross, Miss. The Life and Memoirs of the Late Miss Ann Catley, the Celebrated Actress. London: J. Bird, 1790.

C54.   Anderson, Chester G. James Joyce and His World. New York: Viking Press, 1968.

C55.   Anderson, Garland. From Newsboy to Bellhop to Playwright. San Francisco: n. p., 1925.

C56.   Anderson, James R. An Actor's Life. Ed. W. E. Adams. London: Walter Scott, 1902.

C57.   _____. Diary, 1847. Source Materials in the Field of Theatre, No. 29, Reel 5. Ann Arbor, Mich.: University Microfilms, 1959.

C58.   Anderson, Jean. Late Joys at the Players' Theatre. London: T. V. Boardman, 1943.

C59.   Anderson, John. Box Office. New York: Jonathan Cape and H. Smith, 1929.

C60.   Anderson, Hugh A. Out without My Rubbers. New York: Library Publishers, 1954.

C61.   Anderson, Mary. A Few Memories. New York: Harper and Company, 1896.

C62.   _____. A Few More Memories. London: Hutchinson, 1936.

C63.   Anderson, Maxwell. Dramatist in America: The Letters of Maxwell Anderson. Ed. Laurence G. Avery. Chapel Hill: University of North Carolina Press, 1967.

C64.   Anderson, Sherwood. Letters. Ed. H. M. Jones and W. R. Rideout. Boston: Little, Brown and Company, 1953.

C65.   _____. Memoirs. New York: Harcourt, Brace and Company, 1942.

C66.   _____. A Story Teller's Story. New York: B. W. Huebsch, 1924.

C67.   Andrews, Clarence E. Richard Brome: A Study of His Life and Works. New York: Henry Holt, 1913.

C68.   Andrews, Gertrude. The Romance of a Western Boy: The Story of Corse Payton. New York: Andrews Press, 1901.

C69.   Anfuso, Bernice S. "The Passing Star: Eleonora Duse in America." Unpublished master's thesis, University of California at Los Angeles, 1956.

C70.   Angelo, Henry. Angelo's Picnic: or Table Talk.... London: J. Ebers, 1834.

C71.   Angelo, Henry. Reminiscences of Henry Angelo, 2 vols. London: H.
        Colburn, 1828-30.

C72.   Anthony, Gordon. Beryl Grey. London: Phoenix House, 1952.

C73.   _____. John Gielgud. London: G. Bles, 1938.

C74.   Antoine, Le Roi. Achievement: The Life of Laura Bowman. New
        York: Pageant Press, 1961.

C75.   An Apology for the Life of Mr. Theophilus Cibber, Comedian. Lon-
        don: J. Mechell, 1740.

C76.   Appleton, William W. Charles Macklin: An Actor's Life. Cam-
        bridge: Harvard University Press, 1960.

C77.   _____. Madame Vestris and the London Stage. New
        York: Columbia University Press, 1974.

C78.   Arant, F. Fairlie. "A Biography of the Actor Thomas Abthorpe
        Cooper (1775-1849)." Unpublished doctoral dissertation, Uni-
        versity of Minnesota, 1971.

C79.   Archer, Charles. William Archer: His Life, Work and Friendships.
        London: Allen and Unwin, 1931.

C80.   Archer, Frank. An Actor's Notebooks: Being Some Memories,
        Friendships, Criticisms and Experiences. London: S. Paul,
        1912.

C81.   Archer, William and Robert W. Lowe. The Fashionable Tragedian
        [Henry Irving]: A Criticism. Edinburgh: T. Gray and Company,
        1877.

C82.   _____. Henry Irving: Actor and Manager. London: Field
        and Tuer, 1883.

C83.   _____. William Charles Macready. London: K. Paul,
        Trench, Trübner and Company, 1890.

C84.   Arditi, Luigi. My Reminiscences. London: Skeffington, 1896.

C85.   Aria, Eliza D. My Sentimental Self. London: Chapman and Hall,
        1922.

C86.   Arliss, George. George Arliss: By Himself. London: J. Murray,
        1940.

C87.   _____. On the Stage: An Autobiography. London: John
        Murray, 1928.

C88.   _____. Up the Years from Bloomsbury. Boston: Little,
        Brown and Company, 1927.

C89.   Armens, Sven M. John Gay: Social Critic. New York: King's Crown
        Press, 1954.

C90.   Armitage, Merle. Accent on America. New York: E. Weyhe, 1944.

C91.   _____. George Gershwin: Man and Legend. New York: Duell, Sloan, and Pearce, 1938.

C92.   Armstrong, Margaret N. Fanny Kemble: A Passionate Victorian. New York: The Macmillan Company, 1938.

C93.   Arnold, Edward and F. F. Dubuc. Lorenzo Goes to Hollywood: The Autobiography of Edward Arnold. New York: Horace Liveright, 1940.

C94.   Arnold, S. J. Forgotten Facts in the Memoirs of Charles Mathews, Comedian, Recalled in a Letter to Mrs. Mathews. London: Ridgway, 1839.

C95.   Aronson, Rudolf. Theatrical and Musical Memoirs. New York: McBride, Nast and Company, 1913.

C96.   Arthur, George. From Phelps to Gielgud: Reminiscences of the Stage through Sixty-Five Years. London: Chapman and Hall, 1936.

C97.   Arthur, George C. Sarah Bernhardt. London: William Heinemann, 1923.

C98.   Arundell, D. D. Dryden and Howard, 1664-68. Cambridge: Cambridge University Press, 1929.

C99.   Arvin, Neil C. Eugène Scribe and the French Theatre, 1815-1860. Cambridge: Harvard University Press, 1924.

C100. Asche, Oscar. Oscar Asche: His Life. London: Hurst, 1929.

C101. Ashley, Elizabeth and Ross Firestone. Actress: Postcards from the Road. New York: M. Evans, 1978.

C102. Ashwell, Lena. Modern Troubadours: A Record of the Concerts at the Front. London: Gyldendal, 1922.

C103. _____. Myself a Player. London: M. Joseph, 1936.

C104. _____. The Stage. London: G. Bles, 1929.

C105. Asquith, Cynthia. Portrait of [James M.] Barrie. London: James Barrie, 1954.

C106. Astaire, Fred. Steps in Time. New York: Harper and Company, 1959.

C107. Astor, Mary. My Story: An Autobiography. Garden City, N. Y.: Doubleday and Company, 1959.

C108. Atkins, John A. Graham Greene. London: Calder and Boyars, 1966.

C109. Aughtry, Charles E. "Lynn Riggs, Dramatist: A Critical Biography." Unpublished doctoral dissertation, Brown University, 1959.

C110. Austin, Louis F. _Henry Irving in England and America, 1838-1884_. London: T. F. Unwin, 1884.

C111. Austin, Mary H. _Earth Horizon_. Boston: Little, Brown and Company, 1932.

C112. _Authentic Narrative of Mr. [John Philip] Kemble's Retirement from the Stage_. London: John Miller, 1817.

C113. Averill, Esther. _Eyes on the World: The Story and Work of Jacques Callot_. New York: Funk and Wagnalls, 1969.

C114. Avery, Burneice. _Walk Quietly through the Night and Cry Softly_. Detroit, Mich.: Balamp, 1977.

C115. Bablet, Denis. _Edward Gordon Craig_. Trans. Daphne Woodward. New York: Theatre Arts Books, 1966.

C116. Bacall, Lauren. _Lauren Bacall by Myself_. New York: Alfred A. Knopf, 1978.

C117. Badal, Robert S. "Kate and Ellen Bateman: A Study in Precocity." Unpublished doctoral dissertation, Northwestern University, 1971.

C118. Bagnold, Enid. _Autobiography_. London: William Heinemann, 1969.

C119. Bagot, Alec. _Coppin the Great: Father of the Australian Stage_. London: Cambridge University Press, 1965.

C120. Bagster-Collins, Jeremy F. _George Colman the Younger, 1762-1836_. New York: King's Crown Press, 1946.

C121. Bailey, Leon E. "The Acting Career of Walter Huston." Unpublished doctoral dissertation, University of Illinois, 1972.

C122. Bailey, Mark. "Lawrence Barrett." Unpublished doctoral dissertation, University of Michigan, 1942.

C123. Bailey, Pearl. _The Raw Pearl_. New York: Harcourt, Brace and World, 1968.

C124. _____. _Talking to Myself_. New York: Harcourt, Brace and Jovanovich, 1971.

C125. Baily, Leslie. _The Gilbert and Sullivan Book_. London: Cassell, 1952.

C126. _____. _Gilbert and Sullivan: Their Lives and Times_. London: Thames and Hudson, 1974.

C127. Bairnsfather, Bruce. _Wide Canvas: An Autobiography_. London:

J. Long, 1939.

C128. Bakeless, John. Christopher Marlowe: The Man in His Time. New
       York: William Morrow, 1937.

C129. Baker, Herschel C. John Philip Kemble: The Actor in His Theatre.
       Cambridge: Harvard University Press, 1942.

C130. Baker, John Milton. Henry Crabb Robinson of Bury, Jena, "The
       Times," and Russell Square. London: G. Allen and Unwin, 1937.

C131. Baker, Josephine and Jo Bouillon. Josephine. Trans. Mariana
       Fitzpatrick. New York: Harper and Row, 1977.

C132. Balaban, Carrie. Continuous Performance: The Story of A. J. Bal-
       aban. New York: G. P. Putnam, 1942.

C133. Balakian, Anna. André Breton, Magus of Surrealism. New York:
       Oxford University Press, 1971.

C134. Ball, William T. Life and Memoirs of William Warren [II], Bos-
       ton's Favorite Comedian. Boston: Daly, 1888.

C135. Bamborough, J. B. Ben Jonson. London: Longmans, Green and Com-
       pany, 1959.

C136. Bancroft, George P. Stage and Bar: Recollections. London: Faber
       and Faber, 1939.

C137. Bancroft, Squire. Empty Chairs. New York: Frederick A. Stokes
       Company, 1925.

C138. _____ and Marie. Mr. and Mrs. Bancroft On and Off the
       Stage, 2 vols. London: Richard Bentley and Son, 1885.

C139. _____. Recollections of Sixty Years. New
       York: E. P. Dutton, 1909.

C140. Bandmann, Daniel E. An Actor's Tour: or Seventy Thousand Miles
       with Shakespeare. New York: Brentano's, 1886.

C141. Bangs, Francis H. John Kendrick Bangs: Humorist of the Nineties.
       New York: Alfred A. Knopf, 1941.

C142. Bangs, John Kendrick. From Pillar to Post: Leaves from a Lectur-
       er's Note-book. New York: Century Publishing Company, 1916.

C143. Banister, Douglas. Life of Mr. John Reeve. London: Richardson,
       1838.

C144. Bankhead, Tallulah. Tallulah: My Autobiography. New York: Harp-
       er and Brothers, 1952.

C145. Bankson, Budd. I Should Live So Long. Philadelphia: J. B. Lip-
       pincott, 1952.

C146. Bannister, Winifred. James Bridie and His Theatre. London: Rock-
         liff, 1955.

C147. Bantock, Granville and F. G. Aflalo. Round the World with "A
         Gaiety Girl." London: John MacQueen, 1896.

C148. Barclay, George L., ed. The Life and Remarkable Career of Adah
         Isaacs Menken. Philadelphia: Barclay and Company, 1868.

C149. Barea, Arturo. Lorca: The Poet and His People. Trans. Ilsa Ba-
         rea. New York: Harcourt, Brace and Company, 1949.

C150. Baring, Maurice. Sarah Bernhardt. London: Peter Davis, 1933.

C151. Barker, Dudley. The Man of Principle: Galsworthy. London: Wil-
         liam Heinemann, 1963.

C152. _____. Writer by Trade: A Portrait of Arnold Bennett.
         New York: Atheneum, 1966.

C153. Barker, Felix. The Oliviers. London: Hamish Hamilton, 1953.

C154. Barker, Richard H. Mr. [Colley] Cibber of Drury Lane. New York:
         Columbia University Press, 1939.

C155. _____. Thomas Middleton. New York: Columbia Univer-
         sity Press, 1958.

C156. Barmam, Christian. Sir John Vanbrugh. London: Ernest Benn, 1924.

C157. Barnes, Elliott. A Tramp Actor. Chicago: Belford, Clarke and
         Company, 1886.

C158. Barnes, Eric W. The Lady of Fashion: The Life and Theatre of
         Anna Cora Mowatt. New York: Charles Scribner's Sons, 1955.

C159. _____. The Man Who Lived Twice: The Biography of Edward
         Sheldon. New York: Charles Scribner's Sons, 1956.

C160. Barnes, Jack B. "Simeon Nash Nye, Pioneer Colorado Theatre Man-
         ager, 1882-1914." Unpublished doctoral dissertation, Univer-
         sity of Denver, 1972.

C161. Barnes, John H. Forty Years on the Stage: Others, (Principally)
         Myself. London: Chapman and Hall, 1914.

C162. Barnum, Phineas T. The Life of P. T. Barnum. New York: Redfield,
         1955.

C163. _____. Struggles and Triumphs: or, Forty Years' Re-
         collections of P. T. Barnum. Hartford, Conn.: J. B. Burr,
         1869.

C164. Baron-Wilson, Margaret, ed. The Life and Correspondence of Mat-
         thew Gregory Lewis, 2 vols. London: H. Colburn, 1839.

C165. Baron-Wilson, Margaret. Memoirs of Harriot, Duchess of St. Albans, 2 vols. London: H. Colburn, 1839.

C166. Barrault, Jean-Louis. Memories for Tomorrow: The Memoirs of Jean-Louis Barrault. Trans. Jonathan Griffin. New York: E. P. Dutton, 1974.

C167. _____. Reflections on the Theatre. Trans. Barbara Wall. London: Rockliff, 1951.

C168. _____. The Theatre of Jean-Louis Barrault. Trans. Joseph Chiari. London: Barrie and Rockliff, 1961.

C169. Barrett, Lawrence. Charlotte Cushman: A Lecture. New York: Dunlap Society, 1889.

C170. Barrett, Lawrence. Edwin Forrest. Boston: J. R. Osgood and Company, 1881.

C171. Barrett, William A. [Michael W.] Balfe: His Life and Work. London: W. Reeves, 1883.

C172. Barrett, Wilson. On Stage for Notes: The Story of the Wilson Barrett Company. Edinburgh: Blackwood, 1954.

C173. Barrie, James M. The Greenwood Hat. New York: Charles Scribner's Sons, 1938.

C174. _____. Letters. Ed. Viola Meynell. New York: Charles Scribner's Sons, 1947.

C175. Barrington, Rutland. Rutland Barrington: A Record of Thirty-Four Years' Experience on the English Stage. London: Grant Richards, 1908.

C176. _____. More Rutland Barrington. London: Grant Richards, 1911.

C177. Barron, Elwyn A. Lawrence Barret: A Professional Sketch. Chicago: Knight and Leonard, 1889.

C178. Barry, John Daniel. Julia Marlowe. Boston: R. G. Badger, 1899.

C179. Barrymore and Gerold Frank. Too Much Too Soon. New York: Henry Holt, 1957.

C180. Barrymore, Elaine and Dody Sanford. All My Sins Remembered. New York: Appleton-Century Company, 1964.

C181. Barrymore, Ethel. Memories: An Autobiography. New York: Harper and Brothers, 1955.

C182. Barrymore, John. Confessions of an Actor. Indianapolis: Bobbs-Merrill, 1926.

C183. Barrymore, Lionel and Cameron Shipp. We Barrymores. New York:

Appleton-Century-Crofts, 1951.

C184. Barrymore, Lionel, Ethel, and John. We Three. Akron, Oh.: Saal-
        field, 1935.

C185. Bartlett, Basil H. Jam Tomorrow: Some Early Reminiscences. Lon-
        don: Granada, 1978.

C186. Barton, Margaret. [David] Garrick. London: Faber and Faber,
        1948.

C187. Barton, Mike A. "Aline Bernstein: A History and Evaluation." Un-
        published doctoral dissertation, Indiana University, 1971.

C188. Bates, Finis L. The Escape and Suicide of John Wilkes Booth: or
        The First True Account of Lincoln's Assassination.... Naper-
        ville, Ill.: J. L. Nichols, 1907.

C189. Bates, Helen M. Lotta's Last Season. Brattleboro, Vt.: E. L.
        Hildreth, 1940.

C190. Bates, Scott. Guillaume Apollinaire. New York: Twayne Publish-
        ers, 1967.

C191. Bates, William N. Euripides: A Student of Human Nature. New
        York: A. S. Barnes, 1930.

C192. _____. Sophocles, Poet and Dramatist. New York: Rus-
        sell and Russell, 1969 [1940].

C193. Batters, Jean. Edith Evans: A Personal Memoir. London: Hart-
        Davis, MacGibbon, 1977.

C194. Bauer, Karoline. Memoirs, 4 vols. 2d ed. London: Remington,
        1885.

C195. Baum, Frank J. and Russell P. MacFall. To Please a Child: A Bio-
        graphy of L. Frank Baum, Royal Historian of Oz. Chicago:
        Reilly and Lee, 1961.

C196. Bax, Clifford, ed. Florence Farr, Bernard Shaw, and W. B. Yeats:
        A Correspondence. Dublin: T. M. MacGlinchey, 1971 [1941].

C197. _____. Pretty Witty Nell: An Account of Nell Gwyn and
        Her Environment. London: Chapman and Hall, 1932.

C198. _____. Some I Knew Well. London: Phoenix House, 1951.

C199. Baxter, Anne. Intermission: A True Tale. New York: G. P. Putnam,
        1976.

C200. Bazaldua, Charles, Jr. "'Going to the People': The Career of Sol
        Smith Russell." Unpublished doctoral dissertation, University
        of Missouri, 1975.

C201. Beal, George B. Through the Back Door of the Circus. Spring-

C238.   Bennett, Charles F. His Memoirs and Poetry. Holt: J. Shalders, 1817.

C239.   Bennett, Cleon V. "James Robinson Planché: Victorian Craftsman." Unpublished doctoral dissertation, University of Wisconsin, 1971.

C240.   Bennett, Dorothy C. Arnold Bennett: A Portrait Done at Home, Together with 170 Letters from Arnold Bennett. London: Jonathan Cape, 1935.

C241.   B., E. C. The Life of William Robert Grossmith, the Celebrated Infant Roscius. Reading: M. Cowslade, 1825.

C242.   Bennett, Joan and Lois Kibbee. The Bennett Playbill. New York: Holt, Rinehart and Winston, 1970.

C243.   Bennett, Marguerite. My Arnold Bennett. London: Nicholson and Watson, 1932.

C244.   Benny, Mary L. Jack Benny. Garden City, N. Y.: Doubleday and Company, 1978.

C245.   Benois, Alexander. Memoirs, 2 vols. Trans. Moura Budberg. London: Chatto and Windus, 1964.

C246.   Benson, Constance. Mainly Players: Bensonian Memories. London: T. Butterworth, 1926.

C247.   Benson, Frank R. My Memoirs. London: Ernest Benn, 1930.

C248.   Benstock, Bernard. Sean O'Casey. Lewisburg, Penn.: Bucknell University Press, 1970.

C249.   Bentley, Gerald E. Shakespeare: A Biographical Handbook. New Haven, Conn.: Yale University Press, 1961.

C250.   Berg, Gertrude and Cherney Berg. Molly and Me. New York: McGraw-Hill Company, 1961.

C251.   Bergman, Herbert. "Augustus Thomas, Dramatist of His Age." Unpublished doctoral dissertation, University of Wisconsin, 1953.

C252.   Bergman, Ingrid and Alan Burgess. Ingrid Bergman: My Story. New York: Delacorte Press, 1982.

C253.   Berkowitz, Hyman C. Benito Pérez Galdós: Spanish Liberal Crusader. Madison: University of Wisconsin Press, 1948.

C254.   Berkson, Michael A. "Morris Carnovsky: Actor and Teacher." Unpublished doctoral dissertation, University of Illinois, 1975.

C255.   Berle, Milton and Haskel Frankel. An Autobiography. New York: Delacorte Press, 1974.

C256. Berle, Milton. Laughingly Yours. Ed. S. S. Simon. New York:
       Samuel French, 1939.

C257. _____. Out of My Trunk. Garden City, N. Y.: Blue Ribbon
       Books, 1945.

C258. Bernard, John. Retrospections of America, 1797-1811. Ed. Mrs.
       Bayle Bernard. New York: Harper and Company, 1886.

C259. _____. Retrospections of the Stage, 2 vols. Ed. W. Bayle
       Bernard. London: H. Colburn and R. Bentley, 1830.

C260. Bernard, Marc. Zola. Trans. Jean M. Leblon. New York: Grove
       Press, 1960.

C261. Bernardi, Jack. My Father [Berel Bernardi], the Actor. New York:
       W. W. Norton, 1971.

C262. Bernhardt, Lysiane S. Sarah Bernhardt: My Grandmother. Trans.
       Vyvyan Holland. London: Hurst and Blackett, 1949.

C263. Bernhardt, Sarah. Memories of My Life. New York: D. Appleton,
       1923.

C264. _____. My Double Life: Memoirs. London: William
       Heinemann, 1907.

C265. Bernstein, Aline F. An Actor's Daughter. New York: Alfred A.
       Knopf, 1941.

C266. Berry, William Henry. Forty Years in the Limelight. London:
       Hutchinson, 1939.

C267. Berton, Thérèse. Sarah Bernhardt as I Knew Her. London: Hurst
       and Blackett, 1923.

C268. Besterman, Theodore. Voltaire. New York: Harcourt, Brace and
       Company, 1969.

C269. Bettany, F. G. Stewart Headlam: A Biography. London: John Mur-
       ray, 1926.

C270. Betterton, Charles. The Life of Mr. Charles Betterton, 2 vols.
       Portsea: G. Moxon, 1829.

C271. Bettisworth, Denny L. "The Life and Career of Zelda Sears." Un-
       published doctoral dissertation, University of Georgia, 1974.

C272. Betty, William H. W. Memoirs. London: B. D. Cousins, 1848.

C273. Bickford, Charles. Bulls, Balls, Bicycles and Actors. New York:
       Paul S. Eriksson, 1965.

C274. Bierley, Paul E. John Philip Sousa: American Phenomenon. New
       York: Appleton-Century-Crofts, 1973.

C275. Bielschowsky, Albert. The Life of Goethe, 3 vols. Trans. W. A. Cooper. New York: G. P. Putnam's Sons, 1905-8.

C276. Bierstadt, Edward H. Dunsany the Dramatist. Boston: Little, Brown and Company, 1917.

C277. Bingham, Madeleine. The Great Lover: The Life and Art of Herbert Beerbohm Tree. New York: Atheneum, 1979.

C278. _____. Henry Irving: The Greatest Victorian Actor. New York: Stein and Day, 1978.

C279. _____. Sheridan: The Track of a Comet. London: George Allen and Unwin, 1972.

C280. Binns, Archie. Mrs. Fiske and the American Theatre. New York: Crown Publishers, 1955.

C281. Bird, Mary Mayer. Life of Robert Montgomery Bird. Ed. C. Seymour Thompson. Philadelphia: University of Pennsylvania Press, 1945.

C282. Bishop, George W. Barry Jackson and the London Theatre. London: A. Barker, 1932.

C283. _____. My Betters. London: William Heinemann, 1957.

C284. Bishop, Jim. The Golden Ham: A Candid Biography of Jackie Gleason. New York: Simon and Schuster, 1956.

C285. _____. The Mark Hellinger Story: A Biography of Broadway and Hollywood. New York: Appleton-Century-Crofts, 1952.

C286. Bispham, David. A Quaker Singer's Recollections. New York: The Macmillan Company, 1922.

C287. Bithell, Jethro. The Life and Writings of Maurice Maeterlinck. London: Walter Scott Publishing Company, 1913.

C288. Black, Helen C. Pen, Pencil, Baton, and Mask: Biographical Sketches. London: Spottiswoode, 1896.

C289. Blakelock, Denys. Finding My Way. London: Hollis and Carter, 1958.

C290. _____. Round the Next Corner. London: Victor Gollancz, 1967.

C291. Blanchard, Edward L. The Life and Reminiscences of E. L. Blanchard, 2 vols. Ed. Clement Scott and Cecil Howard. London: Hutchinson, 1891.

C292. Bland, Robert Henderson. Actor, Soldier, Poet. London: Heath Cranton, 1939.

C293. Blesh, Rudi. [Buster] Keaton. New York: The Macmillan Company,

1966.

C294.   Blesi, Marius. The Life and Letters of Anna Cora Mowatt. Char-
        lottesville: University of Virginia Press, 1952.

C295.   Bloom, Claire. Limelight and After: The Education of an Actress.
        New York: Harper and Row, 1982.

C296.   Bloom, Sol. The Autobiography of Sol Bloom. New York: G. P. Put-
        nam's Sons, 1948.

C297.   Blow, Sydney. The Ghost Walks on Fridays: In and Out of the
        Stage Door. London: Heath, Cranton, 1935.

C298.   Blumenthal, George. My Sixty Years in Show Business. New York:
        F. C. Osberg, 1936.

C299.   Blyth, Harry. My Sweetheart!: The Life and Adventures of Minnie
        Palmer. London: Hansard Publishing Union, 1883.

C300.   Boaden, James. The Life of Mrs. [Dorothy] Jordan, 2 vols. Lon-
        don: E. Bull, 1831.

C301.   _____. Memoirs of the Life of John Philip Kemble, 2
        vols. London: Longman, Hurst, Rees, Orme, Browne, and Green,
        1825.

C302.   _____, ed. Memoris of Mrs. [Elizabeth] Inchbald, 2 vols.
        London: Richard Bentley, 1833.

C303.   _____. Memoirs of Mrs. [Sarah] Siddons, 2 vols. London:
        H. Colburn, 1827.

C304.   _____. The Private Correspondence of David Garrick. Lon-
        don: H. Colburn and R. Bentley, 1831-2.

C305.   Boardman, William H. Vaudeville Days. Ed. David Whitelaw. Lon-
        don: Jarrolds, 1935.

C306.   Boas, Frederick S. Christopher Marlowe: A Biographical and Crit-
        ical Study. Oxford: Clarendon Press, 1940.

C307.   _____. Marlowe and His Circle: A Biographical Sur-
        vey. Oxford: Clarendon Press, 1929.

C308.   Bobbé, Dorothie de B. Fanny Kemble, Actress 1809-93. London:
        Elkin Mathews, 1932.

C309.   Bolitho, Hector. Marie Tempest: Her Biography. London: Cobden-
        Sanderson, 1936.

C310.   Bond, Richard W. The Complete Works of John Lyly, with Biograph-
        ical and Critical Introduction, 3 vols. Oxford: Clarendon
        Press, 1902.

C311.   Booth, John Bennion. The Days We Knew. London: T. W. Laurie,

1943.

C312.   Booth, John Bennion. <u>Old Pink 'Un Days</u>. London: Grant Richards, 1924.

C313.   _____. <u>Pink Parade</u>. London: T. Butterworth, 1933.

C314.   _____. <u>Pink 'Un Remembers</u>. London: T. W. Laurie, 1937.

C315.   _____. <u>Sporting Times: The Pink 'Un World</u>. London: T. W. Laurie, 1938.

C316.   Bordeux, Vahdah J. <u>Eleonora Duse: The Story of Her Life</u>. London: Hutchinson and Company, 1924.

C317.   Bordman, Gerold. <u>Jerome Kern: His Life and Music</u>. New York: Oxford University Press, 1980.

C318.   Borgman, Albert S. <u>The Life and Death of William Mountfort</u>. Cambridge: Harvard University Press, 1935.

C319.   _____. <u>Thomas Shadwell: His Life and Comedies</u>. New York: New York University Press, 1928.

C320.   Bostock, Edward H. <u>Menageries, Circuses and Theatres</u>. New York: Frederick A. Stokes, 1928.

C321.   Bosworth, Patricia. <u>Montgomery Clift</u>. New York: Harcourt, Brace and Jovanovich, 1978.

C322.   Bottomley, Gordon and Paul Nash. <u>Poet and Painter: Being the Correspondence between Gordon Bottomley and Paul Nash, 1910-1946</u>. London: Oxford University Press, 1955.

C323.   Boulton, Agnes. <u>Part of a Lifetime: Eugene O'Neill as a Young Man in Love</u>. Garden City, N. Y.: Doubleday and Company, 1958.

C324.   Bourgeois, Maurice. <u>John Millington Synge and the Irish Theatre</u>. London: Constable and Company, 1913.

C325.   Bournonville, August. <u>My Theatre Life</u>. Trans. Patricia N. McAndrew. Middletown, Conn.: Wesleyan University Press, 1979.

C326.   Bowen, Croswell and Shane O'Neill. <u>The Curse of the Misbegotten: A Tale of the House of O'Neill</u>. New York: McGraw-Hill Company, 1959.

C327.   Bowyer, John W. <u>The Celebrated Mrs. [Susanna] Centlivre</u>. Durham: University of North Carolina Press, 1952.

C328.   Boyd, Frank M. <u>A Pelican's Tale: Fifty Years of London and and Elsewhere</u>. Philadelphia: J. B. Lippincott, 1919.

C329.   Boyer, William. <u>The Romantic Life of Maurice Chevalier</u>. London: Hutchinson and Company, 1937.

C330.   Bradner, Leicester. The Life and Poems of Richard Edwards. New
        Haven: Yale University Press, 1927.

C331.   Brady, William A. The Fighting Man. Indianapolis: Bobbs-Merrill,
        1916.

C332.   _____. Showman. New York: E. P. Dutton, 1937.

C333.   Bradley, Edward S. George Henry Boker: Poet and Patriot. London:
        Oxford University Press, 1927.

C334.   Brady, James J. Life of Denman Thompson (Joshua Whitcomb). New
        York: E. A. McFarland and Alex. Comstock, 1888.

C335.   Bragdon, Claude F. The Secret Springs. London: A. Dakers, 1938.

C336.   Brahms, Caryl. Gilbert and Sullivan: Lost Chords and Discords.
        Boston: Little, Brown and Company, 1975.

C337.   Brailsford, Henry N. Voltaire. London: Oxford University Press,
        1935.

C338.   Brainard, Charles H. John Howard Payne. Boston: Cupples, Upham
        and Company, 1885.

C339.   Brambell, Wilfred. All above Board: An Autobiography. London:
        W. H. Allen, 1976.

C340.   Brandes, Georg. Henrik Ibsen: Björnstjerne Björnson. Trans. Jes-
        se Müir and Mary Morison. London: William Heinemann, 1899.

C341.   _____. Reminiscences of My Childhood and Youth. New
        York: Arno Press, 1975 [1906].

C342.   Brando, Anna K. and E. P. Stein. Brando for Breakfast. New York:
        Crown Publishers, 1979.

C343.   Brandon-Thomas, Jevan. Charley's Aunt's Father. London: Douglas
        Saunders, 1955.

C344.   Brandreth, Gyles. John Gielgud: A Celebration. Boston: Little,
        Brown and Company, 1984.

C345.   Brasol, Boris. Oscar Wilde: The Man, Artist, and Martyr. New
        York: Charles Scribner's Sons, 1938.

C346.   Braybrooke, Patrick. The Amazing Mr. Noël Coward. London: D.
        Archer, 1933.

C347.   Brée, Germaine. Albert Camus. New York: Columbia University
        Press, 1964 [1959].

C348.   Brereton, Austin. Cyril Maude: A Memoir. London: Eyre and Spot-
        tiswoode, 1914.

C349.   _____. "H. B." and Laurence Irving. London: Grant

Richards, 1922.

C350. Brereton, Austin. Henry Irving: A Biographical Sketch. London: D. Bogne, 1883.

C351. _____. The Lyceum and Henry Irving. New York: Mc-Clure, Phillips and Company, 1903.

C352. _____. Sir Henry Irving. London: Treherne, 1905.

C353. Brereton, Geoffrey. Jean Racine: A Critical Biography. London: Cassell, 1951.

C354. Brewster, Dorothy. Aaron Hill: Poet, Dramatist, Projector. New York: Columbia University Press, 1913.

C355. Brian, Dennis. Tallulah, Darling: A Biography of Tallulah Bankhead. New York: The Macmillan Company, 1980.

C356. Bridel, Oscar. Pirandello. London: Bowes, 1969 [1966].

C357. Bridges-Adams, W. The Lost Leader [Harley Granville Barker]. London: Sidgwick and Jackson, 1954.

C358. Bridie, James. One Way of Living. London: Constable, 1939.

C359. Brink, Carol R. Harps in the Wind: The Story of the Singing Hutchinsons. New York: The Macmillan Company, 1947.

C360. Brinkley, Robert F. Nathan Field, the Actor-Playwright. New Haven: Yale University Press, 1928.

C361. Broadbent, R. J. Elizabeth Farren, Countess of Derby. Edinburgh: J. Ballantyne, Hanson, and Company, 1910.

C362. _____. Stage Whispers. London: Simpson, Marshall, Hamilton, Kent, 1901.

C363. Brogna, John J. "Michael Gold: Critic and Playwright." Unpublished doctoral dissertation, University of Georgia, 1982.

C364. Bronson Howard: In Memoriam. New York: Marion Press, 1910.

C365. Brookfield, Charles H. E. Random Reminiscences. London: E. Arnold, 1902.

C366. Brooks, John L. "Alexander Brome: His Life and Works." Unpublished doctoral dissertation, Harvard University, 1934.

C367. Brough, Jean Webster. Prompt Copy: The Brough Story. London: Hutchinson and Company, 1952.

C368. Brougham, John. Life, Stories, and Poems of John Brougham. Ed. William Winter. Boston: J. R. Osgood, 1881.

C369. Brouse, Albert J. "Charles Reade, Dramatist." Unpublished doctoral dissertation, Case Western Reserve University, 1956.

C370. Browder, Clifford. André Breton: Arbiter of Surrealism. Geneva: Droz, 1967.

C371. Brown, Alice. Mercy Warren. New York: Charles Scribner's Sons, 1896.

C372. Brown, Catherine H. Letters to Mary [about Helen Hayes]. New York: Random House, 1940.

C373. Brown, Frank C. Elkanah Settle: His Life and Works. Chicago: University of Chicago Press, 1910.

C374. Brown, Frederick. An Impersonation of Angels: A Biography of Jean Cocteau. New York: Viking Press, 1968.

C375. Brown, Frederick J. A Sketch of the Life of Dr. James McHenry. Baltimore: J. Murphy, 1877.

C376. Brown, Ivor J. C. Shakespeare. Garden City, N. Y.: Doubleday and Company, 1949.

C377. _____. The Way of the World. London: Collins, 1954.

C378. Brown, Joe E. and Ralph Hancock. Laughter Is a Wonderful Thing. New York: Barnes, 1956.

C379. Brown, John Mason. The Ordeal of a Playwright: Robert E. Sherwood and the Challenge of War. New York: Harper and Row, 1970.

C380. _____. The Worlds of Robert E. Sherwood: Mirror to His Times, 1896-1939. New York: Harper and Row, 1965.

C381. Brown, Maria W. The Life of Dan Rice. Long Branch, N. J.: privately printed, 1901.

C382. Brown, Tom. The Life of the Late Famous Comedian, Jo Hayns. London: J. Nutt, 1701.

C383. Browne, Edith A. W. S. Gilbert. New York: John Lane Company, 1907.

C384. Browne, Elliott M. and Henzie Raeburn. Two in One. Cambridge: Cambridge University Press, 1981.

C385. Browne, Maurice. Too Late to Lament: An Autobiography. London: Victor Gollancz, 1955.

C386. Bruford, Walter H. Anton Chekhov. London: Bowes and Bowes, 1957.

C387. Brustein, Robert. Making Scenes: A Personal History of the Turbulent Years at Yale, 1966-1979. New York: Random House, 1981.

C388. Bryan, George B. Ethelwold and Medieval Music-Drama at Winchester: The Easter Play, Its Author, and Its Milieu. European University Studies, Ser. XXX, Vol. 10. Bern: Peter Lang, 1981.

C389.   Bryant, Billy. Children of Ol' Man River: The Life and Times of a Show-Boat Trouper. New York: L. Furman, 1936.

C390.   Buchanan-Taylor, W. One More Shake. London: Heath, Cranton, 1944.

C391.   _____. Shake It Again. London: Heath, Cranton, 1943.

C392.   _____. Shake the Bottle. London: Heath, Cranton, 1942.

C393.   Buckle, Richard, ed. Katherine Dunham: Her Dancers, Singers, Musicians. London: Ballet Publications, 1949.

C394.   Bull, Peter. I Know the Face, But.... London: Peter Davies, 1959.

C395.   _____. I Say, Look Here!: The Rather Random Reminiscences of a Round Actor in the Square. London: Peter Davies, 1965.

C396.   Bulliet, Clarence J. Robert Mantell's Romance. Boston: J. W. Luce, 1910.

C397.   Bulman, Joan. Jenny Lind: A Biography. London: J. Barrie, 1956.

C398.   Bunn, Alfred. The Stage: Both Before and Behind the Curtain. London: Richard Bentley, 1840.

C399.   Burbank, Rex. Thornton Wilder. New York: Twayne Publishers, 1961.

C400.   Burke, Billie and Cameron Shipp. With a Feather on My Nose. New York: Appleton-Century-Crofts, 1949.

C401.   _____. With Powder on My Nose. New York: Coward-McCann, 1959.

C402.   Burke, John. Duet in Diamonds: The Saga of Diamond Jim Brady and Lillian Russell. New York: G. P. Putnam's Sons, 1972.

C403.   Burnand, Francis C. Records and Reminiscences, Personal and General, 2 vols. London: Methuen, 1904.

C404.   Burns, George. Living It Up: or They Still Love Me in Altoona! New York: G. P. Putnam's Sons, 1976.

C405.   Burns, Wayne. Charles Reade: A Study in Victorian Authorship. New York: Bookman Associates, 1961.

C406.   Burroughs, Patricia L. "The Career of Jed Harris in New York, 1925-1956." Unpublished doctoral dissertation, Louisiana State University, 1978.

C407.   Burrows, Abe. Honest Abe: Is There Really No Business Like Show
        Business? Boston: Little, Brown, and Company, 1980.

C408.   Burton, Belle. A Simple Life. Great Neck, N. Y.: Todd and Honey-
        well, 1981.

C409.   Burton, Percy and Lowell Thomas. Adventures among Immortals:
        Percy Burton--Impresario. New York: Dodd, Mead and Company,
        1937.

C410.   Burton, Philip. Early Doors: My Life and the Theatre. New York:
        Dial Press, 1969.

C411.   Byng, Douglas. As You Were: Reminiscences. London: Duckworth,
        1970.

C412.   Cady, Edwin H. The Realist at War: The Mature Years, 1885-1920,
        of William Dean Howells. Syracuse, N. Y.: Syracuse University
        Press, 1958.

C413.   _____. The Road to Realism: The Early Years, 1837-1885,
        of William Dean Howells. Syracuse, N. Y.: Syracuse University
        Press, 1956.

C414.   Cagney, James. Cagney by Cagney. Garden City, N. Y.: Doubleday
        and Company, 1976.

C415.   Cahn, William. Good Night, Mrs. Calabash: The Secret of Jimmy
        Durante. New York: Duell, Sloan, and Pearce, 1963.

C416.   Caine, Thomas H. Hall. My Story. London: William Heinemann,
        1908.

C417.   Calthrop, Dion C. My Own Trumpet: Being the Story of My Life.
        London: Hutchinson and Company, 1935.

C418.   Calvert, Adelaide. Sixty-Eight Years on the Stage. London: Mills
        and Boon, 1911.

C419.   Calvert, Louis. Problems of the Actor. New York: Henry Holt and
        Company, 1918.

C420.   Calvert, Walter. Souvenir of Miss Ellen Terry. London: H. J.
        Drane, 1897.

C421.   _____. Souvenir of Sir Henry Irving. London: H. J.
        Drane, 1895.

C422.   Cameron, James. Point of Departure: Experiment in Biography.
        London: Barker, 1967.

C423.   Campbell, Beatrice Stella. My Life and Some Letters. New York:
        Dodd, Mead and Company, 1922.

C424.   Campbell, Charles, ed. Some Materials to Serve for a Brief Memoir of John Daly Burk. Albany, N. Y.: J. Munsell, 1868.

C425. Campbell, G. A. Strindberg. London: Duckworth, 1933.

C426. Campbell, Thomas. Life of Mrs. [Sarah] Siddons, 2 vols. London:
E. Wilson, 1834.

C427. The Candidate [Jimmy Durante]. New York: Simon and Schuster,
1952.

C428. Canning, Beverly E. "Henry Taylor Parker: Drama Critic." Unpublished doctoral dissertation, University of Michigan, 1960.

C429. Cantor, Eddie. Caught Short: A Saga of Wailing Wall Street. New
York: Simon and Schuster, 1929.

C430. _____ and David Freedman. My Life Is in Your Hands. New
York: Harper and Brothers, 1928.

C431. _____ and Jane Kesner. Take My Life. Garden City, N. Y.:
Doubleday and Company, 1957.

C432. _____. The Way I See It. Englewood Cliffs, N. J.: Prentice-Hall, 1959.

C433. _____ and David Freedman. Ziegfeld, the Great Glorifier.
New York: A. H. King, 1934.

C434. Capper, Alfred O. Rambler's Recollections. London: G. Allen and
Unwin, 1915.

C435. Caputi, Anthony F. John Marston, Satirist. Ithaca, N. Y.: Cornell University Press, 1961.

C436. Cardus, Neville. Autobiography. London: Collins, 1947.

C437. Carey, Gary. Judy Holliday: An Intimate Life. New York: Seaview
Books, 1982.

C438. Carhart, M. S. The Life and Works of Joanna Baillie. New Haven,
Conn.: Yale University Press, 1923.

C439. Carlyle, Thomas. Life of Friedrich Schiller. London: Taylor and
Hessey, 1825.

C440. Carmichael, Ian. Will the Real Ian Carmichael...: An Autobiography. London: The Macmillan Company, 1979.

C441. Carpenter, Humphrey. W. H. Auden, Biography. Boston: Houghton
Mifflin, 1981.

C442. Carr, Alice Comyns. Mrs. J. Comyns Carr's Reminiscences. Ed. Eve
Adam. London: Hutchinson and Company, 1926.

C443. Carson, William G. B. Dear Josephine [Hull]. Norman: University
of Oklahoma Press, 1963.

C444. Carstairs, John P. "Bunch": A Biography of Nelson Keys. London:
       Hurst and Blackett, 1941.

C445. Carter, Everett. Howells and the Age of Realism. Philadelphia:
       J. B. Lippincott, 1954.

C446. Carter, Huntly. The Theatre of Max Reinhardt. London: F. and C.
       Palmer, 1914.

C447. Carter, Jacob. My Drunken Life. Boston: privately printed,
       1848.

C448. Carter, Randolph. The World of Flo Ziegfeld. New York: Praeger,
       1974.

C449. Caskey, John H. The Life and Works of Edward Moore. New Haven,
       Conn.: Yale University Press, 1927.

C450. Casson, John. Lewis [Casson] and Sybil [Thorndike]: A Memoir.
       London: Collins, 1972.

C451. Castle, Charles. Noël [Coward]. London: W. H. Allen, 1972.

C452. Castle, Irene. My Husband [Vernon Castle]. New York: Charles
       Scribner's Sons, 1919.

C453. Cave, Joseph A. A Jubilee of Dramatic Life and Incident. Ed.
       Robert Soutar. London: T. Vernon, 1894.

C454. Cecil, David. Max [Beerbohm]: A Biography. London: Constable,
       1964.

C455. Cellier, François and Cunningham Bridgman. Gilbert, Sullivan,
       and D'Oyly Carte: Reminiscences of the Savoy and the Savoy-
       ards. London: Pitman, 1914.

C456. Centlivre, Susanna. Works, with a New Account of Her Life, 3
       vols. London: J. Knapton, 1760-61.

C457. Chambers, Edmund K. Sir Henry Lee: An Elizabethan Portrait. Lon-
       don: Oxford University Press, 1936.

C458. _____. William Shakespeare: A Study of Facts and
       Problems, 2 vols. Oxford: Clarendon Press, 1930.

C459. Chambers, Jessie. D. H. Lawrence: A Personal Record, 2 vols. New
       York: Barnes and Noble, 1965.

C460. Chaplin, Charles S. Charlie Chaplin's Own Story. Indianapolis:
       Bobbs-Merrill, 1916.

C461. _____. My Autobiography. London: Bodley Head, 1964.

C462. Chapman, Graham. A Liar's Autobiography. London: Methuen, 1981.

C463. Chapman, Hester W. Great Villiers: A Study of George Villiers,

Second Duke of Buckingham. London: Secker and Warburg, 1949.

C464. Chapman, Percy A. The Spirit of Molière. London: H. Milford, 1940.

C465. Charters, Ann and Samuel. I Love: The Story of Vladimir Mayakovsky and Lili Brik. London: Deutsch, 1979.

C466. _____. Nobody: The Story of Bert Williams. New York: The Macmillan Company, 1970.

C467. Chase, Ilka. The Carthagenian Rose. Garden City, N. Y.: Doubleday and Company, 1961.

C468. _____. Free Admission. Garden City, N. Y.: Doubleday and Company, 1948.

C469. _____. Past Imperfect. Garden City, New York: Doubleday and Company, 1942.

C470. Chatfield-Taylor, H. C. Goldoni: A Biography. London: Chatto and Windus, 1914.

C471. _____. Molière: A Biography. New York: Duffield, 1906.

C472. Chekhov, Anton. The Life and Letters of Anton Chekhov. Trans. S. S. Koteliansky and Philip Tomlinson. New York: George B. Doran, 1925.

C473. _____. Literary and Theatrical Reminiscences. Trans. and ed. S. S. Koteliansky. London: Routledge, 1927.

C474. Cherkasov, Nikolai. Notes of a Soviet Actor. Moscow: Foreign Languages Publishing House, 1955.

C475. Chester, Alan G. "Thomas May: Man of Letters." Unpublished doctoral dissertation, University of Pennsylvania, 1932.

C476. Chesterton, Gilbert K. George Bernard Shaw. London: John Lane, 1909.

C477. Chetwood, William Rufus, ed. Memoirs of the Life and Writings of [Ben] Jonson. Dublin: W. R. Chetwood, 1756.

C478. Chevalier, Albert and Brian Daly. Albert Chevalier: A Record by Himself. London: J. Macqueen, 1895.

C479. _____. Before I Forget: The Autobiography of a Chevalier d'Industrie. London: T. F. Unwin, 1901.

C480. Chevalier, Maurice. Bravo, Maurice! London: Allen and Unwin, 1973.

C481. _____. I Remember It Well. New York: The Macmillan Company, 1970.

C482.   Chevalier, Maurice. The Man in the Straw Hat: My Story. New York: Thomas Y. Crowell, 1949.

C483.   _____. With Love. Boston: Little, Brown, and Company, 1960.

C484.   Child, Harold H. A Poor Player: The Story of a Failure. Cambridge: Cambridge University Press, 1939.

C485.   Chiles, Rosa P. John Howard Payne: American Poet, Actor, Playwright, Consul, and the Author of "Home, Sweet Home." Washington, D. C.: W. F. Roberts, 1930.

C486.   Chorley, Henry F. Autobiography, Memoirs and Letters, 2 vols. Ed. Henry G. Hewlett. London: Richard Bentley, 1873.

C487.   Christopher, Milbourne. Houdini: The Untold Story. New York: Thomas Y. Crowell, 1969.

C488.   Churchill, Sarah. Keep on Dancing. Ed. Paul Medlicott. New York: Coward-McCann, 1981.

C489.   _____. A Thread in the Tapestry. New York: Dodd, Mead and Company, 1967.

C490.   Chute, Marchette. Ben Jonson of Westminster. London: Robert Hale, 1954.

C491.   _____. Shakespeare of London. New York: E. P. Dutton, 1949.

C492.   Cibber, Colley. An Apology for the Life of Mr. Colley Cibber. Dublin: G. Faulkner, 1740.

C493.   Cibber, Theophilus. Life and Character of That Excellent Actor, Barton Booth, Esq. London: n. p., 1753.

C494.   Cima, Mary G. "Elizabeth Robins: Ibsen Actress-Manageress." Unpublished doctoral dissertation, Cornell University, 1978.

C495.   Clapp, Henry Austin. Reminiscences of a Dramatic Critic. Boston: Houghton Mifflin, 1902.

C496.   Clarence, Oliver B. No Complaints. London: Jonathan Cape, 1943.

C497.   Clark, Alexander F. B. Jean Racine. Cambridge: Harvard University Press, 1939.

C498.   Clark, Arthur M. Thomas Heywood: Playwright and Miscellanist. Oxford: Basil Blackwell, 1931.

C499.   Clark, Barrett H. Eugene O'Neill: The Man and His Plays. New York: McBride, 1933.

C500.   Clark, David M. "John Corbin: Dramatic Critic." Unpublished doctoral dissertation, University of Nebraska, 1976.

C501.   Clark, Mary Ellen M. Maeterlinck: Poet and Philosopher. London:
        G. Allen and Unwin, 1915.

C502.   Clark, Susie C. John McCullough as Man, Actor, and Spirit. Bos-
        ton: Murray and Emery, 1905.

C503.   Clarke, Asia Booth. Booth Memorials: Passages, Incidents and
        Anecdotes in the Life of Junius Brutus Booth. New York: Carle-
        ton, 1866.

C504.   _____. The Elder and the Younger Booth. Boston:
        J. R. Osgood, 1882.

C505.   _____. The Unlocked Book: A Memoir of John Wilkes
        Booth. London: Faber and Faber, 1938.

C506.   Clarke, Joseph I. C. My Life and Memories. New York: Dodd, Mead
        and Company, 1925.

C507.   Claus, Horst. The Theatre Director Otto Brahm. Ann Arbor, Mich.:
        UMI Research Press, 1982.

C508.   Clement, Clara E. Charlotte Cushman. Boston: J. R. Osgood, 1882.

C509.   Clurman, Harold. All People Are Famous (Instead of an Autobio-
        graphy). New York: Harcourt, Brace and Company, 1974.

C510.   Cleugh, James. Charles Blake Cochran: Lord Bountiful. London:
        Pallas Publishing Company, 1938.

C511.   Coad, Oral S. William Dunlap: A Study of His Life and Works and
        of His Place in Contemporary Culture. New York: Dunlap Socie-
        ty, 1917.

C512.   Coats, Robert H. John Galsworthy as a Dramatic Artist. London:
        Duckworth, 1926.

C513.   Cochran, Charles B. Cock-a-Doodle-Do. London: J. M. Dent, 1941.

C514.   _____. I Had Almost Forgotten. London: Hutchinson
        and Company, 1932.

C515.   _____. Secrets of a Showman. London: William Heine-
        mann, 1925,

C516.   _____. Showman Looks On. London: J. M. Dent, 1945.

C517.   Cocroft, Thoda. Great Names and How They Are Made. Chicago:
        Dartnell, 1941.

C518.   Cocteau, Jean. Professional Secrets: An Autobiography. New York:
        Farrar, Strauss, and Giroux, 1970.

C519.   Cody, William F. The Life of Hon. William F. Cody, Known as Buf-
        falo Bill, the Famous Hunter, Scout, and Guide. Hartford,
        Conn.: F. E. Bliss, 1879.

C520. Coffin, Charles Hayden. <u>Hayden Coffin's Book, Packed with Acts</u>
<u>and Facts</u>. London: Alston Rivers, 1930.

C521. Cohan, George M. <u>Twenty Years on Broadway and the Years It Took</u>
<u>to Get There</u>. New York: Harper and Company, 1925.

C522. Cohen, Robert C. <u>Giraudoux: Three Faces of Destiny</u>. Chicago: University of Chicago Press, 1969.

C523. Cohn, Art. <u>The Joker [Joe E. Lewis] Is Wild</u>. New York: Random
House, 1955.

C524. _____. <u>The Nine Lives of Michael Todd</u>. New York: Random
House, 1958.

C525. Colbourne, Maurice. <u>The Real Bernard Shaw</u>. London: J. R. Dent,
1949.

C526. Cole, John W. <u>The Life and Theatrical Times of Charles Kean</u>, 2
vols. London: Richard Bentley, 1859.

C527. Cole, Marion. <u>Fogie: The Life of Elsie Fogerty, C. B. E.</u> London:
Peter Davies, 1967.

C528. Coleman, Arthur P. and Marion M. <u>Wanderers Twain: Modjeska and</u>
<u>Sienkiewicz</u>. Cheshire, Conn.: Cherry Hill Press, 1964.

C529. Coleman, John. <u>Charles Reade as I Knew Him</u>. London: Treherne and
Company, 1903.

C530. _____. <u>Fifty Years of an Actor's Life</u>, 2 vols. London:
Hutchinson and Company, 1904.

C531. _____ and Edward. <u>Memoirs of Samuel Phelps</u>. London: Remington and Company, 1886.

C532. _____. <u>Players and Playwrights I Have Known</u>, 2 vols.
London: Chatto and Windus, 1888.

C533. Coleman, Marion M. <u>Fair Rosalind: The American Career of Helena</u>
<u>Modjeska</u>. Cheshire, Conn.: Cherry Hill Books, 1969.

C534. Collier, Constance. <u>Harlequinade: The Story of My Life</u>. London:
John Lane, 1929.

C535. Collier, John Payne. <u>Memoirs of Edward Alleyn, Founder of Dul-</u>
<u>wich College</u>. London: Shakespeare Society, 1841.

C536. _____. <u>An Old Man's Diary, Forty Years Ago (For</u>
<u>the First Six Months of 1832)</u>. London: Thomas Richards, 1871.

C537. Collins, Herbert F. <u>Talma: A Biography of an Actor</u>. New York:
Hill and Wang, 1964.

C538. Collins, Horace F. <u>My Best Riches: Story of a Stone Rolling</u>
<u>Round the World and the Stage</u>. London: Eyre and Spottiswoode,

1941.

C539. Collins, José. The Maid of the Mountains, Her Story: The Remi-
       niscences of José Collins. London: Hutchinson and Company,
       1932.

C540. Colman, George (the Younger). Random Records, 2 vols. London:
       H. Colburn and R. Bentley, 1830.

C541. Colman, Juliet B. Ronald Colman: A Very Private Person. New
       York: William Morrow, 1975.

C542. Colum, Mary M. Our Friend James Joyce. Garden City, N. Y.: Dou-
       bleday and Company, 1958.

C543. Combe, William. The Life of Arthur Murphy. London: J. Faulder,
       1811.

C544. Compton, Fay. Rosemary: Some Remembrances. London: Alston Riv-
       ers, 1926.

C545. Congreve, Francis A. Authentic Memoirs of the Late Mr. Charles
       Macklin. London: J. Barker, 1798.

C546. Connell, Charles. They Gave Us Shakespeare: John Heminge and
       Henry Condell. London: Routledge and Kegan Paul, 1982.

C547. Connelly, Marc. Voices Offstage: A Book of Memoirs. New York:
       Holt, Rinehart and Winston, 1968.

C548. Connely, Willard. Sir Richard Steele. London: Charles Scribner's
       Sons, 1934.

C549. _____. Young George Farquhar: A Restoration Drama at
       Twilight. London: Cassell, 1949.

C550. Conrad, Earl. Billy Rose: Manhattan Primitive. Cleveland, Oh.:
       World Publishing Company, 1968.

C551. Conrad, John. Joseph Conrad: Times Remembered. New York: Cam-
       bridge University Press, 1981.

C552. Constanduros, Mabel T. Shreds and Patches. London: Lawson and
       Dunn, 1946.

C553. Constantini, Angelo. The Birth, Life and Death of Scaramouch.
       Trans. C. W. Beaumont. London: C. W. Beaumont, 1924.

C554. Cook, Doris E. Sherlock Holmes and Much More: or Some of the
       Facts about William Gillette. Hartford: Connecticut Historical
       Society, 1970.

C555. Cook, Gary D. "David Warfield: A Theatrical Biography." Unpub-
       lished doctoral dissertation, University of Nebraska, 1975.

C556. Cook, Mabel C. The Story of Helena Modjeska. London: W. H. Allen and Company, 1883.

C557.   Cook, R. A. Fire from the Flint: The Amazing Career of Thomas
        Dixon. Winston-Salem, N. C.: John F. Blair, 1968.

C558.   Cook, Theodore A. and Guy Nickolls. Thomas Doggett, Deceased: A
        Famous Comedian. London: A. Constable, 1908.

C559.   Cooke, William. Memoirs of Charles Macklin. London: J. Asperne,
        1804.

C560.   _____. Memoirs of Samuel Foote, 3 vols. London: R.
        Phillips, 1805.

C561.   Cooper, Charles W. "John Lacy, the Comedian: A Study in the Ear-
        ly Restoration Theatrical Tradition." Unpublished doctoral
        dissertation, University of California, 1931.

C562.   Cooper, Diana Manners. The Light of Common Day. London: Rupert
        Hart-Davis, 1959.

C563.   _____. The Rainbow Comes and Goes. London:
        Rupert Hart-Davis, 1958.

C564.   _____. Trumpets from the Steep. Boston: Houghton
        Mifflin, 1960.

C565.   _____. You'll Never Be Bored. London: Hammond,
        Hammond and Company, 1965.

C566.   Cooper, Gladys. Gladys Cooper: An Autobiography. London: Hutch-
        inson and Company, 1931.

C567.   Copeland, Charles T. Edwin Booth. Boston: Small, Maynard and
        Company, 1901.

C568.   Corbett, James J. The Roar of the Crowd: The True Tale of the
        Rise and Fall of a Champion. New York: G. P. Putnam's Sons,
        1925.

C569.   Cordell, Richard A. Henry Arthur Jones and the Modern Drama. New
        York: R. Long and R. R. Smith, 1932.

C570.   _____. Somerset Maugham: A Biographical and Criti-
        cal Study, 2d ed. Bloomington: Indiana University Press, 1969.

C571.   Corin. The Truth about the Stage. London: Wyman and Sons, 1885.

C572.   Corliss, Lamont. Remembering John Masefield. Rutherford, N. J.:
        Farleigh Dickinson University Press, 1978.

C573.   Cornell, Katharine and Ruth W. Sedgwick. I Wanted to Be an Ac-
        tress: The Autobiography of Katharine Cornell. New York: Ran-
        dom House, 1939.

C574.   Cornish, Nellie C. Miss Aunt Nellie: The Autobiography of Nellie

C. Cornish. Ed. Ellen Van Volkenburg Browne and Edward N. Beck. Seattle: University of Washington Press, 1964.

C575.   Cortez, Jerry V. "Fanny Janauschek: America's Last Queen of Tragedy." Unpublished doctoral dissertation, University of Illinois, 1973.

C576.   Cosgrave, Luke. Theatre Tonight. Hollywood, Cal.: House-Warren, 1952.

C577.   Costello, Peter. James Joyce. Dublin: Gill and Macmillan, 1980.

C578.   Cottrell, John. Laurence Olivier. Englewood Cliffs, N. J.: Prentice-Hall, 1975.

C579.   _____ and Fergus Cashin. Richard Burton: A Biography: London: Coronet, 1974.

C580.   Courthope, William John. Addison. English Men of Letters Series. London: The Macmillan Company, 1884.

C581.   Courtneidge, Cicely. Cicely. London: Hutchinson and Company, 1953.

C582.   Courtneidge, Robert. I Was an Actor Once. London: Hutchinson and Company, 1930.

C583.   Courtney, Marguerite. Laurette [Taylor]. New York: Rinehart Publishing Company, 1955.

C584.   Coward, Noël. Present Indicative. Garden City, N. Y.: Doubleday, Doran and Company, 1937.

C585.   _____. Future Indefinite. Garden City, N. Y.: Doubleday and Company, 1954.

C586.   _____. The Noël Coward Diaries. Ed. Graham Payn and Sheridan Morley. London: Weidenfeld and Nicolson, 1982.

C587.   Cowasjee, Saros. Sean O'Casey: The Man behind the Plays. New York: St. Martin's, 1964.

C588.   Cowell, Joseph L. Thirty Years Passed among the Players of England and America. New York: Harper and Company, 1843.

C589.   Cowie, Peter. Ingmar Bergman: A Critical Biography. New York: Charles Scribner's Sons, 1982.

C590.   Cox, Kenneth D. "Nat Goodwin: A Theatrical Biography." Unpublished doctoral dissertation, University of Nebraska, 1975.

C591.   Craig, Edward. Gordon Craig: The Story of His Life. New York: Alfred A. Knopf, 1968.

C592.   Craig, Edward Gordon. Ellen Terry and Her Secret Self. New York: E. P. Dutton, 1932.

C593.   Craig, Edward Gordon. Henry Irving. New York: Longmans, Green
        and Company, 1930.

C594.   _____. Index to The Story of My Days. London:
        Hulton Press, 1957.

C595.   Cran, Mrs. George. Herbert Beerbohm Tree. London: John Lane,
        1907.

C596.   Crane, Harvey. Playbill: A History of the Theatre in the West
        Country. Plymouth: MacDonals and Evans, 1980.

C597.   Crane, William H. Footprints and Echoes. New York: E. P. Dutton,
        1927.

C598.   Crauford, Alfred L. Sam and Sallie: A Romance of the Stage.
        London: Cranley and Day, 1933.

C599.   Crauford, Russell. The Ramblings of an Old Mummer. London:
        Greening, 1909.

C600.   Craven, Elizabeth B. Memoirs of the Margravine of Anspach, 2
        vols. London: Henry Colburn, 1826.

C601.   Crawford, Cheryl. One Naked Individual: My Fifty Years in the
        Theatre. Indianapolis: Bobbs-Merrill, 1977.

C602.   Crawford, Elisabeth R. "Alfred Kerr, a Critic of the Drama." Un-
        published doctoral dissertation, Yale University, 1938.

C603.   Creahan, John. The Life of Laura Keene: Actress, Artist, Man-
        ager, and Scholar. Philadelphia: Rodgers, 1897.

C604.   Cremer, Robert. Lugosi: The Man behind the Cape. Chicago: Henry
        Regnery, 1976.

C605.   Cressy, Will M. Continuous Vaudeville. Boston: R. G. Badger,
        1914.

C606.   Creswick, William. An Autobiography: A Record of Fifty Years of
        the Professional Life of the Late William Creswick. London: J.
        Henderson, 1885.

C607.   Crichton, Kyle. The Marx Brothers. Garden City, N. Y.: Doubleday
        and Company, 1950.

C608.   Crocker, Lester G. Diderot: The Embattled Philosopher. Rev. ed.
        New York: Free Press, 1966.

C609.   Croft-Cooke, Rupert and W. S. Meadmore. Buffalo Bill: The Le-
        gend, the Man of Action, the Showman. London: Sidgwick and
        Jackson, 1952.

C610.   Crosland, Margaret. Jean Cocteau. London: P. Nevill, 1955.

C611.   Cross, Wilbur L. The History of Henry Fielding, 3 vols. New

Haven, Conn.: Yale University Press, 1918.

C612. Croxton, Arthur. Crowded Nights and Days: An Unconventional Pageant. London: S. Low, Marston and Company, 1931.

C613. Croy, Homer. Country Cured. New York: Harper and Company, 1943.

C614. _____. Our Will Rogers. New York: Duell, Sloan and Pearce, 1953.

C615. Cruickshank, Alfred H. Philip Massinger. Oxford: Basil Blackwell, 1920.

C616. Cruickshank, Joseph. Montherlant. Edinburgh: Oliver and Boyd, 1964.

C617. Cullman, Marguerite. Occupation: Angel. New York: W. W. Norton, 1963.

C618. Culver, Roland. Not Quite a Gentleman. London: Kimber, 1979.

C619. Cumberland, Richard. Memoirs. New York: D. and C. Bruce, 1800.

C620. _____. Memoirs: Supplement and Index. Boston: D. Carlisle, 1806.

C621. Cunningham, Peter. The Story of Nell Gwyn and the Sayings of Charles the Second. London: Bradbury and Evans, 1852.

C622. Curll, Edmund. The Life of Mr. John Dennis, the Renowned Critick. London: J. Roberts, 1734.

C623. _____. Life of Mr. John Gay. London: Edmund Curll, 1733.

C624. _____. The Life of That Eminent Comedian, Robert Wilks. London: Edmund Curll, 1733.

C625. Curran, C. P. James Joyce Remembered. New York: Oxford University Press, 1968.

C626. Curry, Wade C. "Steele Mackaye, Producer and Director." Unpublished doctoral dissertation, University of Illinois, 1958.

C627. Curtin, Robert G. Edgar Wallace--Each Way. London: John Long, 1932.

C628. Curtis, Anthony. The Patter of [W. Somerset] Maugham: A Critical Portrait. London: Hamish Hamilton, 1974.

C629. Curtis, James. Between Flops: A Biography of Preston Sturges. New York: Harcourt-Brace-Jovanovich, 1982.

C630. Dale, Alzina S. The Outline of Sanity: A Biography of G. K. Chesterton. Grand Rapids, Mich.: Eerdmans, 1982.

C631. Dale, James L. _Pulling Faces for a Living_. London: Victor Gol-
       lancz, 1970.

C632. Dalrymple, Jean. _From the Last Row_. Clifton, N. J.: James T.
       White, 1975.

C633. _____. _September Child: The Story of Jean Dalrymple_.
       New York: Dodd, Mead and Company, 1963.

C634. Dalsème, René. _Beaumarchais, 1732-1799_. Trans. Hannaford Ben-
       nett. New York: G. P. Putnam's Sons, 1929.

C635. Daly, Augustin. _Woffington: A Tribute to the Actress and the Wo-
       man_. Philadelphia: Globe Printing House, 1888.

C636. Daly, Joseph F. _The Life of Augustin Daly_. New York: The Macmil-
       lan Company, 1917.

C637. Daniel, George. _Garrick in the Green Room!_ London: Southgate,
       1829.

C638. Daniels, Robert L. _Laurence Olivier: Theater and Cinema_. San Di-
       ego, Cal.: A. S. Barnes, 1980.

C639. Darbyshire, Alfred. _An Architect's Experiences: Professional,
       Artistic, and Theatrical_. Manchester: J. E. Cornish, 1897.

C640. Dardis, Tom. _Keaton: The Man Who WOuldn't Lie Down_. New York:
       Charles Scribner's Sons, 1979.

C641. Dare, Phyllis. _From School to Stage_. London: Collier, 1907.

C642. Dark, Sidney and Rowland Grey. _W. S. Gilbert: His Life and
       Works_. London: Methuen and Company, 1923.

C643. Darlington, William A. _I Do What I Like_. London: MacDonald,
       1947.

C644. _____. _J. M. Barrie_. London: Blackie and Son,
       1938.

C645. _____. _Laurence Olivier_. London: Morgan Grampian
       Books, 1968.

C646. _____. _Sheridan_. London: Longmans, Green and
       Company, 1951.

C647. _____. _6001 Nights: Forty Years a Critic_.
       London: G. G. Harrap, 1960.

C648. _____. _The World of Gilbert and Sullivan_. New
       York: Thomas Y. Crowell, 1950.

C649. Darlow, Michael and Gillian Hodson. _Terence Rattigan: The Man
       and His Work_. London: Quartet Books, 1979.

C650.   Darton, Frederick J. H.   J. M. Barrie. London: Nisbet and Company, 1929.

C651.   Dasent, Arthur I.   Nell Gwynne, 1650-87.   London: Macmillan and Company, 1924.

C652.   Datas.   Datas: The Memory Man.   London: Wright and Brown, 1932.

C653.   Daubeny, Peter. Stage by Stage. London: John Murray, 1952.

C654.   Daughrity, Kenneth L. "The Life and Work of Nathaniel Parker Willis." Unpublished doctoral dissertation, University of Virginia, 1934.

C655.   D'Auvergne, Edmund. Lola Montez: Adventuress of the 'Forties. New York: Brentano's, 1924.

C656.   David, Lester and Jhan Robbins. Richard [Burton] and Elizabeth [Taylor]. New York: Funk and Wagnalls, 1977.

C657.   Davidge, William P. Footlight Flasher. New York: American News Company, 1866.

C658.   Davidson, Arthur F. Alexandre Dumas, père: His Life and Works. Philadelphia: J. B. Lippincott, 1902.

C659.   Davies, Acton. Maude Adams. New York: Frederick A. Stokes, 1901.

C660.   Davies, Thomas. A Genuine Narrative of the Life and Theatrical Transactions of Mr. John Henderson, Commonly Called the Bath Roscius. London: T. Evans, 1777.

C661.   _____. Memoirs of the Life of David Garrick, 2 vols. Dublin: J. Hill, 1780.

C662.   _____. Some Account of the Life and Writings of Philip Massinger. London: Thomas Davies, 1789.

C663.   Davis, Bette. The Lonely Life: An Autobiography. New York: E. P. Dutton, 1962.

C664.   Davis, Charles B., ed. The Adventures and Letters of Richard Harding Davis. New York: Charles Scribner's Sons, 1917.

C665.   Davis, Esmé. Esmé of Paris. New York: Appleton-Century-Crofts, 1944.

C666.   Davis, Nuel Pharr. Life of Wilkie Collins. Urbana: University of Illinois Press, 1956.

C667.   Davis, Owen. I'd Like to Do It Again. New York: Farrar and Rinehart, 1931.

C668.   _____. My First Fifty Years in the Theatre. Boston: Walter H. Baker, 1950.

C669. Davis, Richard Beale. George Sandys, Poet-Adventurer. London:
       Bodley Head, 1955.

C670. Dawson, Giles E. The Life of William Shakespeare. Ithaca, N. Y.:
       Cornell University Press, 1963.

C671. Dawson, James. The Autobiography of James Dawson. Truro: J. R.
       Netherton, 1865.

C672. Day, William Charles. Behind the Footlights: or The Stage as I
       Knew It. London: Frederick Warne and Company, 1885.

C673. Déak, Frantisek J. "Antonin Artaud, A Critical Biography, 1896-
       1930." Unpublished doctoral dissertation, Carnegie-Mellon Uni-
       versity, 1973.

C674. Deam, William L. "A Biographical Study of Miss Laura Justine
       Bonstelle-Stuart Together with an Evaluation of Her Own Con-
       tributions to the Modern Theatre World." Unpublished doctoral
       dissertation, University of Michigan, 1954.

C675. Dean, Basil. Mind's Eye: An Autobiography, 1927-1972. London:
       Hutchinson and Company, 1973.

C676. _____. Seven Ages. London: Hutchinson and Company, 1970.

C677. De Angelis, Jefferson and Alvin F. Harlow. A Vagabond Trouper.
       New York: Harcourt, Brace and Company, 1931.

C678. Deans, Mickey and Ann Pinchot. Weep No More, My Lady [Judy Gar-
       land]. New York: Hawthorn, 1972.

C679. De Boer, Fredrik E. "George Lillo." Unpublished doctoral disser-
       tation, University of Wisconsin, 1965.

C680. Debusscher, Gilbert. Edward Albee: Tradition and Renewal.
       Trans. Anne D. Williams. Brussels: American Studies Center,
       1967.

C681. De Casseres, Benjamin. Don Marquis. New York: Beyold Press,
       1938.

C682. De Castro, Jacob. The Memoirs of De Castro, Comedian. Ed. R.
       Humphreys. London: Sherwood, Jones and Company, 1824.

C683. De Cordova, Rudolph. Mr. H. B. Irving and Miss Dorothea Baird.
       Parts I Have Played Series. Westminster: Abbey Press, 1909.

C684. _____. Mr. Lewis Waller: A Photographic and De-
       scriptive Biography. Parts I Have Played Series. Westminster:
       Abbey Press, 1909.

C685. _____. Mr. Martin Harvey: A Biography. Parts I
       Have Played Series. Westminster: Abbey Press, 1909.

C686. _____. Mr. Matheson Lang and Miss Hutin Britton.

Parts I Have Played Series. Westminster: Abbey Press, 1909.

C687. De Cordova, Rudolph. A Photographic and Descriptive Biography of Mr. Cyril Maude. Parts I Have Played Series. Westminster: Abbey Press, 1909.

C688. _____. Pure Folly [H. G. Pelissier]. Westminster: Abbey Press, 1909.

C689. De Courville, Albert. I Tell You. London: Chapman and Hall, 1928.

C690. De Fontaine, Felix G. Birds of a Feather Flock Together: or Talks with [Edward A.] Sothern. New York: G. W. Carleton, 1878.

C691. De Freece, Matilda A. Recollections of Vesta Tilley. London: Hutchinson and Company, 1934.

C692. De Korte, Juliann. Ethel Waters: Finally Home. Old Tappan, N. J.: Revell, 1978.

C693. De Koven, Mrs. Reginald. A Musician and His Wife. New York: Harper and Brothers, 1927.

C694. De Leine, M. A. Lilian Adelaide Neilson: A Memorial Sketch, Personal and Critical. London: Newman and Company, 1881.

C695. Dell, Floyd. Homecoming: An Autobiography. New York: Farrar and Rinehart, 1933.

C696. De Mille, Agnes. Dance to the Piper. Boston: Little, Brown and Company, 1952.

C697. _____. Where the Wings Grow. Garden City, N. Y.: Doubleday and Company, 1978.

C698. De Mille, Cecil B. The Autobiography of Cecil B. De Mille. Ed. Donald Hayne. Englewood Cliffs, N. J.: Prentice-Hall, 1959.

C699. De Mott, Josephine. The Circus Lady. New York: Thomas Y. Crowell, 1926.

C700. Dempsey, David and Raymond P. Baldwin. The Triumphs and Trials of Lotta Crabtree. New York: William Morrow, 1968.

C701. Denham, Reginald. Stars in My Hair. London: T. Werner Laurie, 1958.

C702. Dent, Alan, ed. Bernard Shaw and Mrs. Patrick Campbell: Their Correspondence. London: Victor Gollancz, 1952.

C703. _____. Mrs. Patrick Campbell. London: Museum Press, 1961.

C704. _____. Vivien Leigh--A Bouquet. London: Hamish Hamilton, 1969.

C705. Derleth, August W. Still Small Voice: The Biography of Zona
       Gale. New York: Appleton, 1940.

C706. Derwent, Clarence. The Derwent Story. New York: Henry Schuman,
       1953.

C707. Desmond, Florence. Florence Desmond. London: G. G. Harrap, 1953.

C708. De Valois, Ninette. Come Dance with Me. London: Hamish Hamilton,
       1957.

C709. De Wolfe, Elsie. After All. New York: Harper and Brothers, 1935.

C710. Dibdin, Charles. Professional and Literary Memoirs. London:
       Society for Theatre Research, 1956.

C711. Dibdin, Thomas J. The Reminiscences of Thomas Dibdin, of the
       Theatres Royal, Covent-Garden, Drury-Lane, Haymarket, etc.,
       2 vols. London: Henry Colburn, 1827.

C712. Dickens, Charles, ed. Memoirs of Joseph Grimaldi, 2 vols. Lon-
       don: Richard Bentley, 1838.

C713. Dickinson, Donald C. A Bio-Bibliography of Langston Hughes. Ham-
       den, Conn.: Archon Books, 1967.

C714. Dier, Caroline. The Lady of the Gardens: Mary Elitch Long. Hol-
       lywood, Cal.: Hollycrofters, 1932.

C715. Diers, Herman H. "Fritz Leiber: Actor and Producer of Shake-
       speare." Unpublished doctoral dissertation, University of Il-
       linois, 1965.

C716. Dietz, Howard. Dancing in the Dark with Howard Dietz. New York:
       Quadrangle, 1974.

C717. Dillon, William A. Life Doubles in Brass. Ithaca, N. Y.: Nollid,
       1944.

C718. Dimnet, Ernest. Paul Bourget. London: Constable, 1913.

C719. Di Orio, Al. Barbara Stanwyck: A Biography. New York: Coward-
       McCann, 1983.

C720. Di Orio, Al, Jr. Little Girl Lost: The Life and Hard Times of
       Judy Garland. New Rochelle, N. Y.: Arlington House, 1973.

C721. Disher, Maurice Willson, ed. The Cowells in America. London: Ox-
       ford University Press, 1934.

C722. _____. The Last Romantic: Sir John Martin-
       Harvey. London: Hutchinson and Company, 1948.

C723. _____. Mad Genius: A Life of Edmund Kean and
       the Women Who Made and Unmade Him. London: Hutchinson and Com-
       pany, 1950.

C724. Dobson, Austin. Henry Fielding. Rev. ed. New York: Dodd, Mead
       and Company, 1883.

C725. _____. The Life of Oliver Goldsmith. London: W. Scott,
       1888.

C726. Dodds, John W. Thomas Southerne, Dramatist. New Haven, Conn.:
       Yale University Press, 1933.

C727. Dodge, John Mason and William H. Holcomb. "Jack" Dodge (John
       Mason Dodge), the Friend of Every Man: His Life and His Times.
       Los Angeles, Cal.: Sherman Danby, 1937.

C728. Doherty, Edward J. Rain Girl: The Tragic Story of Jeanne Ea-
       gels. Philadelphia: Macrae Smith Company, 1930.

C729. Dole, Nathan H. Joseph Jefferson at Home. Boston: Estes and
       Lauriat, 1898.

C730. Dolin, Anton. Ballet-Go-Round. London: M. Joseph, 1938.

C731. _____. Divertissement. London: S. Low, Marston, and Com-
       pany, 1931.

C732. Donaldson, Frances. Freddy [Lonsdale]: A Biography. Philadelph-
       ia: J. B. Lippincott, 1957.

C733. Donaldson, Walter. Fifty Years of Green-Room Gossip: or Recol-
       lections of an Actor. London: Maxwell, 1881.

C734. _____. Recollections of an Actor. London: Maxwell,
       1865.

C735. Doney, Paul H. "The Life and Works of Richard Flecknoe." Unpub-
       lished doctoral dissertation, Harvard University, 1928.

C736. Donisthorpe, G. Sheila. Show Business: A Book of the Theatre.
       London: Fortune Press, 1943.

C737. Doty, Gresdna. The Career of Mrs. Anne Brunton Merry in the
       American Theatre. Baton Rouge: Louisiana State University
       Press, 1971.

C738. Douglas, Alfred. My Friendship with Oscar Wilde. New York: Cov-
       entry House, 1932.

C739. _____. Without Apology. London: M. Secker and Com-
       pany, 1938.

C740. Douglas, Helen G. A Full Life. Garden City, N. Y.: Doubleday and
       Company, 1982.

C741. Douglass, Albert. Footlight Reflections: The Musings of One Who
       Has Spent Sixty Years in the Theatrical Profession. London:
       Samuel French, 1934.

C742.   Douglass, Albert. Memoirs of Mummers and the Old Standard The-
        atre. London: Era Publishing Company, 1924.

C743.   Downer, Alan S. The Eminent Tragedian: William Charles Macready.
        Cambridge, Mass.: Harvard University Press, 1966.

C744.   _____, ed. Memoir of John Durang: American Actor, 1785-
        1816. Pittsburgh: University of Pittsburgh Press, 1966.

C745.   Downey, Fairfax D. Richard Harding Davis: His Day. New York:
        Charles Scribner's Sons, 1933.

C746.   Drake, Fabia. Blind Fortune. London: William Kimber, 1978.

C747.   Draper, Ruth. The Letters of Ruth Draper, 1920-1956: A Self-Por-
        trait of a Great Actress. Ed. Neilla Warren. New York: Charles
        Scribner's Sons, 1979.

C748.   Draper, Walter H. "George L. Fox, Comedian, in Pantomime and
        Travesty." Unpublished doctoral dissertation, University of
        Illinois, 1958.

C749.   Dreier, Katherine S. Shawn, the Dancer. New York: Museum of Mod-
        ern Art, 1933.

C750.   Dressler, Marie. The Life Story of an Ugly Duckling. New York:
        Robert M. McBride, 1924.

C751.   Dressler, Marie and Mildred Harrington. My Own Story. Boston:
        Little, Brown, and Company, 1934.

C752.   Dithmar, Edward A. John Drew. New York: Frederick A. Stokes,
        1900.

C753.   Drew, John. My Years on the Stage. New York: E. P. Dutton, 1922.

C754.   Drew, Louisa Lane. Autobiographical Sketch of Mrs. John Drew.
        London: Chapman and Hall, 1900.

C755.   Drinkwater, John and Albert Rutherston. Claud Lovat Fraser. Lon-
        don: William Heinemann, 1923.

C756.   _____. Discovery: Being the Second Book of an Autobi-
        ography, 1897-1913. London: Ernest Benn, 1932.

C757.   _____. Inheritance: Being the First Book of an Auto-
        biography. London: Ernest Benn, 1931.

C758.   Driver, Leota S. Fanny Kemble. Chapel Hill: University of North
        Carolina Press, 1933.

C759.   Drummond, David T. K. Memoir of Montague Stanley.   Edinburgh:
        W. P. Kennedy, 1848.

C760.   Drutman, Irving. Good Company: A Memoir, Mostly Theatrical.
        Boston: Little, Brown and Company, 1976.

C761. Duclaux, Agnes M. The Life of Racine. London: T. F. Unwin, 1925.

C762. Dudden, F. Homes. Henry Fielding: His Life, Works, and Times, 2 vols. Oxford: Clarendon Press, 1952.

C763. Dudley, Ernest. The Gilded Lily [Lillie Langtry]. London: Odhams Press, 1958.

C764. Duffy, Susan. "Elmer Bernard Kenyon: An Examination of the Career of a Press Agent." Unpublished doctoral dissertation, University of Pittsburgh, 1979.

C765. Dukes, Ashley. The Scene Is Changed: Autobiographical Reminiscences. London: The Macmillan Company, 1942.

C766. Du Maurier, Angela. It's Only the Sister. London: Peter Davies, 1951.

C767. Du Maurier, Daphne. Gerald [Du Maurier]: A Portrait. London: Victor Gollancz, 1934.

C768. Dunbar, Howard H. The Dramatic Career of Arthur Murphy. New York: Modern Language Association, 1946.

C769. Dunbar, Janet. Flora Robson. London: George G. Harrap, 1960.

C770. _____. Mrs. G. B. S. New York: Harper and Row, 1963.

C771. Duncan, Irma and Allan R. Macdougall. Isadora Duncan's Russian Days and Her Last Years in France. London: Victor Gollancz, 1929.

C772. Duncan, Isadora. My Life. Garden City, N. Y.: Garden City Publishing Company, 1927.

C773. Dundy, Elaine. Finch, Bloody Finch: A Life of Peter Finch. New York: Holt, Rinehart and Winston, 1980.

C774. Dunkel, Wilbur D. Sir Arthur Pinero: A Critical Biography with Letters. Chicago: University of Chicago Press, 1941.

C775. Dunlap, William. Diary of William Dunlap, 1766-1839: The Memoirs of a Dramatist, Theatrical Manager, Painter, Critic, Novelist, and Historian. New York: New York Historical Society, 1930.

C776. _____. The Life of George Frederick Cooke, 2 vols. London: Henry Colburn, 1813.

C777. _____. Thirty Years Ago: or Memoirs of a Water-Drinker. New York: Bancroft and Holley, 1836.

C778. Dunn, Thomas A. Philip Massinger: The Man and the Playwright. London: T. Nelson, 1957.

C779. Dunsany, Edward John. Patches of Sunlight. London: William Heinemann, 1938.

C780.   Dunsany, Edward John. The Sirens Wake. London: Hutchinson and
        Company, 1945.

C781.   _____. While Sirens Slept. London: Jarrold's,
        1944.

C782.   Durham, Frank. Du Bose Heyward, the Man Who Wrote "Porgy." Co-
        lumbia: University of South Carolina Press, 1954.

C783.   Dyer, Robert. Nine Years of an Actor's Life. London: Longman,
        Rees, Orme, Brown and Company, 1833.

C784.   East, Napoleon B. "John Bernard, Actor-Manager: 1756-1828." Un-
        published doctoral dissertation, University of Kansas, 1970.

C785.   Eccles, Mark. Shakespeare in Warwickshire. Madison: University
        of Wisconsin Press, 1961.

C786.   Edel, Leon. Henry James, 3 vols. London: Rupert Hart-Davis,
        1953, 1962.

C787.   Edgar, George. Martin Harvey: Some Pages of His Life. London:
        Grant Richards, 1912.

C788.   Edge, Turner W. "James E. Murdoch, American Actor." Unpublished
        doctoral dissertation, University of Illinois, 1964.

C789.   Edgett, Edwin F., ed. Edward Loomis Davenport. New York: Dunlap
        Society, 1901.

C790.   _____. I Speak for Myself.   New York: The Macmillan
        Company, 1940.

C791.   Edmonstone, Wayne E. Nathan Cohen: The Making of a Critic. To-
        ronto, Ont.: Lester and Orpen, 1977.

C792.   Edwards, Anne. Vivien Leigh: A Biography. New York: Simon and
        Schuster, 1977.

C793.   Edwards, Herbert J. and Julie A. Herne. James A. Herne: Rise of
        Realism in the American Drama. Orono: University of Maine
        Press, 1964.

C794.   Edwards, Samuel. Victor Hugo: A Tumultuous Life. New York: Mc-
        Kay, 1971.

C795.   Eels, George. Cole Porter: The Life That Late He Led. New York:
        G. P. Putnam's Sons, 1967.

C796.   _____ and Stanley Musgrove. Mae West: A Biography. New
        York: Morrow, 1982.

C797.   Egan, Pierce. The Life of an Actor. London: Methuen and Company,
        1904.

C798. Egerton, William. Faithful Memoirs of the Life, Amours, and Per-
       formances of Mrs. Anne Oldfield. London: n. p., 1731.

C799. Ellerslie, Blanche. The Diary of an Actress: or The Realities of
       Stage Life. Ed. H. C. Shuttleworth. London: Griffith, Farren
       and Company, 1885.

C800. Elliot, William Gerald. In My Anecdotage. London: P. Allan and
       Company, 1925.

C801. Ellis, S. M. The Life of Michael Kelly 1762-1826. London: Vic-
       tor Gollancz, 1930.

C802. Ellis, William A. 1849: A Vindication [Richard Wagner]. London:
       Kegan Paul, 1892.

C803. _____. Life of Richard Wagner, 6 vols. London: Kegan
       Paul, Trench and Trübner, 1900-08.

C804. Ellis-Fermor, Una. Christopher Marlowe. London: Methuen and Com-
       pany, 1927.

C805. Ellison, Reuben Y. "Sacha Guitry, Virtuoso of the Theatre." Un-
       published doctoral dissertation, University of Wisconsin,
       1940.

C806. Ellsler, John Adam. The Stage Memories of John A. Ellsler. Ed.
       Effie Ellsler Weston. Cleveland, Oh.: Rowfant Club, 1950.

C807. Elwin, Malcolm. Charles Reade: A Biography. London: Jonathan
       Cape, 1931.

C808. Elwood, Muriel. Pauline Frederick: On and Off the Stage. Chi-
       cago: A. Kroch, 1940.

C809. Emboden, William A. Sarah Bernhardt. New York: The Macmillan
       Company, 1975.

C810. Emery, John P. Arthur Murphy, An Eminent English Dramatist of
       the Eighteenth Century. Philadelphia: University of Pennsyl-
       vania Press, 1946.

C811. Endrey, Eugene. Beg, Borrow and Squeal. New York: Pageant Press,
       1963.

C812. Engel, Lehman. Words with Music. New York: The Macmillan Compa-
       ny, 1972.

C813. Enters, Angna. First Person Plural. New York: Stackpole Sons,
       1937.

C814. _____. Silly Girl: A Portrait of Personal Remembrance.
       Cambridge, Mass.: Houghton Mifflin, 1944.

C815. Esslin, Martin. Brecht: A Choice of Evils. London: Eyre and
       Spottiswoode, 1959.

C816.   Evans, Gareth L. _J. B. Priestley: The Dramatist_. London: Willi-
        am Heinemann, 1964.

C817.   Everard, Edward Cape. _Memoirs of an Unfortunate Son of Thespis_.
        Edinburgh: J. Ballantyne and Company, 1818.

C818.   Everson, William K. _The Art of W. C. Fields_. Indianapolis:
        Bobbs-Merrill, 1967.

C819.   Ewen, David. _A Journey to Greatness: The Life and Music of
        George Gershwin_. New York: Henry Holt and Company, 1956.

C820.   _____. _The Story of Irving Berlin_. New York: Henry Holt
        and Company, 1950.

C821.   _____. _The Story of Jerome Kern_. New York: Henry Holt and
        Company, 1953.

C822.   _____. _With a Song in His Heart: The Story of Richard Rod-
        gers_. New York: Holt, Rinehart and Winston, 1963.

C823.   Ewen, Frederic. _Bertolt Brecht: His Life, His Art and His Time_.
        New York: Citadel Books, 1967.

C824.   Eytinge, Rose. _The Memories of Rose Eytinge_. New York: Frederick
        A. Stokes, 1905.

C825.   Fagan, Elisabeth, ed. _From the Wings, By "The Stage Cat."_ Lon-
        don: W. Collins' Sons, 1922.

C826.   Fairbrother, Sydney. _Through an Old Stage Door_. London: Muller,
        1939.

C827.   Fairweather, Virginia. _Cry God for Larry_. London: Calder and
        Boyars, 1969. American title: _Olivier: An Informal Portrait_.

C828.   Faith, William R. _Bob Hope: A Life in Comedy_. New York: G. P.
        Putnam's Sons, 1982.

C829.   Falb, Carl B. "A World Elsewhere: The Stage Career of Anew Mc-
        Master." Unpublished doctoral dissertation, Ohio State Univer-
        sity, 1974.

C830.   Falk, Bernard. _The Naked Lady: or Storm over Adah_ [Isaacs Menk-
        en]. London: Hutchinson and Company, 1934.

C831.   _____. _Rachel, the Immortal_. London: Hutchinson and Com-
        pany, 1935.

C832.   Fallon, Gabriel. _Sean O'Casey: The Man I Knew_. London: Rout-
        ledge, 1965.

C833.   Farjeon, Eleanor. _Portrait of a Family_. New York: Frederick A.
        Stokes, 1936.

C834.   Farmer, Patrick A. "Moss Hart: American Playwright/Director."
         Unpublished doctoral dissertation, Kent State University,
         1980.

C835.   Farrar, J. Maurice. Mary Anderson: The Story of Her Life and
         Professional Career. London: D. Bogue, 1884.

C836.   Farson, Daniel. The Man Who Wrote "Dracula": A Biography of Bram
         Stoker. New York: St. Martin's, 1975.

C837.   Faulkner, Trader. Peter Finch: A Biography. New York: Taplinger,
         1980.

C838.   Favorini, Attilio A. "The Last Tragedian: Robert Bruce Mantell
         and the American Theatre." Unpublished doctoral dissertation,
         Yale University, 1969.

C839.   Fay, Frank. How to Be Poor. New York: Prentice-Hall, 1945.

C840.   Fay, William G., Frank Fay, and C. Carswell. The Fays of the Ab-
         bey Theatre: An Autobiographical Record. London: Rich and Cow-
         an, 1935.

C841.   Fein, Irving A. Jack Benny: An Intimate Biography. New York:
         G. P. Putnam's Sons, 1975.

C842.   Felheim, Marvin. The Theatre of Augustin Daly. Cambridge, Mass.:
         Harvard University Press, 1956.

C843.   Fellows, Dexter W. and Andrew A. Freeman. This Way to the Big
         Show: The Life of Dexter Fellows. New York: Viking Press,
         1936.

C844.   Fennell, James. An Apology for the Life of James Fennell. Phila-
         delphia: Moses Thomas, 1814.

C845.   Ferber, Edna. A Kind of Magic. Garden City, N. Y.: Doubleday and
         Company, 1963.

C846.   _____. A Peculiar Treasure: An Autobiography. New York:
         Literary Guild of America, 1939.

C847.   Fernandez-Azabel, Lilie B. The Countess from Iowa. New York:
         G. P. Putnam's Sons, 1936.

C848.   Ferrier, Winifred. Kathleen Ferrier: Her Life. Harmondsworth,
         Eng.: Penguin Books, 1959.

C849.   Ferris, Paul. Richard Burton: An Arm's Length Biography. New
         York: Coward, McCann and Geoghegan, 1981.

C850.   ffrench, Yvonne. Mrs. Siddons: Tragic Actress. London: Cobden-
         Sanderson, 1936.

C851.   Field, Alfred G. Watch Yourself Go By. Columbus, Oh.: Spohr and
         Glenn, 1912.

C852. Field, Andrew. Djuna: The Life and Times of Djuna Barnes. New
       York: G. P. Putnam's Sons, 1983.

C853. Field, Isobel. This Life I've Loved. New York: Longmans, Green
       and Company, 1937.

C854. Field, Kate. Adelaide Ristori: A Biography. New York: John A.
       Gray and Green, 1867.

C855. _____. Charles Albert Fechter. Boston: J. R. Osgood and
       Company, 1882.

C856. Fields, W. C. W. C. Fields by Himself. Ed. Ronald J. Fields.
       Englewood Cliffs, N. J.: Prentice-Hall, 1973.

C857. Fike, Duane J. "Frank Mayo: Actor, Playwright, and Manager." Un-
       published doctoral dissertation, University of Nebraska at
       Lincoln, 1980.

C858. Finch, Christopher. Rainbow: The Stormy Life of Judy Garland.
       New York: Grosset and Dunlap, 1975.

C859. Finch, Yolanda. Finchy [Peter Finch]. New York: Wyndham Books,
       1981.

C860. Finck, Herman. My Melodious Memories. London: Hutchinson and
       Company, 1937.

C861. Findlater, Richard. Emlyn Williams. New York: The Macmillan Com-
       pany, 1956.

C862. _____. Grimaldi: King of Clowns. London: MacGibbon
       and Kee, 1955.

C863. _____. Lilian Baylis: The Lady of the Old Vic. Lon-
       don: Allen Lane, 1975.

C864. _____. Michael Redgrave, Actor. London: William
       Heinemann, 1956.

C865. Finley, John H., Jr. Pindar and AEschylus. Cambridge, Mass.:
       Harvard University Press, 1955.

C866. Finney, Brian. Christopher Isherwood: A Critical Biography.
       London: Faber and Faber, 1979.

C867. Fiore, Carlo. Bud: The Brando I Knew. New York: Delacorte Press,
       1974.

C868. Fisher, John. What a Performance: The Life of Sid Field. London:
       Seeley, Service and Company, 1975.

C869. Fitch, Clyde. Some Correspondence and Six Conversations. New
       York: Stone and Kimball, 1896.

C870. Fitton, Doris. Not without Dust and Heat: My Life in Theatre.

Sydney: Harper and Row, 1981.

C871. Fitzallen, Allen. Memoirs of Miss [Margaret Ann] Somerville. London: J. Lowndes, 1819.

C872. Fitzball, Edward. Thirty-Five Years of a Dramatic Author's Life, 2 vols. London: T. C. Newby, 1859.

C873. Fitzgerald, Percy. Henry Irving: A Record of Twenty Years at the Lyceum. London: Chapman and Hall, 1893.

C874. _____. The Kembles: An Account of the Kemble Family, 2 vols. London: Tinsley Brothers, 1871.

C875. _____. The Life of Mrs. Catherine Clive, Together with Her Correspondence. London: A. Reader, 1888.

C876. _____. The Life of David Garrick, 2 vols. London: Tinsley Brothers, 1868.

C877. _____. The Lives of the Sheridans, 2 vols. London: Richard Bentley and Son, 1886.

C878. _____. Memoirs of an Author, 2 vols. London: Richard Bentley and Son, 1895.

C879. _____. Samuel Foote: A Biography. London: Chatto and Windus, 1910.

C880. Fitzgerald, S. J. Adair. Dickens and the Drama: Being an Account of Charles Dickens' Connection with the Stage and the Stage's Connection with Him. London: Chapman and Hall, 1910.

C881. Fitzmaurice-Kelly, James. Miguel de Cervantes Saavedra: A Memoir. Oxford: Clarendon Press, 1913.

C882. Fitzsimons, Raymund. Barnum in London. London: Geoffrey Bles, 1969.

C883. _____. The Baron of Picadilly: The Travels and Entertainments of Albert Smith. London: Geoffrey Bles, 1967.

C884. _____. Edmund Kean: Fire from Heaven. London: Hamish Hamilton, 1978.

C885. Fleetwood, Frances and Betty Conquest. Conquest: The Story of a Theatre Family. London: W. H. Allen and Company, 1953.

C886. Fleischer, Nathaniel S. Reckless Lady: The Life Story of Adah Isaacs Menken. New York: C. J. O'Brien, 1941.

C887. Fletcher, Tom. One Hundred Years of the Negro in Show Business. New York: Burdge and Company, 1954.

C888. Flower, Newman, ed. The Journals of Arnold Bennett, 3 vols. London: Cassell and Company, 1932-3.

C889.   Fonda, Henry and Howard Teichman. My Life. New York: New Ameri-
        can Library, 1981.

C890.   Forbes, Bryan. Dame Edith Evans: Ned's Girl. Boston: Little,
        Brown and Company, 1977.

C891.   _____. Notes for a Life. London: Everest, 1974.

C892.   Forbes-Robertson, Diana. My Aunt Maxine: The Story of Maxine
        Elliott. New York: Viking Press, 1964.

C893.   Forbes-Robertson, Johnston. A Player under Three Reigns. Boston:
        Little, Brown and Company, 1925.

C894.   Ford, George D. These Were Actors: The Story of the Chapmans and
        the Drakes. New York: Library Publishers, 1955.

C895.   Ford, Thomas. A Peep behind the Curtain by a Boston Supernumer-
        ary. Boston: Redding and Company, 1850.

C896.   Forde, Gladys I. "David Belasco: An Evaluation of the Man and
        His Contributions to American Theatre History." Unpublished
        doctoral dissertation, Western Reserve University, 1955.

C897.   Fordham, Hallam, comp. John Gielgud: An Actor's Biography in
        Pictures. London: J. Lehmann, 1952.

C898.   Forrest, Sam. Variety of Miscellanea. New York: privately print-
        ed, 1939.

C899.   Forrester, Izola L. This One Mad Act: The Unknown Story of John
        Wilkes Booth and His Family, by His Granddaughter. Boston:
        Cushman and Flint, 1937.

C900.   Forster, John. The Life of Charles Dickens, 3 vols. London:
        Chapman and Hall, 1872-4.

C901.   Forsyth, James. Tyrone Guthrie. London: Hamish Hamilton, 1976.

C902.   Foss, Kenelm. Here Lies Richard Brinsley Sheridan. London: M.
        Secker, 1939.

C903.   Foster, George. Spice of Life: Sixty-Five Years in the Glamour
        World. London: Hurst and Blackett, 1939.

C904.   Foust, Clement. The Life and Dramatic Works of Robert Montgomery
        Bird. New York: Knickerbocker Press, 1919.

C905.   Fowler, Gene. Good Night, Sweet Prince [John Barrymore]. Phila-
        delphia: Blackiston, 1945.

C906.   _____. Minutes of the Last Meeting [W. C. Fields]. New
        York: Viking Press, 1954.

C907.   _____. Schnozzola: The Story of Jimmy Durante. New York:
        Viking Press, 1951.

C908. Fowler, Roy A. Orson Welles. London: Pendulum, 1946.

C909. Fowlie, Wallace. Paul Claudel. New York: Hillary House, 1957.

C910. Fox, W. J. and John Fowler, eds. The Life and Literary Remains
       of Charles Reece Pemberton. London: n. p., 1843.

C911. Foy, Eddie and Alvin F. Harlow. Clowning through Life. New York:
       E. P. Dutton, 1928.

C912. France, Richard. The Theatre of Orson Welles. Lewisburg, Penn.:
       Bucknell University Press, 1977.

C913. Francis, Arlene. Arlene Francis: A Memoir. New York: Simon and
       Schuster, 1978.

C914. Francis, Basil. Fanny Kelly of Drury Lane. London: Rockliff,
       1950.

C915. Francisco, Virginia R. "Charles Kean's Acting Career, 1827-1867,
       and the Development of His Style." Unpublished doctoral dis-
       sertation, Indiana University, 1974.

C916. Frank, Gerold. Judy [Garland]. New York: Harper and Row, 1975.

C917. Franken, Rose. When All Is Said and Done. London: W. H. Allen,
       1962.

C918. Fraser, Pamela Maude. Worlds Away [Cyril Maude]. London: J.
       Baker, 1964.

C919. Freedland, Michael. Irving Berlin. New York: Stein and Day,
       1974.

C920. _____. Jerome Kern: A Biography. New York: Stein
       and Day, 1981.

C921. _____. Jolson. New York: Stein and Day, 1972.

C922. Freedley, George. The Lunts: An Illustrated Study of Their Work.
       New York: The Macmillan Company, 1958.

C923. Freeman, Arthur. Thomas Kyd: Facts and Problems. Oxford: Claren-
       don Press, 1967.

C924. Freeman, Benjamin P., Jr. "The Stage Career of Charles D. Co-
       burn." Unpublished doctoral dissertation, Tulane University,
       1970.

C925. Freeman, William. Oliver Goldsmith. London: H. Jenkins, 1951.

C926   French, Harold. I Swore I Never Would. London: Secker and War-
       burg, 1970.

C927. Frewin, Leslie. Dietrich. New York: Stein and Day, 1967.

C929. Frey, Albert Romer. Mary Anderson in Her Dramatic Roles. New
       York: W. J. Kelly, 1892.

C930. Frick, Constance. The Dramatic Criticism of George Jean Nathan.
       Ithaca, N. Y.: Cornell University Press, 1943.

C931. Friede, Donald. The Mechanical Angel: His Adventures and Enter-
       prises in the Glittering '20's. New York: Alfred A. Knopf,
       1948.

C932. Friedman, Muriel S. "The Theatrical Career of John O'Keeffe."
       Unpublished doctoral dissertation, Loyola University of Chica-
       go, 1974.

C933. Friedman, Robert. "The Contributions of Harry Bache Smith (1860-
       1936) to the American Musical Theatre." Unpublished doctoral
       dissertation, New York University, 1976.

C934. Fripp, Edgar I. Shakespeare, Man and Artist. New York: Oxford
       University Press, 1964.

C935. Frischauer, Paul. Beaumarchais: Adventurer in the Century of Wo-
       men. Trans. Margaret Goldsmith. New York: Viking Press, 1935.

C936. Frohman, Daniel. Daniel Frohman Presents: An Autobiography. New
       York: C. Kendall and W. Sharp, 1935.

C937. _____. Encore. New York: L. Furman, 1937.

C938. _____. Memories of a Manager. Garden City, N. Y.: Dou-
       bleday, Page and Company, 1911.

C939. From Theatre to Convent: Memories of Mother Isabel Mary, C. S.
       M. V. [Isabel Bateman]. London: S. P. C. K., 1936.

C940. Fry, F. Charlton. Charles Fry: His Life and Work. London: J. M.
       Baxter and Company, 1932.

C941. Fuller, Loie. Fifteen Years of a Dancer's Life, with Some Ac-
       count of Her Distinguished Friends. Boston: Small, Maynard and
       Company, 1913.

C942. Funke, Lewis. The Curtain Rises: The Story of Ossie Davis. New
       York: Grosset and Dunlap, 1971.

C943. Furnas, Joseph C. Fanny Kemble: Leading Lady of the Nineteenth
       Century Stage. New York: Dial Press, 1982.

C944. Furnivall, Frederick J. Shakespeare: Life and Work. New York:
       Cassell and Company, 1908.

C945. Fyfe, Henry H. Arthur Wing Pinero, Playwright. London: Greening
       and Company, 1902.

C946.   Gaffney, Paul J. "Allen Crafton: A Theatrical Pioneer." Unpublished doctoral dissertation, University of Kansas, 1979.

C947.   Gaige, Crosby. Footlights and Highlights. New York: E. P. Dutton, 1948.

C948.   Gale, Zona. When I Was a Little Girl. New York: The Macmillan Company, 1913.

C949.   Galsworthy, Ada. Over the Hills and Far Away [John Galsworthy]. New York: Charles Scribner's Sons, 1938.

C950.   Ganthony, Robert. Random Recollections. London: H. J. Drane, 1899.

C951.   Gardner, Fitzroy. Days and Ways of an Old Bohemian. London: John Murray, 1921.

C952.   Gardner, Robert M. "International Rag: The Theatrical Career of John Howard Lawson." Unpublished doctoral dissertation, University of California at Berkeley, 1977.

C953.   Garland, Henry B. Lessing, the Founder of Modern German Literature. Cambridge: Bowes and Bowes, 1937.

C954.   _____. Schiller. New York: McBride, 1950.

C955.   Garnett, Edward. Turgenev. London: Collins, 1927.

C956.   Garten, Hugh F. Gerhart Hauptmann. New Haven, Conn.: Yale University Press, 1954.

C957.   Gatch, K. H. "Robert Wilson, Actor and Dramatist." Unpublished doctoral dissertation, Yale University, 1928.

C958.   Gay, Maisie. Laughing through Life. London: Hurst and Blackett, 1931.

C959.   Gay, Phoebe F. John Gay: His Place in the Eighteenth Century. London: Collins, 1938.

C960.   Gayley, Charles M. Francis Beaumont: Dramatist. London: Duckworth, 1914.

C961.   Geddes, Norman Bel. Miracle in the Evening: An Autobiography. Ed. William Kelley. Garden City, N. Y.: Doubleday and Company, 1960.

C962.   Gelb, Arthur and Barbara. O'Neill. New York: Harper and Brothers, 1962.

C963.   Gerson, Noel B. Because I Loved Him: The Life and Loves of Lillie Langtry. New York: Morrow, 1971.

C964.   Gibbs, Henry. Affectionately Yours, Fanny: Fanny Kemble and the Theatre. London: Jarrolds, 1947.

C965.   Gibbs, Lewis. Sheridan: His Life and His Theatre, 2 vols. New
        York: William Morrow, 1948.

C966.   Gibson, Margaret B. Clifford Odets: American Playwright. New
        York: Atheneum, 1981.

C967.   Gielgud, John. Early Stages. New York: The Macmillan Company,
        1939.

C968.   _____. Gielgud: An Actor and His Time. New York: Clark-
        son N. Potter, 1979.

C969.   _____. Stage Directions. London: William Heinemann,
        1964.

C970.   Gielgud, Kate Terry. An Autobiography. London: Max Reinhardt,
        1953.

C971.   Gielgud, Val. One Year of Grace: A Fragment of Autobiography.
        New York: Longmans, Green and Company, 1950.

C972.   _____. Years in a Mirror. London: Bodley Head, 1965.

C973.   Gilbert, Anne H. The Stage Reminiscences of Mrs. [G. H.] Gil-
        bert. New York: Charles Scribner's Sons, 1901.

C974.   Gilbert, Julie G. Ferber: A Biography. Garden City, N. Y.: Dou-
        bleday and Company, 1978.

C975.   Gilder, Rosamond. John Gielgud's Hamlet. New York: Oxford Uni-
        versity Press, 1937.

C976.   Gildon, Charles. Life of Mr. Thomas Betterton, the Late Eminent
        Tragedian. London: R. Gosling, 1710.

C977.   Gill, Brendan. Cole [Porter]. Ed. Robert Kimball. New York:
        Holt, Rinehart and Winston, 1971.

C978.   Gill, Maud. See the Players. Birmingham: Ronald, 1948.

C979.   Gillmore, Margalo. Four Flights Up. Boston: Houghton Mifflin,
        1964.

C980.   Gingold, Hermione. My Own Unaided Work. London: Werner Laurie,
        1952.

C981.   _____. Sirens Should Be Seen and Not Heard. Phila-
        delphia: J. B. Lippincott, 1963.

C982.   _____. The World Is Square. London: Home and Van
        Thal, 1945.

C983.   Gipson, Alice E. John Home: A Study of His Life and Works. Cald-
        well, Id.: Caxton Printers, 1917.

C984.   Gish, Lillian and Ann Pinchot. The Movies, Mr. Griffith, and Me.

New York: Prentice-Hall, 1969.

C985. Gittleman, Sol. Frank Wedekind. New York: Twayne Publishers, 1969.

C986. Giuliano, William P. "The Life and Work of Jacinto Grau." Unpublished doctoral dissertation, University of Michigan, 1950.

C987. Glasgow, Alice. Sheridan of Drury Lane: A Biography. New York: Frederick A. Stokes, 1940.

C988. Glaspell, Susan. The Road to the Temple [George Cram Cook]. London: Ernest Benn, 1926.

C989. Glover, James M. Hims, Ancient and Modern. London: T. F. Unwin, 1926.

C990. _____. Jimmy Glover, His Book. London: Methuen and Company, 1911.

C991. _____. Jimmy Glover and His Friends. London: Chatto and WIndus, 1913.

C992. Goding, Stowell C. "Henry Bernstein: The Evolution of a Playwright." Unpublished doctoral dissertation, 1943.

C993. Godwin, William. The Lives of Edward and John Phillips, Nephews and Pupils of Milton. London: Longmans, Hurst, Rees, Orme and Brown, 1815.

C994. Goldberg, Isaac. George Gershwin: A Study in American Music. New York: Simon and Schuster, 1931.

C995. _____. Major [Mordecai M.] Noah: American-Jewish Pioneer. Philadelphia: Jewish Publication Society of America, 1936.

C996. _____. Queen of Hearts: The Passionate Pilgrimage of Lola Montez. New York: John Day, 1936.

C997. _____. The Story of Gilbert and Sullivan: or The "Compleat" Savoyard. New York: Simon and Schuster, 1928.

C998. Golden, John and Viola B. Shore. Stage-Struck John Golden. New York: Samuel French, 1930.

C999. Goldoni, Carlo. Memoirs. Trans. John Black. London: Alfred A. Knopf, 1926.

C1000. Goldsmith, Berthold H. Arnold Daly. New York: James T. White, 1927.

C1001. Gooch, Elizabeth. The Life of Mrs. Gooch, 3 vols. London: C. and G. Kearsley, 1792.

C1002. Goodale, Katherine. Behind the Scenes with Edwin Booth. Boston:

Houghton Mifflin, 1931.

C1003. Goodman, Walter. The Keeleys [Robert and Mary Ann], on the Stage and at Home. London: Richard Bentley and Son, 1895.

C10.04. Goodwin, Nat C. Nat Goodwin's Book. Boston: Richard G. Badger, 1914.

C1005. Goodwin, Thomas. Sketches and Impressions, Musical, Theatrical and Social (1799-1885).... New York: G. P. Putnam's Sons, 1887.

C1006. Gordon, Max and Lewis Funke. Max Gordon Presents. New York: Geis, 1963.

C1007. Gordon, Ruth. Myself among Others. New York: Atheneum, 1971.

C1008. _____. My Side: The Autobiography of Ruth Gordon. New York: Harper and Row, 1976.

C1009. _____. Ruth Gordon: An Open Book. Garden City, N. Y.: Doubleday and Company, 1980.

C1010. Goreau, Angeline. Reconstructing Aphra: A Social Biography of Aphra Behn. New York: Dial Press, 1980.

C1011. Gorky, Maxim. Reminiscences of Leonid Andreyev. Trans. Katherine Masefield and S. S. Koteliansky. London: William Heinemann, 1922.

C1012. Gorman, Herbert S.. James Joyce: His First Forty Years. Folcroft: Penn.: Folcroft, Press, 1971.

C1013. Gosse, Edmund. Ibsen. London: Hodder and Stoughton, 1907.

C1014. _____. Life of William Congreve. London: William Heinemann, 1924 [1888].

C1015. Gotch, J. A. Inigo Jones. London: Methuen and Company, 1928.

C1016. Gottfried, Martin. Jed Harris: The Curse of Genius. Boston: Little, Brown and Company, 1984.

C1017. Gottlied, Nora and Raymond Chapman, eds. Letters to an Actress: The Story of Turgenev and Savina. London: Allison and Busby, 1973.

C1018. Gould, Thomas R. The Tragedian: An Essay on the Histrionic Genius of Junius Brutus Booth. New York: Hurd and Houghton, 1868.

C1019. Gourlay, Logan, ed. Olivier. London: Weidenfeld and Nicolson, 1973.

C1020. Gozzi, Carlo. The Memoirs of Count Carlo Gozzi, 2 vols. Trans. John A. Symonds. London: J. C. Nimmo, 1890.

C10 21. Grabish, Richard F. "Montrose Jonas Moses: Critic of American Drama." Unpublished doctoral dissertation, Kent State University, 1979.

C10 22. Graham, Diana M. "The Dreamer and the Maker: A Study of Lewis Casson's Work in the Theatre." Unpublished doctoral dissertation, University of Minnesota, 1972.

C10 23. Graham, Joseph F. An Old Stock Actor's Memories. London: John Murray, 1930.

C10 24. Graham, Shirley. Paul Robeson, Citizen of the World. New York: Julian Messner, 1946.

C10 25. Grain, Richard C. Corney Grain. London: John Murray, 1888.

C10 26. Granach, Alexander. There Goes an Actor. Trans. Willard Trask. Garden City, N. Y.: Doubleday, Doran and Company, 1945.

C10 27. Granlund, Nils Thor, Sid Feder, and Ralph Hancock. Blondes, Brunettes and Bullets. New York: David McKay, 1957.

C10 28. Grant, Elliott M. The Career of Victor Hugo. Cambridge, Mass.: Harvard University Press, 1945.

C10 29. Grattan, Thomas Colley. "My Acquaintance with the Late Edmund Kean," New Monthly Magazine, XXXIX (1833), 7-16, 143-151. [Separately printed]

C10 30. Grau, Robert. The Business Man in the Amusement World. New York: Broadway Publishing Company, 1910.

C10 31. _____. Forty Years of Observation of Music and the Drama. New York: Broadway Publishing Company, 1909.

C10 32. Graves, Charles. The [Charles B.] Cochran Story: The Life and Times of the Century's Greatest Showman. London: W. H. Allen, 1951.

C10 33. Graves, George. Gaities and Gravities. London: Hutchinson and Company, 1931.

C10 34. Gray, George. Vagaries of a Vagabond. London: Heath, Cranton, 1930.

C10 35. Gray, Ronald. Bertolt Brecht. Edinburgh: Oliver and Boyd, 1961.

C10 36. Greacen, Robert. The Art of Noël Coward. Aldington: Hand and Flower Press, 1953.

C10 37. Grebanier, Bernard. Thornton Wilder. Minneapolis: University of Minnesota Press, 1964.

C10 38. Green, Hugh H. Opportunity Knocked. London: Frederick Muller, 1965.

C1039. Green, Joseph G. "Joseph Wood Krutch: Critic of the Drama." Unpublished doctoral dissertation, Indiana University, 1965.

C1040. Green, Martyn. Here's a How-De-Do: My Life in Gilbert and Sullivan. New York: W. W. Norton, 1952.

C1041. Greene, David H. and Edward M. Stephens. John Millington Synge, 1871-1909. New York: The Macmillan Company, 1959.

C1042. Greene, Edward J. H. Marivaux. Toronto, Ont.: University of Toronto Press, 1965.

C1043. Greene, Graham. A Sort of Life. New York: Simon and Schuster, 1971.

C1044. Greene, Naomi. Antonin Artaud: Poet without Words. New York: Simon and Schuster, 1970.

C1045. Greenwall, Harry J. The Strange Life of Willy Clarkson: An Experiment in Biography. London: J. Long, 1936.

C1046. Gregory, Augusta. Journals of Lady Gregory: Irish Theatre, 1916-30. Ed. Lennox Robinson. London: G. P. Putnam's Sons, 1947.

C1047. _____. Lady Gregory: Interviews and Recollections. Ed. E. H. Mikhail. Totowa, N. J.: Rowman and Littlefield, 1977.

C1048. _____. Seventy Years, 1852-1922: Being the Autobiography of Lady Gregory. Ed. Colin Smythe. Gerrards Cross: Colin Smythe, 1974.

C1049. Grenfell, Joyce. Joyce Grenfell Requests the Pleasure. New York: St. Martin's, 1976.

C1050. Gresham, William L. Houdini: The Man Who Walked through Walls. New York: Manor Books, 1975.

C1051. Gressler, Thomas H. "John Murray Anderson: Director of Revues." Unpublished doctoral dissertation, Kent State University, 1973.

C1052. Greville, Fulke. Life of the Renowned Sir Philip Sidney. Ed. N. Smith. Norwood, Penn.: Norwood Editions, 1978 [1907].

C1053. Gribble, Francis. Rachel: Her Stage Life and Her Real Life. London: Chapman and Hall, 1911.

C1054. Griffenhoofe, Arthur. Memoirs of the Life, Public and Private Adventures, of Madame Vestris. London: John Duncombe, 1836.

C1055. Griffith, Frank C. Mrs. Fiske. New York: Neale Publishing Company, 1912.

C1056. Grock. Life's a Lark. Ed. Eduard Behrens. Trans. Madge Pemberton. London: William Heinemann, 1931.

C1057. Gronowicz, Antoni. Modjeska: Her Life and Loves. New York: Thomas Yoseloff, 1956.

C1058. Grossman, Edwina Booth. Edwin Booth: Recollections by His Daughter. New York: Century Company, 1894.

C1059. Grossmith, George, Sr. Piano and I. Bristol: J. W. Arrowsmith, 1910.

C1060. _____. A Society Clown: Reminiscences. Bristol: J. W. Arrowsmith, 1888.

C1061. Grossmith, George, Jr. "G. G." London: Hutchinson and Company, 1933.

C1062. Grossmith, Walter Weedon. From Studio to Stage: Reminiscences. London: John Lane, 1913.

C1063. Grover, Charles A. "James Forbes: His Works and His Career in the American Theatre." Unpublished doctoral dissertation, University of California at Davis, 1976.

C1064. Guest, Ivor. Adeline Genée: A Lifetime of Ballet under Six Reigns. London: A. and C. Black, 1958.

C1065. _____. Fanny Elssler. London: A. and C. Black, 1970.

C1066. Guilbert, Yvette. The Song of My Life: My Memories. Trans. Béatrice de Halthoir. London: George G. Harrap, 1929.

C1067. _____ and Harold Simpson. Yvette Guilbert: Struggles and Victories. London: Miles and Boon, 1910.

C1068. Guiles, Fred L. Marion Davies: A Biography. New York: McGraw-Hill, 1972.

C1069. Guitry, Sacha. If I Remember It Right. Trans. Lewis Gallantière. London: Methuen and Company, 1935. American title: If Memory Serves.

C1070. Guizot, François P. G. Corneille and His Times. New York: Harper and Company, 1852.

C1071. Gustafson, Zadel B. Genevieve Ward: A Biographical Sketch from Original Material Derived from Her Family and Friends. Boston: James R. Osgood, 1882.

C1072. Guthrie, Thomas A. A Long Retrospect [F. Anstey]. London: Oxford University Press, 1936.

C1073. Guthrie, Tyrone. In Various Directions. New York: The Macmillan Company, 1965.

C1074. _____. A Life in the Theatre. London: Hamish Hamilton, 1972.

C1075. Gutman, Robert W. <u>Richard Wagner: The Man, His Mind, and His Music</u>. New York: Harcourt, Brace and World, 1968.

C1076. Haas, Willy. <u>Bert Brecht</u>. Trans. Max Knight and Joseph Fabry. New York: F. Ungar, 1970.

C1077. Haddon, Archibald. <u>Green Room Gossip</u>. London: S. Paul and Company, 1922.

C1078. _____. <u>Hullo, Playgoers</u>. London: C. Palmer, 1924.

C1079. Hagen, Uta. <u>Sources: A Memoir</u>. New York: Performing Arts Journal Publications, 1982.

C1080. Haggard, Stephen. <u>I'll Go to Bed at Noon: A Soldier's Letter to His Son</u>. London: Faber and Faber, 1944.

C1081. Hagler, Nevis E. "William A. Brady: Theatrical Entrepreneur." Unpublished doctoral dissertation, University of Florida, 1976.

C1082. Hahn, Reynaldo. <u>Sarah Bernhardt</u>. Trans. Ethel Thompson. London: E. Matthews and Marrot, 1932.

C1083. Haldane, Charlotte. <u>Alfred: The Passionate Life of Alfred de Musset</u>. New York: Roy, 1961.

C1084. Hall, Peter. <u>Peter Hall's Diaries</u>. Ed. John Goodwin. New York: Harper and Row, 1984.

C1085. Halliwell-Phillips, James O. <u>Life of William Shakespeare</u>. New York: AMS, 1973 [1848].

C1086. _____. <u>Tarlton's Jests and News out of Purgatory</u>. London: Shakespeare Society, 1844.

C1087. Halls, W. D. <u>Maurice Maeterlinck: A Study of His Life and Thought</u>. Oxford: Clarendon Press, 1960.

C1088. Halpern, Martin. <u>William Vaughn Moody</u>. New York: College and University Press, 1964.

C1089. Halpern, Susan. <u>Austin Clarke: His Life and Works</u>. Dublin: Dolmen Press, 1974.

C1090. Halverson, Bruce P. "Arthur Hopkins: A Theatrical Biography." Unpublished doctoral dissertation, University of Washington, 1971.

C1091. Ham, Roswell G. <u>Otway and Lee: A Biography from a Baroque Age</u>. New Haven, Conn.: Yale University Press, 1931.

C1092. Hamilton, Cosmo. <u>Unwritten History</u>. Boston: Little, Brown and Company, 1924.

C1093. Hamilton, Edward W. "The Life of John Gay." Unpublished doctoral dissertation, University of Minnesota, 1940.

C1094. Hammelmann, Hanns A. Hugo von Hofmannsthal. New Haven, Conn.: Yale University Press, 1957.

C1095. Hammerton, John A. Barrie: The Story of a Genius. New York: Dodd, Mead and Company, 1929.

C1096. Hancock, Freddie and David Nathan. Hancock. London: William Kimber, 1969.

C1097. Hancock, Ralph and Letitia Fairbanks. Douglas Fairbanks: The Fourth Musketeer. London: Peter Davies, 1953.

C1098. Handy, William C. Father of the Blues: An Autobiography. New York: The Macmillan Company, 1941.

C1099. Haney, Lynn. Naked at the Feast: A Biography of Josephine Baker. New York: Dodd, Mead and Company, 1981.

C1100. Hanff, Helene. Underfoot in Show Business. New York: Harper and Row, 1962.

C1101. Hanley, Peter. Random Recollections of the Stage. London: Diprose and Bateman, 1883.

C1102. Hanners, John. "The Adventures of an Artist: John Banvard and His Mississippi Panorama." Unpublished doctoral dissertation, Michigan State University, 1979.

C1103. Hanson, Willis T., Jr. The Early Life of John Howard Payne. Boston: Bibliophile Society, 1913.

C1104. Hapgood, Hutchins. A Victorian in the Modern World. New York: Harcourt, Brace and Company, 1939.

C1105. Hapgood, Norman. The Changing Years: Reminiscences of Norman Hapgood. New York: Farrar and Rinehart, 1930.

C1106. Harbage, Alfred. Sir William Davenant, Poet Venturer. Philadelphia: University of Pennsylvania Press, 1935.

C1107. _____. Thomas Killigrew, Cavalier Dramatist, 1612-83. Philadelphia: University of Pennsylvania Press, 1930.

C1108. Harbin, Billy Joe. "The Career of John Hodginson in the American Theatre." Unpublished doctoral dissertation, Indiana University, 1971.

C1109. Harcourt, Frederick C. Vernon. From Stage to Cross: The Record of a Rolling Stone. London: S. W. Partridge and Company, 1901.

C1110. Harding, Bertita. Age Cannot Wither: The Story of Duse and D'Annunzio. Philadelphia: J. B. Lippincott, 1947.

C1111. Harding, Bertita. Hungarian Rhapsody: The Portrait of an Actress [Camille Feher de Vernet]. Indianapolis: Bobbs-Merrill, 1940.

C1112. Harding, James. Sacha Guitry: The Last Boulevardier. London: Methuen and Company, 1968.

C1113. Hardwicke, Cedric. Let's Pretend: Recollections and Reflections of a Lucky Actor. London: Grayson and Grayson, 1932.

C1114. _____. A Victorian in Orbit. London: Methuen and Company, 1961.

C1115. Hare, Arnold. George Frederick Cooke. London: Society for Theatre Research, 1980.

C1116. Hare, G. Van. Fifty Years of a Showman's Life: or The Life and Travels of Van Hare. London: W. H. Allen and Company, 1888.

C1117. Hargreaves, Henry A. "The Life and Plays of Mrs. Aphra Behn." Unpublished doctoral dissertation, Duke University, 1960.

C1118. Harker, Joseph C. Studio and Stage. London: Nisbet, 1924.

C1119. Harlan, Earl. "Elijah Fenton, 1683-1730." Unpublished doctoral dissertation, University of Pennsylvania, 1937.

C1120. Harley, George D. An Authentic Biographical Sketch of the Life of W. H. West Betty. London: Hughes, 1804.

C1121. Harper, Charles H. "Mrs. Leslie Carter: Her Life and Acting Career." Unpublished doctoral dissertation, University of Nebraska at Lincoln, 1978.

C1122. Harriman, Margaret C. Blessed Are the Debonair. New York: Rinehart, 1956.

C1123. Harris, Charles K. After the Ball: Forty Years of Melody. New York: Frank-Maurice, 1926.

C1124. Harris, Frank. Frank Harris on Bernard Shaw. London: Victor Gollancz, 1931.

C1125. _____. Oscar Wilde. London: Constable and Company, 1938.

C1126. _____. Oscar Wilde: His Life and Confessions. New York: privately printed, 1916.

C1127. Harris, Jed. A Dance on the High Wire. New York: Crown Publishers, 1980.

C1128. Harris, Jesse W. John Bale: A Study in the Minor Literature of the Reformation. Urbana: University of Illinois Presss, 1940.

C1129. Harrison, Elizabeth R. Love, Honour, and Dismay. London: Weidenfeld and Nicolson, 1976.

C1130. Harrison, Gabriel. Edwin Forrest: The Actor and the Man. Brooklyn, N. Y.: n. p., 1889.

C1131. _____. The Life and Trials of John Howard Payne. Albany, N. Y.: J. Munsell, 1875.

C1132. Harrison, Gilbert A. The Enthusiast: The Life of Thornton Wilder. New York: Ticknor and Field, 1983.

C1133. Harrison, Rex. Rex: An Autobiography. New York: William Morrow, 1975.

C1134. Harrity, Richard. The World Famous Harrity Family. New York: Trident Press, 1968.

C1135. Hart, Dorothy. Thou Swell, Thou Witty: The Life and Lyrics of Lorenz Hart. New York: Harper and Row, 1976.

C1136. Hart, Jerome A. Sardou and the Sardou Plays. London: J. B. Lippincott, 1913.

C1137. Hart, Moss. Act One. New York: Random House, 1959.

C1138. Hart, William S. My Life East and West. Boston: Houghton Mifflin, 1929.

C1139. Hartnoll, Phyllis, ed. Welcome, Good Friends [Kenneth R. Barnes]. London: Peter Davies, 1958.

C1140. Harvey, Joel. "American Burlesque as Reflected through the Career of Kitty Madison, 1916-1931." Unpublished doctoral dissertation, Florida State University, 1980.

C1141. Harvey, John Martin. The Autobiography of Sir John Martin-Harvey. London: S. Low, Marston and Company, 1933.

C1142. Harvey, John Martin. The Book of Martin-Harvey. London: H. Walker, 1930.

C1143. Harwood, Ronald. Sir Donald Wolfit, C. B. E. London: Secker and Warburg, 1971.

C1144. Haskell, Arnold L. and Walter Nouvel. Diaghileff: His Artistic and Private Life. New York: Simon and Schuster, 1935.

C1145. Hassall, Christopher V. The Timeless Quest [Stephen Haggard]. London: A. Barker, 1948.

C1146. Hastings, George E. The Life and Work of Francis Hopkinson. Chicago: University of Chicago Press, 1926.

C1147. Hatton, Joseph. Henry Irving's Impressions of America, 2 vols. Boston: J. R. Osgood and Company, 1884.

C1148. _____. With a Show in the North: Reminiscences of Mark Lemon. London: W. H. Allen and Company, 1871.

C1149. Havoc, June. Early Havoc. New York: Simon and Schuster, 1959.

C1150. _____. More Havoc. New York: Harper and Row, 1980.

C1151. Hawes, David S. "John Brougham as American Playwright and Man of
the Theatre." Unpublished doctoral dissertation, Stanford University, 1954.

C1152. Hawkins, Anthony Hope. Memories and Notes. London: Hutchinson
and Company, 1927.

C1153. Hawkins, F. W. The Life of Edmund Kean, 2 vols. London: Tinsley
Brothers, 1869.

C1154. Hawkins, Jack. Anything for a Quiet Life. London: Hamish Hamilton, 1973.

C1155. Hawkins, John A. "A Critical Biography of Alan Schneider." Unpublished doctoral dissertation, Tufts University, 1978.

C1156. Hawtrey, Charles H. The Truth at Last. Ed. W. Somerset Maugham.
Boston: Little, Brown and Company, 1924.

C1157. Haycraft, Molly C. First Lady of the Theatre: Sarah Siddons.
Chicago: Kingston House, 1958.

C1158. Hayes, Helen and Lewis Funke. A Gift of Joy. New York: Evans,
1965.

C1159. _____ and Sandford Dody. On Reflection. New York: Evans,
1968.

C1160. Hayman, Ronald. Harold Pinter. London: William Heinemann, 1968.

C1161. _____. John Gielgud. London: William Heinemann, 1971.

C1162. Hazlitt, William Carew. Four Generations of a Literary Family:
The Hazlitts in England, Ireland, and America, 1725--1896.
London: n. p., 1897.

C1163. _____. Shakespear. London: B. Quaritch, 1902.

C1164. Hecht, Ben. Actor's Blood. New York: Covici, Friede and Company,
1936.

C1165. _____. Charlie: The Improbable Life and Times of Charles
MacArthur. New York: Harper and Company, 1957.

C1166. _____. A Child of the Century. New York: Simon and Schuster, 1954.

C1167. Hedgcock, Frank A. A Cosmopolitan Actor: David Garrick and His
French Friends. New York: Duffield and Company, 1912.

C1168. Heiseler, Bernt von. Schiller. Trans. John Bednall. Philadelphia, Penn.: Dufour Editions, 1963.

C1169. Helburn, Theresa. _A Wayward Quest_. Boston: Little, Brown and Company, 1960.

C1170. Hellman, Lillian. _Pentimento_. Boston: Little, Brown and Company, 1973.

C1171. _____. _An Unfinished Woman: A Memoir_. Harmondsworth, Eng.: Penguin Books, 1972.

C1172. Hemmings, Frederick W. _Émile Zola_. Oxford: Clarendon Press, 1953.

C1173. Henderson, Archibald. _Bernard Shaw: His Life and Works_, 2 vols. London: Hurst and Blackett, 1911.

C1174. _____. _Bernard Shaw: Playboy and Prophet_. New York: D. Appleton-Century, 1932.

C1175. Henderson, Donald. _Diary of a Stage-Struck_. London: Houghton, 1932.

C1176. Henry, David D. _William Vaughn Moody: A Study_. Boston: Bruce Humphries, 1934.

C1177. Henslowe, Philip. _The Diary of Philip Henslowe_. Ed. John Payne Collier. London: Shakespeare Society, 1845.

C1178. Henson, Leslie. _My Laugh Story: The Story of My Life, Up to Date_. London: Hodder and Stoughton, 1926.

C1179. _____. _Yours Faithfully: An Autobiography_. London: John Long, 1948.

C1180. Heppner, Sam. _"Cockie"_ [Charles B. Cochran]. London: Leslie Frewin, 1969.

C1181. Herbstruth, Grant M. "Benedict De Bar and the Grand Opera House in St. Louis, Missouri, from 1855 through 1879." Unpublished doctoral dissertation, University of Iowa, 1954.

C1182. Herold, Amos L. _James Kirke Paulding: Versatile American_. New York: Columbia University Press, 1926.

C1183. Herr, John H. "Thomas Wignell and the Chestnut Street Theatre." Unpublished doctoral dissertation, Michigan State University, 1969.

C1184. Heston, Charlton. _The Actor's Life: Journals 1956-1976_. Ed. Hollis Alpert. New York: E. P. Dutton, 1978.

C1185. Hiatt, Charles. _Ellen Terry and Her Impersonations_. London: G. Bell, 1898.

C1186. _____. _Henry Irving: A Record and Review_. London: G. Bell, 1899.

C1187. Hibbard, George R. Thomas Nashe: A Critical Introduction. Cambridge, Mass.: Harvard University Press, 1962.

C1188. Hibbert, Christopher. Gilbert and Sullivan and Their Victorian World. London: G. P. Putnam's Sons, 1976.

C1189. Hibbert, Henry George. A Playgoer's Memories. London: Grant Richards, 1920.

C1190. Hicks, Seymour. Between Ourselves. London: Cassell and Company, 1930.

C1191. _____. Hail Fellow, Well Met! London: Staples Press, 1949.

C1192. _____. Me and My Missus (Fifty Years on the Stage). London: Cassell and Company, 1939.

C1193. _____. Twenty-Four Years of an Actor's Life. London: Alston Rivers, 1910.

C1194. Higham, Charles. Charles Laughton: An Intimate Biography. Garden City, N. Y.: Doubleday and Company, 1976.

C1195. _____. Kate: The Life of Katherine Hepburn. New York: W. W. Norton, 1981.

C1196. _____. Marlene: The Life of Marlene Dietrich. New York: W. W. Norton, 1977.

C1197. _____. Ziegfeld. Chicago: Regnery, 1972.

C1198. Hill, Benson E. Playing About: or Theatrical Anecdotes and Adventures..., 2 vols. London: privately printed, 1840.

C1199. Hill, Charles R. "The Pemberton Technique: A Study of Brock Pemberton's Activities in the American Theatre, 1920-1950." Unpublished doctoral dissertation, University of Kansas, 1971.

C1200. Hill, George H. Scenes from the Life of an Actor. New York: Garrett and Company, 1853.

C1201. Hillebrand, Harold N. Edmund Kean. New York: Columbia University Press, 1933.

C1202. Hilliam, Bentley Collingwood. Flotsam's Follies. London: A. Barron, 1948.

C1203. Hilton, Della. Who Was Kit Marlowe?: The Story of the Poet and Playwright. New York: Taplinger, 1977.

C1204. Hind, A. M. Giovanni Battists Piranesi: A Critical Study. London: Holland Press, 1967 [1922].

C1205. Hingley, Ronald. Chekhov: A Biographical and Critical Study. London: Unwin and Company, 1950.

C1206. Hingley, Ronald. A New Life of Anton Chekhov. New York: Alfred A. Knopf, 1976.

C1207. Hirsch, Foster. Laurence Olivier. Boston: Twayne Publishers, 1979.

C1208. Hirsen, Ronald B. "The Stage Career of Holbrook Blinn." Unpublished doctoral dissertation, University of Illinois, 1975.

C1209. Hitchman, Janet. Such a Strange Lady: A Biography of Dorothy L.. Sayers. New York: Harper and Row, 1975.

C1210. Hodgdon, Samuel Kahler. Town Hall, To-Night: or Show Life on the Cross Roads. N. P.: n. p., 1891.

C1211. Hobson, Harold. Indirect Journey: An Autobiography. London: Weidenfeld and Nicolson, 1978.

C1212. _____. Ralph Richardson: An Illustrated Study of Sir Ralph's Work. London: Rockliff, 1958.

C1213. Hodges, John C. William Congreve, the Man: A Biography from New Sources. London: Oxford University Press, 1941.

C1214. Hodgson, Geraldine. The Life of James Elroy Flecker. Oxford: Basil Blackwell, 1925.

C1215. Hogan, Robert G. Dion Boucicault. New York: Twayne Publishers, 1969.

C1216. Holbrook, Ann Catherine. Memories of an Actress: Comprising a Faithful Narrative of Her Theatrical Career from 1798 to the Present Period.... Manchester: J. M. Harrop, 1807.

C1217. Holcroft, Thomas. Memoirs, 3 vols. London: Longman, Hurst, Rees, Orme and Brown, 1816.

C1218. Holdredge, Helen. The Woman in Black [Lola Montez]. New York: G.P. Putnam's Sons, 1955.

C1219. Holliday, Robert C. Booth Tarkington. Garden City, N. Y.: Doubleday, Page and Company, 1918.

C1220. Hollinshed, John. Footlights. London: Chapman and Hall, 1883.

C1221. _____. My Lifetime, 2 vols. London: Sampson Low, 1895.

C1222. Holloway, Laura C. Adelaide Neilson: A Souvenir. New York: Funk and Wagnalls, 1885.

C1223. Holloway, Stanley. Wiv a Little Bit o' Luck. New York: Stein and Day, 1967.

C1224. Holman, L. E. Lamb's "Barbara S--": The Life of Frances Maria Kelly. London: Methuen and Company, 1935.

C1225. Holme, Timothy. A Servant of Many Masters: The Life and Times of Carlo Goldoni. London: Jupiter Books, 1976.

C1226. Holtzman, Filia. The Young Maxim Gorky, 1869-1902. New York: Columbia University Press, 1948.

C1227. Home, William D. Half-Term Report: An Autobiography. London: Longmans, Green and Company, 1954.

C1228. Honig, Edwin. García Lorca. London: Jonathan Cape, 1968 [1944].

C1229. Hoover, Marjorie L. Meyerhold: The Art of Conscious Theater. Amherst: University of Massachusetts Press, 1974.

C1230. Hope, Bob and Pete Martin. Have Tux, Will Travel. New York: Simon and Schuster, 1954.

C1231. _____. I Never Left Home. New York: Simon and Schuster, 1944.

C1232. _____. I Owe Russia $1200. Garden City, N. Y.: Doubleday and Company, 1963.

C1233. _____. They Got Me Cornered. Hollywood: n. p., 1941.

C1234. Hopkins, Arthur. Reference Point. New York: Samuel French, 1948.

C1235. _____. To a Lonely Boy. Garden City, N. Y.: Doubleday, Doran and Company, 1937.

C1236. Hopkins, R. Thurston. Oscar Wilde: A Study of the Man and His Work. London: Lynwood, 1913.

C1237. Hopper, De Wolf and Wesley W. Stout. Once a Clown, Always a Clown. Boston: Little, Brown and Company, 1927.

C1238. Horne, David H. The Life and Minor Works of George Peele. Westport, Conn.: Greenwood Press, 1978 [1952].

C1239. Hosking, George. Life and Times of Edward Alleyn, Actor, Master of the King's Bears.... London: Jonathan Cape, 1952.

C1240. Hossalla, Richard J. "Henry E. Abbey, Commerial Manager: A Study of Producing Management in the Theatre of the Late Nineteenth Century (1870-1900)." Unpublished doctoral dissertation, Kent State University, 1972.

C1241. Hostetler, Paul S. "James H. Caldwell: Theatre Manager." Unpublished doctoral dissertation, University of Louisville, 1964.

C1242. Hotson, Leslie. The Death of Christopher Marlowe. Cambridge, Mass.: Harvard University Press, 1925.

C1243. _____. George Jolly: Actor Manager: New Light on the Restoration Stage. N. P.: n. p., 1923. [Reprinted from Studies in Philology, XX, 4 (Oct. 1923).

C1244. Houseman, John. _Final Dress_. New York: Simon and Schuster, 1983.

C1245. _____ . _Front and Center_. New York: Simon and Schuster, 1979.

C1246. _____ . _Run-Through: A Memoir_. New York: Simon and Schuster, 1972.

C1247. Housman, Laurence. _The Unexpected Years_. London: Jonathan Cape, 1937.

C1248. Houssaye, Arsène. _Man about Paris: The Confessions of Arsène Houssaye_. Ed. and trans. Henry Knepler. New York: William Morrow, 1970.

C1249. Houston, James. _Autobiography of Mr. James Houston, Scottish Comedian_. Glasgow: John Mengies and Company, 1889.

C1250. Howard, J. Bannister. _Fifty Years a Showman_. London: Hutchison and Company, 1938.

C1251. Howard, Leslie Ruth. _A Quite Remarkable Father_ [Leslie Howard]. New York: Harcourt, Brace and Company, 1959.

C1252. Howard, Ronald. _In Search of My Father_ [Leslie Howard]. New York: St. Martin's, 1982.

C1253. Howe, J. Burdette. _A Cosmopolitan Actor: His Adventures All over the World_. London: Bedford, 1888.

C1254. Howe, Percival P. _Bernard Shaw: A Critical Study_. London: M. Secker, 1915.

C1255. _____ . _John Millington Synge: A Critical Study_. London: M. Secker, 1912.

C1256. _____ . _The Life of William Hazlitt_. London: Hamish Hamilton, 1922.

C1257. Howells, Mildred, ed. _Life in Letters of William Dean Howells_, 2 vols. Garden City, N. Y.: Doubleday, Doran and Company, 1928.

C1258. Hoyt, Edwin P. _Alexander Woollcott: The Man Who Came to Dinner_. Radnor, Penn.: Chilton, 1973.

C1259. _____ . _Paul Robeson: The American Othello_, Cleveland, Oh.: World Publishing Company, 1967.

C1260. Hubbard, Elbert. _In the Spotlight: Personal Experiences of Elbert Hubbard on the American Stage_. East Aurora, N. Y.: The Roycrofters, 1917.

C1261. Hudson, Jack. _James Young_. Belfast: Blackstaff Press, 1975.

C1262. Hughes, Alan. _Henry Irving, Shakespearean_. Cambridge: Cambridge University Press, 1981.

C1263. Hughes, Elinor. Passing through to Broadway. Boston: Waverly House, 1948.

C1264. Hugo, Victor. Memoirs. Trans. John W. Harley. New York: G. W. Dillingham, 1899.

C1265. Humble, Alberta L. "Matilda Heron, American Actress." Unpublished doctoral dissertation, University of Illinois, 1959.

C1266. Huneker, James Gibbons. Intimate Letters. Ed. Josephine Huneker. New York: Boni and Liveright, 1924.

C1267. Hunt, Douglas L. The Life and Work of Charles H. Hoyt. Birmingham, Ala.: Birmingham College, 1946.

C1268. Hunt, Leigh. Autobiography. Ed. R. Ingpen. London: Constable, 1903.

C1269. Hunter, G. K. John Lyly: The Humanist as Courtier. London: Routledge and Kegan Paul, 1962.

C1270. Hunter, Ruth. Come Back on Tuesday. New York: Charles Scribner's Sons, 1945.

C1271. Hurlbut, Gladys. Next Week East Lynne! New York: E. P. Dutton, 1950.

C1272. Hurok, Sol and Ruth Goode. Impresario. New York: Random House, 1946.

C1273. _____. Sol Hurok Presents: A Memoir of the Dance World. New York: Hermitage House, 1953.

C1274. Hurst, Lulu. Lulu Hurst (The Georgia Wonder) Writes Her Autobiography and for the First Time Explains and Demonstrates the Great Secret of Her Marvelous Power. Rome, Ga.: Lulu Hurst Book Company, 1897.

C1275. Huss, Roy. "Max Beerbohm: Critic of the Edwardian Theatre." Unpublished doctoral dissertation, University of Chicago, 1960.

C1276. Hutcheson, Maud M. "Mercy Warren: A Study of Her Life and Works." Unpublished doctoral dissertation, American University, 1951.

C1277. Hutchinson, John Wallace. Story of the Hutchinsons, 2 vols. Ed. Charles E. Mann. Boston: Lee and Shepard, 1896.

C1278. Hutchison, Percy. Masquerade. London: George G. Harrap and Company, 1936.

C1279. Hutton, Laurence. Edwin Booth. New York: Harper and Brothers, 1893.

C1280. Hyams, Joe. Bogie: The Biography of Humphrey Bogart. New York: New American Library, 1966.

C1281. Iacuzzi, A. The European Vogue of [Charles Simon] Favart: The Diffusion of the Opéra Comique. New York: Institute of French Studies, 1932.

C1282. Ibsen, Bergliot. The Three Ibsens: Memories of Henrik Ibsen, Suzannah Ibsen, and Sigurd Ibsen. Trans. Gerik Schjelderup. London: Hutchinson and Company, 1951.

C1283. Idman, Niilo. Charles Robert Maturin: His Life and Works. London: Constable and Company, 1923.

C1284. Inchbald, Elizabeth. A Simple Story. Ed. J. M. S. Tompkins. London: Oxford University Press, 1967.

C1285. Ingram, William. A London Life in the Brazen Age: Francis Langley, 1548-1602. Cambridge, Mass.: Harvard University Press, 1978.

C1286. In Memory of John McCullough. New York: Devenine Press, 1889.

C1287. Ireland, John, ed. Letters and Poems by the Late John Henderson. London: J. Johnson, 1786.

C1288. Ireland, Joseph N., ed. Fifty Years of a Playgoer's Journal: or Annals of the New York Stage from A. D. 1798 to A. D. 1848. New York: Samuel French, 1860.

C1289. _____. A Memoir of the Professional Life of Thomas Abthorpe Cooper. New York: Dunlap Society, 1888.

C1290. _____. Mrs. [Mary Ann] Duff. Boston: J. R. Osgood, 1882.

C1291. Irvin, Eric. Gentleman George [Darrell], King of Burlesque. St. Luica, Queensland: University of Queensland Press, 1980.

C1292. Irving, Gordon. Great Scot: The Life Story of Sir Harry Lauder. London: Frewin, 1968.

C1293. Irving, John. Mary Shaw: Actress, Suffragist, Activist. New York: Arno Press, 1982.

C1294. Irving, Laurence. Henry Irving: The Actor and His World. London: Faber and Faber, 1951.

C1295. _____. The Successors [H. B. and Laurence Irving]. London: Rupert Hart-Davis, 1967.

C1296. _____. Precarious Crust. London: Chatto and Windus, 1971.

C1297. Irving, William H. John Gay: Favorite of the Wits. Durham, N. C.: Duke University Press, 1940.

C1298. Isaac, Winifred F. Alfred Wareing: A Biography. London: privately printed, 1951.

C1299. Isaac, Winifred F. Ben Greet and the Old Vic: A Biography of Sir Phillip Ben Greet. London: Greenbank Press, 1964.

C1300. Isherwood, Christopher. Lions and Shadows: An Education in the '20's. London: Hogarth Press, 1938.

C1301. Isman, Felix. Weber and Fields: Their Tribulations, Triumphs and Their Associates. New York: Boni and Liveright, 1924.

C1302. Israel, Lee. Miss Tallulah Bankhead. New York: G. P. Putnam's Sons, 1972.

C1303. Ives, Burl. The Wayfaring Stranger: An Autobiography. New York: Whittlesey House, 1948.

C1304. Jackson, Anne. Early Stages. Boston: Little, Brown and Company, 1979.

C1305. Jackson, Holbrook. Bernard Shaw. Philadelphia: G. W. Jacobs and Company, 1907.

C1306. Jacob, Naomi. Our Marie [Lloyd]: A Biography. London: Hutchinson and Company, 1936.

C1307. James, William R. "Clay Meredith Greene: A Case Study of an American Journeyman Playwright." Unpublished doctoral dissertation, University of Iowa, 1969.

C1308. Janis, Elsie. So Far, So Good! New York: E. P. Dutton and Company, 1932.

C1309. Jeffares, A. Norman. William Butler Yeats: Man and Poet. London: Routledge and Kegan Paul, 1949.

C1310. Jefferson, Caleb. Life and History of P. T. Barnum, the Greatest of Living Showmen. London: Hansard Publishing Union, 1889.

C1311. Jefferson, Eugenie P. Intimate Recollections of Joseph Jefferson. New York: Dodd, Mead and Company, 1909.

C1312. Jefferson, Joseph. The Autobiography of Joseph Jefferson [III]. New York: Century Publishing Company, 1890.

C1313. _____. Rip Van Winkle: The Autobiography of Joseph Jefferson. New York: Appleton-Century-Crofts, 1950.

C1314. Jeffs, Rae. Brendan Behan: Man and Showman. London: Hutchinson and Company, 1966.

C1315. Jenkins, Harold. The Life and Works of Henry Chettle. London: Sidgwick and Jackson, 1934.

C1316. Jerome, Jerome K. My Life and Times. New York: Harper and Brothers, 1926.

C1317. Jerome, Jerome K. On the Stage and Off: The Brief Career of a Would-Be Actor. London: Simpkin, Marshall and Hamilton Kent, 1885.

C1318. Jerrold, Clare A. The Story of Dorothy Jordan. London: E. Nash, 1914.

C1319. Jerrold, Walter. Douglas Jerrold: Dramatist and Wit, 2 vols. New York: Hodder and Stoughton, 1914.

C1320. Jerrold, William Blanchard. The Life and Remains of Douglas Jerrold. Boston: Ticknor and Fields, 1859.

C1321. Jessel, George. Jessel, Anyone? Englewood Cliffs, N. J.: Prentice-Hall, 1960.

C1322. _____. So Help Me. New York: Random House, 1943.

C1323. _____. This Way, Miss. New York: Henry Holt and Company, 1955.

C1324. _____ and John Austin. The World I Lived In. Chicago: Regnery, 1975.

C1325. Joad, C. E. M. [George Bernard] Shaw. London: Victor Gollancz, 1949.

C1326. Johnson, Edgar. Charles Dickens: His Tragedy and Triumph, 2 vols. London: Victor Gollancz, 1953.

C1327. Johnson, Rossiter. Dora Knowlton Ranous, Author, Editor, Translator: A Simple Record of a Noble Life. New York: Publishers Printing Company, 1916.

C1328. Johnston, Alva. The Legendary Mizners [Wilson and Addison]. New York: Farrar, Straus and Young, 1953.

C1329. Jolson, Harry and Alban Emley. Mistah Jolson. Hollywood, Cal.: House-Warven, 1952.

C1330. Jones, Charles I. Memoirs of Miss [Eliza] O'Neill. London: D. Cox, 1816.

C1331. Jones, Doris A. The Life and Letters of Henry Arthur Jones. London: Victor Gollancz, 1930.

C1332. Jones, Henry Arthur. The Shadow of Henry Irving. London: Grant Richards, 1931.

C1333. Jordan, John. Original Memoirs and Historical Accounts of the Families of Shakespeare and Hart (to 1790). London: T. Richards, 1865.

C1334. Jordan, John C. Robert Greene. New York: Columbia University Press, 1915.

C1335. Jordan, René. The Greatest Star: The Barbra Streisand Story. New York: G. P. Putnam's Sons, 1975.

C1336. Josephson, Matthew. [Émile] Zola and His Time. Garden City, N. Y.: Garden City Publishing Company, 1928.

C1337. Joyce, James. Letters of James Joyce. Ed. Stuart Gilbert. New York: Viking Press, 1966.

C1338. Joyce, Peggy Hopkins. Men, Marriage, and Me. New York: Macaulay, 1930.

C1339. Judith, Julie Bernat. My Autobiography. Ed. Paul G. Sell. Trans. Mrs. Arthur Bell. London: Eveleigh, 1912.

C1340. Jupp, James. The Gaiety Stage Door: Thirty Years' Reminiscences of the Theatre. London: Jonathan Cape, 1923.

C1341. Kahn, E. J., Jr. The Merry Partners: The Age and Stage of [Edward] Harrigan and [Tony] Hart. New York: Random House, 1955.

C1342. Kaminska, Ida. My Theatre. Ed. and trans. Curt Leviant. New York: The Macmillan Company, 1973.

C1343. Kane, Whitford. Are We All Met? London: E. Mathews and Marrot, 1931.

C1344. Kanin, Garson. Remembering Mr. [W. Somerset] Maugham. New York: Atheneum, 1966.

C1345. Kaough, Joseph B., III. "Henry Placide, American Comedian." Unpublished doctoral dissertation, University of Kansas, 1970.

C1346. Karl, Frederick. Joseph Conrad, The Three Lives: A Biography. New York: Farrar, Straus and Giroux, 1979.

C1347. Katkov, Norman. The Fabulous Fanny [Brice]. New York: Alfred A. Knopf, 1953.

C1348. Kaufmann, Ralph J. Richard Brome, Cavalier Playwright. New York: Columbia University Press, 1962.

C1349. Kaye, Joseph. Victor Herbert: The Biography of America's Greatest Composer of Romantic Music. New York: G. H. Watt, 1931.

C1350. Kean, Charles. Emigrant in Motley: The Journey of Charles and Ellen Kean in Quest of a Theatrical Fortune in Australia and America. Ed. J. M. D. Hardwick. London: Rockliffe, 1954.

C1351. Keaton, Buster. My Wonderful World of Slapstick. Garden City, N. Y.: Doubleday and Company, 1960.

C1352. Keeler, Ralph. Vagabond Adventure. Boston: Fields, Osgood and Company, 1870.

C1353. Keese, William Linn. William E. Burton, Actor, Author, and Manager. New York: G. P. Putnam's Sons, 1885.

C1354. Kellar, Harry. A Magician's Tour Up and Down and Round about the Earth: Being the Life and Adventures of the American Nostradamus, Harry Kellar. Chicago: R. R. Donnelley and Sons, 1886.

C1355. Kellock, Harold. [Harry] Houdini: His Life Story. New York: Harcourt, Brace and Company, 1928.

C1356. Kellog, Charles. Charles Kellog, the Nature Singer. Morgan Hill: Pacific Science Press, 1929.

C1357. Kellogg, Clara Louise. Memories of an American Prima Donna. New York: G. P. Putnam's Sons, 1913.

C1358. Kelly, Fred C. George Ade: Warmhearted Satirist. Indianapolis, Ind.: Bobbs-Merrill, 1947.

C1359. Kelly, Jonathan Falconbridge. Dan Marble: A Biographical Sketch. New York: Dewitt and Davenport, 1851.

C1360. Kelly, Linda. The Kemble Era: John Philip Kemble, Sarah Siddons and the London Stage. New York: Random House, 1980.

C1361. Kelly, Michael. Reminiscences of of the King's Theatre, and Theatre Royal, Drury Lane, including a Period of Nearly a Half Century, 2 vols. London: Henry Colburn, 1826.

C1362. Kelly, Richard M. Douglas Jerrold. New York: Twayne Publishers, 1972.

C1363. Kelly, Walter C. Of Me I Sing: An Informal Autobiography. New York: Dodd, Mead and Company, 1953.

C1364. Kemble, Frances Anne. Further Records, 1848-83. London: Richard Bentley and Son, 1890.

C1365. _____. Journal, 2 vols. Philadelphia: Carey, Lea, and Blanchard, 1835.

C1366. _____. Record of a Girlhood, 3 vols. London: Richard Bentley and Son, 1878.

C1367. _____. Records of Later Life, 3 vols. London: Richard Bentley and Son, 1882.

C1368. Kendal, Margaret. Dame Madge Kendal. Ed. Rudolph De Cordova. London: John Murray, 1933.

C1369. _____. Dramatic Opinions [Madge Kendal]. Boston: Little, Brown and Company, 1890.

C1370. Kendall, Harry. I Remember Romano's: The Autobiography of Henry Kendall. London: MacDonald, 1960.

C1371. [Carlo] Goldoni and the Venice of His Time. New York: The Macmillan Company, 1920.

C1372. Kennard, Nina A. Mrs. [Sarah] Siddons. Boston: Roberts Brothers, 1887.

C1373. _____. Rachel. Boston: Roberts Brothers, 1885.

C1374. Kennedy, Bart. Footlights. London: H. Walker, 1928.

C1375. Kenney, Charles Lamb. A Memoir of Michael William Balfe. London: Tinsley Brothers, 1875.

C1376. Keown, Eric. Margaret Rutherford. London: Rockliff, 1956.

C1377. _____. Peggy Ashcroft. London: Rockliff, 1955.

C1378. Kerr, Frederick. Recollections of a Defective Memory. London: T. Butterworth, 1930.

C1379. Kerr, Laura N. Footlights to Fame: The Life of Fanny Kemble. New York: Funk and Wagnalls, 1962.

C1380. Ketchum, Richard M. Will Rogers: His Life and Times. New York: American Heritage, 1973.

C1381. Kiernan, Thomas. Sir Larry: The Life of Laurence Olivier. New York: New York Times Books, 1981.

C1382. Kildare, Owen F. My Mamie Rose: An Autobiograph. New York: Grosset and Dunlap, 1903.

C1383. Kimber, Edward. Juvenile Adventures of David Ranger (Garrick). 2 vols. London: P. Stevens, 1757.

C1384. Kimmel, Stanley P. The Mad Booths of Maryland. Indianapolis, Ind.: Bobbs-Merrill, 1940.

C1385. Kingston, Gertrude. Curtsey While You're Thinking--. London: Williams and Norgate, 1937.

C1386. Kinne, Wisner Payne. George Pierce Baker and the American Theatre. Cambridge, Mass.: Harvard University Press, 1954.

C1387. Kirchner, Louis P. "George Chapman: Translator, Poet, and Dramatist." Unpublished doctoral dissertation, Niagara University, 1945.

C1388. Kirkman, James Thomas. Memoirs of the Life of Charles Macklin, 2 vols. London: Lockington, Allen and Company, 1799.

C1389. Kisch, Cecil. Alexander Blok, Prophet of Revolution. London: Weidenfeld and Nicolson, 1960.

C1390. Kitt, Eartha. Thursday's Child. Toronto, Ont.: Longman's, 1956.

C1391. Klein, Arthur. "A Study of Elizabeth Rachel Félix (1821-1858)." Unpublished doctoral dissertation, University of Michigan, 1948.

C1392. Klein, Carol. Aline [Bernstein]. New York: Harper and Brothers, 1979.

C1393. Kleinfield, H. L. "The Theatrical Career of David Belasco." Unpublished doctoral dissertation, Harvard University, 1956.

C1394. Knapp, Bettina L. Antonin Artaud, Man of Vision. New York: D. Lewis, 1969.

C1395. _____. Louis Jouvet: Man of the Theatre. New York: Columbia University Press, 1958.

C1396. Knef, Hildegard. The Gift Horse: Report on a Life. Trans. David A. Palastanga. New York: McGraw-Hill, 1971.

C1397. Knight, Arthur H. J. George Büchner. New York: Barnes and Noble, 1974 [1951].

C1398. Knight, Esmond. Seeking the Bubble. London: Hutchinson and Company, 1943.

C1399. Knight, Joseph. David Garrick. London: K. Paul, Trench, Trübner and Company, 1894.

C1400. Knoblock, Edward. Round the Room: An Autobiography. London: Chapman and Hall, 1939.

C1401. Knowles, James Sheridan. The Life of Edmund Kean. London: n. p., 1833.

C1402. Knowles, Richard Brinsley. The Life of James Sheridan Knowles. London: Chiswick Press, 1872.

C1403. Kobler, John. Damned in Paradise: The Life of John Barrymore. New York: Atheneum, 1977.

C1404. Kochno, Boris. [Sergei] Diaghilev and the Ballets Russes. Trans. Adrienne Fouke. New York: Harper and Row, 1970.

C1405. Koht, Halvdan. The Life of [Henrik] Ibsen, 2 vols. London: Allen and Unwin, 1931.

C1406. Koller, Ann M. B. "George II, Duke of Saxe-Meiningen, and the German Stage." Unpublished doctoral dissertation, Stanford University, 1965.

C1407. Kommisarjevsky, Theodor. Myself and the Theatre. London: William Heinemann, 1929.

C1408. Kops, Bernard. The World Is a Wedding. New York: Coward-McCann, 1963.

C1409. Kotsilibas-Davis, James. Great Times, Good Times: The Odyssey of
Maurice Barrymore. Garden City, N. Y.: Doubleday and Company,
1977.

C1410. Krause, David. Sean O'Casey and His World. New York: Charles
Scribner's Sons, 1976.

C1411. Kreymborg, Alfred. Troubadour: An Autobiography. New York: Horace Liveright, 1925.

C1412. Kunzog, John C. The One-Horse Show. Jamestown, N. Y.: privately
printed, 1962.

C1413. Kyasht, Lydia. Romantic Recollections. Ed. Erica Beale. New
York: Brentano's, 1929.

C1414. Laceby, Arthur and Helen Giblo. Footlights and Fistfights, and
Femmes: The Jimmy Lake Story. New York: Vantage Press, 1957.

C1415. Lacey, Alexander. [René G. de] Pixérécourt and the French Romantic Drama. Toronto, Ont.: University of Toronto Press, 1928.

C1416. Lafitte, Sophie. [Anton] Chelhov. Trans. Moura Budberg and Gordon Latta. New York: Charles Scribner's Sons, 1973.

C1417. La Guardia, Robert. Monty: A Biography of Montgomery Clift. New
York: Arbor House, 1977.

C1418. Lahr, John. Notes on a Cowardly Lion [Bert Lahr]. New York: Alfred A. Knopf, 1970.

C1419. Lait, Jack. Our Will Rogers. New York: Greenberg, 1935.

C1420. Lamborn, Edmund A. G. and G. B. Harrison. Shakespeare the Man
and His Stage. London: Oxford University Press, 1959.

C1421. Lamm, Martin. August Strindberg. Trans. Harry G. Carlson. New
York: Benjamin Blom, 1971.

C1422. Lammel, Earl L. "Paul Osborn: A Professional Biography." Unpublished doctoral dissertation, Ohio State University, 1973.

C1423. Lancaster, Marie-Jacqueline, ed. Brian Howard: Portrait of a
Failure. London: Blond, 1968.

C1424. Lanchester, Elsa. Charles Laughton and I. New York: Harcourt,
Brace and Company, 1938.

C1425. _____. Elsa Lanchester, Herself. New York: St. Martin's Press, 1983.

C1426. Landau, Penny M. "The Career of Mary Ann Duff, the American Siddons, 1810-1839." Unpublished doctoral dissertation, Bowling
Green State University, 1979.

C1427. Landis, Jessie Royce. You Won't Be So Pretty (But You'll Know More). London: W. H. Allen, 1954.

C1428. Landstone, Charles. I Gate-Crashed. London: Stainer and Bell, 1975.

C1429. Lane, Margaret. Edgar Wallace: The Biography of a Phenomenon. Rev. ed. London: William Heinemann, 1964 [1938].

C1430. Lanfford, Gerald. The Richard Harding Davis Years. New York: Henry Holt and Company, 1961.

C1431. Lang, Anton. Reminiscences. Trans. Anton Lang, Jr. Munich: Carl Aug. Seyfried, 1930.

C1432. Lang, Matheson. Mr. Wu Looks Back. London: S. Paul and Company, 1940.

C1433. Lang, William A., II. "The Career of Alice Brady, Stage and Screen Actress." Unpublished doctoral dissertation, University of Illinois, 1971.

C1434. Langford, Laura H. Adelaide Neilson. New York: Funk and Wagnalls, 1885.

C1435. Langner, Lawrence. The Magic Curtain. New York: E. P. Dutton, 1951.

C1436. Langtry, Lillie. The Days I Knew. New York: George H. Doran, 1925.

C1437. Lano, David. A Wandering Showman, I. East Lansing: Michigan State University Press, 1957.

C1438. Larowe, Nina C. An Account of My Life's Journey So Far: Its Property, Its Adversity, Its Sunshine and Its Clouds. Portland, Ore.: n. p., 1917.

C1439. Larsen, June B. "Margo Jones: A Life in the Theatre." Unpublished doctoral dissertation, City University of New York, 1982.

C1440. Larson, Harold. Björnstjerne Björnson: A Study in Norwegian Nationalism. New York: King's Crown Press, 1944.

C1441. Lasky, Jesse L., Jr., and Pat Silver. Love Scene: The Story of Laurence Olivier and Vivien Leigh. New York: Thomas Y. Crowell, 1978.

C1442. Latham, Jean L. On Stage, Mr. [Joseph] Jefferson! New York: Harper and Company, 1958.

C1443. Lauder, Harry. A Minstrel in France. New York: Hearst's International Library, 1918.

C1444. _____. Roamin' in the Gloamin'. London: Hutchinson and

Company, 1928.

C1445. Laurent, Eugene M. "Walter Hampden: Actor-Manager." Unpublished doctoral dissertation, University of Illinois, 1969.

C1446. Lauriston, Victor. Arthur Stringer, Son of the North: Biography and Anthology. Toronto, Ont.: Ryerson Press, 1941.

C1447. Lavrin, Janko. Nikolai Gogol: A Centenary Survey. London: Sylvan Press, 1951.

C1448. Lawrence, Arthur. Sir Arthur Sullivan: Life Story, Letters, and Reminiscences. Chicago: H. S. Stone, 1900.

C1449. Lawrence, Gertrude. A Star Danced. Garden City, N. Y.: Double-day, Doran and Company, 1945.

C1450. Lawrence, William J. Barry Sullivan: A Biographical Sketch. London: W. and G. Baird, 1893.

C1451. _____. The Life of Gustavus Vaughan Brooke. Belfast: W. and G. Baird, 1892.

C1452. Laye, Evelyn. Boo, to My Friends. London: Hurst and Blackett, 1959.

C1453. Lazarovich-Hrebelianovich, Eleanor C. Pleasures and Palaces: The Memoirs of Princess Lazarovich-Hrebelianovich. New York: Century Publishing Company, 1915.

C1454. Leabo, Karl, ed. Martha Graham. New York: Theatre Arts Books, 1961.

C1455. Leathes, Edmund. An Actor Abroad: or Gossip Dramatic, Narrative and Descriptive. London: Hurst and Blackett, 1880.

C1456. Leavitt, Michael B. Fifty Years in Theatrical Management. New York: Broadway Publishing Company, 1912.

C1457. Lee, Gypsy Rose. Gypsy: A Memoir. New York: Harper and Brothers, 1957.

C1458. Lee, Henry. Memoirs of a Manager: or, Life's Stage with New Scenery. Taunton: W. Bragg, 1830.

C1459. Lee, Sidney. A Life of William Shakespeare. London: Smith, Elder and Company, 1898; 2d ed., 1916.

C1460. Leech, Clifford. John Ford and the Drama of His Time. London: Chatto and Windus, 1957.

C1461. Le Gallienne, Eva. At 33. New York: Longmans, Green and Company, 1934.

C1462. _____. The Mystic in the Theatre: Eleonora Duse. New York: Farrar, Straus and Giroux, 1966.

C1463. Le Gallienne, Eva. With a Quiet Heart. New York: Viking Press, 1953.

C1464. Leja, Alfred E. "Aphra Behn, Tory." Unpublished doctoral dissertation, University of Texas, 1962.

C1465. Lejeune, C. A. Thank You for Having Me. London: Hutchinson and Company, 1964.

C1466. Lemaître, Georges E. Beaumarchais. New York: Alfred A. Knopf, 1949.

C1467. Lemaître, Jules. Theatrical Impressions. Trans. Frederic Whyte. London: H. Jenkins, 1924.

C1468. Leman, Walter M. Memories of an Old Actor. San Francisco, Cal.: A. Roman, 1886.

C1469. Lennig, Arthur. The Count: The Life and Films of Bela "Dracula" Lugosi. New York: G. P. Putnam's Sons, 1974.

C1470. Leno, Dan. Dan Leno: Hys Booke. London: Greening and Company, 1899.

C1471. Leonard, Eddie. What a Life I'm Telling You. New York: privately printed, 1934.

C1472. Leonard, James M. "The Letters of William Duffy, Albany Theatre Manager, 1830-1835." Unpublished doctoral dissertation, Cornell University, 1971.

C1473. Leonard, William E. "The Professional Career of George Becks in the American Theatre of the Nineteenth Century." Unpublished doctoral dissertation, Ohio State University, 1969.

C1474. Lerner, Alan J. The Street Where I Live. New York: W. W. Norton, 1978.

C1475. Le Sage, Laurent. Jean Giraudoux: His Life and Works. University Park: Pennsylvania State University Press, 1959.

C1476. Lesch, Edward C. A. "Thomas Killigrew: Courtier, Playwright, and Manager." Unpublished doctoral dissertation, Princeton University, 1928.

C1477. Lesley, Cole. Remembered Laughter: The Life of Noël Coward. New York: Alfred A. Knopf, 1976.

C1478. Lesser, Allen. Enchanting Rebel [Adah Isaacs Menken]. New York: Beechhurst Press, 1947.

C1479. Letters, Francis J. H. The Life and Work of Sophocles. London: Sheed and Ward, 1953.

C1480. Letters of an Unsuccessful Actor [Anonymous]. Boston: Small, Maynard and Company, 1924.

C1481. Leung, George K. <u>Lan-Fang, Foremost Actor in China</u>. Shanghai: Commercial Press, 1929.

C1482. Leverton, William Henry and John B. Booth. <u>Through the Box-Office Window</u>. London: T. W. Laurie, 1932.

C1483. Levin, Don. <u>Stormy Petrel: The Life and Work of Maxim Gorky</u>. New York: Appleton-Century, 1965.

C1484. Levinson, André. <u>The Story of Léon Bakst's Life</u>. London: Alexander Kogan, 1922.

C1485. Levy, Edward Lawrence. <u>Birmingham Theatrical Reminiscences: Jubilee Recollections (1870-1920)</u>. Birmingham: J. G. Hammond and Company, 1920.

C1486. Lewes, Charles L. <u>Memoirs of Charles Lee Lewes</u>, 4 vols. London: R. Phillips, 1805.

C1487. Lewes, George Henry. <u>Life and Works of Goethe: With Sketches of His Age and Contemporaries</u>, 2 vols. London: n. p., 1855.

C1488. Lewis, Jim G. "The Southern Career of William H. Crisp: Actor/Manager 1844-1874." Unpublished doctoral dissertation, University of Texas, 1981.

C1489. Lewis, Paul. <u>Queen of the Plaza: A Biography of Adah Isaacs Menken</u>. New York: Funk and Wagnalls, 1964.

C1490. Lewis, Robert. <u>Slings and Arrows: Theater in My Life</u>. New York: Stein and Day, 1984.

C1491. Lifar, Serge. <u>Sergei Diaghilev: His Life, His Work, His Legend</u>. London: G. P. Putnam's Sons, 1940.

C1492. <u>Life and Adventures of John Edwin, Comedian</u>. London: n. p., 1791.

C1493. <u>The Life and Amours of Mrs. [Harriet] Waylett, of the Haymarket, Adelphi, and Olympic Theatres</u>. London: W. P. Chubb, 1830.

C1494. <u>Life and Memoirs of William Warren....</u> Boston: James Daly, 1882.

C1495. <u>Life and Theatrical Excursions of William Robert Grossmith, the Juvenile Actor</u>. Reading: n. p., 1827.

C1496. <u>The Life of James Quin, Comedian</u>. London: S. Bladon, 1766.

C1497. <u>The Life of John Philip Kemble</u>. London: J. Johnston, 1809.

C1498. <u>The Life of Lavinia Beswick, alias Fenton, alias Polly Peachum</u>. London: n. p., 1728.

C1499. <u>The Life of Miss Anne Catley, Celebrated Singing Performer of the Last Century</u>. London: n. p., 1888.

C1500. Life of Mr. Richard Savage...Who Was Condemned with Mr. J. Gregory.... London: n. p., 1727.

C1501. The Life of Mrs. [Frances] Abingdon (Formerly Miss Barton), Celebrated Comic Actress. London: Reader, 1888.

C1502. The Life of Tomaso the Wanderer: An Attack upon Thomas Killigrew. Ed. Richard Flecknoe. London: P. J. and A. E. Dobell, 1925 [1667].

C1503. Lillie, Beatrice and John Philip. Every Other Inch a Lady. Garden City, N. Y.: Doubleday and Company, 1972.

C1504. Lindford, Viveca. Viveka...Viveca: An Actress, A Woman, A Life. New York: Everest House, 1982.

C1505. Lindsay, Hugh. History of the Life, Travels and Incidents of Col. Hugh Lindsay, the Celebrated Comedian for a Period of Thirty-Seven Years. Philadelphia: n. p., 1859.

C1506. Lion, Leon M. The Surprise of My Life: The Lesser Half of an Autobiography. London: Hutchinson and Company, 1948.

C1507. Liptzin, Solomon. Arthur Schnitzler. New York: Prentice-Hall, 1932.

C1508. Lister, Raymond. The Muscovite Peacock: A Study of the Art of Léon Bakst. Medlreth, Eng.: Golden Head Press, 1954.

C1509. Little, Stuart. Enter Joseph Papp: In Search of a New American Theatre. New York: Coward, McCann and Geoghan, 1974.

C1510. Littleton, R. H. Biography of William Charles Macready, Tragedian. London: Vickers, 1851.

C1511. Littlewood, Samuel R. Elizabeth Inchbald and Her Circle: The Life Story of a Charming Woman. London: D. O'Connor, 1921.

C1512. Litto, Frederick M. "Edmund Simpson of the Park Theatre, New York." Unpublished doctoral dissertation, Indiana University, 1969.

C1513. Livingstone, Belle. Belle of Bohemia. London: John Hamilton, 1927.

C1514. _____. Belle out of Order. New York: Henry Holt and Company, 1959.

C1515. Lloyd, James. My Circus Life: Being the Life and Adventures and World Travels...of an Artist and Circus Proprietor Now Aged Seventy-Nine Years. London: Noel Douglas, 1925.

C1516. Locke Richardson's Tour around the World with Shakespeare: Some Information as to His Remarkable Career in Many Lands. New York: n. p., c. 1889.

C1517. Lockridge, Richard. Darling of Misfortune: Edwin Booth. New York: Century Publishing Company, 1932.

C1518. Lockwood, Margaret. Lucky Star: The Autobiography of Margaret Lockwood. London: Odhams Press, 1955.

C1519. Loewenstein, Fritz E., ed. The Pictorial Record of the Life of Bernard Shaw. London: Pitkin Press, 1951.

C1520. Loftis, John C. [Richard] Steele at Drury Lane. Berkeley: University of California Press, 1952.

C1521. Logan, Joshua. Josh: My Up and Down and In and Out Life. New York: Delacorte, 1976.

C1522. Logan, Olive. Before the Footlights and Behind the Scene. Philadelphia: Parmelee and Company, 1870.

C1523. _____. The Mimic World and Public Exhibitions. Philadelphia: New World Publishing Company, 1871.

C1524. Long, Mary V. "An Account of the Life and Works of John Westland Marston, including a Stage-History of His Plays." Unpublished doctoral dissertation, Radcliffe College, 1932.

C1525. Loraine, Winifred. Head Wind: The Story of Robert Loraine. New York: William Morrow, 1939.

C1526. _____. Robert Loraine: Soldier, Actor, Airman. London: Collins, 1938.

C1527. Lord, George de F. Homeric Renaissance: The Odyssey of George Chapman. New Haven, Conn.: Yale University Press, 1956.

C1528. Lowe, Robert W. Thomas Betterton. London: Kegan Paul, Trench, Trüber and Company, 1891.

C1529. Lowndes, Marie A. Belloc. "I, Too, Have Lived in Arcadia": A Record of Love and Childhood. London: The Macmillan Company, 1941.

C1530. Lubbock, Percy. George Calderon: A Sketch from Memory. London: Grant Richards, 1921.

C1531. Lucey, Janet C. Lovely Peggy: The Life and Times of Margaret Woffington. London: Hurst and Blackett, 1952.

C1532. Lucia, Ellis. Klondike Kate: The Life and Legend of Kitty Rockwell, the Queen of the Yukon. New York: Hastings House, 1962.

C1533. Ludlow, Noah M. Dramatic Life as I Found It. St. Louis, Mo.: G. I. Jones, 1880.

C1534. Ludwig, Richard M. "A Critical Biography of William Winter." Unpublished doctoral dissertation, Harvard University, 1950.

C1535. Lunn, Hugh K. Frank Harris. London: Jonathan Cape, 1932.

C1536. Lupino, Stanley. From the Stocks to the Stars: An Unconventional Autobiograph. London: Hutchinson and Company, 1934.

C1537. Luttrell, Gladys. Letters of an Actress. New York: Frederick A. Stokes Company, 1902.

C1538. Lyde, Elsie Leslie. Trustable and Preshus Friends, ed. Jane Douglas. New York: Harcourt, Brace and Jovanovich, 1977.

C1539. Lynch, Kathleen M. Roger Boyle, First Earl of Orrery. Knoxville: University of Tennessee Press, 1965.

C1540. Lyons, Charles R. Bertolt Brecht. Carbondale: University Press of Southern Illinois, 1968.

C1541. Lytton, Edward R. The Life, Letters, and Literary Remains of Edward Bulwer, Lord Lytton, 2 vols. New York: Harper and Brothers, 1883.

C1542. Lytton, Henry A. The Secrets of a Savoyard. London: Jarrolds, 1922.

C1543. _____. A Wandering Minstrel. London: Jarrolds, 1933.

C1544. MacArthur, David E. "A Study of the Theatrical Career of Winthrop Ames from 1904 to 1929." Unpublished doctoral dissertation, Ohio State University, 1963.

C1545. Macaulay, George C. Francis Beaumont: A Critical Study. London: Kegan Paul, Trench and Company, 1883.

C1546. _____. James Thomson. London: The Macmillan Company, 1908.

C1547. MacCarthy, Desmond. [George Bernard] Shaw. London: McGibbon and Kee, 1951.

C1548. Macchetta, Blanche R. Victorien Sardou: Poet, Author, and Member of the Academy of France: A Personal Study. London: Kegan Paul, Trench, Trübner and Company, 1892.

C1549. MacClintock, Lander. The Age of Luigi Pirandello. Bloomington: Indiana University Press, 1951.

C1550. MacFall, Haldane. Sir Henry Irving. London: T. N. Foulis, 1906.

C1551. MacGaw, Charles J. William Winter: Critic of the Brown Decades. Ann Arbor, Mich.: University Microfilms, 1945.

C1552. MacGeorge, Ethel. Life and Reminiscences of Jessie Bond, the Old Savoyard. London: John Lane, 1930.

C1553. MacGhee, Mildred M. The Acting of Ada Rehan. Canton, Mo.: Culver-Stockton, 1927.

C1554. Machlin, Milt. Libby [Holman]. New York: Tower Books, 1980.

C1555. Mackail, Denis G. Barrie: The Story of James M. Barrie. New York: Charles Scribner's Sons, 1941.

C1556. Mackaye, Percy. Epoch: A Memoir of Steele Mackaye, 2 vols. New York: Boni and Liveright, 1927.

C1557. MacKenzie, Charles and Edward, eds. Memoirs of Henry Compton. London: Tinsley Brothers, 1879.

C1558. Mackenzie, Henry. An Account of the Life and Writings of John Home. London: A. Constable, 1822.

C1559. Mackintosh, Matthew. Stage Reminiscences: Being Recollections Chiefly Personal, of Celebrated Theatrical and Musical Performers during the Last Forty Years.... Glasgow: James Hedderwick, 1866.

C1560. MacLiammoir, Micheal. All for Hecuba. London: Methuen and Company, 1947.

C1561. _____. Each Actor on His Ass. London: Routledge and Kegan Paul, 1961.

C1562. MacMahon, Donald H. "Charles Reade as a Dramatist." Unpublished doctoral dissertation, Cornell University, 1936.

C1563. Macqueen-Pope, Walter. Edmund Kean. Edinburgh: Nelson, 1960.

C1564. _____. Ivor [Novello]: The Story of an Achievement. London: W. H. Allen, 1951.

C1565. Macready, William C. The Diaries of William Charles Macready, 1833-1851, 2 vols. Ed. William Toynbee. New York: G. P. Putnam's Sons, 1912.

C1566. _____. Macready's Reminiscences and Selections from His Diaries and Letters. Ed. Frederick Pollock. New York: Harper and Brothers, 1875.

C1567. Maeder, Clara F. Autobiography of Clara Fisher Maeder. Ed. Douglas Taylor. New York: Dunlap Society, 1897.

C1568. Magarshack, David. [Nikolai] Gogol: A Life. New York: Grove Press, 1957.

C1569. _____. [Alexander S.] Pushkin: A Biography. New York: Grove Press, 1968.

C1570. _____. [Konstantin] Stanislavsky: A Life. London: MacGibbon and Kee, 1950.

C1571. _____. [Ivan S.] Turgenev: A Life. London: Faber

and Faber, 1954.

C1572. Mahoney, Ella V. Sketches of Tudor Hall and the Booth Family.
Belair, Md.: Tudor Hall, 1925.

C1573. Makover, Abraham B. Mordecai M. Noah: His Life and Work from the
Jewish View. New York: Bloch Publishing Company, 1917.

C1574. Makower, Stanley V. Richard Savage: A Mystery in Biography.
London: Hutchinson and Company, 1909.

C1575. Mallet, Charles E. Anthony Hope and His Books: Being the Author-
ised Life of Sir Anthony Hope Hawkins. London: Hutchinson and
Company, 1935.

C1576. Malone, Mary. Actor in Exile: The Life of Ira Aldridge. New
York: Crowell-Collier, 1969.

C1577. Maltby, Henry F. Ring up the Curtain. London: Hutchinson and
Company, 1950.

C1578. Malvern, Gladys. Curtain Goin Up: The Story of Katharine Cornell. New York: Julian Messner, 1944.

C1579. _____. Good Troupers All: The Story of Joseph Jefferson. Philadelphia: Macrae Smith, 1945.

C1580. Maney, Richard. Fanfare: The Confessions of a Press Agent. New
York: Harper and Company, 1957.

C1581. Mankowitz, Wolf. Mazeppa: The Lives, Loves, and Legend of Adah
Isaacs Menken. New York: Stein and Day, 1982.

C1582. Manvell, Roger. Sarah Siddons: Portrait of an Actress. New York:
G. P. Putnam's Sons, 1970.

C1583. Marbury, Elizabeth. My Crystal Ball: Reminiscences. New York:
Boni and Liveright, 1923.

C1584. March, Richard. Heinrich von Kleist. New Haven, Conn.: Yale University Press, 1954.

C1585. Marchant, William. The Privilege of His Company: Noël Coward Remembered. Indianapolis, Ind.: Bobbs-Merrill, 1975.

C1586. Marcosson, Isaac F. and Daniel Frohman. Charles Frohman: Manager
and Man. New York: Harper and Brothers, 1916.

C1587. Margetts, Ralph E. "A Study of the Theatrical Career of Julia
Dean Hayne." Unpublished doctoral dissertation, University of
Utah, 1959.

C1588. Markham, Pauline. The Life of Pauline Markham. New York: n. p.,
1871.

C1589. Marrot, Harold V. The Life and Letters of John Galsworthy. London: William Heinemann, 1935.

C1590. Marshall, Dorothy. Fanny Kemble. New York: St. Martin's Press, 1978.

C1591. Marshall, Frank A. Henry Irving, Actor and Manager: A Criticism of a Critic's Criticism. London: G. Routledge and Sons, 1883.

C1592. Marshall, Herbert and Mildred Stock. Ira Aldridge: The Negro Tragedian. London: Rockliff, 1958.

C1593. Marshall, Michael. Top Hat and Tails: The Story of Jack Buchanan. London: Elm Tree Books, 1978.

C1594. Marston, John Westland. Our Recent Actors: Being Recollections Critical, and, in Many Cases, Personal of Late Distinguished Performers of Both Sexes with Some Incidental Notices of Living Actors, 2 vols. Boston: Roberts Brothers, 1888.

C1595. Marston, William M. and John H. Feller. F. F. Proctor: Vaudeville Pioneer. New York: Richard R. Smith, 1943.

C1596. Martin, Burns. Allan Ramsay: A Study of His Life and Works. Cambridge, Mass.: Harvard University Press, 1931.

C1597. Martin, Mary. My Heart Belongs. New York: William Morrow, 1976.

C1598. Martin, Theodore. Helena Faucit (Lady Martin). London: W. Blackwood and Sons, 1900.

C1599. _____. Monographs: Garrick, Macready, Rachel, and Baron Stockmar. London: John Murray, 1906.

C1600. Martyn, William Carlos. John B. Gough: The Apostle of Cold Water. New York: Funk, 1893.

C1601. Marx, Arthur. Life with Groucho. New York: Simon and Schuster, 1954.

C1602. Marx, Groucho. Groucho and Me. New York: Bernard Geis, 1959.

C1603. Marx, Harpo and Rowland Barber. Harpo Speaks! London: Victor gollancz, 1961.

C1604. Marx, Maxine. Growing up with Chico [Marx]. Englewood Cliffs, N. J.: Prentice-Hall, 1980.

C1605. Marx, Samuel and Jan Clayton. Rodgers and Hart: Bewitched, Bothered, and Bewildered. New York: G. P. Putnam's Sons, 1976.

C1606. Maschivitz, Eric. No Chip on My Shoulder. London: H. Jenkins, 1957.

C1607. Mason, Alfred E. W. Sir George Alexander and the St. James's Theatre. London: The Macmillan Company, 1935.

C1608. Mason, James. Before I Forget: Autobiography and Drawings. London: Hamish Hamilton, 1981.

C1609. Mason, Rufus O. Sketches and Impressions, Musical, Theatrical, and Social (1799-1885). New York: G. P. Putnam's Sons, 1887.

C1610. Massett, Stephen C. What "Jeems Pipes of Pipesville" Saw-and-Did Drifting About. New York: Carleton, 1863.

C1611. Massey, Raymond. A Hundred Different Lives. Boston: Little, Brown and Company, 1979.

C1612. _____. When I Was Young. Boston: Little, Brown and Company, 1976.

C1613. Mathews, Anne [Mrs. Charles]. Tea-Table Talk, Ennobled Actresses, and Other Miscellanies, 2 vols. London: T. C. Newby, 1857.

C1614. _____. Memoirs of Charles Mathews, Comedian, 4 vols. Philadelphia: Lee and Blanchard, 1838-9.

C1615. Mathews, Charles J. The Life of Charles James Mathews, 2 vols. Ed. Charles Dickens, Jr. London: The Macmillan Company, 1879.

C1616. Mathews, John. Bow! Wow!! Wow!!!: Life and Theatrical Career of John Mathews..., 4 vols. London: n. p., 1874.

C1617. Matthews, Alfred E. Matty: An Autobiography. London: Hutchinson and Company, 1952.

C1618. Matthews, J. H. André Breton. New York: Columbia University Press, 1967.

C1619. Matthews, James Brander. Molière: His Life and His Works. New York: Charles Scribner's Sons, 1910.

C1620. _____. Rip Van Winkle Goes to the Play. New York: Charles Scribner's Sons, 1926.

C1621. _____. These Many Years: Recollections of a New Yorker. New York: Charles Scribner's Sons, 1917.

C1622. Matthews, Jessie. Over My Shoulder. Ed. Muriel Burgess. Westport, Conn.: Arlington House, 1975.

C1623. Matthison, Arthur L. Art, Paint and Vanity. London: Heath Cranton, 1934.

C1624. Maude, Cyril. Behind the Scenes with Cyril Maude. London: John Murray, 1927.

C1625. _____ and Ralph. The Haymarket Theatre: Some Records and Reminiscences. London: Grant Richards, 1903.

C1626. _____. Lest I Forget. New York: J. H. Sears, 1928.

C1627. Maugham, William M. The Summing Up [W. Somerset Maugham]. London: William Heinemann, 1938.

C1628. Maurois, André. The Titans: A Three-Generation Biography of the Dumas. Trans. Gerald Hopkins. New York: Harper and Brothers, 1957.

C1629. Maxwell, Gilbert. Helen Morgan: Her Life and Legend. New York: Hawthorn Books, 1974.

C1630. Mayer, Edwin J. A Preface to Life. New York: Boni and Liveright, 1923.

C1631. Mayer, Sylvain. Reminiscences of a K. C., Theatrical and Legal. London: Selwyn and Blount, 1924.

C1632. Maynadier, Howard. The First American Novelist? [Charlotte Lennox]. Freeport, N. Y.: Books for Libraries Press, 1968 [1940].

C1633. Mayor, Alpheus H. The Bibiena Family. New York: Bittner, 1945.

C1634. _____. Giovanni Battista Piranesi. New York: Bittner, 1952.

C1635. McBride, Joseph. Orson Welles: Actor and Director. New York: Harvest Books, 1977.

C1636. McCabe, John. George M. Cohan: The Man Who Owned Broadway. Garden City, N. Y.: Doubleday and Company, 1973.

C1637. McCallum, Colin W. "The Man Who Broke the Bank": Memories of the Stage and Music Hall [Charles Coborn]. London: Hutchinson and Company, 1930.

C1638. McCambridge, Mercedes. The Quality of Mercy: An Autobiography. New York: New York Times Books, 1981.

C1639. McCarthy, Imogene. Anna Cora Mowatt and Her American Audience. College Park: University of Maryland Press, 1952.

C1640. McCarthy, Justin H. Cissie Loftus: An Appreciation. New York: R. H. Russell, 1899.

C1641. McCarthy, Lillah. Myself and My Friends. London: Thornton Butterworth, 1933.

C1642. McClintic, Guthrie. Me and Kit [Katharine Cornell]. Boston: Little, Brown and Company, 1955.

C1643. McConnell, Margaret E. "William Warren II, the Boston Comedian." Unpublished doctoral dissertation, Indiana University, 1963.

C1644. McCord, David. H. T. P.: Portrait of a Critic [Henry Taylor Parker]. New York: Coward-McCann, 1935.

C1645. McCowen, Alec. Double Bill. New York: Atheneum, 1980.

C1646. McCowen, Alec. Young Gemini. New York: Atheneum, 1979.

C1647. McCullough, Bruce W. The Life and Writings of Richard Penn Smith. Menasha, Wis.: George Banta Publishing Company, 1917.

C1648. McCusker, Honor. John Bale, Dramatist and Antiquary. Bryn Mawr, Penn.: Bryn Mawr College, 1942.

C1649. McFall, Haldane. The Book of Claud Lovat Fraser. London: J. M. Dent and Sons, 1923.

C1650. McGarry, Celestine. "William Hunnis: Elizabethan Playwright and Poet." Unpublished doctoral dissertation, St. John's University, 1947.

C1651. McGill, Vivian J. August Strindberg: The Bedeviled Viking. New York: Brentano's, 1930.

C1652. McKelway, St. Clair. Gossip: The Life and Times of Walter Winchell. New York: Viking Press, 1940.

C1653. McKenna, Virginia. Some of My Friends Have Tails. New York: Harcourt, Brace and Company, 1970.

C1654. McLain, Michael S. "Nikolai P. Oklopkov: A Critical Life in the Soviet Theatre." Unpublished doctoral dissertation, University of Washington, 1982.

C1655. McNeal, Violet. Four White Horses and a Brass Band. New York: Doubleday and Company, 1947.

C1656. Meade, Edwards Hoag. Doubling Back: Autobiography of an Actor, Serio-Comical. Chicago: Hammond Press, 1916.

C1657. Meeks, Leslie H. Sheridan Knowles and the Theatre of His Time. Bloomington, Ind.: Principia Press, 1933.

C1658. Melford, Mark. Life in a Booth. London: Henderson's, 1913.

C1659. Melville, Lewis. Nell Gwyn: The Story of Her Life. London: Hutchinson and Company, 1923.

C1660. Melton, David. Judy [Garland]: A Remembrance. New York: Random House, 1972.

C1661. Memoir and Theatrical Career of Ira Aldridge, the African Roscius. London: Onwhyn, 1848.

C1662. Memoirs of the Celebrated Mrs. [Margaret] Woffington. 2d ed. London: J. Swan, 1760.

C1663. Memoirs of John Howard Payne, the American Roscius. London: J. Miller, 1815.

C1664. Memoirs of Junius Brutus Booth from His Birth to the Present Time...from the Journals Kept by Mr. Booth during His Theatrical Tour of the Continent. London: Chapple and Company, 1817.

C1665. Memoirs of the Life and Writing of Samuel Foote, the English Aristophanes. London: J. Bell, 1777.

C1666. Memoirs of the Life of Madame [Lucia Eliza] Vestris. London: privately printed, 1830.

C1667. Memoirs of Miss [Harriot] Mellon, afterwards Duchess of St. Albans, 2 vols. London: n. p., 1886.

C1668. Memoirs of That Celebrated Comedian, and Very Singular Genius, Thomas Weston. London: S. Bladon, 1776.

C1669. Memoirs of the Celebrated Miss Ann C----y [Catley]. London: n. p., 1773.

C1670. Menard, Wilson. Somerset Maugham. Los Angeles, Cal.: Sherbourne Press, 1965.

C1671. Mendelsohn, Michael J. Clifford Odets: Humane Dramatist. Deland, Fla.: Everett/Edwards, 1969.

C1672. Menpes, Mortimer. Henry Irving. London: A. and C. Black, 1906.

C1673. Meredith, Scott. George S. Kaufman and His Friends. Garden City, N. Y.: Doubleday and Company, 1974.

C1674. Merivale, Herman C. Bar, Stage and Platforms: Autobiographical Memories. London: Chatto and Windus, 1902.

C1675. Merman, Ethel and George Eels. Merman: An Autobiography. New York: Simon and Schuster, 1978.

C1676. _____. Who Could Ask for Anything More? Garden City, N. Y.: Doubleday and Company, 1955.

C1677. Merrill, John. Son of Salem. New York: Vantage Press, 1953.

C1678. Meserve, Walter J. Robert E. Sherwood: Reluctant Moralist. New York: Pegasus, 1970.

C1679. Meyendorff, Stella Z. Through Terror to Freedom: The Dramatic Story of an Englishwoman's Life and Adventures in Russia before, during, and after the Revolution. London: Hutchinson and Company, 1929.

C1680. Meyer, John. Heartbreaker [Judy Garland]. Garden City, N. Y.: Doubleday and Company, 1983.

C1681. Meyer, Michael. Ibsen: A Biography. Garden City, N. Y.: Doubleday and Company, 1971.

C1682. Michael, Edward and John B. Booth. Tramps of a Scamp. London: T. W. Laurie, 1928.

C1683. Middleton, George. Circus Memories: Reminiscences of George Middleton. Los Angeles, Cal.: G. Rice and Sons, 1913.

C1684. Middleton, George M. These Things Are Mine: The Autobiography of a Journeyman Playwright. New York: The Macmillan Company, 1947.

C1685. Miles, Henry D. The Life of Joseph Grimaldi. London: C. Harris, 1838.

C1686. Miller, Charles R. D. Alfieri: A Biography. Williamsport, Penn.: Bayard Press, 1936.

C1687. Miller, David P. The Life of a Showman. London: E. Avery, 1849?.

C1688. Miller, Ernest C. John Wilkes Booth--Oilman. New York: Exposition Press, 1947.

C1689. Miller, Philip B., ed. An Abyss Deep Enough: Letters of Heinrich von Kleist. New York: E. P. Dutton, 1982.

C1690. Miller, Ralph E. "William Seymour, American Director." Unpublished doctoral dissertation, Wayne State University, 1973.

C1691. Miller, Ruby. Believe Me or Not! London: John Long, 1933.

C1692. Mills, John. Up in the Clouds, Gentlemen, Please. New Haven, Conn.: Ticknor and Fields, 1981.

C1693. Millward, Jessie and John B. Booth. Myself and Others. London: Hutchinson and Company, 1923.

C1694. Miln, Louise J. When We Were Strolling Players in the East. London: Osgood, McIlvane and Company, 1894.

C1695. Milne, Alan A. Autobiography. New York: E. P. Dutton, 1939.

C1696. Milne, Tom. Rouben Mamoulian. Bloomington: Indiana University Press, 1969.

C1697. Milsten, David R. An Appreciation of Will Rogers. San Antonio, Tex.: The Naylor Company, 1935.

C1698. Mirsky, D. [Alexander] Pushkin. London: Routledge, 1926.

C1699. Miss Phyllis Dare: An Appreciation. Popular Favourites, No. 2. Manchester: n. p., 1921.

C1700. Mistinguett. Mistinguett and Her Confessions. Trans. Hubert Griffith. London: Hurst and Blackett, 1938.

C1701. Mistinguett, Queen of the Paris Night. Trans. Lucienne Hill. London: Elek Books, 1954.

C1702. Mrs. [Dorothy] Jordan and Her Family: Being the Unpublished Correspondence of Mrs. Jordan and the Duke of Clarence, later

William IV. Ed. A. Aspinall. London: Arthur Barker, 1951.

C1703. Mitchell, Yvonne. Actress. London: Routledge and Kegan Paul, 1957.

C1704. Mitford, Mary R. Letters of Mary R. Mitford, 2 vols. 2d ser. Ed. H. Chorley. London: Richard Bentley, 1872.

C1705. _____. Life of Mary R. Mitford. Ed. W. Harness and A. G. L'Estrange. London: Richard Bentley, 1870.

C1706. _____. Recollections of a Literary Life: or, Books, Places and People. London: Richard Bentley, 1852.

C1707. Modjeska, Helena. Memories and Impressions of Helena Modjeska: An Autobiography. New York: The Macmillan Company, 1910.

C1708. Molloy, Joseph F. The Life and Adventures of Edmund Kean. London: Downey, 1897.

C1709. _____. The Life and Adventures of Peg Woffington, 2 vols. London: Hurst and Blackett, 1884.

C1710. Molnar, Ferenc. Companion in Exile: Notes for an Autobiography. trans. Barrows Mussey. New York: Gaer Associates, 1950.

C1711. Moody, Richard. Edwin Forrest: First Star of the American Stage. New York: Alfred A. Knopf, 1960.

C1712. _____. Lillian Hellman. New York: Bobbs-Merrill, 1972.

C1713. _____. Ned Harrigan: From Corlear's Hook to Herald Square. New York: Nelson-Hall, 1980.

C1714. Moody, William Vaughn. Letters to Harriet. Ed. Percy Mackaye. Boston: Houghton Mifflin, 1935.

C1715. Moore, Eva. Exits and Entrances. London: Chapman and Hall, 1923.

C1716. Moore, Mary. Charles Wyndham and Mary Moore. Edinburgh: privately printed, 1925.

C1717. Moore, Thomas. Memoirs, Journals, and Correspondence of Thomas Moore, 8 vols. Ed. John Russell. New York: D. Appleton, 1853-1856.

C1718. _____. Memoirs of the Life of the Rt. Hon. Richard Brinsley Sheridan. London: Longman, Hurst, Rees, Orme, Brown and Green, 1825.

C1719. More, Kenneth. Happy Go Lucky. London: Robert Hale, 1959.

C1720. _____. More or Less. London: Hodder and Stoughton, 1978.

C1721. Morehouse, Ward. George M. Cohan, Prince of the American Theatre. New York: J. B. Lippincott, 1943.

C1722. Morehouse, Ward. _Just the Other Day: From Yellow Pines to Broadway_. New York: McGraw-Hill, 1953.

C1723. Morell, Parker. _Lillian Russell: The Era of Plush_. New York: Random House, 1940.

C1724. Morgan, Ted. [W. Somerset] _Maugham: A Biography_. New York: Simon and Schuster, 1980.

C1725. Moriarty, Eileen M. "John B. Keane: Kerry Dramatist." Unpublished doctoral dissertation, University of Washington, 1980.

C1726. Morley, Edith J. _The Life and Times of Henry Crabb Robinson_. London: J. M. Dent, 1935.

C1727. Morley, Henry. _The Journal of a London Playgoer: From 1851-1866_. London: G. Routledge, 1866.

C1728. Morley, Margaret. _Larger than Life: The Biography of Robert Morley_. London: Robson, 1979.

C1729. Morley, Robert. _Morley Marvels: Memoirs, Notes and Essays_. South Brunswick, N. J.: A. S. Barnes, 1979.

C1730. _____ and Sewell Stokes. _Responsible Gentleman_. London: William Heinemann, 1966.

C1731. Morley, Sheridan. _Gertrude Lawrence: A Biography_. New York: McGraw-Hill, 1981.

C1732. _____. _Gladys Cooper: The Biography of an Actress_. New York: McGraw-Hill, 1979.

C1733. _____. _Marlene Dietrich_. New York: McGraw-Hill, 1976.

C1734. _____. _A Talent to Amuse: A Biography of Noël Coward_. London: William Heinemann, 1969.

C1735. Morosco, Helen M. and Leonard P. Dugger. _Life of Oliver Morosco, the Oracle of Broadway_. Caldwell, Id.: Caxton Printers, 1944.

C1736. Morris, Clara. _Life on the Stage: My Personal Experiences and Recollections_. London: Isbister, 1902.

C1737. _____. _The Life of a Star_. New York: McClure, Phillips and Company, 1906.

C1738. _____. _Some Recollections of John Wilkes Booth_. New York: n. p., 1896.

C1739. _____. _Stage Confidences: Talks about Players and Play Acting_. Boston: Lothrop, 1902.

C1740. Morris, Felix. _Reminiscences_. New York: International Telegram Company, 1892.

C1741. Morrissey, James W. Noted Men and Women, Containing the Humor, Wit, Sentiment, and Diplomacy in the Social, Artistic, and Business Lives of the People Herein Set Forth. N. P.: Klebold Press, 1910.

C1742. Morrison, Peggy. Rachel: An Interpretation. London: Collins, 1947.

C1743. Morse, Frank P. Backstage with Henry Miller. New York: E. P. Dutton, 1938.

C1744. Mortensen, Brita M. and Brian W. Downs. Strindberg: An Introduction to His Life and Work. Cambridge: Cambridge University Press, 1949.

C1745. Mortimer, John. Clinging to the Wreckage: A Part of Life. New Haven, Conn.: Ticknor and Fields, 1982.

C1746. Morton, W. H. and Henry C. Newton. Sixty Years of Stage Service: Being a Record of the Life of Charles Morton. London: Gale and Polden, 1905.

C1747. Morton, William. I Remember: A Feat of Memory. Hull: Goddard, Walker and Brown, 1934.

C1748. Mosel, Tad and Gertrude Macy. Leading Lady: The World and Theatre of Katharine Cornell. Boston: Little, Brown and Company, 1978.

C1749. Moses, Marilyn A. "Lydia Thompson and the 'British Blondes' in the United States." Unpublished doctoral dissertation, University of Oregon, 1978.

C1750. Moses, Montrose J. and Virginia Gerson. Clyde Fitch and His Letters. Boston: Little, Brown and Company, 1924.

C1751. _____. The Fabulous [Edwin] Forrest: The Record of an American Actor. Boston: Little, Brown and Company, 1929.

C1752. _____. Henrik Ibsen: The Man and His Plays. New York: M. Kennerley, 1908.

C1753. _____. The Life of Heinrich Conried. New York: Thomas Y. Crowell, 1916.

C1754. Moss, Alfred. Jerome K. Jerome: His Life and Work. London: Selwyn and Blount, 1929.

C1755. Moss, Lynda T. "A Historical Study of Katharine Cornell as an Actress-Producer, 1931-1960." Unpublished doctoral dissertation, University of Southern California, 1974.

C1756. Mostel, Kate, Madeline Gilford, Jack Gilford, and Zero Mostel. One Hundred Seventy Years of Show Business. New York: Random House, 1978.

C1757. Mott, Edward S. A Mingled Yard: The Autobiography of Edward S. Mott. London: E. Arnold, 1898.

C1758. Moult, Thomas. [James M.] Barrie. New York: Charles Scribner's Sons, 1928.

C1759. Mozart, George. Limelight. London: Hurst and Blackett, 1938.

C1760. Mudford, William. The Life of Richard Cumberland, Esq. London: Sherwood, Neely and Jones, 1812.

C1761. Muir, Dorothy E. [Niccolo] Machiavelli and His Times. London: William Heinemann, 1936.

C1762. Muir, Kenneth. John Milton. London: Longmans, Green and Company, 1955.

C1763. Mullen, Barbara. Life Is My Adventure. New York: Coward-McCann, 1937.

C1764. Muller, Otto. Charlotte Ackerman: A Theatrical Romance Founded upon Interesting Facts in the Life of a Young Artist of the Last Century. Philadelphia: Porter and Coates, 1871.

C1765. Munden, Thomas S. Memoirs of Joseph Shepherd Munden, Comedian. London: Richard Bentley, 1844.

C1766. Munshin, Jules. Dear Anybody. New York: Crown Publishers, 1957.

C1767. Murdoch, James E. The Stage: Recollections of Actors and Acting from an Experience of Fifty Years. With a biographical sketch by J. Bunting. Philadelphia: J. M. Stoddart, 1880.

C1768. Murphy, Arthur. David Garrick. Dublin: Wogan, Burnet and Company, 1801.

C1769. Murray, Gilbert. AEschylus, the Creator of Tragedy. Oxford: Clarendon Press, 1940.

C1770. _____. Euripides and His Age. New York: Oxford University Press, 1955.

C1771. _____. An Unfinished Autobiography. Ed. Jean Smith and Arnold Toynbee. London: Allen and Unwin, 1960.

C1772. Murray, Ken. The Body Beautiful: The Story of Earl Carroll. Pasadena, Cal.: Ward Ritchie, 1976.

C1773. _____. Life on a Pogo Stick. Philadelphia: John C. Winston, 1960.

C1774. Murray, William H. The Farewell and Occasional Addresses Delivered by W. H. Murray...in the Theatre Royal and Adelphi, Edinburgh. Edinburgh: J. G. Bertram, 1851.

C1775. Musser, Paul H. James Nelson Barker. Philadelphia: University of

Pennsylvania Press, 1929.

C1776. Musset, Paul de. The Biography of Alfred de Musset. Trans. Harriet W. Preston. Boston: Roberts Brothers, 1877.

C1777. Myers, Clarence. "A Descriptive Biography of Henry James Finn, Nineteenth Century Actor, Manager, Playwright." Unpublished doctoral dissertation, University of Michigan, 1977.

C1778. Nabokov, Vladimir V. Nikolai Gogol. Norfolk, Conn.: New Directions, 1944.

C1779. Nadeau, Albert H. "James Robinson Planché, Craftsman of Extravaganza." Unpublished doctoral dissertation, University of Michigan, 1955.

C1780. Napier, Diana. Richard Tauber. Glasgow: Art and Educational Publishers, 1949.

C1781. Nares, Owen. Myself and Some Others: Pure Egotism. London: Duckworth, 1925.

C1782. A Narrative of the Life of Mrs. [Charlotte] Charke. London: W. Reeve, 1755.

C1783. Nason, Arthur H. James Shirley, Dramatist: A Biographical and Critical Study. New York: A. H. Nason, 1915.

C1784. Nason, Elias. A Memoir of Mrs. Susanna Rowson. Albany, N. Y.: J. Munsell, 1870.

C1785. Naylor, S. Gaiety and George Grossmith: Random Recollections on the Serious Business of Enjoyment. London: Stanley Paul, 1913.

C1786. Nash, George. Edward Gordon Craig, 1872-1966. London: Her Majesty's Stationer's Office, 1967.

C1787. Nash, Mary. The Provoked Wife: The Life and Times of Susannah Cibber. Boston: Little, Brown and Company, 1977.

C1788. Nathan, Hans. Dan Emmett and the Rise of Negro Minstrelsy. Norman: University of Oklahoma Press, 1962.

C1789. Neagle, Anna. Anna Neagle Says, "There's Always Tomorrow": An Autobiography. London: W. H. Allen, 1975.

C1790. Neebe, Frederick L. "William Whitehead: A Study of His Life, His Place in His Day, and His Works." Unpublished doctoral dissertation, University of Missouri, 1947.

C1791. Neilson, Julia. This for Remembrance. London: Hurst and Blackett, 1941.

C1792. Nelson, Benjamin. Arthur Miller: Portrait of a Playwright. New

York: McKay, 1970.

C1793. Nelson, Benjamin. Tennessee Williams: His Life and Work. London: P. Owen, 1961.

C1794. Nemirovich-Danchenko, V. I. My Life in the Russian Theatre. Trans. John Cournos. Boston: Little, Brown and Company, 1936.

C1795. Nesbitt, Cathleen. A Little Love and Good Company. London: Faber and Faber, 1975.

C1796. Nethercot, Arthur H. Abraham Cowley: The Muse's Hannibal. London: Oxford University Press, 1931.

C1797. _____. Sir William D'Avenant, Poet-Laureate and Playwright-Manager. Chicago: University of Chicago Press, 1938.

C1798. Newcastle, Margaret. A True Relation of the Birth, Breeding and Life of Margaret Cavendish, Duchess of Newcastle. Kent: privately printed, 1814.

C1799. _____. The Life of William Cavendish, Duke of Newcastle. Ed. C. H. Firth. London: Routledge, 1906.

C1800. Newlin, Claude M. The Life and Writings of Hugh Henry Brackenridge. Princeton, N. J.: Princeton University Press, 1932.

C1801. Newman, Ernest. The Life of Richard Wagner, 4 vols. New York: Alfred A. Knopf, 1933-60.

C1802. Newman, Shirlee P. Ethel Barrymore: Girl Actress. Indianapolis, Ind.: Bobbs-Merrill, 1966.

C1803. Newmark, Maxim. Otto Brahm: The Man and the Critic. New York: G. E. Stechert, 1938.

C1804. Newton, Henry Chance. Cues and Curtain Calls. London: John Lane, 1927.

C1805. Nichols, Beverley. Twenty-Five. London: Penguin Books, 1926.

C1806. _____. The Unforgiving Minute: Some Confessions from Childhood to the Outbreak of the Second World War. London: W. H. Allen, 1978.

C1807. Nicholson, Watson. Anthony Aston: Stroller and Adventurer. South Haven, Mich.: privately printed, 1920.

C1808. Nirdlinger, Charles F. Masques and Mummers. New York: De Witt Publishing House, 1899.

C1809. Noble, Iris. Great Lady of the Theatre: Sarah Bernhardt. New York: Julian Messner, 1960.

C1810. Noble, Peter. The Fabulous Orson Welles. London: Hutchinson and

Company, 1956.

C1811. Noble, Peter. Ivor Novello: Man of the Theatre. London: Falcon
       Press, 1951.

C1812. Nobles, Milton. "Shop Talk": Stories, Anecdotes of the Theatre,
       Reminiscences. Milwaukee, Wis.: Riverside Printing Company,
       1889.

C1813. Nolan, Fred. The Sound of Their Music: The Story of Rodgers and
       Hammerstein. New York: Walker, 1978.

C1814. Norman, Charles. So Worthy a Friend: William Shakespeare. New
       York: Rinehart, 1947.

C1815. Northall, William K. Before and Behind the Curtain: Fifty Years'
       Observations among the Theatres of New York. New York: W. F.
       Burgess, 1851.

C1816. _____, ed. Life and Recollections of Yankee Hill.
       New York: W. F. Burgess, 1850.

C1817. Norton, Sally O. "A Historical Study of Actor Will Geer, His
       Life and Work in the Context of 20th-Century American Social,
       Political, and Theatrical History." Unpublished doctoral dis-
       sertation, University of Southern California, 1981.

C1818. Norton, Sandra K. "William Henry West Betty: Romantic Child Act-
       or." Unpublished doctoral dissertation, University of Missouri
       at Columbia, 1976.

C1819. Nugent, Elliott. Events Leading up to the Comedy: An Autobio-
       graphy. New York: Trident, 1965.

C1820. Nugent, John C. It's a Great Life. New York: Dial Press, 1940.

C1821. Nunn, Curtis. Marguerite Clark: America's Darling of Broadway
       and the Silent Screen. Fort Worth, Tex.: Texas Christian Uni-
       versity Press, 1982.

C1822. Oberstein, Bennet T. "The Broadway Directing Career of Rouben
       Mamoulian." Unpublished doctoral dissertation, Indiana Uni-
       versity, 1977.

C1823. O'Brady, Frederick. All Told. New York: Simon and Schuster,
       1964.

C1824. O'Brien, P. J. Will Rogers: Ambassador of Good Will, Prince of
       Wit and Wisdom. Chicago: John C. Winston, 1936.

C1825. O'Brien, Pat. The Wind at My Back. Garden City, N. Y.: Doubleday
       and Company, 1966.

C1826. O'Bryan, Daniel. Authentic Memoirs: or, The Life and Character
       of That Most Celebrated Comedian, Robert Wilks. London: S.

Slow, 1732.

C1827. O'Casey, Eileen. Eileen/Eileen O'Casey. Ed. J. C. Trewin. London: The Macmillan Company, 1976.

C1828. O'Casey, Sean. Drums under the Window. London: The Macmillan Company, 1945.

C1829. _____. The Green Crow. New York: Braziller, 1956.

C1830. _____. I Knock on Any Door: Swift Glances Back at Things That Made Me. London: Readers' Union, 1943.

C1831. _____. Inishfallen Fare Thee Well. London: The Macmillan Company, 1949.

C1832. _____. Pictures in the Hallway. London: The Macmillan Company, 1942.

C1833. _____. Rose and Crown. London: The Macmillan Company, 1952.

C1834. _____. Sunset and Evening Star. London: The Macmillan Company, 1954.

C1835. O'Connor, Garry. Ralph Richardson: An Actor's Life. New York: Atheneum, 1982.

C1836. O'Connor, Richard. Heywood Broun. New York: G. P. Putnam's Sons, 1975.

C1837. O'Hara, Constance M. Heaven Was not Enough. Philadelphia, Penn.: J. B. Lippincott, 1955.

C1838. O'Keeffe, John. Recollections of the Life of John O'Keeffe, 2 vols. London: Henry Colburn, 1826.

C1839. Olcott, Rita. Song in His Heart [Chauncey Olcott]. New York: House of Field, 1939.

C1840. Oldys, W. Memoirs of Mrs. Anne Oldfield. London: n. p., 1741.

C1841. Oliver, Harold J. Sir Robert Howard: A Critical Biography. Durham, N. C.: Duke University Press, 1963.

C1842. Oliver, Victor. Mr. Showbusiness. London: G. G. Harrap, 1954.

C1843. Olivier, Laurence. Confessions of an Actor: An Autobiography. New York: Simon and Schuster, 1982.

C1844. O'Neil, Colette. After Ten Years: A Personal Record. London: Jonathan Cape, 1931.

C1845. Oppenheimer, George. A View from the Sixties: Memories of a Spent Life. New York: David McKay, 1966.

C1846. Orme, Michael. J. T. Grein: The Story of a Pioneer. London: John Murray, 1936.

C1847. Orr, Lynn E. "Dion Boucicault and the 19th-Century Theatre." Unpublished doctoral dissertation, Louisiana State University, 1953.

C1848. Osborn, James Marshall. John Dryden: Some Biographical Facts and Problems. New York: Columbia University Press, 1965 [1940].

C1849. Ould, Hermon. John Galsworthy. London: Chapman and Hall, 1934.

C1850. Outerbridge, David. Without Makeup: Liv Ullman. New York: William Morrow, 1979.

C1851. Overmyer, Grace. America's First Hamlet: John Howard Payne. New York: New York University Press, 1957.

C1852. Owens, Mary S. [Mrs. John E.]. Memories of the Professional and Social Life of John E. Owens. Baltimore, Md.: John Murphy, 1892.

C1853. Page, Eugene R. George Colman the Elder: Essayist, Dramatist and Theatrical Manager. New York: Columbia University Press, 1935.

C1854. Palmer, John. Ben Jonson. London: Routledge and Kegan Paul, 1934.

C1855. Palmer, John L. Molière: His Life and Works. London: G. Bell and Sons, 1930.

C1856. Palmer, Lilli. Change Lobsters and Dance: An Autobiography. New York: The Macmillan Company, 1975.

C1857. Palmeri, Joseph. "Luigi Riccoboni, Actor-Critic of the 18th Century." Unpublished doctoral dissertation, University of Wisconsin, 1938.

C1858. Papich, Stephen. Remembering Josephine [Baker]. Indianapolis, Ind.: Bobbs-Merrill, 1976.

C1859. Paradise, Nathaniel B. Thomas Lodge: The History of an Elizabethan. New Haven, Conn.: Yale University Press, 1933.

C1860. Parish, James R. and Steven Whitney. Vincent Price Unmasked: A Biography. New York: Drake, 1974.

C1861. Parker, Louis N. Several of My Lives. London: Chapman and Hall, 1928.

C1862. Parry, Edward A. Charles Macklin. London: Kegan Paul, Trench, Trübner and Company, 1891.

C1863. Parry, John O. Victorian Swansdown: Extracts from the Early Travel Diaries of John Orlando Parry, the Victorian Entertainer.

Ed. C. B. Andrews and J. A. Orr-Ewing. London: John Murray, 1935.

C1864. Parsons, Florence M. David Garrick and His Circle. New York: G. P. Putnam's Sons, 1906.

C1865. _____. The Incomparable [Sarah] Siddons. London: Methuen and Company, 1909.

C1866. Parsons, Samuel. Poetical Trifles, Being a Collection of Songs and Fugitive Pieces...with a Sketch of the Life of the Actor. York: R. Johnson, 1822.

C1867. Partridge, Paul W., Jr. "John Blake White, Southern Dramatic Painter and Playwright." Unpublished doctoral dissertation, University of Pennsylvania, 1951.

C1868. Pasquin, Anthony, ed. Eccentricities of John Edwin, Comedian, 2 vols. London: J. Hamilton, 1791.

C1869. Patch, Blanche. Thirty Years with G[eorge] B[ernard] S[haw]. London: Victor Gollancz, 1951.

C1870. Paterson, Peter. The Confessions of a Strolling Player: or, Three Years' Experience in Theatres Rural. London: Bertram and Company, 1852.

C1871. _____. Glimpses of Real Life, as Seen in the Theatrical World and in Bohemia. Edinburgh: W. P. Nimmo, 1864.

C1872. Patterson, Ada and Victory Bateman. By the Stage Door. New York: Grafton, 1902.

C1873. _____. Maude Adams: A Biography. New York: Meyer Brothers, 1907.

C1874. Paul, Harry G. John Dennis: His Life and Criticism. New York: Columbia University Press, 1911.

C1875. Paulding, James Kirke. Letters. Ed. Ralph A. Aderman. Madison: University of Wisconsin Press, 1962.

C1876. Paulding, William I. Literary Life of James Kirke Paulding. New York: Charles Scribner's Sons, 1867.

C1877. Paxton, Sydney. Stage See-Saws: The Ups and Downs of an Actor's Life. London: Mills, 1917.

C1878. Payne, Ben Iden. A Life in a Wooden O: Memoirs of the Theatre. New Haven, Conn.: Yale University Press, 1977.

C1879. Payne, Robert. [George] Gershwin. New York: Pyramid Books, 1960.

C1880. Payne, William Morton. Björnstjerne Björnson. Chicago: A. C. McClurg, 1910.

C1881. Peabody, Josephine Preston. Diary and Letters. Ed. Christina H. Baker. Boston: Houghton Mifflin, 1925.

C1882. Peake, Richard B. Memoirs of the Colman Family, 2 vols. London: Richard Bentley, 1841.

C1883. Pearce, Charles E. The Jolly Duchess: Harriot Mellon, afterwards Mrs. Coutts and the Duchess of St. Albans. London: S. Paul, 1915.

C1884. _____. Madame [Lucia Eliza] Vestris and Her Time. London: Stanley Paul, 1923.

C1885. _____. "Polly Peachum": Being the Story of Lavinia Fenton (Duchess of Bolton) and The Beggar's Opera. New York: Brentano's, 1913.

C1886. Pearson, Hesketh. Beerbohm Tree: His Life and Laughter. London: Methuen and Company, 1956.

C1887. _____. G. B. S.: A Full-Length Portrait. New York: Harper and Brothers, 1942.

C1888. _____. G. B. S.: A Postscript. London: Victor Gollancz, 1951.

C1889. _____. Gilbert and Sullivan. London: Hamish Hamilton, 1935.

C1890. _____. Oscar Wilde: His Life and Wit. New York: Harper and Brothers, 1946.

C1891. Peile, Frederick K. Candied Peel: Tales without Prejudice. London: A. and C. Black, 1931.

C1892. Pelissier, H. G. Potted Pelissier. London: Martin Secker, 1913.

C1893. Pemberton, Thomas Edgar. Ellen Terry and Her Sisters. New York: Dodd, Mead and Company, 1902.

C1894. _____. John Hare, Comedian, 1865-1895. London: Routledge, 1895.

C1895. _____. The Kendals [Madge and William H.]. New York: Dodd, Mead and Company, 1900.

C1896. _____. The Life and Writings of T. W. Robertson. London: Richard Bentley and Son, 1893.

C1897. _____. Lord Dundreary: A Memoir of Edward Askew Sothern, with a Brief Sketch of the Career of E. H. Sothern. New York: Knickerbocker Press, 1908.

C1898. _____. A Memoir of Edward Askew Sothern. London: Richard Bentley and Son, 1889.

C1899. Pemberton, Thomas Edgar. Sir Charles Wyndham: A Biography. London: Hutchinson and Company, 1904.

C1900. Penley, William Sydney. Penley on Himself: The Confessions of a Conscientious Artist. Bristol: J. W. Arrowsmith, 1896.

C1901. Pennington, W. H. Sea, Camp, and Stage: Incidents in the Life of a Survivor of the Balaclava Light Brigade. Bristol: J. W. Arrowsmith, 1906.

C1902. Penuelas, Marcelino C. Jacinto Benavente. Trans. Kay Engler. New York: Twayne Publishers, 1968.

C1903. Peple, Edward H. An Auto-Biography: A Tale of Truth--and Ruth. New York: Moffat, Yard and Company, 1915.

C1904. Peppard, Murray. Friedrich Duerrenmatt. New York: Twayne Publishers, 1969.

C1905. Percy Hammond: A Symposium (In Tribute). Garden City, N. Y.: Doubleday, Doran and Company, 1936.

C1906. Perrie, George W. Buckskin Mose: or Life from the Lakes to the Pacific, as Actor, Circus Rider, Detective, Ranger, Gold-Digger, Indian Scout, and Guide. New York: H. L. Hinton, 1873.

C1907. Perry, Hamilton D. Libby Holman. Boston: Little, Brown and Company, 1983.

C1908. Perry, John. James A. Herne: The American Ibsen. Chicago: Nelson Hall, 1978.

C1909. Pertwee, Roland. Master of None. London: Peter Davies, 1940.

C1910. Peters, Margot. Mrs. Pat: The Life of Mrs. Patrick Campbell. New York: Alfred A. Knopf, 1984.

C1911. Petrova, Olga. Butter with My Bread. Indianapolis, Ind.: Bobbs-Merrill, 1942.

C1912. Peyrouse, John C., Jr. "Oliver Taylor--A Pioneer Theatre Man in Southern Appalachia." Unpublished doctoral dissertation, University of Nebraska at Lincoln, 1978.

C1913. Phelps, W. May and John Forbes-Robertson. The Life and Lifework of Samuel Phelps. London: S. Low, Marston, Searle and Rivington, 1886.

C1914. Phillips, Emma Watts. Watts Phillips: Artist and Playwright. London: Cassell and Company, 1891.

C1915. Phillips, Francis C. My Varied Life. London: Eveleigh Nash, 1914.

C1916. Phippen, Francis. Authentic Memoirs of Edmund Kean. London: J. Roach, 1814.

C1917. Pickles, Wilfred. Wilfred Pickles Invites You to Have Another Go. N. Pomfret, Vt.: Newton Abbot, 1978.

C1918. Picon, Molly and Jean B. Grillo. Molly!: An Autobiography. New York: Simon and Schuster, 1980.

C1919. _____ and Eth C. Rosenberg. So Laugh a Little. New York: Julian Messner, 1962.

C1920. Pinero, Arthur Wing. The Collected Letters of Sir Arthur Pinero. Ed. J. P. Wearing. London: Oxford University Press, 1974.

C1921. Pinto, Vivian de Sola and A. E. Rodway. Enthusiast in Wit: A Portrait of John Wilmot, Earl of Rochester. London: Routledge and Kegan Paul, 1962.

C1922. _____. Sir Charles Sedley: A Study in the Life and Literature of the Restoration. London: Constable, 1927.

C1923. Pitcher, Harvey J. Chekhov's Leading Lady: A Portrait of the Actress, Olga Knipper. New York: Franklin Watts, 1980.

C1924. Pitou, Augustus. Masters of the Show. New York: Neale Publishing Company, 1914.

C1925. Planché, James R. Recollections and Reflections, 2 vols. London: Sampson Low, 1872.

C1926. Playfair, Giles W. [Edmund] Kean. New York: E. P. Dutton, 1939.

C1927. _____. My Father's Son. London: Bles, 1937.

C1928. _____. The Prodigy: A Study of the Strange Life of Master Betty. London: Secker and Warburg, 1967.

C1929. Playfair, Nigel. Hammersmith Hoy: A Book of Minor Revelations. London: Faber and Faber, 1930.

C1930. Plotnicki, Rita M. "The Evolution of a Star: The Career of Viola Allen, 1882-1918." Unpublished doctoral dissertation, City University of New York, 1979.

C1931. Plowman, Thomas F. Fifty Years of a Showman's Life. New York: John Lane Company, 1919.

C1932. Pogson, Rex. Miss [Annie E. F.] Horniman and the Gaiety Theatre, Manchester. London: Rockliff, 1952.

C1933. Poindexter, Betty. "Ted Shawn: His Personal Life, His Professional Career, and His Contributions to the Development of Dance in the U. S. A. from 1891 to 1963." Unpublished doctoral dissertation, Texas Women's University, 1958.

C1934. Poitier, Sidney. This Life. New York: Alfred A. Knopf, 1980.

C1935. Polinger, Elliott H. Pierre Charles Roy, Playwright and Satir-

ist. New York: Columbia University Press, 1930.

C1936. Pollock, Channing. The Footlights, Fore and Aft. Boston: R. G. Badger, 1911.

C1937. _____. Harvest of My Years. Indianapolis, Ind.: Bobbs-Merrill, 1943.

C1938. Pollock, Juliet. [William Charles] Macready as I Knew Him. London: Remington, 1884.

C1939. Pollock, Walter H. Impressions of Henry Irving. London: Longmans, 1908.

C1940. Pontavice de Heussey, Robert du. Villiers de l'Isle Adam: His Life and Works. Trans. Mary Lloyd. London: William Heinemann, 1894.

C1941. Pontiero, Giovanni, ed. and trans. [Eleonora] Duse on Tour: Guido Noccioli's Diaries, 1906-7. Amherst: University of Massachusetts Press, 1982.

C1942. Poole, John. Sketches and Recollections, 2 vols. London: Richard Bentley, 1835.

C1943. Power, Tyrone. Impressions of America, During the Years 1833, 1834, and 1835, 2 vols. London: Richard Bentley, 1836.

C1944. Power-Waters, Alma. John Barrymore, the Legend and the Man. New York: Julian Messner, 1941.

C1945. _____. The Story of Young Edwin Booth. New York: E. P. Dutton, 1955.

C1946. Powers, James T. Twinkle Little Star: Sparkling Memories of Seventy Years. New York: G. P. Putnam's Sons, 1939.

C1947. Préjean, Albert. The Sky and the Stars. Trans. Virginia Graham. London: Harvil, 1956.

C1948. Preston, Harry. Memories. London: Constable and Company, 1928.

C1949. Price, Nancy. Shadows on the Hills. London: Allen and Unwin, 1938.

C1950. Price, Vincent. I Like What I Know. Garden City, N. Y.: Doubleday and Company, 1959.

C1951. _____. Vincent Price: His Movies, His Plays, and His Life. Garden City, N. Y.: Doubleday and Company, 1978.

C1952. Price, William T. A Life of Charlotte Cushman. New York: Brentano's, 1894.

C1953. _____. A Life of William Charles Macready. New York: Brentano's, 1894.

C1954. Prideaux, Tom. Love or Nothing: The Life and Times of Ellen Terry. New York: Charles Scribner's Sons, 1975.

C1955. Priestley, John Boynton. Instead of the Trees: A Final Chapter of Autobiography. New York: Stein and Day, 1977.

C1956. _____. Midnight on the Desert: A Chapter of Autobiography. London: William Heinemann, 1937.

C1957. Prince, Harold S. Contradictions: Notes on Twenty-Six Years in the Theatre. New York: Dodd, Mead and Company, 1974.

C1958. Prinz, Johannes. John Wilmot, Earl of Rochester: His Life and Writings. Leipzig: Mayer and Müller, 1927.

C1959. Prior, James. Life of Edmund Malone, Editor of Shakespeare. London: Smith, Elder and Company, 1860.

C1960. _____. The Life of Oliver Goldsmith, 2 vols. London: John Murray, 1837.

C1961. Privitera, Joseph F. Charles Chevillet de Champmeslé, Actor and Dramatist, with a Critical Edition of His Hitherto Unpublished Play, La Veuve. Baltimore, Md.: Johns Hopkins University Press, 1938.

C1962. Procter, Bryan W. The Life of Edmund Kean, 2 vols. London: E. Moxon, 1835.

C1963. Prouty, Charles Tyler. George Gascoigne: Elizabethan Courtier, Soldier, and Poet. New York: Columbia University Press, 1942.

C1964. Pryce-Jones, David. Graham Greene. Edinburgh: Oliver and Boyd, 1963.

C1965. The Public and Private Life of That Celebrated Actress, Miss Bland, Mrs. Ford, or, Mrs. [Dorothy] Jordan. London: n. p., 1886.

C1966. Purdom, Charles B. Harley Granville Barker: Man of the Theatre, Dramatist, and Scholar. Cambridge, Mass.: Harvard University Press, 1956.

C1967. _____. Life over Again: An Essay in Autobiography. London: J. M. Dent, 1951.

C1968. Purdy, Claire L. Victor Herbert: American Music Master. New York: Julian Messner, 1944.

C1969. Pyper, George D. The Romance of an Old Playhouse. Salt Lake City, Ut.: Deseret News Press, 1937.

C1970. Quinn, Anthony. The Original Sin: A Self-Portrait. Boston: Little, Brown and Company, 1972.

C1971. Quinn, Germain. Fifty Years Back Stage: Being the Life Story of a Theatrical Stage Mechanic. Minneapolis, Minn.: Stage Publishing Company, 1926.

C1972. Quinn, John F. Charles Reade: Social Crusader. New York: New York University Press, 1946.

C1973. Quintero, José. If You Don't Dance, They Beat You. Boston: Little, Brown and Company, 1974.

C1974. Raby, Peter. Fair Ophelia: The Life of Harriet Smithson Berlioz. New York: Cambridge University Press, 1982.

C1975. Rae, William Fraser. [Richard Brinsley] Sheridan: A Biography, 2 vols. London: Richard Bentley, 1896.

C1976. Ramsey, Stanley C. Inigo Jones. London: Ernest Benn, 1924.

C1977. Randall, Harry. Harry Randall, Old Time Comedian. 2d ed. London: Sampson Low, Marston and Company, 1930.

C1978. Ranous, Dora K. The Diary of a Daly Debutante. New York: Duffield and Company, 1910.

C1979. Raphael, Frederic. W. Somerset Maugham and His World. New York: Charles Scribner's Sons, 1977.

C1980. Rathbone, Basil. In and Out of Character. Garden City, N. Y.: Doubleday and Company, 1962.

C1981. Rattray, R. F. Bernard Shaw: A Chronicle. Luton, Eng.: Leagrave Press, 1951.

C1982. Rawson, Claude J. Henry Fielding. New York: Humanities Press, 1968.

C1983. Raymond, Ernest. Good Morning, Good People: An Autobiography, Past and Present. London: Cassell and Company, 1970.

C1984. _____. Please You, Draw Near: Autobiography 1922-1968. London: Cassell and Company, 1969.

C1985. _____. The Story of My Days: An Autobiography, 1888-1922. London: Cassell and Company, 1968.

C1986. Raymond, George, ed. The [Robert W.] Elliston Papers. London: Cunningham and Mortimer, 1842.

C1987. _____. The Life and Enterprises of Robert William Elliston, Comedian, 2 vols. New York: G. Routledge and Company, 1857.

C1988. Reade, Charles L. and Compton Reade. Charles Reade, D. C. L., Dramatist, Novelist, and Journalist: A Memoir. New York: Harper and Brothers, 1887.

C1989. Rede, William Leman. The Late John Reeve. London: n. p., 1938.

C1990. Redfield, William. Letters from an Actor. London: Cassell and Company, 1966.

C1991. Redgrave, Deirdre and Danaë Brook. To Be a Redgrave: Surviving amidst the Glamour. New York: Simon and Schuster, 1982.

C1992. Redgrave, Michael. In My Mind's I: An Actor's Autobiography. New York: Viking Press, 1983.

C1993. _____. Mask or Face: Reflections in an Actor's Mirror. New York: Theatre Arts Books, 1958.

C1994. Reed, Joseph V. The Curtain Falls. New York: Harcourt, Brace and Company, 1935.

C1995. Reeder, Louise. Currer Lyle: or The Stage in Romance and the Stage in Reality. New York: E. D. Long, 1850.

C1996. Rees, James. The Life of Edwin Forrest. Philadelphia, Penn.: T. B. Peterson and Brothers, 1874.

C1997. Reese, Max M. Shakespeare: His World and His Work. London: Arnold, 1953.

C1998. Reeve, Ada. Take It for a Fact: A Record of My Seventy-Five Years on the Stage. London: William Heinemann, 1954.

C1999. Reeve, Franklin D. "Between Image and Icon: The Poetry of Alexander Blok." Unpublished doctoral dissertation, Columbia University, 1958.

C2000. Reeve, Wybert. From Life. London: G. Robertson, 1891.

C2001. Reeves, John S. My Jubilee: or Fifty Years of Artistic Life. London: Simpkin, Marshall and Company, 1889.

C2002. _____. Sims Reeves: His Life and Recollections. London: Simpkin, Marshall and Company, 1888.

C2003. Reid, Norman M. "Edward Loomis Davenport: A Study in Acting Versatility." Unpublished doctoral dissertation, University of Michigan, 1941.

C2004. Reignolds-Winslow, Catherine M. Yesterdays with Actors. Boston: Cupples and Hurd, 1887.

C2005. Reilly, Mary A. "Sir Max Beerbohm, Satirist." Unpublished doctoral dissertation, University of Pittsburgh, 1945.

C2006. Reinhardt, Gottfried. The Genius: A Memoir of Max Reinhardt. New York: Alfred A. Knopf, 1979.

C2007. Relph, Harry. Little Tich. London: John Lane, 1927.

C2008. Rendle, Thomas M. Swings and Roundabouts: A Yokel in London. London: Chapman and Hall, 1919.

C2009. Rennert, Hugo A. The Life of Lope de Vega. London: Gowans and Gray, 1904.

C2010. Ressler, Kathleen. "Jeremy Collier." Unpublished doctoral dissertation, University of Cincinnati, 1935.

C2011. Reynolds, Frederic. The Life and Times of Frederic Reynolds, 2 vols. London: Henry Colburn, 1826.

C2012. Reynolds, Harry. Minstrel Memories: The Story of Burnt Cork Minstrelsy in Great Britain from 1836 to 1927. London: Alston Rivers, 1928.

C2013. Rheinhardt, Emil A. The Life of Eleonora Duse. Trans. Willa and Edwin Muir. London: M. Secker, 1930.

C2014. Rhodes, R. Crompton. Harlequin Sheridan: The Man and the Legends. Oxford: Basil Blackwell, 1933.

C2015. Rhys, Horton. A Theatrical Trip for a Wager: Through Canada and the United States. London: C. Dudley, 1861.

C2016. Ribalow, Harold U. Arnold Wesker. New York: Twayne Publishers, 1965.

2017. Rice, Elmer. Minority Report. New York: Simon and Schuster, 1963.

C2018. Richardson, Joanna. Rachel. London: Max Reinhardt, 1956.

C2019. _____. Sarah Bernhardt. London: Max Reinhardt, 1959.

C2020. _____. Victor Hugo. New York: St. Martin's Press, 1978.

C2021. Richek, Roslyn G. "Thomas Randolph: Christian Humanist, Scholar, and London Theater Playwright." Unpublished doctoral dissertation, University of Oklahoma, 1982.

C2022. Richel, Veronica C. Luise Gottsched: A Reconsideration. Bern: Peter Lang, 1973.

C2023. Richman, Harry and Richard Gehman. A Hell of a Life. New York: Duell, Sloan and Pearce, 1966.

C2024. Richtman, Jack. Adrienne Lecouvreur. Englewood Cliffs, N. J.: Prentice-Hall, 1971.

C2025. Ridolfi, Roberto. The Life of Niccolo Machiavelli. Trans. Cecil Grayson. Chicago: University of Chicago Press, 1963.

C2026. Riewald, J. G. Sir Max Beerbohm, Man and Writer. The Hague: Nij-
        hoff, 1953.

C2027. Rinehart, Mary Roberts. My Story. New York: Farrar and Rinehart,
        1931.

C2028. Ringler, William A. Stephen Gosson: A Biographical Study.
        Princeton, N. J.: Princeton University Press, 1942.

C2029. Ristori, Adelaide. Memoirs and Artistic Studies of Adelaide Ris-
        tori. Trans. G. Mantellini. New York: Doubleday, Page and Com-
        pany, 1907.

C2030. Ritchie, Anna Cora M. Autobiography of an Actress: or Eight
        Years on the Stage. Boston: Ticknor, Reed and Fields, 1854.

C2031. _____. Mimic Life: or Before and Behind the Cur-
        tain. Boston: Ticknor and Fields, 1856.

C2032. Rivers, John. Figaro: The Life of Beaumarchais. London: Hutchin-
        son and Company, 1922.

C2033. Robbins, Phyllis. Maude Adams: An Intimate Portrait. New York:
        G. P. Putnam's Sons, 1956.

C2034. _____. The Young Maude Adams. Francestown, N. H.:
        Marshall Jones, 1959.

C2035. Roberts, Arthur and Richard Morton. The Adventures of Arthur Ro-
        berts by Rail, Road, and River. Bristol: J. W. Arrowsmith,
        1895.

C2036. _____. Fifty Years of Spoof. London: John Lane, 1927.

C2037. Roberts, J. W. Richard Boleslavsky: His Life and Work in the
        Theatre. Ann Arbor, Mich.: UMI Research Press, 1981.

C2038. Roberts, Joan. Never Alone. New York: The Macmillan Company,
        1954.

C2039. Robertson, John George. The Life and Work of Goethe. London: G.
        Routledge and Sons, 1932.

C2040. Robertson, Thomas W. S. Memoir. In The Principal Dramatic Works
        of T. W. Robertson. London: Sampson Low, Marston, Searle and
        Rivington, 1889.

C2041. Robertson, Walford Graham. Letters from Graham Robertson. Ed.
        Kerrison Preston. London: Hamish Hamilton, 1953.

C2042. _____. Time Was. London: Hamish Hamilton,
        1931.

C2043. Robeson, Dave. Al G. Barnes, Master Showman. Caldwell, Id.: Cax-
        ton Printers, 1935.

C2044. Robeson, Eslanda G. Paul Robeson, Negro. London: Victor Gollancz, 1930.

C2045. Robey, George. Looking Back on Life. London: Constable and Company, 1933.

C2046. _____. My Life up till Now: A Naughtibiography. London: Greening, 1908.

C2047. Robins, Edward. The Palmy Days of Nance Oldfield. Chicago: H. S. Stone and Company, 1898.

C2048. Robins, Elizabeth. Both Sides of the Curtain. London: William Heinemann, 1940.

C2049. Robinson, Edward G. and Leonard Spiegelgass. All My Yesterdays: An Autobiography. New York: Hawthorn Books, 1973.

C2050. Robinson, Gil. Old Wagon Show Days. Cincinnati, Oh.: Brockwell, 1925.

C2051. Robinson, Henry Crabb. Diary, Reminiscences, and Correspondence of H. Crabb Robinson, 3 vols. Ed. Thomas Sadler. Boston: Fields, Osgood and Company, 1869.

C2052. Robinson, Jay and Jim Hardiman. The Comeback. Lincoln, Va.: Chosen Books, 1979.

C2053. Robinson, John R. and Hunter H. Robinson. Life of Robert Coates, Better Known as "Romeo" and "Diamond" Coates. London: Sampson Low, Marston and Company, 1891.

C2054. Robinson, Kenneth. Wilkie Collins. London: Davis Poynter, 1974.

C2055. Robinson, Lennox. Curtain Up. London: M. Joseph, 1942.

C2056. Robinson, Mary. Memoirs of Mary Robinson, "Perdita." Ed. Mary Robinson II. Intro. J. Fitzgerald Molloy. London: Gibbings and Company, 1894.

C2057. _____. Memoirs of the Late Mrs. Robinson. Ed. Mary Robinson II. London: R. Phillips, 1801.

C2058. Robson, William. The Old Playgoer. London: J. Masters, 1846.

C2059. Robyns, Gwen. Light of a Star. London: Leslie Frewin, 1968.

C2060. Rodgers, Richard. Musical Stages. New York: Random House, 1975.

C2061. Rodney, Peter M. "Robert Ardrey: A Biographical and Critical Analysis." Unpublished doctoral dissertation, Case Western Reserve University, 1980.

C2062. Rodway, Philip and C. F. Slingsby. Philip Rodway and a Tale of Two Theatres. Birmingham: Cornish Brothers, 1934.

C2063. Rogers, Betty. Will Rogers: His Wife's Story. New York: Bobbs-Merrill, 1941.

C2064. Rogers, Henry Munroe. Memories of Ninety Years: One Man and Many Friends. Boston: Houghton Mifflin, 1928.

C2065. Rogers, Will. Autobiography. Ed. Donald Day. Boston: Houghton Mifflin, 1949.

C2066. Rolfe, William James. A Life of William Shakespeare. Boston: D. Estes and Company, 1905.

C2067. Romer, Frank. P. T. Barnum. Washington, D. C.: Judd and Detweiler, 1933.

C2068. Root, Harvey Woods. The Unknown [P. T.] Barnum. New York: Harper and Brothers, 1927.

C2069. _____. The Ways of the Circus: Being the Memories and Adventures of George Conklin, Tamer of Lions. New York: Harper and Brothers, 1921.

C2070. Rose, Billy. Wine, Women and Words. New York: Simon and Schuster, 1948.

C2071. Rose, Clarkson. Red Plush and Greasepaint. London: Museum Press, 1964.

C2072. Rose, Enid. Gordon Craig and the Theatre. London: Sampson Low, Marston and Company, 1931.

C2073. Rosenberg, Charles G. Jenny Lind in America. New York: Stringer and Townsend, 1851.

C2074. Rosenfeld, Lulla. Bright Star of Exile: Jacob Adler and the Yiddish Theatre. New York: Thomas Y. Crowell, 1977.

C2075. Rosmond, Babette. Robert Benchley: His Life and Good Times. Garden City, N. Y.: Doubleday and Company, 1970.

C2076. Ross, Frederick G. The Actor from Point Arena: Excerpts Taken from the Memories of an Old Theatrical Man. Ed. Travis Bogard. Berkeley: University of California Press, 1977.

C2077. Rosslyn, James F. My Gamble in Life. London: Cassell and Company, 1928.

C2078. Roth, Lillian. Beyond My Worth. New York: Frederick Fell, 1958.

C2079. _____, Mike Connolly, and Gerold Frank. I'll Cry Tomorrow. New York: Frederick Fell, 1954.

C2080. Rourke, Constance. Troupers of the Gold Coast: or The Rise of Lotta Crabtree. New York: Harcourt, Brace and Company, 1928.

C2081. Row, Arthur W. Sarah [Bernhardt] the Divine. New York: Comet

Press, 1957.

C2082. Rowland, Mabel, ed. Bert Williams, Son of Laughter: A Symposium of Tribute to the Man and His Work. New York: Negro University Press, 1969.

C2083. Rowse, Alfred L. Christopher Marlowe: His Life and Work. New York: Harper and Row, 1964.

C2084. _____. Shakespeare, the Man. New York: Harper and Row, 1973.

C2085. _____. William Shakespeare: A Biography. New York: Harper and Row, 1963.

C2086. Roy, James A. James Matthew Barrie: An Appreciation. New York: Charles Scribner's Sons, 1938.

C2087. Royde-Smith, Naomi. The Private Life of Mrs. [Sarah] Siddons. London: Victor Gollancz, 1933.

C2088. Royle, Edwin M. Edwin Booth as I Knew Him. New York: Players' Club, 1933.

C2089. Rubin, Benny. Come Backstage with Me. Bowling Green, Oh.: Bowling Green University Popular Press, 1972.

C2090. Rueff, Suze. I Knew Sarah Bernhardt. London: Frederick Muller, 1951.

C2091. Ruggles, Eleanor. Prince of Players [Edwin Booth]. New York: W. W. Norton, 1953.

C2092. Rushmore, Robert. Fanny Kemble. New York: Crowell-Collier, 1970.

C2093. Russell, Charles E. Julia Marlowe: Her Life and Art. New York: D. Appleton, 1926.

C2094. Russell, Edward R. [Henry] Irving as Hamlet. London: H. S. King and Company, 1875.

C2095. Russell, Henry. The Passing Show. Boston: Little, Brown and Company, 1926.

C2096. Russell, Percy. Sir Henry Irving. London: S. Champness, 1896.

C2097. Rutherford, Margaret and Gwyn Robyns. Margaret Rutherford. London: W. H. Allen, 1972.

C2098. Ryan, Kate. Old Boston Museum Days. Boston: Little, Brown and Company, 1915.

C2099. Ryan, Patricia C. "John Golden: American Theatrical Producer." Unpublished doctoral dissertation, New York University, 1972.

C2100. Ryan, Patrick M., Jr. "Albert M. Palmer, Producer: A Study of

Management, Dramaturgy, and Stagecraft in the American Theatre, 1872-1946." Unpublished doctoral dissertation, Yale University, 1959.

C2101. Ryley, Samuel W. The Itinerant: or, Memoirs of an Actor, 9 vols.
Vols. 1-3. London: Taylor and Hessey, 1808.
Vols. 4-6. London: Sherwood, Neely, and Jones, 1816-7.
Vols. 7-9. London: Sherwood and Company, 1827.

C2102. Sackville-West, Victoria. Aphra Behn: The Incomparable Astrea.
London: G. Howe, 1927.

C2103. Sadleir, Michael. [Edward] Bulwer: A Panorama. Boston: Little,
Brown and Company, 1931.

C2104. _____. [Edward] Bulwer and His Wife: A Panorama,
1803-36. London: Constable and Company, 1933.

C2105. Sagar, Keith. The Life of D. H. Lawrence. New York: Pantheon
Books, 1980.

C2106. St. Denis, Ruth. Unfinished Life: An Autobiography. London:
George G. Harrap, 1939.

C2107. St. Denis, Teddie. Almost a Star. London: F. Muller, 1940.

C2108. St. John, Christopher. Ellen Terry. New York: John Lane, 1907.

C2109. _____. Henry Irving. London: The Green Sheaf,
1905.

C2110. St. Leger, Heyward J. Reminiscences of [Michael W.] Balfe. London: A. Nimmo, 1871.

C2111. Saintsbury, H. A. and Cecil Palmer. We Saw Him Act: A Symposium
on the Art of Sir Henry Irving. London: Hurst and Blackett,
1939.

C2112. Sala, George A. Life and Adventures of George Augustus Sala, 2
vols. London: Cassell and COmpany, 1895.

C2113. _____. [Frederick] Robson: A Sketch. London: J. C. Hot-
ten, 1864.

C2114. Salvini, Tommaso. Leaves from the Autobiography of Tommaso Salvini. New York: Century Publishing Company, 1893.

C2115. Samples, Gordon. Lust for Fame: The Stage Career of John Wilkes
Booth. Jefferson, N. C.: McFarland, 1982.

C2116. Sanders, Ronald. The Days Grow Short: The Life and Music of Kurt
Weill. New York: Holt, Rinehart and Winston, 1980.

C2117. Sands, Mollie. [Frederick] Robson of the Olympic. London: Society for Theatre Research, 1979.

C2118. Sanger, George. Seventy Years a Showman: My Life and Adventures in Camp and Caravan the World Over. London: J. M. Dent, 1926.

C2119. Sarcey, Francisque. Recollections of Middle Life. Trans. Elizabeth L. Carey. London: William Heinemann, 1893.

C2120. Sargeaunt, Margaret Joan. John Ford. Oxford: Basil Blackwell, 1935.

C2121. Sarlos, Robert K. Jig [George Cram] Cook and the Provincetown Players: Theatre in Ferment. Amherst: University of Massachusetts Press, 1982.

C2122. Saroyan, Aram. William Saroyan. New York: Harcourt-Brace-Jovanovich, 1983.

C2123. Saroyan, William. Chance Meetings: A Memoir. New York: W. W. Norton, 1978.

C2124. Sartain, John. The Reminiscences of a Very Old Man. New York: D. Appleton, 1889.

C2125. Sarton, May. I Knew a Phoenix. New York: W. W. Norton, 1954.

C2126. Savage, Richard. Memoirs of the Life of Mr. Theophilus Keene, the Late Eminent Tragedian. London: William Chetwood, 1718.

C2127. Savin, Maynard. T. W. Robertson: His Plays and Stagecraft. Providence, R. I.: Brown University Press, 1950.

C2128. Savo, Jimmy. I Bow to the Stones. New York: Frisch, 1963.

C2129. Sayler, Oliver M. Max Reinhardt and His Theatre. New York: Brentano's, 1924.

C2130. Schaffner, Neil E. and Vance Johnson. The Fabulous Toby and Me. Englewood Cliffs, N. J.: Prentice-Hall, 1968.

C2131. Schallit, Leon. John Galsworthy: A Survey. New York: Charles Scribner's Sons, 1929.

C2132. Schanke, Robert A. "Eva Le Gallienne: First Lady of Repertory." Unpublished doctoral dissertation, University of Nebraska, 1975.

C2133. Schildkraut, Joseph. My Father and I. New York: Viking Press, 1959.

C2134. Schoenbaum, Samuel. William Shakespeare: A Documentary Life. New York: Oxford University Press, 1975.

C2135. Schwartz, Charles. Cole Porter. New York: Dial Press, 1977.

C2136. Schwarz, Henry S. Alexandre Dumas, fils, Dramatist. New York: New York University Press, 1927.

C2137. Scott, A. C. Mei Lan-Fang, Leader of the Pear Garden. Hong Kong: Hong Kong University Press, 1959.

C2138. Scott, Clement W. Ellen Terry: An Appreciation. New York: Frederick A. Stokes, 1900.

C2139. _____ . Thirty Years at the Play and Dramatic Table Talk. London: Railway and General Automatic Library, 1890.

C2140. Scott, Cyril. My Years of Indiscretion. London: Mills and Boon, 1924.

C2141. Scott, Janette. Act One. New York: Nelson, 1953.

C2142. Scott, Margaret C. Old Days in Bohemian London: Recollections of Clement Scott. New York: Frederick A. Stokes, 1919.

C2143. Scott, Marion G. Chatauqua Caravan. New York: Appleton-Century, 1939.

C2144. Scott-Thomas, Herbert F. "The Life and Works of Nahum Tate." Unpublished doctoral dissertation, Johns Hopkins University, 1932.

C2145. Scriptor, Veritatis. Memoirs of the Present Countess of Derby (Late Miss Farren). London: Lee and Hurst, 1797.

C2146. Scurr, Helem M. "Henry Brooke." Unpublished doctoral dissertation, University of Minnesota, 1922.

C2147. Searle, Townley. Sir William Schwenck Gilbert: A Topsy-Turvy Adventure. London: Alexander-Ousley, 1931.

C2148. Seaver, Richard E. "Douglas Campbell: A Study of His Artistic Accomplishments as an Actor and Dramatist at Selected Theatres in England, Canada, and the United States to 1979." Unpublished doctoral dissertation, Wayne State University, 1981.

C2149. Sedgwick, Henry D. Alfred de Musset. Indianapolis, Ind.: Bobbs-Merrill, 1931.

C2150. _____ . Horace: A Biography. New York: Russell and Russell, 1967 [1947].

C2151. Sein, Kenneth and Joseph A. Withey. The Great Po Sein: A Chronicle of the Burmese Theatre. Bloomington: Indiana University Press, 1966.

C2152. Selby-Lowndes, Joan. The Blue Train: The Story of Anton Dolin. London: Collins, 1953.

C2153. _____ . The [Italia] Conti Story. London: Collins, 1954.

C2154. Seldes, Marian. The Bright Lights: A Theatre Life. New York: Houghton Mifflin, 1978.

C2155. Selig, Edward I. The Flourishing Wreath: A Study of Thomas Carew's Poetry. New Haven, Conn.: Yale University Press, 1958.

C2156. Sell, Henry B. and Victor Weybright. Buffalo Bill and the Wild West. New York: Oxford University Press, 1955.

C2157. Selznick, Irene M. A Private View. New York: Alfred A. Knopf, 1983.

C2158. Senior, Francesca D. The Life and Times of Colley Cibber. London: Constable and Company, 1928.

C2159. Sergeant, Philip W. Mrs. [Dorothy] Jordan: Child of Nature. London: Hutchinson and Company, 1913.

C2160. Seroff, Victor. The Real Isadora [Duncan]. New York: Dial Press, 1971.

C2161. Seymour, John. Memoirs of the Life of Elinor Gwyn. London: F. Stamper, 1752.

C2162. Shapiro, Leonard B. [Ivan] Turgenev: His Life and Times. New York: Random House, 1978.

C2163. Shattuck, Charles W., ed. Bulwer and Macready: A Chronicle of the Early Victorian Theatre. Urbana: University of Illinois Press, 1958.

C2164. Shaw, George Bernard. Sixteen Self-Sketches. London: Constable and Company, 1949.

C2165. _____. To a Young Actress: The Correspondence between Bernard Shaw and an American Artist [Molly Tompkins] from 1921 through 1948. Ed. Peter Tompkins. New York: C. N. Potter, 1960.

C2166. Shaw, Martin F. Up to Now. London: Oxford University Press, 1929.

C2167. Sheean, Vincent. Oscar Hammerstein I: The Life and Exploits of an Impresario. New York: Simon and Schuster, 1956.

C2168. Sheldon, Esther K. Thomas Sheridan of Smock Alley. Princeton, N. J.: Princeton University Press, 1967.

C2169. Shelley, Henry C. The Life and Letters of Edward Young. Boston: Little, Brown and Company, 1914.

C2170. Shelton, George. It's Smee. London: Ernest Benn, 1928.

C2171. Sherard, Robert H. Émile Zola: A Biographical and Critical Study. London: Chatto and Windus, 1893.

C2172. _____. The Life of Oscar Wilde. New York: Dodd, Mead and Company, 1928 [1906].

C2173. _____. The Real Oscar Wilde. London: T. Werner Laurie, 1917.

C2174. Sherk, Herman Dennis. William Gillette: His Life and Works. Bloomington, Ind.: Gaslight, 1983.

C2175. Sherk, Warren A. Agnes Moorehead: A Very Private Person. Philadelphia, Penn.: Dorrance, 1976.

C2176. Sherriff, Robert Cedric. No Leading Lady. London: Victor Gollancz, 1968.

C2177. Sherwood, John. No Golden Journey: A Biography of James Elroy Flecker. London: William Heinemann, 1973.

C2178. Sherwood, Robert Edmund. Here We Are Again: Recollections of an Old Circus Clown. Indianapolis, Ind.: Bobbs-Merrill, 1926.

C2179. _____. Hold Yer Horses! The Elephants Are Coming! New York: The Macmillan Company, 1932.

C2180. Shore, Florence T. Sir Charles Wyndham. London: John Lane, 1908.

C2181. Sichel, Pierre. The Jersey Lily: The Story of the Fabulous Mrs. Langtry. New York: Prentice-Hall, 1958.

C2182. Sichel, Walter S. [Richard Brinsley] Sheridan, 2 vols. London: Constable and Company, 1909.

C2183. Sieben, Pearl. The Immortal [Al] Jolson. New York: Frederick Fell, 1962.

C2184. Siegfried, David A. "Claude Bragdon, Artist-in-the-Theatre." Unpublished doctoral dissertation, University of Illinois, 1979.

C2185. Signorelli, Olga R. Eleonora Duse. London: Thames and Hudson, 1959.

C2186. Signoret, Simone. Nostalgia Isn't What It Used to Be. New York: Harper and Row, 1978.

C2187. Silin, Charles I. [Isaac de] Bensérade and His Ballets de Cour. London: Oxford University Press, 1940.

C2188. Sillard, Robert M. Barry Sullivan and His Contemporaries: A Histrionic Record. London: T. F. Unwin, 1901.

C2189. Sillman, Leonard. Here Lies Leonard Sillman, Straightened out at Last. New York: Citadel Press, 1959.

C2190. Silvers, Phil and Robert Saffron. This Laugh Is on Me: The Phil Silvers Story. Englewood Cliffs, N. J.: Prentice-Hall, 1973.

C2191. Simmons, Ernest J. [Anton] Chekhov: A Biography. London: Jonathan Cape, 1963.

C2192. Simon, Barbara A. "Twentieth-Century American Performing Arts as Viewed through the Career of Peggy Wood." Unpublished doctoral dissertation, New York University, 1981.

C2193. Simond, Ike. Old Slack's Reminiscences and Pocket History of the Colored Performer from 1865 to 1891. Chicago: n. p., 1892.

C2194. Simonov, Ruben N. Stanislavsky's Protégé, Eugene Vakhtangov. Trans. Miriam Goldina. New York: DBS Publications, 1969.

C2195. Simonson, Lee. Untended Grave. New York: Duell, Sloan and Pearce, 1946.

C2196. Sims, George R. My Life: Sixty Years' Recollections of Bohemian London. London: Eveleigh Nash, 1917.

C2197. Sinden, Donald. A Touch of the Memoirs. London: Hodder and Stoughton, 1982.

C2198. Singer, Kurt. The Laughton Story: An Intimate Story of Charles Laughton. Philadelphia, Penn.: J. C. Winston, 1954.

C2199. Sketch of the Life of George Holland, the Veteran Comedian, with Dramatic Reminiscences, Anecdotes, etc. New York: T. H. Morrell, 1871.

C2200. A Sketch of the Life of James William Wallack, Late Actor and Manager. New York: T. H. Morrell, 1865.

C2201. A Sketch of the Life of Miss Clara Fisher, the Lilliputian Actress. London: n. p., 1819.

C2202. A Sketch of the Theatrical Life of the Late Mr. John Palmer ("Plausible Jack"). London: n. p., 1798.

C2203. Sketches from the Life of Dan Rice, the Shakespearian Jester and Original Clown. Albany, N. Y.: E. James, 1849.

C2204. Skinner, Cornelia Otis. Happy Family. London: Constable and Company, 1950.

C2205. _____. Life with [Howard] Lindsay and [Russel] Crouse. Boston: Houghton Mifflin, 1976.

C2206. _____. Madame Sarah [Bernhardt]. Boston: Houghton Mifflin, 1967.

C2207. _____ and Emily Kimbrough. Our Hearts Were Young and Gay. New York: Dodd, Mead and Company, 1942.

C2208. _____. That's Me All Over. New York: Dodd, Mead and Company, 1948 [1941].

C2209. Skinner, Laurence H. Collin d'Harleville, Dramatist. New York: Columbia University Press, 1933.

C2210. Skinner, Maud and Otis. One Man in His Time: The Adventures of Harry Watkins, Strolling Player, 1845-1863. Philadelphia: University of Pennsylvania Press, 1938.

C2211. Skinner, Otis. Footlights and Spotlights. Indianapolis, Ind.: Bobbs-Merrill, 1924.

C2212. _____. The Last Tragedian: [Edwin] Booth Tells His Own Story. New York: Dodd, Mead and Company, 1939.

C2213. Skinner, Richard D. Eugene O'Neill: A Poet's Quest. New York: Longman's, 1935.

C2214. Slezak, Walter. What Time's the Next Swan? New York: Doubleday and Company, 1962.

C2215. Small, Miriam R. Charlotte Ramsay Lennox: An Eighteenth Century Lady of Letters. New Haven, Conn.: Yale University Press, 1935.

C2216. Smedley, Constance. Crusaders: The Reminiscences of Constance Smedley. London: Duckworth, 1929.

C2217. Smith, Constance B. John Masefield: A Life. Oxford: Oxford University Press, 1978.

C2218. Smith, George C. M. Thomas Randolph. London: Oxford University Press, 1927.

C2219. Smith, Harry B. First Nights and First Editions. Boston: Little, Brown and Company, 1931.

C2220. Smith, Jane S. Elsie de Wolfe: A life in the High Style. New York: Atheneum, 1982.

C2221. Smith, Kate. Upon My Lips a Song. New York: Funk and Wagnalls, 1960.

C2222. Smith, Mortimer B. The Life of Ole Bull. Westport, Conn.: Greenwood Press, 1973 [1943].

C2223. Smith, Sol. Theatrical Apprenticeship. Philadelphia, Penn.: Carey and Hart, 1848.

C2224. _____. The Theatrical Journey-work and Anecdotal Recollections of Sol Smith. Philadelphia, Penn.: T. B. Peterson, 1854.

C2225. _____. Theatrical Management in the West and South for Thirty Years. New York: Harper and Brothers, 1868.

C2226. Smithers, Peter. Life of Joseph Addison. Oxford: Clarendon Press, 1954.

C2227. Smyth, Ethel. Female Pipings in Eden. London: Peter Davies, 1933.

C2228. Smyth, James. David Garrick. London: Reeves, 1807.

C2229. Smyth, William. Memoir of Mr. [Richard B.] Sheridan. Leeds: J. Cross, 1840.

C2230. Smythe, Arthur J. The Life of William Terriss, Actor. Westminster: A. Constable, 1898.

C2231. Snagg, Thomas. Recollections of Occurrences. London: Dropmore Press, 1951.

C2232. Soldene, Emily. My Theatrical and Musical Recollections. London: Downey and Company, 1897.

C2233. Sollers, John Ford. "The Theatrical Career of John T. Ford." Unpublished doctoral dissertation, Stanford University, 1963.

C2234. Some Account of the Life and Experience of James Pack, Late Celebrated Actor.... London: privately printed, 1819.

C2235. Some Particulars of the Life of the Late George Coleman. London: T. Cadell and W. Davies, 1795.

C2236. Sommer, Sally R. "Loie Fuller: From the Theatre of Popular Entertainment to the Parisian Avant-Garde." Unpublished doctoral dissertation, New York University, 1979.

C2237. Sonneck, Oscar G. Francis Hopkinson, the First American Poet-Composer and James Lyon, Patriot, Preacher, and Psalmodist. Washington, D. C.: H. L. McQueen, 1905.

C2238. Sorel, Cécile. Cécile Sorel: An Autobiography. Trans. Philip J. Stead. London: Staples Press, 1953.

C2239. Sorel, Walter. Hanya Holm: The Biography of an Artist. Middletown, Conn.: Wesleyan University Press, 1969.

C2240. Sothern, Edward H. Julia Marlowe's Story. Ed. Fairfax Downey. New York: Rinehart, 1954.

C2241. _____. The Melancholy Tale of "Me." New York: Charles Scribner's Sons, 1916.

C2242. Sothern, Georgia. Georgia: My Life in Burlesque. New York: New American Library, 1972.

C2243. Sousa, John Philip. Marching Along: Recollections of Men, Women, and Music. Boston: Hale, Cushman, and Flint, 1928.

C2244. Southard, Andrea C. "The Artistic Career of Nikolai P. Okhlopkov." Unpublished doctoral dissertation, University of Kansas, 1980.

C2245. Spada, James. [Barbra] Streisand: The Woman and the Legend. New York: Simon and Schuster, 1983.

C2246. Speaight, Robert. The Property Basket: Recollections of a Divided Life. London: Collins, 1970.

C2247. Speaight, Robert. William Poel and the Elizabethan Revival. London: William Heinemann, 1954.

C2248. Spector, Susan J. "Uta Hagen: The Early Years, 1919-1951." Unpublished doctoral dissertation, New York University, 1982.

C2249. Spence, Edward F. Bar and Buskin: Being Memories of Life, Law and the Theatre. London: E. Mathews and Marrot, 1930.

C2250. Spencer, Hazleton. The Art and Life of William Shakespeare. New York: Harcourt, Brace and Company, 1940.

C2251. Sprigge, Elizabeth. The Strange Life of August Strindberg. London: Hamish Hamilton, 1949.

C2252. _____. Sybil Thorndike Casson. London: Victor Gollancz, 1971.

C2253. Stagg, Jerry. The Brothers Shubert. New York: Random House, 1968.

C2254. Stallbaumer, Virgil R. "Thomas Holcroft: Radical and Man of Letters." Unpublished doctoral dissertation, Johns Hopkins University, 1934.

C2255. Stanford, Derek. Christopher Fry. London: Longmans, 1954.

C2256. _____. Christopher Fry Album. London: P. Nevill, 1952.

C2257. Stanislavsky, Konstantin. My Life in Art. Trans. J. J. Robbins. Boston: Little, Brown and Company, 1924.

C2258. Starkie, Walter F. Jacinto Benavente. London: Oxford University Press, 1924.

C2259. _____. Luigi Pirandello. New York: E. P. Dutton, 1926.

C2260. Starr, Blaze and Hugh Perry. Blaze Starr: My Life. New York: Praeger, 1974.

C2261. Starr, Wilmarth H. "Florent Carton Dancourt: His Life and Dramatic Works." Unpublished doctoral dissertation, Johns Hopkins University, 1937.

C2262. Stayley, George. The Life and Opinions of an Actor, 2 vols. Dublin: n. p., 1762.

C2263. Stebbins, Emma. Charlotte Cushman: Her Letters and Memories of Her Life. Boston: Houghton, Osgood and Company, 1879.

C2264. Steegmuller, Francis. [Guillaume] Apollinaire: Poet among the Painters. New York: Farrar and Straus, 1963.

C2265. _____. [Jean] Cocteau. Boston: Little, Brown and Company, 1970.

C2266. Steegmuller, Francis, ed. Yours, Isadora: The Love Story of Isadora Duncan and Gordon Craig..... New York: Random House, 1974.

C2267. Steel, Byron. O Rare Ben Jonson. New York: Alfred A. Knopf, 1927.

C2268. Steele, Elizabeth. Memoirs of Mrs. Sophia Baddeley, 6 vols. London: privately printed, 1787.

C2269. Steen, Marguerite. A Pride of Terrys: Family Saga. London: Longmans, 1962.

C2270. Steiger, Brad. Judy Garland. New York: Ace Books, 1969.

C2271. Stein, Elizabeth P. David Garrick, Dramatist. New York: The Macmillan Company, 1934.

C2272. Stern, Ernest. My Life, My Stage. Trans. Edward Fitzgerald. London: Victor Gollancz, 1951.

C2273. Stern, Madeline B. Purple Passage: The Life of Mrs. Frank Leslie. Norman: University of Oklahoma Press, 1953.

C2274. Stern, Philip V. The Man Who Killed Lincoln [John Wilkes Booth]. New York: Random House, 1939.

C2275. Stevens, George Alexander. The Dramatic History of Master Edward, Miss Ann, Mrs. Llwhuddwhydd and Others: The Extraordinaries of These Times [Edward Shuter]. London: T. Waller, 1763.

C2276. Stewart, Nellie. My Life's Story. Sydney, Aust.: John Sands, 1923.

C2277. Stewart, Walter P. "The Dramatic Career of James Miller." Unpublished doctoral dissertation, University of Texas, 1939.

C2278. Stickney, Dorothy. Openings and Closings. Garden City, N. Y.: Doubleday and Company, 1979.

C2279. Stirling, Edward. Old Drury Lane: Fifty Years' Recollections of Author, Actor, and Manager, 2 vols. London: Chatto and Windus, 1881.

C2280. Stirling, W. Edward. Something to Declare: The Story of My English Theatre Abroad. London: Travel Book Company, 1942.

C2281. Stoddart, Dayton. Lord Broadway: Variety's Sime [Silverman]. New York: W. Funk, 1941.

C2282. Stoddart, James H. Recollections of a Player. New York: Century, 1902.

C2283. Stoker, Bram. Personal Reminiscences of Henry Irving. New York: The Macmillan Company, 1906.

C2284. Stokes, Sewell. Personal Glimpses. London: T. Werner Laurie, 1924.

C2285. _____. Without Veils: The Intimate Biography of Gladys Cooper. London: P. Davies, 1953.

C2286. Stoll, Elmer E. John Webster: The Periods of His Work as Determined by His Relations to the Drama of His Day. Boston: A. Mudge, 1905.

C2287. Stolp, Dorothy E. "Mrs. John Drew, American Actress-Manager, 1820-1897." Unpublished doctoral dissertation, Louisiana State University, 1953.

C2288. Stone, Ezra and Weldon Melick. Coming, Major! Philadelphia, Penn.: J. B. Lippincott, 1944.

C2289. Stone, Fred. Rolling Stone. New York: Whittlesey House, 1945.

C2290. Stone, George W. and George M. Kahrl. David Garrick: A Critical Biography. Carbondale: Southern Illinois University Press, 1979.

C2291. Stone, Henry D. Personal Recollections of the Drama: or Theatrical Reminiscences. Albany, N. Y.: C. Van Benthuysen and Sons, 1873.

C2292. Strange, Michael. Who Tells Me True. New York: Charles Scribner's Sons, 1944.

C2293. Strasberg, Susan. Bittersweet. New York: G. P. Putnam's Sons, 1980.

C2294. Strindberg, Frida Uhl. Marriage with Genius [August Strindberg]. London: Jonathan Cape, 1937.

C2295. Strode, Scott K. "Sir Johnston Forbes-Robertson: A Study and Assessment of His Theatrical Career." Unpublished doctoral dissertation, Indiana University, 1974.

C2296. Strong, Leonard A. The Minstrel Boy: A Portrait of Tom Moore. London: Hodder and Stoughton, 1937.

C2297. Styan, John L. Max Reinhardt. Cambridge: Cambridge University Press, 1982.

C2298. Sullivan, Edward D. The Fabulous Wilson Mizner. New York: Henkle Company, 1935.

C2299. Sullivan, Herbert and W. N. Flower. Sir Arthur Sullivan: His Life, Letters, and Friends. London: Cassell and Company, 1927.

C2300. Summerson, John N. Inigo Jones. London: Oxford University Press, 1965.

C2301. Sutherland, James M. From Stage to Pulpit: Life of "Senator" Bob

Hart, J. M. Sutherland, Twenty-Eight Years an Actor and Minstrel. New York: Charles S. Hamilton and Company, 1883.

C2302. Sutro, Alfred. Celebrities and Simple Souls. London: Duckworth, 1933.

C2303. Sutton, William H. "The Life and Works of Jean Richepin." Unpublished doctoral dissertation, Columbia University, 1961.

C2304. Swaffer, Hannen. Really Behind the Scenes. London: G. Newnes, 1929.

C2305. Swart, Jacobus. Thomas Sackville: A Study in Sixteenth Century Poetry. Groningen: J. B. Walters, 1949.

C2306. Swears, Herbert. When All's Said and Done. London: Bles, 1937.

C2307. Swindell, Larry. Charles Boyer: The Reluctant Lover. Garden City, N. Y.: Doubleday and Company, 1983.

C2308. Symons, Arthur. Eleonora Duse. London: E. Mathews, 1926.

C2309. Taber, Edward M. Stowe Notes, Letters, and Verses. Boston: Houghton Mifflin, 1913.

C2310. Taft, Kendall B. "Samuel Woodworth." Unpublished doctoral dissertation, University of Chicago, 1936.

C2311. Tanselle, G. Thomas. Royall Tyler. Cambridge, Mass.: Harvard University Press, 1967.

C2312. Taranow, Gerda. Sarah Bernhardt: The Art within the Legend. Princeton, N. J.: Princeton University Press, 1972.

C2313. Tasch, Peter A. The Dramatic Cobbler: The Life and Works of Isaac Bickerstaff. Lewisburg, Penn.: Bucknell University Press, 1972.

C2314. Taylor, Deems. Some Enchanted Evenings: The Story of Rodgers and Hammerstein. New York: Harper and Brothers, 1953.

C2315. Taylor, Dwight. Blood and Thunder [Charles A. Taylor]. New York: Atheneum, 1962.

C2316. _____. Joy Ride. New York: G. P. Putnam's Sons, 1959.

C2317. Taylor, Frank A. The Theatre of Alexandre Dumas, fils. Oxford: Clarendon Press, 1937.

C2318. Taylor, John. Records of My Life. London: E. Bull, 1832.

C2319. Taylor, John Russell. Alec Guinness: A Celebration. Boston: Little, Brown and Company, 1984.

C2320. Taylor, Justus H. Joe Taylor, Barnstormer: His Travels, Troubles, and Triumphs during Fifty Years in Footlight Flashes. New York: William R. Jenkins, 1913.

C2321. Taylor, Robert Lewis. The Running Pianist [Bobby Clark]. Garden City, N. Y.: Doubleday and Company, 1950.

C2322. _____. W. C. Fields: His Follies and Fortunes. New York: Doubleday and Company, 1949.

C2323. Teichmann, Howard. George S. Kaufman: An Intimate Portrait. New York: Atheneum, 1972.

C2324. Tellegen, Lou. Women Have Been Kind. New York: Vanguard Press, 1931.

C2325. Tennant, Roger. Joseph Conrad. New York: Atheneum, 1981.

C2326. Tenney, Edward A. Thomas Lodge. Ithaca, N. Y.: Cornell University Press, 1935.

C2327. Terriss, Ellaline. Ellaline Terriss. London: Cassell and Company, 1928.

C2328. _____. Just a Little Bit of String. London: Hutchinson and Company, 1955.

C2329. Terry, Ellen. Ellen Terry and Bernard Shaw: A Correspondence. Ed. Christopher St. John. London: Reinhardt and Evans, 1949.

C2330. _____. The Heart of Ellen Terry: A Selection of Letters. London: Mills and Boon, 1928.

C2331. _____. Memoirs. New York: G. P. Putnam's Sons, 1932.

C2332. _____. The Story of My Life. New York: McClure, 1908.

C2333. Terry, Walter. Isadora Duncan: Her Life and Her Legacy. New York: Dodd, Mead and Company, 1964.

C2334. _____. The King's Ballet Master: A Biography of Denmark's August Bournonville. New York: Dodd, Mead and Company, 1979.

C2335. Thesiger, Ernest. Practically True. London: William Heinemann, 1927.

C2336. Thomas, Augustus. The Print of My Remembrance. New York: Charles Scribner's Sons, 1922.

C2337. Thomas, Bob. Walter Winchell: The Man and the Myth. Garden City, N. Y.: Doubleday and Company, 1971.

C2338. Thomson, Christopher B. Autobiography of an Artisan. London: J. Chapman, 1847.

C2339. Thorndike, Russell. Sybil Thorndike. London: T. Butterworth,

1929.

C2340. Thorndike, Sybil and Russell. Lilian Baylis. London: Chapman and Hill, 1938.

C2341. Thurston, Howard. My Life of Magic. Philadelphia, Penn.: Dorrance and Company, 1929.

C2342. Tillinghast, John K. "Guthrie McClintic, Director." Unpublished doctoral dissertation, Indiana University, 1964.

C2343. Tillman, Frances N. A Little Girl Goes Barnstorming. Baltimore, Md.: Barton-Gillet, 1939.

C2344. Timberlake, Craig. The Life and Work of David Belasco, the Bishop of Broadway. New York: Library Publishers, 1954.

C2345. Tischler, Nancy M. Tennessee Williams: Rebellious Puritan. New York: Citadel Press, 1961.

C2346. Todd, Ann. The Eighth Veil. New York: G. P. Putnam's Sons, 1981.

C2347. Todd, Michael, Jr. and Susan M. A Valuable Property: The Life Story of Michael Todd. New York: Arbor House, 1983.

C2348. Toller, Ernst. I Was a German: The Autobiography of Ernst Toller. Trans. Edward Crankshaw. New York: William Morrow, 1934.

C2349. Tolles, Winton. Tom Taylor and the Victorian Drama. New York: Columbia University Press, 1940.

C2350. Tolson, Julius H. "Dion Boucicault." Unpublished doctoral dissertation, University of Pennsylvania, 1951.

C2351. Tomkins, Simon. The Adventures of a Strolling Player: An Autobiography. Ed. Susarion. London: Charles Griffin, 1868.

C2352. Toole, John L. and Joseph Hatton. Reminiscences of J. L. Toole, 2 vols. London: Hurst and Blackett, 1889.

C2353. Torme, Mel. The Other Side of the Rainbow with Judy Garland on the Dawn Patrol. New York: William Morrow, 1970.

C2354. Torrens-McCullagh, William. Memoirs of the Right Honourable Richard Lalor Sheil, 2 vols. London: Hurst and Blackett, 1855.

C2355. Torrents, John E. "Booth Tarkington: A Man of the Theatre." Unpublished doctoral dissertation, Indiana University, 1974.

C2356. Toth, John W. "The Actor-Manager Career of Sir Frank Robert Benson in Perspective: An Evaluation." Unpublished doctoral dissertation, Ohio State University, 1971.

C2357. Townsend, George A. The Life, Crime, and Capture of John Wilkes Booth.... New York: Dick and Fitzgerald, 1865.

C2358. Tracy, Clarence R. The Artificial Bastard: A Biography of Richard Savage. Cambridge, Mass.: Harvard University Press, 1953.

C2359. Trainer, James. Ludwig Tieck: From Gothic to Romantic. The
Hague: Mouton, 1964.

C2360. Tree, Herbert B. Thoughts and Afterthoughts. London: Cassell and
Company, 1913.

C2361. Tree, Viola. Castles in the Air: The Story of My Singing Days.
London: Hogarth Press, 1926.

C2362. Trewin, John C. Alec Clunes. London: Rockliff, 1958.

C2363. _____. [Frank R.] Benson and the Bensonians. London:
Barrie and Rockliff, 1960.

C2364. _____. Edith Evans. London: Rockliff, 1954.

C2365. _____. Mr. [William Charles] Macready, a Nineteenth
Century Tragedian and His Theatre. London: George G. Harrap,
1955.

C2366. _____. Paul Scofield. London: Rockliff, 1956.

C2367. _____. Robert Donat: A Biography. London: William Heinemann, 1968.

C2368. _____. Sybil Thorndike. London: Rockliff, 1955.

C2369. _____. Up from the Lizard. London: Carroll and Nicholson, 1948.

C2370. Trewin, Wendy. All on Stage: Charles Wyndham and the Alberys.
London: George G. Harrap, 1980.

C2371. Trommer, Marie. Ira Aldridge, American Negro Tragedian, and
Taras Shvchenko, Poet of the Ukraine: Story of a Friendship.
Brooklyn, N. Y.: M. Trommer, 1939.

C2372. Trowbridge, John T. My Own Story: With Recollections of Noted
Persons. Boston: Houghton Mifflin, 1904.

C2373. Truax, Sarah. A Woman of Parts: Memories of a Life on Stage. New
York: Longmans, Green and Company, 1949.

C2374. Tucker, Sophie. Some of These Days. Garden City, N. Y.: Doubleday, Doran and Company, 1945.

C2375. Tully, Jim. Circus Parade. Garden City, N. Y.: Garden City Publishing Company, 1927.

C2376. Tweedie, Ethel B. Behind the Footlights. London: Hutchinson and
Company, 1904.

C2377. _____. Me and Mine: A Medley of Thoughts and Memories. London: Hutchinson and Company, 1932.

C2378. Tweedie, Ethel B. My Table-Cloths: A Few Reminiscences. London: Hutchinson and Company, 1916.

C2379. _____. Thirteen Years of a Busy Woman's Life. London: John Lane, 1912.

C2380. _____. Tight Corners of My Adventurous Life. London: Hutchinson and Company, 1933.

C2381. Tyler, George C. and J. C. Furnas. Whatever Goes Up. Indianapolis, Ind.: Bobbs-Merrill, 1934.

C2382. Tynan, Kenneth. Alec Guinness. London: Rockliff, 1953.

C2383. Uddgren, Gustaf. [August] Strindberg the Man. Trans. Axel J. Uppvall. London, C. W. Daniel, 1920.

C2384. Ullman, Liv. Changing. New York: Alfred A. Knopf, 1977.

C2385. Underwood, Peter. Horror Man: The Life of Boris Karloff. London: Leslie Frewin, 1972.

C2386. Ure, Peter. [William Butler] Yeats, the Playwright. New York: Barnes and Noble, 1963.

C2387. Ustinov, Peter. Dear Me. Boston: Little, Brown and Company, 1977.

C2388. Vachell, Horace A. Distant Fields: A Writer's Autobiography. London: Cassell and Company, 1937.

C2389. _____. Fellow Travelers. London: Cassell and Company, 1938.

C2390. Vail, Robert W. G. Susanna Haswell Rowson, the Author of Charlotte Temple. Worcester, Mass.: American Antiquarian Society, 1933.

C2391. Vallee, Rudy. Let the Chips Fall.... Harrisburg, Penn.: Stackpole Books, 1975.

C2392. _____ and Gil McKean. My Time Is Your Time. New York: Ivan Obolensky, 1962.

C2393. _____. Vagabond Dreams Come True. New York: E. P. Dutton, 1930.

C2394. Vanbrugh, Irene. To Tell My Story. London: Hutchinson and Company, 1949.

C2395. Vanbrugh, Violet. Dare to Be Wise. London: Hodder and Stoughton, 1925.

C2396. Vandenhoff, George. Dramatic Reminiscences: or Actors and Actresses in England and America. London: T. W. Cooper, 1860.

C2397. _____ . Leaves from an Actor's Notebook. New York: D. Appleton, 1860.

C2398. Van Doren, Mark. Shakespeare. New York: Henry Holt and Company, 1939.

C2399. Van Druten, John. This Way to the Present: A Personal Record. London: M. Joseph, 1938.

C2400. Varconi, Victor and Ed Honeck. It's not Enough to Be Hungarian. Denver, Col.: Graphic Impressions, 1976.

C2401. Varney, George Leon, ed. Reminiscences of Henry Clay Barnabee. Boston: Chapple Publishing Company, 1913.

C2402. Veiller, Bayard. The Fun I've Had. New York: Raynal and Hitchcock, 1941.

C2403. Verneuil, Louis. The Fabulous Life of Sarah Bernhardt. Trans. Ernest Boyd. New York: Harper and Brothers, 1942.

C2404. Victor, Benjamin. Memoirs of the Life of Barton Booth. London: J. Watts, 1733.

C2405. Victoria and Albert Museum. Claud Lovat Fraser. Ed. Grace Lovat Fraser. London: V. A. M., 1969.

C2406. Victoria and Albert Museum. Edward Gordon Craig. Ed. George Nash. London: V. A. M., 1967.

C2407. Villari, Pasquale. The Life and Times of Niccolo Machiavelli. Trans. Linda Villari. New York: Haskell House, 1969 [1892].

C2408. Vincent, Howard P. "The Life and Writings of George Colman the Younger." Unpublished doctoral dissertation, Harvard University, 1933.

C2409. Vincent, William T. Recollections of Fred Leslie, 2 vols. London: Kegan Paul, Trench and Trübner, 1894.

C2410. Vizetelly, Ernest A. Émile Zola, Novelist and Reformer: An Account of His Life and Work. London: John Lane, 1904.

C2411. Volbach, Walther R. Adolphe Appia, Prophet of the Modern Theatre. Middletown, Conn.: Wesleyan University Press, 1968.

C2412. Volker, Klaus. [Bertolt] Brecht: A Biography. Trans. John Nowell. New York: Seabury Press, 1978.

C2413. Waal, Carla R. "Johanne Dybwad, Norwegian Actress." Unpublished doctoral dissertation, Indiana University, 1964.

C2414. Wadlington, Mary E. "Mrs. Frances Sheridan: Her Life and Works, Including a Study of Her Influence on R. B. Sheridan's Plays, and an Edition of Her Comedy, The Discovery." Unpublished doctoral dissertation, Yale University, 1914.

C2415. Wagner, Charles L. Seeing Stars. New York: G. P. Putnam's Sons, 1940.

C2416. Wagner, Harr. Joaquin Miller and His Other Self. San Francisco, Cal.: Harr Wagner Publishing Company, 1929.

C2417. Waife-Goldberg, Marie. My Father, Sholom Aleichem. New York: Simon and Schuster, 1968.

C2418. Waite, Richard J. "James R. Waite: Pioneer of 'The Ten-Twenty-Thirty' Repertory." Unpublished doctoral dissertation, Texas Technical University, 1979.

C2419. Waitzkin, L. The Witch of Wych Street: A Study of the Theatrical Reforms of Madame Vestris. Cambridge, Mass.: Harvard University Press, 1933.

C2420. Walbrook, Henry M. J. M. Barrie and the Theatre. London: F. V. White, 1922.

C2421. _____. A Playgoer's Wanderings. London: Leonard Parsons, 1926.

C2422. Waldman, Max. Zero by Mostel. New York: Horizon Press, 1965.

C2423. Walker, Katherine S. Robert Helpmann. London: Rockliff, 1957.

C2424. Wallace, Ethel V. Edgar Wallace by His Wife. London: Hutchinson and Company, 1932.

C2425. Wallace, Irving. The Fabulous Showman [P. T. Barnum]. New York: Alfred A. Knopf, 1959.

C2426. Wallace, Malcolm W. The Life of Sir Philip Sidney. Cambridge: Cambridge University Press, 1915.

C2427. Wallack, John Lester. Memories of Fifty Years. New York: Charles Scribner's Sons, 1889.

C2428. Wallett, William Frederick. The Public Life of W. F. Wallett, the Queen's Jester. Ed. J. Luntley. London: Derby, 1870.

C2429. Walsh, Richard J. The Making of Buffalo Bill: A Study in Heroics. Indianapolis, Ind.: Bobbs-Merrill, 1928.

C2430. Walsh, Townsend. The Career of Dion Boucicault. New York: Dunlap Society, 1915.

C2431. Wann, Jack K. "The Career of Owen Davis in the American Theatre." Unpublished doctoral dissertation, Louisiana State University, 1978.

C2432. Ward, Charles E. The Life of John Dryden. Chapel Hill: University of North Carolina Press, 1961.

C2433. Ward, Genevieve and R. Whiteing. Both Sides of the Curtain. London: Cassell and Company, 1918.

C2434. Ward, Kathryn M. P. "George Powell, Playwright-Actor." Unpublished doctoral dissertation, George Washington University, 1948.

C2435. Warde, Frederick B. Fifty Years of Make-Believe. New York: International Press Syndicate, 1920.

C2436. Wardle, Irving. The Theatres of George Devine. London: Jonathan Cape, 1978.

C2437. Wardle, Ralph M. Life of [Oliver] Goldsmith. Lawrence: University of Kansas, 1957.

C2438. Warner, Oliver. John Gay. London: Longmans, Green and Company, 1964.

C2439. Warren, Doug. Betty Grable. New York: St. Martin's Press, 1981.

C2440. Waterbury, Ruth. Richard Burton. New York: Pyramid Books, 1965.

C2441. Watermeier, Daniel J., ed. Between Actor and Critic: Selected Letters of Edwin Booth and William Winter. Princeton, N. J.: Princeton University Press, 1971.

C2442. Waters, Clara E. Charlotte Cushman. Boston: James R. Osgood, 1882.

C2443. Waters, Edward N. Victor Herbert: A Life in Music. New York: The Macmillan Company, 1955.

C2444. Waters, Ethel and Charles Samuels. His Eye Is on the Sparrow. Garden City, N. Y.: Doubleday and Company, 1951.

C2445. Waters, Walter K., Jr. "George L. Baker and the Baker Stock Company." Unpublished doctoral dissertation, Stanford University, 1964.

C2446. Waterston, Mrs. R. C. Adelaide Phillips: A Record. Boston: A. Williams and Company, 1883.

C2447. Watkins, John. Memoirs of the Public and Private Life of the Rt. Hon. Richard Brinsley Sheridan, 2 vols. London: Henry Colburn, 1817.

C2448. Watson, Alfred E. T. A Sporting and Dramatic Career. London: The Macmillan Company, 1918.

C2449. Watson, Vera. Mary Russell Mitford. London: Evans Brothers, 1949.

C2450. Waxman, Samuel M. [André] Antoine and the Théâtre Libre. Cambridge, Mass.: Harvard University Press, 1926.

C2451. Weales, Gerald. Clifford Odets, Playwright. New York: Pegasus, 1971.

C2452. Webb, Bernice L. Poetry on the Stage: William Poel, Producer of Verse Drama. Salzburg: University of Salzburg, 1979.

C2453. Webster, Margaret. Don't Put Your Daughter on the Stage. New York: Alfred A. Knopf, 1972.

C2454. _____. The Same Only Different. New York: Alfred A. Knopf, 1969.

C2455. Weigel, Helene. Helene Weigel, Actress. Leipzig: VEB, 1961.

C2456. Weir, Molly. Walking into the Lyons' Den. London: Hutchinson and Company, 1977.

C2457. Welland, Dennis. Arthur Miller. Edinburgh: Oliver and Boyd, 1961.

C2458. Wellington, Marjorie. "The Life and Works of John Tobin." Unpublished doctoral dissertation, University of Southern California, 1933.

C2459. Wells, Mary. Memories of the Life of Mrs. Sundel, Late Wells of the Theatre Royal Drury Lane, and Haymarket, 3 vols. London: C. happle, 1811.

C2460. Wemyss, Francis C. Twenty-Six Years of the Life of an Actor and Manager. New York: Burgess, Stringer and Company, 1847.

C2461. Werner, Morris R. [P. T.] Barnum. New York: Harcourt, Brace and Company, 1923.

C2462. West, Mae. Goodness Had Nothing to Do with It. Englewood Cliffs, N. J.: Prentice-Hall, 1959.

C2463. Wettach, Adrien. Grock, King of Clowns. Trans. Basil Creighton. London: Methuen and Company, 1957.

C2464. Wewitzer, Ralph. Dramatic Reminiscences, Anecdotes, Comical Sayings and Doings. London: T. H. Lacy, c. 1812.

C2465. Wheatley, Henry B. Notes on the Life of John Payne Collier, with a Complete List of His Works. London: E. Stock, 1884.

C2466. Whicher, George F. The Life and Romances of Mrs. Eliza Haywood. New York: Columbia University Press, 1915.

C2467. Whiffen, Blanche. Keeping off the Shelf. New York: E. P. Dutton, 1928.

C2468. Whistler, Laurence. The Initials in the Heart [Judith Furse].

Boston: Houghton Mifflin, 1964.

C2469. Whistler, Laurence. Sir John Vanbrugh: Architect and Dramatist. London: Cobden-Sanderson, 1938.

C2470. White, Arthur F. John Crowne: His Life and Dramatic Works. Cleveland, Oh.: Western Reserve University Press, 1922.

C2471. White, Pearl. Just Me. New York: George H. Doran, 1919.

C2472. Whitfield, John H. [Niccolo] Machiavelli. Oxford: Basil Blackwell, 1947.

C2473. Whiting, Lilian. Kate Field: A Record. Boston: Little, Brown and Company, 1900.

C2474. Whitridge, Arnold. Alfred de Vigny. London: Oxford University Press, 1933.

C2475. Wilcox, Herbert. 25,000 Sunsets. London: Bodley Head, 1967.

C2476. Wild, Samuel. The Original, Complete and Only Authentic Story of a Nursery of Strolling Players. Ed. W. B. Megson. London: G. Vickers, 1888.

C2477. Wilder, Marshall P. The People I've Smiled With: Recollections of a Merry Little Life. New York: Cassell and Company, 1886.

C2478. _____. The Sunny Side of the Street. New York: Funk and Wagnalls, 1908.

C2479. Wiley, David W. "Philip Moeller of the Theatre Guild: An Historical and Critical Study." Unpublished doctoral dissertation, Indiana University, 1973.

C2480. Wilkinson, Alfred O. "Thomas Holcroft: Perfectability's Playwright." Unpublished doctoral dissertation, Stanford University, 1956.

C2481. Wilkinson, Tate. Memoirs of His Own Life, 4 vols. York: Wilson, Spence and Mawman, 1790.

C2482. _____. The Wandering Patentee: or, A History of Yorkshire Theatres from 1770 to the Present Time, 4 vols. York: Wilson, Spence, and Mawman, 1795.

C2483. Willans, Geoffrey. Peter Ustinov. London: Peter Owen, 1957.

C2484. Willcocks, Mary P. A True-Born Englishman: Being the Life of Henry Fielding. London: George Allen and Unwin, 1947.

C2485. William Poel and His Stage Productions, 1880-1932. London: n. p., 1932.

C2486. Williams, Bransby. An Actor's Story. London: Chapman and Hall, 1909.

C2487. Williams, Bransby. Bransby Williams. London: Hutchinson and Company, 1954.

C2488. Williams, Clifford J. Madame Vestris: A Theatrical Biography. London: Sidgwick and Jackson, 1973.

C2489. Williams, Dakin and Shepheard Mead. Tennessee Williams: An Intimate Biography. New York: Arbor House, 1983.

C2490. Williams, Edwina D. and Lucy Freeman. Remember Me to Tom [Tennessee Williams]. New York: G. P. Putnam's Sons, 1963.

C2491. Williams, Ernest G. H. Four Years at the Old Vic, 1929-1933. London: G. P. Putnam's Sons, 1935.

C2492. _____, ed. "Vic-Wells": The Work of Lilian Baylis. London: Cobden-Sanderson, 1938.

C2493. Williams, Emlyn. Emlyn: An Early Autobiography, 1927-35. New York: Viking Press, 1973.

C2494. _____. George: An Early Biography. New York: Random House, 1961.

C2495. Williams, Henry L. The "Queen of the Drama," Mary Anderson: Her Life on and off the Stage.... New York: Williams and Company, 1885.

C2496. Williams, John A. Memoirs of John Philip Kemble. London: J. B. Wood, 1817.

C2497. Williams, Montagu. Later Leaves: Being the Further Reminiscences of Montagu Williams, Q. C. London: The Macmillan Company, 1891.

C2498. _____. Leaves of a Life: Being the Reminiscences of Montagu Williams, 2 vols. London: The Macmillan Company, 1890.

C2499. Williams, Stanley T. Richard Cumberland: His Life and Dramatic Works. New Haven, Conn.: Yale University Press, 1917.

C2500. Williams, Tennessee. Memoirs. Garden City, N. Y.: Doubleday and Company, 1975.

C2501. Williamson, Audrey. Paul Rogers. London: Rockliff, 1956.

C2502. Williamson, Jane. Charles Kemble: Man of the Theatre. Lincoln: University of Nebraska Press, 1970.

C2503. Wills, Freeman. W. G. Wills: Dramatist and Painter. New York: Longmans, Green and Company, 1898.

C2504. Willson, Meredith. But He Doesn't Know the Territory. New York: G. P. Putnam's Sons, 1959.

C2505. _____. Eggs I Have Laid. New York: Henry Holt and

Company, 1955.

C2506. Willson, Meredith. There I Stood with My Piccolo. Garden City,
N. Y.: Doubleday and Company, 1948.

C2507. Wilmeth, Don B. George Frederick Cooke, Machiavel of the Stage.
Westport, Conn.: Greenwood Press, 1980.

C2508. Wilson, Albert E. Playgoer's Pilgrimage. London: S. Paul, 1948.

C2509. Wilson, Charles. Memoirs of the Life, Writings, and Amours of
William Congreve. London: n. p., 1730.

C2510. Wilson, Eloise. "Lynn Riggs, Oklahoma Dramatist." Unpublished
doctoral dissertation, University of Pennsylvania, 1957.

C2511. Wilson, Francis. Francis Wilson's Life of Himself. Boston:
Houghton Mifflin, 1924.

C2512. _____. John Wilkes Booth: Fact and Fiction of Lincoln's Assassination. Boston: Houghton Mifflin, 1929.

C2513. _____. Joseph Jefferson: Reminiscences of a Fellow
Player. New York: Charles Scribner's Sons, 1906.

C2514. _____. Recollections of a Player. New York: De Vinne
Press, 1897.

C2515. Wilson, John H. Nell Gwyn: Royal Mistress. New York: Pellegrini
and Cudahy, 1952.

C2516. _____. A Rake and His Times: George Villiers, 2nd Duke
of Buckingham. New York: Farrar, Straus, and Young, 1954.

C2517. Wilson, Mona. Sir Philip Sidney. 2d ed. London: Rupert Hart-
Davis, 1950.

C2518. Wilson, Sandy. This Is Sylvia: Her Lives and Loves. London: Max
Parrish, 1954.

C2519. Wilstach, Paul. Richard Mansfield: The Man and the Actor. New
York: Charles Scribner's Sons, 1908.

C2520. Winn, Peter C. "The 'Terrible Fitzball': The Work of a Hack Dramatist." Unpublished doctoral dissertation, Cornell University, 1979.

C2521. Winston, James. Drury Lane Journal: Selections from James Winston's Diaries, 1819-1827. Ed. A. L. Melson and G. B. Cross.
London: Society for Theatre Research, 1974.

C2522. Winter, William. Ada Rehan: A Study. New York: privately printed, 1891.

C2523. _____. Henry Irving. New York: Coombes, 1885.

C2524. Winter, William. In Memory of Frank Worthing, Actor. New York: privately printed, 1911.

C2525. _____. The Jeffersons. Boston: J. R. Osgood, 1881.

C2526. _____. Life and Art of Edwin Booth. New York: The Macmillan Company, 1893.

C2527. _____. Life and Art of Richard Mansfield, with Selections from His Letters, 2 vols. New York: Moffat, Yard and Company, 1910.

C2528. _____. The Life of David Belasco, 2 vols. New York: Moffat, Yard and Company, 1918.

C2529. _____. A Sketch of the Life of John Gilbert. New York: Dunlap Society, 1890.

C2530. _____. Stage Life of Mary Anderson. New York: G. J. Coombes, 1896.

C2531. _____. Tyrone Power. New York: Moffat, Yard and Company, 1913.

C2532. Winton, Calhoun. Captain Steele: The Early Career of Richard Steele. Baltimore, Md.: Johns Hopkins University Press, 1964.

C2533. _____. Sir Richard Steele: The Later Career. Baltimore, Md.: Johns Hopkins University Press, 1970.

C2534. Winwar, Frances. Oscar Wilde and the Yellow 'Nineties. New York: Harper and Brothers, 1940.

C2535. _____. Wingless Victory: A Biography of Gabriele d'Annunzio and Eleonora Duse. New York: Harper and Brothers, 1956.

C2536. Wolf, Simon. Mordecai Manuel Noah. Philadelphia, Penn.: Levy Type Company, 1897.

C2537. Wolfit, Donald. First Interval. London: Odhams Press, 1954.

C2538. Wood, Audrey and Max Wilk. Represented by Audrey Wood. Garden City, N. Y.: Doubleday and Company, 1981.

C2539. Wood, Charles W. Memorials of Mrs. Henry Wood, By Her Son. London: Richard Bentley, 1894.

C2540. Wood, J. Hickory. Dan Leno. London: Methuen and Company, 1905.

C2541. Wood, Lawrence A., Jr. "John W. Marston, LL. D.: Neo-Elizabethan Dramatist in the Victorian Age." Unpublished doctoral dissertation, Western Reserve University, 1955.

C2542. Wood, Peggy. Actors and People: Both Sides of the Footlights. New York: D. Appleton, 1930.

C2543. Wood, Peggy. _Arts and Flowers_. New York: William Morrow, 1963.

C2544. _____ . _How Young You Look: Memoirs of a Middle-Sized Actress_. New York: Farrar and Rinehart, 1941.

C2545. _____ . _A Splendid Gypsy: John Drew_. New York: E. P. Dutton, 1928.

C2546. Wood, William Burke. _Personal Recollections of the Stage_. Philadelphia, Penn.: Henry Carey Baird, 1855.

C2547. Woodress, James L. _Booth Tarkington: Gentleman from Indiana_. Philadelphia, Penn.: J. B. Lippincott, 1955.

C2548. Woollcott, Alexander, ed. _Mrs. Fiske: Her Views on Actors, Acting, and the Problems of Production_. New York: Century, 1917.

C2549. Works, Bernhard. "Norman Bel Geddes, Man of Ideas." Unpublished doctoral dissertation, University of Wisconsin, 1966.

C2550. _The Works of Hugh Kelly, to Which Is Prefixed the Life of the Author_. London: n. p., 1778.

C2551. Worozylski, Wiktor. _The Life of [Vladimir] Mayakovsky_. Trans. Boleslaw Taborski. New York: Orion, 1970.

C2552. Wotton, Mabel E. _H. B. Irving: An Appreciation_. London: Cassell and Company, 1912.

C2553. Wyatt, Edward A. _John Daly Burk: Patriot, Playwright, Historian_. Charlottesville: University of Virginia Press, 1936.

C2554. Wyndham, Horace. _The Magnificent [Lola] Montez: From Courtesan to Convert_. London: Hutchinson and Company, 1935.

C2555. Wynn, Keenan and James Brough. _Ed Wynn's Son_. Garden City, N. Y.: Doubleday and Company, 1959.

C2556. Wynn, Nancy E. "Sophie Treadwell: The Career of a 20th-Century American Feminist Playwright." Unpublished doctoral dissertation, City University of New York, 1982.

C2557. Yablonsky, Lewis. _George Raft_. New York: McGraw-Hill, 1974.

C2558. Yarmolinsky, Avrahm. _[Ivan] Turgenev: The Man, His Art and His Age_. Rev. ed. New York: Orion Books, 1959.

C2559. Yates, Douglas. _Franz Grillparzer: A Critical Biography_, 2 vols. Oxford: Basil Blackwell, 1946.

C2560. Yates, Edmund. _Edmund Yeats: His Recollections and Experiences_, 2 vols. London: Richard Bentley, 1884.

C2561. _____ . _Fifty Years of London Life: Memoirs of a Man of the World_. New York: Harper and Brothers, 1884.

C2562. Yeater, James W. "Charlotte Cushman, American Actress." Unpublished doctoral dissertation, University of Wisconsin, 1955.

C2563. Yeats, William Butler. Autobiographies: Reveries over Childhood and Youth and the Trembling of the Veil. London: The Macmillan Company, 1926.

C2564. _____. Dramatis Personae, 1896-1902. London: The Macmillan Company, 1936.

C2565. _____. [John Millington] Synge and the Ireland of His Times. Churchtown, Dundrum: Cuala Press, 1911.

C2566. York, Zack L. "Lee Simonson, Artist-Craftsman of the Theatre." Unpublished doctoral dissertation, University of Wisconsin, 1950.

C2567. Yorke, Elenor. My Weapon Is Love: An Autobiography. Chicago: Oceanic, 1945.

C2568. Young, Artee F. "Lester Walton: Black Theatre Critic." Unpublished doctoral dissertation, University of Michigan, 1980.

C2569. Young, Julian C. Memoir of Charles Mayne Young, Tragedian, 2 vols. London: The Macmillan Company, 1871.

C2570. Young, Mary J. Memoirs of Mrs. [Anna Maria] Crouch, 2 vols. London: J. Asperne, 1806.

C2571. Young, Roland. Actors and Others. Chicago: P. Covici, 1925.

C2572. Yurka, Blanche. Bohemian Girl: Blanche Yurka's Theatrical Life. Athens: University of Ohio Press, 1970.

C2573. _____. Dear Audience. Englewood Cliffs, N. J.: Prentice-Hall, 1959.

C2574. Zec, Donald and Anthony Fowles. Barbra: A Biography of Barbra Streisand. New York: St. Martin's Press, 1981.

C2575. Zellers, Parker. Tony Pastor: Dean of the Vaudeville Stage. Ypsilanti, Mich.: Eastern University Press, 1971.

C2576. Zeydel, Edwin H. Ludwig Tieck, the German Romanticist: A Critical Study. Princeton, N. J.: Princeton University Press, 1935.

C2577. Ziegler, Philip. Diana Cooper. New York: Alfred A. Knopf, 1982.

C2578. Zolotow, Maurice. Stage Struck: The Romance of Alfred Lunt and Lynn Fontanne. New York: Harcourt, Brace and World, 1965.

C2579. Zucker, A. E. Ibsen: The Master Builder. London: Thornton Butterworth, 1930.

C2580. Zuckerman, Robert S. "Robert Ayres Barnet: American Playwright and Lyricist." Unpublished doctoral dissertation, City Univer-

C2581. Zuckmayer, Carl. A Part of Myself. Trans. Richard and Clara Winston. New York: Harcourt-Brace-Jovanovich, 1970.

C2582. _____. Second Wind. Trans. Elizabeth R. Hapgood. New York: Doubleday, Doran and Company, 1940.

ADDENDA

C2583. Bryan, George B. An Ibsen Companion: A Dictionary-Guide to the Life, Works, and Critical Reception of Henrik Ibsen. Westport, Conn.: Greenwood Press, 1984.

C2584. Christie, Agatha. An Autobiography. New York: Dodd, Mead and Company, 1977.

C2585. Eames, Emma. Some Memories and Reflections. New York: D. Appleton and Company, 1927.

C2586. Fonteyn, Margot. Autobiography. New York: Alfred A. Knopf, 1976.

C2587. Ford, James Lauren. Forty-Odd Years in the Literary Shop. New New York: E. P. Dutton, 1921.

C2588. Kean, Charles and Ellen Tree. Letters of Mr. and Mrs. Charles Kean Relating to Their American Tours. Ed. William G. B. Carson. St. Louis, Mo.: Washington University Press, 1945.

C2589. Kemble, Fanny. The Terrific Kemble: A Victorian Self-Portrait from the Writings of Fanny Kemble. Ed. Eleanor Ransome. London: Hamish Hamilton, 1978.

C2590. Melba, Nellie. Melodies and Memories. London: Thornton Butterworth, 1925.

C2591. Moritzen, Julius. Georg Brandes in Life and Letters. Newark, N. J.: D. S. Colver, 1922.

C2592. Pyros, John A. "Morris Gest, Producer-Impresario in the American Theatre." Unpublished doctoral dissertation, New York University, 1973.

C2593. Robinson, Francis. [Enrico] Caruso: His Life in Pictures. New York: Bramhall House, 1957.

C2594. Ryan, Pat M. Thomas Lodge, Gentleman. Hamden, Conn.: Shoe String Press, 1958.

C2595. Lawton, Mary. [Ernestine] Schumann-Heink, The Last of the Titans. New York: The Macmillan Company, 1928.

C2596. Skinner, Cornelia Otis. Family Circle. Boston: Houghton Mifflin Company, 1948.

C2597. Spada, James. Judy [Garland] and Liza [Minnelli]. Garden City,

N. Y.: Doubleday and Company, 1983.

Part II:
Index of Biographees

A28, I, 119-39; A42, pp. 200-230; A70, pp. 189-208; A81, I, 29-30; A89, pp. 117-56; A91, pp. 48-53; A92, pp. 159-161; A93, pp. 65-70; A97, pp. 109-27; C1501

ABORN, Milton (1864-1933)
American producer: A96, p. 5

ACHURCH, Janet [born Sharp; Mrs. Charles Charrington] (1864-1916)
British actress, producer: A16, II, 31; A50, pp. 386-7; B14, pp. 207-9

ACKERMAN, Charlotte (1757-74)
German actress: C1764

ADAM, Ronald (1896--)
English actor, manager, playwright: C9

ADAMS, Annie A. [born Kiskadden] (1847-1916)
American actress: A16, II, 179; A96, p. 6

ADAMS, Dolly (1904--)
A110, pp. 51-2

ADAMS, Earl P.
A96, pp. 6-7

ADAMS, Edwin (1834-77)
American actor: A81, II, 75-6; A96, p. 7; A122, pp. 137-42; A125, pp. 1-2

ADAMS, Franklin R. (1883-1963)
American lyricist, librettist: A96, p. 7

ADAMS, G. G. (1823-53)
American actor: A96, p. 7

ADAMS, John B. (1830-63)
American actor: A96, p. 7

ADAMS, J. P. (d. 1853)
American Yankee comedian: A96, p. 8

ADAMS, Joey (1911--)
American comedian, producer: C13, C14, C15

ADAMS, Justin F. (1862-1937)
American playwright, actor: A96, p. 8

ADAMS, Leslie (1887-1936)
American actor: A96, p. 8

ADAMS, Maude [born Kiskadden] (1872-1953)
American actress: A1, n. p., por.; A2, n. p.; A3, n. p.; A13, p. 7; A15, p. 55; A16, II, 253; A23, pp. 4-6; A38, n. p.; A44, III, 40-41; A50, pp. 394-6; A55, n. p., por.; A56, pp. 324-46; A61, pp. 3-9; A63, pp. 1-42; A66, n. p.; A79, pp. 88-9; A80, pp. 202-7; A96, p. 8; A103, pp. 32-3; A106, pp. 11-26; A112, pp. 131-54; A115, pp. 89-100; A123, II, 209-61; A125, pp. 3-7; C659; C1873; C2033; C2034

ADAMS, Selby (1872-1943)
American actor: A96, p. 9

ADCOCK, William (fl. 1752-72)
English actor: A96, p. 9

ADDAMS, Augustus A. (d. 1851)
American actor: A96, p. 6; A125, pp. 8-11

ADDIS, John B. (b. 1804)
English actor: A96, p. 9

ADDISON, Joseph (1672-1719)
English playwright: A22, pp. 147-50; C580; C2226

ADDISON, Laura (1822-52)
English actress: A96, p. 9

ADDISON, Thomas
A96, p. 9

ADE, George (1866-1944)
American playwright: A96, pp. 9-10; C1358

ADLER, Jacob P. (1855-1926)
Russian-American actor: A96, p. 10; C2074

ADLER, Luther (1903--)
American actor: A96, p. 10

AESCHYLUS (525-456 B. C.)
Greek playwright: C865; C1769

AGATE, James (1877-1947)
English critic: B20, pp. 11-2;
C22; C23; C24; C25; C26; C27;
C28; C29; C30

AHERN, Will
American performer: A100, pp.
50-55

AHERNE, Brian (1902--)
English actor: A50, pp. 474-6;
C33

AICKIN, James (c. 1735-1803)
English playwright: A93, pp.
97-100

AIGEN, Maye Louise (c. 1874-1919)
American actress: A98, pp. 57-8

AIKEN, Frank Eugene (1840-1910)
American actor, manager: A23,
pp. 6-9; A96, p. 10

AIKEN, George L. (1830-76)
American actor, playwright:
A96, pp. 10-11

AINLEY, Henry (1879-1945)
English actor, producer, director; A9, p. 1, por.; A16, II,
191; A29, pp. 33-4; A50, pp.
433-4; A96, p. 11

AISTON, Arthur C. (1868-1924)
American producer: A96, p. 11

AKED, Muriel (1887-1955)
English actress: A9, p. 2, por.

AKERSTROM, Ullie R. (b. 1863)
American actress, playwright:
A66, n. p.; A96, p. 11; A103,
pp. 250-51

AKINS, Zoë (1886-1958)
American playwright: A96, p.
11; B15, pp. 6-7; B20, pp. 13-4

ALBANESI, Meggie (1899-1923)

C37

ALBANI, Emma [born Marie La Jeun-
esse] (1852-1930)
Canadian singer: C38

ALBAUGH, John W., Sr. (1837-1909)
American actor, manager: A23,
pp. 9-11, A96, p. 12

ALBAUGH, Mary [born Mitchell]
(c. 1834-1908)
American actress: A16, p. 251

ALBEE, Edward (1928--)
American playwright: A65, pp.
3-23; C680

ALBEE, Edward F. (1857-1930)
American producer: A96, p. 12

ALBEE, Portia (b. 1860)
A23, pp. 11-3

ALBERY, James (1838-89)
English playwright: A96, p. 12;
C39

ALDRICH, Louis [born Lyon] (1843-
1901)
American actor, producer: A1,
n. p., por.; A2, n. p.; A23,
pp. 13-5; A50, p. 360; A96,
pp. 12-3

ALDRIDGE, Ira (1804-67)
American actor: A79, pp. 30-31;
A81, II, 58-9; A90, pp.
21-4; C1576; C1592; C1661;
C2371

ALDRIDGE, Michael (1920--)
English actor: A32, pp. 94-5

ALEICHEM, Sholom [Solomon J. Ra-
binowitz] (1859-1916)
Ukranian-American playwright:
B20, p. 1144; C2417

ALEXANDER, George [George A. Sam-
son] (1858-1918)
English actor, manager: A29,
pp. 25-30; A33, pp. 108-22;
A44, IX, 10-11; A50, pp. 379-
80; A81, II, 102-3; A82, pp.
23-32; A83, pp. 74-94; A86,

n. p., por.; A96, p. 13; C1607

ALEXANDER, John Henry (1786-1851)
A81, I, 91; A92, pp. 375-6

ALEXANDER, Sidney (1845-1911)
American actor: A96, p. 13

ALEXANDER, William [Earl of Stir-
ling] (1567?-1640)
English playwright: A22, p. 19

ALFIERI, Vittorio (1749-1803)
Italian playwright: C42; C1686

ALISON, George (1866-1936)
English performer: A16, III,
13; A96, p. 13

ALLAN, Maud (c. 1883-1956)
Canadian dancer: C45

ALLEN, Andrew Jackson ["Dummy"]
(1776-1853)
American actor: A96, p. 14

ALLEN, Charles Leslie (1830-1917)
American performer: A16, p.
135; A23, pp. 15-7

ALLEN, Clarissa (d. 1851)
Actress: A96, p. 14

ALLEN, Fred [John Florence Sulli-
van] (1894-1956)
American performer: A96, pp.
13-4; A126, pp. 265-86; C46;
C47; C48

ALLEN, Gracie [Mrs. George Burns]
(1905-64)
American performer: A96, p. 14

ALLEN, Joseph (1840-1917)
English actor: A96, p. 14

ALLEN, Ricca (1863-1949)
Canadian actress: A16, p. 133

ALLEN, Ruth B.
A16, II, 60

ALLEN, Susanne [born Leonard;
Mrs. Robert Westford] (1865-
1944)
American actress: A96, pp. 14-5

ALLEN, Viola [Mrs. Peter Duryea]
(1867-1948)
American actress: A1, n. p.,
por.; A2, n. p.; A3, n. p.;
A13, p. 19; A15, pp. 52-3; A16,
II, 241; A23, pp. 17-20; A44,
III, 24-5; A50, pp. 393-4; A52,
pp. 137-50; A61, pp. 13-7; A63,
pp. 178-81; A64, pp. 532-5;
A66, n. p.; A96, p. 15; A103,
pp. 8-9; A106, pp. 134-46;
A125, pp. 12-5; C1930

ALLEYN, Edward (1566-1626)
English actor: A17, pp. 25-35;
A81, I, 7-8; A92, pp. 2-3;
C535, C1239

ALLTREE, George W.
British performer: C50

ALSOP, Frances [born Bettesworth]
(d. 1821)
English actress: A96, p. 15

ALTER, Lottie [Charlotte Alice
Alter] (1879-1912)
American actress: A103, pp.
234-5

AMBER, Mabel (1866-1945)
American actress: A96, pp. 15-6

AMECHE, Don [Dominic F. Amici]
(1908--)
American actor: A96, p. 16

AMES, Amy [Mrs. Gus Hennessey]
(d. 1916)
American actress: A96, p. 16

AMES, Percy (1874-1936)
English actor: A96, p. 16

AMES, Winthrop (1871-1937)
American producer: A96, p. 16;
C1544

AMHERST, J. H. (1776-1851)
English playwright, actor: A96,
p. 16

ANDERSON, Addie (1844-84)
American actress: A96, p. 17

ANDERSON, Edith (b. 1816)

American actress: A96, p. 17

ANDERSON, Euphemia [born Jefferson] (d. 1831)
American actress: A96, pp. 20-21

ANDERSON, Garland (c. 1886-1939)
American playwright: C55

ANDERSON, James (b. 1811)
A96, p. 17.

ANDERSON, James Robertson (1811-95)
English actor, manager: A96, p. 18; C56; C57

ANDERSON, Jean
British producer: C58

ANDERSON, John Hargis (1896-1943)
American critic: A96, p. 18; C59

ANDERSON, John Henry ["The Wizard of the North"] (1815-74)
American magician: A96, p. 18

ANDERSON, John Murray (1886-1954)
American producer, director: B15, pp. 10-11; C60; C1051

ANDERSON, Judith (1898--)
Australian actress: A13, p. 98; A50, pp. 461-2; A57, pp. 117-22; A125, pp. 16-9; B15, pp. 12-3

ANDERSON, Mary [Mrs. Antonio F. de Navarro] (1859-1940)
American actress: A1, n. p., por.; A2, n. p.; A8, pp. 26-8; A14, pp. 111-5; A15, pp. 44-6; A16, III, 176; A23, pp. 20-21; A25, pp. 163-72; A30, pp. 163-72; A44, V, 4-5; A50, pp. 381-3; A52, pp. 303-12; A56, pp. 230-64; A66, n. p.; A71, pp. 1-18; A75, pp. 1-18; A77, pp. 51-61; A81, II, 100; A91, pp. 230-33; A96, pp. 19-20; A101, n. p., por.; A112, pp. 44-67; A120, pp. 255-78; A121, I, 90-118; A123, II, 1-46; A125, pp. 20-28; C61; C62; C835; C929;

C2495; C2530

ANDERSON, Max (d. 1943)
American manager: A96, p. 20

ANDERSON, Maxwell (1888-1959)
American playwright: A65, pp. 23-35; B20, 23-4; C63

ANDERSON, Ophelia [born Pelby] (1813-52)
American actress: A96, p. 20

ANDERSON, P. Augustus (1839-1919)
American actor: A96, p. 20

ANDERSON, Robert (1917--)
American playwright: A65, pp. 35-45

ANDERSON, Sherwood (1876-1941)
American playwright: B20, pp. 24-6; C64; C65; C66

ANDRESEN, Hans (b. 1869)
Actor: A16, III, 267

ANDREWS, George H. (1798-1866)
English actor: A96, p. 21

ANDREWS, Jane [Mrs. Greene C. Germon] (fl. 1839-58)
Actress: A96, p. 18.

ANDREWS, Julie [Julia Elizabeth Wells; Mrs. Blake Edwards] (1935--)
English actress: A125, pp. 29-33

ANDREWS, William C. (fl. 1878)
Actor: A96, p. 21

ANDREYEV, Leonid (1871-1919)
Russian playwright: B20, pp. 28-9; C1011

ANGELES, Aimee [Mrs. George Considine] (b. 1880)
Actress: A16, III, 50

ANGELO, Henry (1756-1835)
British performer: C70; C71

ANGLIN, Margaret (1876-1958)
Canadian actress: A3, n. p.;

A13, p. 21; A15, pp. 53-4; A16, II, 92; A50, p. 397; A61, pp. 21-2; A96, pp. 21-2; A103, pp. 118-9; A106, pp. 270-72; A125, pp. 34-8

ANONYMOUS
Actor: C1480

ANSON, Albert Edward (1879-1936)
English actor; A96, p. 22

ANSON, George William (1847-1920)
Scottish actor: A16, II, 261

ANSPACHER, Louis Kaufman (1878-1947)
American playwright: A96, p. 22

ANSTEY, F. [Thomas Anstey Guthrie] (1856-1934)
English playwright: A16, II, 181; B20, pp. 591-2; C1072

ANTOINE, André (1858-1943)
French producer, director, actor: C2450

APOLLINAIRE, Guillaume (1880-1918)
Polish-French critic: C190; C2264

APPIA, Adolphe (1862-1928)
Swiss designer: C2411

ARBUCKLE, Macklyn (1866-1931)
American actor: A3, n. p.; A16, II, 160; A96, p. 22; A103, pp. 112-3

ARBUTHNOT, John (1667-1735)
British playwright: A22, p. 157; C34

ARCHER, Belle [born Mingle] (1860-1900)
American actress: A66, n. p.

ARCHER, Frank (1845-1917)
British actor: A50, p. 361; C80

ARCHER, Thomas (d. 1851)
American singer: A96, p. 22

ARCHER, William (1856-1924)

Scottish critic, playwright: A116, pp. 3-11; B20, pp. 37-8; C79

ARDEN, Edwin Hunter (1864-1918)
American playwright, actor: A16, II, 53; A96, p. 22

ARDITI, Luigi (1822-1903)
Italian composer: C84

ARDREY, Robert (1908-80)
American playwright: C2062

ARGYLE, Fanny Austin (d. 1917)
Actress: A96, p. 23

ARIA, Eliza Davis (b. 1866)
British actress: C85

ARIELL, Anne
British actress: A119, p. 109
(See BRACEGIRDLE, Anne.)

ARLINGTON, Billy (1835-91)
American minstrel: A96, p. 23

ARLINGTON, Nettie Bourne (1877-1947)
American actress: A96, p. 23

ARLISS, George (1868-1946)
English actor: A3, n. p.; A13, p. 33; A96, p. 23; A103, pp. 173-80; A125, pp. 39-44; C86; C87; C88

ARMIN, Robert (c. 1570- c. 1615)
British playwright, actor: A22, p. 19; A27, pp. 190-201

ARMITAGE, Merle (1893-1975)
American impresario: C90

ARMSTRONG, Anna (1863-1948)
Actress: A96, pp. 23-4

ARMSTRONG, Paul (1869-1915)
American playwright: A16, II, 104; A96, p. 24; B20, pp. 41-2

ARMSTRONG, Sydney [Mrs. W. G. Smyth]
Actress: A16, p. 85; A66, n. p.

ARNAUD, Yvonne (1892-1958)

French actress, pianist: A47,
pp. 105-16

ARNOLD, Edward [Guenther Schneider] (1890-1956)
American actor: C93

ARNOLD, Elizabeth [Mrs. William Clendining] (1768-99)
British actress: A96, p. 24

ARNOULD, Sophie (1740-1802)
French actress: A37, I, 150

ARONSON, Rudolph (1856-1919)
American producer: A96, p. 24; C95

ARTAUD, Antonin (1896-1930)
French actor, director: C673;
C1044; C1394

ARTHUR, George C. A.
British writer: C96

ARTHUR, Joseph [Joseph A. Smith] (1848-1906)
American playwright: A1, n. p., por.

ARTHUR, Julia [born Ida Lewis; Mrs. Benjamin P. Cheney, Jr.] (1869-1950)
Canadian actress: A1, n. p., por.; A15, pp. 49-52; A16, III, 117; A23, pp. 21-4; A44, II, 4-5; XII, n. p.; A61, pp. 25-7; A64, pp. 315-7; A66, n. p.; A96, pp. 24-5; A106, pp. 161-73

ARTHUR, Lee (c. 1877-1917)
American playwright: A96, p. 25

ARTHUR, Paul [born McDonough]
American actor: A66, n. p.

ARTSYBASHEV, Mikhail P. (1878-1927)
Russian playwright: B20, pp. 42-3

ASCH, Sholem (1880-1957)
Polish playwright: B20, pp. 45-6

ASHBURY, Joseph (1638-1720)

British actor: A92, pp. 19-20

ASCHE, Oscar [Thomas Stanger Heiss] (1871-1936)
Australian actor: A16, II, 149; A50, pp. 430-31; A82, pp. 65-70; C100

ASHCROFT, Peggy (1907--)
English actress: A9, p. 3; A19, pp. 89-98; A40, pp. 209-27; A50, pp. 503-04; A57, pp. 89-103; C1377

ASHFORD, Harry (1858-1926)
English actor: A96, p. 25

ASHLEY, Elizabeth (1939--)
American actress: C101

ASHLEY, Minnie [born Whitehead; Mrs. William Sheldon; Mrs. W. A. Chanler] (1875-1945)
American actress: A107, pp. 134-46

ASHTON, Florence (1904-73)
American performer: A58, pp. 16-25

ASHTON, Lillian
American performer: A58, pp. 8-15

ASHWELL, Lena [born Pocock; Mrs. Arthur Playfair; Lady Simson]
American actress: A16, III, 222; A86, n. p., por.; C102; C103; C104

ASTAIRE, Adele (1898-1981)
American performer: A35, pp. 48-51; A96, p. 25; B15, pp. 18-9

ASTAIRE, Fred (1899--)
American performer: A35, pp. 48-51; A96, p. 25; B15, pp. 18-9; C106

ASTLEY, Philip (1742-1814)
English equestrian: A81, I, 37; A92, p. 194

ASTON, Anthony (?1682-1749)
British actor: A22, p. 153;

A50, pp. 45-6; A96, pp. 25-6; C1807

ASTOR, Mary [born Lucille Lange-hanke] (1906--)
American actress: C107

ATHELSTON, Edith
Actress: A44, VIII, 24-5

ATKINS, Eileen (1934--)
English actress: A32, pp. 14-5

ATKINS, Robert (1886-1972)
English actor: A9, p. 4; A50, pp. 398-9

ATKINSON, [Justin] Brooks (1894-1984)
American critic: B20, pp. 49-50

ATWELL, Grace [Mrs. Edwin Mordant] (1872-1952)
American actress: A98, pp. 55-6

ATWILL, Lionel (1885-1946)
English actor: A96, p. 27

AUDEN, Wystan Hugh (1907-73)
English playwright: A116, pp. 12-24; C441

AUSTIN, Mary [born Hunter; Mrs. S. W. Austin] (1868-1934)
American playwright: C111

AVERY, Burniece (1908--)
C114

AYMAR, Neva (fl. 1908-10)
Actress: A16, II, 101

AYNESWORTH, Allan [E. Abbot Anderson] (1865-1959)
English actor: A16, II, 99; A47, pp. 75-84

AYRES, Agnes [born Henkle] (1896-1940)
American actress: A35, p. 96, por.

AYRES, James (fl. 1729-44)
Irish playwright: A22, p. 189

BACALL, Lauren (1924--)
American actress: C116

BACKUS, Charles (1831-83)
American minstrel: A96, p. 28

BACON, Frank (1864-1922)
American actor, playwright: A96, p. 28; A102, pp. 295-302

BACON, James (1821-58)
Actor: A96, p. 28

BADDELEY, Angela [Madeleine A. Clinton-Baddeley] (1904-76)
English actress: A9, p. 5

BADDELEY, Robert (1732-94)
British actor: A6, I, 231; A7, I, pp. 301-02; A28, II, 1-20; A81, I, 30; A92, pp. 161-2

BADDELEY, Sophia [born Snow; Mrs. Robert Baddeley] (1745-86)
British actress: A28, II, 1-20; A42, pp. 231-54; A45, II, 217-27; A81, I, 34; A92, pp. 192-4; A93, pp. 77-84; A97, pp. 157-8; C2268

BADEL, Sarah (1943--)
British actress: A32, p. 44

BADLEY, Robert A. (1865-1918)
American producer: A96, p. 28

BAGNOLD, Enid [Lady Roderick Jones] (1889-1981)
British playwright: B20, pp. 59-60; C118

BAILEY, Abraham (fl. 1667)
British playwright: A22, p. 79

BAILEY, Charlotte [born Watson; Mrs. Thomas Bailey] (b. 1815)
English actress: A96, p. 29

BAILEY, Consuelo (fl. 1909-11)
Actress: A16, II, 112

BAILEY, Paul (1937--)
British actor: A76, pp. 156-69

BAILEY, Pearl (1918--)
American singing actress: C123;

C124

BAILEY, William H. (b. 1826)
American actor: A81, II, 87

BAILLIE, Joanna (1762-1851)
Scottish playwright: C438

BAILLIE, John (fl. 1736)
Scottish playwright: A22, p.
191

BAINBRIDGE, A. G. ["Buzz"]
(c. 1886-1936)
American press agent, manager:
A96, p. 29

BAINBRIDGE, Clement
A96, p. 30

BAINTER, Fay (1892-1968)
American actress: A13, p. 91;
A79, pp. 116-7

BAIRD, Dorothea [Mrs. H. B. Irv-
ing] (1875-1933)
English actress: A16, II, 121;
C683

BAIRNSFATHER, Bruce (1887-1959)
British playwright: C127

BAKER, Alexina Fisher [Mrs. John
Lewis] (1822-87)
American actress: A96, p. 30

BAKER, Benjamin A. (1818-90)
American actor, manager, playwright: A96, p. 30

BAKER, George Luis (1868-1941)
American actor, producer: C2445

BAKER, George Pierce (1866-1935)
American educator: B20, p. 63;
C1386

BAKER, Guelma
Actress: A16, II, 223

BAKER, Henry (1698-1774)
British playwright: A22, p. 177

BAKER, Josephine (1906-75)
American performer: A35, p. 15,
por.; A90, pp. 39-44; C131;

C1099; C1858

BAKER, Lee (1880-1948)
American actor: A96, pp. 30-31

BAKER, Peter F. (c. 1851-1923)
American actor: A96, p. 31

BAKER, Phil (1898-1963)
American actor: A96, p. 31

BAKER, Thomas (fl. 1700-09)
British playwright: A22, p. 144

BAKST, Léon [Lev Samuilovich Ros-
enberg] (1866-1924)
Russian designer: C1484; C1508

BALABAN, A. J. (1889-1962)
American theatre executive:
C132

BALDWIN, James (1924--)
American playwright: A65, pp.
45-9

BALDWIN, Joseph (1787-1820)
British burlesque singer: A96,
p. 32

BALDWIN, Silas (1825-67)
American minstrel: A96, p. 32

BALE, John (1495-1563)
British playwright: A22, p.
199; C1128; C1648

BALFE, Louise (b. 1864)
Singing actress: A96, pp. 32-3

BALFE, Michael W. (1808-70)
Irish composer: C171; C1375;
C2110

BALLS, John S. (1799-1844)
English actor: A96, p. 33

BANCROFT, George Pleydell (1868-
1956)
English playwright, actor: C136

BANCROFT, John (d. 1696)
British playwright: A22, p. 105

BANCROFT, Marie [born Wilton]
(1839-1921)

English actress, manager: A33,
pp. 17-44; A75, pp. 19-36; A81,
II, 94; A96, pp. 33-4; B22, pp.
294-303; C138; C139

BANCROFT, Squire (1841-1926)
English actor, manager: A33,
pp. 17-44; A48, I, 297-334;
A71, pp. 19-36; A75, pp. 19-36;
A81, II, 94; B22, pp. 294-303;
C137; C138; C139

BANDMANN, Daniel E. (1840-1905)
German actor: A50, p. 359; A66,
n. p.; A81, II, 91-2; A96, p.
34; C140

BANGS, John Kendrick (1862-1922)
American playwright: A16,   p.
122; B20, pp. 67-8; C141; C142

BANGS, Frank C. (1833-1908)
American performer: A8, pp. 82-
3; A23, pp. 24-6

BANKHEAD, Tallulah (1903-68)
American actress: A9, p. 40;
A13, p. 119; A35, p. 73, por.;
A79, pp. 132-3; A96, p. 34;
A125, pp. 45-50; A126, pp. 12-
81; B15, pp. 20-21; C144; C355;
C1302

BANKS, John (c. 1650-1706)
British playwright: A22, p. 106

BANKS, Leslie (1890-1952)
English actor: A9, p. 3; A50,
p. 455

BANKS, Nathaniel H. (1811-94)
American   actor,   playwright:
A96, p. 34

BANKSON, Budd (1916--)
C145

BANNISTER, Charles (1741-1804)
English actor: A81, I, 34-5;
A92, pp. 181-5

BANNISTER, John ["Jack"] (1760-
1836)
English actor: A6, II, 72-4;
A7, II, 93-6; A81, I, 55-6;
A92, pp. 266-71; C21

BANNISTER, Nathaniel H. (1813-47)
American   actor,   playwright:
A96, p. 35

BANTOCK, Granville (1868-1946)
English composer: C147

BANVARD, John (1815-91)
American painter: C1102

BARAKA,   Amiri   [Leroi   Jones]
(1934--)
American playwright: A65, pp.
49-56

BARBIER, George W. (1865-1945)
American actor: A96, pp. 35-6

BARBOUR, Edwin Wilbur (1841-1914)
American   actor,   playwright:
A96, pp. 36-7

BARCLAY, Delancey (d. 1917)
American actor: A96, p. 36

BARCLAY, William (d. 1677)
British playwright: A22, p. 55

BARD,   Wilkie   [Billie   Smith]
(1870-1944)
English actor: A96, p. 36

BARFORD, William (d. 1792)
British playwright: A22, p. 172

BARKER,   Harley   Granville   (1877-
1946)
English actor, director, playwright: A82, pp. 71-80; A116,
pp.   25-31;   B20,   pp.   564-5;
C357; C1966

BARKER, James Nelson (1784-1858)
American playwright: C1775

BARKER, Reginald (1895-1945)
American   actor,   manager: A96,
p. 37

BARKER, Thomas (fl. 1620)
British playwright: A22, p. 113

BARLOW, Milt G. (1843-1904)
American minstrel: A96, p. 37

BARLOW, Reginald (1867-1943)

American actor: A96, p. 37

BARNABEE, Henry Clay (1833-1917)
American singing actor: A16, p.
252; A44, I, 12-3; X, n. p.;
A66, n. p.; A96, p. 37; A103,
pp. 88-9; A104, pp. 176-88;
C2401

BARNES, Al G. (1862-1931)
American producer: C2043

BARNES, Barnabee (?1569-1609)
British playwright: A22, p. 36

BARNES, Charlotte [Mrs. E. S.
Conner] (1818-63)
English actress, playwright:
A96, p. 38

BARNES, Djuna [born Chappell]
(1892-1982)
American playwright: B20, pp.
72-3; C852

BARNES, Elliott (1843-86)
American actor, playwright:
A96, p. 38; C157

BARNES, John (1761-1841)
British actor: A81, II, 24;
A96, p. 38

BARNES, John H. (1850-1925)
English actor: A50, p. 364;
A96, p. 38; C161

BARNES, Joseph H. (c. 1872-1942)
A44, VI, 38-9

BARNES, Kenneth Ralph (1878-1957)
English educator: C1139

BARNES, Mary [born Greenhill;
Mrs. John Barnes] (1780-1864)
English actress: A81, II, 24;
A96, p. 38

BARNES, William A. (fl. 1870)
American playwright: A96, p. 39

BARNES, William Augustus (1826-
68)
American actor: A96, pp. 38-9

BARNET, Robert Ayres (1853-1933)

American playwright, librettist: A96, p. 39; C2580

BARNUM, Phineas Taylor (1810-91)
American manager: A87, pp. 350-
54; A117, pp. 80-86; B1, pp. 1-
15; B9, pp. 189-220; B23, pp.
18-22; C162; C163; C882; C1310;
C2067; C2068; C2425; C2461

BARON, Robert (b. 1630)
British playwright: A22, p. 62

BARRACLOUGH, Sydney (1869-1930)
Actor: A16, III, 187

BARRAS, Charles M. (1826-73)
American actor, playwright:
A96, p. 35; A117, pp. 87-90

BARRAULT, Jean-Louis (1910--)
French actor, director: C166;
C167; C168

BARRETT, George H. ["Gentleman
George"] (1794-1860)
English actor: A81, II, 35;
A96, pp. 39-40

BARRETT, Lawrence [Larry Branni-
gan] (1838-91)
American actor, manager: A1,
n. p., por.; A2, n. p.; A5, pp.
87-94; A8, pp. 106-7; A50, pp.
356-7; A66, n. p.; A71, pp. 37-
54; A75, pp. 37-54; A77, pp.
62-71; A81, II, 85-7; A91, pp.
196-8; A96, p. 40; A111, pp.
30-32; A120, pp. 231-54; A121,
I, 215-25; II, 195-9; A123, I,
304-39; A125, pp. 51-5; C122;
C177

BARRETT, Louis F. (1843-96)
American actor: A96, p. 40

BARRETT, Wilson (1846-1904)
English actor, manager, playwright: A1, n. p., por.; A2,
n. p.; A44, V, 18-9; A48, I,
117-82; A50, p. 361; A66,
n. p.; A66, n. p.; A81, II,
105; A96, p. 40; A121, II, 339-
58; C172

BARRIE, James Matthew (1860-1937)

Scottish playwright: A16, II, 116; A116, pp. 32-45; B18, pp. 336-52; B20, pp. 79-81; C105; C173; C174; C644; C650; C1095; C1555; C1758; C2086; C2420

BARRINGTON, Rutland [George R. B. Fleet] (1853-1922)
English actor: A48, II, 299-316; C175; C176

BARRISON, Mabel (1882-1912)
American actress: A16, III, 106

BARRON, Charles [Charles Harrison Brown] (1840-1918)
American actor: A23, pp. 26-8; A81, II, 99; A96, pp. 40-41

BARRON, Elwyn A. (1855-1929)
American critic, playwright: A96, p. 41

BARROWS, James O. (1853-1925)
American actor: A16, p. 81; A23, pp. 28-32; A96, p. 41; A98, pp. 105-06

BARRY, Anne [born Street; Mrs. William Dancer; Mrs. Thomas Crawford; Mrs. Spranger Barry] (c. 1734-1801)
British actress: A97, pp. 103-08

BARRY, Clara [born Biddles; Mrs. Thomas Barry; Mrs. William Redmund] (d. 1854)
English actress: A23, pp. 32-4

BARRY, Elizabeth (1658-1713)
English actress: A6, I, 71-3; A7, I, 89-92; A43, pp. 1-13; A45, I, 85-7; A50, pp. 37-8; A81, I, 16; A92, pp. 56-8; A119, pp. 110-17

BARRY, Helen [Mrs. Alexander Rolls] (1853-1904)
American actress: A81, II, 109-10

BARRY, James W. ["Jimmy"] (c. 1866-1931)
American actor: A16, p. 202

BARRY, Mrs. James
American actress: A16, p. 285

BARRY, Lodowick (fl. 1611)
British playwright: A22, p. 38

BARRY, Lydia [Mrs. George Felix] (c. 1876- 1932)
American actress: A96, p. 41

BARRY, Philip (1896-1949)
American playwright: A65, pp. 56-67; B20, pp. 81-2

BARRY, Spranger (1719-77)
Irish actor, playwright: A4, pp. 72-86; A6, I, 204-07; A7, I, 265-9; A70, pp. 123-38; A81, I, 24-5; A92, pp. 127-9; A93, pp. 41-6

BARRYMORE FAMILY: A78, pp. 169-95; C51; C184

BARRYMORE, Diana (1921-60)
American actress: C179

BARRYMORE, Elaine
American actress: C180

BARRYMORE, Ethel (1879-1959)
American actress: A3, n. p.; A13, p. 56; A16, II, 188; A61, pp. 31-2; A63, pp. 43-66; A67, pp. 215-40; A79, pp. 92-3; A102, pp. 97-100; A103, pp. 184-5; A125, pp. 56-60; B15, pp. 23-3; C181; C1802

BARRYMORE, Georgie [born Drew] (1856-93)
American actress: A1, n. p., por.; A25, pp. 311-20; A30, pp. 311-9; A66, n. p.

BARRYMORE, John (1882-1942)
American actor: A3, n. p.; A13, p. 57; A16, II, 54; A35, pp. 61-3; A50, pp. 434-9; A79, pp. 124-5; A102, pp. 61-8; A125, pp. 61-9; B23, 22-7; C182; C905; C1403; C1944

BARRYMORE, Lionel (1878-1954)
American actor: A13, p. 55; A16, II, 106; A35, 60, por.;

A125, pp. 70-74; C183

BARRYMORE, Maurice [Herbert Blythe] (1847-1905)
English actor: A1, n. p., por.; A2, n. p.; A21, pp. 49-51; A23, pp. 34-6; A44, III, 26-7; A64, pp. 385-95; A66, n. p.; A77, pp. 241-8; A81, II, 104; A108, pp. 54-6; A125, pp. 75-81; C1409

BARRYMORE, William Henry (c. 1800-45)
English actor: A96, pp. 43-4

BARTELS, Louis John (1895-1932)
American actor: p. 44

BARTHELMESS, Richard (1895-1963)
American actor: A35, p. 6, por.

BARTHOLOMAE, Philip H. (1880-1947)
American playwright, producer: A96, p. 44

BARTHOLOMEW, William H. (1830-1917)
Actor: A96, p. 44

BARTLEMAN, James (1769-1821)
British singer: A92, pp. 287-8

BARTLETT, Basil H. (1905--)
English actor, playwright: C185

BARTLETT, Josephine [Mrs. Harold Perry] (c. 1862-1910)
American actress: A16, III, 170

BARTLEY, George (1782-1858)
English actor: A12, pp. 4-8; A81, I, 96

BARTLEY, Sarah [born Smith; Mrs. George Bartley] (1783-1850)
English actress: A12, pp. 8-15; A81, I, 74; A92, pp. 337-8

BARTOLETTI, Mlle.
Singer: A110, pp. 45-6

BARTON, Grace (fl. 1900-06)
American actress: A16, III, 201

BARTON, John (1870-1946)
American actor: A96, p. 45

BARTON, May
American actress: A16, III, 207

BASCOMB, A. W. (1880-1939)
English actor: A16, II, 157

BASSHE, Emjo (1900-39)
Russian playwright, director: B20, p. 84

BATCHELDER, Fannie (d. 1933)
Actress: A44, IX, 28-9

BATEMAN, Ellen [Mrs. C. Green, Mrs. Claude Greppo] (1844-1936)
American actress: A81, II, 92; C117

BATEMAN, Hezekiah Linthicum (1812-75)
American manager: A117, pp. 68-71

BATEMAN, Isabel (1854-1934)
American actress, manager: C939

BATEMAN, Jessie (1877-1940)
American actress, manager: A86, n. p., por.

BATEMAN, Kate [Mrs. George Crowe]
American actress: A81, II, 92; A125, pp. 82-3; C117

BATEMAN, Victory (1865-1926)
American actress: A96, p. 45; C1872

BATES, Blanche [Mrs. Milton F. Davis; Mrs. George Creel] (1873-1941)
American actress: A3, n. p.; A13, p. 34; A38, n. p.; A96, pp. 45-6; A103, pp. 208-9; A106, pp. 243-7; A125, pp. 84-7

BATES, Marie (c. 1853-1923)
American actress: A52, pp. 41-52; A96, p. 46

BAUER, Karoline (1807-77)
Actress: C194

BAUM, Lyman Frank (1856-1919)
American playwright: A96, pp.
46-7; B20, p. 89; C195

BAX, Clifford (1886-1962)
English playwright: A116, pp.
45-54; C198

BAXTER, Anne (1923--)
American actress: C199

BAXTER, Keith [Keith Stanley Baxter Wright] (1935--)
Welsh actor: A32, pp. 54-5

BAYES, Nora [Eleanor Goldberg]
(1880-1928)
American performer: A13, p. 41;
A96, p. 46a; A102, pp. 255-62;
B15, pp. 30-31

BAYLIS, Lilian (1874-1937)
English producer: C863; C2340;
C2492

BEACH, William (1874-1926)
American actor: A96, p. 46a

BEAL, George B.
American circus performer: C201

BEALE, Franklin Parkes (1874-
1947)
American performer: A96, pp.
46a-47

BEANE, George A., Sr. (d. 1893)
Actor: A96, p. 47

BEARD, John (1716-91)
British performer: A92, pp.
106-07; C202

BEASLEY, Byron (1872-1927)
American actor: A96, p. 47

BEATON, Cecil (1904--)
English designer: C203; C204;
C205; C206; C207; C208

BEAUDET, Louise (1865-1947)
Canadian actress: A25, pp. 233-
46; A30, pp. 233-45

BEAUMARCHAIS [Pierre A. Caron]
(1732-99)

French playwright: C1466;
C2032

BEAUMONT, Francis (1584-1616)
British playwright: A22, pp.
28-9; C960; C1545

BEAUMONT, Nellie (c. 1870-1938)
American actress: A16, II, 231

BEBAN, George (1873-1928)
American actor: A96, p. 47

BECHTEL, William A. ["Billy"]
(1858-1930)
American actor: A96, p. 47

BECK, Martin (1869-1940)
Czechoslovak-American manager:
A96, pp. 47-8

BECKINGHAM, Charles (1699-1831)
British playwright: A22, p. 167

BECKS, George
American actor: C1473

BEDFORD, Paul John (1792-1871)
English actor: A81, I, 92-3;
A92, pp. 377-9; C214

BEDLOE, William (d. 1680)
British playwright: A22, p. 107

BEERBOHM, Max (1872-1956)
English critic: A16, III, 198;
B20, pp. 102-3; C220; C454;
C1275; C2005; C2026

BEGGS, Lee (1870-1943)
American actor: A96, p. 48

BEHAN, Brendan (1923-64)
Irish playwright: C217; C1314

BEHN, Aphra (1640-89)
English playwright: A22, pp.
89-91; B2, pp. 110-22; C1010;
C1117; C1464; C2102

BEHRMAN, Samuel Nathaniel (1893-
1973)
American playwright: A65, pp.
68-89; B20, pp. 103-4; C219;
C221

BÉJART, Armande (c. 1642-1700)
French actress: A37, I, 1-71;
A118, pp. 1-86

BELASCO, David (1853-1931)
American producer, actor, playwright: A1, n. p., por.; A2,
n. p.; A16, III, 174; A46, pp.
98-103; A65, pp. 90-100; A96,
pp. 49-50; B15, pp. 32-3; B20,
p. 104; C222; C896; C1393;
C2344; C2528

BELASCO, Edward (1874-1937)
American producer: A96, pp. 50-
51

BELCHER, Frank (1869-1947)
American actor: A96, p. 51

BELCHIER, Drawbridge-Court (1580-
1621)
British playwright: A22, p. 40

BELDON, Edwin Leslie (fl. 1900-
20)
American actor: A16, III, 238

BELFRAGE, Bruce (1901-74)
English actor: C223

BELL, Digby (1851-1917)
American actor: A1, n. p.,
por.; A66, n. p.; A85, pp. 117-
25; A96, p. 51; A104, pp. 224-
35

BELL, Gaston (1877-1963)
American actor: A16, p. 212

BELL, Laura Joyce [born Maskell]
(1858-1904)
English actress: A66, n. p.

BELLAMY, Daniel (1687-1788)
British playwright: A22, p. 183

BELLAMY, George Anne
British actress: A6, I, 275-87;
A7, I, 358-74; A11, pp. 241-79;
A41, pp. 76-143; A42, pp. 141-
99; A45, II, 75-118; A70, pp.
209-18; A81, I, 30-32; A92, pp.
165-7; A97, pp. 27-41; A99, pp.
97-156; C227

BELLAMY, Ralph (1904--)
American actor: C228

BELLAMY, William Hoare (1800-66)
Irish actor: A96, pp. 51-2

BELLEW, [Harold] Kyrle (1855-
1911)
English actor: A1, n. p., por.;
A2, n. p.; A3, n. p.; A16, III,
87; A21, pp. 40-44; A38, n. p.;
A44, I, 24-5; A66, n. p.; A81,
II, 96; A96, p. 52; A108, pp.
100-06; A125, pp. 88-90

BELLON, P.
British playwright: A22, p. 135

BELTON, Fred (fl. 1815-71)
British actor: C231

BENAVENTE Y MARTINEZ, Jacinto
(1866-1954)
Spanish playwright: B20, pp.
111-2; C1902; C2258

BENCHLEY, Robert (1889-1945)
American critic, actor: B15,
pp. 36-7; B20, p. 113; C233;
C2075

BENFIELD, Robert (d. 1649)
British actor: A113, pp. 262-4

BENNETT, Arnold (1867-1931)
English playwright: A116, pp.
55-60; B20, pp. 118-9; C152;
C236; C237; C240; C243; C888

BENNETT, Belle [Mrs. F. Winde-
mere] (1891-1932)
American actress: A96, p. 53

BENNETT,   Charles   Frederick
(b. 1775)
English actor: C238

BENNETT, Clarence (1858-1930)
American   actor,   playwright:
A96, p. 53

BENNETT, George John (1800-79)
British actor: A12, pp. 15-6

BENNETT, Gertrude
Actress: A16, p. 231

BENNETT, Johnstone [born Walenton Cronise] (1870-1906)
American actress: A1, n. p., por.; A2, n. p.; A66, n. p.; A96, p. 54; A103, pp. 260-61

BENNETT, Richard (1873-1944)
American actor: A13, p. 59; A16, II, 121; A49, pp. 350-51; A102, pp. 137-40; A125, pp. 91-3; C242

BENNY, Jack [Benjamin Kubelsky] (1894-1974)
American comedian: A20, pp. 98-101; A126, pp. 155-94; C244; C841

BENOIS, Alexandre (1870-1960)
Russian designer: C245

BENRIMO, Joseph Harry (1874-1942)
American actor, playwright, director: A96, pp. 55-6

BENSÉRADE, Isaac de (1613-91)
French dramatist: C2187

BENSLEY, Robert (1742-1817)
English actor: A93, pp. 101-04

BENSLEY, William (1738-1817)
English actor: A81, I, 33-4; A92, pp. 178-81 (See BENSLEY, Robert.)

BENSON, Frank R. (1858-1939)
English actor, manager: A31, pp. 122-7; A50, pp. 377-9; A82, pp. 33-40; A83, pp. 148-51; C246; C247; C2356; C2363

BENSON, Ruth [Mrs. Holbrook Blinn] (1873-1948)
American actress: A16, III, 152

BERESFORD, Russell [Cecil Roberts] (1892--)
English playwright: B20, pp. 1179-80

BERG, Gertrude (1899-1966)
American actress: C250

BERGEN, Edgar (1903-78)
American performer: A100, pp. 38-49

BERGEN, Nella [Mrs. De Wolf Hopper] (1873-1919)
American performer: A16, III, 273

BERGER, Henrietta Newman (1856-1943)
American actress: A96, p. 56

BERGÈRE, Valérie [born de Beaumont] (1872-1938)
French actress: A16, II, 74; A103, pp. 216-7

BERGMAN, Ingmar (1918--)
Swedish director: C589

BERGMAN, Ingrid (1915-82)
Swedish actress: C252

BERGNER, Elizabeth (1900--)
Austrian actress: A96, p. 56

BERINGER, Esmé (1875-1972)
English actress: A16, p. 200

BERK, Sammy
American performer: A100, pp. 63-7

BERLE, Milton (1908--)
American comedian: A20, pp. 109-10; A100, pp. 68-73; C255; C256; C257

BERLEIN, Annie Mack (1850-1935)
Irish actress: A96, pp. 56-7

BERLIN, Irving [born Baline] (1888--)
Russian-American composer, lyricist: A35, p. 57, por.; A124, pp. 136-42; C820; C919

BERNARD, Barney (1877-1924)
American actor, playwright: A16, II, 190; A96, p. 57

BERNARD, John (1756-1828)
English actor, manager: A81, II, 18; A96, p. 57; A124, pp. 94-9; C258; C259; C784

BERNARD, Richard (1566/7-1641)

British playwright: A22, p. 13

BERNARD, Sam [born Barnett]
(1863-1927)
English actor: A85, pp. 171-9;
A96, pp. 57-8

BERNARD, Vivian (d. 1913)
American actress: A96, p. 58

BERNARD, William H. (1833-90)
American minstrel: A96, p. 58

BERNARD-BEERE, Mrs. [born Whitehead; Mrs. A. C. S. Oliver]
(1856-1915)
English actress, manager: A16,
p. 221; A81, II, 101-2

BERNARDI, Berel (?1873-1932)
Actor: C261

BERNHARDT, Sarah [born Rosine
Bernard; Mrs. Jacques Damala]
(1844-1923)
French actress: A1, n. p.,
por.; A2, n. p.; A8, pp. 104-5;
A13, p. 3; A14, pp. 71-82; A37,
II, 273-9; A44, IV, 28-9; A56,
pp. 3-51; A60, pp. 9-29, 135-
201; A64, pp. 149-66; A66,
n. p.; A67, pp. 125-50; A79,
pp. 70-71; A81, II, 90-91; A86,
n. p.; A91, pp. 213-22; A101,
n. p.; A110, pp. 17-8; A114,
pp. 53-90; A121, II, 304-23;
A123, I, 475-544; A124, pp. 10-
18; A125, pp. 100-08; B1, pp.
16-27; B10, pp. 241-82; B23,
pp. 29-31; C32; C97; C150;
C262; C263; C264; C267; C809;
C1082; C1809; C2019; C2081;
C2090; C2206; C2312; C2403

BERNSTEIN, Aline [born Frankau]
(1881-1955)
American designer: C187; C265;
C1392

BERNSTEIN, Henry (1876-1953)
French playwright: B20, pp.
134-5; C992

BERRY, William Henry (1870-1951)
English actor: C266

BERT, Frederic W. (1844-1911)
American minstrel: A96, p. 59

BERTRAM, Helen [born Lulu Mae
Burt; Mrs. Edward J. Morgan]
(b. 1869)
American actress: A1, n. p.,
por.; A2, n. p.; A66, n. p.;
A103, pp. 106-7

BESIER, Rudolf (1878-1942)
British playwright: B20, p. 136

BESWICK, Lavinia (1708-60)
British actress: A11, pp. 33-
50; A42, pp. 27-41 (See FENTON,
Lavinia.)

BETTERTON, Charles (b. ?1804)
English actor: C270

BETTERTON, Mary [Mrs. Sanderson;
Mrs. Thomas Betterton]
(c. 1647-1712)
British actress: A7, p. 83;
A67, pp. 1-22; A81, I, 9; A92,
pp. 12-3; A119, pp. 117-20

BETTERTON, Thomas (1635-1710)
English actor, playwright: A6,
I, 53-9; A7, I, 65-73; A17, pp.
36-54; A22, pp. 107-10; A45, I,
8-23; A50, pp. 32-6; A80, pp.
47-63; A81, I, 9-10; A92, pp.
13-9; A99, pp. 21-42; C7; C976;
C1528

BETTY, William Henry West (1791-
1874)
English actor: A4, pp. 316-26;
A6, II, 185-93; A7, II, 240-51;
A41, pp. 423-42; A73, pp. 297-
314; A81, I, 79; A92, pp. 363-
5; C272; C1120; C1818; C1928

BEVERIDGE, Glen S. (1886-1947)
American actor: A96, p. 60

BIBIENA FAMILY: C1633

BICKERSTAFF, Isaac (c. 1735-
c. 1812)
Irish playwright: C2313

BICKFORD, Charles (1891-1967)
American actor: C273

BIDWELL, David (1820-89)
American manager: A96, p. 60

BIFFIN, Miss (1784-1850)
Freak: A92, pp. 336-7

BIGELOW, Charles A. (1862-1912)
American actor: A16, II, 272;
A85, pp. 157-65; A96, pp. 60-
61; A103, pp. 252-3

BILLINGTON, Elizabeth [born
Weichsel; Mrs. James Billing-
ton] (1768-1818)
British singing actress: A81,
I, 61-2; A92, pp. 291-3

BILLIS, William
British playwright: A22, p. 178

BINGHAM, Amelia [born Swilley;
Mrs. Lloyd Bingham] (1869-
1927)
American actress: A16, II, 79;
A52, pp. 197-210; A96, p. 60;
A103, pp. 98-9

BINGHAM, Lloyd (1865-1915)
American manager: A96, pp. 61-2

BINLEY, Gertrude
Actress: A16, II, 270

BINYON, Laurence (1869-1943)
English playwright: B20, p. 143

BIRCH, William ["Billy"] (1831-
97)
American minstrel: A96, p. 62

BIRD, Robert Montgomery (1806-54)
American playwright: C281;
C904

BISHOP, Charles B. (1833-89)
American manager: A81, II, 108;
A96, pp. 62-3

BISHOP, George Walter (1886-1965)
English critic: C283

BISHOP, Kenyon (c. 1860-1940)
Actress: A16, p. 223

BISPHAM, David S. (1857-1921)
American singer: A16, p. 20;

C286

BJÖRNSON, Björnstjerne (1832-
1910)
Norwegian playwright: A16, III,
280; C340; C1440; C1880

BLACK, Helen C.
British designer: C288

BLACK, Kenneth (b. 1856)
Actor: A16, p. 122

BLACK, Nettie
Actress: A16, II, 141

BLACKMER, Sidney (1895-1973)
American actor: A13, p. 133

BLADEN, Martin (d. 1746)
British playwright: A22, pp.
145-6

BLAIR, Eugenie (1868-1922)
American actress: A66, n. p.;
A96, p. 63; A103, pp. 220-21

BLAISDELL, John W. (1840-1911)
American actor, manager: A96,
pp. 63-4

BLAISDELL, William (1867-1930)
American actor: A96, p. 64

BLAKE, Caroline [born Placide;
Mrs. Leigh Waring; Mrs. William
Rufus Blake] (1798-1881)
American actress: A81, II, 26

BLAKE, William Rufus (1805-63)
Canadian actor: A59, pp. 22-40;
A81, II, 26; A96, p. 64; A117,
pp. 23-6

BLAKELOCK, Denys (1901-70)
English actor: C289; C290

BLANCHARD, Edward Leman (1820-89)
English playwright, critic:
C291

BLANCHARD, Kitty [Mrs. McKee
Rankin] (1847-1911)
American actress: A23, pp. 287-
9; A81, II, 107

BLANCHARD, William (1769-1835)
British actor: A12, pp. 16-8;
A96, p. 64

BLANCHE, Belle [born Minzesheim-
er] (1891-1963)
American performer: A16, II,
132

BLAND, Robert Henderson (d. 1941)
British actor, playwright: C292

BLANDICK, Clara (1881-1962)
American actress: A16, II, 134

BLANEY, Charles Edward (1868-
1944)
American actor, playwright:
A96, p. 65

BLESSINGTON, Murrough Boyle, Lord
(1609-1702)
English playwright: A22, p. 197

BLINN, Holbrook (1872-1928)
American actor: A13, p. 65;
A16, III, 38; C1208

BLISS, James A. (fl. 1917)
A16, III, 57

BLOCH, Jean-Richard (1884-1947)
French playwright: B20, pp.
151-3

BLOCK [Jesse] and SULLY [Eve]
American performers: A100, pp.
74-82

BLOK, Alexander (1880-1921)
Russian playwright: B20, p.
153; C1389; C1999

BLOODGOOD, Clara [born Stephens;
Mrs. William Havemeyer; Mrs.
John Bloodgood, Jr.; Mrs. C. S.
Lalmbeer] (1870-1907)
American actress: A16, p. 189;
A103, pp. 204-05

BLOOM, Claire (1931--)
English actress: C295

BLOOM, Ike
A102, pp. 101-06

BLOOM, Sol (1870-1949)
American actor: A96, p. 66;
C296

BLOSSOM, Henry M., Jr. (1866-
1919)
American playwright: A16, II,
117

BLOW, Sydney [born Jellings-Blow]
(1878-1961)
English playwright, actor: C297

BLUMENTHAL, George (1862-1943)
American producer: C298

BLUNKALL, Ervin J. ["Jack"]
(1875-1943)
American actor: A96, p. 66

BLYTHE, Helen (b. 1861)
Actress: A111, pp. 63-5

BOARDMAN, William H.
British performer: C305

BODENHEIM, Maxwell (1893-1954)
American playwright: B20, pp.
154-5; B23, pp. 32-40

BODENS, Charles (fl. 1732-60)
British playwright: A22, p. 184

BOGART, Andrew (b. 1874)
American actor: A16, II, 212

BOGART, Humphrey (1900-57)
American actor: B15, pp. 40-41;
C1280

BOKER, George Henry (1823-90)
American playwright: C333

BOLAND, Mary (1885-1965)
American actresses: A13, p. 76;
A16, II, 33

BOLESLAVSKY, Richard (1889-1937)
Polish actor, director, educator: C2037

BOND, Frederic (1861-1914)
American actor: A16, III, 213;
A23, pp. 36-40; A66, n. p.

BOND, Jessie (1853-1942)

English actress: A96, pp. 67-8;
C1552

BONEHILL, Bessie [Mrs. William
Seeley] (d. 1902)
American actress: A96, p. 68

BONELLI, William
Actor: A96, p. 68

BONFANTI, Marietta (1847-1921)
Italian dancer: A110, pp. 9-10

BONIFACE, George C. (1833-1912)
American actor: A16, p. 243;
A23, pp. 40-3; A96, p. 67

BONIFACE, George C. (c. 1860-
1917)
American actor: A96, p. 67

BONITA [born Pauline L. Des Lan-
des; Mrs. Lew Hearn] (b. 1885)
Dancer: A16, p. 268

BONSTELLE, Jessie [Laura Justine
Bonesteele] (1872-1932)
American actress, manager: A96,
p. 68; C674

BOOTH FAMILY: A78, pp. 18-55;
C1572

BOOTH, Agnes [born Marian Agnes
Land Rookes; Mrs. Harry Perry;
Mrs. Junius B. Booth II; Mrs.
John B. Schoeffel] (1846-1910)
Australian-American   actress:
A16, p. 220; A23, pp. 43-6;
A25, pp. 173-84; A30, pp. 173-
83; A44, IX, 40-41; A66, n. p.;
A77, pp. 231-7; A81, II, 101;
A96, pp. 68-9; A111, 67-8

BOOTH, Barton (1681-1733)
British actor, playwright:
A6, I, 98-104; A7, I, 125-34;
A22, pp. 160-62; A45, I, 163-
73; A50, pp. 155-7; A80, pp.
69-73; A81, I, 13-4; A92, pp.
54-6; C493; C2404

BOOTH, Edwin Thomas (1833-93)
American actor, manager: A1,
n. p., por.; A2, n. p.; A8, pp.
102-03; A34, pp. 143-88; A44,

I, 16-7; A46, pp. 83-9; A50,
pp. 225-52; A54, pp. 23-38;
A64, pp. 28-44; A66, n. p.;
A71, pp. 55-76; A75, pp. 55-76;
A77, pp. 26-50; A79, pp. 60-61;
A80, pp. 152-61; A81, II, 71-5;
A88, pp. 279-314; A91, pp. 184-
90; A94, pp. 75-93; A95, pp.
25-32; A108, pp. 15-8; A111,
pp. 15-7; A113, pp. 122-53;
A115, pp. 43-56; A121, I, 63-
89; A122, pp. 148-215; A125,
pp. 109-17; B6, pp. 167-202;
B16, pp. 11-3, 48-54; B19, pp.
34-7; C504; C567; C1002; C1058;
C1279; C1384; C1517; C1945;
C2088; C2091; C2212; C2441;
C2526

BOOTH, Hope [Mrs. Rennold Wolf]
(1872-1933)
Canadian actress: A16, III, 278

BOOTH, John Bennion (1880-1961)
British   critic: C311;   C312;
C313; C314; C315

BOOTH, John Wilkes (1838-65)
American actor: A21, pp. 31-4;
A125, pp. 118-21; B19, pp. 34-
7; C188; C505; C899; C1688;
C1738;   C2115;   C2274;   C2357;
C2512

BOOTH,   Junius   Brutus   I   (1796-
1852)
English actor: A28, II, 38-61;
A72, pp. 91-126; A79, pp. 26-7;
A80, pp. 124-9; A81, I, 87-90;
A88, pp. 119-58; A92, pp. 373-
5; A99, pp. 263-84; A117, pp.
1-11; A121, II, 27-37; A123, I,
84-92; A125, pp. 122-7; B23,
pp. 40-41; C503; C1018; C1664

BOOTH, Junius Brutus II (1821-83)
American actor: A81, II, 47-8;
A96, pp. 71-2; B19, pp. 34-7

BOOTH,   Junius   Brutus   III   (1868-
1912)
American actor: A96, p. 72

BOOTH, Rita (d. 1892)
Actress: A96, p. 72

BOOTH, Sarah (1793-1867)
English actress: A12, pp. 18-20

BOOTH, Shirley [born Thelma Booth] (1907--)
American actress: A13, p. 125; A96, p. 72

BOOTHBY, Frances (fl 1665)
British playwright: A22, p. 88

BOOTHE, Clare [Mrs. George T. Brokaw; Mrs. Henry R. Luce; (1903-1971)
American actress, playwright: A96, pp. 72-3; B20, pp. 161-2

BORDONI, Irene (1895-1953)
French performer: A13, p. 97; A102, pp. 289-94; B15, pp. 42-3

BORUP, Doan (1875-1944)
American actor: A96, pp. 73-4

BOSTOCK, Edward H. (1858-1940)
British menagerie owner, producer: C320

BOSWORTH, Hobart (1867-1943)
American actor, director: A96, p. 74

BOTHNER, Gustave (1858-1933)
Manager: A96, p. 74

BOTTOMLEY, Gordon (1874-1948)
English playwright: A116, pp. 61-6; B20, pp. 165-6; C322

BOTTOMLEY, Roland (1879-1947)
English actor: A96, p. 75

BOUCICAULT FAMILY: A78, pp. 114-40

BOUCICAULT, Aubrey (1869-1913)
English actor: A16, III, 151; A44, IX, 46-7; A96, p. 75

BOUCICAULT, Dion (1822-90)
Irish actor, playwright: A8, pp. 52-3; A16, II, 123; A66, n. p.; A68, p. 72; A71, pp. 77-94; A75, pp. 77-94; A77, pp. 81-7; A79, pp. 66-7; A81, II, 49-50; A92, pp. 417-9; A96, pp.

75-6; A120, pp. 124-51; C1215; C1847; C2350; C2430

BOUCICAULT, Nina [Mrs. E. H. Kelly] (1867-1950)
English actress: A96, p. 76

BOURCHIER, Arthur (1863-1927)
English actor: A83, pp. 177-8; A86, n. p., por.; A96, p. 76

BOURGET, Paul C. J. (1852-1935)
French playwright: B20, pp. 166-7; C718

BOURNE, Margaret (b. 1880)
Actress: A16, II, 171

BOURNE, Ruben (fl. 1692)
British playwright: A22, p. 115

BOURNONVILLE, August (1805-79)
Danish choreographer: C325; C2334

BOUTON, Lilie
American actress: C847

BOUTON, Madeleine (fl. 1898)
Actress: A44, VII, 36-7

BOWERS, Charles (b. 1847)
Actor: p. 76

BOWERS, Elizabeth [born Crocker; Mrs. James McCollom; Mrs. D. P. Bowers] (1830-95)
American actress: A5, pp. 119-26; A25, pp. 287-300; A30, pp. 287-99; A66, n. p.; A81, II, 55-6; A96, p. 76

BOWES, Edward E. (1874-1946)
American manager: A96, pp. 76-7

BOWMAN, Laura (1881-1957)
American actress: C74

BOWTELL, Elizabeth [born Ridley] (fl. 1663-96)
British actress: A119, pp. 120-22

BOYD, Archie (1850-1914)
American actor: A96, p. 77

BOYD, Belle [Mrs. Nathaniel R. High] (1843-1900)
American actress: A96, p. 77

BOYD, Frank M. (b. 1863)
British critic: C328

BOYD, William Henry (c. 1890-1935)
American actor: A96, p. 77

BOYER, Abel (1667-1729)
British playwright: A22, p. 142

BOYER, Charles (1899-1978)
French actor: C2307

BOYLE, Roger, Earl of Orrery (1621-79)
British playwright: A22, p. 71; C1539

BOYNE, Leonard (1853-1920)
Irish actor, manager: A16, II, 97; A44, I, 20-21

BRACEGIRDLE, Anne (1663-1748)
British actress: A6, I, 68-71; A7, I, 86-9; A43, pp. 14-33; A50, pp. 38-40; A81, I, 11-2; A89, pp. 3-40; A92, pp. 28-31; A119, pp. 122-7

BRACKENRIDGE, Hugh Henry (1748-1816)
Scottish-American playwright: C1800

BRADBURY, Robert (1774-1831)
British actor: A92, p. 303

BRADFIELD, W. Louis (1866-1919)
Actor: A16, II, 141

BRADFORD, Edith
Actress: A16, III, 151

BRADLEY, Alice M. (b. 1875)
Playwright: A96, p. 78

BRADLEY, Leonora (c. 1855-1935)
American actress: A98, pp. 21-2

BRADY, Alice (1892-1939)
American actress: A13, p. 96; B15, pp. 48-9; C1433

BRADY, William A. (1863-1950)
American actor, manager: A96, p. 78; C331; C332; C1081

BRADY, William J. ["William A. Brady, Jr."] (1900-36)
American producer: A96, pp. 78-9

BRAGDON, Claude (1866-1946)
American designer: C335; C2184

BRAHAM, Henry (c. 1850-1923)
English actor: A96, p. 79

BRAHAM, John (1774-1856)
British singer: A12, pp. 21-4; A81, I, 64-5; A92, pp. 303-08

BRAHM, Otto (1856-1912)
German critic, manager: C507; C1803

BRAITHWAITE, Lilian [Mrs. Gerald Lawrence] (1873-1948)
English actress: A9, p. 6, por.; A47, pp. 56-9; A57, pp. 66-74

BRAMBELL, Wilfred (1912--)
British performer: C339

BRAMWELL, William C. (d. 1928?)
A16, II, 207

BRANDES, Georg Morris (1842-1927)
Danish critic: B20, pp. 183-4; C341; C2591

BRANDO, Marlon (1924--)
American actor: A13, p. 142; C342; C867

BRANDON, Samuel (fl. 1598)
British playwright: A22, p. 18

BRANDT, Sophie (c. 1896-1946)
Actress: A16, II, 156

BRATTON, John W. (1867-1947)
American manager, composer: A16, III, 34; A96, p. 79

BRAWN, John P. (1872-1943)
American actor, manager: A96, pp. 79-80

BRECHT, Bertolt (1898-1956)
German playwright: B20, pp. 186-7; C815; C823; C1035; C1076; C1540; C2412

BREESE, Edmund (1871-1936)
American actor: A3, n. p.; A16, III, 147; A96, p. 80; A98, pp. 101-02

BRENNAN, Jay (c. 1883-1961)
American actor: A102, pp. 113-8

BRERETON, Austin (1862-1922)
English critic, producer: A16, II, 162

BRERETON, Thomas (1691-1722)
British playwright: A22, p. 160

BRETON, André (1896-1966)
French critic: C133; C370; C1618

BRETON, Nicholas (?1555-1625?)
British playwright: A22, p. 4

BRETT, Jeremy [born Huggins] (1933--)
A32, pp. 17, 19

BREVAL, John Durant (d. 1738/9)
British playwright: A22, pp. 165-6

BREWER, Anthony (fl. 1630-55)
British playwright: A22, p. 43

BRIAN, Donald (1877-1948)
Canadian actor: A13, p. 72; A16, II, 55; A96, p. 80

BRICE, Elizabeth [born Bessie Shaler] (d. 1965)
American actress: A16, III, 61

BRICE, Fanny [Fanny Borach] (1891-1951)
American singing actress: A13, p. 99; A20, pp. 33-6; A35, p. 68, por.; A84, pp. 43-50; A102, pp. 221-6; A125, pp. 128-33; C1347

BRIDIE, James [Osborne Henry Mavor] (1888-1951)

Scottish playwright: A116, pp. 66-75; C146; C358

BRIEUX, Eugène (1858-1932)
French playwright: B20, pp. 190-91

BRIGHOUSE, Harold (1882-1958)
English playwright: A116, pp. 75-80; B14, pp. 62-7; B20, pp. 191-2

BRINKER, Una Abell (c. 1874-1952)
American actress: A16, p. 185

BRITTON, Hutin [Mrs. Matheson Lang] (1876-1965)
English actress: C686

BRITTON, Thomas (1644-1714)
British musician: A92, pp. 26-7

BROADBENT, R. J.
C362

BROADHURST, George H. (1865-1951)
English actor, playwright: A96, p. 81; B20, pp. 196-7

BROADHURST, Thomas William (1858-1936)
English playwright: A96, p. 81

BROADHURST, William (c. 1787-1869)
British actor: A12, p. 24

BROCKBANK, Harrison (1867-1947)
English actor: A16, II, 223

BROD, Max (1884-1968)
German playwright: B20, p. 198

BROME, Alexander (1620-66)
British playwright: A22, p. 64; C366

BROME, Richard (c. 1590-1653)
British playwright: A22, pp. 43-4; C67; C1348

BROOK, Clive (1891-1974)
English actor: A9, p. 7, por.

Brooke, Fulke Greville, Baron (1554-1628)

British playwright: A22, pp. 34-5

BROOKE, Gustavus Vaughan (1818-66)
Irish actor: A26, II, 223-47; A69, II, 171-9; A81, II, 46-7; C1451

BROOKE, Henry (1703-83)
Irish playwright: A22, pp. 187-8; C2146

BROOKFIELD, Charles H. E. (1857-1913)
Actor, playwright: A96, p. 82; C365

BROOKLYN, May (d. 1894)
Actress: A44, I, 14-5; A96, pp. 81-2

BROUGH FAMILY: C367

BROUGH, Fanny Whiteside [Mrs. R. S. Boleyn] (1854-1914)
English actress: A50, p. 369

BROUGH, Lionel (1836-1909)
British actor: A48, II, 267-97; A50, p. 369

BROUGHAM, John (1810-80)
Irish actor, manager, playwright: A59, pp. 42-60; A72, pp. 273-96; A81, II, 42-3; A95, pp. 3-10; A117, pp. 12-8; A120, pp. 98-123; A121, II, 95-112; A123, I, 133-46; A125, pp. 134-8; C368; C1151

BROUN, Heywood (1888-1939)
American critic: C1836

BROWN, Albert O. (1872-1945)
American actor, producer: A16, III, 249

BROWN, Alice (1857-1948)
American playwright: B20, pp. 205-06

BROWN, Anthony (d. 1666)
British playwright: A22, p. 189

BROWN, Carrie Clarke Ward (1862-

1926)
American actress: A96, p. 82

BROWN, Clark (1877-1944)
American manager: A96, p. 83

BROWN, Ivor (1891-1974)
British critic: C377

BROWN, James Hutchinson (d. 1930)
Actor, manager: A96, p. 83

BROWN, Joe E. (1892-1973)
American actor: C378

BROWN, John Mason (1900-69)
American critic: B20, pp. 206-7

BROWN, Martin (1885-1936)
Canadian actor, playwright: A96, p. 84

BROWN, Pamela (1917-75)
English actress: A50, pp. 512-3

BROWN, Percy (1883-1919)
Actor: A96, p. 84

BROWN, Thomas (1663-1703)
British playwright: A22, p. 138

BROWN, Thomas Allston (1836-1918)
American manager, author: A96, p. 84

BROWNE, Elliott Martin (1900-80)
English director, actor: C384

BROWNE, Henrietta (d. 1932)
Actress: A16, p. 219

BROWNE, James (1791-1869)
British actor: A12, p. 25

BROWNE, Maurice (1881-1955)
English actor, producer: C385

BRUNA, Eda
Actress: A16, II, 115

BRUNE, Minnie Tittell [Mrs. Clarence M. Brune] (b. 1883)
A103, pp. 102-3

BRUNTON, Louisa [Countess Craven] (1779-1860)

British actress: A6, II, 123;
A81, I, 72-3; A92, pp. 335-6

BRUSTEIN, Robert (1927--)
American director, educator:
C387

BRYAN, George (fl. 1586-c. 1613)
English actor: A27, pp. 129-31

BRYANT, Billy (1888-1948)
English actor, showboat manager: C389

BRYANT, Dan [Daniel Webster
O'Bryan] (1833-75)
American minstrel, actor: A95,
p. 62; A96, p. 85

BRYANT, Sam (1855-1948)
American showboat manager: A96,
p. 85

BRYNNER, Yul (1916--)
American actor: A13, p. 137

BRYTON, Frederick (c. 1856-1902)
Actor: A96, p. 85

BUBBLES, John (1902--)
American actor: A100, pp. 56-62

BUCHANAN, Jack (1891-1957)
Scottish actor, producer: A29,
pp. 76-9; B15, pp. 50-51; C1593

BUCHANAN, McKean (1823-72)
American actor: A81, II, 50;
A96, p. 86

BUCHANAN, Robert W. (1841-1901)
American playwright: A96, p. 85

BUCHANAN, Thompson (1877-1937)
American playwright: A96, p. 86

BUCHANAN, Virginia (1843-1931)
American actress: A16, II, 194

BUCHANAN-TAYLOR, W.
C390; C391; C392

BUCKINGHAM, Fanny Louise [Mrs.
Sallie Ward Pettit] (c. 1866-
1935)
Actress: A96, p. 86

BUCKINGHAM, Samuel (b. 1818)
Actor: A68, pp. 78-85

BUCKLEY, Annie (1872-1916)
American actress: A16, III, 98;
A96, p. 86

BUCKLEY, May [May Uhl] (b. 1875)
Actress: A16, III, 287

BUCKSTONE, John Baldwin (1802-79)
British actor, playwright: A50,
p. 350; A72, pp. 181-96; A81,
I, 98-100; A92, pp. 385-6; A96,
p. 87

BUCKSTONE, John Copeland (1858-
1924)
English actor: A16, II, 205

BUCKSTONE, Rowland (1860-1922)
English actor: A44, IX, 22-3

BUECHNER, Georg (1813-37)
German playwright: C1397

BUFFHAM, Elmer C. (b. 1874)
American actor: A103, pp. 290-
91

BULGER, Harry (1872-1926)
American actor: A16, III, 53;
A96, p. 87

BULL, Ole (1810-80)
Norwegian theatre founder:
C2222

BULL, Peter (1912-84)
English actor: C394; C395

BULLINS, Ed (1935--)
American playwright: A65, pp.
100-11

BUNN, Alfred (1798-1860)
British manager, librettist:
C398

BUNN, Margaret [born Somerville]
(1799-1883)
British actress: A12, pp. 25-8;
A68, pp. 73-8; C871

BUNNY, John (1863-1915)
American actor: A96, p. 88

BURBAGE, Richard (c. 1567-1619)
English actor: A6, I, 19-23;
A17, pp. 9-15; A27, pp. 1-56;
A50, pp. 17-20; A81, I, 8; A92,
p. 4

BURBECK, Frank (1856-1930)
American actor: A96, p. 89

BURGESS, Neil (1846-1910)
American actor, playwright:
A16, III, 154; A23, pp. 46-7;
A96, p. 89; A103, pp. 278-9

BURK, John Daly (c. 1776-1808)
American playwright: C424;
C2553

BURKE, Billie [born Ethel Burke;
Mrs. Florenz Ziegfeld, Jr.]
(1886-1970)
American actress: A3, n. p.;
A13, p. 66; A16, II, 181; A35,
p. 69, por.; A96, pp. 89-90;
B15, pp. 52-3; C400; C401

BURKE, Charles S. T. (1822-54)
British actor, playwright: A96,
p. 90

BURKE, Daniel (1867-1943)
Dancer: A96, p. 90

BURKE, Edwin (1889-1944)
Actor, playwright: A96, pp. 90-
91

BURKE, Joseph ["The Irish Roscius"] (1818-1902)
actor: A96, p. 91

BURKE, William J. (1856-1914)
American minstrel: A96, p. 91

BURKHARDT, Harry (1870-1943)
Actor: A16, II, 217

BURKHEAD, Henry (fl. 1641)
British playwright: A22, p. 61

BURNABY, Charles (fl. 1700-03)
British playwright: A22, p. 140

BURNAND, Francis Cowley (1836-
1917)
British playwright, actor: C403

BURNEL, Henry (fl. 1641)
British playwright: A22, p. 51

BURNETTE, Frances Hobson [Mrs.
Stephen Townsend] (1849-1924)
English playwright: A16, p. 259

BURNHAM, Charles C. (1853-1938)
American producer: A96, p. 91

BURNS, George (1896--)
American comedian: A100, pp.
83-7; C404

BURRESS, William (1867-1948)
American actor: A16, p. 187

BURROUGHS, Marie [born Lillie Ar-
rington; Mrs. R. B. Macpherson]
(1866-1926)
American actress: A1, n. p.,
por.; A2, n. p.; A44, VI, 16-7;
A66, n. p.; A96, p. 92; A106,
pp. 291-8

BURROUGHS, Watkins (1790-1869)
English actor, manager: A96,
p. 92

BURROWS, Abe (1910--)
American playwright, director:
C407

BURROWS, Charles (1864-1947)
American actor: A96, p. 92

BURROWS, James (1842-1926)
American actor: A96, pp. 92-3

BURT, Laura [Mrs. Henry Stanford]
(1875-1952)
English actress: A16, III, 216

BURTON, Belle
C408

BURTON, Henry K. (1886-1947)
American actor: A96, p. 93

BURTON, Percy (1878-1948)
English producer: C409

BURTON, Philip (1904--)
Welsh director: C410

BURTON, Richard [born Jenkins]

(1925-84)
Welsh actor: A18, pp. 13-29;
A50, pp. 515-7; C579; C656;
C849; C2440

BURTON, William E. (1804-60)
English actor, manager: A50,
pp. 350-51; A72, pp. 215-38;
A81, II, 36-7; A88, pp. 353-86;
A125, pp. 138-42; C1353

BURTON, William H. (1845-1926)
American manager: A96, p. 93

BUSBY, Amy (1872-1957)
American actress: A44, IV, 12-3

BUSLEY, Jessie [Mrs. Ernest Joy]
(1869-1950)
American actress: A16, II, 73

BUTLER, Bunny
A102, pp. 277-84

BUTLER, Cecil
A16, II, 150

BUTLER, Charlotte (fl. 1673-95)
English actress: A119, pp. 127-
9

BUTLER, Edward (1882-1943)
Actor: A96, p. 94

BUTLER, Fred [Alfred Joline But-
ler] (1867-1929)
American actor, director: A103,
pp. 244-5

BUTLER, Nellie [born Chute]
(fl. 1894-1912)
Actress: A16, p. 46

BUTLER, Samuel (1820-45)
English actor: A96, p. 94

BUTTERFIELD, Walter S. (c. 1901-
1936)
Actor, manager, playwright:
A96, pp. 94-5

BUXTON, Frederick F. (d. 1858)
English actor: A96, p. 95

BYFORD, Roy (1873-1939)
English performer: A9, p. 48

BYNG, Douglas (1893--)
English actor: C411

BYRNE, Francis M. (1875-1923)
American actor: A16, III, 183

BYRNE, James A. (1868-1927)
American actor, playwright:
A96, p. 95

BYRON, Arthur William (1872-1961)
American actor: A16, p. 86;
A96, p. 95; A103, pp. 182-3

BYRON, Kate [born Mary Kate Rehan; Mrs. Oliver D. Byron]
(1846-1920)
American actress: A66, n. p.;
A96, p. 96

BYRON, Oliver Doud (1842-1920)
American actor: A1, n. p.,
por.; A16, II, 256; A23, pp.
47-51; A66, n. p.

CAGNEY, James (1899--)
American actor, dancer: A20,
pp. 90-93; C414

CAHILL, Marie [Mrs. Daniel V.
Arthur] (1870-1933)
American actress: A3, n. p.;
A13, p. 43; A38, n. p.; A96, p.
96

CAINE, Georgia (1876-1964)
American actress: A16, III, 245

CAINE, Hall (1853-1931)
English playwright: A83, pp.
180-84; A87, pp. 452-4; B14,
pp. 117-27; B15, pp. 54-5; B20,
pp. 235-7; C416

CALDARA, Orme (1875-1925)
American actor: A96, p. 97

CALDER-MARSHALL, Anna (1947--)
A32, pp. 25-7; A76, pp. 188-202

CALDERON, George (1868-1915)
British playwright: C1530

Caldwell,   Ann   (1869-1936)

American playwright, lyricist: A96, p. 97.

CALDWELL, James H. (1793-1863)
English actor, manager: A81, II, 24; A96, p. 97; C1241

CALDWELL, Zoë (1933--)
Australian actress: A50, pp. 517-9

CALEF, Jennie [born Murphy] (d. 1916)
Actress: A110, pp. 19-20

CALHERN, Louis [born Carl Henry Vogt] (1895-1956)
American actor: A125, pp. 143-7

CALHOUN, Eleanor [Princess Lazarovich-Hrebelianovich] (1862-1957)
American actress: A50, p. 390; C1453

CALLADINE, C. (1822-61)
American actor: A96, pp. 96-7

CALLAHAN, Charles E. (1843-1917)
American actor, playwright: A96, p. 97

CALLENDER, Charles (c. 1827-97)
American minstrel: A96, pp. 97-8

CALLOT, Jacques (c. 1592-1635)
French designer: C113; C211

CALTHROP, Dion Clayton (1878-1937)
English playwright, designer: C417

CALVERT, Adelaide [born Biddles; Mrs. Charles Calvert] (1836-1921)
British actress, playwright: C418

CALVERT, Charles A. (1828-79)
English actor, manager: A31, pp. 31-79; A50, pp. 353-4

CALVERT, Louis (1859-1923)
English actor, manager: A50,

pp. 380-81; A96, p. 98; C419

CAMARGO, Marie-Anne de Cupis de (1710-70)
Flemish dancer: A37, I, 257-84; A118, pp. 199-221

CAMBRIDGE, Arthur (b. c. 1840)
Manager, agent: A96, p. 98

CAMERON, Beatrice [born Susan Hegeman; Mrs. Richard Mansfield] (1863-1940)
American actress: A52, pp. 9-24; A66, n. p.; A96, pp. 98-9

CAMERON, Grace [Mrs. Lon C. O'Connor] (b. 1879)
American actress: A103, pp. 110-11

CAMERON, Hugh (1879-1941)
American actor: A96, p. 99

CAMERON, James (1911--)
C422

CAMERON, Violet [Mrs. D. De Bensaude] (1862-1919)
American actress: A16, p. 273

CAMP, Frank E. (1870-1943)
American playwright, musician: A96, p. 99

CAMPBELL, Bartley (1843-88)
American playwright: A96, pp. 99-100

CAMPBELL, Douglas (1922--)
Scottish actor: C2148

CAMPBELL, Mrs. Patrick [Beatrice Stella Tanner] (1865-1940)
English actress, manager: A13, p. 32; A16, p. 44; A47, pp. 45-54; A50, pp. 387-90; A83, pp. 192-3; A123, II, 338-67; A125, pp. 148-54; C423; C702; C703; C1910

CAMPEAU, Frank (1864-1943)
American actor: A96, p. 101

CAMUS, Albert (1913-60)
French playwright, critic: C347

CANNAN, Gilbert (1884-1955)
English playwright: A116, pp.
81-5; B20, pp. 243-4

CANNON, Hughie (1840-1912)
American minstrel, composer:
A96, p. 101

CANTOR, Eddie [born Edward Israel
Iskowitz] (1893-1964)
American singing actor, producer: A13, p. 85; A84, pp. 75-
9; C429; C430; C431; C432

CAPEK, Karel (1890-1938)
Czechoslovakian   playwright:
B20, pp. 246-7

CAPPER, Alfred Octavius (1865-
1921)
English mindreader: C434

CARDUS, Neville (1889-1975)
British   critic,   journalist:
C436

CAREW, Elizabeth (fl. 1613)
British playwright: A22, p. 24

CAREW, James (1876-1938)
American actor: A96, p. 101

CAREW, Thomas (?1595-1640)
British playwright: A22, p. 49;
C2155

CAREY, Eleanor (1852-1915)
Chilean actress: A16, III, 202

CAREY, Henry (1690-1743)
British   playwright: A22,   pp.
166-7

CARHART, James L. (1843-1937)
American actor: A16, II, 280

CARLE, Richard [born Charles N.
Carleton] (1871-1941)
American   actor,   playwright:
A16, III, 163; A49, pp. 342-6;
A96, p. 102; A104, pp. 217-23

CARLELL, Lodowick (fl. 1629-64)
British playwright: A22, p. 55

CARLETON, Henry Guy (1851-1910)

American playwright: A16, II,
147; A96, p. 102

CARLETON, William T. (1859-1930)
American producer: A1, n. p.,
por.; A2, n. p.

CARLILE, James (d. 1691)
British playwright: A22, p. 111

CARLISLE, Alexandra [born Swift]
(1886-1936)
English actress: A35, p. 47,
por.; A96, p. 103

CARLISLE, Sybil (b. 1871)
South African actress: A16, II,
51

CARLYLE, Francis (c. 1868-1916)
English actor: A16, III, 199;
A44, V, 22-3

CARMICHAEL, Ian (1920--)
British actor: C440

CARNOVSKY, Morris (1898--)
American actor: A50, pp. 459-
61; A125, pp. 155-60; C254

CARPENTER, Richard (fl. 1623-70)
British playwright: A22, p. 39

CARR, Alexander (1878-1946)
Russian-American actor, playwright: A96, p. 103

CARR, Alice Comyns [Mrs. Joseph
Comyns Carr] (b. 1850)
English designer: C442

CARR, F. Osmond (1858-1916)
English musician: A16, ii, 103

CARROLL, Earl (1892-1948)
American producer, playwright:
A96, p. 103; C1772

CARROLL, James (b. 1817)
Actor: A96, pp. 103-04

CARROLL, Jean (1909-72)
American performer: A100, pp.
252-9

CARROLL, Paul Vincent (1900-68)

Irish playwright: A96, p. 104;
A116, pp. 85-94; B20, pp. 253-4

CARROLL, Richard Field (1866-1925)
American actor: A96, p. 104

CARSON, David (b. 1837)
American minstrel: A96, pp. 104-5

CARTER, Jacob (b. 1813)
Actor: C447

CARTER, Mrs. Leslie [born Caroline Louise Dudley; Mrs. William L. Payne] (1862-1937)
American actress: A3, n. p.; A13, p. 11; A16, III, 142; A38, n. p.; A44, VIII, 4-5; A61, pp. 35-9; A102, pp. 107-12; A103, pp. 24-5; A106, pp. 193-205; A123, II, 323-32; A125, pp. 161-6; C1121

CARTER, Lincoln J. (1865-1926)
American playwright: A96, p. 105

CARTWRIGHT, Charles M. (1855-1916)
English actor, manager: A16, III, 75; A96, p. 105

CARTWRIGHT, George (fl. 1661)
British playwright: A22, p. 72

CARTWRIGHT, William (1611-43)
British playwright: A22, p. 57

CARUSO, Enrico (1873-1921)
Italian singer: C2593

CASSON, Lewis T. (1875-1969)
English actor, director: A50, pp. 396-7; C450; C1022

CASTLE, Irene (?1893-1969)
American performer: A96, p. 106; B15, pp. 56-7

CASTLE, Egerton (1858-1920)
English playwright: B20, pp. 256-7

CASTLE, Vernon [born Vernon C. Blythe] (1877-1918)
English performer: C452

CASTLETON, Kate (1857-1892)
Actress: A66, n. p.; A96, p. 106

CATLEY, Anne (1745-89)
British actress: A81, I, 36; A92, pp. 195-6; A97, pp. 153-7; C53; C1499; C1669

CAVE, Joseph Arnold (1823-1912)
British actor, manager: C453

CAVENDISH, Ada [Mrs. Frank Marshall] (1847-95)
English actress: A81, II, 112

CAWTHORN, Joseph (1867-1949)
American actor: A96, p. 106

CAYVAN, Georgia (1858-1906)
American actress: A1, n. p., por.; A2, n. p.; A23, pp. 51-2; A25, pp. 139-52; A30, pp. 139-51; A44, III, 32-3; A66, n. p.; A77, pp. 274-85; A96, pp. 106-07; A125, pp. 167-71

CAZAURAN, Augustus R. (1820-89)
Playwright: A96, pp. 107-8

CECIL, Arthur [born A. C. Blunt] (1843-96)
English actor: A48, II, 151-68

CELESTE, Marie [born Martin; Mrs. Henry Elliot] (1811-82)
English actress: A81, II, 43; A103, pp. 276-7; A107, pp. 156-71

CENTLIVRE, Susannah [born Freeman] (?1667-1723)
English playwright: A22, pp. 140-41; A45, I, 121-4; C327; C456

CERVANTES SAAVEDRA, Miguel de (1547-1616)
Spanish playwright: C225; C881

CHAMBERLAIN, Richard (1935--)
American actor: A32, pp. 45-7

(1797-1866)
British actress: A12, pp. 29-30

CHATTERTON, Frederick Balsir (1834-86)
British manager: A26, II, 323-97

CHATTERTON, Ruth (1893-1961)
American actress: A13, p. 84; A35, p. 2, por.

CHAVES, A. (fl. 1705)
British playwright: A22, p. 140

CHAYEFSKY, Paddy (1923-81)
American playwright: A65, pp. 111-7

CHEATHAM, Kitty [Catherine Smiley Bugge] (c. 1865-1946)
American actress: A1, n. p., por.; A2, n. p.; A66, n. p.

CHEKHOV, Anton P. (1860-1904)
Russian playwright: B28, pp. 294-301; C386; C472; C473; C1205; C1206; C1416; C2191

CHERKASOV, Nikolai K. (1903-66)
Russian actor: C474

CHERRY, Andrew (1762-1812)
Irish actor, playwright: A92, pp. 289-90

CHESTER, Eliza (b. 1799)
British actress: A12, pp. 30-32

CHESTER, Kate
American actress: A110, pp. 55-6

CHESTERTON, Gilbert Keith (1874-1936)
English playwright: A116, pp. 101-06; C630

CHETTLE, Henry (c. 1560-1607)
British playwright: C1315

CHETWOOD, William Rufus (d. 1766)
British playwright: A22, p. 181

CHEVALIER, Albert (1861-1923)
English actor: A16, p. 113;

A96, p. 113; C478; C479

CHEVALIER, Maurice (1888-1972)
French singing actor: A35, p. 84, por.; C329; C480; C481; C482; C483

CHILD, Harold Hannyngton (1869-1945)
English critic, actor: C484

CHILDRESS, Alice (1920--)
American playwright: A65, pp. 118-24

CHIPPENDALE, William H. (1801-88)
English actor: A96, p. 114

CHISWICK, William (b. 1813)
Actor: A96, p. 114

CHORLEY, Henry Fothergill (1808-72)
British playwright, critic: C486

CHORPENNING, Charlotte
American playwright: C213

CHRISTIAN, Thomas (1810-67)
American minstrel: A96, p. 114

CHRISTIE, Agatha (1891-1976)
English playwright: C2584

CHRISTY, Dave [born Lyman Van Valer] (1853-1926)
American minstrel: A96, p. 114

CHRISTY, Edwin P. (1815-62)
American minstrel: A96, pp. 114-5

CHRISTY, George N. (1827-68)
American minstrel: A96, p. 115

CHURCHILL, Berton (1876-1940)
Canadian actor: A96, p. 115

CHURCHILL, Sarah (1914-82)
English actress: C488; C489

CIBBER, Colley (1671-1757)
English actor, manager, playwright: A6, I, 74-88; A7, I, 93-112; A22, pp. 122-4; A36,

pp. 155-98; A45, I, 125-49; A50, pp. 41-4; A81, I, 12-3; A92, pp. 43-7; B17, pp. 143-66; C154; C492; C2158

CIBBER, Susannah Maria [born Arne; Mrs. Theophilus Cibber] (1714-66)
British actress: A6, I, 271-5; A7, I, 352-8; A11, pp. 193-240; A43, pp. 65-106; A81, I, 18; A92, pp. 94-8; A97, pp. 14-26; C6; C1787

CIBBER, Theophilus (1703-58)
British actor: A6, I, 109; A7, I, 140-41; A22, pp. 171-2; A92, pp. 83-4; C75

CLAIRE, Ina [born Fagan; Mrs. J. R. Whittaker] (1892--)
American actress: A13, p. 92; A35, p. 29, por.; A102, pp. 55-60; A125, pp. 184-8; B15, pp. 64-5

CLAIRON, Hippolyte [born Claire Joseph Lerys] (1723-1803)
French actress: A37, II, 52-79; A118, pp. 275-352

CLANCY, Michael (fl. 1700-50)
British playwright: A22, p. 192

CLAPP, Henry Austin (1841-1904)
American critic: C495

CLARENCE, Oliver B. (1870-1955)
English actor: A9, p. 8; C496

CLARETIE, Jules [born Arsène Arnaud] (1840-1913)
French playwright, critic, director: A16, II, 268

CLARGES, Verner (1848-1911)
Actor: A16, II, 24; A23, pp. 52-5; A96, pp. 115-6

CLARK, Barrett Harper (1890-1953)
American critic: B20, pp. 284-5

CLARK, Bobby (1888-1960)
American actor: A13, p. 106; C2321

CLARK, George (b. 1840)
A81, II, 106

CLARK, Hilda (c. 1873-1932)
Singing actress: A44, XI, n. p.; A107, pp. 253-9

CLARK, Lois Frances [Mrs. Roger Harding] (c. 1863-1937)
American actress: A16, III, 184

CLARK, Marguerite (1887-1940)
American actress: A3, n. p.; A16, II, 59; A96, p. 116; C1821

CLARK, William H. ["Hulch"] (1863-1913)
Singer: A96, pp. 117-8

CLARKE, Annie M. (1845-1902)
Actress: A23, pp. 56-7; A96, p. 116

CLARKE, Austin (1896-1974)
Irish playwright: A116, pp. 106-11; C1089

CLARKE, Burt G. (1847-1913)
Actor: A96, p. 116

CLARKE, [Charles] Creston (1865-1910)
American actor: A1, n. p., por.; A23, pp. 57-8

CLARKE, George [born O'Neill] (1840-1906)
American actor: A23, pp. 58-62

CLARKE, Harry Corson (c. 1861-1923)
American actor: A16, III, 27; A103, pp. 262-3

CLARKE, John H. (1788-1838)
Actor: A96, p. 116

CLARKE, John Sleeper (1833-99)
American actor, manager: A23, pp. 62-4; A71, pp. 95-112; A75, pp. 95-112; A81, II, 69-70; A96, p. 117; A123, I, 278-82

CLARKE, Joseph I. C. (1846-1925)
Irish-American playwright: A16, III, 177; A96, pp. 116-7; C506

CLARKE, Wilfred (1866-1945)
American actor, producer: A96,
p. 117

CLARKSON, William (1865-1934)
British costumer: C1045

CLAUDEL, Paul (1868-1955)
French playwright: B20, pp.
285-6: C909

CLAXTON, Kate [born Cone; Mrs.
C. A. Stevenson] (1848-1924)
American actress: A23, pp. 64-
6; A44, VI, 24-5; A66, n. p.;
A81, II, 105; A96, p. 118;
A111, pp. 57-9; A125, pp. 189-
92

CLAYTON, Estelle [born Evesson]
(1867-1917)
Actress, playwright: A1, n. p.,
por.; A2, n. p.; A96, p. 118

CLEARY, Mena
Singing actress: A23, II, 36-7

CLEMENS, Henry Cameron (c. 1866-
1932)
Actor: A96, p. 118

CLEMENT, Clay [born Clement Geig-
er] (1863-1910)
American actor: A96, pp. 118-9

CLEMENTS, Colin [born Campbell]
(1894-1948)
American playwright: A96, p.
119

CLEMENTS, John S. (1910--)
English actor, producer: A32,
pp. 48-9

CLEMENTS, Miriam
Actress: A86, n. p., por.

CLEMMONS, Katherine [Viola Dayan]
(1873-1930)
American actress: A66, n. p.

CLEUGH, Sophia [born Sadler; Mrs.
Dennis Cleugh] (?1887--)
English actress: B20, pp. 287-8

CLEVELAND, Bessie

Actress: A66, n. p.

CLIFFE, Alice Belmore [Mrs. H.
Cooper Cliffe] (1870-1943)
Actress: A96, p. 119

CLIFFE, H. Cooper [born H. Clif-
ford Cooper] (1862-1939)
English actor: A16, p. 166;
A44, IX, 30-31

CLIFFORD, Billy ["Single"] (1869-
1930)
American minstrel: A96, pp.
119-20

CLIFFORD, Ed (1845-95)
Actor: A96, p. 120

CLIFFORD, Lucy [born Lane; Mrs.
W. K. Clifford] (d. 1929)
English playwright: B20. pp.
288-9

CLIFT, Montgomery (1920-66)
American actor: C321; C1417

CLIFTON, Genevieve
Actress: A110, pp. 49-50

CLIFTON, Joseph [born Dilks]
(b. 1858)
Actor, playwright: A96, p. 120

CLIFTON, Josephine [born Miller;
Mrs. Robert Place] (1813-47)

CLIFTON, Marion P. (1833-1917)
Actress: A96, p. 120

CLINE, Maggie (1857-1934)
American actress: A96, pp. 120-
21

CLINTON, Katherine (d. 1935)
American actress: A98, pp. 67-8

CLIVE, Catherine ["Kitty"; born
Raftor] (1711-85)
British actress: A6, I, 300-05;
A7, I, 391-7; A11, pp. 51-108;
A42, pp. 74-109; A70, pp. 47-
58; A81, I, 18-9; A92, pp. 98-
102; A93, pp. 25-30; A97, pp.
67-87; C875;

CLIVE, Edward E. (1876-1940)
English actor, producer: A96,
p. 121

CLOWES, Mary Louise
Actress: A16, p. 135

CLUNES, Alec (1912-70)
English actor: C2362

CLURMAN, Harold (1901-80)
American director, critic: C509

COATES, Robert ["Romeo"] (1772-
1848)
British actor: A50, pp. 342-3;
B23, pp. 75-6; C2053

COBB, Lee J. [born Leo Jacoby]
(1911-76)
A125, pp. 193-7

COBORN, Charles (1852-1945)
British performer: C1637

COBURN, Charles Douville (1877-
1961)
American actor: A50, p. 397;
A96, p. 121; C924

COBURN, John Arthur (1869-1943)
American mistrel: A96, p. 121

COCHRAN, Charles Blake (1872-
1951)
English producer: A29, pp. 61-
2; C510; C513; C514; C515;
C516; C1032; C1180

COCROFT, Thoda (1893-1943)
American actress, press agent:
A96, pp. 121-2; C517

COCTEAU, Jean (1889-1963)
French playwright: B15, pp. 66-
7; B20, pp. 293-4; C374; C518;
C610; C2265

CODY, Eleanor
American performer: A58, pp.
44-53

CODY, William F. ["Buffalo Bill"]
1846-1917)
American producer, performer:
A8, pp. 88-9; C519; C609;

C2156; C2429

COE, Isabelle [Mrs. I. C. McKee]
(1881-1919)
Actress: A1, n. p., por.; A66,
n. p.; A96, p. 122

COFFEY, Charles (d. 1745)
British playwright: A22, p. 176

COFFIN, Charles Hayden (1862-
1935)
English actor: A44, V, 30-31;
A86, n. p., por.; C520

COGHLAN, Charles F. (1842-99)
English actor: A23, pp. 66-9;
A44, III, 6-7; A50, p. 359;
A66, n. p.; A81, II, 96; A123,
I, 423-38

COGHLAN, Gertrude [Mrs. Augustus
Pitou, Jr.] (1876-1952)
English actress: A3, n. p.

COGHLAN, Rose [Mrs. Clinton Ed-
gerly; Mrs. John T. Sullivan]
(1851-1932)
English actress: A1, n. p.,
por.; A2, n. p.; A3, n. p.; A5,
pp. 159-60; A15, pp. 39-40;
A16, p. 75; A23, pp. 69-70;
A25, pp. 69-82; A30, pp. 69-81;
A38, n. p.; A44, V, 20-21; A66,
n. p.; A77, pp. 249-58; A81,
II, 96; A106, pp. 258-69; A111,
pp. 32-5; A125, pp. 198-201

COHAN, Cal (1859-1944)
American minstrel: A96, p. 122

COHAN, George M. (1878-1942)
American actor, director, producer, dancer, singer, playwright: A3, n. p.; A13, p. 49;
A16, III, 160; A20, pp. 52-4;
A64, pp. 605-07; A80, pp. 255-
7; A115, pp. 101-12; A125, pp.
202-08; C521; C1636; C1721

COHAN, Jerry [born Jere J. Cohan]
(1848-1917)
American performer: A96, p. 123

COHAN, Josephine [Mrs. Fred
Niblo] (1876-1916)

American performer: A16, II, 281

COHAN, Timothy (1846-1914)
Actor: A96, p. 123

COHEN, Nathan (1923-71)
Canadian critic: C791

COKAYNE, Aston (1608-84)
British playwright: A22, p. 56

COLBERT, Claudette (1905--)
French-American actress: A96, pp. 123-4; B15, pp. 68-9

COLE, Robert (c. 1868-1911)
Comedian: A96, p. 124

COLEMAN, E. B. (1838-97)
English actor: A96, pp. 124-5

COLEMAN, John (1831-1904)
British actor, manager, playwright: C530; C532

COLEMAN, John J. (b. 1860)
Actor, manager: A96, p. 125

COLLETTE, Charles (1843-1924)
British actor: A16, p. 170

COLLIER, Constance [born Hardie; Mrs. Julian L'Estrange] (1878-1955)
English actress: A13, p. 47; A50, p. 398; A86, n. p., por.; C534

COLLIER, James Walter (1836-1920)
American actor: A96, pp. 125-6

COLLIER, Jeremy (1650-1726)
British writer: C2010

COLLIER, John Payne (1789-1883)
British critic: C536; C2465

COLLIER, Lizzie Hudson [Mrs. J. Walter Collier] (c. 1864-1924)
Actress: A66, n. p.
(See HUDSON, Lizzie.)

COLLIER, William (1868-1944)
American actor, playwright: A3, n. p.; A13, pp. 44; A16,

III, 259; A85, pp. 77-84; A96, p. 126; A102, pp. 87-96; A103, pp. 140-41

COLLIN D'HARVILLE, Jean-François (1755-1806)
French playwright: C2209

COLLINGBOURNE, Florence
Singing actress: A86, n. p., por.

COLLINGE, Patricia (1884-1974)
Irish actress: A13, p. 115; A102, pp. 285-8

COLLINS, Charles W. (1880-1964)
American critic: A96, p. 126

COLLINS, Horace (1875-1964)
British manager: C538

COLLINS, José (1887-1958)
English actress: C539

COLLINS, Lottie (1866-1910)
Actress: A1, n. p., por.; A2, n. p.; A66, n. p.

COLLINS, Wilkie (1824-89)
English playwright: B24, pp. 156-64; C666; C2054

COLMAN, George, Sr. (1732-94)
British playwright, manager: C1853; C1882; C2235

COLMAN, George, Jr. (1762-1836)
British playwright, manager: C120; C540; C2408

COLMAN, Ronald (1891-1958)
English actor: A35, p. 21, por.; A96, p. 128; C541

COLVILLE, Samuel (1825-86)
Actor, manager: A96, p. 129

COMER, Thomas (1790-1862)
English actor: A96, p. 129

COMPSON, Betty (1897-1974)
American actress: A35, p. 28, por.

COMPTON, Fay (1894-1978)

English actress: A9, p. 9; A29, pp. 87-8; A32, p. 88; A35, p. 1, por.; A50, p. 457; C544

COMPTON, Henry [born Charles Mackenzie] (1805-77)
Scottish actor: C1557

COMSTOCK, Nanette [Mrs. Frank Burbeck] (1873-1942)
American actress: A16, II, 164; A96, p. 129; A103, pp. 246-7

CONCANNEN, Matthew (1701-49)
British playwright: A22, pp. 170-1

CONDELL, Henry (?1556-1627)
British actor: A27, pp. 132-50; C546

CONDUIT, Mauvaise [born Ribbon; Mrs. Benedict De Bar] (1805-51)
English actress: A96, pp. 129-30

CONGREVE, William (1670-1729)
English playwright: A22, pp. 114-5; C1014; C1213; C2509

CONKLIN, George (1845-1924)
American circus performer: C2069

CONNELLY, Edward J. (1859-1928)
American actor: A16, II, 285

CONNELLY, Marcus Cook (1890-1980)
American playwright: A35, p. 100, por.; A65, pp. 124-30; B20, pp. 306-7; C547

CONNER, Edmon Sheppard (1809-91)
American actor: A81, II, 37; A96, p. 131

CONNOLLY, Elise
A110, pp. 37-8

CONNOLLY, Walter (1888-1940)
American actor: A96, p. 131

CONNOR, Charles (d. 1826)
British actor: A12, pp. 34-5

CONNOR, James (1824-67)

Irish actor: A96, p. 131

CONQUEST FAMILY: C885

CONQUEST, Ida [born Moriner; Lady Riccardo Bertelli] (1876-1937)
American actress: A3, n. p.; A61, pp. 43-4; A103, pp. 66-7; A106, pp. 69-71

CONRAD, Edith
A16, III, 214

CONRAD, Joseph (1851-1924)
British playwright: A116, pp. 111-5; C551; C1346; C2325

CONRIED, Heinrich (1848-1909)
Austrian producer: A16, p. 204; C1753

CONSIDINE, John, Sr. (1862-1943)
Manager: A96, p. 131

CONSTANDUROS, Mabel [born Tilling] (1880-1957)
English actress, playwright: C552

CONTAT, Louise (1760-1813)
French actress: A37, II, 80-101

CONTI, Italia (1874-1946)
English actress, educator: C2153

CONWAY, Fred B. (1819-74)
English actor, manager: A81, II, 132; A96, p. 132

CONWAY, George W. (d. 1918)
Actor: A96, p. 132

CONWAY, H. J. (1800-60)
Actor, playwright: A96, p. 132

CONWAY, William A. [born Rugg] (1780-1828)
English actor: A81, II, 104

CONY, Burkham ["The Dog Star"] (1802-58)
English actor, dog trainer: A96, p. 133

COOK, Augustus (1859-1904)

Actor: A44, V, 42-3

COOK, George Cram (1873-1924)
American playwright, producer:
B20, pp. 310-11; C988; C2121

COOK, James M. (b. 1825)
English actor: A96, pp. 133-4

COOK, John (fl. 1599-1604)
A22, pp. 19-20

COOKE, Alexander [also Sander
Cooke] (d. 1613)
British actor: A27, pp. 182-8

COOKE, Eddie G. (1869-1942)
American manager, press agent:
A96, p. 133

COOKE, Edward (fl. 1678)
A22, p. 104

COOKE, George Frederick (1756-
1812)
English actor: A4, pp. 102-15;
A6, II, 52-71; A7, II, 67-92;
A41, pp. 331-60; A45, II, 192-
216; A73, pp. 1-22; A77, pp.
209-12; A79, pp. 22-3; A80, pp.
107-15; A81, I, 46-8; A92, pp.
234-8; A93, pp. 115-20; A96, p.
133; A99, pp. 207-32; C776;
C1115; C2507

COOKE, Joe (1890-1959)
American actor: A96, p. 134

COOKE, Sarah (d. 1688)
British actress: A119, pp. 130-
31

COOKE, Thomas (1703-56)
A22, p. 183

COOKE, Thomas Potter (1786-1864)
English actor: A12, pp. 37-41

COOKE, Thomas Simpsom (1782-1848)
English actor: A12, pp. 35-7;
A81, I, 72; A92, pp. 334-5

COOMBS, Jane [Mrs. F. A. Brown]
A96, p. 134

COOPER, Diana Manners (b. 1892)

English actress: C562; C563;
C564; C565; C2577

COOPER, Frank Kemble (1857-1918)
English actor: A16, p. 119

COOPER, Gladys (1888-1971)
English actress: A29, pp. 52-3;
A35, p. 94, por.; A57, pp. 133-
4; C566; C1732; C2285

COOPER, Priscilla Elizabeth
(d. 1889)
Actress: A96, pp. 134-5

COOPER, Thomas Abthorpe (1776-
1849)
English actor: A73, pp. 235-52;
A81, II, 18-9; A96, p. 135;
A125, pp. 213-7; C78; C1289

COOTE, Bert (1868-1938)
English comedian: A96, p. 136

COOTE, Henry (c. 1880-1949)
Actor: A16, III, 74

COPPIN, George Selth (1819-1906)
Australian manager: C119

COQUELIN, Benoît Constant (1841-
1909)
French actor: A1, n. p., por.;
A2, n. p.; A8, pp. 70-71; A16,
p. 32; A44, VIII, 6-7; A81, II,
92; A86, n. p., por.; A91, pp.
207-12; A121, II, 324-9; A123,
I, 398-413

CORBETT, Harry H. (1925--)
English actor: A18, pp. 31-60

CORBETT, James J. (1866-1933)
American actor, pugilist: A16,
p. 197; A21, pp. 68-9; C568

CORBIN, John (1870-1959)
American critic: C500

CORCORAN, Jane [Mrs. J. Emmett
Baxter]
Actress: A16, II, 187

CORDEN, Juliet
Actress: A44, IX, 16-7

CORELLI, Alan
  American performer: A100, pp.
  83-95

COREY, Katherine [born Mitchell;
  Mrs. John Corey] (b. c. 1635)
  British actress: A119, pp. 132-
  4

COREY, Madison W. (1873-1952)
  American manager: A49, pp. 336-
  7

CORIN [born Lind]
  English actor: C571

CORINNE [born Corinne Belle de
  Brion; Mrs. Corinne Kimball]
  (1873-1937)
  American actress: A1, n. p.,
  por.; A2, n. p.; A66, n. p.

CORNEILLE, Pierre (1606-84)
  French playwright: C1070

CORNELL, Katharine [Mrs. Guthrie
  McClintic]   (1898-1974)
  American actress: A13, p. 109;
  A35, p. 56, por.; A50, pp. 462-
  3; A79, pp. 126-7; A80, pp.
  234-8; A115, pp. 123-32; A125,
  pp. 218-23; B15, pp. 76-7;
  C573; C1578; C1642; C1748;
  C1755

CORNISH, Nellie C. (1876-1956)
  American educator: C574

CORRIGAN, Emmett (1868-1932)
  Dutch actor: A16, III, 140;
  A96, p. 136

CORT, John (1859-1929)
  American manager: A96, pp. 136-
  7

CORTHELL, Herbert (1878-1947)
  American actor: A16, III, 34;
  A96, p. 137

COSGRAVE, Luke (1862-1949)
  American actor: C576

COTEY, John
  British playwright: A22, p. 93

COTTON, Charles (1630-87)
  British playwright: A22, p. 88

COTTRELLY, Mathilde [born Meyer;
  Mrs. Wilson] (1851-1933)
  German actress, manager: A44,
  VI, 40-41; A96, p. 137

COULDOCK, Charles Walter (1815-
  98)
  English actor: A66, n. p.; A68,
  pp. 130-31; A81, II, 44; A96,
  pp. 137-8

COURTAINE, Henry (d. 1899)
  Performer: A111, pp. 39-42

COURTENAY, Tom (1937--)
  English actor: A32, pp. 30-31

COURTENAY, William L. (1875-1933)
  American actor: A16, III, 148

COURTLEIGH, William Louis, Sr.
  [born Flynn] (1869-1930)
  Canadian actor: A16, II, 150;
  A44, VIII, 14-5; A96, p. 138;
  A98, pp. 87-8

COURTNEIDGE, Charles (d. 1935)
  British actor, manager: A35, p.
  46, por.

COURTNEIDGE, Cicely (1893-1980)
  Australian actress: A35, p. 46,
  por.; A57, pp. 162-78; C581

COURTNEIDGE, Robert (1859-1939)
  Scottish manager, playwright,
  actor: C582

COURTNEY, Fay (1868-1941)
  American actress: A96, p. 138

COWARD, Noël (1899-1973)
  English actor, director, playwright, composer: A19, pp. 164-
  77; A29, pp. 89-98; A35, pp.
  41-5, por.; A116, pp. 116-29;
  A125, pp. 224-9; B15, pp. 80-
  81; B20, pp. 319-20; C346;
  C451; C584; C585; C586; C1036;
  C1477; C1585; C1734

COWELL, Anna [born Cruise; Mrs.
  William Cowell] (b. 1824)

A96, p. 138

COWELL, Joe (1792-1863)
English actor: A96, pp. 138-9;
A125, pp. 230-2; C588

COWELL, Sam (1820-64)
English actor: C721

COWELL, Sydney (1846-1925)
English actress: A23, pp. 71-4

COWELL, William (1820-68)
Irish actor: A96, p. 139

COWELS, Charles O. (1861-1916)
American actor: A96, p. 139

COWIE, Laura (1892-1969)
Scottish actress: A9, p. 10,
por.

COWL, Jane [born Cowles] (1884-
1950)
American actress: A13, p. 74;
A35, p. 4, por.; A50, pp. 451-
5; A102, pp. 303-8; A125, pp.
233-8; B15, pp. 82-3

COWLES, Eugene (1860-1948)
Canadian singing actor: A44, I,
28-9, XI, n. p.; A66, n. p.;
A96, p. 139

COWLEY, Abraham (1618-67)
British playwright: A22, pp.
50-51; C1796

COWLEY, Richard (d. 1619)
British actor: A27, pp. 159-64

COX, Elizabeth (?1639-88?)
British actress: A119, pp. 134-
5

COX, Robert (1580-1648)
British actor: A22, p. 64; A81,
I, 8; A92, pp. 5-6

CRABTREE, Charlotte ["Lotta"]
(1847-1924)
American actress: A8, pp. 86-7;
A14, pp. 18-25; A16, II, 249;
A23, pp. 75-7; A25, pp. 93-
105; A30, pp. 95-103; A44, III,
12-3; A46, pp. 42-8; A66,

n. p.; A77, pp. 321-7; A81, II,
92; A125, pp. 239-42; C189;
C700; C2080

CRAFTON, Allen (1890-1966)
American producer: C946

CRAIG, Edith [born Wardell]
(1869-1947)
English actress, designer: A16,
p. 273; A47, pp. 29-42; C19

CRAIG, Edward Gordon (1872-1966)
English designer, actor: A47,
pp. 29-42; B14, pp. 202-3; B20,
p. 324; C115; C591; C594;
C1786; C2072; C2406

CRAIG, John (1868-1932)
American actor, manager: A96,
p. 141; A98, pp. 27-8

CRAIG, Laura (1880-1947)
Actress: A96, p. 141

CRAMPTON, Charlotte (1816-68)
American actress: A96, p. 141

CRANE, Edith [Mrs. Tyrone Power
II] (1865-1912)
Actress: A96, p. 142

CRANE, Gardner (1874-1939?)
American performer: A16, p. 157

CRANE, Harvey
C596

CRANE, Madge [born Margaret; Mrs.
Gardner Crane] (1875-1963)
American performer: A16, p. 52

CRANE, William H. (1845-1928)
American actor: A1, n. p.,
por.; A2, n. p.; A3, n. p.;
A16, II, 107; A23, pp. 77-9;
A44, III, 22-3; A52, pp. 291-
302; A61, pp. 47-50; A64, pp.
430-36; A66, n. p.; A77, pp.
341-51; A81, II, 88; A96, p.
142; A103, pp. 30-31; A105, pp.
149-65; A111, pp. 62-3; A125,
pp. 243-9; C597

CRAUFORD, David
British playwright: A22, p. 144

CRUMIT, Frank (1889-1943)
American actor: A96, p. 145

CULLMAN, Marguerite [born Sanders] (1908--)
American investor: C617

CULVER, Roland (1900-84)
English actor: C618

CUMBERLAND, Richard (1732-1811)
English playwright: C619; C620; C1760; C2499

CUMMINGS, Tony
Actor: A98, pp. 111-2

CURRER, Elizabeth (fl. 1673-1743)
British actress: A119, pp. 135-6

CURTIS, Brownie
A102, pp. 277-84

CUSHING, Sidney (d. 1912)
Actor: A16, III, 170

CUSHMAN, Adelaide (c. 1873-1904)
American actress: A98, pp. 65-6

CUSHMAN, Charlotte (1816-76)
American actress: A5, pp. 166-71; A28, II, 182-204; A46, pp. 35-41; A67, pp. 79-96; A74, pp. 137-54; A79, pp. 44-7; A81, II, 40; A87, pp. 315-8; A89, pp. 343-78; A91, pp. 145-51; A92, pp. 408-09; A112, pp. 17-43; A120, pp. 152-77; A121, I, 206-14, II, 119-34; A123, I, 159-76; A125, pp. 255-62; B8, pp. 95-124; B25, pp. 21-6; C169; C508; C1952; C2263; C2442; C2562

CUSHMAN, Pauline (1833-93)
Actress: A45, pp. 26-30

CUSHMAN, Susan Webb (1822-59)
American actress: A96, p. 147

CUTTING, Robert Livingstone (c. 1869-1910)
Actor: A44, VII, 16-7

DAILEY, Peter F. (1868-1908)
American actor: A16, II, 22; A85, pp. 199-207; A104, pp. 256-64

DAILEY, Robert L. (d. 1934)
Actor: A16, III, 35

DAIROLLES, Adrienne (fl. 1888-97)
Actress: A44, VIII, 8-9

DALE, Gretchen [Mrs. Howard Estabrook] (b. 1886)
Actress: A16, p. 67

DALE, James (b. 1886)
English actor: C631

DALE, Teresa
Actress: A16, II, 18

DALLAS, Merwyn (c. 1824-1911)
Actor: A96, p. 148

DALRYMPLE, Jean (1910--)
American performer, producer, press agent: A100, pp. 96-102; C632; C633

DALTON, Charles (1864-1942)
English actor: A96, p. 148; A103, pp. 286-7

D'ALTON, Louis (1900-51)
British playwright: A116, pp. 129-33

DALTON, M.
British playwright: A22, p. 188

DALY, Arnold [born Peter Christopher Arnold] (1875-1927)
American actor: A3, n. p.; A16, II, 225; A80, pp. 207-12; A96, p. 148; A102, pp. 147-52; C1000

DALY, Augustin (1838-99)
American manager: A5, pp. 218-20; A96, pp. 148-9; A122, pp. 216, 281; A123, I, 348-58; C636; C842

DALY, Blythe (1902--)
Actress: A102, pp. 9-14

DALY, Dan (1858-1904)
American actor: A64, pp. 580-82; A104, pp. 168-75

DALY, Henry F. (1828-1905)
Actor: A96, p. 149

DALY, Julia [Mrs. Wayne Olwine; Mrs. Warren Edgarton] (1833-87)
Actress: p. 149

DALY, Vinie (b. 1883)
Dancer, singer: A16, II, 36

DALZELL, Davidson (b. 1858)
Actor: A96, pp. 149-50

DANCE, George C. (c. 1855-1932)
English playwright, director: A96, p. 150

DANCER, John (fl. 1660-75)
British playwright: A22, p. 171

DANCOURT, Florent Carton (1661-1725)
French playwright: C2261

DANDY, Jess [born Jesse A. Danzig] (1871-1923)
American actor: A16, II, 250

DANE, Clemence [born Winifred Ashton] (1888-1965)
English playwright, actress: A116, pp. 133-8; B20, pp. 346-7

DANE, Essex [born Findon; Mrs. Arthur Lewis] (c. 1866-1962)
English actress, playwright: A16, II, 48

DANIEL, Samuel (c. 1562-1619)
British playwright: A22, pp. 35-6

DANIELS, Frank Albert (1860-1935)
American actor: A3, n. p.; A66, n. p.; A85, pp. 131-8; A96, pp. 150-51; A103, pp. 104-05; A104, pp. 141-53

D'ANNUNZIO, Gabriele (1863-1938)
Italian playwright: B20, pp. 31-2; C2535

DARBYSHIRE, Alfred (1839-1908)
British designer: C639

DARCY, James (fl. 1732-49)
British playwright: A22, p. 182

DARE, Leona [born Stuart] (1855-1922)
Actress: A8, pp. 38-9

DARE, Phyllis (1890-1975)
British actress: C641; C1699

DARLEY, John (c. 1756-1819)
British actor: A81, II, 20

DARLEY, John, Jr. (c. 1779-1853)
British actor: A96, p. 151

DARLINGTON, William A. (1890-1979)
English critic: C643; C647

DARRELL, Charles (1858-1932)
Playwright: A16, II, 151

DARRELL, George (1841-1921)
Australian actor: C1291

D'ARVILLE, Camille [born Neeltya Dykstra; Mrs. C. W. Crelin] (1863-1932)
Dutch actress: A16, III, 149; A44, V, 40-41; A66, n. p.; A96, p. 151; A103, pp. 242-3

DATAS (b. 1875)
English performer: C652

DAUBENY, Peter (1921-75)
English manager: C653

DAUBORNE, Robert
British playwright: A22, p. 39

DAUVRAY, Helen [born Nellie Williams, "Little Nell, the California Diamond"] (1858-1923)
American actress: A5, pp. 126-33; A44, VIII, 36-7; A66, n. p.; A96, pp. 151-2

DAVENANT, Charles (1656-1714)
British playwright: A22, p. 103

D'AVENANT, William (1606-68)

A22, pp. 58-9; B17, pp. 33-54; C1106; C1797

DAVENPORT FAMILY: A78, pp. 226-54

DAVENPORT, Adolphus H. [born Hoyt; "Dolly"] (1828-73)
American actor: A96, p. 152

DAVENPORT, Allen
Actor: A16, p. 94

DAVENPORT, Edgar Longfellow (1862-1918)
American actor: A44, VII, 23-4; A103, pp. 202-3

DAVENPORT, Edward Loomis (1815-77)
English actor: A23, pp. 81-3; A50, pp. 352-3; A74, pp. 119-36; A81, II, 44; A96, p. 152; A125, pp. 263-7; C789; C2003

DAVENPORT, Fanny Lily Gypsy (1850-98)
American actress: A8, pp. 68-9; A14, pp. 83-6; A16, II, 97; A25, pp. 83-92; A30, pp. 83-93; A44, V, 16-7; A64, pp. 351-60; A66, n. p.; A77, pp. 108-18; A81, II, 98-9; A101, n. p., por.; A111, pp. 23-6 (Caution: some of these references may be to the mother, Fanny Elizabeth Vining Davenport.)

DAVENPORT, Harry G. B. (1866-1949)
American actor: A16, II, 33

DAVENPORT, Hester [Countess of Oxford; Mrs. Peter Holt] (c. 1641-1717)
British actress: A119, pp. 137-9

DAVENPORT, Jean Margaret (1829-1903)
Actress, playwright: A96, p. 153 (See LANDER, Jean M.)

DAVENPORT, Mary Ann [born Harvey; Mrs. George G. Davenport] (1759-1843)

A12, p. 43; A81, I, 54-5; A92, pp. 265-6

DAVENPORT, May [Mrs. William Seymour] (1856-1927)
American actress: A23, pp. 83-5

DAVENPORT, Robert (fl. 1623-39)
British playwright: A22, p. 63

DAVEY, Thomas W. (c. 1830-79)
Actor, manager: A96, p. 155

DAVIDGE, William P. (1814-88)
English actor: A68, pp. 174-85; A81, II, 107; A96, p. 153; C657

DAVIDSON, Dore (1850-1930)
American actor, playwright: A96, p. 153; A103, pp. 240-41

DAVIES, Marion [born Marion C. Douras] (1898-1961)
American actress: A35, p. 24, por.; C1068

DAVIES, Phoebe [Mrs. Joseph R. Grismer] (1867-1912)
Actress: A16, II, 83; A23, pp. 85-8; A103, pp. 176-7

DAVIES, Thomas (c. 1710-85)
British biographer: A92, pp. 90-92

DAVIOT, Gordon [Elizabeth Mackintosh] (1896-1952)
British playwright: A116, pp. 139-41

DAVIS, Bertha (d. 1916)
Actress: A16, III, 274

DAVIS, Bette [born Ruth E. Davis] (1908--)
American actress: C663

DAVIS, Charles Lindsay ["Jumbo"] (1848-1900)
American actor, playwright: A96, p. 154

DAVIS, Esmé (c. 1898-1950)
Dancer: C665

DAVIS, Fay [Mrs. Gerald Lawrence]

American actress: A16, p. 276; A106, pp. 273-84

DAVIS, Jessie Bartlett (1861-1905)
American actress: A1, n. p., por.; A44, I, 22-3, X, n. p.; A66, n. p.; A96, p. 154; A103, pp. 94-5; A107, pp. 88-103

DAVIS, Mary ["Moll"] (d. 1726)
British actress: A7, pp. 59-60; A119, pp. 139-41

DAVIS, Ossie (1917--)
American actor, playwright: A65, pp. 144-7; C942

DAVIS, Owen (1874-1956)
American playwright: B20, pp. 354-5; C667; C668; C2431

DAVIS, Rae
American performer: A58, pp. 6-7

DAVIS, Richard Harding (1864-1916)
American playwright: A16, II, 101; B20, pp. 355-6; C664; C745; C1430

DAVIS, Thomas H. (1859-1911)
Actor, manager: A96, p. 154

DAVIS, William James (1844-1919)
Manager: A16, p. 44; A96, pp. 154-5

DAVISON, Maria [born Duncan] (1783-1858)
British actress: A12, pp. 44-6

DAVY, Samuel (fl. 1737-9)
British playwright: A22, p. 187

DAWISON, Bogumil (1818-72)
German actor: A123, I, 183-5

DAWN, Hazel (b. c. 1891)
Actress: A13, p. 102

DAWSON, James (1779-1878)
English actor, manager: C671

DAY, Edmund (1866-1923)

Playwright: A96, p. 156

DAY, John (?1574-1640?)
British playwright: A22, p. 36

DAY, William Charles (c. 1822-95)
British actor: C672

DAYNE, Blanche [Mrs. Will M. Cressy] (c. 1871-1944)
American actress: A16, p. 283

DAZEY, Charles Turner (1853-1938)
American playwright: A16, p. 181; A96, p. 156

DAZIAN, Henry (1854-1937)
American manager, costumer: A49, pp. 309-10

DAZIE, Mlle. [Daisy Peterkin; Mrs. Mark A. Luescher; Mrs. Cornelius Fellowes] (1882-1952)
A16, II, 211

DEAN, Alfred (b. 1830)
Actor: A96, p. 156

DEAN, Basil (1888-1978)
English actor, manager, director, playwright: C675; C676

DEAN, Doris (b. 1889)
Actress: A16, II, 148

DEAN, Edwin (b. 1805)
Actor, manager: A96, p. 156

DEAN, Julia [Mrs. Hayne; Mrs. James Cooper] (1830-68)
American actress: A14, pp. 63-6; A81, II, 62; A96, p. 156; C1587

DEAN, Julia (1880-1952)
American actress: A13, p. 60; A16, III, 123; A96, p. 156; A125, pp. 273-6

DEANE, Barbara [born Katie Davies; Mrs. Basil Loder] (b. 1886)
Actress: A16, p. 53

DE ANGELIS, Jefferson (1859-1933)

American actor: A16, III, 270;
A44, VIII, 34-5; A85, pp. 51-9;
A96, p. 157; A103, pp. 84-5;
A104, pp. 236-55; C677

DE BAR, Benedict (1812-77)
English actor, manager: A81,
II, 43; A96, p. 155; C1181

DE BELLEVILLE, Frederic (1857-
1923)
Belgian actor: A44, IV, 38-9;
A66, n. p.; A81, II, 111

DE CASTRO, Jacob (1758-1835)
British actor: C682

DE COURVILLE, Albert P. (1887-
1960)
English manager, director: C689

DE FILLIPPE, Dora
Actress: A16, II, 235

DÉJAZET, Pauline (1798-1875)
French actress: A91, pp. 119-28

DEKKER, Thomas (c. 1572-c. 1632)
English playwright: A22, p. 24

DE KOVEN, Reginald (1859-1920)
American composer: C693

DELANE, Dennis (1700-73)
British actor: A92, pp. 81-2

DELEHANTY, William H. (1846-80)
American minstrel: A96, p. 158

DELL, Floyd (1887-1969)
American playwright: B20, pp.
369-70; C695

DELMORE, Ralph (1853-1923)
American actor: A16, p. 277;
A96, p. 158

DE LUSSAN, Zélie (c. 1854-1949)
American singing actress: A44,
IV, 44-5

DE MAR, Carrie (c. 1876-1963)
Actress: A16, II, 90

DEMAY, Florence
American performer: A58, pp.

26-31

DE MILLE, Agnes (1905--)
American dancer, choreographer:
C696; C697

DE MILLE, Cecil Blount (1881-
1959)
American actor, director, producer: A35, p. 20, por.; A96,
pp. 158-9; C698

DE MILLE, Henry C. (1850-93)
American playwright, actor:
A96, p. 159

DE MILLE, William C. (1878-1955)
American playwright: A96, p.
159

DEMING, Will J. (1871-1926)
Actor: A96, p. 159

DE MOTT, Josephine [Mrs. John
Robinson] (d. 1948)
American circus performer: C699

DENCH, Judi (1934--)
English actress: A50, pp.
519-20

DENHAM, John (1615-69)
British playwright: A22, pp.
72-3

DENHAM, Reginald (1894-1983)
English actor, director, producer: C701

DENIER, Tony (1839-1917)
Actor: A96, pp. 159-60

DENIN, Susan [Mrs. F. Woodward;
Mrs. Harry Huntingdon; Mrs.
Frank Banoll] (1835-75)
American actress: A81, II, 76

DENNIS, John (1657-1734)
British critic, playwright:
C622; C1874

DENNISTON, Reynolds (1881-1943)
New Zealand actor: A96, p. 160

DERWENT, Clarence (1884-1959)
English actor, playwright, pro-

ducer: C706

DESMOND, Florence (1905--)
English actress: C707

DE TREVILLE, Yvonne (1881-1954)
Singer: A16, II, 193

DEVAL, Jacques (1893-1972)
French playwright: B20, pp.
376-7

DE VALOIS, Ninette [Edris Stannus] (1898--)
Irish dancer, producer: C708

DE VERE, George F. (c. 1835-1915)
Actor: A16, II, 114

DEVINE, George (1910-66)
English actor, producer: C2436

DE WALDEN, Thomas B. (1811-73)
English actor, playwright: A96,
p. 161

DE WOLFE, Drina [born Alexandrina
Waters; Mrs. Charteris De
Wolfe] (b. 1880)
Actress: A16, II, 180; A38,
n. p.

DE WOLFE, Elsie [Lady Mendl]
(1865-1950)
American actress: A16, III,
290; A44, IV, 16-7; A52, pp.
53-66; A61, pp. 53-4; A106, pp.
248-57; C232; C709; C2220

DIAGHILEV, Sergei (1872-1929)
Russian impresario: C1144;
C1404; C1491

DIARD, Fatmah
Actress: A66, n. p.

DIBDIN, Charles (1745-1814)
British playwright, composer:
A81, I, 39; A92, pp. 198-200;
C710

DIBDIN, Thomas John (1771-1841)
British actor, manager, playwright: C711

DICKENS, Charles (1812-70)

English playwright, performer:
C880; C900; C1326

DICKINSON, Thomas H. (1877-1960)
American writer: A46, pp. 130-5

DICKSON, Charles S. (1862-1927)
American actor, manager, playwright: A44, II, 26-7; A66,
n. p.; A96, pp. 161-2

DIDEROT, Denis (1713-84)
French playwright, critic: C608

DIETRICH, Marlene (1904--)
German singing actress: B15,
pp. 9203; C927; C1196; C1733

DIETZ, Howard (1896-1983)
American lyricist, playwright:
C716

DIGBY, George, Earl of Bristol
(d. 1676)
British playwright: A22, p. 134

DIGGES, Dudley (1879-1947)
Irish actor: A125, pp. 277-80

DIGGES, West (1720-86)
British actor: A81, I, 26-7;
A92, pp. 130-31

DIGNUM, Charles (c. 1765-1827)
British actor: A81, I, 59-60;
A92, pp. 283-4

DILKE, Thomas (d. c. 1698)
British playwright: A22, p. 124

DILLINGHAM, Charles Bancroft
(1868-1934)
American manager, producer:
A96, p. 162

DILLON, Charles (1819-81)
English actor, manager: A26,
II, 248-94; A69, II, 180-92;
A81, II, 47; A123, I, 186-93

DILLON, John [born John Daily
Marum] (1831-1913)
Actor: A96, p. 163

DILLON, William Austin (1877-
1966)

American performer: C717

DITRICHSTEIN, Leo J. (1865-1928)
Hungarian-American actor, playwright: A16, III, 23; A96, p.
163; A102, pp. 15-22; A103, pp.
174-5

DIXEY, Henry E. (1859-1943)
American actor, manager: A1,
n. p.; A2, n. p.; A3, n. p.;
A21, pp. 6204; A23, pp. 88-90;
A44, III, 10-11; A66, n. p.;
A81, II, 110; A96, pp. 163-4;
A104, pp. 189-207

DIXON, Dorothy (1875-1947)
Actress: A96, p. 164

DIXON, George Washington (1795-
1861)
American actor: A96, p. 164

DIXON, Thomas (1864-1946)
American actor, manager, playwright: A16, p. 25; A96, pp.
164-5; B20, p. 387: C557

DOCKSTADER, Lew [George C. Clapp]
(1856-1924)
American minstrel: A85, pp. 65-
72; A96, p. 165

DODD, James William (1734-96)
British actor: A6, pp. 232-3;
A7, I, 303-04; A28, I, 186-205;
A81, I, 35-6; A92, pp. 189-91;
A93, pp. 71-6

DODGE, Jack [born John Mason
Dodge]
C727

DODSLEY, Robert (1703-64)
British playwright: A22, p. 186

DODSON, John E. (1857-1931)
English actor: A3, n. p.; A16,
III, 220; A23, pp. 90-91; A103,
pp. 62-3; A105, pp. 278-87

DOEBLIN, Alfred (1878-1957)
German playwright: B20, pp.
389-90

DOGGETT, Thomas (c. 1670-1721)

British actor, manager: A6, I,
89-90; A7, I, 113-5; A22, pp.
124-5; A45, I, 150-62; A81, I,
13; A92, pp. 47-8; C558

DOLIN, Anton [born Patrick Healey-Kay] (1904-83)
English dancer: C730; C731;
C2152

DOLLY, Jenny (1893-1941)
Hungarian-American performer:
A35, pp. 86-8, por.

DOLLY, Rosie (1892-1970)
Hungarian-American performer:
A35, pp. 86-8, por.

DONALDSON, Arthur (1869-1955)
Swedish-American actor, director, playwright, producer:
A103, pp. 300-01

DONALDSON, Walter (1793-1877)
British actor: C733; C734

DONAT, Robert (1905-58)
English actor: A9, p. 11, por.;
C2367

DONISTHORPE, Sheila (1898-1946)
English playwright: C736

DONNELLY, Dorothy Agnes (1880-
1928)
American actress, playwright:
A16, III, 40; A63, pp. 237-43

DONNELLY, Henry Grattan (1850-
1931)
Actor, playwright: A96, p. 166

DONNELLY, Leo (1878-1935)
American actor, playwright:
A96, p. 166

DONOHUGH, Jack (b. 1892)
American actor: A96, p. 166

DORO, Marie [born Marie K. Stewart] (1882-1956)
American actress: A3, n. p.;
A13, p. 48; A16, III, 131

DORR, Dorothy [Mrs. H. J. W. Dam]
(b. 1867)

Actress: A16, II, 280

D'ORSAY, Lawrence [born Dorset William Lawrence] (1860-1931) English actor: A96, p. 167

DOTRICE, Roy (1923--) English actor: A32, pp. 16, 18

DOUGHARTY, Houghline (1844-1919) American minstrel: A96, p. 167

DOUGLAS, Helen Gahagan (1900-80) American actress: A96, pp. 167-8; C740

DOUGLAS, Melvyn (1901-81) American actor: A125, pp. 281-6

DOUGLASS, Albert (1864-1940) British manager: C741; C742

DOUGLASS, David (c. 1730-86) British actor, manager: A36, pp. 255-69; A96, p. 167

DOVER, John (d. 1725) British playwright: A22, p. 128

DOVEY, Alice (1885-1969) American actress, manager: A16, III, 200

DOWLING, Joseph J. (1848-1928) American actor, playwright: A96, p. 168

DOWNING, Robert L. (1857-1944) American actor: A5, pp. 182-3; A16, II, 242; A23, pp. 91-2; A44, VII, 10-11; A66, n. p.; A81, II, 108; A96, p. 169

DOWTON, William (1765-1846) English actor: A12, pp. 47-8; A81, I, 58-9; A92, pp. 277-8; A96, p. 169

D'OYLY CARTE, Richard (1844-1901) English manager: C455

DRAKE FAMILY: C894

DRAKE, Alexander (1800-93) American actor, manager: A81, II, 34; A96, p. 169

DRAKE, Alfred [born Capurro] (1914--) American singing actor: A13, p. 131; A50, pp. 509-10; A125, pp. 287-91

DRAKE, Fabia (1904--) English actress: C746

DRAKE, Frances Ann [born Denny; Mrs. Alexander Drake; Mrs. Cutter] (1797-1875) American actress: A81, II, 34

DRAKE, James (1667-1706/7) British playwright: A22, p. 127

DRAKE, Julia [Mrs. Thomas Fosdick; Mrs. Edmund Dean] (b. 1801) American actress: A96, p. 169

DRAKE, Julia (1856-88) Actress: A96, p. 170

DRAKE, Samuel (1768-1854) English actor, manager: A46, pp. 11-4; A96, pp. 170-71

DRAKE, Samuel, Jr. (d. 1888) American actor: A125, pp. 292-6

DRAPER, Ruth (1884-1956) American performer: B15, pp. 94-5; C747

DRESSER, Louise [born Louise J. Kerlin] (1882-1965) American actress: A16, II, 226

DRESSLER, Marie [born Leila Koerber] (1869-1934) Canadian actress: A13, p. 37; A16, III, 254; A96, pp. 171-2; A103, pp. 264-5; A107, pp. 181-91; C750; C751

DREW FAMILY: A78, pp. 169-95

DREW, Frank Nelson (1831-1932) Actor: A96, p. 172

DREW, John, I (1827-62) Irish actor: A81, II, 61; A117, pp. 44-8; A125, pp. 297-9

DREW, John, II (1853-1927)
American actor: A1, n. p.,
por.; A2, n. p.; A3, n. p.; A8,
pp. 28-9; A13, p. 6; A16, II,
255; A21, pp. 72-5; A23, pp.
92-4; A44, III, 34-5; A55,
n. p., por.; A61, pp. 57-61;
A62, pp. 1-32; A66, n. p.; A77,
pp. 154-8; A81, II, 105; A96,
pp. 172-3; A102, pp. 1-8; A103,
pp. 18-9; A105, pp. 84-93;
A124, pp. 150-57; A125, pp.
306-15; C752; C753; C2545

DREW, Louisa [born Lane; Mrs. John
Drew I]
American actress: A1, n. p.,
por.; A2, n. p.; A44, III, pp.
20-21; A66, n. p.; A77, pp.
127-34; A81, II, 60-61; C754;
C2287

DREW, Louise [Mrs. Jack Dever-
eau] (c. 1882-1954)
American actress: A16, II, 226

DREW, Margaret (c. 1856-1963)
Actress: A16, II, 127

DREW, Sidney [born White] (1868-
1919)
American actor: A96, p. 173

DREWITT, Stanley (b. 1878)
Actor: A16, p. 230

DRINKWATER, John (1882-1937)
English playwright: A116, pp.
142-7; B20, pp. 399-401; C756;
C757

DROUET, Robert M. (1870-1914)
American actor, playwright:
A103, pp. 162-3

DRURY, Thomas (fl. 1732-41)
British playwright: A22, p. 184

DRUTMAN, Irving (1910--)
American composer: C760

DRYDEN, John (1631-1700)
English playwright: A22, pp.
82-7; B17, pp. 55-78; C98;
C1848; C2432

DRYDEN, John II (1667/8-1701)
English playwright: A22, p. 121

DUERRENMATT, Friedrich (1921--)
Swiss playwright: C1904

DUFF, John R. (1787-1831)
Irish actor: A81, II, 23; A96,
p. 173

DUFF, Mary [Mrs. A. A. Adams;
Mrs. Joseph Gilbert; Mrs. J. G.
Porter] (c. 1816-52)
Irish actress: A96, p. 174

DUFF, Mary Ann [born Dyke] (1794-
1857)
English actress: A50, p. 346;
A72, pp. 77-90; A81, II, 23-4;
A96, p. 173; A121, II, 19-26;
A123, I, 63-9; C1290; C1426

DUFFETT, Thomas (fl. 1674-8)
British playwright: A22, p. 97

DUFFY, William (fl. 1830-35)
American manager: C1472

DUGAZON, Louise-Rosalie [born Le-
fèvre] (1753-1821)
French actress: A37, II, 22-51

DUHAMEL, Georges (1884-1966)
French playwright: B20, pp.
403-05

DUKES, Ashley (1885-1959)
English critic, playwright,
producer: A116, pp. 148-52;
C765

DUMAS FAMILY: C1628

DUMAS, Alexandre, père (1802-70)
French playwright: C658

DUMAS, Alexandre, fils (1824-95)
French playwright: C2136; C2317

DU MAURIER, Angela
English actress: C766

DU MAURIER, Gerald (1873-1934)
English actor, manager: A16,
II, 82; A29, pp. 39-48; A33,
pp. 168-83; A47, pp. 75-84;

C767

DUMONT, Frank (c. 1848-1919)
Actor: C96, pp. 174-5

DUNCAN, Isadora (1878-1927)
American actress: A79, pp.
110-11; A114, pp. 139-60; B23,
pp. 118-20; B28, pp. 522-32;
C771;   C772;   C2160;   C2266;
C2333

DUNCAN, Malcolm (1878-1942)
American actor: A16, II, 212

DUNCAN, Rosetta (1902-59)
American performer: A102, pp.
69-74

DUNCAN, Vivien (1899--)
American performer: A102, pp.
69-74

DUNHAM, Katherine (c. 1910--)
American dancer, choreographer:
C393

DUNLAP, William (1766-1839)
American actor, manager, playwright, theatre historian: A96,
p. 175; C511; C775; C777

DUNSANY, Edward John, Lord (1878-
1957)
Irish   playwright: A116,   pp.
152-62; B20, p.   407; C276;
C779; C780; C781

DUPREE, Minnie (1873-1947)
American actress: A16, III, 33

DURANG, John (1786-1822)
American dancer: A79, pp. 18-9;
C744

DURANT, Alexia
American actress: A98, pp. 25-6

DURANT, Jack
American performer: A100, pp.
103-14

DURANTE, Jimmy (1893-1980)
American performer: A20, pp.
106-08; A126, pp. 82-134; C20;
C415; C427; C907

D'URFEY, Thomas (1653-1723)
English playwright: A22, pp.
101-03

DURRIVAGE, John E. (1813-61)
American   actor,   playwright:
A96, p. 177

DURUSET, John (1796-1843)
British actor: A12, p. 49

DUSE, Eleonora (1859-1924)
Italian actress: A14, pp. 87-
95; A16, III, 228; A44, II, 12-
3; A56, pp. 171-202; A60, pp.
204-24; A66, n. p.; A67, pp.
153-84; A79, pp. 84-5; A124,
pp. 39-52; A125, pp. 316-23;
C69; C316; C1110; C1462; C1940;
C2013; C2185; C2308; C2535

DU SOUCHET, Henry A. (1852-1922)
American playwright: A96, p.
177

DYBWAD, Johanne (1867-1950)
Norwegian actress: C2413

DYER, Robert
British actor, writer: C783

EAGELS, Jean (1894-1929)
American actress: A13, p. 80;
A35, pp. 26-7, por.; A79, pp.
122-3; A125, pp. 324-8; B15,
pp. 96-7; C728

EAMES, Emma (1865-1952)
American singer: C2585

EARLE, Clara [Mrs. George Howard]
English actress: A16, II, 117

EARLE, Erminie
Actress: A16, II, 26

EARLE, Virginia (1875-1937)
American   actress: A16,   III,
186; A96, p. 178; A107, pp. 21-
9

EASTLAKE, Mary (1856-1911)
Actress: A66, n. p.; A81, II,
109

EATON, Charles Henry (1813-43)
American actor: A96, p. 179

EATON, Mary (1902-48)
American actress: A96, p. 179;
B15, pp. 168-9

EATON, Walter P. (1878-1957)
American critic: B20, pp. 410-11

EATON, Will D. (fl. 1878-97)
A96, p. 179

EBERLE, Eugene A. (1840-1917)
American actor: A16, p. 92

EBERLE, Robert M. (1840-1912)
Actor, manager: A96, pp. 179-80

EBERT, Franz
Actor: A44, III, 42-3

ECCLESTONE, Edward (fl. 1679)
A22, p. 106

ECCLESTONE, William (d. c. 1652)
British actor: A27, pp. 245-8

ECHARD, Laurence (1671-1730)
British playwright: A22, p. 117

ECHEGARAY, José (1832-1916)
Spanish playwright: A16, p. 93

EDDINGER, Wallace (1881-1929)
American actor: A16, III, 167

EDDY, Edward (1822-75)
American actor: A96, p. 180

EDESON, Robert (1868-1931)
American actor: A3, n. p.; A16,
II, 133; A52, pp. 251-66; A96,
pp. 180-81

EDGETT, Edwin Francis (1867-1946)
American critic: C790

EDISS, Connie (1872-1934)
English actress: A16, II, 185;
A86, n. p., por.

EDMISTON, Miss (b. 1801)
British actress: A12, p. 50

EDOUIN, Willie [born William
Frederick Bryer] (1846-1908)
British actor, manager: A86,
n. p., por.

EDWARDES, Paula (b. 1878)
Actress: A16, p. 213; A107, pp.
113-9

EDWARDS, Emilie Frances [Mrs.
George Edwards] (d. 1885)
Actress: A1, n. p., por.

EDWARDS, Gus [born Simon] (1879-1945)
German-American actor, producer: A20, pp. 11-5; A96, p. 181

EDWARDS, Henry (1831-91)
English actor: A81, II, 68-9;
A111, pp. 68-70

EDWARDS, Julian (1855-1910)
English composer: A16, III, 282

EDWARDS, Richard (?1523-66)
British playwright: A22, pp. 4,
22; C330

EDWIN, John (1749-90)
British actor: A6, II, 75-7;
A81, II, 42-3; A92, pp. 214-6;
C1492; C1868

EGAN, Pierce (1772-1849)
Irish playwright: C797

EGERTON, Daniel (1772-1835)
British actor: A12, pp. 50-51

EGERTON, George [born Mary C.
Dunne Golding Bright] (1860-1945)
Australian playwright: B20, pp.
192-3

EGERTON, Sarah [born Fisher]
(1782-1847)
British actor: A12, pp. 51-3

ELDER, Lonne III (1931--)
American playwright: A65, pp.
148-51

ELDRIDGE, Florence (1901--)
American actress: A35, p. 59,

por.

ELDRIDGE, Louisa [born Harwood or Mortimer] (1829-1905)
American actress: A23, pp. 94-5

ELEN, Gus [born Ernest Augustus Elen] (1862-1940)
English actor: A16, II, 167

ELIOT, Thomas Stearns (1888-1965)
Anglo-American playwright: A65, pp. 151-72; A116, pp. 163-85

ELISCU, Fernanda (1880-1968)
Rumanian actress: A16, II, 104

ELITCH, Mary (d. 1936)
American manager, theatre owner: C714

ELLAR, Thomas (1780-1842)
British pantomimist: A68, pp. 117-25

"ELLERSLIE, Blanche"
British actress: C799

ELLIOT, Robert Wallace (c. 1864-1905)
Actor: A98, pp. 95-6

ELLIOT, William Gerald (b. 1858)
C800

ELLIOTT, Gertrude [born Dermot; Mrs. Johnston Forbes-Robertson] (1874-1950)
American actress: A16, III, 285

ELLIOTT, Maxine [born Jessie Dermot; Mrs. Nat C. Goodwin] (1871-1940)
American actress: A3, n. p.; A13, p. 17; A16, III, 49; A44, V, 24-5; A52, pp. 313-26; A61, pp. 95-6; A63, pp. 182-3; A96, pp. 181-2; A103, pp. 16-7; A106, pp. 104-12; A125, pp. 329-33; C892

ELLIS, Florence (d. 1944)
Actress: A110, pp. 11-2

ELLISTON, Grace [born Rutter] (1881-1950)

American actress: A3, n. p.

ELLISTON, Robert William (1774-1831)
British actor, manager: A6, II, 194-213; A7, II, 252-78; A12, pp. 53-61; A41, pp. 361-400; A73, pp. 159-90; A81, I, 62-3; A92, pp. 294-300; C1986; C1987

ELLSLER, Effie E. [Mrs. Frank Weston] (1855-1942)
American actress: A25, pp. 273-86; A30, pp. 273-86; A44, II, 28-9; A66, n. p.; A96, p. 182; A103, pp. 180-81

ELLSLER, John Adam (1822-1903)
American actor, manager: A23, pp. 95-6; C806

ELRINGTON, Thomas (1688-1732)
British actor: A92, pp. 62-4

ELSIE, Lily (1886-1962)
English performer: A29, pp. 3-19

ELSSLER, Fanny (1810-84)
Austrian dancer: A79, pp. 54-5; C1065

ELTINGE, Julian [born William Dalton] (1883-1941)
American performer: A13, p. 70; A96, p. 182

ELTON, Edmund (1871-1952)
English actor: A16, II, 47

ELTON, Edward William (1794-1843)
British actor: A50, pp. 346-7; A68, pp. 149-58

EMERSON, William P. [born William E. Redman] (1836-1932)
American minstrel: A96, pp. 182-3

EMERY, John (1777-1822)
British actor: A6, II, 237-9; A7, II, 310-13; A45, II, 289-93; A81, I, 70-71; A92, pp. 327-9

EMERY, Winifred [Mrs. Cyril

Maude] (1862-1924)
English actress: A86, n. p.,
por.

EMMET, Joseph K. (1841-91)
American actor: A66, n. p.;
A81, II, 105; A96, p. 183;
A111, pp. 56-7

EMMETT, Daniel Decatur (1815-
1904)
American minstrel: A96, p. 183;
C1788

EMMETT, Katie [born Katherine]
(c. 1882-1960)
American actress: A66, n. p.

EMNEY, Fred (1865-1917)
Performer: A16, p. 64

ENDREY, Eugene (1891-1967)
American director, choreographer, producer: C811

ENGEL, Lehman (1910--)
American composer, conductor:
C812

ENTERS, Angna (1907--)
American mime, dancer: A79, pp.
136-7; C813; C814

ERLANGER, Abraham L. (1860-1930)
American manager: A16, p. 107;
A96, pp. 184-5

ERROLL, Leon (1881-1951)
Australian actor: A96, p. 185

ERSKINE, James [born James Francis Rosslyn]
English actor: C2077

ERSKINE, Wallace (1862-1943)
English actor: A16, III, 187

ERVINE, St. John Greer (1883-
1971)
Irish playwright, critic: A116,
pp. 186-93; B20, pp. 428-9

ESTCOURT, Richard (1668-1712)
British actor, playwright: A6,
I, 64-5; A7, I, 81-2; A22, pp.
146-7; A92, pp. 36-8

ESTELLE, Fred
American performer: A58, pp.
32-5

ETHEL, Agnes (1853-1903)
Actress: A23, pp. 361-3; A125,
pp. 334-9

ETHELWOLD, Bishop of Winchester
(?908-84)
Playwright: C388

ETHEREGE, George (1634-91)
British playwright: A22, p. 81

EURIPIDES (c. 486-407 B. C.)
Greek playwright: C191; C1770

EUSTACE, Jennie A. (1865-1936)
American actress: A16, III,
240; A103, pp. 298-9

EVANS, Alice
Actress: A66, n. p.

EVANS, Charles Evan (1856-1945)
American actor, manager: A16,
II, 204; A96, p. 186; A103, pp.
236-7

EVANS, Edith (1888-1976)
English actress: A9, p. 12,
por.; A19, pp. 111-35; A32, p.
24; A40, pp. 193-208; A50, pp.
446-9; A57, pp. 75-88; C193;
C890; C2364

EVANS, John (1692-1734)
British actor: A92, pp. 69-70

EVANS, Lizzie [Mrs. Harry Mills;
Mrs. Jefferson Lloyd] (c. 1857-
1940)
American actress: A66, n. p.;
A103, pp. 268-9

EVANS, Maurice (1901--)
English actor: A13, p. 122;
A50, pp. 470-72; A79, pp. 148-
9; A125, pp. 339-44

EVARTS, William H. [born William
Hentz] (1867-1940)
American actor: A96, p. 186

EVELYN, Judith (1913-67)

American actress: A13, p. 135

EVERARD, Edward Cape (b. 1755)
Scottish actor: C817

EVEREST, Barbara (1890-1968)
English actress: A9, p. 13

EVESSON, Isabelle [born Mensing]
(1863-1914)
American actress: A66, n. p.;
A96, p. 187; A103, pp. 122-3

EYTINGE, Rose [Mrs. Barnes; Mrs.
George H. Butler; Mrs. Cyril
Searle] (1835-1911)
American actress: A16, III,
266; A23, pp. 96-100; A81, II,
77; A111, pp. 42-44; A125, pp.
345-9; C824

FABER, Leslie (1879-1929)
English actor: A47, pp. 117-28

FABER, Mary (c. 1890-1945)
Actress: A16, III, 256

FABIAN, Thomas (fl. 1735)
British playwright: A22, p. 183

FAGAN, Elisabeth
British actress: C825

FAIRBANKS, Douglas [born Douglas
E. Elman; also known as Elton
Thomas] (1883-1939)
American actor: A3, n. p.; A16,
III, 130; A96, p. 187; C1097

FAIRBROTHER, Leon (d. 1903)
Conductor: A98, pp. 123-4

FAIRBROTHER, Sydney [born Sydney
Parselle Cowell; Mrs. S. But-
ler] (1872-1941)
English actress: A16, II, 174;
C826

FALCONER, Edmund (c. 1825-79)
British actor, playwright: A96,
pp. 187-8

FALKLAND, Henry Cary, Viscount
(1634-63)
British playwright: A22, p. 76

FALLON, Thomas
A16, III, 211

FANE, Francis (d. c. 1689)
British playwright: A22, p. 98

FANSHAWE, Richard (1608-66)
British playwright: A22, 61-2

FARJEON, Benjamin L. (1838-1903)
English playwright: C833

FARKOA, Maurice (1864-1916)
A16, III, 107

FARLEY, Charles (1771-1859)
British actor, playwright: A12,
pp. 61-2

FARLEY, Elizabeth [Mrs. James
Weaver] (fl. 1665)
A119, pp. 142-4

FARNUM, Dustin (1874-1929)
American actor: A16, III, 132;
A96, p. 188

FARNUM, William (1875-1953)
American actor: A96, p. 188;
A103, pp. 100-01

FARQUHAR, George (1678-1707)
Irish playwright: A22, pp. 129-
31; A45, I, 174-82; C549

FARQUHARSON, Robert (1877-1966)
English singing actor: A47, pp.
95-104

FARR, Florence (1860-1917)
British actress: C196

FARRELL, John J. (b. 1865)
Actor: A16, II, 131

FARREN, Elizabeth [Countess of
Derby] (?1759-1829)
British actress: C6, II, 122-3;
A42, pp. 255-73; A45, II, 228-
33; A73, pp. 117-32; A81, I,
53-4; A92, pp. 261-4; A97, pp.
179-95; C361; C2145

FARREN, George Francis (c. 1861-
1935)
American actor: A16, p. 205

FARREN, Nellie [Mrs. Robert Soutar] (1848-1904)
English actress: B22, pp. 322-6

FARREN, William (1786-1861)
British actor: A12, pp. 63-5; A28, II, 89-111; A69, I, 151-67; A81, I, 74; A92, pp. 339-41

FASSETT, Edna
Actress: A16, II, 258

FAUCIT, Helen [born Diddear] (1789-1847)
English actress: A12, pp. 66-8; A97, pp. 326-40

FAUCIT, Helen [born Helena Saville; Lady Theodore Martin] (1817-98)
English actress: A31, pp. 130-32; A72, pp. 171-88; A81, II, 40-41; A92, pp. 409-14; C1598

FAUST, Lotta [Mrs. Richie Ling] (1880-1910)
American actress: A16, II, 49

FAVART, Charles Simon (1710-92)
French manager, playwright: C1281

FAVART, Justine [born Duronceray] (1726-72)
French actress: A37, I, 100-49; A118, pp. 225-72

FAVERSHAM, William (1868-1940)
English actor: A3, n. p.; A13, p. 46; A16, III, 54; A21, p. 80; A44, VI, 30-31; A50, p. 392; A61, pp. 65-7; A96, p. 189; A103, pp. 96-7; A105, pp. 94-109; A125, pp. 349-51

FAWCETT, George D. (1860-1939)
American actor: A16, III, 198

FAWCETT, John (1769-1837)
British actor: A12, pp. 68-70; A81, I, 60; A92, pp. 290-91

FAWCETT, Owen S. (1838-1904)
Actor: A23, pp. 100-05; A66, n. p.; A81, II, 87

FAY, Elfie (d. 1927)
Actress: A16, II, 27

FAY, Frank (1870-1931)
Irish actor: C840

FAY, Frank (1897-1961)
American actor: A126, pp. 195-219; C839

FAY, William George (1872-1947)
Irish actor, manager: A9, p. 14, por.; C840

FEALY, Maude [Mrs. Louis F. Sherwin; Mrs. James Durkin] (1883-1971)
American actress: A16, II, 59

FEATHERSTONE, Vane [born Featherstonhaugh] (1864-1948)
English actress: A86, n. p., por.

FECHTER, Charles Albert (1824-79)
English actor, manager: A8, pp. 44-5; A21, p. 45; A26, II, 295-322; A28, II, 256-63; A69, II, 193-8; A74, pp. 207-28; A81, II, 61-2; A88, pp. 315-52; A91, pp. 165-71; A92, pp. 419-21; A123, I, 222-7; A125, pp. 352-7; B22, pp. 246-52; C855

FEIFFER, Jules (1929--)
American playwright: A65, pp. 172-8

FELDER, Al and Harriet
American performers: A58, pp. 142-5

FELLOWS, Dexter (1871-1937)
American press agent: C843

FENNELL, James (1766-1816)
English actor, playwright: A50, p. 341; A81, II, 17; A96, p. 190; A125, pp. 358-62; C844

FENTON, Elijah (1683-1730)
British playwright: A22, p. 173; C1119

FENTON, Lavinia [born Beswick;

Duchess of Bolton] (1708-60)
British actress: A81, I, 16-7;
A92, pp. 86-7; C1498; C1885

FENTON, Mabel [born Ada Towne;
Mrs. Charles J. Kelly; Mrs.
Charles J. Rose] (1868-1931)
American actress: A16, II, 84

FENWICK, Irene [born Frizzel]
(1887-1936)
American actress: A35, p. 60,
por.

FERBER, Edna (1887-1968)
American   playwright: C845;
C846; C974

FERGUSON, Elsie (1883-1961)
American actress: A3, n. p.;
A13, p. 64; A16, III, 195;
A102, pp. 23-8

FERGUSON, Robert V. (c. 1860-
1913)
Actor: A16, II, 91; A96, pp.
190-91

FERGUSON, William J. (1849-1930)
American actor: A16, III, 141;
A23, pp. 105-08; A44, VI, 22-3;
A96, p. 191

FERNANDEZ, Bijou [Mrs. W. C.
Abingdon] (1877-1961)
American actress: A16, III, 251

FERRER, José (1912--)
Puerto Rican actor: A13, p. 134

FERRIER, Kathleen (1912-53)
British singer: C848

ffrangcon-Davies, Gwen (b. 1896)
English actress: A50, pp. 458-9

FIELD, Alfred Griffith (1852-
1921)
American minstrel: C851

FIELD, Betty (1913-73)
American actress: A13, p. 130

FIELD, Isobel Osbourne (1858-
1953)
American playwright: C853

FIELD, Kate [born Mary Katherine
Keemle] (1838-96)
American actress, playwright:
A96, p. 192; B25, pp. 79-83;
C2473

FIELD, Nathaniel (1587-1633)
British playwright: A22, p. 38;
A27, pp. 206-23; C360

FIELD, Sid (1904-50)
English comedian: C868

FIELDING, Fenella (1934--)
English actress: A32, pp. 86-7

FIELDING, Henry (1707-54)
English playwright: A22, pp.
174-5; B24, pp. 5-57; C611;
C724; C762; C1982; C2484

FIELDS, Joseph H. (1798-1856)
English actor: A96, p. 192

FIELDS, Lew M. [born Lewis M.
Schanfields] (1867-1941)
American actor, manager: A3,
n. p.; A13, p. 14; A16, p. 17;
A36, pp. 213-22; A61, pp. 287-
8; A125, pp. 1153-1161; C1301

FIELDS, W. C. [born Claude William Dukenfield] (1879-1946)
American juggler, actor: A13,
p. 100; A20, pp. 29-32; A84,
pp. 51-8; A125, pp. 363-9;
B23, pp. 125-34; C818; C856;
C906; C2322

FILKINS, Grace [born Sweetman;
Mrs. Adolph Marix] (1865-1962)
American actress: A3, n. p.

FILMER, Edward (fl. 1675-1707)
British playwright: A22, p. 127

FINCH, Peter (1916-77)
Australian actor: C773; C837;
C859

FINCK, Herman (1872-1939)
English composer, musical director: C860

FINLAY, Frank (1926--)
English actor: A32, p. 76

FINN, Henry James (1787-1840)
Australian actor, playwright:
A50, p. 344; C1777

FINNEY, Albert (1936--)
English actor: A18, pp. 61-98;
A32, p. 50

FINNEY, Jameson Lee (1863-1911)
British actor: A16, II, 279

FIRBANK, [A. A.] Ronald (1886-
1926)
English playwright: B20, pp.
455-6

FISCHER, Alice [Mrs. William K.
Harcourt] (1869-1947)
American actor: A16, II, 31;
A44, VIII, 28-9

FISHER, Charles (1816-91)
English actor: A59, pp. 76-91;
A77, pp. 204-20; A81, II, 44;
A121, I, 367-73

FISHER, Charles J. B. (1804-59)
Actor, manager: A96, p. 193

FISHER, Perkins D. (1860-1930)
Actor, manager: A96, p. 194

FISHER, Sallie (1881-1950)
American actress: A16, II, 183

FISKE, Harrison Grey (1861-1942)
American playwright, manager,
publisher: A16, II, 174; A96,
p. 194

FISKE, Minnie Maddern [Mrs. Harrison G. Fiske] (1865-1932)
American actress, manager: A3,
n. p.; A13, p. 5; A16, III,
289; A23, pp. 108-12; A38,
n. p.; A44, IX, 4-5; A52, pp.
67-78; A56, pp. 265-98; A61,
pp. 71-5; A63, pp. 139-62; A64,
pp. 105-22; A66, n. p.; A67,
pp. 185-214; A77, pp. 328-40;
A79, pp. 80-81; A80, pp. 194-
202; A102, pp. 309-18; A103,
pp. 12-3; A106, pp. 50-68;
A112, pp. 81-100; A123, II,
262-308; A124, pp. 102-15;
A125, pp. 375-82; C280; C1055;

C2548

FITCH, [William] Clyde (1865-
1909)
American playwright: A16, III,
116; A65, pp. 178-88; C224;
C869; C1750

FITTON, Doris (b. 1897)
Australian actress: C870

FITZBALL, Edward (1792-1973)
British playwright: C872; C2520

FITZGERALD, Marie G.
Actress: A16, II, 170

FITZGERALD, Percy Hetherington
(1834-1925)
Irish writer: C878

FITZHENRY, Elizabeth [born Flan-
nagan; Mrs. John Gregory]
(d. 1790)
British actress: A97, pp. 140-
43

FITZWILLIAM, Edward (1788-1852)
British actor: A12, pp. 78-9;
A81, II, 77-8

FITZWILLIAM, Fanny Elizabeth
[born Copeland; Mrs. Edward
Fitzwilliam] (1802-54)
British actress: A12, pp. 79-80

FLAVIN, Martin [born Archer]
(1883-1967)
American playwright: B20, pp.
463-4

FLECKER, James Elroy (1884-1915)
English playwright: B20, pp.
464-5; C1214; C2177

FLECKNOE, Richard (c. 1600-
c. 1678)
British playwright: A22, p. 64;
C735

FLETCHER, John (1579-1625)
English playwright: A22, pp.
29-31

FLETCHER, Tom (b. 1873)
American performer: C887

FLORENCE, Katherine [born Rogers; Mrs. Frederick Williams] (c. 1874-1952)
English actress: A16, II, 279; A44, V, 28-9; A103, pp. 126-7

FLORENCE, Kathleen
Actress: A23, pp. 112-3

FLORENCE, Malvina [born Pray; Mrs. William J. Florence] 1834-1906)
American actress: A66, n. p.; A75, pp. 113-30

FLORENCE, William J. [born Bernard Conlin] (1831-91)
American actor: A8, pp. 92-3; A66, n. p.; A71, pp. 113-30; A75, pp. 113-30; A77, pp. 94-107; A81, II, 52-4; A95, pp. 35-40; A117, pp. 49-56; A121, I, 159-77; A123, I, 233-9; A125, pp. 383-6

FOGERTY, Elsie (1866-1945)
English actress, educator: C527

FOLLINE, Miriam Florence [Mrs. Frank Leslie] (1851-1914)
American actress: C2273

FONDA, Henry (1905-82)
American actor: C889

FONTANNE, Lynn [Mrs. Alfred Lunt] (?1887-1983)
English actress: A13, p. 94; A35, pp. 100-01, por.; A79, pp. 164-5; A80, pp. 257-63; A102, pp. 193-200; A115, pp. 113-22; A125, pp. 704-15; B15, pp. 188-9; C922; C2578

FONTEYN, Margot [born Hooker] (1919--)
British dancer: C2586

FOOTE, James
British playwright: A22, p. 190

FOOTE, Maria (1798-1867)
British actress: A6, II, 247-50; A7, II, 323-7; A12, pp. 80-81; A81, I, 84-5; A92, pp. 376-7

FOOTE, Phil
American performer: A58, pp. 54-65

FOOTE, Samuel (1720-77)
British actor, manager, playwright: A6, I, 234-56; A7, I, 305-34; A45, I, 290-315; A70, pp. 139-60; A81, I, 25-6; A92, pp. 134-41; A117, pp. 121-36; C560; C879; C1665

FORBES, Bryan (1926--)
English actor, director: C891

FORBES, James (1871-1938)
Canadian actor, playwright: A96, p. 196; C1063

FORBES-ROBERTSON, Jean (1905-62)
English actress: A9, p. 15, por.

FORBES-ROBERTSON, Johnston (1853-1937)
English actor, manager: A13, p. 23; A17, pp. 234-41; A33, pp. 123-40; A39, pp. 147-63; A50, pp. 330-40; A82, pp. 1-8; A83, pp. 132-5; A86, n. p., por.; A122, pp. 340-420; A125, pp. 387-94; B24, pp. 165-74; C893; C2295

FORD, James Lauren (1854-1928)
American writer: C2587

FORD, John (c. 1586-c. 1639)
English playwright: A22, p. 49; C1460; C2120

FORD, John T. (1829-94)
American manager: A96, p. 196; C2233

FORD, Thomas (fl. 1664)
British playwright: A22, p. 59

FORD, Thomas (1829-94)
American actor: C895

FORNES, Maria Irene (1930--)
American playwright: A65, pp. 188-91

FORREST, Arthur (1859-1933)

German actor: A16, II, 189

FORREST, Edwin (1806-72)
American actor: A5, pp. 68-74;
A8, pp. 48-9; A50, pp. 208-24;
A74, pp. 33-68; A79, pp. 32-5;
A81, II, 28-32; A88, pp. 159-
206; A91, pp. 129-35; A94, pp.
11-45; A95, pp. 19-22; A113,
pp. 93-121; A115, pp. 13-26;
A117, pp. 27-35; A121, II, 47-
80; A123, I, 101-27; A125, pp.
395-401; B27, pp. 291-312; C43;
C170; C1130; C1711; C1751;
C1996

FORREST, Sam (1870-1944)
American actor, director, playwright: A96, p. 197; C898

FORREST, William (b. 1800)
Actor, manager: A96, p. 198

FOSTER, George (b. 1864)
English manager: C903

FOUNTAIN, John (d. c. 1669)
British playwright: A22, p. 72

FOWLER, Ned Howard (c. 1875-1904)
American actor: A98, pp. 99-100

FOX, Charles Kemble (1833-75)
American actor, manager: A96,
p. 198

FOX, Della [Mrs. Jacob D. Levy]
American actress: A1, n. p.,
por.; A2, n. p.; A44, III, 8-
9; A64, pp. 566-7; A66, n. p.;
A96, p. 198; A107, pp. 192-207

FOX, George L. (1825-77)
American actor: A50, p. 353;
A95, pp. 55-8; C748

FOX, Grace (d. 1946)
Actress: A16, III, 168

FOY, Eddie [born Edwin Fitzger-
ald] (1856-1928)
American actor: A13, p. 29;
A16, II, 73; A96, pp. 198-9;
C911

FRANCE, Abraham

British playwright: A22, p. 8

FRANCE, Charles Vernon (1868-
1949)
English actor: A9, p. 16, por.

FRANCE, Richard (1930--)
American playwright: A65, pp.
191-6

FRANCIS, Arlene (1908--)
American actress: C913

FRANCIS, Emma (fl. 1874-89)
Actress: A16, p. 184

FRANKEN, Rose D. [born Lewin;
Mrs. William B. Meloney]
(b. 1895)
American playwright: B20, pp.
491-2; C917

FRANKLIN, Irene (1876-1941)
American actress: A96, p. 199

FRASER, Claud Lovat (1890-1921)
British designer: C755; C1649;
C2405

FRASER, Robert (1842-96)
Actor, playwright: A96, p. 199

FRAWLEY, T. Daniel (1864-1936)
American actor, manager: A96,
p. 199

FRAWLEY, William (1887-1966)
American actor: B23, pp. 140-42

FRAYNE, Frank I. (c. 1863-1938)
American actor, manager, playwright: A96, p. 200

FREDERICK, Pauline (1885-1938)
American actress: A16, II, 186;
A96, p. 200; C808

FREEAR, Louie (1873-1939)
English actress: A16, p. 260;
A86, n. p., por.

FREEMAN, Maurice ["Max"]
(d. 1912)
Actor, manager: A96, p. 200

FREEMAN, Ralph (d. 1655)

British playwright: A22, pp. 64-5

FRENCH, Harold (b. 1897)
English actor, producer: C926

FRENCH, Lena G.
Actress: A110, pp. 47-8

FRIEDE, Donald (1901-65)
American investor: C931

FRIGANZA, Trixie [born Della O'Callahan] (1870-1955)
American actress: A16, II, 263

FRODSHAM, Bridge ["The Garrick of the North"] (1734-68)
British actor: A26, II, 202-22

FROHMAN, Charles (1860-1915)
American producer: A16, III, 147; A46, pp. 119-24; A96, p. 201; C1586

FROHMAN, Daniel (1851-1940)
American producer: A1, n. p., por.; A2, n. p.; A46, pp. 119-24; A96, p. 201; C936; C937; C938

FROOS, Sylvia (1914--)
American performer: A100, pp. 115-20

FROWDE, Phillip (d. 1738)
British playwright: A22, p. 174

FRY, Charles (1845-1928)
British producer: C940

FRY, Christopher (1907--)
English playwright: C2255; C2256

FULDA, Ludwig (1862-1939)
German playwright: A16, p. 205

FULLER, Loie (1862-1928)
American dancer, actress: A1, n. p., por.; A2, n. p.; A66, n. p.; A79, pp. 82-3; C941; C2236

FULLER, Margaret [born Witter] (1872-97)

Actress: A16, II, 36

FULLER, Molly [Mrs. Frederick Hallen] (1865-1933)
American actress: A1, n. p., por.; A2, n. p.; A66, n. p.

FULTON, Charles J. [born Foss] (1857-1938)
Actor: A16, III, 172

FULWELL, Ulpian (b. 1556)
British playwright: A22, p. 7

FURSE, Judith (1912-44)
English actress, producer: C2468

FYFFE, Charles J. (1830-1910)
Actor: A16, p. 206

FYLES, Franklin (1847-1911)
Playwright: A96, p. 202

GABRIEL, Master [born Gabriel Wiegel] (c. 1883-1929)
A16, II, 146

GAIGE, Crosby (1882-1949)
American producer: C947

GALE, George (1800-50)
English actor: A96, p. 202

GALE, Minna K. [Mrs. Archibald C. Haynes] (1869-1944)
Actress: A66, n. p.; A81, II, 109; A96, p. 202

GALE, Zona [Mrs. William L. Breese] (1874-1938)
American playwright: B20, pp. 509-10; C705; C948

GALLAND, Bertha (1876-1932)
American actress: A3, n. p.; A16, II, 256

GALLATIN, Alberta (c. 1861-1948)
American actress: A16, II, 94; A103, pp. 284-5

GALSWORTHY, John (1867-1933)
English playwright: A24, pp. 27-44; A116, pp. 194-206; B15,

pp. 110-111; B20, pp. 510-12;
C151; C512; C949; C1589; C1849;
C2131

GANNON, Mary (1829-68)
American actress: A96, p. 203

GANTHONY, Richard (c. 1857-1924)
Actor, playwright: A16, III,
212

GANTHONY, Robert (1849-1931)
British playwright: C950

GARCÍA LORCA, Federico (1899-
1936)
Spanish playwright: B20, pp.
513-5; C149; C1228

GARDINER, Matthew (fl. 1740-41)
British playwright: A22, p. 189

GARDNER, Amelia (c. 1866-1947)
Actress: A16, III, 208

GARDNER, Charles A. [also known
as Karl Gardner] (c. 1848-1924)
Actor, composer: A96, p. 203

GARDNER, Fitzroy (b. 1855)
English manager: C951

GARDNER, Grace
Actress: A16, II, 70

GAREY, James R. (1861-1943)
Actor, playwright: A96, p. 203

GARLAND, Judy [born Frances Gumm]
(1922-69)
American singing actress: A20,
pp. 127-9; B26, pp. 279-90;
C678; C720; C858; C916; C1660;
C1680; C2270; C2353; C2597

GARRICK, David (1717-79)
English actor, manager, playwright: A4, pp. 8-71; A6, I,
133-73; A7, I, 171-225; A17,
pp. 55-95; A22, p. 188; A39,
pp. 24-48; A45, I, 247-89; A50,
pp. 94-111; A70, pp. 59-100;
A80, pp. 84-94; A81, I, 21-3;
A88, pp. 3-38; A91, pp. 33-9;
A92, pp. 107-19; A93, pp. 33-
44; A113, pp. 3-29; C186; C304;

C637; C661; C876; C1167; C1383;
C1399; C1599; C1768; C1864;
C2228; C2271; C2290

GARRICK, Henry Walter (b. 1871)
English journalist, press
agent: A16, II, 193

GARSON, Greer (1908--)
Irish actress: A96, pp. 204-5

GASCOIGNE, George (?1525-77)
British playwright: A22, p. 5;
C1963

GATTIE, Henry (1774-1844)
British actor: A12, p. 81;
A81, I, 73-4

GAXTON, William [born Arturo Gax-
iola] (1893-1963)
American actor: A13, p. 101

GAY, John (1685-1732)
English playwright: A22, pp.
157-8; C89; C235; C623; C959;
C1093; C1297; C2438

GAY, Maisie [born Munro-Noble]
English actress: C958

GAYER, Echlin (1878-1926)
Actor: A96, p. 205

GAYLER, Charles (1820-92)
American actor, playwright:
A96, pp. 205-06

GAZZOLO, Frank A. P. (1871-1959)
American manager: A96, p. 206

GEARY, John J.
Stage manager: A98, pp. 47-8

GEDDES, Barbara Bel (1922--)
American actress: A13, p. 139

GEDDES, Norman Bel (1893-1958)
American designer: C961; C2549

GEDDES, Virgil (b. 1897)
Playwright: B20, pp. 519-20

GEER, Will (1902-79)
American actor: C1817

II, 228

GILLETTE, William H. (1855-1937)
American actor, playwright: A3,
n. p.; A13, p. 10; A16, III,
172; A23, pp. 118-21; A44, IV,
34-5; A46, pp. 125-9; A55,
n. p., por.; A61, pp. 83-8;
A62, pp. 33-70; A64, pp. 302-
14; A86, n. p., por.; A103, pp.
22-3; A105, pp. 174-89; A125,
pp. 426-31; C554; C2174

GILLINGWATER, Claude (1870-1939)
American actor: A16, II, 178

GILLMORE, Frank (1867-1943)
American actor: A16, II, 118;
A23, pp. 121-5

GILLMORE, Margalo (b. 1897)
English actress: C979

GILMAN, Ada (c. 1854-1921)
American actress: A16, III,
230; A23, pp. 121-5

GILMAN, Mabelle [Mrs. W. E. Cor-
ey] (b. 1880)
American actress: A103, pp.
142-3; A107, pp. 56-66

GILMORE, Paul (b. 1873)
American actor: A103, pp. 218-9

GILMOUR, John H. (c. 1857-1922)
American actor, producer: A98,
pp. 85-6

GILPIN, Charles S. (1878-1930)
American actor: A96, p. 211;
A125, pp. 432-5

GILROY, Frank D. (1925--)
American playwright: A65, pp.
208-15

GILSON, Lottie [born Lydia Dea-
gon] (1867-1912)
American actress: A16, p. 17;
A96, p. 211

GINGOLD, Hermione (born 1897)
English actress: C980; C981;
C982

GIOSEFFI, Andrew ["Mighty Andy"]
American performer: A58, pp.
146-53

GIRARDOT, Étienne (1856-1939)
English actor: A16, III, 61;
A96, p. 211

GIRAUDOUX, Jean (1882-1944)
French playwright: B20, pp.
537-9; C522; C1475

GISH, Dorothy (1898-1968)
American actress: A13, p. 113;
A35, p. 80, por.; A125, pp.
436-8

GISH, Lillian (1896--)
American actress: A13, p. 114;
A29, pp. 122-31; A35, pp. 102-
04, por.; A125, pp. 439-43;
C984

GISH, Mary R. (c. 1860-1948)
Actress: A96, p. 212

GLADKOV, Fedor V. (1883-1958)
Russian playwright: B20, p. 539

GLAPTHORNE, Henry (c. 1610-
c. 43)
British playwright: A22, pp.
54-5

GLASER, Lulu [Mrs. R. C. Herz]
(1874-1958)
American actress: A3, n. p.;
A16, III, 137; A66, n. p.;
A103, pp. 60-61; A107, pp. 120-
33

GLASON, Billy (1904--)
American performer: A100, pp.
30-37

GLASPELL, Susan [Mrs. George Cram
Cook; Mrs. Norman H. Matson]
American playwright: A65, pp.
215-23; B20, pp. 541-2

GLASSFORD, Andrew L. (d. 1918)
Actor, manager: A96, p. 212

GLASSFORD, David (1866-1935)
Australian actor: A96, p. 212

GLEASON, Jackie (1916--)
American comedian: C284

GLEASON, Lucille [born Webster]
(1888-1947)
American actress: A96, p. 212

GLENDINNING, Ernest (1884-1936)
English actor: A16, III, 60;
A96, p. 212

GLENDINNING, John (1857-1916)
English actor, manager: A16,
II, 264

GLICK, Joseph (1880-1943)
American actor, manager: A96,
pp. 212-3

GLOVER, Amelia [Mrs. John H. Russell; Mrs. Al Lawrence] (1870-
1910)
American dancer: A66, n. p.

GLOVER, James M. (1861-1931)
British conductor, composer,
manager: C989; C990; C991

GLOVER, Julia [born Betterton]
(1783-1850)
British actress: A6, II, 250-
51; A12, pp. 83-4; A28, II,
112-32; A43, pp. 284-97; A69,
I, 260-73; A81, I, 71-2; A92,
pp. 333-4

GLYN, Isabel [Mrs. E. S. Dallas]
(1823-89)
Scottish actress: A81, II, 61

GNITO, Leonora [born von Ottin-
ger]
Singing actress: A98, pp. 77-8

GOETHE, Johann Wolfgang von
(1749-1832)
German playwright, director:
B21, pp. 100-08; C275; C1487;
C2039

GOFFE, Thomas (1591-1629)
British playwright: A22, p. 37

GOGOL, Nikolai (1809-52)
Russian playwright: C1447;
C1568; C1778

GOLD, Michael [born Irving Gran-
ich] (1893-1967)
American playwright: B20, p.
547; C363

GOLDBERG, Dick (1947--)
American playwright: A65, pp.
224-7

GOLDEN, Beatrice Wiley (d. 1919)
A16, III, 71

GOLDEN, Grace (d. 1903)
American singer: A44, II, 32-3;
A66, n. p.

GOLDEN, John (1874-1955)
American   actor,   playwright,
producer: A96, p. 213; C998;
C2099

GOLDEN, Richard (1854-1909)
American   actor,   playwright:
A16, III, 161; A66, n. p.; A96,
p. 213; A103, pp. 68-9; A104,
pp. 91-102

GOLDONI, Carlo (1707-93)
Italian playwright: C470; C999;
C1225; C1371

GOLDSMITH, Francis (d. 1655)
British playwright: A22, p. 56

GOLDSMITH, Oliver (1728-74)
Irish playwright: C725; C925;
C1960; C2437

GOLDTHWAITE, Jennie (fl. 1887)
American actress: A44, IV, 20-
21

GOMERSAL, Robert (1600-46?)
British playwright: A22, p. 48

GOOCH, Elizabeth (born E. Villa
Real; Mrs. William Gooch] (fl.
1775-96)
British actress: C1001

GOODFRIEND,   Ida   Jeffreys
(c. 1856-1926)
American actress: A16, II, 227

GOODRICH, Edna [born Stephens;
Mrs. Nat C. Goodwin] (1883-

1971)
American actress: A16, III, 291

GOODMAN, Cardell (?1649-99)
British actor: A50, pp. 40-41

GOODWIN, J. Cheever (1850-1912)
American actor, playwright:
A96, p. 214

GOODWIN, Nat C. (1857-1919)
American actor: A1, n. p.,
por.; A2, n. p.; A3, n. p.; A8,
pp. 36-7; A13, p. 16; A16, II,
169; A23, pp. 125-9; A44, II,
10-11; A52, pp. 313-26; A61,
pp. 91-4; A64, pp. 255-83; A66,
n. p.; A77, pp. 377-88; A81,
II, 99-100; A103, pp. 14-5;
A105, pp. 119-35; A125, pp.
444-7; C590; C1004

GOODWIN, Thomas (1799-1886)
English actor: C1005

GORDON, Margaret (fl. 1890-1900)
A16, II, 276

GORDON, Max (1892-1978)
American actor, manager: A96,
p. 215; C1006

GORDON, Ruth (1896--)
American actress: A13, p. 108;
A35, p. 22, por.; C1007; C1008;
C1009

GORDONE, Charles (1925--)
American playwright: A65, pp.
227-31

GORING, Charles (fl. 1687-1708)
British playwright: A22, p. 153

GORKY, Maxim [born Aleksei M.
Peshkov] (1868-1936)
Russian playwright: A24, pp. 1-
26; B20, pp. 553-5; C1226;
C1483

GOSSON, Stephen (1554-1624)
English playwright: C2028

GOTTSCHALK, Ferdinand (1858-1944)
English actor, playwright:
A23, pp. 129-31; A44, IX, 42-3

GOTTSCHED, Luise (1713-62)
German playwright: C2022

GOUGH, John B. (1817-86)
American temperance lecturer:
A87, pp. 3-6; B1, pp. 45-58;
C1600

GOUGHE, Robert (d. 1624)
British actor: A27, pp. 265-7

GOULD, Harold W. (c. 1873-1951)
American actor: A23, pp. 131-2

GOULD, Howard (1867-1938)
American actor: A16, III, 83;
A96, p. 217; A103, pp. 248-9

GOULD, Robert (fl. 1696-1737)
British playwright: A22, p. 118

GOZZI, Carlo (1720-1806)
Italian playwright: C1020

GRABLE, Betty [Mrs. Harry James]
(1916-1973)
American singing actress: C2439

GRAHAM, Anna (b. 1837)
American actress: A81, II, 87

GRAHAM, George (1875-1939)
English actor: A96, p. 218

GRAHAM, Joseph F. (1851-1933)
British actor, manager: C1023

GRAHAM, Martha (?1900--)
American dancer, choreographer:
B15, pp. 122-3; C1454

GRAHAM, Robert E. (1858-1916)
American actor: A16, II, 275

GRAIN, Richard Corney (1844-95)
English singer: C1025

GRANACH, Alexander (1890-1945)
Russian actor: C1026

GRANGER, Maude [born Anna Brain-
erd] (1846-1928)
Actress: A111, pp. 61-2

GRANLUND, Nils Thor (1882-1957)
Swedish producer: C1027

GRANVILLE, Charlotte [born Stuart; Mrs. Synge] (1863-1942)
Actress: A86, n. p., por.

GRANVILLE, Wilfred
Actor: A1, n. p., por.

GRATTAN, Emma [Mrs. William Henry Courtaine] (fl. 1854-69)
English actress: A111, pp. 38-9

GRATTAN, Lawrence (1870-1941)
American actor, playwright: A96, p. 218

GRATTAN, Stephen
A44, IX, 26-7

GRAU, Jacinto (1877-1958)
Spanish playwright: C986

GRAU, Jacob F. (1817-77)
Austrian manager: A96, pp. 218-9

GRAU, Robert (d. 1916)
American manager: C1030; C1031

GRAVES, George (1876-1949)
English actor: C1033

GRAY, Dulcie (1919--)
British actress: A76, pp. 56-68

GRAY, George ["The Fighting Parson"]
C1034

GREBER, James
British playwright: A22, p. 76

GREEN Dorothy [Mrs. Norman November; Mrs. Alfred A. Harris] (1886-1961)
English actress: A50, p. 446

GREEN, Hughie (1920--)
British performer: C1038

GREEN, Martyn (1899-1975)
English actor: C1040

GREEN, Paul (1894-1981)
American playwright: A65, pp. 231-42; B20, pp. 570-71

GREENE, Clay M. (1850-1933)
American playwright: A96, p. 219; C1307

GREENE, Evie [Mrs. Richard Temple, Jr.] (1876-1917)
American actress: A16, II, 29; A86, n. p., por.

GREENE, Graham (1904--)
English playwright: C108; C1043; C1964

GREENE, John (1795-1860)
American actor, manager: A96, pp. 219-20

GREENE, Robert (?1560-92)
English playwright: A22, p. 19; C1334

GREENFIELD, Caroline
Actress: A16, III, 284

GREENSTREET, Sydney H. (1879-1954)
English actor: A96, p. 220

GREENWALD, Joseph (1879-1938)
American actor: A96, p. 220

GREENWALL, Henry W. (1832-1913)
Manager: A96, p. 220

GREENWOOD, Charlotte (1893-1978)
American actress: A13, p. 78

GREENWOOD, Walter (1903-74)
British playwright: A116, pp. 206-08; B20, pp. 573-4

GREET, [Philip] Ben (1857-1936)
English actor, manager: A50, p. 376; C1299

GREGORY, Augusta, Lady (1852-1932)
Irish manager, playwright: A116, pp. 208-12; B20, pp. 575-6; C12; C1046; C1047; C1048

GREIN, Jacob Thomas (1862-1935)
Anglo-Dutch producer, critic: C1846

GREINER, Alvin G. (1911--)

American performer: A58, pp. 66-71

GRENFELL, Joyce (1910-79)
English actress: C1049

GREVILLE, Alexander
British playwright: A22, p. 76

GREY, Beryl (1927--)
English dancer: C72

GREY, Jane [born Mary E. Tyrrell] (1883-1944)
American actress: A96, p. 221

GREY, Katherine (1873-1950)
American actress: A16, II, 282; A44, IV, 24-5; A96, p. 221

GRIBBIN, Marie Louise
Actress: A16, III, 118

GRIFFIN, Benjamin (1680-1740)
British actor, playwright: A22, p. 158

GRIFFIN, Gerald (1804-40)
American playwright: A41, pp. 401-22

GRIFFITHS, George H. (1822-88)
English actor: A81, II, 87

GRILLPARZER, Franz (1791-1872)
Austrian playwright: C2559

GRIMALDI, Joseph (1778-1837)
English actor: A4, pp. 371-80; A12, pp. 85-90; C712; C862; C1685

GRIMSTON, William, Viscount (c. 1692-1756)
British playwright: A22, p. 146

GRISMER, Joseph R. (1849-1922)
American actor, manager, playwright: A96, p. 219

GROCK [born Charles A. Wettach] (1880-1959)
Swiss clown: A35, p. 16, por.; C1056; C2463

GROODY, Louise (1897-1961)

American actress: B15, pp. 124-5

GROSSMITH, George, Sr. (1847-1912)
English actor: A48, II, 229-44; C1059; C1060

GROSSMITH, George, Jr. (1874-1935)
English actor: C1061; C1785

GROSSMITH, [Walter] Weedon (1852-1919)
English actor: A16, II, 139; A86, n. p., por.; C1062

GROSSMITH, William Robert (1818-99)
British actor: C241; C1495

GROVER, Leonard (1835-1926)
American actor, manager: A96, p. 222

GROVER, Leonard, Jr. (1859-1947)
American actor: A96, p. 222

GROVES, Charles (1843-1909)
English actor: A86, n. p., por.

GUARE, John (1938--)
American playwright: A65, pp. 243-6

GUERRE, Johnny
American performer: A58, pp. 134-41

GUILBERT, Yvette [Mrs. Max Schiller] (1865-1944)
French actress: B14, pp. 47-9; B15, pp. 126-7; C1066; C1067

GUIMARD, Madeleine (1743-1816)
French actress: A37, II, 1-21

GUINAN, "Texas" [born Mary Louise Cecelia] (1884-1933)
American hostess, entertainer: B23, pp. 164-72

GUINNESS, Alec (1914--)
English actor: A32, p. 9; A50, p. 509; A125, pp. 448-52; C2319; C2382

GUITRY, Sacha (1885-1957)
Russian-French actor, playwright: B20, pp. 586-7; C805; C1069; C1112;

GUNTER, Archibald Clavering (1847-1907)
English playwright: A96, p. 223

GUTHRIE, Tyrone (1900-71)
English director, actor, producer: A50, pp. 467-70; C901; C1073; C1074

GWYNNE or GWYN, Eleanor ["Nell"]
English actress: A6, I, 44-7; A7, I, 55-9; A45, I, 69-75; A81, I, 10-11; A92, pp. 22-5; A99, pp. 43-74; A119, pp. 146-8; C197; C621; C651; C1659; C2161; C2515

HABINGTON, William (1605-54)
British playwright: A22, p. 56

HACKETT FAMILY: A78, pp. 142-66

HACKETT, James Henry (1800-71)
American actor, manager: A72, pp. 157-69; A81, II, 33; A96, p. 223; A121, II, 38-46; A123, I, 93-100; A125, pp. 453-8

HACKETT, James K. (1869-1926)
Canadian actor: A3, n. p.; A13, p. 8; A16, III, 210; A21, pp. 76-8; A23, pp. 132-5; A44, VIII, 30-31; A50, p. 393; A52, pp. 237-50; A61, pp. 99-102; A96, p. 224; A103, pp. 38-9; A105, pp. 200-10; A125, pp. 459-62

HACKETT, Jeanette (d. 1979)
American performer: A100, pp. 182-7

HACKETT, Norman H. (b. 1874)
Canadian actor, manager: A49, pp. 348-9

HACKETT, Walter (1876-1944)
American director, playwright, producer: A96, p. 224

HADAWAY, Thomas H. (1801-92)
English actor: A96, p. 224

HADDON, Archibald (1871-1942)
English critic: C1077; C1078

HADING, Jane [born Jeanette Hadingue] (1859-1941)
French actress: A16, p. 79; A44, IV, 4-5; A64, pp. 523-31; A66, n. p.; A81, II, 110-11; A86, n. p., por.; A96, p. 224; A101, n. p., por.

HAGAN, James P. (1888-1947)
American actor, manager, playwright: A96, p. 225

HAGEN, Uta (1919--)
German-American actress: A13, p. 132; C1079; C2248

HAGENBECK, Carl (1844-1913)
German animal trainer: A8, pp. 56-7

HAGGARD, Stephen (1911-43)
British actor: C1080; C1145

HAINES or HAYNS, Joseph (1638-1701)
British actor: A6, I, 40-43; A7, I, 50-53; A22, pp. 119-21; A45, I, 30-42; A92, pp. 21-2; C382

HAINES, Robert T. (1870-1943)
American actor, playwright, producer: A16, III, 48; A96, p. 225; A103, pp. 186-7

HALE, Helen (fl. 1902-7)
American actress: A16, II, 232

HALE, John [born Jesse Hay] (1859-1947)
American actor, manager: A96, p. 225

HALE, Walter (1869-1917)
American actor: A16, II, 179

HALEY, Jack (1899-1979)
American actor: A100, pp. 129-34

HALL, Henry (1876-1954)
American actor: A16, III, 251

HALL, Howard [Charles Sumner] (1867-1921)
American actor, playwright: A98, p. 128

HALL, Josephine (d. 1920)
American actress: A66, n. p.; A107, pp. 46-55

HALL, Laura Nelson [born Barnhurst; Mrs. Frederick Truesdell] (b. 1876)

HALL, Mary [born Mary Hall Ledoux] (c. 1876-1960)
English actress: A98, pp. 49-50

HALL, Pauline [born Schmidgall; Mrs. Edmund R. White] (1860-1919)
American actress: A16, III, 66; A25, pp. 247-58; A30, pp. 247-57; A44, IX, 32-3; A64, pp. 608-11; A66, n. p.; A96, p. 226; A103, pp. 168-9; A107, pp. 239-52

HALL, Peter (1930--)
English director, producer: C1084

HALLAM, Lewis (1714-56)
English actor, manager: A46, pp. 3-10; A70, pp. 243-52; A81, II, 17; A96, p. 226

HALLAM, Mrs. Lewis, Sr. [Mrs. David Douglass] (c. 1712-74)
British actress: A81, II, 17

HALLAM, Lewis, Jr. (1740-1808)
British actor: A81, II, 17; A96, p. 226; A125, pp. 463-5

HALLAM, Nancy (fl. 1759-61)
British actress: A79, pp. 16-7

HALLAM, William (c. 1712-c. 1758)
English manager: A96, pp. 226-7

HALLEN, Fred (c. 1860-1920)
Canadian actor: A66, n. p.

HAMBLIN, Elizabeth [born Blanchard; Mrs. Thomas Hamblin; Mrs. Charles] (d. 1849)
English actress: A81, II, 35

HAMBLIN, Thomas S. (1800-53)
English actor, manager: A50, pp. 347-8; A81, II, 35; A96, p. 227

HAMILTON, Cicely (1872-1952)
British playwright: A116, pp. 212-5

HAMILTON, Clayton [born Meeker] (1881-1946)
American playwright, critic: A96, p. 227; B20, pp. 604-05

HAMILTON, Cosmo [born Gibbs] (1872-1942)
English playwright: B20, pp. 605-06; C1092

HAMILTON, Esther [Mrs. George Bland; Mrs. John Hamilton; Mrs. Sweeny] (1730-87)
British actress: A92, pp. 151-3; A97, pp. 145-50

HAMILTON, Hale (1880-1942)
American actor: A96, pp. 227-8

HAMILTON, Newburgh (fl. 1715-43)
British playwright: A22, p. 159

HAMILTON, Patrick (1904-62)
English playwright: A116, pp. 216-8

HAMILTON, Theodore (1830-1916)
American actor: A16, p. 244; A23, pp. 136-7; A44, IX, 6-7; A96, p. 228

HAMILTON, William Bishop (1810-68)
English actor, manager: A96, p. 228

HAMMERSTEIN, Oscar, I (1847-1919)
German-American manager: A96, p. 228; C2167

HAMMERSTEIN, Oscar, II (1895-1960)

American lyricist, librettist, producer: C1813; C2314

HAMMOND, Percy (1873-1936)
American critic: B20, pp. 608-09; C1905

HAMMOND, William (fl. 1740)
British playwright: A22, p. 189

HAMPDEN, Walter [born Walter H. Dougherty] (1879-1955)
American actor, producer: A13, p. 61; A16, II, 151; A35, p. 10, por.; A50, pp. 431-3; A79, pp. 112-3; A125, pp. 466-73; B15, pp. 128-9; C1445

HAMPTON, Louise (1876-1954)
English actress: A9, p. 18, por.

HAMPTON, Mary (c. 1868-1931)
American actress: A66, n. p.

HANCHETT, David (1821-1902)
American actor, manager: A96, p. 229

HANCOCK, Freddie [born Anthony John Hancock] (1924-68)
British performer: C1096

HANDY, William Christopher (1873-1958)
American minstrel, composer: C1098

HANFF, Helene
American playwright: C1100

HANFORD, Charles B. (1859-1926)
American actor, manager: A16, p. 108; A23, pp. 138-9; A44, VII, 14-5; A96, pp. 229-30; A103, pp. 258-9

HANKIN, St. John (1869-1909)
British playwright: A16, II, 215; A116, pp. 218-26

HANLEY, Martin W. (1843-1905)
Actor, manager: A96, p. 230

HANLEY, Peter
British writer: C1101

HANNEN, Nicholas (1881-1972)
English actor, producer: A9, p. 19, por.

HANSBERRY, Lorraine (1930-65)
American playwright: A65, pp. 247-54

HAPGOOD, Hutchins (1869-1944)
American critic: C1104

HAPGOOD, Norman (1868-1937)
American critic: C1105

HARCOURT, Frederick C. Vernon (b. 1845)
English actor: C1109

HARDIE, James W. (d. 1912)
Actor, manager: A96, p. 231

HARDING, Ann (1902-81)
American actress: A35, p. 76, por.

HARDING, Lyn (1867-1952)
Welsh actor: A50, pp. 390-91

HARDWICKE, Cedric (1893-1964)
English actor, director: A47, pp. 117-28; A50, p. 456; C1113; C1114

HARDY, Sam B. (1883-1935)
American actor: A16, II, 80

HARE, Doris (1905--)
Welsh actress: A32, pp. 32-3

HARE, G. Van (b. 1815)
English circus manager: C1116

HARE, John [born Fairs] (1844-1921)
English actor: A16, II, 119; A48, II, 13-38; A123, I, 439-47; C1894

HARE, [Francis] Lumsden (1875-1964)
Irish actor, director: A16, II, 105

HARKER, Joseph (1855-1927)
English designer: C1118

HARKER, Lizzie A. [born Watson]
(1863-1933)
English playwright: B20, p. 617

HARKINS, Daniel H. (1835-1902)
American actor: A5, pp. 100-04;
A23, pp. 139-42; A96, p. 231

HARLAN, Otis (1865-1940)
American actor: A104, pp. 208-
16

HARLEY, John Pritt (1786-1858)
British actor: A12, pp. 92-4;
A92, p. 341

HARLOWE, Sarah [Mrs. Francis G.
Waldron] (1765-1852)
British actress: A12, p. 95

HARNED, Virginia [Mrs. E. H.
Sothern]
American actress: A3, n. p.;
A16, III, 133; A44, VI, 32-3;
A52, pp. 9-24; A61, pp. 273-4;
A62, pp. 109-50; A66, n. p.;
A103, pp. 48-9; A106, pp. 125-
34

HARRIGAN, Edward (1845-1911)
American actor, manager, playwright: A16, II, 240; A44, II,
30-31; A52, pp. 91-102; A64,
pp. 520-22; A66, n. p.; A77,
pp. 395-9; A125, pp. 474-8;
C1341; C1713

HARRIMAN, Margaret C. (d. 1966)
American writer: C1122

HARRIS, Charles Kassell (1865-
1930)
American composer: C1123

HARRIS, Frank (1855-1931)
Irish writer, playwright: C1535

HARRIS, Henry B. (1866-1912)
American manager: A16, II, 267;
A96, p. 233

HARRIS, Jed [born Jacob Hirsch
Horowitz] (1900-79)
American producer: A126, pp.
220-64; B15, pp. 134-5; C406;
C1016; C1127

HARRIS, Joseph (fl. 1661-99)
British playwright: A22, p. 126

HARRIS, Julie (1925--)
American actress: A13, p. 138;
A115, pp. 143-7

HARRIS, Rosemary (1930--)
English actress: A51, pp. 13-26

HARRIS, Sam H. (1872-1941)
American manager: A96, p. 233

HARRIS, William (1839-1916)
Actor: A96, pp. 233-4

HARRISON, Alice Maude (1850-96)
American actress: A96, p. 234

HARRISON, Elizabeth R.
English writer: C1129

HARRISON, Lee [born Louis Harris]
(1866-1916)
A96, p. 234

HARRISON, Louis (1859-1936)
American actor, playwright:
A66, n. p.; A96, pp. 234-5

HARRISON, Maud [Mrs. Edward M.
Bell] (1854-1907)
American actress: A66, n. p.

HARRISON, Rex (1908--)
English actor: A125, pp. 479-
86; C1133

HARRISON, William Bristow (1812-
81)
English actor, manager: A96, p.
235

HARRISSON, William (fl. 1701)
British playwright: A22, p. 153

HARRITY, Richard (1907-73)
American actor, playwright:
C1134

HART, Bob ["Senator"; born James
Sutherland] (1835-88)
American minstrel: C2301

HART, Charles (c. 1630-83)
British actor: A45, I, 5-7;

A81, II, 12; C1333

HART, Joseph (1858-1921)
American actor: A66, n. p.

HART, Lorenz (1895-1943)
American lyricist: B15, pp.
242-3; C1135; C1605

HART, Moss (1904-61)
American playwright: A65, pp.
254-62; B20, pp. 623-4; C834;
C1137

HART, Tony [born Anthony Cannon]
(1855-91)
American actor: A125, pp. 474-
8; C1341; C1713

HART, William S. (1870-1946)
American actor: A96, pp. 235-6;
C1138

HARTLEY, Elizabeth White (1751-
1824)
English actress: A68, pp. 112-
7; A81, I, 43-4; A92, pp. 221-
3

HARVEY, John Martin (1863-1944)
English actor, manager: A16, p.
143; A29, pp. 36-8; A50, pp.
384-6; A82, pp. 47-54; C685;
C722; C787; C1141; C1142

HARVEY, Laurence [born Skikne]
(1928-73)
Lithuanian actor: A32, pp. 35-7

HARWOOD, John E. (1771-1809)
English actor: A81, II, 18;
A96, p. 236

HASSON, William J.
American actor: A98, pp. 45-6

HASWELL, Percy [Mrs. George Faw-
cett] (1871-1945)
American actress: A16, III,
111; A23, pp. 143-4

HATTON, Joseph (b. 1801)
Playwright: A96, p. 236

HAUCK, Minnie (?1852-1929)
American singer: A8, pp. 34-5;

A16, p. 253

HAUPTMANN, Gerhart (1862-1946)
German playwright: B20, pp.
625-7; C956

HAUSTEAD, Peter (d. 1645)
British playwright: A22, p. 48

HAVARD, William (1710-78)
British actor, playwright: A22,
p. 185; A92, pp. 92-3

HAVERLY, Jack H. [born Chris-
topher] (1837-1901)
American manager: A96, p. 237

HAVOC, June (1916--)
American actress: C1149; C1150

HAWKES, John (1925--)
American playwright: A65, pp.
263-8

HAWKINS, Jack (1910-73)
English actor: C1154

HAWKINS, William (fl. 1627-34)
British playwright: A22, p. 194

HAWLEY, Curtis B. [born George W.
Perrie]
American   actor,   performer:
C1906

HAWORTH, Joseph (1858-1903)
American actor: A23, pp. 144-6;
A44, VII, 34-5; A64, pp. 536-8;
A66, n. p.; A81, II, 108-09;
A96, p. 237; A103, pp. 132-3;
A105, pp. 311-25

HAWTREY, Charles (1858-1923)
English actor, manager, playwright: A16, III, 218; A29, pp.
34-5; A47, pp. 75-84; A86,
n. p., por.; C1156

HAY, Ian [born John Hay Beith]
(1876-1952)
Scottish playwright: B20, p.
104

HAYE, Helen (1874-1957)
English actress: A50, p. 396

HAYES, Helen [Mrs. Charles Mac-
Arthur] (1900--)
American actress: A13, p. 107;
A35, pp. 98-9, por.; A79, pp.
182-3; A80, pp. 244-8; A102,
pp. 249-54; A115, pp. 133-42;
A125, pp. 487-95; B15, pp. 136-
7; C372; C1158; C1159

HAYNES, Minnie [born Gale; Mrs.
Archibald C. Haynes] (1867-
1944?)
Actress: A23, pp. 146-8 (See
GALE, Minna K.)

HAYWOOD, ELiza (?1693-1756)
British actress, playwright:
C2466

HAZLITT FAMILY: C1162

HAZLITT, William (1778-1830)
English critic: C1256

HEAD, Richard (?1637-86?)
British playwright: A22, pp.
75-6

HEADLAM, Stewart Duckworth (1847-
1924)
English: C269

HEATH, Tom K. (1853-1938)
American minstrel: A53, pp. 35-
7

HECHT, Ben (1894-1964)
American playwright: A65, pp.
268-74; B20, pp. 631-2; C1164;
C1166

HEDMONDT, Emmanuel Christian
(1857-1940)
American singer: A16, II, 239

HEIMAN, Marcus (1883-1957)
American producer: A96, p. 239

HELBURN, Theresa (1887-1959)
American producer, playwright:
C1169

HELD, Anna [Mrs. Florenz Ziegfeld, Jr.] (1873-1918)
French actress: A3, n. p.; A13,
p. 38; A16, II, 78; A44, XII,

n.p.; A61, pp. 107-09; A84, pp.
33-6; A96, p. 239; A103, pp.
134-5; A125, pp. 494-9

HELLINGER, Mark (1903-47)
American writer: A96, pp. 239-
40; C285

HELLMAN, Lillian (1906-84)
American playwright: A65, pp.
275-95; B20, p. 634; C1170;
C1171; C1712

HELPMANN, Robert (1909--)
Australian actor, dancer: A50,
p. 508; C2423

HEMINGE, John (c. 1556-1630)
English actor: A6, I, 24-5;
A27, pp. 57-78; C546

HEMINGE, William (1602-32?)
British playwright: A22, p. 60

HEMPLE, Sam (1833-92)
American actor: A117, pp. 72-9

HENDERSON, David (1853-1908)
Scottish manager, playwright,
critic: A96, p. 240

HENDERSON, Donald L. (1905--)
English playwright: C1175

HENDERSON, John (1747-85)
English actor: A4, pp. 87-101;
A6, I, 213-5; A7, I, 278-80;
A45, II, 21-36; A70, pp. 253-
66; A81, I, 40-41; A92, pp.
205-07; C660; C1287

HENDRICKS, Amanda (d. 1935)
A16, III, 258

HENGLER, Flora (c. 1897-1965)
A16, II, 172

HENGLER, May (c. 1884-1952)
A16, II, 113

HENLEY, Edward J. (1861-98)
English actor: A66, n. p.; A96,
p. 240

HENSHAW, Thomas E. (d. 1914)
Actor: A96, p. 241

HENSLOWE, Philip (?1550-1616)
British manager: A34, pp. 19-
62; C1177

HENSON, Leslie Lincoln (1891-
1957)
English actor, producer: C1178;
C1179

HEPBURN, Katherine (1909--)
American actress: A13, p. 127;
A125, pp. 500-05; C1195

HERBERT, Alan Patrick (1890-1971)
British playwright: A116, pp.
226-31

HERBERT, Henry (1879-1947)
English actor, producer: A96,
p. 241

HERBERT, Sidney (d. 1927)
Actor: A1, n. p., por.

HERBERT, Victor (1859-1924)
Irish-American composer: C1349;
C1968; C2443

HERMAN, Selma (1876-1972)
American actress: A16, II, 126;
A103, pp. 238-9

HERNE, Chrystal [Mrs. Harold S.
Pollard] (1883-1950)
American actress: A3, n. p.;
A16, II, 143

HERNE, James A. [born Ahearn]
(1839-1901)
American actor, playwright:
A23, pp. 148-51; A44, II, 42-3;
A61, pp. 113-7; A64, pp. 379-
84; A80, pp. 170-74; A103, pp.
42-3; A105, pp. 18-35; A125,
pp. 506-11; B16, pp. 65-89;
C793; C1908

HERNE, Julie (1880-1955)
American actress, playwright:
A16, II, 244

HERON, Bijou [born Hélène Stoep-
el; Mrs. Henry Miller] (1863-
1937)
American actress: A23, pp. 246-
9

HERON, Matilda [Mrs. Robert Stoe-
pel] (1830-77)
Irish actress, playwright: A14,
pp. 96-9; A74, pp. 229-46; A80,
pp. 145-52; A81, II, 107-08;
A122, pp. 59-72; A125, pp. 512-
5; C1265

HESTON, Charlton (1923--)
American actor: A13, p. 140;
C1184

HEWITT, John (fl. 1729-34)
British playwright: A22, p. 187

HEYWARD, Dorothy (1890-1961)
American playwright: A65, pp.
295-301

HEYWARD, Du Bose (1885-1940)
American playwright: A65, pp.
295-301; B20, p. 648; C782

HEYWOOD, Elizabeth (?1693-1756)
British actress, playwright:
A22, p. 171 (See HAYWOOD,
Eliza.)

HEYWOOD, Jasper (1535-98)
British playwright: A22, p. 7

HEYWOOD, John (c. 1497-1580)
British playwright: A22, pp. 2-
3

HEYWOOD, Thomas (c. 1570-1641)
British actor, playwright: A22,
pp. 31-2; A81, I, 8; A92, pp.
6-7; C498

HIBBERT, Henry George (1862-1924)
English critic: C1189

HICKS, [Edward] Seymour (1871-
1949)
English actor, manager, playwright: A86, n. p., por.;
C1190; C1191; C1192; C1193

HIGDEN, Henry (fl. 1693)
British playwright: A22, p. 115

HIGGENS, Bevil
British playwright: A22, p. 112

HILDRETH, Sarah [Mrs. Benjamin

Butler] (1810-76)
American actress: A96, p. 244

HILL, Aaron (1685-1750)
British playwright: A22, p. 152; C354

HILL, [C.] Barton (1828-1911)
English actor: A23, pp. 151-8; A81, II, 87

HILL, Benson Earle (1796-1845)
English actor: C1198

HILL, George Handel ["Yankee"] (1798-1849)
American actor: A125, pp. 516-24; C1200; C1816

HILL, Gus [born Gustave H. Metz] (1860-1937)
American actor, manager, playwright: A96, p. 245

HILL, J. M. (d. 1912)
Manager: A96, p. 245

HILLIAM, Bentley Collingwood (born 1890)
British composer: C1202

HILLIARD, Harry S. (d. 1966)
American actor: A16, III, 241

HILLIARD, Robert C. (1857-1927)
American actor, manager: A16, II, 126; A38, n. p.; A44, IV, 26-7; A66, n. p.; A96, pp. 245-6; A103, pp. 266-7

HIPPISLEY, John (1696-1748)
British playwright, actor: A22, p. 177

HITCHCOCK, Raymond (1865-1929)
American actor: A3, n. p.; A13, p. 51; A16, p. 232; A102, pp. 201-08

HITE, Mabel [Mrs. Mike Donlin] (c. 1885-1912)
American actress: A16, III, 134

HOADLY, Benjamin (1706-57)
British playwright: A22, p. 192

HOARE, Prince (1755-1834)
British playwright: A68, pp. 86-8

HOBART, George V. [born Hugh Mc-Hugh; also known as John Henry] (1867-1926)
Canadian playwright: A96, p. 247

HOBSON, Harold (1904--)
English critic: C1211

HODGDON, Sam K. (1853-1922)
American manager: C1210

HODGE, William (1874-1932)
American actor, playwright: A3, n. p.; A16, III, 249; A96, p. 247

HODGKINSON, John [born Meadow-croft] (c. 1765-1805)
English actor, manager: A81, II, 18; A125, pp. 525-30; C1108

HODSON, Henrietta [Mrs. Henry La-bouchere] (1841-1910)
British actress, manager: A50, pp. 359-60

HOEY, Josephine [born Shaw; Mrs. John Hoey] (1824-96)
English actress: A81, II, 51; A96, p. 247

HOEY, William F. (1855-97)
Actor, manager: A44, IV, 42-3; A96, pp. 247-8

HOFFMAN, Emma (d. 1960)
A110, pp. 41-2

HOFMANNSTHAL, Hugo von (1874-1929)
Austrian playwright: B20, pp. 657-8; C1094

HOLBROOK, Ann Catherine (1780-1837)
British actress: C1216

HOLCROFT, Thomas (1745-1809)
English actor, playwright: A36, pp. 12-44; A45, II, 153-91; C1217; C2254; C2480

American actor: A1, n. p., por.; A2, n. p.; A3, n. p.; A13, p. 31; A16, II, 85; A44, III, 30-31; A64, pp. 563-5; A66, n. p.; A85, pp. 11-9; A103, pp. 58-9; A104, pp. 63-90; A125, pp. 535-40; C1237

HOPPER, Edna Wallace [also known as Mabel Douglas; Mrs. De Wolf Hopper; Mrs. Albert O. Brown] (1874-1959)
American actress: A16, III, 30; A66, n. p.; A103, pp. 146-7; A107, pp. 104-12

HOPPER, Hedda [born Edna Furry; Mrs. De Wolf Hopper] (1890-1966)
American actress, journalist: A35, p. 25, por.; A96, p. 250

HORATIUS FLACCUS, Quintus [Horace] (65-8 B.C.)
Roman critic: C2150

HORDEN, Hildebrand (d. 1696)
British playwright: A6, I, 110; A7, I, 141-2; A22, p. 129

HORN, Charles E. (1786-1849)
British singer, composer: A12, p. 95

HORN, Eph (1823-77)
American minstrel, actor: A96, pp. 250-51

HORN, Kate [Mrs. John W. Buckland] (1820-96)
Actress: A96, p. 251

HORNBLOW, Arthur (1865-1942)
English critic: A96, p. 251

HORNIMAN, Annie E. F. (1860-1937)
English investor, producer: B14, pp. 209-11; C1932

HOROVITZ, Israel (1939--)
American playwright: A65, pp. 301-8

HORVATH, Odön von (1901-38)
Hungarian-German playwright: B20, p. 667-8

HOUDINI, Harry [born Ehrien Weiss] (1874-1926)
Hungarian-American magician: C487; C1050; C1355

HOUGHTON, [William] Stanley (1881-1813)
British playwright: A116, pp. 231-4; B14, pp. 55-62; B20, pp. 669-70

HOUSEMAN, John (1902--)
American director, actor, educator: C1244; C1245; C1246

HOUSMAN, Laurence (1865-1959)
English playwright: A16, II, 165; A116, pp. 235-42; B20, pp. 673-4; C1247

HOUSSAYE, Arsène (1815-96)
French producer: C1248

HOUSTON, James
Scottish actor: C1249

HOWARD, Brian (1905-58)
British writer: C1423

HOWARD, Bronson [born Crocker]
American playwright: A1, n. p., por.; A2, n. p.; C364

HOWARD, Charles D. S. (1800-58)
Actor: A96, pp. 253-4

HOWARD, Edward (1624-c. 1700)
British playwright: A22, pp. 79-80

HOWARD, Frank (1850-1915)
American minstrel: A96, p. 253

HOWARD, Harold (1870-1944)
Actor: A16, II, 192

HOWARD, Henry (1820-53)
British actor: A68, pp. 222-31

HOWARD, J. Bannister (1867-1946)
English manager: C1250

HOWARD, James (fl. 1666-7)
British playwright: A22, pp. 79-80

HOWARD, Joseph E. (1868-1961)
American performer, composer:
A96, p. 253

HOWARD, Keble [born John Keble
Bell] (1875-1928)
English playwright: C226

HOWARD, Leslie [born Stainer]
(1893-1943)
English actor, playwright: A13,
p. 39; A35, p. 47, por.; A47,
pp. 67-9; A50, pp. 456-7; A80,
pp. 239-42; A125, pp. 541-6;
C1251; C1252

HOWARD, Mabel (b. 1879)
American actress: A16, p. 198;
A103, pp. 200-01

HOWARD, May (b. c. 1845)
American actress: A96, pp. 253-
4

HOWARD, Robert (1626-98)
British playwright: A22, pp.
78-9; C98; C1841

HOWARD, Sidney (1891-1939)
American playwright: A24, pp.
179-226; A65, pp. 308-14; B20,
pp. 674-5

HOWE, Buddy (d. 1981)
American performer: A100, pp.
18-22

HOWE, Henry [born H. H. Hutchin-
son] (1812-96)
Actor: A96, p. 254

HOWE, J. Burdette (1828-1908)
English actor: A96, p. 254;
C1253

HOWELL, James (?1594-1666)
British playwright: A22, p. 41

HOWELLS, Ursula (1922--)
English actress: A9, p. 14,
por.

HOWELLS, William Dean (1837-1920)
American playwright: C412;
C413; C445; C1257

HOWES, Bobby (1895-1972)
English actor: A29, pp. 79-80

HOWITT, Belle (fl. 1869)
A110, pp. 53-4

HOWSON, Albert S. (1881-1960)
American actor: A16, II, 81

HOWSON, Charles Edwin (d. 1916)
Actor: A96, p. 255

HOWSON, John (1844-87)
Tasmanian actor: A81, II, 90

HOYT, Caroline [born Miskel; Mrs.
Charles H. Hoyt] (1873-98)
American actress: A44, VII, 12-
3

HOYT, Charles Hale (1860-1900)
American playwright, manager:
C1267

HOYT, Flora [born Walsh; Mrs.
Charles H. Hoyt] (1870-93)
American actress: A66, n. p.

HUBBARD, Elbert (1856-1915)
American performer: C1260

HUDSON, Alfred (1879-1914)
Actor: A96, p. 255

HUDSON, James (1811-78)
Irish actor: A81, II, 45-6

HUFF, Forrest (1876-1947)
American actor: A96, p. 255

HUGHES, Elinor (1906--)
American critic: C1263

HUGHES, Hatcher (1883-1945)
American playwright: B20, p.
683

HUGHES, Henry (1828-1914)
American minstrel: A96, p. 255

HUGHES, J. C. (1789-1840)
British actor: A12, p. 96

HUGHES, John (1667-1720)
British playwright: A22, pp.
154-5

HUGHES, Langston (1902-67)
American playwright: A65, pp.
314-24; B15, pp. 154-5; B20,
pp. 683-4; C713

HUGHES, Margaret (?1643-1719)
British actress: A119, pp. 149-
51

HUGHES, Richard A. W. (1900-76)
English playwright: B20, pp.
684-5

HUGHES, Rupert (1872-1956)
American playwright: A16, II,
41; B20, pp. 685-6

HUGHSTON, Regan (c. 1875-1951)
A16, II, 202

HUGO, Victor (1802-85)
French playwright: C794; C1028;
C1264; C2020

HULET, Charles (1701-36)
British actor: A92, pp. 82-3

HULETTE, Gladys
A35, p. 6, por.

HULL, Henry (1890-1977)
American actor: A13, p. 110;
A35, p. 59, por.

HULL, Josephine [born Sherwood]
(1886-1957)
American actress: A13, p. 111;
C443

HUMPHREY, William (d. 1921)
Actor: A98, pp. 97-8

HUNEKER, James Gibbons (1860-
1921)
American critic: C1266

HUNNIS, William (fl. 1566-97)
British playwright: C1650

HUNT, Leigh (1784-1859)
English critic: C1268

HUNT, Martita (1900-69)
English actress: A9, p. 21,
por.; A50, p. 467

HUNT, William (fl. 1713)
British playwright: A22, p. 170

HUNTER, Glenn (1893-1945)
American actor: A13, p. 79

HUNTER, N. C. (1908-71)
British playwright: A116, pp.
242-7

HUNTER, Ruth (1902-76)
American wardrobe supervisor:
C1270

HUNTINGTON, Agnes (fl. 1889)
American singing actress: A1,
n. p., por.; A66, n. p.

HUNTLEY, Francis (1787-1831)
British actor: A12, pp. 96-8

HURLBUT, Gladys
American actress, playwright:
C1271

HURLBUT, William J. (b. 1883)
American playwright: A96, p.
256

HUROK, Sol (1888-1974)
American producer: C1272; C1273

HURST, Lulu ["The Georgia Wonder"]
American mindreader: C1274

HUSTON, Walter (1884-1950)
Canadian actor: A13, p. 87;
A96, pp. 256-7; A125, pp. 547-
53; C121

HUTCHINS, Miriam
A16, p. 246

HUTCHINSON FAMILY: C359; C1277

HUTCHINSON, Kathryn (b. 1883)
American actress: A16, II, 208

HUTCHINSON, Percy (1875-1945)
English actor, manager: C1278

HYMAN, Emma
American performer: A58, pp.
82-3

IBSEN, Henrik (1828-1906)
Norwegian dramatist: B28, pp. 113-20; C340; C1013; C1282; C1405; C1681; C1752; C2579; C2583

ILLINGTON, Margaret [born Light; Mrs. Daniel Frohman] (1881-1934)
American actress: A16, III, 84; A96, p. 258

INCHBALD, Elizabeth [born Simpson] (1753-1821)
English actress: A43, pp. 169-97; A81, I, 44; A97, pp. 159-62; C302; C1284; C1511

INCLEDON, [Benjamin] Charles (1757-1826)
English actor: A81, I, 59; A92, pp. 278-83

INGE, William (1913-73)
American playwright: A65, pp. 325-37

INGELAND, Thomas (fl. 1560s)
British playwright: A22, p. 5

INGERSOLL, William (1860-1936)
American actor: A16, III, 233

INTROPIDI, Ethel (c. 1896-1946)
American actress: A96, p. 258

IRELAND, Joseph Norton (1817-98)
American writer: C1288

IRISH, Annie [Mrs. J. E. Dodson; Lady Fladgate] (1865-1947)
English actress: A16, p. 94; A44, IX, 24-5

IRVING FAMILY: C1295

IRVING, Henrietta (1855-91)
American actress: A96, p. 259

IRVING, Henry [born John Henry Brodribb] (1838-1905)
English actor, manager: A1, n. p.; A2, n. p.; A17, pp. 187-233; A31, pp. 80-115; A33, pp. 45-107; A35, I, 30-46, 119-29, 178-84, 226-42, 348-66, II,

277-91; A39, pp. 120-46; A39, pp. 120-46; A44, I, 4-5; A48, I, 2-116; A50, pp. 277-316; A54, pp. 39-47; A61, pp. 127-31; A64, pp. 123-48; A66, n. p.; A71, pp. 131, 152; A75, pp. 131-52; A79, pp. 72-3; A80, pp. 184-8; A81, II, 80-82; A87, pp. 312-4; A91, pp. 199-206; A108, pp. 132-4; A109, pp. 140-67; A113, pp. 154-85; A122, pp. 282-339; A125, pp. 554-62; B12, pp. 199-212; C81; C82; C110; C278; C350; C351; C352; C421; C593; C873; C1147; C1186; C1262; C1294; C1332; C1550; C1591; C1672; C1939; C2094; C2096; C2109; C2111; C2283; C2523

IRVING, Henry B. (1870-1919)
English actor, manager: A16, III, 185; A82, pp. 55-60; A83, pp. 203-04; A86, n. p., por.; C349; C683; C2552

IRVING, Isabel [Mrs. W. H. Thompson] (1871-1944)
American actress: A1, n. p., por.; A2, n. p.; A3, n. p.; A16, III, 67; A23, pp. 161-2; A44, III, 16-7; A61, pp. 135-6; A66, n. p.; A96, p. 259; A103, pp. 138-9; A106, pp. 98-103

IRVING, Jane (d. 1913)
Actress: A98, pp. 17-8

IRVING, Laurence [born Sydney Brodribb] (1871-1914)
English actor, manager: A82, pp. 61-4; A83, pp. 203-04; A123, II, 368-404; C349; C1296

IRVING, Sidney [Mrs. Maurice H. Hoffmann] (d. 1900)
Actress: A16, II, 165 (See CUSHING, S.)

IRWIN, May [born Ada Campbell; Mrs. Kurt Eisfeldt]
Canadian actress: A3, n. p.; A13, p. 22; A16, III, 153; A23, pp. 162-5; A44, VI, 36-7; A61, pp. 139-42; A64, pp. 593-8; A66, n. p.; A103, pp. 196-7;

A106, pp. 174-86; A125, pp. 563-6

IRWIN, Selden (1831-91)
American actor: A96, p. 260

ISAACS, Mr. (b. 1791)
British actor: A12, pp. 98-9

ISHERWOOD, Christopher (1904--)
English playwright: B20, pp. 707-08; C866; C1300

ISHERWOOD, Harry (d. 1840)
Actor, scene-painter: A96, p. 260

IVES, Alice (1883-1930)
American playwright: A96, p. 261

IVES, Burl (1909--)
American actor, singer: C1303

JACK, John Henry (1836-1913)
American actor, manager: A23, pp. 165-7

JACKSON, Albert (d. 1913)
English actor: A96, p. 261

JACKSON, Anne (1926--)
American actress: C1304

JACKSON, Barry (1879-1961)
English producer, playwright: C282

JACKSON, Ethel (1877-1957)
American actress: A16, II, 46

JACOB, Giles (1686-1744)
British playwright: A22, p. 197

JACOB, Hildebrand (fl. 1664)
British playwright: A22, pp. 172-3

JAMES, Henry (1843-1916)
American playwright: C786

JAMES, Louis (1842-1910)
American actor, manager: A1, n. p., por.; A2, n. p.; A3, n. p.; A16, II, 224; A23, pp.

167-71; A44, VIII, 18-9; A50, p. 360; A66, n. p.; A81, II, 106; A96, pp. 261-2; A108, pp. 39-53. 156-60

JAMES, Millie [Mrs. Edgar Seidenberg] (b. 1876)
Actress: A16, II, 115

JAMIESON, George W. (1810-68)
American actor, playwright: A81, II, 113-8; A123, I, 128-32

JANAUSCHEK, Fanny [born Franziska M. Romance] (1830-1904)
Czechoslovakian actress: A16, II, 166; A23, pp. 171-4; A44, VIII, 20-21; A66, n. p.; A77, pp. 18-25; A81, II, 64-5; A111, pp. 11-4; A125, pp. 568-71; B25, pp. 55-60; C575

JANIS, Elsie [born Bierbower] (1889-1956)
American performer: A3, n. p.; A13, p. 69; A16, III, 81; A102, pp. 81-6; A124, pp. 143-9; A125, pp. 572-6; C1308

JANIS, Percy (d. 1907)
American actor: A16, p. 29

JANSELL, Sadie
A16, III, 231

JANSEN, Marie [born Hattie Johnson] (1864-1914)
American singing actress: A1, n. p., por.; A2, n. p.; A25, pp. 205-22; A30, pp. 205-21; A44, III, 28-9; A66, n. p.; A96, pp. 262-3

JANVIER, Emma (d. 1924)
Actress: A16, II, 111

JARBEAU, Vernona [Mrs. Jefferson Bernstein] (c. 1864-1914)
American singing actress: A66, n. p.

JARRETT, Henry C. (1828-1903)
American actor, manager: A96, p. 263

JAY, Isabel [Mrs. H. S. H. Caven-

dish; Mrs. Frank Curzon]
(1879-1927)
English actress: A16, II, 235

JEANS, Isabel (b. 1891)
English actress: A9, p. 22,
por.

JEFFERSON FAMILY: A78, pp. 58-87

JEFFERSON, Cornelia F. [Mrs. Joseph Jefferson I] (1796-1849)
American actress: A96, p. 263

JEFFERSON, Cornelia (b. 1835)
American actress: A96, p. 263

JEFFERSON, Elizabeth [born May;
Mrs. Thomas Jefferson I] (1733-
76)
British actress: A81, I, 30;
A92, pp. 164-5

JEFFERSON, John (d. 1831)
American actor: A96, pp. 263-4

JEFFERSON, Joseph I (1778-1832)
English actor: A81, II, 18;
A96, p. 264; A125, pp. 577-81

JEFFERSON, Joseph II (1804-42)
American actor, scene-painter:
A96, p. 264

JEFFERSON, Joseph III (1829-1905)
American actor: A1, n. p.,
por.; A2, n. p.; A8, pp. 84-5;
A23, pp. 174-84; A44, I, 32-3;
A46, pp. 75-82; A52, pp. 267-
80; A54, pp. 3-22; A61, pp.
145-50; A64, pp. 284-96; A66,
n. p.; A71, pp. 153-74; A75,
pp. 153-74; A77, pp. 1-17; A79,
pp. 64-5; A80, pp. 161-7; A81,
II, 54-5; A87, p. 305; A91, pp.
172-7; A103, pp. 6-7; A105, pp.
11-7; A111, pp. 9-11; A113, pp.
186-213; A120, pp. 64-97; A121,
I, 130-58; A125, pp. 582-95;
B11, pp. 93-115; C729; C1311;
C1312; C1313; C1442; C1579;
C2513; C2525

JEFFERSON, Thomas L. (1857-1932)
American actor: A16, p. 203

JEFFREYS, Ellis [Mrs. Frederic
Curzon; Mrs. Herbert Sleath]
(1868-1943)
English actress: A16, p. 117;
A86, n. p., por.; A96, p. 265

JEFFRIES, Maud [Mrs. James Nott
Osborne] (1869-1946)
American actress: A16, p. 141;
A23, pp. 184-5; A86, n. p.,
por.; A96, p. 265

JELLICOE, Ann (1927--)
British playwright: A76, pp.
106-19

JENKS, Fred C. (1871-1944)
American manager: A96, p. 265

JEROME, Clara Belle
A16, p. 284

JEROME, Jerome Klapka (1859-1927)
English playwright, actor:
A116, pp. 247-52; B20, pp. 724-
5; C1316; C1317; C1754

JERROLD, Douglas W. (1803-57)
British playwright: C1319;
C1320; C1362

JESSE, Friniwyd T. [Mrs. H. M.
Harwood] (1889-1958)
British playwright: B20, pp.
725-6

JESSEL, George (1898-1981)
American performer: A100, pp.
23-9; C1321; C1322; C1323;
C1324

JESSEL, Joseph (b. 1859)
Playwright: A96, p. 266

JESSOP, George H. (d. 1915)
Irish playwright, actor: A96,
p. 266

JEVON, Thomas (1652-88)
British playwright: A22, p. 112

JEWELL, Izetta [born Kenney; Mrs.
Miller] (1883-1981)
American actress: A16, II, 260;
A98, pp. 23-4

JEWETT, Henry (1863-1930)
Australian actor, producer:
A44, IX, 38-9; A86, pp. 185-8;
A103, pp. 194-5; A105, pp. 211-
22

JOHNSON, Benjamin (1665-1742)
British actor: A92, pp. 31-2

JOHNSON, Celia (1908-82)
English actress: A32, pp. 82-3

JOHNSON, Charles (1679-1748)
British playwright: A22, p. 145

JOHNSON, John (1759-1819)
English actor: A96, pp. 266-7

JOHNSON, Owen (1878-1952)
American playwright: A16, II,
194

JOHNSON, Roy L. (1867-1943)
American minstrel: A96, p. 267

JOHNSON, Samuel (1709-84)
English playwright: A22, p. 193

JOHNSON, Selene
Actress: A16, II, 58

JOHNSTON, Dennis (1901--)
British playwright: A116, pp.
253-8

JOHNSTON, Henry (c. 1750-99)
British actor: A81, I, 41; A92,
pp. 216-8

JOHNSTON, Henry Erskine (1777-
1845)
Scottish actor: A96, p. 268

JOHNSTON, T. B. (1815-61)
American actor: A96, p. 268

JOHNSTONE, Jack (1750-1828)
British actor: A81, I, 42; A92,
pp. 218-21

JOHNSTONE, Justine (b. 1899)
American singing actress: A102,
pp. 233-42

JOLLY, George (fl. 1640-73)
British actor: C1243

JOLSON, Al [born Asa Yoelson]
(1886-1950)
Russian-American singing actor:
A13, p. 81; A20, pp. 42-7; A35,
p. 89, por.; A96, pp. 268-9;
A102, pp. 185-92; A125, pp.
595-602; B15, pp. 160-61; B23,
pp. 207-08; B26, pp. 49-62;
C921; C2183

JOLSON, Harry [born Yoelson]
(1882-1953)
American performer: C1329

JONES, Avonia Stanhope [Mrs. Gustavus V. Brooke] (1839-67)
American actress: A96, p. 270

JONES, Franklin
A16, II, 262

JONES, Henry Arthur (1851-1929)
English playwright: A16, p.
207; A116, pp. 259-68; B14, pp.
203-05; C569; C1331

JONES, Inigo (1573-1652)
English designer, playwright:
A22, p. 200; C1015; C1976;
C2300

JONES, John (fl. 1635)
British playwright: A22, p. 52

JONES, Joseph Stevens (1809-77)
American actor, manager, playwright: A96, p. 271

JONES, Julia [born Wagstaff; Mrs.
Benjamin Deanes; Mrs. J. M.
Cooke; Mrs. W. G. Jones] (1829-
1907)
English actress: A16, p. 92;
A23, pp. 188-91; A63, pp. 176-
8; A96, p. 271

JONES, Margo (1913-55)
American producer: C1439

JONES, Preston (1936-79)
American playwright: A65, pp.
337-44

JONES, Richard ["Gentleman
Jones"] (1778-1851)
British actor: A12, pp. 99-104;

A81, I, 63-4; A92, pp. 332-3

JONES, Walter (1874-1922)
Actor: A44, II, 38-9; A64, pp.
577-9; A85, pp. 89-97; A96, pp.
271-2; A104, pp. 54-62

JONSON, Ben (c. 1573-1637)
English playwright: A22, pp.
25-8; B17, pp. 20-32; C135;
C477; C490; C1854; C2267

JORDAN, Dorothy [born Dorothea
Bland] (1762-1816)
Irish actress: A6, II, 98-121;
A7, II, 127-64; A10, pp. 197-
280; A42, pp. 356-98; A45, II,
234-49; A73, pp. 133-58; A81,
I, 56-7; A89, pp. 197-232; A92,
pp. 272-6; A97, pp. 196-217;
A99, pp. 177-206; C300; C1318;
C1702; C1965; C2159

JORDAN, Kate [Mrs. Frederick M.
Vermilye] (1862-1926)
Irish actress, playwright: A16,
II, 271

JORDAN, Thomas (?1612-85?)
British playwright, actor: A22,
p. 65

JOUVET, Louis (1891-1951)
French actor, director, producer: C1395

JOYCE, James (1882-1941)
Irish playwright: A116, pp.
268-78; C54; C542; C577; C625;
C1012; C1337

JOYCE, Peggy Hopkins [born Margaret Upton] (1893-1957)
American performer: C1338

JOYNER, William (d. 1706)
British playwright: A22, p. 92

JUCH, Emma [Mrs. Francis L. Well-
man] (1863-1939)
Austrian-American singing actress: A25, pp. 195-204; A30,
pp. 195-204

JUDITH, Madame [born Julie Ber-
nat] (1827-1912)

French actress: C1339

JUPP, James
British stage doorkeeper: C1340

KADISON, Harry
American performer: A58, pp.
84-9

KAHN, Florence [Lady Beerbohm]
(1878-1951)
American actress: A16, p. 62;
A103, pp. 280-81

KAISER, Georg (1878-1945)
German playwright: B20, pp.
742-3

KALICH, Bertha (1874-1939)
Polish actress: A3, n. p.;
A16, II, 205; A125, pp. 603-08

KAMINSKA, Ida (1899-1980)
Actress, playwright, producer:
C1342

KANE, Whitford (1882-1956)
British actor: C1343

KANIN, Garson (1912--)
American playwright: A65, II,
3-11

KARL, Tom [born Carroll] (1846-
1916)
Irish singing actor: A66, n. p.

KARLOFF, Boris [born William Henry Pratt] (1887-1969)
English actor: C8; C2385

KARNO, Fred (1866-1941)
British actor, manager: C18

KATAEV, Valentin P. (b. 1897)
Russian playwright: B20, p.
747

KAUFMAN, George S. (1889-1961)
American actor, director, play-
wright: A35, p. 100. por.; A65,
II, 11-26; B20, pp. 748-9;
C1673; C2323

KEAN, Charles (1811-68)

English actor, manager: A4, pp. 288-315; A26, I, 65-116; A28, II, 232-55; A31, pp. 12-9; A69, I, 168-215; A74, pp. 91-118; A81, I, 100-02; A92, pp. 402-03; A125, pp. 609-14; C526; C915; C1350; C2588

KEAN, Edmund (1787-1833)
English actor: A4, pp. 146-219; A6, II, 127-74; A7, II, 165-226; A12, pp. 104-44; A17, pp. 108-59; A21, pp. 27-30; A39, pp. 72-93; A50, pp. 166-90; A72, pp. 1-36; A79, pp. 24-5; A80, pp. 115-24; A81, I, 75-7; A88, pp. 75-118; A91, pp. 101-08; A92, pp. 341-52; A93, pp. 129-38; A99, pp. 233-62; A113, pp. 30-54; A125, pp. 615-20; B2, pp. 234-61; C723; C884; C1029; C1153; C1201; C1401; C1563; C1708; C1916; C1926; C1962

KEANE, Doris (1881-1945)
American actress: A3, n. p.; A13, p. 67; A16, III, 283; A96, p. 275

KEANE, James A.
American actor: A98, pp. 113-4

KEANE, John B. (1928--)
Irish playwright: C1725

KEATON, Buster [born Joseph F. Keaton] (1895-1966)
American actor: C293; C640; C1351

KEELER, Ralph (1840-73)
American minstrel : C1352

KEELEY, Mary Ann (1806-99)
British actress: C1003

KEELEY, Robert (1794-1869)
British actor, manager: A12, pp. 144-5; A68, pp. 91-108; A81, I, 85-6; A92, pp. 372-3; B22, pp. 278-83; C1003

KEENAN, Frank [born James Francis] (1858-1929)
American actor: A3, n. p.

KEENE, Laura [born Lee or Moss; Mrs. John Taylor] (c. 1820-73)
English actress: A14, pp. 67-70; A81, II, 56-7; A96, p. 276; A122, pp. 46-58; A125, pp. 621-5; B25, pp. 45-9; C603

KEENE, Theophilus (d. 1718)
British actor: C2126

KEENE, Thomas W. [born Thomas R. Eagleson] (1840-98)
American actor: A44, II, 22-3; A50, p. 358; A64, pp. 373-8; A66, n. p.; A81, II, 109; A96, p. 276

KEIM, Adelaide (b. c. 1880)
American actress: A16, p. 50

KEITH, Benjamin Franklin (1846-1914)
American manager: A96, pp. 276-7

KELCEY, Herbert [born Lamb] (1855-1917)
English actor: A1, n. p., por.; A3, n. p.; A16, II, 230; A23, pp. 191-4; A44, II, 18-9; A61, pp. 153-5; A66, n. p.; A103, pp. 50-51; A105, pp. 326-33

KELLAR, Harry (1849-1922)
American magician: C1354

KELLERD, John E. (1863-1929)
English actor: A23, pp. 194-7

KELLERMANN, Annette (1888-1975)
American performer: A16, III, 162

KELLEY, Desmond (b. 1884)
American actress: A16, p. 110

KELLOG, Charles (c. 1869-1949)
American performer: C1356

KELLOGG, Clara Louise [Mrs. Max Strakosch] (1842-1916)
American singer: C1357

KELLY, Frances Harriet (b. 1805)
English actress: A12, pp. 145-50

American actor: A85, pp. 143-51; A103, pp. 210-11

KENDALL, Harry (1897-1962)
English actor: C1370

KENDRICK, Alfred (b. 1869)
English actor: A16, II, 180

KENDRICK, Jennie [Mrs. James L. Seeley]
American actress: A98, pp. 79-80

KENNARK, Jane [Mrs. Charles E. Lothian] (1863-1938)
American actress: A103, pp. 90-91

KENNEDY, Bart (1861-1930)
British actor: C1374

KENNEDY, Charles Rann (1871-1950)
English actor, playwright: B20, p. 753-4

KENT, Stanley
American actor: A98, pp. 115-6

KENYON, Elmer Bernard (d. 1949)
American press agent: C764

KERN, Jerome (1885-1945)
American composer: C317; C821; C920

KERR, Alfred (c. 1868-1948)
Critic: C602

KERR, Fred [born Frederick G. Keen] (1858-1933)
English actor: C1378

KEYES, Katherine
A16, II, 114

KEYS, Nelson (1886-1939)
British actor: C444

KIDDER, Edward E. (?1849-1927)
American playwright: A96, p. 283

KIDDER, Kathryn [Mrs. Louis K. Anspacher] (1867-1939)
American actress: A16, III,

292; A23, p. 198; A44, VI, pp. 28-9; A66, n. p.; A106, pp. 299-305

KILDARE, Owen Frawley (1864-1911)
American playwright: C1382

KILLIGREW, Henry (1612-1700)
British playwright: A22, p. 54

KILLIGREW, Thomas (1612-83)
British actor, manager, playwright: A22, p. 77; A81, I, 8-9; A92, pp. 7-9; C1107; C1476; C1502

KILLIGREW, William (1606-95)
British playwright: A22, p. 79

KIMBALL, Grace [Mrs. M. D. McGuire] (b. 1870)
American actress: A16, p. 51; A44. V, 36-7

KIMBALL, Jennie (1848-96)
American actress, manager: A96, p. 284

KING, Ada (c. 1862-1940)
English actress: A47, pp. 85-94

KING, Dennis (1897-1971)
English actor: A13, p. 95

KING, Thomas (1730-1804)
English actor, playwright: A6, I, 224-7; A7, I, 293-6; A28, I, 97-118; A45, II, 128-52; A81, I, 29; A92, pp. 157-8; A93, pp. 59-62

KINGDON, Edith [Mrs. George J. Gould] (1862-1921)
American actress: A44, VII, 24-5

KINGSBURY, Lillian [Mrs. Robert G. Hutchins]
Actress: A16, III, 109

KINGSLEY, Sidney (1906--)
American playwright: A65, II, 31-41; B20, p. 764

KINGSTON, Gertrude [born Konstam] (1887-1937)

English actress, manager: C1385

KIRALFY, Imre (1845-1919)
Hungarian manager: A96, p. 285

KIRBY, J. Hudson (1819-48)
American actor: A96, pp. 285-6

KIRK, John (d. 1643)
British playwright: A22, p. 54

KIRK, John R. (c. 1866-1948)
American actor, manager, director: A49, pp. 346-7

KITT, Eartha (1930--)
American singing actress: C1390

KLAW, Marc (1858-1936)
American manager: A16, p. 123

KLEIN, Cecil (b. 1875)
American actor: A16, 149

KLEIN, CHarles (1867-1915)
English actor, playwright: A16, III, 24; A96, p. 286

KLEIST, Heinrich von (1777-1811)
German playwright: C1584; C1689

KLIMT, George (1861-1942)
American actor, playwright: A96, p. 286

KNEF, Hildegard
German performer: C1396

KNEPP, Mary (d. 1677)
British actress: A119, pp. 154-6

KNEVET, Ralph (fl. 1631)
British playwright: A22, p. 45

KNIGHT, Edward (1774-1826)
British actor: A12, pp. 160-70; A81, I, 64; A92, pp. 300-02

KNIGHT, Esmond (1906--)
English actor: C1398

KNIGHT, Frances Maria (17th century)
British actress: A119, pp. 156-9

KNIPE, Charles (fl. 1715)
British playwright: A22, p. 159

KNIPPER, Olga [Mrs. Anton Chekhov] (1868-1959)
Russian actress: C1923

KNOBLOCK, Edward (1874-1945)
Actor, playwright: A116, pp. 279-88; C1400

KNOWLES, James Sheridan (1784-1862)
British playwright: A69, II, 122-38; A81, II, 22; C1402; C1657

KNOWLES, Richard George (1858-1919)
Canadian actor: A16, p. 224

KNOWLTON, Maude (fl. 1900-10)
American actress: A16, III, 48

KOBER, Arthur (1900-75)
American playwright, producer: B20, pp. 771-2

KOLB, Matt B., Sr. (d. 1947)
American actor, producer: A96, p. 287

KOMMISARJEVSKY, Theodor (1882-1954)
Russian director, producer: C1407

KOPIT, Arthur (1937--)
American playwright: A65, II, 41-9

KOPS, Bernard (1926--)
English playwright: C1408

KREMER, Theodore (1871-1923)
German playwright: A16, II, 68

KREYMBORG, Alfred (1883-1966)
American playwright: B20, pp. 775-6; C1411

KRUTCH, Joseph Wood (1893-1970)
American critic: C1039

KYASHT, Lydia (1886-1959)
Russian dancer: C1413

KYD, Thomas (1558-94?)
English playwright: A22, p. 18;
C923

KYLE, Howard [born Kyle A. Vanda-
grift] (1861-1950)
American actor: A102, pp. 274-5

KYNASTON, Edward (?1640-1706)
British actor: A6, I, 60-61;
A7, I, 75-6; A45, I, 24-9; A81,
I, 9; A92, pp. 9-11

LACEY, Catherine (1904-79)
English actress: A9, p. 23,
por.

LACEY or LACY, John (1622-81)
British playwright: A22, pp.
9203; A92, pp. 11-2

LACKAYE, Wilton (1862-1932)
American actor: A3, n. p.; A16,
II, 219; A21, pp. 65-7; A23,
pp. 199-202; A44, VI, 14-5;
A66, n. p.; A103, pp. 80-81;
A105, pp. 166-73

LACY, Frances [born Cooper; Mrs.
Thomas Hailes Lacy] (1819-72)
Actress: A68, pp. 199-222

LACY, Harry B. (c. 1890-1944)
Actor: A66, n. p.

LACY or LACEY, John (1622-81)
British actor, playwright: C561

LACY, Walter (1809-98)
English actor: A92, pp. 397-400

LA HARTE, Rose (c. 1891-1958)
Actress: A16, p. 66

LAHR, Bert (1895-1967)
American actor: A13, p. 117;
A125, pp. 642-9; C1418

LAKE, Jimmy [born Arthur Laceby]
(1879-1967)
American comedian: C1414

LANCHESTER, Elsa [Mrs. Charles
Laughton] (1902--)
English actress: C1424; C1425

LANDA, Frank
Actor: A1, n. p., por.

LANDER, Jean [born Davenport;
Mrs. Fred W. Lander] (1829-
1903)
English actress: A23, pp. 202-
04; A81, II, 62-3; A121, II,
151; A123, I, 228-32; A125, pp.
650-54; B25, pp. 50-54 (See
DAVENPORT, Jean.)

LANDIS, Jessie Royce (1904-72)
American actress: C1427

LANDSTONE, Charles (b. 1891)
British business manager: C1428

LANE, Samuel (1804-71)
British actor: C598

LANE, Sarah ["Sallie"] (1823-99)
British actress: C598

LANG, Anton (1875-1938)
German actor: C1431

LANG, [Alexander] Matheson (1877-
1948)
Canadian   actor,   playwright,
producer: A50, pp. 397-8; C686;
C1432

LANGLEY, Francis (1548-1602)
English theatre owner: C1285

LANGNER, Lawrence (1890-1962)
American producer, playwright:
B20, pp. 788-9; C1435

LANGRISH, John S. (1830-95)
Irish actor, manager: A96, p.
290

LANGTRY, Lillie [born Emily Le
Breton; Mrs. Edward Langtry;
Mrs. Frederick Gebhardt] (1852-
1929)
English actress, manager: A5,
pp. 175-8; A8, pp. 72-3; A14,
pp. 56-62; A16, III, 235; A25,
pp. 153-62; A30, p. 153; A44,
IV, 32-3; A50, pp. 367-9; A64,
pp. 396-415; A66, n. p.; A81,
II, 101; A101, n. p.; por.;
A123, II, 576-7; A125, pp. 655-

A91, pp. 26-32; A118, pp. 129-96; C2024

LEDERER, George W. (1861-1938)
American manager: A96, pp. 292-3

LEE, Gypsy Rose [born Hovick] (1914-70)
American performer: C1457

LEE, Henry (1533-1611)
British playwright: C457; C1458

LEE, Mary [born Aldridge; Lady Slingsby] (17th century)
A119, pp. 159-62

LEE, Mary Ann (1823-99)
American dancer: A79, pp. 52-3

LEE, Nathaniel (?1653-92)
British playwright: A22, pp. 97-8; C1091

LEFFLER, John (1875-1944)
Manager: A96, p. 293

LE GALLIENNE, Eva (1899--)
English actress: A13, p. 90; A35, p. 12, por.; A80, pp. 250-53; A125, pp. 671-7; B15, pp. 174-5; C1461; C1463; C2132

LE HAY, John [born Healy] (1854-1926)
Irish actor: A16, II, 82

LEHMANN, Beatrix (1903-79)
English actress: A9, p. 25, por.; A32, pp. 66-7

LEIBER, Fritz (1883-1949)
American actor, producer: C715

LEICESTER, Ernest (1866-1939)
A16, II, 140

LEIGH, Alice (d. 1913)
Actress: A16, II, 258

LEIGH, Anthony (d. 1692)
English actor: A7, I, 80

LEIGH, Elinor (17th century)
British actress: A119, pp. 162-5

LEIGH, John
British playwright: A22, p. 168

LEIGH, Lisle (c. 1879-1927)
Actress: A44, VIII, 12-3

LEIGH, Vivien (1913-1967)
English actress: A13, p. 136; A47, pp. 70-73; A125, pp. 678-84; C153; C704; C792; C1441; C2059

LEIGHTON, Margaret (1922-76)
English actress: A32, pp. 56-7; A50, p. 513

LEJEUNE, C. A. (1897-1973)
British critic: C1465

LEMAITRE, Jules (1853-1914)
French playwright: B20, pp. 811-2; C1467

LEMAN, Walter Moore (b. 1810)
American actor: C1468

LEMON, Mark (1809-70)
British actor: A81, I, 100; C1148

LE MOYNE, Sarah [born Cowell; Mrs. William J. Le Moyne] (1859-1915)
American actress: A23, pp. 208-11; A61, pp. 163-4; A103, pp. 20-21; A106, pp. 39-49

LE MOYNE, William J. (1831-1905)
American actor: A23, pp. 204-07; A44, VI, 10-11; A66, n. p.; A77, pp. 259-65

LENNOX, Charlotte (1720-1804)
American playwright: C1632; C2215

LENO, Dan [born George Galvin] (1860-1904)
English performer: C1470; C2540

LENORMAND, Henri-René (1882-1951)
French playwright: B20, pp. 813-4

LEONARD, Eddie (1875-1941)
American minstrel: C1471

LEONARD, John
British playwright: A22, p. 104

LEONTINE, Caroline
French dancer: A110, pp. 33-4

LEONTOVICH, Eugenie (1900--)
Russian actress: A125, pp. 685-91

LERNER, Alan Jay (1918--)
American composer: C1474

LESLIE, Elsie [Mrs. William J. Winter] (1881-1966)
American actress: A8, pp. 90-91; A16, II, 187; A23, p. 211; C1538

LESLIE, Fred [born Hobson] (1855-92)
English actor, playwright: C2409

LESLIE, Teddy
American performer: A58, pp. 90-91

LESSING, Gotthold Ephraim (1729-81)
German playwright, critic: C953

LESSING, Madge [Mrs. McClellan] (fl. 1897-1933)
English actress: A107, pp. 81-7

LESTER, Florence
Actress: A16, p. 136

LE SUEUR, Charles (1879-1960)
English singer: A16, II, 124

LEVANT, Oscar (1906-72)
American performer: A126, pp. 135-54

LEVERTON, William Henry (1866-1941)
English box-office manager: C1482

LEVEY, Ethel (1880-1955)
American actress: A16, p. 258

LEVICK, Milnes (1825-97)
English actor: A44, VIII, 46-7

LEVY, Bert (c. 1871-1934)
A16, p. 144

LEVY, Edward Lawrence (b. 1851)
English writer: C1485

LEWERS, William (d. 1926)
A16, III, 100

LEWES, [Charles] Lee (1740-1803)
British actor: A92, pp. 185-6; C1486

LEWIS, Ada (1875-1925)
American actress: A16, III, 82

LEWIS, Annie (1870-96)
American actress: A66, n. p.

LEWIS, Catherine (1854-1942)
Actress: A110, pp. 57-8

LEWIS, Cleo
American performer: A58, pp. 92-9

LEWIS, Eric [born Tuffley] (1855-1935)
English actor: A16, II, 239

LEWIS, Frederick G. (1873-1946)
American actor: A16, II, 53

LEWIS, Horace (d. 1905)
American actor: A23, pp. 211-7; A98, pp. 107-08

LEWIS, James (1839-96)
American actor: A44, III, 18-9; A66, n. p.; A81, II, 85; A121, I, 379-82; A123, I, 340-47

LEWIS, Jeffreys (1857-1926)
English actress: A16, p. 234; A66, n. p.; A96, p. 295

LEWIS, Joe E. (1902-71)
American comedian: C523

LEWIS, Lillian [Mrs. Lawrence Marsden] (d. 1899)
American actress: A66, n. p.

LEWIS, Mary Sybil (1900-41)
American singer: B15, pp. 168-9

LEWIS, Matthew Gregory ["Monk"]
(1775-1818)
British playwright: C164

LEWIS, Robert (1909--)
American actor, director, producer: C1490

LEWIS, Sammy
American performer: A100, pp.
211-8

LEWIS, William ["Gentleman Lewis"] (1748-1811)
British actor, manager: A6, II,
74-5; A81, I, 41-2; A92, pp.
208-09

LILLIE, Beatrice [Lady Robert
Peel] (1898--)
Canadian performer: A13, p.
116; A20, pp. 124-6; A35, pp.
52-5, por.; A125, pp. 692-6;
C1503

LILLO, George (?1693-1739)
English playwright: A22, p.
179; C679

LIND, Jenny [born Johanna Maria
Lind] (1820-87)
Swedish singer: C397; C2073

LINDFORD, Viveca (1920--)
Swedish actress: C1504

LINDSAY, Howard (1889-1968)
American playwright, producer,
director, actor: A46, pp. 136-
43; C2205

LINDSAY, Hugh (b. 1804)
American circus performer:
C1505

LINGARD, James W. (1823-70)
English actor: A53, pp. 25-7

LINGARD, William Horace [born
William Thomas] (c. 1840-1927)
English actor, manager: A53,
pp. 60-64; A96, pp. 295-6

LINLEY, Elizabeth Ann [Mrs. Richard Brinsley Sheridan] (1754-
92)
British actress: A81, I, 44;
A92, pp. 223-5

LINTHICUM, Lotta (d. 1952)
Actress: A44, X, n. p.

LION, Leon M. (1879-1947)
English actor, director, producer: A9, p. 26, por.; C1506

LIPMAN, Clara [Mrs. Louis Mann]
(1869-1952)
American actress: A16, II, 270;
A66, n. p.; A103, pp. 74-5

LIPTON, Thomas
British playwright: A22, p. 79

LISTON, John (1776-1846)
English actor: A6, II, 239-43;
A7, II, 313-7; A12, pp. 171-6;
A73, pp. 253-68; A81, I, 69-70;
A91, pp. 85-91; A92, pp. 322-5

LISTON, Mrs. John (b. c. 1780)
British actress: A12, p. 177

LITTLE TICH [born Harry Relph]
(1869-1928)
English performer: C2007

LITTLEFIELD, Emma [Mrs. Victor
Moore] (1883-1934)
American actress: A16, II, 28

LIVINGSTONE, Belle [born Isabel
Graham; Mrs. Richard Wherry;
Countess Florentino Laltazzi;
Mrs. Edward Mohler; Mrs. Walter
Hutchins] (1875-1957)
American writer: C1513; C1514

LLEWELLYN, Fewlass (1866-1941)
English actor, playwright, director: A16, II, 69

LLOYD, Alice [born Wood] (1873-
1949)
English performer: A16, II, 237

LLOYD, James (1846-1909)
English circus performer: C1515

LLOYD, Marie [born Matilda A. V. Wood] (1870-1922)
English performer: A16, II, 52; C1306

LLOYD, Morris (c. 1891-1974)
American actor: A58, pp. 102-15

LLOYD, Rosie (1897-1944)
Singing actress: A16, II, 135

LLOYD, Violet (1879-1924)
English actress: A16, p. 259

LOCKWOOD, Margaret [born Day] (1916--)
British actress: C1518

LODER, Charles A. (1857-1949)
Actor: A96, p. 297

LODGE, Thomas (?1558-1625)
British playwright: A22, pp. 17-8; C1859; C2326; C2594

LOFTUS, Cissie [born Marie Cecilia M'Carthy] (1876-1943)
Scottish actress: A3, n. p.; A13, p. 40; A16, II, 238; A96, p. 297; B15, pp. 182-3; C1640

LOGAN, Joshua (1908--)
American director, producer: C1521

LOGAN, Olive [Mrs. Wirt Sikes] (1839-1909)
American actress: A36, pp. 270-87; C1522; C1523

LONG, Jane (17th century)
British actress: A119, pp. 165-7

LONSDALE, Frederick [born Leonard] (1881-1954)
English playwright: A116, pp. 294-300; B20, p. 847; C732

LORAINE, Robert (1876-1935)
English actor, producer: A47, pp. 135-42; C1525; C1526

LORBER, Martha
Actress: B15, pp. 168-9

LORD, Pauline (1890-1950)
American actress: A13, p. 88; A35, p. 7, por.; A80, pp. 242-4; A102, pp. 271-6; A124, pp. 82-7; A125, pp. 697-703

LORIMER, Wright (1874-1911)
American actor, playwright, producer: A16, III, 77; A38, n. p.

LOSEE, Frank (1856-1937)
American actor: A16, III, 144; A23, pp. 218-21

LOVE, Emma Sarah [Mrs. Grandby Calcraft] (b. 1801)
English actress: B12, p. 178

LOVE, Mabel [born Watson] (1874-1953)
English actress: A16, p. 229

LOVETT, Josephine
A16, III, 239

LOWIN, John (1576-1658)
British actor: A27, pp. 165-79

LOWNDES, Marie Adelaide Belloc (1868-1947)
British playwright: B20, pp. 855-6; C1529

LOWREY, Gwendolyn
A16, II, 86

LOWRIE, Jeanette [Mrs. Thomas Q. Seabrooke] (1862-1937)
Welsh actress: A16, p. 48

LUBY, Jeanette
A16, p. 227

LUDLOW, Noah Miller (1795-1886)
American actor, manager: C153 ;

LUGOSI, Bela (1884-1956)
Hungarian actor: C604; C1469

LUNT, Alfred (1892-1977)
American actor: A13, p. 93; A79, pp. 164-5; A80, pp. 257-63; A115, pp. 113-22; A125, pp. 704-15; B15, pp. 188-9; C922; C2578

LUPINO, Stanley (1894-1942)
English actor, playwright, producer: A96, pp. 299-300; C1536

"LUTTRELL, GLADYS"
American actress: C1537

LYLY, John (c. 1554-1606)
British playwright: C310; C1269

LYNCH, Francis
British playwright: A22, p. 184

LYTTON, Edward Bulwer, Lord (1803-73)
English playwright: C1541; C2103; C2104; C2163

LYTTON, Harry A. (1867-1936)
English actor: C1542; C1543

MacARTHUR, Charles (1895-1956)
American playwright: A65, II, 49-53; B15, pp. 190-91; B23, pp. 227-30; C1165

MACAULAY, Bernard (1837-87)
American actor, manager: A81, II, 87; A96, p. 300

MacDONALD, Christie (1875-1962)
Canadian actress: A13, p. 42; A16, II, 64; A103, pp. 160-61; A107, pp. 172-80

MacDONALD, Cordelia [Mrs. Edward Wade]
American actress: A98, pp. 81-2

MacDONALD, William H. (d. 1913)
American singing actor: A44, I, 36-7; A66, n. p.

MacDOWELL, [William] Melbourne (1857-1941)
American actor: A16, II, 260; A23, pp. 221-3; A66, n. p.; A105, pp. 238-47

MACHIAVELLI, Niccolo (1469-1527)
Italian playwright: C1761; C2025; C2407; C2472

MACHIN, Lewis

British playwright: A22, p. 51

MACK, Andrew [born McAloon] (1863-1931)
American actor: A103, pp. 198-9

MACK, Charles Emmett (c. 1900-27)
American actor: A96, p. 300

MACK, George E. (c. 1866-1948)
American actor: A98, pp. 37-8

MACK, J. Herbert (1856-1947)
Manager: A96, pp. 300-01

MACK, Willard W. [born Charles W. McLaughlin] (1873-1934)
Canadian actor, manager, playwright: A96, p. 301

MACK, William B. (1872-1955)
A16, III, 99

MACKAY, Charles (1786-1857)
British actor: A81, I, 74-5; A92, pp. 338-9

MACKAY, Charles D. (1867-1935)
American actor: A16, p. 234; A98, pp. 103-04

MACKAY, Frank Finlay (c. 1831-1923)
American actor, playwright: A23, pp. 223-5

MACKAYE, Percy (1875-1956)
American playwright: B20, pp. 881-2

MACKAYE, [James] Steele (1844-94)
American actor, manager, playwright, educator: C626; C1556

MACKINTOSH, Matthew ["An Old Stager"]
Scottish machinist: C1559

MACKINTOSH, William (1855-1929)
A16, II, 167

MacLEAN, Rezin D. [born R. D. Shepherd] (1859-1948)
American actor: A103, pp. 166-7

MacLEISH, Archibald (1892-1982)
American playwright: A65, II, 53-63

MACKLIN, Charles (1699-1797)
Irish actor, playwright: A4, pp. 327-57; A6, I, 174-203; A7, I, 226-64; A22, p. 191; A36, pp. 45-58; A45, II, 1-20; A70, pp. 1-24; A80, pp. 76-80; A81, I, 15-6; A92, pp. 64-8; C76; C545; C559; C1388; C1862

MACKLIN, Mrs. Charles
British actress: A97, pp. 129-30

MACKLIN, Miss
British actress: A97, pp. 130-33

MacLARNIE, Thomas (c. 1871-1931)
American actor: A98, pp. 35-6

MacLIAMMOIR, Micheal (1899-1978)
Irish actor, director, producer: C1560; C1561

MacNAMARA, Brinsley [born John Weldon] (1890-1963)
Irish playwright: A116, II, 3-8

MACNEE, Patrick (1922--)
English actor: A76, pp. 70-76

MacNEICE, Louis (1907-63)
British playwright: A116, II, 8-12

MACPHERSON, Jeanne Culbertson (c. 1887-1946)
A16, III, 126

MACREADY, William Charles (1793-1873)
English actor, manager: A4, pp. 220-87; A6, II, 253-78; A7, II, 330-63; A12, pp. 179-82; A17, pp. 160-71; A26, I, 15-64; A36, pp. 119-35; A39, pp. 94-119; A50, pp. 208-24; A68, pp. 2-36; A69, I, 1-108; A74, pp. 1-32; A79, pp. 36-7; A81, I, 79-82; A88, pp. 207-46; A91, pp. 109-18; A92, pp. 366-70; A113, pp. 55-92; A125, pp. 723-9; C83;

C743; C1510; C1565; C1566; C1599; C1938; C1953; C2163; C2365

MADDEN, Joe
American performer: A58, pp. 100-01

MADDEN, Samuel (1686-1765)
British playwright: A22, p. 106

MADISON, Kitty
American burlesque performer: C1140

MAEDER, Clara [born Fisher] (1811-98)
English actress: A12, pp. 71-8; A72, pp. 259-72; A79, pp. 38-9; A125, pp. 370-74; C1567; C2201 (See FISHER, Clara.)

MAETERLINCK, Maurice (1862-1949)
Belgian playwright: A124, pp. 224-6; B20, pp. 892-5; C287; C501; C1087

MAGINN, Bonnie
Actress: A16, p. 45

MAHER, John B.
A16, II, 67

MAHON, Gertrude (b. 1752)
Actress: B3, pp. 247-94

MAIDWELL, John
British playwright: A22, p. 107

MAINE, Jasper
British playwright: A22, pp. 57-8

MALLESON, Miles (1888-1969)
English actor, playwright: A9, p. 27, por.

MALLET, David (?1705-65)
British playwright: A22, pp. 182-3

MALONE, Edmund (1741-1812)
Irish critic: C1959

MALONE, John
British actor: A23, pp. 225-8;

A44, VI, 34-5

MALTBY, Henry Francis (1880-1963)
South African actor: C1577

MALTZ, Albert (1908--)
American playwight: B20, pp. 899-900

MAMET, David (1947--)
American playwright: A65, II, 63-70

MAMOULIAN, Rouben (1897--)
Russian-American   director: C212; C1696; C1822

MANEY, Richard (1891-1968)
American press agent: C1580

MANLEY, Mary de la Rivière (1663-1724)
British playwright: A22, p. 118

MANN, Louis (1865-1931)
American actor, producer, playwright: A3, n. p.; A16, II, 102; A103, pp. 72-3

MANNERING, Mary [born Florence Friend; Mrs. James K. Hackett] (1876-1953)
English actress: A3, n. p.; A13, p. 9; A16, II, 106; A23, pp. 228-30; A52, pp. 237-50; A55, n. p., por.; A61, pp. 103-04; A103, pp. 40-41; A106, pp. 156-60; A125, pp. 730-32

MANOLA, Marion [Mrs. Mould; Mrs. John Mason; Mrs. George G. Gates] (c. 1866-1914)
American singing actress: A25, pp. 259-72; A30, pp. 259-71; A66, n. p.

MANSFIELD, Richard (1857-1907)
English   actor,   manager: A1, n. p.; A13, p. 2; A16, p. 121; A23, pp. 230-34; A44, I, 40-41; A46, pp. 111-8; A50, pp. 371-6; A52, pp. 25-40; A54, pp. 61-79; A61, pp. 167-70; A62, pp. 71-108; A64, pp. 62-104; A66, n. p.; A77, pp. 135-45; A79, pp. 78-9; A80, pp. 174-9; A81,

II, 103; A103, pp. 10-11; A105, pp. 36-57; A108, pp. 136-8; A113, pp. 214-38; A121, I, 301-14, II, 207-32; A125, pp. 733-9; C2519; C2527

MANTELL, Robert Bruce (1854-1928)
American actor, manager: A3, n. p.; A8, pp. 96-7; A13, p. 4; A16, II, 48; A21, pp. 70-71; A23, pp. 234-7; A44, III, 14-5; A50, pp. 370-71; A66, n. p.; A81, II, 106; A103, pp. 170-71; A105, pp. 288-96; A125, pp. 740-44; C396; C838

MANTLE, [Robert] Burns (1873-1948)
American critic: B20, p. 908

MANUCH, Cosmo
British playwright: A22, p. 63

MARBE, Fay
Actress: A102, pp. 209-14

MARBLE, Danforth (1807-49)
American actor: A125, pp. 745-7; C1359

MARBLE, Mary (1876-1965)
Actress: A16, II, 83

MARBURY, Elizabeth (1856-1933)
American agent: C1583

MARCELINE [born Marceline Orbes]
Spanish clown: A16, p. 115

MARCH, Fredric (1897-1975)
American actor: A13, p. 112

MARINOFF, Fanny (1890-1971)
Actress: A16, p. 76

MARIVAUX [born Pierre de Carlet de Chamblain] (1688-1763)
French playwright: C1042

MARKHAM, Gervase (?1568-1637)
British playwright: A22, p. 41

MARKHAM, Pauline [Mrs. Jean Gravel] (1847-1919)
American actress: A96, pp. 307-08; A110, pp. 25-6; C1588

MARKS, Jeanette Augustus (1875–1964)
American playwright: C20, pp. 910–11

MARLOWE, Christopher (1564–93)
English playwright: A22, p. 8; A109, pp. 1–23; C128; C306; C307;   C804;   C1203;   C1242; C2083

MARLOWE, Julia [born Sarah F. Frost; Mrs. Robert Taber; Mrs. E. H. Sothern] (1866-1950)
Scottish actress, manager: A3, n. p.; A5, pp. 155–9; A8, pp. 76–7; A13, p. 13; A16, III, 194; A23, pp. 237–41; A44, II, 24–5; A50, pp. 423–7; A52, pp. 165–82; A55, n. p., por.; A56, pp. 299–323; A61, pp. 173–6; A63, pp. 67–94; A64, pp. 196–218; A66, n. p.; A77, pp. 159–69; A79, pp. 90–91; A81, II, 101; A101, n. p., por.; A102, pp. 215–20;   A103, pp. 78–9; A106, pp. 27–38; A112, pp. 101–30; A114, pp. 119–38; A115, pp. 77–88; A122, pp. 447–74; A123, II, 73–84, 88–123; A125, pp. 752–6; C178; C2093; C2240

MARMION, Shakerley (1603-39)
British playwright: A22, p. 48

MARQUIS, Don (1878-1937)
American playwright: B20, pp. 913–4; C681

MARS, Mlle. [born Anne F. H. Bontet] (1779-1847)
French actress: A91, pp. 92-100

MARSDEN, Fred [born W. A. Silver] (d. 1888)
American playwright: A96, pp. 308–09

MARSH, Charles
British playwright: C22, p. 189

MARSHALL, Anne [Mrs. Peter Quin] (17th century)
British actress: A119, pp. 168–70

MARSHALL, Rebecca (17th century)
British actress: A119, pp. 170–72

MARSTON, John (1576-1634)
British playwright: A22, p. 37; C435

MARSTON, John Westland (1819-90)
Playwright: C1524; C1594; C2541

MARSTON, Vivian
A16, II, 54

MARTIN, Mary (1913--)
American singing actress: A13, p. 123; A125, pp. 757-60; C1597

MARTIN, Millicent (1934--)
English actress: A32, pp. 77-9

MARTINOT, Sadie [born Sarah Martin; Mrs. Fred Stinson; Mrs. Louis F. Nethersole] (1861-1923)
American actress: A25, pp. 129–38; A30, pp. 129-37; A44, IV, 8-9; A66, n. p.; A96, p. 309; A103, pp. 114-5

MARTYN, Edward (1859-1923)
British playwright: A116, II, 13-6

MARX FAMILY: C607

MARX, Chico (1891-1961)
American performer: C1604

MARX, Groucho [born Julius Henry Marx] (1895-1977)
American performer: A20, pp. 102-05; A125, pp. 761-7; B23, pp. 234-40; C1601; C1602

MARX, Harpo (1893-1964)
American performer: C1603

MASCHIVITZ, Eric (1901-69)
English playwright: C1606

MASEFIELD, John (1878-1967)
English playwright: A116, II, 16-22; B20, pp. 924-7; C572; C2217

MASON, Elizabeth [Mrs. Crooke] (1780-1835)
English actress: A81, II, 20

MASON, Alfred E. W. (1865-1948)
English playwright: B20, p. 927

MASON, James (1909-84)
English actor: C1608

MASON, John B. [born Hill Belcher] (1857-1919)
American actor: A3, n. p.; A16, III, 244; A23, pp. 241-3; A66, n. p.; A105, pp. 110-18

MASON, Rufus O. (1830-1903)
American writer: C1609

MASSEN, Louis F. (1855-1925)
French actor, director: A16, III, 39; A66, n. p.

MASSETT, Stephen C. (1820-98)
British actor: C1610

MASSEY, Raymond (1896-1983)
Canadian actor: A13, p. 120; A125, pp. 768-70; C1611; C1612

MASSINGER, Philip (1583-1640)
English playwright: A22, pp. 42-3; C615; C662; C778

MASSON, William Charles (d. 1933)
American actor: A98, pp. 117-8

MATHER, Margaret [born Finlayson; Mrs. Haberkorn] (1860-98)
Canadian actress: A66, n. p.; A81, II, 104

MATHEWS, Ann [Mrs. Charles Mathews, Sr.] (1782-1869)
English actress: C1613

MATHEWS, Charles (1776-1835)
English actor: A6, II, 214-34; A7, II, 279-306; A12, pp. 182-8; A73, pp. 191-216; A81, I, 66-8; A92, pp. 312-9; A125, pp. 771-5; C94; C1614

MATHEWS, Charles James (1803-78)
English actor, playwright: A4, pp. 381-401; A26, I, 209-44; A28, II, 133-81; A68, pp. 47-56, 187-98; A69, II, 159-70; A72, pp. 197-215; A81, I, 95-6; A88, pp. 247-78; A92, pp. 390-92; A125, pp. 776-9; C1615

MATHEWS, John
English actor: C1616

MATTHEWS, Alfred Edward (1869-1960)
English actor: A47, pp. 75-84; C1617

MATTHEWS, [James] Brander (1852-1929)
American critic: A16, II, 59; C1620; C1621

MATTHEWS, Jessie (1907-81)
English actress, dancer: C1622

MATTHISON, Arthur L. (1826-83)
British actor, playwright: C1623

MATTOCKS, Isabella [born Holland] (1745-1826)
British actress: A81, I, 37; A92, pp. 196-8

MATURIN, Charles Robert (1782-1824)
British playwright: C1283

MAUDE, Cyril (1862-1951)
English actor, manager: A86, n. p., por.; B15, pp. 196-7; C348; C687; C918; C1624; C1625; C1626

MAUGHAM, William Somerset (1874-1965)
English playwright: A116, II, 22-42; B20, pp. 934-6; B23, pp. 240-42; C570; C628; C1344; C1627; C1670; C1724; C1979

MAUREL, Victor (1848-1923)
French singer: A44, VIII, 38-9

MAY, Edna [born Pettie; Mrs. Frederick Titus; Mrs. Oscar Lewisohn] (1875-1948)
American actress: A13, p. 39; A16, III, 206; A61, pp. 179-81;

A96, p. 311; A103, pp. 28-9; A107, pp. 147-55

MAY, Thomas (1595-1650)
British playwright: A22, pp. 40-41; C475

MAYAKOVSKY, Vladimir (1894-1930)
Russian playwright: C465; C2551

MAYCLIFFE, May
A16, II, 277

MAYER, Edwin Justus (1897-1960)
American playwright: C1630

MAYER, Sylvain (1863-1948)
British playwright: C1631

MAYHEW, Kate (1853-1944)
American actress: A96, p. 312

MAYHEW, Stella [born Izetta E. Sadler] (1875-1934)
American actress: A16, III, 265

MAYO, Eleanor
Singing actress: A44, II, 40-41

MAYO, Frank (1839-96)
American actor, manager, playwright: A21, pp. 46-8; A44, IX, 18-9; A66, n. p.; A96, p. 312; C857

MAYWOOD, Augusta [born Williams] (1825-76)
Dancer: A79, pp. 48-9

MAYWOOD, Robert Campbell (1786-1856)
Actor: A81, II, 23

McALISTER, Jessie
Actress: A16, II, 209

McALLISTER, Paul (1875-1955)
American actor: A16, p. 150

McARDELL, Helen
American performer: A58, pp. 102-15

McCAMBRIDGE, Mercedes (1918--)
American actress: C1638

McCarthy, Lillah [Mrs. Harley Granville Barker] (1875-1960)
English actress: A16, p. 209; C1641

McCAULL, Angela
A16, III, 79

McCLINTIC, Guthrie (1893-1961)
American director: C2342

McCLOSKY, J. J. (1826-1913)
Playwright, manager: A96, pp. 314-5

McCOLLOM, James C. (1838-83)
Actor: A81, II, 87

McCOURT, Peter
American actor, manager: C10

McCOWEN, Alec (1925--)
British actor: C1645; C1646

McCRACKEN, Joan (1922-61)
American actress: A13, p. 150

McCULLERS, Carson (1917-67)
American playwright: A65, II, 70-74

McCULLOUGH, John (1832-85)
Irish actor, manager: A7, pp. 204-30; A50, pp. 354-5; A66, n. p.; A74, pp. 265-86; A79, pp. 62-3; A81, II, 65-7; A91, pp. 191-5; A96, pp. 315-6; A111, pp. 44-6; A121, I, 185-205; A123, I, 240-77; A125, pp. 716-22; C502; C1286

McDONOUGH, John Edwin (1825-82)
Actor: A96, p. 316

McEWAN, Geraldine [born McKeown] (1933--)
English actress: A32, pp. 38-9

McHENRY, James (1785-1845)
Playwright: C355

McHENRY, Nellie [Mrs. John Webster] (1853-1935)
Actress: A25, pp. 385-99; A30, pp. 385-99; A66, n. p.

McINTOSH, Burr (1862-1942)
American actor: A16, III, 196;
A44, VI, 26-7; A52, pp. 211-22;
A103, pp. 206-07

McINTOSH, Madge (1875-1950)
British actress: A16, II, 95

McINTYRE, James
Minstrel: A53, pp. 35-7

McKENNA, Virginia
C1653

McKENZIE, Beatrice
Actress: A16, II, 269

McLEAN, R. D. (1859-1948)
American actor: A16, II, 71
(See MacLEAN, R. D.)

McMaster, Anew (1891-1962)
American actor: C889

McNALLY, Terrence (1939--)
American playwright: A65, II,
74-82

McNAUGHTON, Fred (c. 1869-1920)
A16, II, 125

McNAUGHTON, Tom (1867-1923)
English actor: A16, II. 135

McNEAL, Violet
Medicine show actress: C1655

McRAE, Bruce (1867-1927)
British actor: A16, II, 30

McVICKER, James Horace (1822-96)
American actor, manager: A96,
pp. 318-9

McVICKER, Sarah
Actress: A16, III, 95

MEAD, Robert
British playwright: A22, p. 63

MEADE, Edwards Hoag (b. 1863)
American actor: C1656

MEADOWS, Drinkwater (c. 1795-
1869)
British actor: A12, pp. 188-9

MEDBOURNE, Matthew (d. 1679)
British playwright: A22, p. 87

MEDINA, Louise [Mrs. Thomas Ham-
blin] (c. 1795-1838)
American actress, playwright:
A81, II, 35; A96, pp. 319-20

MEDOFF, Mark (1940--)
American playwright: A65, II,
82-6

MEI LAN-FANG (1894-1943)
Chinese actor: C1481; C2137

MEIGHAN, Thomas (1879-1936)
American actor: B15, pp. 200-
01

MELBA, Nellie [born Helen Porter
Mitchell] (1861-1931)
Australian singer: C2590

MELFORD, Mark (d. 1914)
British actor, manager, playwright: C1658

MELLISH, Fuller [born Leclerq]
(1865-1936)
English actor: A16, II, 20

MELLON, Harriot [Duchess of St.
Albans] (1775-1837)
British actress: A6, II, 123-4;
A42, pp. 399-438; A92, pp. 320-
22; C165; C1667; C1883

MELMOTH, Charlotte [Mrs. Courtney
Melmoth] (1749-1823)
English actress: A81, II, 19

MELTZER, Charles Henry (1852-
1936)
English playwright, critic:
A16, p. 132

MELVILLE, Rose (1873-1946)
American actress: A16, II, 40

MENKEN, Adah Isaacs [born Ade-
laide McCord] (1835-68)
American actress: A8, pp. 64-5;
A45, pp. 12-7; A81, II, 76-7;
A125, pp. 780-83; B22, pp. 319-
22; C148; C830; C886; C1478;
C1489; C1581

MERCOURI, Melina (1925--)
Greek actress: A51, pp. 73-82,
97-110

MEREDITH, Burgess (1909--)
American actor, director, producer: A80, pp. 267-8

MERITON, Thomas
British playwright: A22, p. 72

MERIVALE, Herman Charles (1839-
1906)
British playwright: C1674

MERIVALE, Philip (1886-1946)
British actor: B15, pp. 202-03

MERMAN, Ethel [born Ethel Agnes
Zimmerman] (1912-84)
American singing actress: A13,
p. 121; A79, pp. 162-3; A125,
pp. 784-9; A126, pp. 287-305;
B26, pp. 333-42; C1675; C1676

MERRILEES, Carrie
Actress: A16, II, 210

MERRILL, John (b. 1875)
C1677

MERRITT, Grace (1881-1919)
Actress: A16, II, 168

MERRY, Anne [born Brunton; Mrs.
Robert Merry] (1768-1808)
Actress: A81, II, 17-8; A125,
pp. 700-94; C737

MESTAYER, William A. (1844-96)
American actor: A96, p. 322

MEYENDORFF, Stella Z. A.
English actress: C1679

MEYERHOLD, Vsevelod (1874-1942)
Russian director, actor: C1229

MICHAEL, Edward (1853-1950)
British business manager: C1682

MICHELENA, Vera (1884-1961)
Actress: A16, II, 144

MICHELL, Keith (1928--)
Australian actor: A32, pp. 71-3

MIDDLETON, George (1846-1926)
American circus performer:
C1683

MIDDLETON, George (1880-1967)
American playwright: B20, pp.
955-6; C1684

MIDDLETON, Thomas (?1580-1627)
English playwright: A22, pp.
32-3; C155

MIELZINER, Jo (1901-76)
American designer : B15, pp.
204-05

MILDENBERG, Albert (1878-1918)
A16, II, 28

MILES, Sarah (1941--)
English actress: A32, pp. 20-21

MILLARD, Evelyn [Mrs. R. P. Coul-
ter] (1869-1941)
English actress, producer: A16,
p. 207; A50, pp. 429-30

MILLER, Arthur (1915--)
American playwright: A65, II,
86-111; C1792; C2457

MILLER, Charles T. K. (c. 1867-
1911)
American actor, manager: A16,
III, 195

MILLER, David Prince (1808-73)
British manager: C1687

MILLER, Henry (1860-1926)
English actor, manager: A1,
n. p., por.; A3, n. p.; A8, pp.
40-41; A13, p. 25; A16, II, 45;
A21, p. 79; A23, pp. 243-5;
A38, n. p.; A44, I, 44-5; A61,
pp. 185-8; A64, pp. 422-3;
A103, pp. 232-3; A105, pp. 190-
99; A125, pp. 795-9; C1743

MILLER, James (d. 1744)
Playwright: C2277

MILLER, Jason (1939--)
American playwright: A65, II,
112-5

MILLER, Joaquim [born Cincinnatus
H. Miller] (1837-1913)
American playwright: A96, p.
328; C2416

MILLER, Marilyn [born Mary Ellen
Reynolds] (1898-1936)
American performer: A13, p. 86;
A84, pp. 59-66; B15, pp. 206-
07

MILLER, Ruby (1889-1976)
British actress: C1691

MILLETT, Maude [Mrs. Tennant]
(1867-1920)
British actress: A16, II, 250

MILLIKEN, Sandol
A16, p. 260

MILLS, John (1908--)
English actor: A9, p. 28, por.;
C1692

MILLWARD, Jessie [Mrs. John Glen-
dinning] (1861-1932)
English actress: A16, II, 163;
A23, pp. 249-51; A61, pp. 191-
2; A81, II, 110; A96, p. 323;
A103, pp. 82-3; C1693

MILN, Louise Jordan (1864-1933)
British actress: C1694

MILNE, Alan A. (1882-1956)
English playwright: A116, II,
42-5; B20, pp. 964-5; C1695

MILTON, Ernest (1890-1974)
American actor: A50, p. 450

MILTON, John (1608-74)
English playwright: A22, pp.
51-2; C1762

MILTON, Maud (1859-1945)
English actress: A16, p. 79

MILWARD, Dawson (1870-1926)
English actor: A16, p. 163

MINER, Henry Clay (d. 1900)
American manager: A49, pp. 332-
3; A96, pp. 324-5

MINNELLI, Liza (1946--)
American singing actress: C2597

MINZELLI, Helene
Dancer: A110, pp. 21-2

MISHLER, Isaac J. (b. 1862)
American manager: A49, pp. 329-
30

MISTINGUETT [Marie Jeanne Bour-
geois] (1875-1956)
French performer: A35, p. 85,
por.; C1700; C1701

MITCHELL, Dodson (1868-1939)
American actor, playwright:
A16, II, 35

MITCHELL, Joseph (c. 1675-1738)
British playwright: A22, p. 169

MITCHELL, Julian (c. 1844-1926)
American actor, director: A96,
p. 313

MITCHELL, Langdon (1862-1935)
American playwright: A65, II,
115-20

MITCHELL, Maggie [Mrs. Paddock]
(1832-1918)
American actress: A23, pp. 252-
5; A44, I, 54-6; A66, n. p.;
A77, pp. 309-20; A81, II, 65;
A125, pp. 800-03

MITCHELL, Mason (b. 1859)
A44, VIII, 10-11

MITCHELL, Yvonne (1925-79)
English actress, playwright:
A76, pp. 78-90; C1703

MITFORD, Mary (1787-1855)
British playwright: C1704;
C1705; C1706; C2449

MIZNER FAMILY: C1328

MIZNER, Wilson (1876-1933)
American playwright: B23, pp.
246-52; C2298

MODJESKA, Helena [born Modrzejew-
ska] (1840-1909)

Polish actress: A1, n. p., por.; A2, n. p.; A8, pp. 54-5; A14, p. 36; A23, pp. 255-8; A25, pp. 105-16; A30, pp. 105-15; A44, I, 18-9; A46, pp. 104-10; A56, pp. 52-92; A64, pp. 1-27; A66, n. p.; A71, pp. 193-210; A75, pp. 193-210; A77, pp. 72-80; A81, II, 88-9; A91, pp. 223-6; A101, n. p., por.; A103, pp. 130-31; A106, pp. 306-22; A121, II, 330-38; A123, I, 359-97; A125, pp. 804-10; B25, pp. 15-20; C52; C528; C533; C556; C1057; C1707

MOELLER, Philip (1880-1958)
American producer, director: C2479

MOISEIWITSCH, Tanya (1914--)
English designer: C218

MOLIERE [born Jean Baptiste Poquelin] (1622-73)
French actor, manager, playwright: A91, pp. 8-15; A109, pp. 24-52; C464; C471; C1619; C1855

MOLLOY, Charles (d. 1767)
British playwright: A22, p. 159

MOLNAR, Ferenc (1878-1952)
Hungarian playwright: B15, pp. 208-09; B20, pp. 970-71; C1710

MONKHOUSE, Allan N. (1858-1936)
English playwright, critic: A116, II, 46-9; B20, p. 971

MONTAGUE, Henry J. (1844-78)
Actor: A21, pp. 35-9; A44, VI, 6-7; A122, pp. 143-7

MONTAGUE, Joseph
British playwright: A22, p. 60

MONTAGUE, Lee (1927--)
Actor: A76, pp. 138-53

MONTEZ, Lola [born Marie D. E. R. Gilbert] (1818-61)
Irish actress: A14, pp. 2-11; A125, pp. 811-4; C655; C996; C1218; C2554

MONTGOMERY, William
A16, III, 276

MONTGOMERY, David (1870-1917)
Actor, manager: A16, II, 102

MONTHERLANT, Henry de (1896-1972)
French playwright: C616

MOODY, John (1724-1813)
British actor: A81, I, 27; A92, pp. 146-7; A93, pp. 57-8; A96, p. 329

MOODY, William Vaughn (1869-1910)
American playwright: A16, II, 159; A65, II, 120-25; B20, pp. 976-7; C1088; C1176; C1714

MOORE, Decima [Mrs. Walker Leigh; Mrs. Frederick G. Guggisberg] (1871-1964)
Actress: A16, II, 272

MOORE, Edward (1712-57)
British playwright: C449

MOORE, Eva (1870-1955)
English actress: C1715

MOORE, Florence E. [Mrs. John Ogden Kerner] (1886-1935)
American actress: A16, III, 260

MOORE, Frank F. (1855-1931)
Irish playwright: B20, p. 977

MOORE, George (1852-1933)
Irish playwright: A24, pp. 57-154; A116, II, 50-61; B21, pp. 192-203

MOORE, Grace (1901-47)
American singer: B15, pp. 214-5

MOORE, Irene (b. 1890)
A16, II, 218

MOORE, J. H.
Manager: A49, pp. 316-7

MOORE, Mary [Mrs. Albery; Lady Charles Wyndham] (1861-1931)
English actress: A16, II, 156; C1716

MOORE, Maud
A110, pp. 39-40

MOORE, Thomas (1779-1852)
British playwright: A22, p.
165; C1717

MOORE, Tom (1874-1955)
Irish actor: C2296

MOORE, Victor F. (1876-1962)
American actor: A13, p. 68;
A16, II, 61

MOOREHEAD, Agnes (1906-74)
American actress: C2175

MOORES, Clara
A102, pp. 153-8

MORALES, Gabrielle
A110, pp. 27-8

MORDAUNT, Frank [born Arthur H.
Markham] (1841-1906)
American actor: A23, pp. 258-
61; A44, VIII, 42-3; A96, p.
330

MORE, Kenneth (1914-82)
English actor: C1719; C1720

MOREHOUSE, Ward (1898-1966)
American playwright, critic:
C1722

MORETTI, Eleanor [Mrs. Charles P.
Huntington] (d. 1918)
A16, III, 97

MORGAN, Beatrice
A16, III, 141

MORGAN, Edward J.
Actor: A23, pp. 261-4; A61, pp.
195-7

MORGAN, Eloise
Singing actress: A44, III, 36-
7

MORGAN, Helen (1900-41)
American singing actress: A125,
pp. 815-8; B15, pp. 220-21;
C1629

MORGAN, Lizzie
Australian actress: A98, pp.
75-6

MORISON, Lindsay (d. 1917)
English actor: A98, pp. 41-2

MORISON, Rose [born Cummings;
Mrs. Lindsay Morison]
Actress: A98, pp. 83-4

MORLEY, Henry (1822-94)
British playwright, editor,
critic: C1727

MORLEY, Robert (1908--)
English actor, playwright: A9,
p. 29, por.; A76, pp. 34-46;
C1728; C1729; C1730

MOROSCO, Oliver (1875-1945)
American manager, director:
C1735

MORRIS, Clara [born Morrison or
La Montagne; Mrs. Frederick C.
Harriott] (c. 1848-1925)
Canadian actress: A5, pp. 196-
9; A8, pp. 30-31; A14, pp. 107-
10; A16, II, 78; A23, pp. 264-
7; A25, pp. 353-74; A30, pp.
353-73; A44, VII, 4-5; A50, pp.
363-4; A64, pp. 416-21; A66,
n. p.; A71, pp. 211-28; A75,
pp. 211-28; A77, pp. 88-93;
A81, II, 103-4; A111, pp. 18-
20; A121, II, 171-94; A123, I,
562-75; A125, pp. 819-24;
C1736; C1737; C1739

MORRIS, Felix (1850-1900)
English actor: A66, n. p.;
C1740

MORRIS, Mrs. Maesmore
Actress: A86, n. p., por.

MORRIS, Nina
Actress: A98, pp. 63-4

MORRIS, William (1861-1932)
Actor: A66, n. p.; A96, p. 332;
A103, pp. 92-3

MORRISON, Arthur (1863-1945)
English playwright: B20, pp.

988-90

MORRISON, Lewis (1845-1906)
British actor, manager: A16,
II, 203; A23, pp. 267-9; A66,
n. p.; A96, p. 332

MORRISSEY, James W. (c. 1853-
1917)
American manager, press agent:
C1741

MORTIMER, John (1923--)
English playwright, critic:
C1745

MORTON, Charles (1819-1904)
British actor: C1746

MORTON, Teckla
Swedish actress: A66, n. p.

MORTON, William (1838-1938)
British producer: C1747

MOSCONI, Charles
American performer: A100, pp.
140-68

MOSES, Montrose Jonas (1878-1934)
American critic: C1021

MOSS, Edward
British playwright: A22, p. 193

MOSS, Theodore
British playwright: A22, p. 194

MOSSOP, Henry (1729-73)
Irish actor: A6, I, 207-12; A7,
I, 270-76; A41, pp. 228-39;
A70, pp. 171-88; A81, I, 28-9;
A92, pp. 147-51

MOSTEL, Kate
C1639

MOSTEL, Zero [born Sam Joel Mos-
tel] (1915-77)
American actor: A79, pp. 176-7;
A125, pp. 825-30; C1756; C2422

MOTT, Edward Spencer (1844-1910)
English actor: C1757

MOTTEUX, Peter Anthony (1660/63-

1718)
British playwright: A22, pp.
124-5

MOTTLEY, John (1692-1750)
British playwright: A22, pp.
168-9

MOUNEY-SULLY [born Jean Sully
Mounet] (1841-1916)
French actor: A44, VIII, 22-3;
A123, I, 414-22

MOUNTAIN, Rosaman (1771-1840)
British actress: A81, I, 60;
A92, p. 294

MOUNTFORT, Susannah [Mrs. William
Mountfort] (1669-1703)
British actress: A6, I, 66-8;
A7, I, 84-6; A92, pp. 39-41;
A119, pp. 177-81

MOUNTFORT, William (1660-92)
British actor, playwright: A6,
I, 59-60; A7, I, 74-5; A22, p.
112; A28, I, 1-37; A45, I, 76-
80; A92, pp. 27-8; C318

MOWATT, Anna Cora [born Ogden;
Mrs. William F. Ritchie] (1819-
70)
American actress, playwright:
A46, pp. 48-50; A74, pp. 155-
70; A81, II, 27; A125, pp. 831-
6; B25, pp. 68-72; C158; C294;
C1639; C2030; C2031

MOZART, George (1864-1947)
English performer: C1759

MULLE, Ida (1863-1934)
American singing actress: A66,
n. p.; A96, p. 335

MULLEN, Barbara (1914--)
American actress: C1763

MUNDEN, Joseph Shepherd (1758-
1832)
English actor: A4, pp. 358-70;
A6, II, 235-7; A7, II, 307-10;
A12, pp. 189-201; A73, pp. 97-
116; A81, I, 52-3; A92, pp.
256-61; A93, pp. 121-8; C1765

MUNI, Paul [born Weisenfreund]
(1895-1967)
Austrian-American actor: A125,
pp. 837-45

MUNSHIN, Jules (1915-70)
American actor: C1766

MURDOCH, James E. (1812-93)
American actor, manager: A50,
pp. 351-2; A81, II, 41-2; A125,
pp. 846-51; C788; C1767

MURDOCK, John J. (1865-1948)
Manager: A49, pp. 313-5; A96,
pp. 335-6

MURPHY, Arthur (1730-1805)
British actor, playwright: A45,
II, 119-27; A92, pp. 153-4;
C543; C768; C810

MURPHY, John Daly [born J. D.
Conlon] (1873-1934)
Irish actor: A16, p. 42

MURPHY, Joseph (d. 1914)
Actor: A66, n. p.

MURPHY, Tim (1861-1928)
American actor: A3, n. p.; A16,
II, 98; A103, pp. 214-5

MURRAY, Alma (1854-1945)
English actress: A16, II, 259

MURRAY, Gilbert (1866-1957)
Australian playwright, translator: A116, II, 61-71; C1771

MURRAY, Katherine
American performer: A58, pp.
36-43

MURRAY, Ken (1903--)
American performer: A100, pp.
195-202; C1773

MURRAY, William Henry (1790-1852)
British manager, playwright:
C1774

MUSSET, Alfred de (1810-57)
French playwright: C1083;
C1776; C2149

MYERS, Annie [Mrs. Harry Myers]
(c. 1857-1935)
American actress: A44, VI, 20-
21; A66, n. p.

MYNITT, William (1710-63)
British actor: A92, pp. 89-90

NABBES, Thomas (b. 1605)
British playwright: A22, p. 45

NARES, Owen (1888-1943)
English actor, producer: A29,
pp. 35-6; A35, p. 94, por.;
C1781

NASH, Mary (1885-1976)
American actress: A13, p. 103

NASHE, Thomas (1567-1601)
British playwright: A22, p. 16;
C1187

NATHAN, George Jean (1882-1958)
American critic: B4, pp. 197-
207; B20, pp. 1007-08; C930

NAUDAIN, Mary (1880-1923)
American actress: A16, p. 226

NAZIMOVA, Alla (1879-1945)
Russian actress: A3, n. p.;
A13, p. 54; A16, II, 122; A79,
pp. 114-5; A80, pp. 253-4;
A125, pp. 852-7

NEAGLE, Anna (1904--)
English actress, producer: A57,
pp. 145-61; C1789

NEILSEN, Alice (b. 1875)
American singing actress: A103,
pp. 56-7

NEILSON, Adelaide [born Elizabeth
Ann Browne] (1848-80)
English actress: A8, pp. 112-3;
A14, pp. 43-8; A44, VI, 4-5;
A46, pp. 27-31; A50, pp. 361-3;
A66, n. p.; A69, II, 219-50;
A74, pp. 287-304; A81, II, 97-
8; A89, pp. 379-98; A91, pp.
227-9; A101, n. p., por.; A120,
pp. 279-301; A121, I, 47-62,
II, 268-76; A123, I, 544-61;

A125, pp. 858-63; C694; C1222; C1434

NEILSON, Charlotte
Actress: A1, n. p., por.; A2, n. p.

NEILSON, Julia [Mrs. Fred Terry] (1869-1957)
English actress: A16, II, 140; C1791

NEMIROVICH-DANCHENKO, Vladimir I. (1858-1943)
Russian actor, director, producer: C1794

NESBIT, Evelyn (1885-1967)
American performer: B19, pp. 82-5

NESBITT, Cathleen (1888-1982)
English actress: C1795

NETHERSOLE, Olga (1863-1951)
English actress, producer: A3, n. p.; A8, pp. 98-9; A16, II, 32; A44, IV, 36-7; A55, n. p., por.; A61, pp. 201-05; A64, pp. 297-301; A106, pp. 217-31; A123, II, 309-22; A125, pp. 864-72

NEVIL, Alexander
British playwright: A22, p. 6

NEVIL, Robert
British playwright: A22, p. 53

NEVILLE, Henry G. (1837-1910)
Actor: A16, II, 146; A48, II, 247-63

NEVILLE, John (1925--)
A18, pp. 99-130; A32, pp. 40-41

NEWCASTLE, Margaret Lucas Cavendish, Duchess of, (?1624-74)
English playwright: A22, pp. 74-5; C1798

NEWCASTLE, William Cavendish, Duke of (1592-1676)
English playwright: A22, pp. 73-4; C1799

NEWTON, Henry Chance (1854-1931)
English playwright, critic: C1804

NEWTON, Thomas
British playwright: A22, p. 7

NEY, Marie (b. 1895)
English actress: A9, p. 30, por.

NIBLO, Fred (1874-1948)
American actor: A16, II, 17

NICHOLS, Beverley (1899--)
English playwright, critic: B20, pp. 1021-2; C1805; C1806

NICHOLS, Blanche (d. 1947)
A16, II, 72

NICHOLS, Robert M. B. (1893-1944)
English playwright: B20, p. 1022

NICHOLSON, Kenyon (b. 1894)
American playwright: B20, pp. 1022-3

NIELSEN, Alice [Mrs. Benjamin Wentwig] (1876-1943)
American singing actress: A23, pp. 269-70; A44, XI, n. p.; A61, pp. 209-10; A107, pp. 1-20

NILLSON, Carlotta (c. 1878-1951)
Swedish actress: A3, n. p.

NIRDLINGER, Charles Frederic (1863-1940)
American playwright, critic: C1808

NISBETT, Louisa Cranstoun (?1812-58)
Actress: A69, II, 151-8

NOAH, Mordecai Manuel (1785-1851)
American playwright: C995; C1573; C2536

NOBLES, Dollie [Mrs. Milton Nobles] (c. 1863-1930)
American actress: A66, n. p.

NOBLES, Milton [born Tamey]

(1847-1924)
American actor, manager: A16,
II, 217; A44, VII, 30-31; A66,
n. p.; C1812

NOKES, James (d. 1696)
British actor: A6, I, 62-3; A7,
I, 78-80

NOLTE, Charles (1926--)
American actor, playwright:
A13, p. 144

NORMAN, Christine (d. 1930)
A16, III, 286

NORMAN, Mary [born Cope]
(c. 1870-1926)
Actress: A64, pp. 616-7

NORRIS, Henry ["Jubilee Dicky"]
(1665-1734)
British actor: A22, p. 172;
A92, pp. 32-3

NORRIS, William [born W. N.
Block] (1870-1929)
American actor: A3, n. p.; A16,
III, 146; A103, pp. 190-91

NORRIS, Bobby [born Harold Young]
(1881-1936)
A16, II, 46

NORTHALL, William Knight
American playwright: C1815

NORTON, William A. (c. 1880-1940)
American actor: A16, III, 182

NORWORTH, Jack (1879-1959)
American actor, composer: A16,
III, 22

NOSSITER, Miss
A97, pp. 143-4

NOVELLI, Ermete (1852-1919)
Italian actor, producer: A16,
III, 118

NOVELLO, Ivor [born I. N. Davies]
(1893-1951)
Welsh actor, playwright, producer, composer: A29, pp. 80-
84, 85-7; A35, p. 93, por.;

C1564; C1811

NUCE, Thomas
British playwright: A22, pp.
6-7

NUGENT, Elliott (1899-1980)
American actor, playwright,
producer: C1819

NUGENT, John C. (1868-1947)
American actor, playwright:
A96, p. 340; C1820

NYE, Simeon Nash (fl. 1882-1914)
American manager: C160

OAKER, Jane (1880-1960)
Actress: A16, II, 145

OAKES, Percy
American performer: A100, pp.
203-10

O'BRADY, Frederic (1903--)
French actor: C1823

O'BRIEN, Nora
Actress: A16, II, 206; A44, IX,
36-7

O'BRIEN, Pat (1899-1953)
American actor: C1825

O'BRIEN, Susan (d. 1827)
Actress: A28, II, 21-37

O'BRIEN, William (c. 1736-1815)
British actor, playwright: A7,
I, 289-90; A28, II, 21-37

O'CASEY, Eileen [born Katherine
Reynolds]
C1827

O'CASEY, Sean (1884-1964)
Irish playwright: A116, II, 71-
90; C248; C587; C832; C1410;
C1828; C1829; C1830; C1831;
C1832; C1833; C1834

ODELL, Maude (c. 1872-1937)
American actress: A16, III,
255; A98, pp. 59-60; A103, pp.
150-51

ODELL, Thomas (c. 1691-1749)
British playwright: A22, pp. 169-70

ODETS, Clifford (1906-63)
American playwright, director, actor: A65, II, 126-39; B20, pp. 1040-41; C966; C1671; C2451

O'HARA, Constance Marie (fl. 1920-55)
American playwright: A1837

O'HARA, Fiske (1878-1945)
Irish actor: A16, III, 78

O'KEEFE, Anna
American actress: A44, VIII, 16-7; A66, n. p.

O'KEEFFE, John (1747-1833)
Irish playwright: C932; C1838

OKLOPKOV, Nikolai P. (1900-67)
Russian actor, playwright, producer: C1654; C2244

OLCOTT, Chauncey [born John Chancellor] (1860-1932)
American actor: A3, n. p.; A13, p. 35; A16, III, 171; A21, pp. 59-61; A44, VIII, 26-7; A52, pp. 223-6; A103, pp. 158-9; C1839

OLDCASTLE, Flouina [Countess Josephina de Castelvecchio Frabsilis] (c. 1864-1932)
Actress: A16, p. 33

OLDFIELD, Ann ["Nance"] (1683-1730)
English actress: A6, I, 111-4; A7, I, 142-6; A11, pp. 11-32; A43, pp. 34-59; A45, I, 88-92; A81, I, 14-5; A89, pp. 41-76; A92, pp. 58-62; C798; C1840; C2047

OLDMIXON, Georgina [born Sidus; Mrs. John Oldmixon] (1763-1836)
British actress: A81, II, 17; A125, pp. 873-7

OLDMIXON, John (c. 1673-1742)
British playwright: A22, p. 153

OLIVER, Olive (c. 1871-1961)
American actress: A16, II, 147

OLIVER, Vic [born Viktor O. Samek] (1898-1964)
Austrian-English actor: C1842

OLIVIER, Laurence (1907--)
English actor, director, producer: A9, p. 31, por.; A13, p. 128; A17, pp. 274-84; A32, pp. 61-3; A39, pp. 204-37; A50, pp. 478-501; A125, pp. 878-86; C153; C578; C638; C645; C827; C1019; C1207; C1381; C1441; C1843

O'MARA, Joseph (1861-1927)
Singer: A16, II, 164

O'NEIL, Colette [Lady Constance Malleson]
British actress: C1844

O'NEIL, Nance [born Gertrude Lamson] (1874-1965)
American actress: A3, n. p.; A13, p. 36; A15, p. 52; A16, II, 229; A125, pp. 887-93

O'NEILL, Anne (b. 1872)
Actress: A44, V, 32-3; A52, pp. 79-90

O'NEILL, Eliza [Lady William W. Becher] (1791-1872)
British actress: A6, II, 244-7; A7, II, 319-23; A43, pp. 298-312; A50, pp. 345-6; A73, pp. 285-96; A81, I, 82-4; A92, pp. 359-63; A97, pp. 264-72; C1330

O'NEILL, Eugene Gladstone (1888-1953)
American playwright: A65, II, 139-65; A94, pp. 129-54; B4, pp. 175-8; B15, pp. 226-7; B20, pp. 1048-50; B28, pp. 662-8; C323; C326; C499; C962; C2213

O'NEILL, James (1849-1920)
Irish actor: A3, n. p.; A8, pp. 60-61; A16, III, 235; A23, pp. 270-72; A44, VII, 38-9; A61, pp. 213-5; A64, pp. 536-8; A66, n. p.; A77, pp. 299-308;

A94, pp. 94-115; A103, pp. 26-7; A105, pp. 136-48; A125, pp. 894-900

O'NEILL, Maire [born Allgood] (1887-1952)
Irish actress: A102, pp. 37-42

OPP, Julie [Mrs. William Faversham] (1871-1921)
American actress: A3, n. p.; A16, II, 38

OPPENHEIMER, George (1900-77)
American playwright, critic: C1845

O'RAMEY, Georgie (1886-1928)
American actress: A102, pp. 131-6

ORGER, Mary Ann [born Ivers] (1788-1849)
British actress: A12, pp. 203-06

OSBORN, Paul (1901--)
American playwright: C1422

OSTLER, William (d. 1614)
British actor: A27, pp. 202-05

OTERO, Nona
American performer: A58, pp. 36-43

OTIS, Elita Proctor (c. 1851-1927)
American actress: A44, VIII, 44-5

OTWAY, Thomas (1652-85)
English playwright: A22, pp. 98-9; C1091

OVERMAN, Lynne (1887-1943)
American actor: A102, pp. 263-70

OWEN, Cecil (c. 1873-1928)
A16, p. 130

OWEN, William F. (1844-1906)
Irish actor: A23, pp. 272-9

OWENS, John Edward (1823-86)

English actor: A81, II, 50-51; A98, pp. 43-6; A121, II, 142-50; A123, I, 215-21; C1852

OXBERRY, William (1784-1824)
English actor: A12, pp. 206-13

OZELL, John (d. 1743)
British playwright: A22, pp. 162-3

PACK, James
British actor: C2234

PAGE, Geraldine (1924--)
American actress: A125, pp. 901-08

PAGET, ffolliott
A44, VII, 20-21

PALFREY, May [born Lever; Mrs. Weedon Grossmith] (1873-1929)
English actress: A16, p. 105

PALLISER, Esther Walters (b. 1872)
Actress: A66, n. p.

PALMER, Albert M. (1838-1905)
American manager: A96, pp. 344-5; C2100

PALMER, Clara (d. 1938)
Actress: A16, III, 218

PALMER, John ["Plausible Jack"] (1747-98)
British actor: A6, I, 227-30; A7, I, 296-300; A28, I, 139-62; A81, I, 39-40; A92, pp. 201-04; A93, pp. 85-90; C2202

PALMER, Lilli [Mrs. Carlos Thompson] (1911--)
Austrian actress: A76, pp. 48-53; C1856

PALMER, Millicent [Mrs. Daniel Bandmann]
Actress: A16, II, 207

PALMER, Minnie [Mrs. John R. Rogers] (1860-1936)

A16, p. 82; A23, pp. 279-81; A25, pp. 185-94; A30, pp. 185-93; A66, n. p.; A81, II, 100; A110, pp. 7-8; C299

PAPP, Joseph (1921--)
American director, producer: C1509

PARKER, Henry Taylor (1867-1934)
American critic: C428; C1644

PARKER, Lottie Blair (1858-1937)
American actress, playwright: A96, p. 345

PARKER, Louis Napoleon (1852-1944)
English playwright: A16, II, 238; B20, p. 1076; C1861

PARRY, John Orlando (1810-79)
English singer: C1863

PARSONS, Samuel (b. 1762)
English actor: C1866

PARSONS, William (1736-95)
British actor: A6, I, 231-2; A7, I, 302-03; A28, I, 206-30; A92, pp. 172-4; A93, pp. 63-4; C229

PASSMORE, Walter (1867-1946)
English singing actor: A86, n. p., por.

PASTOR, Tony [born Antonio] (1835-1908)
American performer, manager: A16, p. 123; A53, pp. 9-14, 100-02; A93, pp. 71-8; A125, pp. 909-13; C2575

PATERSON, Peter [born James Glass Bertram] (1824-92)
English actor: C1870; C1871

PATON, Mary Anne [Mrs. Joseph Wood] (1802-64)
Scottish actress: A12, pp. 214-7

PATRICK, JOhn (1906--)
American playwright: A65, II, 166-71

PATRICK, Nigel (1913-81)
English actor: A32, pp. 68-9

PAUL, Isabella [born Featherstone; Mrs. Howard Paul] (1833-79)
English actress: A81, II, 75

PAUL, William M. (d. 1901)
A98, pp. 119-20

PAULDING, Frederick [born Dodge] (1859-1937)
American actor: A16, III, 40; A44, V, 10-11; A66, n. p.

PAULDING, James Kirke (1778-1860)
American playwright: C1182; C1875; C1876

PAULINE, J. Robert (d. 1942)
Hypnotist: A16, III, 143

PAXTON, Sydney [born S. P. Hood] (1860-1930)
English actor, producer: A16, p. 145; C1877

PAYNE, Ben Iden (1881-1976)
English actor, producer: C1878

PAYNE, Edmund (1865-1914)
Actor: A86, n. p., por.

PAYNE, John Howard (1791-1852)
American actor, playwright: A72, pp. 37-54; A81, II, 21-2; C338; C485; C1103; C1131; C1663; C1851

PAYTON, Corse (1867-1934)
American actor, manager: C68

PEABODY, Josephine Preston (1874-1922)
American playwright: B20, pp. 1086-7; C1881

PEAPS, William
British playwright: A22, p. 63

PEARSON, Beatrice (1920--)
American actress: A13, p. 143

PEELE, George (1556-96)
English actor, playwright: A22,

p. 17; C1238

PEILE, Frederick Kinsey (1862–1934)
British actor, playwright: C1891

PELISSIER, Harry Gabriel (1874–1913)
English actor, producer: C688; C1892

PEMBERTON, Brock (1885–1950)
American producer, director: C1199

PEMBERTON, Charles Reece (1790–1840)
British actor: C910

PENLEY, William Sydney (1851–1912)
English actor, manager: C1900

PENLEY, William (d. 1838)
British actor: A12, p. 218

PENNINGTON, W. H. (1832–1923)
English actor: C1901

PEPLE, Edward H. (1869–1924)
American playwright: A16, p. 180; C1903

PERCY, Esmé (1887–1957)
English actor, director: A47, pp. 95–104; A50, pp. 449–50

PERÉZ GALDÓS, Benito (1843–1920)
Spanish playwright: C253

PERKINS, Carrie E.
A110, pp. 23–4

PERKINS, Osgood (1892–1937)
American actor: A125, pp. 914–7

PERTWEE, Roland (1885–1963)
English playwright: B20, pp. 1096–6; C1909

PERUGINI [born John Chatterton] (1855–1914)
American singing actor: A66, n. p.

PETRIE, David Hay (1895–1948)
Scottish actor: A50, pp. 457–8

PETROVA, Olga (1886–1977)
English actress, playwright: C1911

PHELPS, Samuel (1804–78)
English actor, manager: A17, pp. 172–86; A26, I, 117–208; A31, pp. 20–30; A50, pp. 264–76; A69, n. p.; A74, pp. 69–90; A81, I, 102–04; A92, pp. 394–5; C531; C1913

PHILLIPS, William (d. 1734)
British playwright: A22, pp. 128–9

PHILLIPS, Adelaide (1833–99)
American actress: C2446

PHILLIPS, Alexandra [Mrs. Milton Fahrney] (c. 1876–1936)
Actress: A16, II, 247

PHILLIPS, Ambrose
British playwright: A22, pp. 155–6

PHILLIPS, Augustine (d. 1605)
British actor: A27, pp. 79–88

PHILLIPS, Augustus (1838–93)
A16, II, 177

PHILLIPS, Catherine
British playwright: A22, pp. 71–2

PHILLIPS, Mrs. E. J. (1830–1904)
Actress: A66, n. p.

PHILLIPS, Edward (1630–96?)
British playwright: A22, p. 183; C993

PHILLIPS, Francis Charles (1849–1921)
English manager, playwright: C1915

PHILLIPS, John (d. 1765)
British playwright: A22, p. 162

PHILLIPS, Margaret (1923––)

Welsh actress: A13, p. 146

PHILLIPS, Stephen (1868-1915)
English actor, playwright:
A116, II, 91-4; B20, pp. 1101-
02

PHILLIPS, Watts (1829-74)
British playwright: C1914

PHILLPOTTS, Eden (1862-1960)
British playwright: A116, II,
94-98

PICKLES, Wilfred (1904-78)
C1917

PICON, Molly [born Pyekoon; Mrs.
Jacob Kalich] (1898--)
American actress: C1918; C1919

PILKINGTON, Letitia
British playwright: A22, p. 193

PINCHOT, Rosamond (1904-38)
American actress: B15, pp. 228-
9

PINERO, Arthur Wing (1855-1934)
English playwright: A16, II,
123; A116, II, 98-110; C774;
C945; C1920

PINTER, Harold (1930--)
English playwright: C1160

PIRANDELLO, Luigi (1867-1936)
Italian playwright: B20, pp.
1107-09; C356; C1549; C2259

PIRANESI, Giovanni Battista
(1720-78)
Italian designer: C1204; C1634

PITMAN, James R. (c. 1843-1914)
American director: A98, pp. 11-
2

PITOU, Augustus (1843-1915)
American manager, playwright:
A16, II, 63; A96, p. 350; C1924

PITT, Fanny Addison (1844-1937)
English actress: A16, II, 267;
A98, pp. 73-4

PIX, Mary
British playwright: A22, pp.
125-6

PIXÉRÉCOURT, René Guilbert de
(1773-1844)
French playwright: C1415

PIXLEY, Annie [born Shea] (1858-
93)
American actress: A66, n. p.;
A81, II, 104

PLACIDE, Henry (1799-1870)
American actor, manager: A50,
p. 347; A59, pp. 3-20; A72, pp.
143-56; A81, II, 32; A125, pp.
918-22; C1345

PLANCHÉ, James Robinson (1796-
1880)
English playwright: C239;
C1779; C1925

PLAYFAIR, Nigel (1874-1934)
English actor, director, playwright, producer: C1927; C1929

PLOWMAN, Thomas Forder (1844-
1919)
British playwright, manager:
C1931

PLOWRIGHT, Joan [Baroness Olivier
of Brighton] (1929--)
English actress: A32, pp. 92-3

PLYMPTON, Eben (1853-1915)
American actor: A23, pp. 281-4;
A66, n. p.

POE, Elizabeth [born Arnold]
(1787-1811)
Actress: A81, II, 20

POEL, William (1852-1934)
English actor, director, producer: C2247; C2452; C2485

POITIER, Sidney (1924--)
American actor: A90, pp. 81-6;
C1934

POLK, Joseph B. (c. 1841-1902)
American actor: A66, n. p.

POLLOCK, CHanning (1880-1946)
American playwright: B20, pp.
1113-4; C1936; C1937

PONISI, Elizabeth [born Hanson;
Mrs. Samuel Wallis] (1818-99)
English actress: A81, II, 107

POOLE, John (1786-1872)
British playwright: C1942

POPE, Alexander (1762-1835)
British actor: A22, p.   157;
A92, pp. 271-2

POPE, Elizabeth [born Younge]
(1740-97)
British actress: A28, I, 231-
55; A43, pp. 160-68; A81, I,
33; A92, pp. 187-9

POPE, Jane (1734-1818)
British actress: A7, I, 401;
A81, I, 38-9

POPE, Thomas (d. 1604)
British actor: A27, pp. 120-28

POPPLE, WIlliam
British playwright: A22, p. 186

PORDAGE, Samuel
British playwright: A22, p. 133

PORTER, Cole (1891-1964)
American composer: B15, pp.
230-31; C795; C977; C2135

PORTER, Eric (1928--)
English actor: A18, pp. 131-58

PORTER, Mary Ann (1683-1765)
British actress: A6, I, 114-6;
A7, I, 146-9; A43, pp. 60-64;
A81, I, 14; A92, pp. 53-4

PO SEIN (?1880-1952)
Burmese actor: C2151

POSSART, Ernst (1841-1921)
German actor, manager: A81, II,
108

POST, Guy Bates (1875-1968)
American actor: A16, II, 213;
A103, pp. 270-71

POST, Lilly [Mrs.   William H.
Morton] (d. 1899)
Actress: A25, pp. 333-44; A30,
pp. 333-44

POTTER, Cora [born Urquhart; Mrs.
James Brown Potter] (1859-1936)
American actress: A16, II, 119;
A25, pp. 57-68; A30, pp. 57-67;
A44, I, 26-7; A64, pp. 329-45;
A66, n. p.; A81, II, 111-2;
A86, n. p., por.; A108, pp. 57-
68; A125, pp. 923-7

POTTER, Henry
British playwright: A22, p. 19

POTTER, Thomas
British playwright: A22, p. 77

POWELL, George (1669-1714)
British actor, playwright: A22,
p. 113; A92, pp. 38-9; C2434

POWELL, William (1736-69)
British actor: A92, pp. 174-5

POWER FAMILY: A78, pp. 281-308

POWER, Jewel
A16, III, 237

POWER, Tyrone I [born William
Grattan Tyrone] (1797-1841)
Irish actor: A12, p. 222; A68,
pp. 128-49; A81, I, 92; A92, p.
377; A96, pp. 353-4; A125, pp.
928-32; C1943

POWER, [Frederick] Tyrone II
(1869-1931)
English actor: A38, n. p.; A50,
pp. 392-3; C2531

POWERS, James Thomas (1862-1943)
American actor: A3, n. p.; A16,
II, 105; A66, n. p.; A103, pp.
144-5; A104, pp. 44-53; C1946

POYNTER, Beulah
A16, II, 136

PRATT, Lynn (1863-1930)
A16, III, 31

PREJEAN, Albert (b. 1898)

French actor: C1947

PRESCOTT, Marie (1853-93)
American actress: A66, n. p.;
A111, pp. 51-2

PRESTON, Harry (1860-1936)
British actor: C1948

PRESTON, Robert (1917--)
American actor: A125, pp. 933-8

PRESTON, Thomas (1537-98)
British playwright: A22, p. 3

PRESTWICK, Edmund
British playwright: A22, p. 58

PRICE, Lizzie [Mrs. H. A. Hanker;
Mrs.   Willie   Wintle;   Mrs.
Charles A. Fechter] (b. 1842)
American actress: A81, II, 89-
90

PRICE, Morton [born Horton Rhys]
(1824-76)
British actor, theatre lessee:
C2015

PRICE, Nancy [Mrs. Charles Maude]
(1880-1970)
English   actress: A9, p. 32,
por.; C1949

PRICE, Stephen (1783-1840)
American manager: A34, pp. 87-
142

PRICE, Vincent (1911--)
American actor: C1860; C1950;
C1951

PRIEST, Janet (b. 1881)
A16, II, 261

PRIESTLEY, John B. (1894--)
English playwright: A116, II,
110-16; B20, pp. 1129-30; C816;
C1955; C1956

PRIMROSE, George H. (1852-1919)
Canadian minstrel: A16, II, 254

PRINCE,   Adelaide   [born Ruben-
stein; Mrs. Creston Clarke]
(1866-1941)

English actress: A16, II, 273;
A66, n. p.

PRINCE, Harold S. (1928--)
American   producer,   director:
C1957

PRINTEMPS, Yvonne [Mrs.   Sacha
Guitry] (1895-1977)
French   actress: A35, p. 5,
por.

PRITCHARD, Hannah [born Vaughan]
(1711-68)
British actress: A6, I, 268-71;
A7, I, 349-52; A11, pp. 109-22;
A43, pp. 107-23; A81, I, 19-20;
A92, pp. 102-06; A97, pp. 88-97

PROBERT, George (d. 1957)
A16, III, 97

PROCTOR, Frederick F. (1876-1929)
American manager: A49, pp. 301-
06; C1595

PROCTOR, Joseph (1816-97)
American actor: A96, pp. 355-6

PURCELL, Alban W. (1844-1913)
American actor, manager, playwright: A98, pp. 121-2

PURDOM, Charles Benjamin (1883-
1965)
English critic: C1967

PUSHKIN, Alexander S. (1799-1837)
Russian   playwright: C1569;
C1698

PYNE, James Frederick (c. 1785-
1857)
British singer: A12, p. 222

PYPER, George D.
American performer: C1969

QUARLES, Francis (1592-1644)
British playwright: A22, pp.
60-61

QUARTERMAINE, Charles (1877-1958)
English actor: A16, III, 295

QUARTERMAINE, Leon (1876-1967)
English actor: A9, p. 33, por.;
A50, p. 431

QUICK, John (1748-1831)
British actor: A6, I, 221-2;
A7, I, 288-9; A81, I, 42; A92,
pp. 210-12

QUIN, James (1693-1766)
British actor: A6, I, 117-30;
A7, I, 150-68; A45, I, 183-214;
A50, pp. 60-61; A70, pp. 25-46;
A80, pp. 73-6; A81, I, 17-8;
A92, pp. 70-76; A99, pp. 75-96;
A117, pp. 108-20; C44; C1496

QUINLAN, Gertrude (1875-1963)
American actress: A16, II, 62

QUINN, Anthony (1915--)
Mexican-American actor: C1970

QUINN, Germain (b. 1866)
American stage mechanic: C1971

QUINTERO, José (1924--)
Panamanian director, producer:
C1973

RABE, David (1940--)
American playwright: A65, II,
172-8

RACHEL [born Elisabeth Félix]
(1821-58)
French actress: A28, II, 205-
31; A36, pp. 136-54; A37, II,
248-72; A60, pp. 30-67, 95-114;
A69, II, 279-89; A81, II, 48-9;
A89, pp. 305-42; A91, pp. 152-
6; A125, pp. 939-42; C31; C210;
C831; C1053; C1373; C1391;
C1599; C1742; C2018

RACINE, Jean (1639-99)
French playwright: C353; C497;
C761

RADCLYFFE, Cecilia
A16, II, 75

RAEBURN, Henzie [Mrs. E. Martin
Brown] (1900-73)
English actress: C384

RAFT, George (1903-80)
American actor: C2557

RAINS, Claude (1889-1967)
English actor: A47, pp. 135-43

RALEIGH, Cecil [born Rowlands]
(1856-1914)
British actor: A16, II, 37

RALEIGH, Isabel ["Saba"; born El-
lissen; Mrs. Cecil Raleigh]
(c. 1866-1923)
British actress: A86, n. p.,
por.

RALPH, James (?1695-1762)
British playwright: A22, p. 181

RAMBEAU, Marjorie (1889-1970)
American actress: A13, p. 62

RAMSAY, Allan (1686-1758)
British playwright: A22, p.
179; C1596

RAND, Rosa (1848-1920)
American actress: A16, p. 35

RANDALL, Harry (1860-1932)
British actor: C1977

RANDOLPH, Louise (c. 1870-1953)
American actress: A16, III, 79

RANDOLPH, Thomas (1605-35)
British playwright: A22, pp.
44-5; C2021; C2218

RANKIN, [Arthur] McKee (1841-
1914)
Canadian actor, manager: A5,
pp. 105-18; A23, pp. 285-7;
A81, II, 106; A96, pp. 355-6;
A125, pp. 943-7

RANKIN, Phyllis [Mrs. Harry
Thompson] (1874-1934)
American actress: A1, n. p.,
por.; A2, n. p.; A16, II, 197

RANOUS, Dora Knowlton (1859-1916)
American actress: C1327; C1978

RATCLIFFE, Edward J. (1863-1948)
English actor: A44, V, 34-5

RATHBONE, Basil (1892-1967)
South African actor: A125, pp.
948-51; C1980

RATTIGAN, Terence (1911--)
English playwright: C649

RAUCOURT, Françoise (1755-1815)
French actress: A37, II, 102-49

RAVENSCROFT, Edward (fl. 1671-97)
British playwright: A22, pp.
94-5

RAWLINGS,   Marjorie   Kinnan
(1906--)
British playwright: A9, p. 34,
por.

RAWLINS, Thomas (?1703-67)
British playwright: A22, pp.
56, 136

RAWSON, Thomas William (b. 1867)
A16, II, 234

RAYMOND, Ernest (1888-1974)
English   playwright: C1983;
C1984; C1985

RAYMOND, John T. [born John
O'Brien] (1836-87)
American actor: A66, n. p.;
A71, pp. 229-46; A75, pp. 229-
46; A81, II, 78-9; A111, pp.
35-8; A121, II, 200-06; A123,
I, 291-303; A125, pp. 361-7

RAYMOND, Maude [Mrs. Gus Rogers]
(c. 1872-1961)
American actress: A16, p. 183;
A107, pp. 233-8

RAYNER, Lionel Benjamin (1787-
1855)
British actor, manager: A12,
pp. 223-30

RAYNORE, Katherine
A16, p. 22

READE, Charles (1814-84)
English playwright: A26, II, 3-
116; C369; C405; C529; C807;
C1562; C1972; C1988

REDDISH, Samuel (1735-85)
British actor: A7, I, 276-7

REDFIELD, William (1927-76)
British   actor,   playwright:
C1990

REDGRAVE FAMILY: C1991

REDGRAVE, Michael (1908--)
English actor: A9, p. 35, por.;
A19, pp. 99-110; A32, p. 34;
A39, pp. 238-63; A50, pp. 504-
08; C864; C1992; C1993

REDGRAVE, Vanessa (1937--)
English actress: A18, pp. 159-
82

REDMUND, William (d. 1915)
English actor: A23, pp. 289-90

REED, Florence (1883-1967)
American actress: A13, p. 73;
A16, II, 251; B15, pp. 232-3

REED, Joseph (c. 1723-87)
British playwright: A22, p. 189

REED, Joseph Verner (1902-73)
American producer: C1994

REED, Roland (1852-1901)
American actor: A1, n. p.,
por.; A2, n. p.; A23, pp. 290-
92; A44, VII, 26-7; A64, pp.
539-40; A66, n. p.; A81, II,
111; A105, pp. 297-310

"REEDER, Louise" (1837-59)
American actress: C1995

REEVE, Ada [Mrs. Bert Gilbert;
Mrs.   Wilfred   Cotton]   (1874-
1966)
English actress: A86, n. p.,
por.; C1998

REEVE, John (1799-1838)
British actor: A12, pp. 230-33;
C143; C1989

REEVE, Wybert (1839-1906)
British actor, manager: C2000

REEVES, John Sims (1818-1900)

British singer: C2001; C2002

REHAN, Ada [born Crehan] (1860-
1916)
Irish actress: A1, n. p., por.;
A2, n. p.; A3, n. p.; A8, pp.
58-9; A14, pp. 49-55; A16, III,
107; A23, pp. 292-4; A25, pp.
301-05; A30, pp. 301-10; A44,
I, 38-9; A50, pp. 383-4; A56,
pp. 203-29; A61, pp. 219-21;
A64, pp. 241-54; A66, n. p.;
A77, pp. 146-53; A81, II, 102;
A101, n. p., por.; A103, pp.
44-5; A106, pp. 113-24; A112,
pp. 68-80; A121, I, 258-68, II,
156-70, 233-67; A123, II, 124-
74; A125, pp. 952-6; C1553;
C2522

REICHER, Hedwig (1884-1971)
German actress: A3, n. p.

REID, Margaret
Singing actress: A44, I, 10-11

REIFFARTH, Jennie (1848-1913)
American singing actress: A16,
p. 87

REIGNOLDS, Kate [Mrs. Henry Farren; Mrs. Erving Winslow]
English actress: A23, pp. 294-
7; A81, II, 65; C2004

REINHARDT, Max [born Goldman]
Austrian actor, director, pro-
ducer: C446; C2006; C2129;
C2297

REJANE, Gabrielle (1857-1920)
French actress: A44, V, 8-9;
A56, pp. 126-70; A64, pp. 167-
72; A86, n. p., por.

RENDLE, Thomas McDonald (1856-
1926)
English critic: C2008

REVELL, Dorothy [Mrs. T. H. Wyndham Walker] (1879-1908)
A16, p. 190

REVELLE, [Arthur] Hamilton [born
Engström] (1872-1958)
Actor: A16, III, 134

REVET, Edward
British playwright: A22, p. 91

REYNOLDS, E. Vivian (1866-1952)
English actor, stage manager:
A16, II, 148

REYNOLDS, Frederic (1764-1841)
British playwright: C2011

REYNOLDS, Harry
British minstrel: C2012

RHEA, Hortense (1844-99)
Belgian actress: A66, n. p.;
A81, II, 110

RICARD, Amy (c. 1878-1937)
A16, II, 19

RICCARDO, Corona (d. 1917)
Italian actress: A98, pp. 61-2;
A106, pp. 147-55

RICCOBONI, Luigi (c. 1675-1753)
Italian actor: C1857

RICE, Dan (1823-1900)
American actor, manager: C381;
C1412; C2203

RICE, Elmer L. [born Reizenstein]
(1892-1967)
American playwright: A65, II,
179-92; B15, pp. 234-5; B20,
pp. 1166-7; C2017

RICE, Fanny [Mrs. G. W. Prudy]
(1866-1936)
American actress: A16, III, 49;
A103, pp. 272-3

RICE, John (b. c. 1596)
British actor: A27, pp. 280-82

RICE, John B. (1809-72)
American actor, manager: A96,
p. 360

RICE, Thomas D. (1808-60)
American actor: A92, pp. 395-6;
A125, pp. 957-63

RICH, John (1681-1761)
English actor, manager: A81, I,
13; A92, pp. 48-52

RICHARDS, Isabel
A16, II, 233

RICHARDS, Nathaniel
British playwright: A22, p. 57

RICHARDSON, Jack (1935--)
American playwright: A65, II, 192-8

RICHARDSON, John (1766-1837)
British actor: A81, I, 61; A92, pp. 285-6

RICHARDSON, Locke
C1516

RICHARDSON, Ralph (1902-83)
English actor, producer: A9, p. 36, por.; A19, pp. 62-88; A50, pp. 502-03; A125, pp. 964-70; C1212; C1835

RICHEPIN, Jean (1849-1926)
French playwright: C2303

RICHINGS, Peter (1797-1871)
English singing actor: A81, II, 25-6; A96, p. 361; A117, pp. 19-22

RICHMAN, Charles J. (1870-1940)
American actor: A3, n. p.; A61, pp. 225-6; A103, pp. 136-7

RICHMAN, Harry (1894-1972)
American performer: C2023

RICHMOND, Dorothy
A16, III, 242

RIDDLE, George (1851-1910)
American actor: A23, pp. 297-9

RIDER, William
British playwright: A22, p. 64

RIGGS, Lynn (1899-1954)
American playwright: B20, pp. 1174-5; C109; C2510

RIGL, Emily
Dancer: A111, pp. 46-8

RIGNOLD, George (1838-1912)
English actor, manager: A66,

n. p.

RINEHART, Mary Roberts (1876-1958)
American playwright: C2027

RING, Blanche [Mrs. Frederick E. McKay] (1876-1961)
American performer: A13, p. 50; A16, III, 108

RINGGOLD, Benjamin T. (c. 1835-1905)
Actor: A23, pp. 300-06

RISTORI, Adelaide (1822-1906)
Italian actress: A8, pp. 80-81; A54, pp. 109-19; A60, pp. 68-94, 115-34; A81, II, 49; A88, pp. 399-431; A91, pp. 157-64; A121, II, 299-303; A125, pp. 970-79; B25, pp. 32-8; C854; C2029

RITCHIE, Adele (1874-1930)
American actress: A16, III, 290; A44, I, 42-3

RITCHIE, Franklyn (d. 1918)
Actor: A98, pp. 89-90

RITZ, Harry (1908--)
American performer: A100, pp. 179-81

ROBE, Annie [Mrs. Daniel P. Griswold] (1864-1922)
Actress: A81, II, 109

ROBERTS, Arthur (1852-1933)
English actor: A16, II, 213; C2035; C2036

ROBERTS, Florence [Mrs. Lewis Morrison] (1871-1927)
Actress: A3, n. p.; A16, III, 56; A103, pp. 302-3

ROBERTS, Franklyn (c. 1849-1907)
A16, p. 208

ROBERTS, James Booth (1818-1901)
American actor: A23, pp. 306-7; A81, II, 65

ROBERTS, Joan (c. 1920--)

American actress: C2038

ROBERTSON, Agnes [Mrs. Dion Bou-
cicault] (1833-1916)
Scottish actress: A23, pp. 307-
10; A75, pp. 77-94; A81, II,
50; A111, pp. 70-73; A125, pp.
980-82

ROBERTSON, Thomas William (1799-
1838)
British playwright: C2040

ROBERTSON, Thomas W. S. (1829-71)
English playwright: A26, II,
140, 64; A31, pp. 135-64;
C1896; C2127

ROBERTSON, Walford Graham (1867-
1948)
English   playwright: C2041;
C2042

ROBESON, Paul (1898-1976)
American singing actor: A50,
pp. 463-5; A70, pp. 158-9; A90,
pp. 95-100; B15, pp. 238-9;
C1024; C1259; C2044

ROBEY, George [born George Edward
Wade] (1869-1954)
English comedian: A50, p. 430;
C2045; C2046

ROBINS, Elizabeth [Mrs. George R.
Parkes; also known as C. E.
Raimond] (1862-1952)
American actress: B14, pp. 178-
9; B20, pp. 1184-5; C494; C2048

ROBINSON, Anna [Countess Rosslyn]
(c. 1870-1917)
American actress: A44, VIII,
40-41

ROBINSON,   Bill   ["Bojangles"]
(1878-1949)
American performer: A90, pp.
105-08

ROBINSON, Edward G. (1893-1973)
American actor: A35, p. 74,
por.; B15, pp. 240-41; C2049

ROBINSON, Frederic C. (1832-1912)
English actor: A23, pp. 310-11;

A66, n. p.

ROBINSON, Gil [born John G. Rob-
inson] (b. 1845)
American circus manager: C2050

ROBINSON, Henry Crabb (1775-1867)
English   writer: C130;   C1726;
C2051

ROBINSON, Jay (1930--)
American actor, producer: C2052

ROBINSON, Lennox (1886-1958)
Irish   playwright,   director:
A116, II, 116-21; B20, pp.
1187-8; C2055

ROBINSON, Mary ["Perdita"; born
Darby] (1758-1800)
English actress: A6, II, 79-97;
A7, II, 102-26; A10, pp. 171-
96; A28, I, 61-96; A42, pp.
274-314; A81, I, 86-7; A89,
pp. 233-68; A92, pp. 291-330;
A97, pp. 135-40; C2056; C2057

ROBINSON, Richard (d. 1647)
British actor: A27, pp. 268-73

ROBSON, Eleanor (1879-1979)
American actress: A3, n. p.;
A13, p. 27; A16, II, 273; A38,
n. p.; A96, p. 365; A103, pp.
70-71; C230

ROBSON, Flora (1902
English actress: A9, p. 37,
por.; A13, p. 129; A50. pp.
476-7; A57, pp. 104-16; A76,
pp. 16-31; C769

ROBSON, Frederick [born Thomas R.
Brownbill] (1821-64)
English actor: A4, pp. 402-10;
A69, II, 261-78; A74, pp. 189-
206; A81, II, 59-60; A98, pp.
414-7; B22, pp. 283-8; C2113;
C2117

ROBSON, May Waldron [born Mary
Robison; Mrs. Stuart R. Rob-
son; Mrs. A. H. Brown] (1865-
1942)
Australian actress: A3, n. p.;
A16, II, 247; A23, pp. 312-3;

A52, pp. 113-24; A61, pp. 229-30; A66, n. p.; A106, pp. 323-38

ROBSON, Stuart [born Henry R. Stuart] (1836-1903)
American actor: A1, n. p., por.; A2, n. p.; A23, pp. 313-6; A44, II, 6-7; A61, pp. 233-6; A64, pp. 430-36; A66, n. p.; A77, pp. 352-60; A81, II, 88; A96, pp. 365-6; A103, pp. 34-5; A105, pp. 223-37; A111, pp. 59-61; A125, pp. 983-7

ROBSON, William ["The Old Playgoer"] (d. 1863)
English writer: C2058

ROBYN, Alfred G. (1860-1935)
American manager: A49, pp. 306-09

ROCHESTER, John Wilmot, Earl of (1647-80)
British playwright: A22, p. 87; C1921; C1958

ROCK, Charles ["Old Bill"; born Arthur C. Rock de Fabeck] (1866-1919)
British actor: A16, II, 127

ROCKWELL, Florence [born Grace Atherton] (1880-1964)
American actress: A16, p. 161; A103, pp. 212-3

ROCKWELL, Kitty [born Kathleen Eloisa Rockwell] (1876-1967)
American actress: C1532

RODGERS, Richard (1902-79)
American composer, producer: B15, pp. 242-3; C822; C1605; C1813; C2061

RODNEY, Frank (1859-1902)
Actor: A50, p. 380

RODWAY, Philip (1877-1932)
British producer: C2062

ROEBUCK, Mabel [Mrs. Pope Washington] (c. 1876-1939)
Actress: A16, II, 196

ROGERS, Gus [born Solomon] (1869-1908)
American performer: A61, pp. 239-40; A103, pp. 152-3

ROGERS, Max [born Solomon] (1873-1932)
American performer: A61, pp. 239-40; A103, pp. 152-5

ROGERS, Henry Munroe (1839-1937)
American writer: C2064

ROGERS, Paul (1917--)
English actor: C2501

ROGERS, Will (1879-1935)
American performer: A20, pp. 135-44; A35, pp. 79-80, por.; A84, pp. 67-74; B20, pp. 1190-91; C209; C614; C1380; C1419; C1697; C1824; C2063; C2065

ROMA, Caro [born Carrie Northey] (1866-1937)
Singing actress: A16, II, 206

ROSA, Patti [Mrs. John Dunne] (d. 1894)
Actress: A66, n. p.

ROSE, Billy [born W. S. Rosenberg] (1899-1966)
American producer, actor: C550; C2070

ROSE, Clarkson [born Arthur Rose] (1890-1968)
English performer: C2071

ROSE, Edward E. (1848-1904)
Actor, playwright: A16, II, 51; A108, pp. 190-95

ROSE MARIE [born Rose Marie Curley]
American performer: A100, pp. 260-66

ROSS, Charles J. [born Charles J. Kelly] (1859-1918)
Canadian actor: A16, II, 56; A64, pp. 583-92; A103, pp. 128-9

ROSS, David (1728-90)

British actor: A7, I, 277

ROSS, Frederick G. (1858-1942)
American actor: C2076

ROSS, Hope
Actress: A98, p. 128

ROSS, Thomas W. (1873-1959)
American actor: A16, II, 35

ROSSI, Ernesto (1829-96)
Italian actor: A81, II, 63-4

ROSTAND, Edmond (1868-1918)
French playwright: B20, pp.
1202-03

ROTH, Lillian (1910--)
American actress: C2078; C2079

ROWE, George Fawcett (1839-89)
English   actor,   playwright:
A81, II, 79

ROWE, Nicholas (1674-1718)
English   playwright: A22,   p.
132; B17, pp. 114-31

ROWE, Samuel
British playwright: A22, p. 48

ROWE, William
British playwright: A22, p. 48

ROWSON, Susanna [born Haswell]
(1762-1824)
American actress, playwright:
C1784; C2390

ROY, Pierre Charles (1683-1764)
French playwright: C1935

ROYLE, Edwin Milton (1862-1942)
American   actor,   playwright:
A16, II, 72; A23, pp. 316-7

ROYLE, Selena [born Fetter, Mrs.
Edwin M. Royle] (1860-1955)

RUBIN, Benny (1899--)
American performer: A100, pp.
169-78; C2089

RUGGERI, Ruggero (1871-1953)
Actor: A50, p. 394

RUSH, Isadore [Mrs. Roland Reed]
(c. 1869-1904)
American   actress: A103,   pp.
156-7

RUSKIN, Sybil [born Raphael]
A16, p. 209

RUSSELL,   Annie   [Mrs.   Oswald
Yorke] (1864-1936)
English   actress: A3,   n.   p.;
A16, III, 27; A23, pp. 318-20;
A44, IV, 40-41; A52, pp. 183-
96; A55, n. p., por.; A61, pp.
243-7; A63, pp. 95-138, 194-8;
A64,   pp.   424-7;   A66,   n.   p.;
A103, pp. 36-7; A106, pp. 82-
97; A125, pp. 988-91

RUSSELL, Dorothy (b. 1881)
A16, p. 113

RUSSELL, Henry (1812-1900)
English actor: A92, pp. 405-06;
C2095

RUSSELL, Lillian [born Helen Louise Leonard] (1861-1922)
American   singing   actress: A1,
n.   p.,   por.;   A2,   n.   p.;   A3,
n.   p.;   A8,   pp.   50-51;   A13,   p.
1;   A14,   pp.   129-33;   A16,   II,
268; A25, pp. 43-57; A30, pp.
43-56; A44, I, 34-5; A61, pp.
251-3; A64, pp. 549-62; A66,
n.   p.;   A107,   pp.   30-45;   A125,
pp. 992-6; C402; C1723

RUSSELL,   Samuel   ["Jerry   Sneak"]
(1766-1845)
British actor: A92, pp. 286-7

RUSSELL, Sol Smith (1848-1902)
American   actor,   manager: A1,
n.   p.,   por.;   A2,   n.   p.;   A16,
II, 142; A23, pp. 320-24; A44,
IV, 30-31; A61, pp. 257-9; A64,
pp. 541-6; A66, n. p.; A77, pp.
368-76; A103, pp. 76-7; A105,
pp.   248-59;   A125,   pp.   997-9;
C200

RUTHERFORD,   Margaret   [Mrs.
Stringer Davies] (1892-1972)
English actress: A56, pp. 123-
32; C1376; C2097

RUTTER, Joseph
British playwright: A22, p. 52

RUTTER, Louise
A16, III, 215

RYAN, John F. (c. 1848-1913)
A16, II, 26

RYAN, Kate (1857-1922)
American actress: C2098

RYAN, Lacy (1694-1770)
British actor, playwright: A22,
p. 181; A45, I, 215-8; A92, pp.
76-8

RYDER, John (1814-85)
Actor: A26, I, 300-29

RYLEY, Madeleine Lucette [Mrs.
J. H. Ryley] (1868-1934)
English actress, playwright:
A16, p. 284

RYLEY, Samuel William (1755-1837)
British actor: C2101

RYMER, Thomas (1641-1713)
British playwright, critic:
A22, p. 105

SACKLER, Howard (1929-82)
American playwright: A65, II,
198-204

SACKVILLE, Thomas, Baron Buck-
hurst (1536-1608)
British playwright: A22, p. 4;
C2305

SAINPOLIS, John M. (1887-1942)
American actor: A98, pp. 29-30

ST. DENIS, Ruth [born Ruth Den-
nis] (1877-1968)
American dancer, choreographer:
A3, n. p.; B15, pp. 252-3;
C2106

ST. DENIS, Teddie (1909--)
British actress: C2107

ST. HUBERTY, Anne [born Clavel]
(1756-1812)

French actress: A37, II, 150-
247

ST. LEONARD, Florence
A16, II, 99

ST. SERSE, Thomas
British playwright: A22, p. 81

SALA, George Augustus (1828-95)
British playwright: C2112

SALIS, Peter (1921--)
Actor: A76, pp. 122-35

SALVINI, Alexander (1861-96)
Italian actor: A1, n. p., por.;
A2, n. p.; A44, II, 34-5; A66,
n. p.; A77, pp. 292-8; A91, pp.
178-83

SALVINI, Maud [born Dixon]
(d. 1944)
Actress: A44, VIII, 32-3

SALVINI, Tommaso (1829-1916)
Italian actor: A8, pp. 32-3;
A44, V, 6-7; A54, pp. 80-108;
A66, n. p.; A81, II, 57-8;
A121, I, 339-47; A123, I, 283-
9; A125, pp. 1000-06; C2114

SAMPSON, William
British playwright: A22, p. 46

SAMUELS, Rae (d. 1979)
American performer: A100, pp.
188-94

SANDERS, Mary
American actress: A23, pp. 324-
5; A98, pp. 19-20; A103, pp.
288-9

SANDERSON, Julia [born Julia
Sackett; Mrs. J. T. Sloan]
(1887-1975)
American actress: A3, n. p.;
A13, p. 71; A16, II, 191

SANDERSON, Sibyl (1865-1903)
Singing actress: A44, III, 4-5

SANDFORD, Samuel (fl. 1661-99)
British actor: A6, I, 61-2;
A45, I, 81-4; A50, pp. 36-7;

A81, I, 12

SANDOW, Eugene (1867-1925)
German strong man: A8, pp. 100-01; A84, pp. 29-32

SANDYS, George (1578-1644)
British playwright: A22, p. 39; C669

SANGER, George ["Lord"] (1827-1911)
British manager: C2118

SANTJE, Susan
A16, III, 227

SANTLEY, Joseph H. (1886-1971)
American actor: A13, p. 77

SANTLEY, Mabel
A110, pp. 13-4

SARCEY, Francisque (1827-99)
French critic: C2119

SARDOU, Victorien (1831-1908)
French playwright: A16, p. 201; C1136; C1548

SARJEANTSON, Kate [born Morris; Mrs. George Power] (d. 1918)
Welsh actress: A86, n. p., por.

SAROYAN, William (1908-81)
American playwright: A65, II, 204-27; B20, pp. 1233-4; C2122; C2123

SARTAIN, John (1808-97)
English stage machinist: C2124

SARTON, May (1912--)
American actress: C2125

SAUNDERS, Charles
British playwright: A22, p. 110

SAUNDERS, Elizabeth (1819-1909)
A16, II, 94

SAUNDERS, Florence (1890-1926)
Chilean actress: A50, pp. 450-51

SAVAGE, Henry W. (1859-1927)

American manager: A96, p. 374

SAVAGE, Richard (?1697-1743)
British playwright: A22, pp. 164-5; A45, I, 93-120; C1500; C1574; C2358

SAVINA, Maria G. (1854-1915)
Russian actress, manager: C1016

SAVO, Jimmy (1895-1960)
American actor: C2128

SAVOY, Bert [born Everett McKenzie] (c. 1888-1923)
American actor: A102, pp. 113-8

SAXE-MEININGEN, Georg II, Duke of (1826-1914)
German director, designer, manager: C1406

SAYERS, Dorothy L. (1893-1957)
English playwright: A116, II, 121-5; C1209

SCANLAN, William J. (1856-98)
American actor: A66, n. p.; A81, II, 106-07

SCARAMOUCH [born Tiberio Fiorelli] (1608-94)
Italian actor: C553

SCHAFFNER, Neil E.
American actor, producer: C2130

SCHEFF, Fritzi [born Anna S. Yager] (1879-1954)
Austrian actress: A3, n. p.; A13, p. 45; A16, III, 202

SCHICKELE, René (1863-1940)
German playwright: B20, pp. 1240-41

SCHILDKRAUT, Joseph (1895-1964)
Austrian actor: A125, pp. 1007-12; C2133

SCHILLER, Friedrich (1759-1805)
German playwright: C439; C954; C1168

SCHNEIDER, Alan (1917--)
American, producer, director:

C1155

SCHNITZLER, Arthur (1862-1931)
Austrian playwright: B20, pp.
1244-5; C1507

SCHOEFFEL, John B. (1846-1918)
American manager: A96, pp. 364-
5

SCHUMANN-HEINK, Ernestine [born
Roessler] (1861-1936)
Austrian singer: C2596

SCOFIELD, Paul (1922--)
English actor: A50, pp. 513-4;
C2366

SCOTT, Agnes [born Elliott]
(d. 1926)
A16, p. 131

SCOTT, Clement William (1841-
1904)
British critic, playwright:
C2139; C2142

SCOTT, Cyril (1866-1945)
Irish actor: A16, II, 50; A96,
pp. 375-6; C2140

SCOTT, Janette (1938--)
English actress: C2141

SCOTT, John R. (1808-56)
American actor: A81, II, 33-4

SCOTT, Louis N.
American manager: A49, pp. 340-
41

SCOTT, Margaretta (1912--)
English actress: A9, p. 38,
por.

SCOTT, Marion G. [born Gallagher]
American actress: C2143

SCOTT, Thomas
British playwright: A22, p. 121

SCRIBE, [Augustin] Eugène (1791-
1861)
French playwright: C99

SEABROOKE, Thomas Q. [born T. J.

Quigley] (1860-1913)
American actor: A1, n. p.,
por.; A2, n. p.; A44, IV, 10-
11; A66, n. p.; A104, pp. 118-
40

SEARS, Heather (1935--)
English actress: A32, p. 96

SEARS, Zelda [born Paldi] (1873-
1935)
American actress, playwright:
A16, II, 34; C271

SEDLEY, CHarles (1639-1701)
British playwright: A22, pp.
80-81; C1922

SEELEY, James L. (c. 1867-1943)
American actor: A98, pp. 33-4

SELBINI, Lalla
A16, II, 195

SELDES, Marion (1928--)
American actress: C2154

SELIGMAN, Minnie [Mrs. Eugene
Kaufmann; Mrs. R. L. Cutting;
Mrs.   William   Bromwell]
(c. 1869-1919)
American actress: A16, III, 20;
A44, VII, 16-7; A66, n. p.

SELZNICK, Irene [born Mayer]
(1907--)
American producer: C2157

SERRANO, Vincent (1896-1935)
American actor: A103, pp. 254-5

SETTLE, Elkanah (1648-1724)
British playwright: A22, pp.
95-7; C373

SEWELL, George
British playwright: A22, p. 168

SEYLER, Athene (b. 1889)
English actress: A9, p. 39,
por.

SEYMOUR, Kate (c. 1874-1903)
Actress: A86, n. p., por.

SEYMOUR, William G. (1855-1933)

American actor, director: A15,
pp. 34-7; A23, pp. 325-9; C1690

SHADWELL, Charles (d. 1726)
British playwright: A22, p. 154

SHADWELL, George
British playwright: A22, p. 168

SHADWELL, Thomas (?1642-92)
British playwright: A22, pp.
81-2; B17, pp. 79-96; C319

SHAIRP, Mordaunt (1887-1939)
English playwright: A116, II,
125-8

SHAKESPEARE, William (1564-1616)
English actor, playwright: A22,
pp. 8-17; A91, pp. 1-7; B11,
pp. 75-92; C16; C41; C249;
C376; C458; C491; C670; C785;
C934; C944; C1085; C1163;
C1420; C1459; C1814; C1997;
C2066; C2084; C2085; C2134;
C2250; C2398

SHALEK, Bertha (b. 1884)
A16, II, 20

SHANCKE, John (d. 1635)
British actor: A27, pp. 274-9

SHANNON, Effie [Mrs. Herbert Kel-
cey] (1867-1954)
American actress: A3, n. p.;
A16, II, 118; A23, pp. 330-32;
A44, II, 20-21; A61, pp. 153-5;
A64, pp. 428-9; A66, n. p.;
A103, pp. 52-3; A106, pp. 187-
92

SHANNON, Lavinia [Mrs. Giles
Shine] (c. 1876-1945)
Actress: A98, pp. 51-2

SHANNON, Walter
A16, II, 184

SHARP, Lewis
British playwright: A22, p. 57

SHARPHAM, Edward (c. 1576-1608)
British playwright: A22, p. 39

SHATTUCK, Truly [born Claire

Etrulia; Mrs. Stephen A. Doug-
las] (1876-1954)
American actress: A16, p. 169

SHAW, George Bernard (1856-1950)
Irish playwright, critic, di-
rector: A16, III, 174; A116,
II, 129-48; B4, pp. 189-92;
B14, pp. 11-21; B15, pp. 260-
61; B16, pp. 428-42; B20, pp.
1268-70; B23, pp. 336-8; B24,
pp. 237-60; B28, pp. 247-61;
B83, pp. 7-32; C196; C476;
C525; C770; C1124; C1173;
C1174; C1254; C1305; C1325;
C1519; C1547; C1869; C1887;
C1888; C1981; C2164; C2165

SHAW, Glen Byam (1904--)
English actor: A9, p. 40, por.

SHAW, Martin F. (1875-1958)
English musician: C2166

SHAW, Mary (1860-1929)
American actress: A15, pp. 41-
3; A23, pp. 332-3; A44, IX, 8-
9; A106, pp. 206-16; C1293

SHAWN, Ted [born Edwin M. Shawn]
(1891-1972)
American dancer, choreographer:
B15, pp. 252-3; C749; C1933

SHEA, Michael
American manager: A49, pp. 315-
6

SHEFFIELD, John
British playwright: A22, pp.
178-9

SHEIL, Richard L. (1791-1851)
British playwright: C2354

SHELDON, Edward Brewster (1886-
1946)
A24, pp. 45-56; A65, II, 228-
31; B20, pp. 1274-5; C159

SHELDON, Suzanne [Mrs. Henry Ain-
ley] (1875-1924)
American actress: A16, p. 33

SHELTON, George (1852-1932)
British actor: C2170

SIDNEY, Philip (1554-86)
English critic: A22, pp. 5-6;
C1052; C2426; C2517

SIGNORET, Simone (1921--)
French actress: C2186

SILLMAN, Leonard (1908-82)
American director, producer:
C2189

SILLY, Lea
A110, pp. 35-6

SILSBEE, Joshua (1815-53)
American actor: A96, p. 382;
A125, pp. 1013-7

SILVERMAN, Sime (1873-1933)
American editor, publisher:
C2281

SILVERS, Phil (1911--)
American actor: C2190

SIM, Alistair (1900-76)
Scottish actor: A9, p. 41,
por.; A32, p. 70

SIMON, Neil (1927--)
American playwright: A65, II,
252-62

SIMMS, Willard (c. 1864-1917)
American actor: A16, III, 263

SIMOND, Ike
American minstrel: C2193

SIMONSON, Lee (1888-1967)
American designer: C2195; C2566

SIMPSON, Edmund (1784-1848)
English actor, manager: C1512

SIMPSON,   [John]   Palgrave
(d. 1885)
Playwright: A26, II, 165-76

SIMS, George R. (1847-1922)
English playwright: C2196

SINCLAIR, Arthur [born McDonnell]
(1883-1951)
Irish actor: A102, pp. 37-42

SINCLAIR, Catherine [born Norton;
Mrs. Edwin Forrest] (1818-91)
English actress, manager: A14,
pp. 31-5; A81, II, 40

SINCLAIR, John (1790-1857)
Scottish singer: A12, pp. 235-
41

SINDEN, Donald (1923--)
English actor: C2197

SITGREAVES, Beverly (1867-1943)
American actress: A16, II, 100

SKELTON, Red (1910--)
American comedian: A20, pp.
111-4

SKINNER, Cornelia Otis (1901-79)
American   actress: C2204;
C2207; C2208

SKINNER, Otis (1858-1942)
American actor: A3, n. p.; A8,
pp. 110-11; A13, p. 20; A16,
III, 153; A23, pp. 335-6; A35,
p. 9, por.; A44, III, 38-9;
A50, pp. 376-7; A52, pp. 281-
90; A61, pp. 263-5; A64, pp.
318-28; A66, n. p.; A79, pp.
118-9; A103, pp. 54-5; A105,
pp. 260-77; A125, pp. 1018-22;
B15, pp. 262-3; C2211; C2596

SLAYTON, H. L.
American manager: A49, pp. 310-
11

SLEZAK, Walther (1902-83)
Austrian actor: C2214

SLOANE,   Alfred   Baldwin   (1872-
1925)
American playwright, composer:
A16, p. 192

SLOMAN, Mrs. John [born Whitaker;
Mrs. H. Darnton] (1799-1858)
English actress: A92, p. 379

SLY, William (1587-1608)
British actor: A27, pp. 151-8

SMALL, Andrew J.
American   manager: A49,   pp.

311-2

SMEDLEY, Constance [Mrs. Arm-
field] (1881-1941)
British playwright: C2216

SMITH, A. T.
Actor: A32, pp. 28-9

SMITH, Albert (1816-60)
English actor: A92, pp. 403-04;
C883

SMITH, C. Aubrey (1863-1948)
English actor: A16, II, 166

SMITH, Dodie (b. 1896)
British playwright: A116, II,
158-62

SMITH, Edgar McPhail (1857-1938)
American actor, playwright, librettist: A16, II, 271

SMITH, Edmund
British playwright: A22, pp.
151-2

SMITH, George (1777-1836)
British actor: A12, pp. 242-3

SMITH, Harry Bache (1860-1936)
American lyricist, librettist:
A16, II, 283; C933; C2219

SMITH, Henry
British playwright: A22, p. 111

SMITH, Joe (c. 1900-52)
American performer: A100, pp.
239-51

SMITH, John (d. 1612)
British playwright: A22, pp.
104, 130

SMITH, Kate [born Kathryn Elizabeth Smith] (1910--)
American performer: C2221

SMITH, Maggie (1934--)
English actress: A18, pp. 183-
204; A32, p. 60

SMITH, Mark (1829-84)
American actor: A16, II, 60;

A23, pp. 336-8; A81, II, 60;
A122, pp. 126-36

SMITH, Richard Penn (1799-1854)
Playwright: C1647

SMITH, Solomon F. (1801-69)
American actor: A36, pp. 59-
118; A81, II, 34-5;   C2223;
C2224; C2225

SMITH,   William   ["Gentleman"]
(1730-1819)
British actor: A6, I, 223-4;
A7, I, 291-3; A22, p. 40; A28,
I, 163-85; A81, I, 28; A92, pp.
155-7

SMITHSON, Harriet [Mrs. Hector
Berlioz] (1800-54)
Irish actress: A12, p. 243;
A28, II, 62-87; A50, pp. 348-
50; A92, pp. 379-80; C1974

SMYTH, Ethel (1858-1944)
British composer: C2227

SMYTH, James Moore (c. 1702-34)
British playwright: A22, pp.
173-4

SNAGG, Thomas (1746-1812)
British actor: C2231

SNYDER, Ella
A16, p. 222

SOFAER, Abraham (b. 1896)
A9, p. 42, por.

SOLDENE, Emily (1840-1912)
English performer: C2232

SOMMERS, Harry J. (1869-1935)
American manager: A49, pp. 333-
5

SOPHOCLES (c. 496-406 B. C.)
Greek playwright: C192; C1479

SOREL, Cécile (1875-1966)
French actress: C2238

SOTHERN FAMILY: A78, pp. 90-112

SOTHERN, Edward Askew [born Doug-

English actor: A23, pp. 353-5; A44, IV, 14-5; A64, pp. 361-72; A66, n. p.; A77, pp. 238-40; A111, pp. 65-7; C2282

STOKER, Bram (1847-1912)
Irish business manager: B20, pp. 1350-51; C836

STOKES, Sewell (1902--)
English playwright: C2284

STONE, Amelia F. (b. 1879)
A16, p. 271

STONE, Carol (1915--)
American actress: A13, p. 141

STONE, Ezra C. (1917--)
American   actor,   director: C2288

STONE, Fred A. (1873-1959)
American actor: A13, p. 52; A16, II, 190; B15, pp. 266-7; C2289

STONE, Henry Dickinson
American writer: C2291

STOWE, Vira
A16, II, 173

STRANGE, Michael [born Blanche Oelrichs] (1890-1950)
Actress, playwright: C2292

STRASBERG, Lee (1901-82)
Austrian-American   educator, actor: C11; C2293

STRAWBERRY
American   performer: A58, pp. 120-23

STREISAND, Barbra (1942--)
American singing actress: A51, pp. 177-86; A79, pp. 190-91; B26, pp. 358-64; C1335; C2445; C2574

STRINDBERG, August (1849-1912)
Swedish playwright: B20, pp. 1359-61; B21, pp. 259-67; C425; C1421; C1651; C1744; C2251; C2294; C2383

STRINGER, Arthur J. A. (1874-1950)
Canadian playwright: B20, pp. 1361-2; C1446

STRODE, William (1602-45)
British playwright: A22, p. 55

STUART, Jane L.
American actress: A66, n. p.

STUART, Leslie [born Thomas A. Barrett] (1864-1928)
English composer: A16, II, 76

STUART, Otho [born Otto S. Andrae] (1865-1930)
Actor, producer: A16, II, 182

STUDELY, John
British playwright: A22, p. 7

STUDHOLME, Marie [Mrs. Harold Giles Borrell] (1875-1930)
English singing actress: A86, n. p., por.

STURGES, Preston [born Edward P. Biden] (1898-1959)
American playwright: C629

SUCKLING, John (1609-42)
British   playwright: A22, pp. 52-3

SUDERMANN, Hermann (1857-1928)
German playwright: A16, p. 214; B20, pp. 1368-60

SUETT, Richard (1758-1805)
British actor: A6, II, 77-8; A81, I, 51-2; A92, pp. 253-6

SUGDEN, Charles (1850-1921)
English actor: A16, p. 282

SULLIVAN, Arthur (1842-1900)
English composer: B12, pp. 242-52; C125; C126; C336; C648; C997; C1188; C1448; C1889; C2299

SULLIVAN, Barry (1824-91)
Irish actor: A50, pp. 264-76; A53, pp. 78-81; A81, II, 54; C1450; C2188

SULLIVAN, Edward J. (1880-1958)
American manager: A49, pp. 341-2

SULLIVAN, James R.
American manager: A49, pp. 337-9

SULLY, Daniel [born Sullivan] (1855-1910)
American actor, playwright: A16, II, 249; A103, pp. 224-5

SUMMERVILLE, Amelia [born Amelia M. Shaw] (1862-1934)
Irish actress: A66, n. p.

SURRATT, Valeska (c. 1882-1962)
Actress: A16, p. 147

SUTHERLAND, Annie [Mrs. Charles Harding] (1867-1942)
American actress: A16, p. 61; A44, XII, n. p.; A66, n. p.

SUTHERLAND, Evelyn G. [born Baker] (1855-1908)
American playwright: A16, II, 208

SUTRO, Alfred (1863-1933)
English playwright: A16, p. 179; A116, II, 163-8; B20, pp. 1373-4; C2302

SWAFFER, Hannen (1879-1962)
English critic: C2304

SWEARS, Herbert (1869-1946)
British playwright: C2306

SWINEY, Owen (?1675-1754)
British playwright: A22, p. 154

SWINHOE, Gilbert
British playwright: A22, p. 65

SWINLEY, Ion (1891-1937)
English actor, playwright: A50, p. 455

SYKES, Jerome (1868-1903)
American actor: A103, pp. 108-9; A104, pp. 154-67

SYNGE, John Millington (1871-1909)
Irish playwright: A116, II, 168-84; B20, pp. 1378-80; C324; C1041; C1255; C2565

TABER, Edward Martin (1863-96)
American designer: C2309

TABER, Lulu (d. 1917)
Actress: A44, VII, 32-3

TABER, Robert
A44, IV, 18-19

TABER, Robert Schell (1865-1904)
American actor: A23, pp. 355-9; A96, p. 391

TAGLIONI, Amalia (1801-81)
Italian dancer: A79, pp. 50-51

TAGLIONI, Paul (1808-84)
Italian dancer: A79, pp. 50-51

TALBOT, Montague (1778-1831)
British actor: A92, pp. 330-32

TALIAFERRO, Mabel (1887-1979)
Actress: A3, n. p.; A16, III, 128

TALMA, François Joseph (1763-1826)
French actor: A81, I, 78-9; A91, pp. 77-84; C537

TANDY, Jessica [Mrs. Hume Cronyn] (1909--)
English actress: A50, pp. 508-9

TANGUAY, Eva (1878-1947)
Canadian performer: A96, p. 392

TANNER, Cora (fl. 1880-98)
American actress: A23, pp. 359-60; A66, n. p.

TARKINGTON, Booth (1869-1946)
American playwright: A124, pp. 116-23; B20, pp. 1384-5; C1219; C2355; C2547

TARLTON or TARLETON, Richard (1530-88)
English actor: A6, I, 14-7;

A17, pp. 16-20; A81, I, 7; A98, pp. 1-2; C1086

TATE, Nahum (1652-1715)
Irish playwright: A22, pp. 104-05; B17, pp. 97-113; C2144

TATEHAM, John (1632-64)
British playwright: A22, p. 63

TAUBER, Richard (1891-1948)
Austrian singing actor, composer: C1780

TAVERNER, William
English playwright: A22, pp. 156-7

TAYLOR, Billee [born Izetta Estelle Sadler; also known as Stella Mayhew] (c. 1875-1934)
Actress: A16, II, 139

TAYLOR, Charles A. (1864-1942)
American playwright, producer: C2315

TAYLOR, Dwight (1902--)
American playwright: C2316

TAYLOR, Elizabeth (1932--)
British actress: C656

TAYLOR, Eve (1895-1977)
American actress: A98, pp. 53-4

TAYLOR, John (1758-1832)
British critic: C2318

TAYLOR, Joe [born Justus Hurd Taylor] (b. 1834)
American actor: C2320

TAYLOR, Joseph (1585-c. 1650)
British actor: A27, pp. 249-61

TAYLOR, Laurette [Laura Cooney; Mrs. Charles A. Taylor; Mrs. J. Hartley Manners] (1884-1946)
American actress: A13, p. 63; A67, pp. 241-68; A102, pp. 119-24; A125, pp. 1041-53; C583

TAYLOR, Oliver (1862-1923)
American manager: C1912

TAYLOR, Robert
British playwright: A22, p. 37

TAYLOR, Tom (1817-80)
English playwright: A26, II, 117-39; C2349

TEARLE, Conway (1878-1938)
American actor: A16, II, 120

TEARLE, Godfrey (1884-1953)
American actor: A9, pp. 44, por.

TEARLE, [George] Osmond (1852-1901)
English actor, manager: A50, p. 366; A81, II, 111

TELLEGEN, Lou [born Isador L. B. van Dammeler] (1883-1934)
Dutch-American actor: C2324

TEMPEST, Marie [born Etherington; Mrs. C. Cosmo Gordon-Lennox] (1864-1942)
English actress: A1, n. p., por.; A2, n. p.; A8, pp. 46-7; A13, p. 24; A16, III, 168; A44, II, 8-9; A47, pp. 105-16; A57, pp. 41-56; A66, n. p.; A107, pp. 222-32; A125, pp. 1054-61; C309

TEMPLETON, Fay [Mrs. William Patterson] (1865-1939)
American singing actress: A8, pp. 67-80; A13, p. 30; A44, IX, 20-21; A64, pp. 618-24; A66, n. p.; A103, pp. 230-31

TENNANT, Dorothy (c. 1865-1942)
Actress: A16, II, 161

TERRISS, Ellaline [Mrs. Seymour Hicks] (1871-1971)
British actress: A16, II, 98; A86, n. p., por.; C2327; C2328

TERRISS, William [born William C. J. Lewin] (1847-97)
English actor: A44, V, 38-9; A48, II, 207-26; A66, n. p.; A81, II, 96-7; C2230

TERRY FAMILY: C2269

THOMPSON, [Frank] Hallett (c. 1871-1938)
Actor: A98, pp. 93-4

THOMPSON, Lydia [Mrs. Alexander Henderson] (1836-1908)
English actress: A8, pp. 94-5; A16, II, 57; A66, n. p.; A81, II, 78; A125, pp. 1075-9; B22, pp. 317-21; C1749

THOMPSON, Thomas (1783-1869)
British playwright: A22, p. 81

THOMSON, Christopher Birdwood (b. 1799)
British actor: C2338

THOMSON, James (1700-48)
Scottish playwright: A22, pp. 180-81; C1546

THORNDIKE, Sybil [Mrs. Lewis Casson] (1882-1976)
English actress: A9, p. 46, por.; A19, pp. 49-61; A32, pp. 51-3; A40, pp. 174-92; A50, pp. 441-3; A57, pp. 24-40; C450; C2252; C2339; C2368

THORNE, Ann Maria [born Mestayer; Mrs. Charles R. Thorne, Sr.] (1815-81)
American actress: A81, II, 45

THORNE, Charles R. , Sr. (1814-93)
American actor, manager: A81, II, 45; A96, p. 398

THORNE, Charles R., Jr. (1840-83)
American actor: A77, pp. 221-30; A81, II, 97

THORNE, Thomas (d. 1864)
Actor: A48, II, 171-203

THURMOND, John (1700-49)
British actor: A92, pp. 80-81

THURSBY, Emma (1845-1931)
Singer: A16, p. 53

THURSTON, Howard (1869-1936)
American magician: C2341

THURSTON, [Ernest] Temple (1879-1933)
English playwright: B14, pp. 205-07; B20, pp. 1405-06

TIDEN, Frederick L. ["Fritz"] (c. 1877-1931)
Actor: A16, III, 132

TIECK, Ludwig (1733-1853)
German playwright: C2359; C2576

TIFFANY, Annie Ward (d. 1918)
Actress: A52, pp. 103-12

TILBURY, Zeffie [Mrs. L. D. Woodthrope] (1863-1950)
English actress: A16, II, 259

TILLEY, Vesta [born Matilda Ball; Lady Walter de Freece] (1864-1952)
English performer: A16, p. 114; A64, pp. 605-07; C691

TILLMAN, Frances Nelson
American actress: C2343

TOBIN, John (1770-1804)
British playwright: C234; C2458

TODD, Ann (1910--)
English actress: A9, p. 47, por.; C2346

TODD, Michael [born Avron Hirsh Goldbogen] (1909-58)
American producer: C525; C2347

TOLER, Sidney [born H. G. Toler, Jr.] (1874-1947)
American actor: A16, p. 99; A103, pp. 294-5

TOLLER, Ernst (1893-1939)
German playwright: B20, pp. 1410-11; C2348

TOLSTOY, Alexey N. (1882-1945)
Russian playwright: B20, pp. 1411-2

TOMKINS, Simon
British actor: C2351

TOMPKINS, Molly [born Arthur]

A16, p. 176

TUCKER, Sophie [born Abuza] (1884-1966)
Russian-American singing actress: A102, pp. 141-6; C2374

TUKE, Richard
British playwright: A22, p. 93

TUKE, Samuel (d. 1674)
British playwright: A22, p. 75

TULLY, Jim (1891-1947)
American writer: C2375

TURGENEV, Ivan (1818-83)
Russian playwright: C955; C1017; C1571; C2162; C2558

TURNER, Carrie (1858-97)
American actress: A66, n. p.

TUTCHIN, John
British playwright: A22, p. 111

TUTIN, Dorothy (1930--)
English actress: A18, pp. 231-56

TWEEDIE, Ethel B. [Mrs. Alec Tweedie] (d. 1940)
British writer: C2376; C2377; C2378; C2379; C2380

TYARS, Frank (1848-1918)
English actor: A16, II, 170

TYLER, George C. (1867-1946)
American producer: A16, III, 102; C2381

TYLER, Odette [born Elizabeth Lee Kirkland; Mrs. R. D. Shepherd] (1869-1936)
American actress: A1, n. p., por.; A2, n. p.; A16, p. 211; A44, VII, 44-5; A66, n. p.; A96, p. 402; A103, pp. 164-5; A106, pp. 285-90

TYLER, Royall (1757-1826)
American playwright: C2311

TYREE, Elizabeth (d. 1952)
Actress: A23, pp. 363-4; A44,

V, 8-9

TZARA, Tristan (1896-1963)
Rumanian theorist: B23, pp. 374-7

ULLMAN, Liv (1938--)
Swedish actress: C1850; C2384

ULRIC, Lenore [born Ulrich] (1892-1970)
Actress: A13, p. 83; A125, pp. 1095-8

UNDERHILL, Cave (?1634-1710?)
British actor: A6, I, 63-4; A7, I, 80-81

UNDERWOOD, John (?1590-1624)
British actor: A27, pp. 224-32

UNRUH, Fritz von (1885-1971)
German playwright: B20, p. 1435

URQUHART, Isabelle (1865-1907)
American actress: A25, pp. 117-28; A30, pp. 117-28; A66, n. p.

USTINOV, Peter (1921--)
Anglo-Russian actor, playwright: A32, pp. 89-91; C2387; C2483

VACHELL, Horace A. (1861-1955)
English playwright: A16, II, 244; B20, pp. 1436-7; C2388; C2389

VAKHTANGOV, Eugene (1883-1922)
Russian actor, director, producer: C2194

VALLEE, Rudy (1901--)
American singing actor: A100, pp. 229-38; C2391; C2392; C2393

VALLI, Valli [born Knust; Mrs. Louis Dreyfus] (1882-1927)
German actress: A16, III, 53

VANBRUGH, Irene [Mrs. Dion Boucicault, Jr.] (1872-1949)
English actress: A9, p. 48,

A57, pp. 57-65; A83, pp. 196-7; A86, n. p., por.; C2394

VANBRUGH, John (1664-1726)
English playwright: A22, pp. 127, 195; C156; C2469

VANBRUGH, Violet [Mrs. Arthur Bourchier] (1867-1942)
English actress: A9, p. 48, por.; A16, p. 134; A50, pp. 391-2; C2395

VAN BUREN, A. H. (c. 1879-1965)
A16, III, 99

VANCE, Clarice (d. 1961)
A16, II, 76

VANDENHOFF, George C. (1820-84)
British actor: A50, pp. 344-5; A125, pp. 1099-1103; C2396; C2397

VANDENHOFF, John (1790-1861)
English actor: A81, I, 78; A92, pp. 357-8

VAN DRUTEN, John (1901-57)
English director, playwright: A116, II, 189-200; B20, pp. 1444-5; C2399

VANE, Sutton (1888-1963)
British playwright: A116, II, 200-03; B20, p. 1446

VAN ITALLIE, Jean-Claude (1936--)
American playwright: A65, II, pp. 290-300

VAN STUDDIFORD, Grace [born Quivey; Mrs. Charles Van Studdiford] (1873-1927)
American actress: A16, II, 25

VARCONI, Victor (1891-1976)
C2400

VAUGHN, Theresa [born Ott; Mrs. William H. Mestayer] (c. 1860-1903)
Singing actress: A44, I, 30-31

VEGA CARPIO, Lope Felix de (1562-1635)

Spanish playwright: C2009

VEGERIUS, Paul
British playwright: A22, p. 132

VEILLER, Bayard (1869-1943)
American playwright: B20, pp. 1452-3; C2402

VERNET, Camille Feher de
Hungarian actress: C1111

VERNON, Jane [born Fisher; Mrs. George Vernon] (1796-1869)
Actress: A81, II, 24-5

VERNON, Marie
Actress: A102, pp. 181-4

VESTRIS, Lucia Eliza [born Bartolozzi; Mrs. Charles Mathews, Jr.] (1797-1856)
English actress, manager: A6, II, 251-2; A12, pp. 256-9; A26, I, 245-62; A68, pp. 37-56; A72, pp. 127-42; A81, II, 26-7; A125, pp. 1104-07; C77; C1054; C1666; C1884; C2419; C2488

VEZIN, Hermann (1829-1910)
American actor: A16, II, 67; A81, II, 93

VEZIN, Jane Elizabeth [Mrs. Charles Young; Mrs. Hermann Vezin] (c. 1828-1902)
English actress: A81, II, 93-4

VICKERS, Mattie [Mrs. Charles S. Rogers]
Actress: A66, n. p.; A110, pp. 43-4

VIGNY, Alfred Victor de (1797-1863)
French playwright: C2474;

VILLIERS, George, Duke of Buckingham (1628-87)
English playwright: C463; C2516

VILLIERS DE L'ISLE ADAM, Philippe (1838-89)
French playwright: C1940

VINCENT, Mary Ann [born Farley;

Mrs. Wilson; Mrs. J. R. Farley]
(1818-87)
English actress: A77, pp. 194-
203; A81, II, 47

VINING, Frederick (1790-1871)
British actor: A12, pp. 259-60

VINING, Mrs. Frederick (d. 1853)
British actress: B12, p. 261

VIVIAN,   Charles   Algernon
(b. 1830)
Actor: A96, p. 407

VOKES, Rosina [Mrs. Cecil Clay]
(1854-94)
English actress: A25, pp. 375-
84; A30, pp. 375-83; A66,
n. p.; A81, II, 110; A108, pp.
88-99

VOLLMER, Lula (1898-1955)
American playwright: B20, pp.
1459-60

VOLTAIRE [born François Marie
Arouet] (1694-1778)
French playwright: A91, pp. 16-
25; B7, pp. 23-60; B21, pp.
278-87; C268; C337

VOORHEES, Winifred
A16, II, 93

WADE, Edward
American actor: A98, pp. 39-40

WADSWORTH, William (1874-1950)
A16, II, 137

WAGENHALS, Lincoln A. (1869-1931)
American manager: A16, p. 90

WAGER, Lewis
British playwright: A22, p. 5

WAGNER, Charles L. (c. 1869-1956)
American director, producer:
C2415

WAGNER, Richard (1813-83)
German   librettist,   composer,
theorist: B28, pp. 12-25; C802;
C803; C1075; C1801

WAINWRIGHT, Marie [born Marie W.
Page; Mrs. James; Mrs. Henry W.
Slaughter; Mrs. Franklyn Ro-
berts] (1853-1923)
American actress: A16, II, 116;
A23, pp. 365-6; A25, pp. 223-
32; A30, pp. 223-32; A44, II,
44-5; A66, n. p.; A81, II, 106

WAITE, James R.
American actor: C2418

WAKEMAN, Keith (1866-1933)
American actress: A16, II, 95

WALBROOK, Henry Mackinnon (1864-
1941)
English   playwright,   critic:
C2421

WALCOT, Charles Melton (1816-68)
English   actor,   playwright:
A23, pp. 366-8; A81, II, 48

WALCOT,   Charles   Melton,   Jr.
(1840-1921)
American actor: A16, III, 159;
A81, II, 94

WALCOT, Isabella [born Nickinson;
Mrs. Charles M. Walcot, Jr.]
(1847-1906)
American actress: A23, pp. 368-
9

WALDRON, Georgia [Mrs. Edward
Emery] (1872-1950)
American actress: A16, II, 120

WALDRON, Harriet
American   performer: A58,   pp.
36-43, 44-53

WALDROP, Oza
A16, III, 93

WALKER, Charlotte (1878-1958)
Actress: A3, n. p.; A16, II,
284

WALKER, Mildred
Actress: A102, pp. 43-8

WALKER, Thomas (1698-1744)
British actor: A22, p. 178;
A92, pp. 78-9

A57, pp. 4-6; A81, I, 315-21;
A83, p. 200; A121, I, 315-21;
C1071; C2433

WARD, Henry
British playwright: A22, p. 193

WARD, Simon (1941--)
English actor: A32, pp. 64-5

WARDE, Frederick B. (1851-1935)
English actor: A5, pp. 94-9;
A16, p. 54; A23, pp. 372-4;
A50, pp. 365-6; A66, n. p.;
A96, p. 411; A105, pp. 228-9;
C2435

WARE, Helen [born Remer] (1877-
1924)
American actress: A16, III, 236

WAREING, Alfred (1876-1942)
English producer: C1298

WARFIELD, David (1866-1951)
American actor: A3, n. p.; A13,
p. 18; A16, III, 269; A38,
n. p.; A50, p. 390; A52, pp.
125-36; A64, pp. 599-600; A85,
pp. 185-93; A102, pp. 159-64;
A123, II, 175-91; A125, pp.
1133-40; C555

WARING, Herbert [born H.W. Rutty]
English actor: A16, II, 257;
A86, n. p., por.

WARNER, Charles [born Lickfold]
(1846-1909)
English actor: A16, p. 225;
A48, II, 113-50

WARNER, Henry Byron [born Lick-
fold] (1876-1958)
English actor: A16, p. 235

WARNER, Mary Amelia (1804-54)
British actress: A69, I, 274-
88; A81, I, 95; A92, pp. 392-3

WARREN, Mercy Otis (1728-1814)
American   playwright: C371;
C1276

WARREN, William I (1767-1832)
English   actor: A81,   II,   18;

A125, pp. 1141-3

WARREN, William II (1812-88)
American actor: A44, VII, 6-7;
A66, n. p.; A77, pp. 178-93;
A81, II, 38-9; A91, pp. 136-44;
A122,   pp.   17-45;   A125,   pp.
1144-7; C134; C1494; C1643

WARRILOW, Maude
A16, p. 90

WARRINGTON, Ann (c. 1864-1934)
A16, II, 216

WATERS, Ethel (1900-77)
American singing actress: A13,
p. 126; A125, pp. 1148-52; B26,
pp. 80-96; C692; C2444

WATKINS, Harry (1825-94)
American actor, manager, playwright: C2210

WATKINS, Rosina [born Shaw; Mrs.
Charles Howard; Mrs. Harry Wat-
kins] (d. 1904)
A16, II, 284

WATSON, Alfred E. T. (1849-1922)
British critic: C2448

WATSON, Douglas (1921--)
American actor: A13, p. 149

WATSON, Henrietta [Mrs. Walter T.
Radcliffe] (1873-1964)
A16, p. 69

WAVER, Robert
British playwright: A22, p. 4

WAYER, William
British playwright: A22, p. 5

WAYLETT,   Harriet   Cooke   (1798-
1851)
British actress: A12, pp. 266-
7; C1493

WEATHERSBY, Eliza (1850-87)
Actress: A8, pp. 108-09

WEATHERSBY, Jennie (d. 1931)
Actress: A16, p. 162

WEAVER, Harry A., Sr. (c. 1832-
1903)
Actor: A23, pp. 374-8

WEAVER, Harry A., Jr.
Actor: A23, pp. 378-80

WEAVER, John (1673-1760)
British   playwright,   dancer:
A22, p. 160

WEBB, Clifton [born Webb Parmalee
Hollenbeck] (1893-1966)
American actor, dancer: A13, p.
104; A79, pp. 128-9; B15, pp.
284-5

WEBB, Nella (c. 1876-1954)
American actress: A16, III, 209

WEBER, Joe M. (1867-1942)
American actor, manager: A13,
p. 14; A16, p. 181; A36, pp.
213-22; A61, pp. 287-8; A85,
pp. 103-11; A125, pp. 1153-61;
C1301

WEBSTER, Benjamin (1864-1947)
English actor: A50, p. 386

WEBSTER, Benjamin N. (1799-1882)
English actor, manager, playwright: A26, I, 279-93; A69, I,
233-59; A72, pp. 169-80; A81,
I, 97-8; A92, pp. 381-2; B22,
pp. 288-93

WEBSTER, John (?1580-1625?)
British playwright: A22, p. 38;
C2286

WEBSTER, Margaret (1905-72)
English actress, director, producer: C2453; C2454

WEDEKIND, Frank (1864-1918)
German actor, playwright, producer: B20, pp. 1488-9; C985

WEIGEL, Helene [Mrs. Bertolt
Brecht] (1900-71)
German actress: C2455

WEILL, Kurt (1900-50)
German composer: C2116

WEIR, George R. (1853-1909)
A50, p. 366

WEIR, Molly
C2456

WELFORD, Dallas (1872-1946)
English actor: A16, p. 120

WELLES, Orson (1915--)
American actor, director, producer: A50, pp. 510-12; A125,
pp. 1162-5; C908; C912; C1635;
C1810

WELLS, Mary ["Becky"] (1759-
1826?)
British actress: A42, pp. 315-
55; C2459

WELSTEAD, Leonard
British playwright: A22, p. 174

WEMYSS, Francis C. (1797-1859)
English actor: A125, pp. 1166-
70; C2460

WERFEL, Franz V. (1890-1945)
Czechoslovakian   playwright:
B20. pp. 1497-8

WESKER, Arnold (1932--)
English playwright: C2016

WEST, Mae (1893-1980)
American singing actress, playwright: A35, p. 72, por.; A125,
pp. 1171-4; B23, pp. 402-07;
C796; C2462

WEST, Paul ["Dick"] (1871-1965)
A16, II, 37

WEST, Richard
British playwright: A22, p. 190

WEST, William H. [born Flynn]
(1853-1902)
American minstrel: A103, pp.
296-7

WEST, W. (b. 1796)
British actor: A12, pp. 268-9

WEST, Mrs. W. (d. 1876)
British actress: A12, pp. 270-

71

WESTERN, Helen [Mrs. James Herne] (1843-68)
American actress: A81, II, 99

WESTERN, Lucille [Mrs. James H. Meade] (1843-77)

WESTON, John
British playwright: A22, p. 79

WESTON, Thomas (1737-76)
British actor: A6, I, 218-21; A7, I, 285-8; A45, I, 232-46; A81, I, 27-8; A92, p. 142; C1668

WETHERBY, James
British playwright: A22, p. 179

WETHERILT, Robert (1708-45)
British actor: A92, pp. 84-6

WEWITZER, Ralph (1748-1825)
English actor: A92, pp. 212-4; C2464

WHEAT, Lawrence (1876-1963)
A16, III, 238

WHEATCROFT, Nelson (1852-97)
English actor: A44, II, 46-7; A66, n. p.; A96, p. 417

WHEATCROFT, Stanhope (1888-1966)
A16, III, 122

WHEATLEY, Alan (1907--)
English actor: A9, p. 50, por.

WHEATLEY, William (1816-76)
American actor, manager: A81, II, 135-40; A98, pp. 65-8; A117, pp. 137-264; A121, II, 135-40; A123, I, 177-82

WHEELOCK, Joseph F. (1839-1908)
American actor: A81, II, 109

WHIFFEN, Mrs. Thomas [born Blanche Galton] (1845-1936)
English actress: A16, II, 75; A23, pp. 380-81; A44, IX, 12-3; C2467

WHINCOP, Thomas (d. 1730)
British playwright: A22, p. 192

WHITAKER, William
British playwright: A22, p. 107

WHITE, Charles T. (1821-91)
American minstrel: A95, pp. 61-2

WHITE, John Blake (1781-1859)
American playwright: C1867

WHITE, Maude Valerie (1855-1937)
A16, p. 116

WHITE, Pearl (1889-1938)
American actress: C2471

WHITEHEAD, William (1715-85)
British playwright: C1790

WHITELAW, Billie (1932--)
English actress: A32, pp. 10-11

WHITEMORE, Hugh (1936--)
A76, pp. 172-86

WHITESIDE, Walker (1869-1942)
American actor: A1, n. p., por.; A2, n. p.; A3, n. p.; A16, II, 77; A44, VII, 18-9; A66, n. p.; A96, p. 418; A102, pp. 222-3

WHITFORD, Annabelle [born Annabelle W. Buchan] (c. 1878-1961)
A16, II, 157

WHITING, Joseph E. (d. 1910)
American actor: A23, pp. 381-3

WHITMAN, Helen
A16, II, 138

WHITNEY, Edith
A16, p. 39

WHITTLESEY, [Charles] White (d. 1940)
American actor: A16, III, 155; A23, pp. 383-5

WHITTY, May [Mrs. Ben Webster] (1865-1948)

English actress: A57, pp. 1-3

WIGAN, Alfred Sydney (1814-78)
Actor: A26, I, 263-78; A69,
II, 251-61

WIGAN, Horace (d. 1885)
Actor: A26, I, 263-78

WIGNELL, Thomas (1753-1803)
English actor, manager: A125,
pp. 1175-8; C1183

WILBUR, Albert L. (c. 1842-1917)
American actor, manager: A49,
pp. 330-32

WILCOX, Herbert (b. 1892)
British playwright: C2475

WILD, Robert
British playwright: A22, p. 113

WILD, Samuel (1815-83)
British actor, manager: C2476

WILDE, Oscar (1856-1900)
Irish playwright: A8, pp. 74-5;
A116, II, 204-18; B13, pp. 163-
292; C345; C738; C739; C1126;
C1236; C1890; C2172; C2173;
C2534

WILDE, Percival (1887-1953)
American playwright: B20, p.
1518

WILDER, Marshall P. (1859-1915)
American performer: A44, IX,
34-5; A49, pp. 349-50; C2477;
C2478

WILDER, Thornton (1897-1975)
American playwright: A65, II,
304-19; B20, pp. 1518-9; C399;
C1037; C1132

WILKINS, George
British playwright: A22, p. 53

WILKINSON, Tate (1736-1803)
English actor, manager: A6, I,
257-67; A7, I, 335-48; A12, pp.
272-5; A34, pp. 63-86; A41, pp.
144-218; A70, pp. 219-42; A81,
I, 33; A92, pp. 169-71; A99,

pp. 157-76; C2481; C2482

WILKINSON, William
British playwright: A22, p. 131

WILKS, Robert (1665-1732)
British actor, manager: A6, I,
90-94; A7, I, 115-9; A45, I,
43-68; A92, pp. 41-3; C624;
C1826

WILLAN, Leonard
British playwright: A22, p. 63

WILLARD, Edward S. (1853-1915)
English actor: A1, n. p., por.;
A2, n. p.; A16, III, 25; A44,
IV, 6-7; A48, I, 241-94; A64,
pp. 346-50; A66, n. p.; A86,
n. p., por.; A96, p. 420; A121,
I, 322-38, II, 292-8; A123, I,
598-633

WILLIAMS, Barney [born Bernard
O'Flaherty] (1823-76)
Irish actor: A81, II, 51-2;
A125, pp. 1179-81

WILLIAMS, Bert [born Egbert Austin Williams] (1875-1922)
West Indian actor: A20, pp. 48-
51; A84, pp. 37-42; A102, pp.
227-32; A125, pp. 1182-8; C466;
C2082

WILLIAMS, Bransby (1870-1961)
English actor: A16, p. 182;
C2486; C2487

WILLIAMS, Emlyn (1905--)
Welsh actor, playwright: A9,
p. 51, por.; A125, pp. 1188-91;
C861; C2493; C2494

WILLIAMS, Espy [born William Hen-
dricks] (1852-1908)
Actor, playwright: A16, p. 36

WILLIAMS, Eva
Actress: A16, p. 175

WILLIAMS, Fritz (1865-1930)
American actor: A16, II, 192;
A23, pp. 385-6; A44, IX, 14-5;
A103, pp. 124-5

WILLIAMS, Gus [born Leweck]
(1848-1915)
American actor: A66, n. p.;
A103, pp. 282-3

WILLIAMS, [Ernest G.] Harcourt
(1880-1957)
English actor, director: A16,
p. 82; C2491

WILLIAMS, Hattie (1870-1942)
American actress: A3, n. p.

WILLIAMS, Maria K. [born Pray;
Mrs. Barney Williams] (c. 1826-
1911)
Actress: A23, pp. 386-92; A81,
II, 51-2

WILLIAMS, Marie (1921-67)
Actress: A110, pp. 31-2

WILLIAMS, Montagu (1834-92)
British   playwright: C2497;
C2498

WILLIAMS, Odell (1853-1902)
American actor: A103, pp. 148-9

WILLIAMS, Tennessee [born Thomas
Lanier Williams] (1911-83)
A65, II, 320-50; C1793; C2345;
C2489; C2490; C2500

WILLIAMS, Zenaide
Actress: A16, p. 188

WILLIS, Nathaniel Parker (1806-
67)
American playwright: C216; C654

WILLS, William Gorman (1828-91)
British playwright: C2503

WILLSON, Meredith [born Robert
Meredith Reiniger] (1902-84)
American playwright, composer:
C2504; C2505; C2506

WILMOT, Robert (fl. 1568-1600)
British playwright: A22, p. 17

WILSON, Albert Edward (1885-1960)
English critic: C2508

WILSON, Al H. (c. 1888-1964)

A16, III, 73

WILSON, Benjamin F. (c. 1876-
1930)
A16, II, 158

WILSON, Francis (1854-1935)
American   actor,   playwright:
A3, n. p.; A13, p. 28; A16,
III, 50; A23, pp. 393-4; A44,
II, 14-5; A52, pp. 151-64; A61,
pp. 291-4; A62, pp. 151-78;
A66, n. p.; A85, pp. 37-45;
A103, pp. 178-9; A104, pp. 18-
43; C2511; C2514

WILSON, George W. (1849-1931)
American   actor: A16, p. 210;
A23, pp. 394-9; A81, II, 109

WILSON, John [also known as
Christopher North] (1785-1854)
British playwright: A22, p. 75

WILSON, Lanford (1937--)
American playwright: A65, II,
350-68

WILSON, Robert (1579-1610)
British actor, playwright: A22,
p. 17; C957

WILSON, Sandy (1924--)
British playwright: C2518

WINCHELL, Walter (1897-1972)
American   performer: C1652;
C2337

WINCHELSEA, Countess
British playwright: A22, p. 155

WINSLOW, Leah
Actress: A16, III, 268

WINSTON, James (1773-1843)
British manager: C2521

WINSTON, Jennie [born Jeanette
Webster Bruce] (c. 1845-1929)
Actress: A66, n. p.

WINTER, Dale
Actress: A102, pp. 165-72

WINTER, [John] Keith (1906--)

Welsh playwright: B20, pp. 1533-4

WINTER, Percy C. (1861-1928)
Canadian actor, stage manager: A16, II, 257; A23, pp. 396-8

WINTER, William (1836-1917)
American critic: A87, pp. 306-11; C1534; C1551

WINTNER, Helene
Actress: A16, III, 264

WINWOOD, Estelle (1883-1984)
English actress: A35, p. 3, por.; A50, pp. 443-4; A125, pp. 1192-4

WISE, Thomas A. (1865-1928)
English actor: A16, III, 85

WITHERS, Clarice
American performer: A58, pp. 124-33

WOFFINGTON, Margaret ["Peg"] (1720-40)
Irish actress: A6, I, 292-300; A7, I, 380-91; A11, pp. 151-92; A28, I, 38-60; A42, pp. 110-40; A45, I, 219-31; A67, pp. 23-50; A70, pp. 101-22; A81, I, 26; A89, pp. 77-116; A91, pp. 40-47; A92, pp. 123-7; A93, pp. 47-56; A197, pp. 42-66; C635; C1531; C1662; C1709

WOLF, Friedrich (1888-1953)
German playwright: B20, pp. 1539-40

WOLFIT, Donald (1902-68)
English actor, producer: A9, p. 50, por.; A50, pp. 472-4; C1143; C2537

WOLHEIM, Louis R. (1881-1931)
American actor: A102, pp. 125-30; B15, pp. 292-3

WOOD, Audrey (1905--)
American literary agent: C2538

WOOD, Mrs. Henry [born Ellen Price] (1814-87)

British playwright: C2539

WOOD, Joseph (1801-70)
English actor: A81, I, 93

WOOD, Juliana [born Westray; Mrs. William B. Wood] (d. 1836)
Actress: A81, II, 21

WOOD, Marjorie (1887-1955)
English actress: A16, II, 203

WOOD, Mary Ann [born Paton] (1802-64)
British singer: A79, pp. 42-3; A92, pp. 386-8

WOOD, Nathaniel
British playwright: A22, p. 6

WOOD, Peggy (1894-1978)
American actress: A13, p. 105; A35, p. 95, por.; A125, pp. 1195-1201; C2192; C2542; C2543; C2544

WOOD, Susannah [born Paton; Mrs. Joseph Wood] (1802-64)
Scottish actress: A81, I, 93-4

WOOD, William B. (1779-1861)
American actor: A79, pp. 20-21; A81, II, 21; A125, pp. 1202-05; C2546

WOODRUFF, Henry I. (1869-1916)
American actor: A16, III, 137; A23, pp. 399-401; A44, VI, 42-3

WOODS, Albert Herman ["Al"] (c. 1870-1951)
American manager: A102, pp. 29-36

WOODWARD, Henry (1717-77)
British actor: A7, I, 281-2; A81, I, 20-21; A92, pp. 119-23; A93, pp. 31-2

WOODWORTH, Samuel (1785-1842)
American playwright: C2310

WOOLGAR, Sarah Jane [Mrs. Sarah Jane Mellon] (1824-1909)
Actress: A68, pp. 167-73

Appendix: Necrological Annals

Dekker, Thomas (?1572-1632?)
Denham, John (1615-69)
Digby, George, Earl of Bristol (d. 1676)
Dilke, Thomas (d. c. 1698)
Ecclestone, William (d. c. 1652)
Etherege, George (1634-91)
Falkland, Henry Cary, Viscount (1634-63)
Fane, Francis (d. c. 1689)
Fanshawe, Richard (16-8-66)
Field, Nathaniel (1587-1633)
Flecknoe, Richard (?1600-78?)
Fletcher, John (1579-1625)
Ford, John (?1586-1639?)
Fountain, John (d. c. 1669)
Freeman, Ralph (d. 1655)
Glapthorne, Henry (?1610-43?)
Goffe, Thomas (1591-1629)
Goldsmith, Francis (d. 1655)
Gomersal, Robert (1600-46?)
Goodman, Cardell (?1649-99)
Gosson, Stephen (1554-1624)
Goughe, Robert (d. 1624)
Gwynne, Eleanor (1650-87)
Habington, William (1605-54)
Hart, Charles (?1630-83)
Haustead, Peter (d. 1645)
Head, Richard (?1637-86?)
Heminge, William (1602-32?)
Hemings, John (?1556-1630)
Henslowe, Philip (?1550-1616)
Heywood, Thomas (?1570-1641)
Horden, Hildebrand (d. 1696)
Howard, Robert (1626-98)
Howell, James (?1594-1666)
Jevon, Thomas (1652-88)
Jones, Inigo (1573-1652)
Jonson, Ben (1573-1637)
Jordan, Thomas (?1612-85?)
Killigrew, Thomas (1612-83)
Killigrew, William (1606-95)
Kirk, John (d. 1643)
Knepp, Mary (d. 1677)
Lacy, John (1622-81)
Langley, Francis (1548-1602)
Lee, Henry (1533-1611)
Lee, Nathaniel (?1653-92)
Leigh, Anthony (d. 1692)
Lodge, Thomas (?1558-1625)
Lowin, John (1576-1658)
Lyly, John (?1554-1606)
Markham, Gervase (?1568-1637)
Marmion, Shakerley (1603-39)
Marston, John (1576-1634)
Massinger, Philip (1583-1640)

May, Thomas (1595-1650)
Medbourne, Matthew (d. 1679)
Middleton, Thomas (?1580-1627)
Milton, John (1608-74)
Molière (1622-73)
Mountfort, William (1660-92)
Nabbes, Thomas (d. 1605)
Nashe, Thomas (1567-1601)
Newcastle, Margaret Cavendish, Duchess of (?1624-74)
Newcastle, William Cavendish, Duke of (1592-1676)
Nokes, James (d. 1696)
Ostler, William (d. 1614)
Otway, Thomas (1652-85)
Phillips, Augustine (d. 1605)
Phillips, Edward (1630-96?)
Quarles, Francis (1592-1644)
Racine, Jean (1639-99)
Randolph, Thomas (1605-35)
Rochester, John Wilmot, Earl of (1647-80)
Sackville, Thomas (Baron Buckhurst) (1536-1608)
Sandys, George (1578-1644)
Scaramouch (1608-94)
Shadwell, Thomas (?1642-92)
Shakespeare, William (1564-1616)
Shancke, John (d. 1635)
Shirley, James (1596-1666)
Smith, John (d. 1612)
Stapleton, Robert (d. 1669)
Strode, William (1602-45)
Suckling, John (1609-42)
Tateham, John (1632-64)
Taylor, Joseph (1585-1650?)
Tooley, Nicholas (?1575-1623)
Tourneur, Cyril (?1575-1626)
Tuke, Samuel (d. 1674)
Underwood, John (?1590-1624)
Vega Carpio, Lope de (1562-1635)
Webster, John (?1580-1625)
Wilson, Robert (1579-1610)

1700

Béjart, Armande (c. 1642)
Dryden, John (1631)
Hopkins, Charles
Howard, Edward (1624)
Killigrew, Henry (1612)

1701

Champmeslé, Charles de (1642)
Dryden, John II (1667)
Haines, Joseph (1638)
Sedley, Charles (1639)

1702

Blessington, Murrough Boyle, Lord
 (1609)

1703

Crowne, John (1640?)
Mountfort, Susannah (1669)

1704

Brown, Thomas (1663)

1706

Banks, John (1650?)
Drake, James (1667)
Joyner, William
Kynaston, Edward (1640?)

1707

Farquhar, George (1678)

1710

Betterton, Thomas (1635)
Underhill, Cave (1634?)

1712

Betterton, Mary S. (1647?)
Estcourt, Richard (1668)

1713

Barry, Elizabeth (1658)
Rymer, Thomas (1641)

1714

Britton, Thomas (1644)
Davenant, Charles (1656)
Powell, George (1668)

1715

Tate, Nahum (1652)

1716

Wycherley, William (1640?)

1717

Davenport, Hester (1641?)

1718

Keene, Theophilus
Motteux, Peter (1660?)
Rowe, Nicholas (1674)

1719

Addison, Joseph (1692)
Hughes, Margaret (1643?)

1720

Ashbury, Joseph
Hughes, John (1667)

1721

Doggett, Thomas (1670?)

1722

Brereton, Thomas (1691)

1723

Centlivre, Susannah (1667?)
D'Urfey, Thomas (1653)

1724

Gildon, Charles (1665)
Manley, Mary D. (1663)
Settle, Elkanah (1648)

1725

Dancourt, Florent C. (1661)
Dover, John

1726

Collier, Jeremy (1650)
Davis, Mary
Shadwell, Charles
Vanbrugh, John (1664)

1729

Boyer, Abel (1667)
Congreve, William (1670)
Steele, Richard (1672)

1730

Echard, Laurence (1671)
Fenton, Elijah (1683)
Lecouvreur, Adrienne (1692)
Oldfield, Anne (1683)
Spiller, James (1692)
Whincop, Thomas

1731

Beckingham, Charles (1699)
Ward, Edward (1667)

1732

Elrington, Thomas (1688)
Gay, John (1685)
Wilks, Robert (1665)

1733

Booth, Barton (1681)

1734

Dennis, John (1657)
Evans, John (1692)
Norris, Henry (1665)
Philips, William
Smyth, James M. (1702?)

1735

Arbuthnot, John
Granville, George, Marquess of
Lansdowne (1667)

1736

Hulet, Charles (1701)

1738

Breval, John D.
Frowde, Phillip
Mitchell, Joseph (1675?)

1739

Lillo, George (1693)

1740

Griffin, Benjamin (1680)

1742

Johnson, Benjamin (1665)
Oldmixon, John (1673?)

1743

Bibiena, Ferdinando (1657)
Carey, Henry (1690)
Ozell, John
Savage, Richard (1697)

1744

Jacob, Giles (1686)
Miller, James
Theobald, Lewis (1688)
Walker, Thomas (1698)

1745

Coffey, Charles
Wetherilt, Robert (1708)

1746

Blades, Martin
Southerne, Thomas (1660)

1747

Aston, Anthony (1682)

1748

Bracegirdle, Anne (1663)
Hippisley, John (1696)
Johnson, Charles (1679)
Thomson, James (1700)

1749

Concannen, Matthew (1701)
Odell, Thomas (1691?)
Thurmond, John (1700)

1750

Hill, Aaron (1685)
Mottley, John (1692)

1751

Kelly, John

1753

Riccoboni, Luigi (1675?)

1754

Fielding, Henry (1707)
Swiney, Owen (1675?)

1756

Cooke, Thomas (1703)
Grimston, William (1692?)
Hallam, Lewis (1714)
Heywood, Elizabeth (1693?)

1757

Cibber, Colley (1671)
Hoadly, Benjamin (1706)
Holliday, Barton (1706)
Moore, Edward (1712)

1758

Cibber, Theophilus (1703)
Hallam, William (1712?)
Ramsay, Allan (1685?)

1760

Charke, Charke (1713)
Fenton, Lavinia Beswick (1708)
Weaver, John (1673)
Woffington, Margaret (1720?)

1761

Rich, John (1681)

1752

Gottsched, Luise (1713)
Ralph, James (1695?)

1763

Marivaux (1688)
Mynitt, William (1710)

1764

Dodsley, Robert (1703)
Roy, Pierre C. (1683)

1765

Madden, Samuel (1686)
Mallet, David (1705?)

Wignell, Thomas (1753)
Wilkinson, Tate (1739)

1804

Bannister, Charles (1741)
King, Thomas (1730)
Lennox, Charlotte (1720)
Tobin, John (1770)

1805

Crouch, Anna M. (1763)
Hodgkinson, John (1765?)
Murphy, Arthur (1727?)
Schiller, Friedrich (1759)
Suett, Richard (1758)

1806

Gozzi, Carlo (1720)

1808

Burk, John Daly (1776?)
Collin   d'Harleville,   Jean   F.
   (1755)
Hallam, Lewis, Jr. (1740)
Home, John (1722)
Murry, Anna B. (1769)

1809

Harwood, John E. (1771)
Holcroft, Thomas (1745)

1810

Stanley, Charlotte

1811

Cumberland, Richard (1732)
Kleist, Heinrich von (1777)
Lewis, William (1748)
Poe, Elizabeth (1787)

1812

Bickerstaff, Isaac (1735?)
Cherry, Andrew (1762)
Cooke, George Frederick (1756)
Malone, Edmund (1741)
St. Huberty, Anne (1756)
Snagg, Thomas (1746)

1813

Contat, Louise (1760)
Moody, John (1728)

1814

Astley, Philip
Dibdin, Charles (1745)
Warren, Mercy Otis (1728)

1815

Abingdon, Frances (1737)
O'Brien, William (1736?)
Raucourt, Françoise (1755)

1816

Brackenridge, Hugh Henry (1748)
Durang, John (1785)
Fennell (1766)
Guimard, Madeleine (1743)
Jordan, Dorothy (1762)
Sheridan, Richard Brinsley (1751)

1817

Bensley, Robert (1742?)
Bensley, William (1738)
Holman, Joseph G. (1764)

1818

Billington, Elizabeth (1768)
Lewis, Matthew Gregory (1775)
Pope, Jane (1734)

1819

Darley, John (1756?)
Johnson, John (1759)

Smith, William (1730)

1820

Baldwin, Joseph (1787)

1821

Alsop, Frances
Bartleman, James (1769)
Dugazon, Louise (1753)
Inchbald, Elizabeth (1753)

1822

Emery, John (1777)
Kemble, Stephen (1758)
Wroughton, Richard (1748)

1823

Kemble, John Philip (1757)

1824

Hartley, Elizabeth W. (1751)
Melmoth, Charlotte (1749)
Oxberry, William (1784)
Rowson, Susanna (1762)

1825

Wewitzer, Ralph (1748)

1826

Connor, Charles
Incledon, Charles (1757)
Kelly, Michael (1762)
Knight, Edward (1774)
Mattocks, Isabella (1745)
Talma (1763)
Tyler, Royall (1757)
Wells, Mary S. (1759)

1827

Dignum, Charles (1765?)

O'Brien, Susan

1828

Bernard, John (1756)
Conway, William A. (1780)
Johnstone, Jack (1750)

1829

Farren, Elizabeth (1759)
Terry, Daniel (1789)
Wright, Thomas (1763)

1830

Chapman, Samuel (1799)
Hazlitt, William (1778)
Sherwin, Ralph (1799)

1831

Anderson, Euphemia
Bradbury, Robert (1774)
Duff, John R. (1787)
Elliston, Robert W. (1774)
Huntley, Francis (1787)
Jefferson, John
Quick, John (1748)
Siddons, Sarah (1755)
Talbot, Montague (1778)

1832

Goethe, Johann Wolfgang von
(1749)
Jefferson, Joseph I (1778)
Munden, Joseph S. (1758)
Taylor, John (1758)
Warren, William I (1767)

1833

Dibden, Charles (1768)
Kean, Edmund (1787)
O'Keeffe, John (1747)

1834

Hoare, Prince (1755)

1835

Angelo, Henry (1756)
Blanchard, William (1769)
Castro, Jacob de (1758)
Egerton, Daniel (1772)
Mason, Elizabeth (1780)
Mathews, Charles (1776)
Pope, Alexander (1762)

1836

Bannister, John (1760)
Colman, George II (1762)
Lee, Henry (1765)
Oldmixon, Georgina (1863)
Smith, George (1777)
Wood, Juliana

1837

Büchner, George (1813)
Grimaldi, Joseph (1778)
Mellon, Harriot (1777)
Pushkin, Alexander S. (1799)
Richardson, John (1766)
Ryley, Samuel W. (1755)

1838

Clarke, John H. (1788)
Fawcett, John (1769)
Kemble, Theresa (1773)
Penley, William
Reeve, John (1799)

1839

Chapman, William S. I (1764)
Dunlap, William (1766)

1840

Finn, Henry J. (1787)
Griffin, Gerald (1804)
Hughes, J. C. (1789)
Isherwood, Harry
Mountain, Rosamon (1771)

Pemberton, Charles R. (1790)
Price, Stephen (1783)

1841

Barnes, John (1761)
Conduit, Mauvaise (1805)
Dibdin, Thomas J. (1771)
Power, Tyrone I (1797)
Reynolds, Frederic (1764)

1842

Ellar, Thomas (1780)
Jefferson, Joseph II (1804)
Woodworth, Samuel (1785)
Yates, Frederick H. (1797)

1843

Abbott, William
Davenport, Mary Ann (1759)
Duruset, John (1796)
Eaton, Charles (1813)
Elton, Edward W. (1794)
Wrench, Benjamin (1776)

1844

Balls, John S. (1799)
Gattie, Henry (1774)
Gibbs, Mary (1772)
Pixérécourt, René Guilbert de
   (1773)
Stanley, Montague (1809)

1845

Barrymore, William H. (1800?)
Butler, Samuel (1820)
Hopkins, Priscilla (1756)
Johnston, Henry E. (1777)
McHenry, James (1785)
Russell, Samuel (1766)

1846

Dowton, William (1765)
Liston, John (1776)

1847

Bannister, Nathaniel H. (1813)
Clifton, Josephine (1813)
Egerton, Sarah (1782)
Faucit, Helen (1789)
Mars, Mlle. (1779)

1848

Coates, Robert (1772)
Cooke, Thomas S. (1782)
Kirby, J. Hudson (1819)
Simpson, Edmund (1784)

1849

Charles, James (1808)
Cooper, Thomas A. (1775)
Egan, Pierce (1772)
Hamblin, Elizabeth
Hill, George H. (1798)
Horn, Charles E. (1786)
Jefferson, Cornelia F. (1796)
Marble, Danforth (1807)
Orger, Mary Ann (1788)

1850

Bartley, Sarah (1783)
Biffin, Miss (1784)
Gale, George (1800)
Glover, Julia (1781?)

1851

Addams, Augustus A.
Alexander, John Henry (1796)
Allen, Clarissa
Amherst, J. H.   (1776)
Archer, Thomas
Baillie, Joanna (1762)
Jones, Richard (1778)
Noah, Mordecai M. (1785)
Sheil, Richard L. (1791)
Waylett, Harriet C. (1798)

1852

Addison, Laura (1822)

Anderson, Ophelia (1813)
Booth, Junius Brutus I (1796)
Duff, Mary (1816?)
Gogol, Nikolai (1809)
Harlowe, Sarah (1765)
Moore, Thomas (1779)
Murray, William H. (1790)
Payne, John Howard (1791)

1853

Adams, G. G. I (1823)
Adams, J. P.
Allen, Andrew J. (1776)
Darley, John, Jr. (1779?)
Hamblin, Thomas S. (1800)
Howard, Henry (1820)
Silsbee, Joshua (1815)
Tieck, Ludwig (1773)
Vining, Mrs. Frederick

1854

Barry, Clara P.
Bird, Robert M. (1806)
Burke, Charles S. T. (1822)
Drake, Samuel (1768)
Fitzwilliam Fanny E. (1802)
Kemble, Charles (1854)
Smith, Richard P. (1799)
Smithson, Harriet (1800)
Warner, Mary A. (1804)
Wilson, John (1785)

1855

Mitford, Mary R. (1787)
Rayner, Lionel L. (1787)

1856

A'Beckett, Gilbert (1811)
Braham, John (1774)
Fields, Joseph H. (1798)
Maywood, Robert C. (1786)
Scott, John R. (1808)
Vestris, Lucia Eliza (1797)
Young, Charles Mayne (1777)

1857

Chapman, William B. (1799)
Duff, Mary Ann (1794)
Jerrold, Douglas (1803)
Mackay, Charles (1786)
Musset, Alfred de (1810)
Pyne, James F. (1785?)
Sinclair, John (1790)

1858

Abbott, Elizabeth B. (1820)
Bacon, James
Barber, James Nelson (1784)
Bartley, George (1782)
Brixton, Frederick F.
Cony, Burkham (1802)
Davison, Maria (1783)
Fitzwilliam, Edward (1788)
Harley, John P. (1786)
Howard, Charles D. S. (1800)
Nisbett, Louisa C. (1812?)
Rachel (1821)
Sloman, Mrs. John (1799)

1859

Cushman, Susan W. (1822)
Farley, Charles (1771)
Fisher, Charles J. B. (1804)
Hunt, Leigh (1784)
Wemyss, Francis C. (1797)
White, John B. (1781)

1860

Barrett, George H. (1794)
Brunton, Louisa (1779)
Bunn, Alfred (1798)
Burton, William E. (1804)
Conway, H. J. (1800)
Greene, John (1795)
Paulding, James K. (1778)
Rice, Thomas D. (1808)
Smith, Albert (1816)

1861

Calladine, C. (1822)
Dixon, George W. (1795)
Durrivage, John E. (1813)
Farren, William II (1786)
Johnston, T. B. (1815)

Montez, Lola (1818)
Scribe, Eugène (1791)
Vandenhoff, John (1790)
Wood, William B. (1779)

1862

Christy, Edwin P. (1815)
Comer, Thomas (1790)
Drew, John I (1827)
Knowles, James Sheridan (1784)
Tree, Maria (1802)

1863

Adams, John B. (1830)
Barnes, Charlotte (1818)
Blake, William Rufus (1805)
Caldwell, James H. (1793)
Cowell, Joseph L. (1792)
Robson, William (1785?)
Vigny, Alfred de (1797)

1864

Barnes, Mary G. (1780)
Cooke, Thomas P. (1786)
Cowell, Sam (1820)
Paton, Mary Anne (1802)
Robson, Frederick I (1821)
Thorne, Thomas
Wallack, James W. (1791)
Wood, Mary Ann (1802)
Wood, Susannah (1802)

1865

Booth, John Wilkes (1838)
Chapman, Henry (1822)

1866

Andrews, George H. (1798)
Bellamy, William H. (1800)
Brooke, Gustavus V. (1818)
Chatterley, Louisa (1797)

1867

Aldridge, Ira (1807)

Baldwin, Silas (1825)
Booth, Sarah (1793)
Christian, Thomas (1810)
Connor, James (1824)
Foote, Maria (1798)
Jones, Avonia S. (1839)
Robinson, Henry C. (1775)
Willis, Nathaniel P. (1806)

1868

Barnes, William A. (1826)
Christy, George N. (1827)
Cowell, William (1820)
Crampton, Charlotte (1816)
Dean, Julia (1830)
Gannon, Mary (1829)
Hamilton, William B. (1810)
Jamieson, George W. (1810)
Kean, Charles (1811)
Menken, Adah Isaacs (1835)
Walcot, Charles M. (1816)
Western, Helen (1843)

1869

Broadhurst, William (1787?)
Browne, James (1791)
Burroughs, Watkins (1790)
Keeley, Robert (1793)
Meadows, Drinkwater (1795?)
Smith, Sol (1801)
Thompson, Thomas (1783)
Vernon, Jane (1796)

1870

Balfe, Michael W. (1808)
Dickens, Charles (1812)
Dumas, Alexandre père (1802)
Holland, George (1791)
Lemon, Mark (1809)
Lingard, James W. (1823)
Mowatt, Anna C. (1819)
Placide, Henry (1799)
Thayer, Edward N. (1798)
Wallack, Henry J. (1790)
Wood, Joseph (1801)

1871

Bedford, Paul J. (1792)

Hackett, James H. (1800)
Lane, Samuel (1804)
Richings, Peter (1797)
Robertson, Thomas W. (1829)
Vining, Frederick (1790)

1872

Buchanan, McKean (1823)
Chorley, Henry F. (1808)
Conquest, Benjamin O. (1804)
Forrest, Edwin (1806)
Grillparzer, Franz (1791)
Lacy, Mrs. Thomas H. (1819)
O'Neill, Eliza (1792)
Rice, John B. (1809)

1873

Barras, Charles M. (1826)
Davenport, A. H. (1828)
De Walden, Thomas B. (1811)
Fitzball, Edward (1792)
Keeler, Ralph (1840)
Keene, Laura (1820?)
Lytton, Edward Bulwer, Lord
  (1803)
Macready, William Charles (1793)
Miller, David P. (1808)
Thayer, Agnes
Wallack, James W. II (1818)

1874

Anderson, John Henry (1815)
Betty, William H. W. (1791)
Conway, Fred B. (1791)
Phillips, Watts (1829)

1875

Bateman, Hezekiah L. (1812)
Bryant, Dan (1833)
Déjazet, Pauline (1798)
Denin, Susan (1835)
Drake, Frances Ann (1797)
Eddy, Edward (1822)
Fox, Charles K. (1833)

1876

Aiken, George L. (1830)
Cushman, Charlotte (1816)
Hildreth, Sarah (1810)
Maywood, Augusta (1825)
Price, Morton (1824)
Wheatley, William (1816)
Williams, Barney (1823)

1877

Adams, Edwin (1834)
Bauer, Karoline (1807)
Compton, Harry (1805)
Davenport, Edward L. (1815)
De Bar, Benedict (1814)
Donaldson, Walter (1793)
Fox, George L. (1825)
Grau, Jacob F. (1817)
Heron, Matilda (1830)
Horn, Eph (1823)
Jones, Joseph S. (1809)
Western, Lucille (1843)

1878

Hudson, James (1811)
Mathews, Charles James (1803)
Montague, Henry J. (1844)
Phelps, Samuel (1804)
Wigan, Alfred S. (1814)

1879

Bennett, George John (1800)
Bournonville, August (1805)
Buckstone, John B. (1802)
Calvert, Charles A. (1828)
Davey, Thomas W. (1830?)
Falconer, Edmund (1825?)
Fechter, Charles A. (1824)
Paul, Isabella (1833)

1880

Brougham, John (1810)
Bull, Ole (1880)
Delehanty, William H. (1846)
Neilson, Adelaide (1848)
Planché, James R. (1796)
Taylor, Tom (1817)
Tree, Ellen (1806)

1881

Blake, Caroline (1798)
Dillon, Charles (1819?)
Harrison, William B. (1812)
Sothern, Edward A. (1826)
Taglioni, Amalia (1801)
Thorne, Ann Maria (1815)

1882

Celeste, Marie (1811)
Kelly, Frances M. (1790)
McDonough, John E. (1825)
Stephens, Kitty (1794)
Webster, Benjamin N. (1797)

1883

Backus, Charles (1831)
Booth, Junius Brutus II (1821)
Bunn, Margaret A. (1799)
Collier, John Payne (1789)
McCollom, James C. (1838)
Somerville, Margaret A. (1799)
Thorne, CHarles R., Jr. (1840)
Turgenev, Ivan (1818)
Wagner, Richard (1813)

1884

Anderson, Addie (1844)
Chanfrau, Frank S. (1824)
Elssler, Fanny (1810)
Reade, Charles (1814)
Smith, Mark (1829)
Taglioni, Paul (1808)
Vandenhoff, George (1820)

1885

Edwards, Emilie F.
Hugo, Victor (1802)
McCullough, John E. (1832)
Ryder, John (1814)
Simpson, Palgrave
Wigan, Horace

1886

Barnes, Elliott (1843)
Chatterton, Frederick B. (1834)
Colville, Samuel (1825)
Gough, John B. (1817)
Ludlow, Noah M. (1795)
Owens, John E. (1823)
Woolgar, William

1887

Baker, Alexina F. (1822)
Daly, Julia (1833)
Howson, John (1844)
Lind, Jenny (1820)
Macaulay, Bernard (1837)
Raymond, John T. (1836)
Sherman, William E. (1839)
Vincent, Mary Ann (1818)
Wood, Ellen P. (1814)

1888

Campbell, Bartley (1843)
Chippindale, William H. (1801)
Creswick, William (1813)
Davidge, William P. (1814)
Drake, Julia (1856)
Drake, Samuel, Jr.
Griffiths, George H. (1822)
Marsden, Fred
Wallack, Lester (1820)
Warren, William II (1812)

1889

Albery, James (1838)
Bidwell, David (1820)
Bishop, Charles B. (1833)
Blanchard, E. L. (1820)
Cazauran, Augustus R. (1820)
Collins, Wilkie (1824)
Cooper, Priscilla E.
Gilbert, John I (1810)
Glyn, Isabel (1823)
Rowe, George F. (1839)
Villiers de l'Isle Adam, Philippe
  (1838)

1890

A'Beckett, Thomas (1808)
Baker, Benjamin A. (1818)

Bernard, William H. (1833)
Boker, George Henry (1823)
Boucicault, Dion (1822)
Chapman, Elizabeth (1810)
Marston, John W. (1819)

1891

Abbott, Emma (1850)
Arlington, Billy (1835)
Barnum, Phineas T. (1810)
Banvard, John (1815)
Barrett, Lawrence (1838)
Conner, Edmon S. (1809)
Davenport, Fanny E. V. (1829)
Edwards, Henry
Emmet, Joseph K. (1841)
Fisher, Charles (1816)
Florence, William J. (1831)
Hart, Tony (1855)
Irving, Henrietta (1855)
Irwin, Selden (1831)
Lesthes, Edmund (1847)
Sinclair, Catherine N. (1818)
Sullivan, Barry (1824)
White, Charles T. (1821)
Wills, William G. (1828)

1892

Booth, Rita
Castleton, Kate (1857)
Gayler, Charles (1820)
Hadaway, Thomas H. (1801)
Hemple, Sam (1833)
Leslie, Fred (1855)
Paterson, Peter (1824)
Wallett, William F. (1808)
Williams, Montague (1834)

1893

Barrymore, Georgie Drew (1856)
Beane, George A., Sr.
Booth, Edwin (1833)
Cushman, Pauline (1833)
De Mille, Henry C. (1850)
Drake, Alexander (1800)
Hooley, Richard M. (1822)
Hoyt, Flora W. (1870)
Kemble, Fanny (1809)
Murdock, James E. (1812)
Phillips, Augustus (1838)

Pixley, Annie (1858)
Prescott, Marie (1853)
Thorne, Charles R. (1814)

1894

Banks, Nathaniel H. (1811)
Brooklyn, May
Ford, John T. (1829)
Mackaye, Steele (1844)
Morley, Henry (1822)
Rosa, Patti
Stirling, Edward (1809)
Vokes, Rosina (1854)
Watkins, Harry (1825)
Yates, Edmund (1832)

1895

Anderson, James R. (1811)
Bowers, Elizabeth (1830)
Cavendish, Ada (1847)
Clifford, Ed (1845)
Day, William Charles (1823?)
Dumas, Alexandre fils (1824)
Langrish, John S. (1830)
Sala, George A. (1828)
Sterling, Fanny (1815)

1896

Abbey, Henry E. (1846)
Barrett, Louis F. (1843)
Cecil, Arthur (1843)
Field, Kate (1838)
Fraser, Robert (1842)
Harrison, Alice M. (1850)
Hoey, Josephine (1824)
Horn, Kate (1826)
Houssaye, Arsène (1815)
Howe, Henry (1812)
Kimball, Jennie (1848)
Lewis, Annie (1870)
Lewis, James (1839)
Mayo, Frank (1839)
McVicker, James H. (1822)
Mestayer, William A. (1844)
Rossi, Ernesto (1829)
Salvini, Alexander (1861)
Siddons, Mary F. Scott (1844)
Taber, Edward M. (1863)
Terry, FLorence (1854)

1897

Birch, William (1831)
Callender, Charles (1827?)
Coleman, E. B. (1838)
Drew, Louisa Lane (1820)
Fuller, Margaret (1872)
Hoey, William F. (1855)
Kelly, J. W. (1857)
Levick, Milnes (1825)
Proctor, Joseph (1816)
Terriss, William (1847)
Turner, Carrie (1858)
Wheatcroft, Nelson (1852)

1898

Couldock, CHarles W. (1815)
Davenport, Fanny L. G. (1850)
Faucit, Helen (1817)
Henley, Edward J. (1861)
Hoyt, Caroline M. (1873)
Ireland, Joseph N. (1817)
Keene, Thomas W. (1840)
Lacy, Walter (1809)
Maeder, Clara F. (1811)
Mather, Margaret (1860)
Scanlan, William J. (1856)
Thompson, Charlotte (1843)

1899

Clarke, John S. (1833)
Coghlan, Charles F. (1842)
Courtaine, Henry
Creese, Elizabeth (1843)
Daly, Augustin (1839)
Keeley, Mary Ann (1806)
Lane, Sarah (1823)
Lee, Mary Ann (1823)
Lewis, Lillian
Phillips, Adelaide (1833)
Ponisi, Elizabeth (1818)
Post, Lilly
Rhea, Hortense (1844)
Sarcey, Francisque (1827)
Waller, Emma (1820)

1900

Archer, Belle (1860)
Boyd, Belle (1843)

Brough, Lionel (1836)
Davis, Charles L. (1848)
Hoyt, Charles H. (1860)
Irving, Sidney
Miner, Henry C.
Morris, Felix (1850)
Rice, Dan (1823)
Russell, Henry (1812)
Sullivan, Arthur (1842)
Wilde, Oscar (1854)

1901

Aldrich, Louis (1843)
Buchanan, Robert W. (1841)
Conquest, George A. O. (1837)
D'Oyly Carte, Richard (1844)
Haverly, Jack H. (1837)
Herne, James A. (1839)
Paul, William M.
Reed, Roland (1852)
Roberts, James B. (1818)
Tearle, Osmond (1852)

1902

Bonehill, Bessie
Bryton, Frederick (1856?)
Burke, Joseph (1818)
Clarke, Annie M. (1845)
Hanchett, David (1821)
Harkins, Daniel H. (1835)
Polk, Joseph B. (1841?)
Rodney, Frank (1859)
Russell, Sol Smith (1848)
Vezin, Jane E. (1828?)
West, William H. (1853)
Williams, Odell (1853)
Zola, Émile (1840)

1903

Arditi, Luigi (1822)
Davenport, Jean M. (1829)
Ellsler, John A. (1822)
Ethel, Agnes (1853)
Fairbrother, Leon
Farjeon, Benjamin L. (1838)
Germaine, Katherine (1873)
Golden, Grace
Haworth, Joseph (1858)
Jarrett, Henry C. (1828)
Lander, Jean M. D. (1829)

Robson, Stuart (1836)
Sanderson, Sibyl (1865)
Seymour, Kate (1874?)
Vaughn, Theresa (1867?)
Weaver, Henry A., Sr. (1832?)

1904

Barlow, Milt G. (1843)
Barrett, Wilson (1846)
Barry, Helen (1853)
Bell, Laura J. (1858)
Chekhov, Anton (1864)
Clapp, Henry A. (1841)
Coleman, John (1831)
Cook, Augustus (1859)
Cushman, Adelaide (1873?)
Daly, Dan (1858)
Emmett, Daniel D. (1815)
Farren, Nellie (1848)
Fawcett, Owen S. (1838)
Fowler, Ned H. (1875?)
Gilbert, Anne H. (1821)
Hollingshead (1827)
Janauschek, Fanny (1830)
Leno, Dan (1860)
Morton, Charles (1819)
Rose, Edward E. (1848)
Rush, Isadore (1869?)
Scott, Clement W. (1841)
Stevens, Sara (1834?)
Sykes, Jerome (1868)
Taber, Robert S. (1865)
Watkins, Rosina

1905

Bandmann, Daniel E. (1840)
Barrymore, Maurice (1847)
Craven, John T. (1849?)
Daly, Henry F. (1828)
Davis, Jessie B. (1861)
Eldridge, Louisa (1829)
Elliot, Robert (1864?)
Hanley, Martin W. (1843)
Irving, Henry (1838)
Jefferson, Joseph III (1829)
Le Moyne, William J. (1831)
Lewis, Horace
Palmer, Albert M. (1838)
Ringgold, Benjamin T. (1835?)
Shubert, Sam S. (1875)

1906

Arthur, Joseph (1848)
Bennett, Johnstone (1870)
Cayvan, Georgia (1858)
Clarke, George (1840)
Coppin, George S. (1819)
Crisp, Henry (1847)
Florence, Malvina (1834)
Ibsen, Henrik (1828)
Merivale, Herman C. (1839)
Mordaunt, Frank (1841)
Morgan, Edward J. (1871)
Morrison, Lewis (1845)
Owen, William F. (1844)
Reeve, Wybert (1839)
Ristori, Adelaide (1821)
Stephens, Robert N. (1867)
Toole, John L. (1830)
Walcot, Isabella (1847)
Yeamans, Jennie (1862)

1907

Bloodgood, Clara (1870)
Gunter, Archibald C. (1847)
Harrison, Maud (1854)
Janis, Percy
Jones, Julia D. (1829)
Mansfield, Richard (1857)
Roberts, Franklyn (1849?)
Stoddart, James H. (1827)
Urquhart, Isabelle (1865)

1908

Albaugh, Mary M. (1834?)
Bangs, Frank C. (1833)
Dailey, Peter F. (1868)
Darbyshire, Alfred (1839)
Edouin, Willie (1846)
Henderson, David (1853)
Howard, Bronson (1842)
Howe, J. Burdette (1828)
Pastor, Tony (1837)
Revell, Dorothy (1879)
Rogers, Gus (1869)
Sardou, Victorien (1831)
Sutherland, Evelyn G. (1855)
Thompson, Lydia (1836)
Wheelock, Joseph F. (1839)
Williams, Espy

1909

A'Beckett, Arthur W. (1844)
Albaugh, John W., Sr. (1837)
Brough, Lionel (1836)
Conried, Heinrich (1855)
Coquelin, Benoît C. (1841)
Crompton, William H. (1843)
Fitch, Clyde (1865)
Germon, Jane A. (1822)
Golden, Richard (1854)
Graves, Charles (1843)
Hankin, St. John (1869)
Logan, Olive (1840)
Modjeska, Helena (1840)
Saunders, Elizabeth (1819)
Synge, John Millington (1871)
Warner, Charles (1846)
Weir, George R. (1853)
Woolgar, Sarah J. (1824)
Young, Emma (1847?)

1910

Aiken, Frank E. (1840)
Bartlett, Josephine (1862?)
Björnson, Björnstjerne (1832)
Booth, Agnes (1846)
Burgess, Neil (1846)
Carleton, Henry G. (1851)
Clarke, Creston (1865)
Clement, Clay (1863)
Collins, Lottie (1866)
Cutting, Robert L. (1869?)
Edwards, Julian (1855)
Faust, Lotta (1880)
Fyffe, Charles J. (1830)
Glover, Amelia (1870?)
Hodson, Henrietta (1841)
Holland, George II (1846)
James, Louis (1842)
Kendall, Ezra F. (1861)
Moody, Willian Vaughn (1869)
Neville, Henry G. (1837)
Riddle, George (1851)
Sully, Daniel (1855)
Vezin, Hermann (1829)
Whiting, Joseph E.
Worthing, Frank (1866)

1911

Alexander, Sidney (1845)
Bellew, Kyrle (1855)
Bert, Frederic W. (1844)
Blaisdell, John W. (1840)

Blanchard, Kitty (1847)
Brough, Sydney (1869)
Clarges, Verner (1848)
Cole, Robert (1868)
Crox, Elvia
Dallas, Merwyn (1824?)
Davis, Thomas H. (1859)
Eastlake, Mary (1856)
Eytinge, Rose (1835)
Finney, Jameson L. (1863)
Fyles, Franklin (1847)
Gilbert, William S. (1836)
Harrigan, Edward (1845)
Hill, Barton (1828)
Kildare, Owen F. (1864)
Lorimer, Wright (1874)
Miller, Charles T. K. (1867?)
Reignolds, Kate (1832)
Sanger, George (1827)
Thompson, Denman (1833)
Williams, Maria K. (1826?)

1912

Alter, Lottie (1879)
Barrison, Mabel (1882)
Bigelow, Charles A. (1862)
Boniface, George C., Sr. (1833)
Booth, Junius Brutus III (1868)
Brahm, Otto (1856)
Cannon, Hughie (1840)
Cave, Joseph A. (1823)
Crane, Edith (1865)
Cushing, Sidney
Davies, Phoebe (1867)
Eberle, Robert M.
Freeman, Maurice
Gilson, Lottie (1867)
Goodwin, J. Cheever (1850)
Grossmith, George, Sr. (1847)
Hardie, James W.
Harris, Henry B. (1866)
Hill, James M.
Judith, Mme. (1827)
Penley, William S. (1851)
Rignold, George (1838)
Robinson, Frederic C. (1832)
Shine, Giles (1860?)
Soldene, Emily (1840)
Stoker, Bram (1847)
Strindberg, August (1849)
Terry, Edward O. (1844)
Yale, Francis
Yeamans, Annie (1835)

1913

Bernard, Vivian
Boucicault, Aubrey (1869)
Brookfield, Charles H. E. (1857)
Claretie, Jules (1840)
Clark, William H. (1863)
Clarke, Burt G. (1847)
Dillon, John (1831)
Ferguson, Robert V. (1860?)
Fox, Della (1872)
Greenwall, Henry W. (1832)
Holland, Edmund N. (1848)
Houghton, Stanley (1881)
Irving, Jane
Jack, John H. (1836)
Jackson, Albert
Law, Arthur (1844)
Leigh, Alice
MacDonald, William H.
McCloskl, James J. (1826)
Miller, Joaquin (1837)
Pelissier, Harry G. (1874)
Purcell, Alban W. (1844)
Reiffarth, Jennie (1848)
Ryan, John F. (1848?)
Seabrooke, Thomas Q. (1860)

1914

Barbour, Edwin W. (1841)
Bond, Frederic (1861)
Boyd, Archie (1850)
Brough, Fanny W. (1854)
Burke, William J. (1856)
Cohan, Timothy (1846)
Drouet, Robert M. (1870)
Evesson, Isabelle (1863)
Folline, Miriam F. (1851)
Germon, Effie (1845)
Hagenbeck, Carl (1844)
Henshaw, Thomas E.
Hudson, Alfred (1879)
Hughes, Henry (1828)
Irving, Laurence (1871)
Jansen, Marie (1864)
Jarbeau, Vernona (1861?)
Keith, Benjamin F. (1846)
Lemaître, Jules (1853)
Manola, Marion (1866?)
Melford, Mark
Murphy, Joseph
Payne, Edmund (1865)
Perugini (1855)

Pitman, James R. (1843?)
Raleigh, Cecil (1856)
Rankin, McKee (1841)
Saxe-Meiningen, Georg II, Duke of
   (1826)
Thomas, Brandon (1856)
Young, James

1915

Armstrong, Paul (1869)
Beere, Mrs. Bernard (1856)
Bingham, Lloyd (1865?)
Bunny, John (1859)
Calderon, George (1868)
Carey, Eleanor (1852)
De Vere, George F. (1835?)
Flecker, James E. (1884)
Frohman, Charles (1860)
Geiwitz, Emma C. (1817)
Howard, Frank (1850)
Jessop, George H.
Klein, Charles (1867)
Le Moyne, Sarah C. (1859)
Phillips, Stephen (1868)
Pitou, Augustus (1843)
Plympton, Eben (1853)
Redmund, William
Savina, Maria G. (1854)
Waller, Lewis (1860)
Walsh, Blanche (1873)
Wilder, Marshall P. (1859)
Willard, Edward S. (1853)
Williams, Gus (1848)

1916

Achurch, Janet (1864)
Adams, Annie A. (1847)
Aleichem, Sholom (1859)
Ames, Amy
Buckley, Annie (1872)
Calef, Jennie
Carlyle, Francis (1868?)
Carr, F. Osmond (1858)
Cartwright, Charles M. (1855)
Cohan, Josephine (1876)
Cowels, Charles O. (1861)
Davis, Bertha
Davis, Richard Harding (1864)
Echegaray, José (1832)
Farkoa, Maurice (1864)
Glendinning, John (1857)
Graham, Robert E. (1858)

Grau, Robert
Hamilton, Theodore (1830)
Harris, William (1839)
Harrison, Lee (1866)
Howson, Charles E.
James, Henry (1843)
Karl, Tom (1846)
Mounet-Sully (1841)
Ranous, Dora K. (1859)
Rehan, Ada (1860)
Robertson, Agnes (1833)
Salvini, Tommaso (1829)
Trowbridge, John T. (1827)
Woodruff, Henry I. (1869)

1917

Allen, Charles L. (1830)
Allen, Joseph (1840)
Archer, Frank (1845)
Argyle, Fanny A.
Arthur, Lee (1877?)
Barclay, Delancey
Barnabee, Henry C. (1833)
Bartholomew, William H. (1830)
Bateman, Kate (1843)
Bell, Digby V. (1851)
Boniface, George C., Jr. (1860?)
Burnand, Francis C. (1836)
Callahan, Charles E. (1843)
Clayton, Estelle (1867)
Clifton, Marion P. (1833)
Cody, William F. (1846)
Cohan, Jere J. (1848)
Denier, Tony (1839)
Eberle, Eugene A. (1844)
Emney, Fred (1865)
Farr, Florence (1860)
Greene, Evie (1876)
Hale, Walter (1869)
Kelcey, Herbert (1855)
Kendal, William H. (1843)
Montgomery, David (1870)
Morison, Lindsay
Morrissey, James W, (1853?)
Riccardo, Corona
Robinson, Anna (1870?)
Simms, Willard (1867?)
Taber, Lulu
Tree, H. Beerbohm (1853)
Wilbur, Albert L.
Winter, William (1836)

1918

Alexander, George (1858)
Apollinaire, Guillaume (1880)
Arden, Edwin (1864)
Badley, Robert A. (1865)
Barron, Charles (1840)
Brown, Thomas A. (1836)
Castle, Vernon (1877)
Conway, George W.
Cooper, Frank K. (1857)
Davenport, Edgar L. (1862)
Glassford, Andrew L.
Held, Anna (1873)
Mildenberg, Albert (1878)
Mitchell, Maggie (1832)
Moretti, Eleanor
Ritchie, Franklyn
Ross, Charles J. (1859)
Rostand, Edmond (1868)
Sarjeantson, Kate
Schoeffel, John B. (1846)
Stanley, Charles H. (1857?)
Tiffany, Annie Ward
Tyars, Frank (1848)
Wedekind, Frank (1864)

1919

Abbott, Bessie (1878)
Abeles, Edward S. (1869)
Aigen, May Louise (1874?)
Anderson, P. Augustus (1839)
Andreyev, Leonid (1871)
Aronson, Rudolph (1836)
Baum, L. Frank (1856)
Bergen, Nella (1873)
Blossom, Henry M., Jr. (1866)
Bradfield, W. Louis (1866)
Brown, Percy (1883)
Cameron, Violet (1862)
Coe, Isabelle (1881)
Davis, William J. (1844)
Dougharty, Houghline (1844)
Drew, Sidney (1868)
Dumont, Frank (1848?)
Golden, Bernice W.
Goodwin, Nat C. (1857)
Grossmith, Weedon (1852)
Hall, Pauline (1860)
Hammerstein, Oscar I (1847)
Irving, Henry B. (1870)
Kiralfy, Imre (1845)
Knowles, Richard G. (1858)
Markham, Pauline (1847)
Mason, John B. (1857)
Merritt, Grace (1881)

Novelli, Ermete (1852)
Plowman, Thomas F. (1844)
Primrose, George H. (1852)
Rock, Charles (1866)
Seligman, Minnie (1869?)
Thompson, Frederick W. (1872)
Wyndham, Charles (1837)

1920

Anson, George W. (1847)
Boyne, Leonard (1853)
Byron, Kate (1846)
Byron, Oliver Doud (1842)
Castle, Egerton (1858)
Collier, James W. (1836)
Crawford, Clifton (1870)
De Koven, Reginald (1859)
Hall, Josephine
Hallen, Fred (1860?)
Howells, William D. (1837)
Lawrence, Walter N. (1858?)
McNaughton, Fred (1869?)
Millett, Maude (1867)
O'Neill, James (1849?)
Pérez Caldós, Benito (1843)
Rand, Rosa (1848)
Réjane, Gabrielle (1857)

1921

Bancroft, Marie W. (1839)
Bispham, David S. (1857)
Blok, Alexander (1880)
Bonfanti, Marietta (1847)
Calvert, Adelaide (1836)
Chambers, Charles Haddon (1860)
Darrell, George (1841)
Field, Alfred G. (1852)
Fraser, Claud Lovat (1890)
Gilman, Ada (1854?)
Hall, Howard (1867)
Hare, John (1844)
Hart, Joseph (1858)
Humphrey, William
Huneker, James G. (1860)
Kingdon, Edith (1862)
Larowe, Nina (1838)
Opp, Julie (1871)
Phillips, Francis C. (1849)
Possart, Ernst (1841)
Sugden, Charles (1850)
Walcot, Charles M., Jr. (1840)

1922

Bacon, Frank (1864)
Bangs, John K. (1862)
Barrington, Rutland (1853)
Blair, Eugenie (1868)
Brereton, Austin (1862)
Buckstone, Rowland (1860)
Dare, Leona (1855)
Du Souchet, Henry A. (1852)
Gilmour, John H. (1857?)
Grismer, Joseph R. (1849)
Hodgdon, Sam K. (1853)
Jones, Walter (1874)
Kelly, John T. (1855)
Lloyd, Marie (1870)
Peabody, Josephine P. (1874)
Robe, Annie (1864)
Russell, Lillian (1861)
Ryan, Kate (1857)
Sims, George R. (1847)
Vakhtangov, Eugene (1883)
Ward, Genevieve (1838)
Watson, Alfred E. T. (1849)
Williams, Bert (1876)

1923

Albanesi, Meggie (1899)
Baker, Peter F. (1852?)
Bates, Maried (1853?)
Bernhardt, Sarah (1844)
Braham, Harry
Byrne, Francis M. (1875)
Calvert, Louis (1859)
Chevalier, Albert (1861)
Clarke, Harry C. (1861?)
Dandy, Jess (1871)
Dauvray, Helen (1858)
Day, Edmund (1866)
De Belleville, Frederic (1857)
Delmore, Ralph (1853)
Hawtrey, Charles (1858)
Kremer, Theodore (1871)
Mackay, Frank F. (1831?)
Martinot, Sadie (1861)
Martyn, Edward (1859)
Maurel, Victor (1848)
McNaughton, Tom (1867)
Naudain, Mary (1880)
Raleigh, Isabel (1866?)
Savoy, Bert (1888?)
Stevens, Edwin (1860)
Taylor, Oliver (1862)

Trench, Herbert (1865)
Wainwright, Marie (1853)

1924

Aiston, Arthur C. (1868)
Archer, William (1856)
Bakst, Léon (1866)
Bernard, Barney (1877)
Buckstone, John C. (1858)
Burnette, Frances H. (1849)
Claxton, Kate (1848)
Collette, Charles (1843)
Collier, Lizzie H. (1864?)
Conklin, George (1845)
Conrad, Joseph (1851)
Cook, George Cram (1873)
Crabtree, Charlotte (1847)
Dockstader, Lew (1856)
Duse, Eleonora (1859)
Emery, Winifred (1862)
Ganthony, Richard (1857?)
Gardner, Charles A. (1848?)
Gielgud, Kate T. (1844)
Headlam, Stewart D. (1847)
Herbert, Victor (1859)
Hibbert, Henry G. (1862)
Janvier, Emma
Lloyd, Violet (1879)
Nobles, Milton (1847)
Peple, Edward H. (1869)
Sheldon, Suzanne (1875)
Terry, Kate (1844)
Tracy, Helen (1850?)
Ware, Helen (1877)

1925

Barnes, John H. (1850)
Barrows, James O. (1853)
Caldara, Orme (1875)
Carroll, Richard F. (1866)
Clarke, Joseph I. C. (1846)
Cowell, Sydney (1846)
Lewis, Ada (1875)
Massen, Lewis F. (1858?)
Morris, Clara (1848)
Sandow, Eugene (1867)
Sloane, Alfred B. (1872)

1926

Adler, Jacob P. (1855)

Ashford, Harry (1858)
Bancroft, Squire (1841)
Bateman, Victory (1865)
Beach, William (1874)
Brown, Carrie C. W. (1862)
Bulger, Harry (1872)
Burroughs, Marie (1866)
Burrows, James (1842)
Burton, William H. (1845)
Carter, Lincoln J. (1865)
Christy, Dave (1853)
Deming, Will J. (1871)
Firbank, Ronald (1886)
Gayer, Echlin (1878)
Goodfriend, Ida J. (1856?)
Grover, Leonard (1835)
Hackett, James K. (1869)
Hanford, Charles B. (1859)
Hobart, George V. (1867)
Holland, Joseph J. (1860)
Houdini, Harry (1874)
Jordan, Kate (1862)
Lawrence, Lillian (1868)
Le Hay, John (1854)
Lewers, William
Lewis, Jeffreys (1857)
Miller, Henry (1860)
Milward, Dawson (1870)
Mitchell, Julian (1844?)
Norman, Mary (1870?)
Rendle, Thomas M. (1856)
Richepin, Jean (1849)
Saunders, Florence (1890)
Scott, Agnes E.
Walkley, Arthur B. (1855)
Zangwill, Israel (1864)

1927

Artsybashev, Mikhail P. (1878)
Beasley, Byron (1872)
Bernard, Sam (1863)
Bingham, Amelia (1869)
Bourchier, Arthur (1863)
Brandes, Georg (1842)
Byrne, James A. (1868)
Daly, Arnold (1875)
Davenport, May (1856)
Dickson, Charles S. (1862)
Drew, John II (1853)
Duncan, Isadora (1878)
Fay, Elfie
Harker, Joseph (1855)
Herbert, Sidney
Hilliard, Robert C. (1857)

Jay, Isabel (1879)
Jerome, Jerome K. (1859)
Kidder, Edward E. (1849?)
Leigh, Lisle (1879?)
Lingard, William H. (1840?)
Mack, Charles E. (1900?)
Marceline (1873)
McRae, Bruce (1867)
O'Mara, Joseph (1861)
Otis, Elita P. (1851?)
Roberts, Florence (1871)
Savage, Henry W. (1859)
Valli, Valli (1882)
Studdiford, Grace Van (1873?)

1928

Appia, Adolphe (1862)
Arthur, Paul (1859)
Bayes, Nora (1880)
Beban, George (1873)
Blinn, Holbrook (1872)
Connelly, Edward J. (1859)
Crane, William H. (1845)
Ditrichstein, Leo J. (1865)
Donnelly, Dorothy (1880)
Dowling, Joseph J. (1848)
Ford, James L. (1854)
Foy, Eddie (1856)
Fry, Charles (1845)
Fuller, Loie (1870)
Granger, Maude (1846)
Howard, Keble (1875)
Little Tich (1869)
Mantell, Robert B. (1854)
Murphy, Tim (1861)
O'Ramey, Georgie (1886)
Owen, Cecil (1873?)
Stevens, Emily (1882)
Stuart, Leslie (1864)
Sudermann, Hermann (1857)
Terry, Ellen (1847)
Winter, Percy (1861)
Wise, Thomas A. (1865)

1929

Barron, Elwyn A. (1855)
Butler, Fred J. (1867)
Clifford, Lucy
Cort, John (1859)
Diaghilev, Sergei (1872)
Eagels, Jeanne (1894)
Eddinger, Wallace (1881)

Faber, Leslie (1879)
Farnum, Dustin (1874)
Gabriel, Master (1883?)
Hauck, Minnie (1852?)
Hitchcock, Raymond (1865)
Hofmannsthal, Hugo von (1874)
Jones, Henry Arthur (1851)
Keenan, Frank (1858)
Kellerd, John E. (1863)
Langtry, Lillie (1853)
Mackintosh, William (1855)
Matthews, Brander (1852)
Norris, William (1870)
Palfrey, May (1873)
Proctor, Frederick F. (1851)
Shaw, Mary (1854)
Stevenson, Charles A. (1852)
Stewart, Grant (1866?)
Winston, Jeannie (1845?)

1930

Albani, Emma (1852)
Albee, Edward F. (1857)
Artaud, Antonin (1896)
Barraclough, Sydney (1870?)
Bechtel, William A. (1858)
Bennett, Clarence (1858)
Blaisdell, William (1867)
Brown, James H.
Burbeck, Frank (1856)
Carleton, William T. (1859)
Clemmons, Katherine (1873)
Clifford, Billy (1869)
Courtleigh, William L., Sr. (1869)
Crauford, J. Russell (1848?)
Cressy, Will M. (1863)
Davidson, Dore (1850)
Erlanger, Abraham L. (1860)
Ferguson, William J. (1849)
Fisher, Perkins D. (1860)
Gilpin, Charles S. (1878)
Ives, Alice (1883)
Jewett, Henry (1863)
Kennedy, Bart (1861)
Lawrence, D. H. (1885)
Mayakovsky, Vladimir (1894)
Nobles, Dollie (1863?)
Norman, Christine
Paxton, Sydney (1860)
Pratt, Lynn (1863)
Ritchie, Adele (1874)
Stuart, Otho (1865)
Studholme, Marie (1875)

Terry, Marion (1856)
Williams, Fritz (1865)
Wilson, Benjamin F. (1876?)

1931

Arbuckle, Macklyn (1866)
Barnes, Al G. (1862)
Barry, James W. (1866?)
Belasco, David (1853)
Bennett, Arnold (1867)
Buchanan, Virginia (1843)
Caine, Hall (1853)
Dodson, John E. (1857)
Donnelly, Henry G. (1850)
D'Orsay, Lawrence (1860)
Edeson, Robert (1868)
Fay, Frank (1870)
Fenton, Mabel (1868)
Ganthony, Robert (1849)
Glover, James M. (1861)
Hampton, Mabel (1868?)
Harris, Frank (1855)
Mack, Andrew (1863)
MacLarnie, Thomas (1871?)
Mann, Louis (1865)
Moore, Frank F. (1855)
Moore, Mary (1861)
Newton, Henry Chance (1854)
Power, Tyrone II (1869)
Schnitzler, Arthur (1862)
Shipman, Ernest (1871)
Stewart, Nellie (1860)
Thursby, Emma (1845)
Tiden, Frederick L. (1877?)
Wagenhals, Lincoln A. (1869)
Weathersby, Jennie
Wilson, George W. (1849)
Wolheim, Louis R. (1881)

1932

Abbe, Charles S. (1859)
Barry, Lydia (1876?)
Bartels, Louis J. (1895)
Bennett, Belle (1891)
Bernardi, Berel (1873?)
Bonstelle, Jessie (1872)
Brieux, Eugène (1858)
Brown, Henrietta
Clark, Hilda (1873?)
Clemens, Henry C. (1866?)
Coghlan, Rose (1851)
Corrigan, Emmett (1868?)

Craig, John (1868)
Dance, George C. (1855?)
Darrell, Charles (1858)
D'Arville, Camille (1863)
Drew, Frank N. (1831)
Emerson, William P. (1836)
Fiske, Minnie M. (1865)
Galland, Bertha (1876)
Gregory, Lady Augusta (1852)
Hodge, William T. (1874)
Jefferson, Thomas L. (1857)
Lackaye, Wilton (1862)
Millward, Jessie (1861)
Morris, William (1861)
Olcott, Chauncey (1860)
Oldcastle, Flouina (1864?)
Randall, Harry (1860)
Rodway, Philip (1877)
Rogers, Max (1873?)
Shelton, George (1852)
Sousa, John Philip (1854)
Spence, Edward F. (1860)
Wallace, Edgar (1875)
Waring, Herbert (1857)
Ziegfeld, Florenz, Jr. (1869)

1933

Aborn, Milton (1864)
Baird, Dorothea (1875)
Barnet, Robert A. (1853)
Batchelder, Fanny
Booth, Hope (1872)
Bothner, Gustave (1858)
Cahill, Marie (1870)
Corbett, James J. (1866)
Cottrelly, Mathilde (1851)
Courtenay, William L. (1875)
De Angelis, Jefferson (1859)
Forrest, Arthur (1859)
Fuller, Molly (1865)
Galsworthy, John (1867)
Graham, Joseph F. (1851)
Greene, Clay M. (1850)
Guinan, "Texas" (1884)
Harker, Lizzie A. (1863)
Hope, Anthony (1863)
Kerr, Fred (1858)
Marbury, Elizabeth (1856)
Masson, William C.
Miln, Louise J. (1864)
Mizner, Wilson (1876)
Moore, George (1852)
Roberts, Arthur (1852)
Seymour, William G. (1855)

Shipman, Louis E. (1869)
Silverman, Sime (1873)
Sothern, E. H. (1859)
Sutro, Alfred (1863)
Terry, Fred (1863)
Thurston, Temple (1879)
Ticker, Jac
Wakeman, Keith (1866)

1934

Anstey, F. (1856)
Austin, Mary H. (1868)
Bateman, Isabel (1854)
Clarkson, Willy (1865)
Cline, Maggie (1857)
Dailey, Robert L.
Dillingham, Charles B. (1868)
Dressler, Marie (1873)
Du Maurier, Gerald (1873)
Ediss, Connie (1872)
Illington, Margaret (1881)
Levy, Bert (1871?)
Littlefield, Emma (1883)
Mack, Willard (1873)
Mayhew, Stella (1875)
Moses, Montrose J. (1878)
Mulle, Ida (1863)
Murphy, John D. (1873)
Parker, Henry T. (1867)
Payton, Corse (1867)
Peile, Frederick K. (1862)
Pinero, Arthur W. (1855)
Playfair, Nigel (1874)
Poel, William (1852)
Rankin, Phyllis (1874)
Ryley, Madeleine L. (1868)
Summerville, Amelia (1862)
Taylor, Billie (1875?)
Tellegen, Lou (1883)
Thomas, Augustus (1857)
Warrington, Ann (1864?)

1935

Baker, George P. (1866)
Berlein, Annie M. (1850)
Bourget, Paul C. J. (1852)
Boyd, William H. (1890?)
Bradley, Leonora (1855?)
Buckingham, Fanny L. (1866?)
Chambers, Kellett (1867)
Clinton, Katherine
Coffin, Hayden (1862)
Courtneidge, Charles

Daniels, Frank (1860)
Donnelly, Leo (1878)
Farren, George F. (1861?)
Glassford, David (1866)
Grein, J. T. (1862)
Grossmith, George, Jr. (1874)
Hardy, Sam B. (1883)
Hendricks, Amanda
Hopper, De Wolf (1858)
Kemble, Madge (1848)
Leavitt, Michael B. (1843)
Lewis, Eric (1855)
Loraine, Robert (1876)
Mackay, Charles D. (1867)
McHenry, Nellie (1853?)
Mitchell, Langdon (1862)
Moore, Florence E. (1886)
Meyers, Annie (1857?)
Robyn, Alfred G. (1860)
Rogers, Will (1879)
Sears, Zelda (1873)
Serrano, Vincent (1866)
Sommers, Harry J. (1869)
Warde, Frederick B. (1851)
Wilson, Francis (1854)

1936

Aarons, Alfred E. (1865)
Adams, Leslie (1887)
Alison, George (1866)
Ames, Percy (1874)
Anson, Albert E. (1879)
Asche, Oscar (1872)
Bainbridge, A. G.
Bateman, Ellen (1844)
Brady, William A., Jr. (1900)
Breese, Edmund (1871)
Broadhurst, Thomas W. (1858)
Brown, Martin (1885)
Butterfield, Walter S. (1901?)
Caldwell, Ann (1869)
Carlisle, Alexandra (1886)
Chesterton, G. K. (1874)
Elitch, Mary
Eustace, Jennie A. (1865)
Fenwick, Irene (1887)
Frawley, T. Daniel (1864)
García Lorca, Federico (1899)
Glendinning, Ernest (1884)
Gorky, Maxim (1868)
Greet, Phillip Ben (1857)
Hammond, Percy (1873)
Harrison, Louise (1859)
Ingersoll, William (1860)

Klaw, Marc (1858)
Lytton, Henry A. (1867)
Meighan, Thomas (1879)
Mellish, Fuller (1865)
Meltzer, Charles H. (1852)
Miller, Marilyn (1898)
Monkhouse, Alan N. (1858)
North, Bobby (1881)
Palmer, Minnie (1860)
Phillips, Alexandra (1876?)
Pirandello, Luigi (1867)
Potter, Cora U. (1859)
Preston, Henry (1860)
Rice, Fanny (1866)
Russell, Annie (1864)
Smith, Harry B. (1860)
Tyler, Odette (1869)
Whiffin, Mrs. Thomas (1845)

1937

Abbott, Marion (1866)
Adams, Justin F. (1862)
Ames, Winthrop (1870)
Barrie, James M. (1860)
Baylis, Lilian (1874)
Belasco, Edward (1874)
Boleslavsky, Richard (1889)
Buchanan, Thompson (1877)
Calthrop, Dion C. (1878)
Carhart, James L. (1843)
Carter, Mrs. Leslie (1862)
Clark, Lois F. (1863?)
Conquest, Ida (1876)
Dazian, Henry (1854?)
Drinkwater, John (1882)
Earle, Virginia (1875)
Fellows, Dexter (1871)
Forbes-Robertson, Johnston (1853)
Gershwin, George (1898)
Gillette, William H. (1853)
Heron, Bijou (1863)
Hill, Gus (1860)
Horniman, Annie E. F. (1860)
Kimball, Corinne (1873)
Kingston, Gertrude (1881)
Laughlin, Anna (1885)
Losee, Frank (1856)
Lowrie, Jeanette (1862)
Marquis, Don (1878)
Odell, Maude (1872?)
Parker, Lottie B. (1858)
Paulding, Frederick (1859)
Perkins, Osgood (1892)
Pitt, Fanny A. (1844)

Ricard, Amy (1878?)
Rogers, Henry M. (1839)
Roma, Caro (1866)
Russell, Henry (1871)
Standing, Guy (1873)
Swinley, Ion (1891)
Thurston, Howard (1869)
Tree, Maud (1863)
Truesdell, Frederick (1873?)
White, Maude V. (1855)

1938

Abercrombie, Lascelles (1881)
Beaumont, Nellie (1870?)
Bergère, Valérie (1872)
Burnham, Charles C. (1858?)
Capek, Karel (1890)
Carew, James (1876)
Coote, Bert (1868)
D'Annunzio, Gabriele (1863)
Dazey, Charles T. (1853)
Forbes, James (1871)
Frayne, Frank I. (1863?)
Frederick, Pauline (1885)
Fulton, Charles J. (1857)
Gale, Zona (1874)
Gould, Howard (1867)
Greenwald, Joseph (1879)
Heath, Tom K. (1853)
Horvath, Odön von (1901)
Irwin, May (1862)
Kennark, Jane (1863)
Lang, Anton (1875)
Lederer, George W. (1861)
Morton, William (1838)
Palmer, Clara
Pinchot, Rosamond (1904)
Sheridan, Emma V. (1866?)
Smith, Edgar M. (1857)
Stanislavsky, Konstantin (1863)
Tearle, Conway (1878)
Thompson, Hallett (1871?)
Tree, Viola (1884)
White, Pearl (1889)
Yohe, May (1869)

1939

Anderson, Garland (1886?)
Bascomb, A. W. (1880)
Basshe, Emjo (1900)
Benson, Frank R. (1858)
Brady, Alice (1892)

Broun, Heywood (1888)
Byford, Roy (1873)
Cliffe, H. Cooper (1862)
Courtneidge, Robert (1859)
Fairbanks, Douglas (1883)
Fawcett, George D. (1860)
Finck, Herman (1872)
Freear, Louie (1873)
Fulda, Ludwig (1862)
Gillingwater, Claude (1870)
Girardot, Étienne (1856)
Graham, George (1875)
Howard, Sidney (1891)
Juch, Emma (1863)
Kalich, Bertha (1874)
Kelly, Walter C. (1873)
Keys, Nelson (1886)
Kidder, Kathryn (1867)
Leicester, Ernest (1866)
Mitchell, Dodson (1868)
Roebuck, Mabel (1876?)
Shairp, Mordaunt (1887)
Templeton, Fay (1865)
Toller, Ernst (1893)
Yeats, William Butler (1865)

1940

Anderson, Mary (1859)
Ayres, Agnes (1896)
Bateman, Jessie (1877)
Beck, Martin (1869)
Bishop, Kenyon (1860?)
Bostock, Edward H. (1858)
Cameron, Beatrice (1863)
Campbell, Mrs. Patrick (1865)
Churchill, Berton (1876)
Clark, Marguerite (1887)
Connolly, Walter (1888)
Douglass, Albert (1864)
Elen, Gus (1862)
Elliott (1871)
Evans, Lizzie (1857?)
Evarts, William H. (1867)
Faversham, William (1868)
Frohman, Daniel (1851)
Harlan, Otis (1865)
Hedmondt, Emmanuel C. (1857)
Heyward, Du Bose (1885)
King, Ada (1862?)
Nirdlinger, Charles F. (1863)
Norton, William A. (1880?)
Richman, Charles J. (1870)
Ruskin, Sybil (1880)
Schickele, René (1863)

Tweedie, Ethel B.
Whittlesey, White

1941

Anderson, Sherwood (1876)
Baker, George L. (1868)
Bates, Blanche (1873)
Bland, R. Henderson
Cameron, Hugh (1879)
Carle, Richard (1871)
Chapman, Ada B. (1851)
Courtney, Fay (1868)
Dolly, Jenny (1893)
Eltinge, Julian (1883)
Fairbrother, Sydney (1872)
Fields, Lew M. (1867)
Franklin, Irene (1876)
Grattan, Lawrence (1870)
Hading, Jane (1859)
Harris, Sam H. (1872)
Joyce, James (1882)
Karno, Fred (1866)
Leonard, Eddie (1875)
Leverton, William H. (1866)
Lewis, Mary S. (1900)
Llewellyn, Fewlass (1866)
MacDowell, Melbourne (1857)
Millard, Evelyn (1869)
Morgan, Helen (1900)
Prince, Adelaide (1866)
Smedley, Constance (1881)
Walbrook, Henry M. (1864)

1942

Abbott, Harry (1861)
Barnes, Joseph H. (1872?)
Barrymore, John (1882)
Benrimo, Joseph H. (1874)
Besier, Rudolf (1878)
Bond, Jessie (1853)
Cohan, George M. (1878)
Comstock, Nanette (1873)
Cooke, Eddie G. (1869)
Crews, Laura H. (1880)
Dalton, Charles (1864)
Duncan, Malcolm (1878)
Ellsler, Effie E. (1855)
Fiske, Harrison G. (1861)
Gest, Morris (1871)
Granville, Charlotte (1863)
Haddon, Archibald (1871)
Hamilton, Cosmo (1872)

Hamilton, Hale (1880)
Hornblow, Arthur (1865)
Klimt, George (1861)
Lewis, Catherine (1854)
Lupino, Stanley (1894)
McIntosh, Burr (1862)
Meyerhold, Vsevelod (1874)
Pauline, J. Robert
Robson, May W. (1865)
Ross, Frederick G. (1858)
Royle, Edwin Milton (1862)
Sainpolis, John M. (1887)
Skinner, Otis (1858)
Stock, Frederick (1872)
Sutherland, Annie (1867)
Taylor, Charles A. (1864)
Tempest, Marie (1866)
Tennant, Dorothy (1865?)
Vanbrugh, Violet (1867)
Wareing, Alfred (1876)
Weber, Joe M. (1867)
Whiteside, Walker (1869)
Williams, Hattie (1870)

1943

Aarons, Alexander A. (1891)
Abbott, Annie (1868)
Adams, Selby (1872)
Anderson, John H. (1896)
Anderson, Max
Antoine, André (1858)
Barlow, Reginald (1867)
Beggs, Lee (1870)
Berger, Henrietta N. (1856)
Binyon, Laurence (1869)
Blumenthal, George (1862)
Blunkall, Ervin J. (1875)
Bosworth, Hobart (1867)
Brown, John P. (1872)
Burke, Daniel (1867)
Burkhardt, Harry (1870)
Butler, Edward (1882)
Camp, Frank E. (1870)
Campeau, Frank (1864)
Charters, Spencer (1875)
Cliffe, Alice B. (1870)
Coburn, John A. (1869)
Cocroft, Thoda (1893)
Considine, John W., Sr. (1862)
Crummit, Frank (1889)
Denniston, Reynolds (1881)
Dixey, Henry E. (1859)
Erskine, Wallace (1862)
Garey, James R. (1861)

Gillmore, Frank (1867)
Glick, Joseph (1880)
Haggard, Stephen (1911)
Hines, Robert T. (1870)
Hart, Lorenz (1895)
Howard, Leslie (1893)
Jeffreys, Ellis (1868)
Johnson, Roy L. (1867)
Loftus, Cissie (1876)
Mei Lan-Fang (1894)
Nares, Owen (1888)
Nemirovich-Danchenko,   Vladimir
    (1858)
Nielsen, Alice (1876)
Overman, Lynne (1887)
Powers, James T. (1862)
Reinhardt, Max (1873)
Seeley, James L. (1867?)
Sheridan, Frank (1869)
Sitgreaves, Beverly (1863?)
Veiller, Bayard (1869)
Woollcott, Alexander (1887)
Wright, Haidée (1868)
Wright, Huntley (1869)

1944

Ade, George (1866)
Allen, Suzanne W. (1865)
Bard, Wilkie (1870)
Bennett, Richard (1873)
Blaney, Charles E. (1868)
Borup, Doan (1875)
Brown, Clark (1877)
Burke, Edwin (1889)
Cohan, Cal (1859)
Collier, William (1868)
Crosman, Henrietta (1865)
Dayne, Blanche (1871?)
Downing, Robert L. (1857)
Ellis, Florence
Forrest, Sam (1870)
Gale, Minna K. (1869)
Giraudoux, Jean (1882)
Gottschalk, Ferdinand (1858)
Grey, Jane (1883)
Guilbert, Yvette (1865)
Hackett, Walter (1876)
Harvey, John Martin (1863)
Haynes, Minnie G. (1867)
Holland, Mildred (1869)
Howard, Harold (1870)
Hutchins, Hapgood (1869)
Irving, Isabel (1871)
Jenks, Fred C. (1871)

Lacy, Harry B. (1890?)
Leffler, John (1875)
Lloyd, Rosie (1897)
Mayhew, Kate (1853)
Nichols, Robert M. B. (1893)
Parker, Louis N. (1852)
Salvini, Maud D.

1945

Abdullah, Achmed (1881)
Ainley, Henry (1879)
Amber, Mabel (1866)
Ashley, Minnie (1875)
Barbier, George W. (1865)
Barker, Reginald (1895)
Benchley, Robert (1889)
Brown, Albert O. (1872)
Child, Harold H. (1869)
Clarke, Wilfred (1866)
Coborn, Charles (1852)
Craven, Frank (1875)
Davis, Fay (1872)
Edwards, Gus (1879)
Egerton, George (1860)
Evans, Charles E. (1856)
Faber, Mary (1890?)
Fogerty, Elsie (1866)
Furse, Judith (1912)
Gay, Maisie (1883)
Granach, Alexander (1890)
Hart, William S. (1874)
Haswell, Percy (1871)
Hughes, Hatcher (1883)
Hunter, Glenn (1893)
Hutchinson, Percy (1875)
Kaiser, Georg (1878)
Keane, Doris (1881)
Kern, Jerome (1885)
Knoblock, Edward (1874)
La Verne, Lucille (1872)
Milton, Maud (1859)
Morosco, Oliver (1875)
Morrison, Arthur (1863)
Murray, Alma (1854)
Nazimova, Alla (1879)
O'Hara, Fiske (1875)
Scott, Cyril (1866)
Shannon, Lavinia (1876?)
Tolstoy, Alexey N. (1882)
Werfel, Franz W. (1890)

1946

Arliss, George (1868)
Atwill, Lionel (1885)
Barker, Harley Granville (1877)
Barton, John (1870)
Bowes, Edward E. (1874)
Bragdon, CLaude (1866)
Brandt, Sophie (1896?)
Carr, Alexander (1878)
Cheatham, Kitty (1865?)
Conti, Italia (1874)
Dixon, Thomas (1864)
Donisthorpe, Sheila (1898)
Edgett, Edwin F. (1867)
Fields, W. C. (1879)
Fox, Grace
Hamilton, Clayton (1881)
Harned, Virginia (1868)
Hart, William S. (1870)
Hauptmann, Gerhart (1862)
Howard, J. Bannister (1867)
Intropidi, Ethel (1896?)
Jeffries, Maud (1869)
Lewis, Frederick G. (1873)
MacPherson, Jennie C. (1887?)
Melville, Rose (1873)
Merivale, Philip (1886)
Passmore, Walter (1867)
Pollock, Channing (1880)
Sheldon, Edward B. (1886)
Sherwood, Robert Edmund (1864)
Swears, Herbert (1869)
Tarkington, Booth (1869)
Taylor, Laurette (1884)
Tyler, George C. (1867)
Welford, Dallas (1872)

1947

Agate, James (1877)
Anspacher, Louis K. (1878)
Arlington, Nettie B. (1877)
Bartholomae, Philip H. (1880)
Beale, Franklin P. (1874)
Beaudet, Louise (1865)
Belcher, Frank (1869)
Beveridge, Glen S. (1886)
Block, Jean-Richard (1884)
Bottomley, Roland (1879)
Bratton, John W. (1867)
Brockbank (1867)
Burrows, Charles (1864)
Burton, Henry K. (1886)
Chambers, Lyster (1876)
Corthell, Herbert (1878)
Craig, Edith (1869)

Craig, Laura (1880)
Digges, Dudley (1879)
Dixon, Dorothy (1875)
Dupree, Minnie (1873)
Fay, William G. (1872)
Fischer, Alice (1869)
Gardner, Amelia (1866?)
Gleason, Lucille (1888)
Grover, Leonard, Jr. (1859)
Hagan, James P. (1888)
Hale, John (1859)
Hellinger, Mark (1903)
Herbert, Henry (1879)
Hollis, William (1867)
Huff, Forrest (1876)
Irish, Annie (1865)
Kolb, Matt B., Sr.
Lion, Leon M. (1879)
Lowndes, Marie Belloc (1868)
Mack, J. Herbert (1856)

Moore, Grace (1900)
Mozart, George (1864)
Nicholas, Blanche
Nugent, John C. (1878)
Tanguay, Eva (1878)
Thomas, Albert E. (1872)
Toller, Sidney (1874)
Tully, Jim (1891)
Webster, Benjamin (1864)

1948

Allen, Viola (1867)
Armstrong, Anna (1863)
Baker, Lee (1880)
Benson, Ruth (1873)
Bottomley, Gordon (1874)
Braithwaite, Lilian (1873)
Brian, Donald (1877)
Brown, Alice (1857)
Bryant, Billy (1888)
Bryant, Sam (1855)
Burress, William (1867)
Burton, Percy (1878)
Carroll, Earl (1892)
Chapman, Edyth (1863)
Clements, Colin (1894)
Cowles, Eugene (1860)
Crawley, Sayre (1867)
Eaton, Mary (1902)
Featherstone, Vane (1864)
Gallatin, Alberta (1861?)
Gish, Mary R. (1860?)
Glaspell, Susan (1882)

Kerr, Alfred (1868?)
Kirk, John R. (1866?)
Lang, Matheson (1879)
Mack, George E. (1866?)
MacLean, Rezin D. (1859)
Mantle, Burns (1873)
Mason, Alfred E. W. (1865)
May, Edna (1875)
Mayer, Sylvain (1863)
Murdock, John J. (1865)
Niblo, Fred (1874)
Petrie, David H. (1895)
Ratcliffe, Edward J. (1863)
Robertson, W. Graham (1867)
Smith, C. Aubrey (1863)
Stirling, W. Edward (1891)
Tauber, Richard (1891)
Whitty, May (1865)

1949

Allen, Ricca (1863)
Barry, Philip (1896)
Bloom, Sol (1949)
Cawthorne, Joseph (1868)
Coote, Henry (1880?)
Cosgrave, Luke (1862)
Davenport, Harry (1866)
De Lussan, Zélie (1854?)
France, Charles V. (1868)
Gaige, Crosby (1882)
Graves, George (1876)
Hicks, Seymour (1871)
Kellog, Charles (1899?)
Kenyon, Elmer B.
Leiber, Fritz (1883)
Lloyd, Alice (1873)
Loder, Charles A. (1857)
Maeterlinck, Maurice (1862)
Robinson, Bill (1878)
Shiels, George (1886)
Vanbrugh, Irene (1872)

1950

Arthur, Julia (1869)
Boucicault, Nina (1867)
Brady, William A. (1863)
Busley, Jessie (1869)
Clive, Edward E. (1876)
Cowl, Jane (1884)
Davis, Esmé (1898?)
De Wolfe, Elsie (1865)
Elliott, Gertrude (1874)

Elliston, Grace (1881)
Field, Sid (1904)
Fisher, Sallie (1881)
Grey, Katherine (1873)
Herne, Chrystal (1883)
Hopkins, Arthur (1878)
Huston, Walter (1884)
Jolson, Al (1886)
Kennedy, Charles Rann (1871)
Kyle, Howard (1861)
Lauder, Harry (1870)
Lord, Pauline (1890)
Marlowe, Julia (1866?)
McIntosh, Madge (1875)
Pemberton, Brock (1885)
Shaw, George Bernard (1856)
Strange, Michael (1890)
Stringer, Arthur J. A. (1874)
Tilbury, Zeffie (1863)
Torrence, Ridgley (1875)
Wadsworth, William (1874)
Waldron, Georgia (1872)
Weill, Kurt (1900)

1951

Berry, William H. (1870)
Brice, Fanny (1891)
Bridie, James (1888)
Broadhurst, George H. (1865)
Cochran, Charles B. (1872)
D'Alton, Louis (1900)
Erroll, Leon (1881)
Gould, Harold W. (1873?)
Homan, Gertie (1880)
Hughston, Regan (1875?)
Jouvet, Louis (1891)
Kahn, Florence (1878)
La Pierre, Irma (1880)
Latham, Hope (1872?)
Lenormand, Henri-René (1882)
Maude, Cyril (1862)
Nethersole, Olga (1863)
Nillson, Carlotta (1878?)
Novello, Ivor (1893)
Sinclair, Arthur (1883)
Warfield, David (1866)
Woods, Albert H. (1870?)

1952

Atwell, Grace (1872)
Banks, Leslie (1890)
Brinker, Una A. (1874?)

Burt, Laura (1875)
Coghlan, Gertrude (1876)
Corey, Madison W. (1873)
Daviot, Gordon (1896)
Dazie, Mlle. (1882)
Dean, Julia (1880)
Elton, Edmund (1871)
Florence, Katherine (1874?)
Hamilton, Cicely (1872)
Harding, Lyn (1867)
Hay, Ian (1876)
Hengler, May (1884?)
Johnson, Owen (1878)
Lawrence, Gertrude (1898)
Linthicum, Lotta
Lipman, Clara (1869)
Molnar, Ferenc (1878)
O'Neill, Maire (1887)
Po Sein (1880?)
Reynolds, E. Vivian (1866)
Robins, Elizabeth (1862)
Smith, Joe (1900?)
Tilley, Vesta (1864)
Tyree, Elizabeth
Ward, Fanny B. (1872)

1953

Adams, Maude (1872)
Bernstein, Henry (1876)
Bordoni, Irene (1895)
Clark, Barrett H. (1890)
Farnum, William (1875)
Ferrier, Kathleen (1912)
Field, Isobel O. (1858)
Jolson, Harry (1882)
Love, Mabel (1874)
Mannering, Mary (1876)
O'Neill, Eugene G. (1888)
Randolph, Louise (1870?)
Ruggeri, Ruggero (1871)
Shubert, Lee (1875)
Spooner, Cecil (1872?)
Spooner, Edna M. (1875?)
Tearle, Godfrey (1884)
Trouncer, Cecil (1898)
Wallis, Gladys (1873?)
Wilde, Percival (1887)
Wolf, Friedrich (1888)
Young, Roland (1887)

1954

Anderson, John Murray (1886)

Barrymore, Lionel (1878)
Benavente y Martinez, Jacinto (1866)
Bodenheim, Maxwell (1893)
De Treville, Yvonne (1881)
Drew, Louise (1882?)
Greenstreet, Sydney (1879)
Hall, Henry (1876)
Hampton, Louise (1876)
Kommisarjevsky, Theodor (1882)
Lonsdale, Frederick (1881)
Riggs, Lynn (1899)
Robey, George (1869)
Scheff, Fritzi (1879)
Shannon, Effie (1867)
Shattuck, Truly
Stern, Ernest (1876)
Webb, Nella (1876?)

1955

Aked, Muriel (1887)
Bernstein, Aline (1881)
Browne, Maurice (1881)
Cannan, Gilbert (1884)
Clarence, Oliver B. (1870)
Claudel, Paul (1868)
Collier, Constance (1878)
De Mille, William C. (1878)
Donaldson, Arthur (1869)
Friganza, Trixie (1870)
Golden, John (1874)
Hampden, Walter (1879)
Herne, Julie (1880)
Jones, Margo (1913)
Kemper, Collin (1870)
Levey, Ethel (1880)
Mack, William B. (1872)
McAllister, Paul (1875)
Moore, Eva (1870)
Moore, Tom (1874)
Royle, Selena F. (1860)
Sherwood, Robert Emmett (1896)
Spong, Hilda (1875)
Stahl, Rose (1870)
Vachell, Horace A. (1861)
Vollmer, Lula (1898)
Walton, Lester (1882)
Wood, Marjorie (1889?)

1956

Allan, Maud (1873?)
Allen, Fred (1894)

Arnold, Edward (1890)
Bancroft, George P. (1868)
Beerbohm, Max (1872)
brecht, Bertolt (1898)
Calhern, Louis (1895)
Charlot, André (1882)
Davis, Owen (1874)
Doro, Marie (1882)
Draper, Ruth (1884)
Hughes, Rupert (1872)
Janis, Elsie (1889)
Kane, Whitford (1882)
Lawton, Thais (1881)
Lugosi, Bela (1884)
MacArthur, Charles (1895)
Mackaye, Percy (1875)
Milne, Alan A. (1882)
Mistinguett (1875)
Wagner, Charles (1869?)
Wycherly, Margaret (1881)

1957

Asch, Sholem (1880)
Ashwell, Lena (1872)
Barnes, Kenneth R. (1878)
Bogart, Humphrey (1900)
Bowman, Laura (1881)
Buchanan, Jack (1891)
Busby, Amy (1872)
Calhoun, Eleanor (1862)
Constanduros, Mabel (1880)
Döblin, Alfred (1878)
Dunsany, Edward, Lord (1878)
Eaton, Walter P. (1878)
Granlund, Nils T. (1882)
Guitry, Sacha (1885)
Haye, Helen (1874)
Heiman, Marcus (1883)
Henson, Leslie (1891)
Hull, Josephine (1886)
Jackson, Ethel (1877)
Joyce, Peggy Hopkins (1893)
Livingstone, Belle (1875)
Murray, Gilbert (1866)
Neilson, Julia (1869)
Percy, Esmé (1887)
Probert, George L.
Sayers, Dorothy L. (1893)
Sherwood, Josephine (1886)
Van Druten, John (1901)
Williams, Harcourt (1880)

1958

Akins, Zoë (1886)
Anglin, Margaret (1876)
Arnaud, Yvonne (1892)
Brighouse, Harold (1882)
Collins, José (1887)
Colman, Ronald (1891)
Crothers, Rachel (1878)
Donat, Robert (1905)
Geddes, Norman Bel (1893)
Gladkov, Fedor V. (1883)
Glaser, Lulu (1874)
Grau, Jacinto (1877)
Handy, William C. (1873)
Howard, Brian (1905)
Jesse, Friniwyd T. (1889)
La Harte, Rose (1891?)
Moeller, Philip (1880)
Nathan, George Jean (1882)
Quartermaine, Charles (1877)
Revelle, Hamilton (1872)
Rinehart, Mary Roberts (1876)
Robinson, Lennox (1886)
Shaw, Martin F. (1875)
Squire, Ronald (1886)
Sullivan, Edward J. (1880)
Todd, Michael (1909)
Walker, Charlotte (1878)
Walker, Wilfrid (1881?)
Warner, Henry B. (1876)

1959

Anderson, Maxwell (1888)
Aynesworth, Allan (1865)
Bairnsfather, Bruce (1887)
Barrymore, Ethel (1879)
Cooke, Joe (1890)
Corbin, John (1870)
De Mille, Cecil B. (1881)
Derwent, Clarence (1884)
Dukes, Ashley (1885)
Duncan, Rosetta (1902)
Gazzolo, Frank A. P. (1871)
Grock (1880)
Helburn, Theresa (1887)
Hopper, Edna W. (1874)
Housman, Laurence (1865)
Knipper, Olga (1868)
Kyasht, Lydia (1886)
Norworth, Jack (1879)
Ross, Thomas W. (1873)
Steger, Julius
Sterling, Richard (1880)
Stone, Fred (1873)
Sturges, Preston (1898)

Trevelyan, Hilda (1879)
Wallace, Edna (1874)
Wallace, Fay (1889?)

1960

Barrymore, Diana (1921)
Benois, Alexandre (1870)
Camus, Albert (1913)
Clark, Bobby (1888)
De Courville, Albert P. (1887)
Dickinson, Thomas H. (1877)
Emmett, Katherine (1882?)
Hall, Mary (1876?)
Hammerstein, Oscar II (1895)
Howson, Albert S. (1881)
Le Sueur, Charles B. (1879)
Matthews, Alfred E. (1869)
Mayer, Edwin J. (1897)
McCarthy, Lillah (1875)
Oaker, Jane (1880)
Phillpotts, Eden (1862)
Savo, Jimmy (1895)
Wilson, Albert E.

1961

Blow, Sydney (1878)
Booth, John B. (1880)
Brennan, Jay (1883?)
Byron, Arthur W. (1872)
Chatterton, Ruth (1893)
Coburn, Charles D. (1877)
Davies, Marion (1897)
Fay, Frank (1897)
Ferguson, Elsie (1883)
Fernandez, Bijou (1877)
George, Grace (1879)
Green, Dorothy (1886)
Groody, Louise (1897)
Hart, Moss (1904)
Heyward, Dorothy (1890)
Howard, Joseph E. (1868)
Jackson, Barry (1879)
Kaufman, George S. (1889)
Marx, Chico (1891)
McClintic, Guthrie (1893)
McCracken, Joan (1922)
Michelena, Vera (1884)
Oliver, Olive (1871?)
Raymond, Maude (1872?)
Ring, Blanche (1876)
Thesiger, Ernest (1879)
Vance, Clarice

Whitford, Annabelle (1878?)
Williams, Bransby (1870)

1962

Balaban, A. J. (1889)
Bax, Clifford (1886)
Blandick, Clara (1881)
Chase, Pauline (1885)
Dane, Essex (c. 1866)
Elsie, Lily (1886)
Filkins, Grace (1865)
Forbes-Robertson, Jean (1905)
Hamilton, Patrick (1904)
Kendall, Henry (1897)
Langner, Lawrence (1890)
Laughton, Charles (1899)
MacDonald, Christie (1875)
McMaster, Anew (1891)
Moore, Victor F. (1876)
Surratt, Valeska (1882?)
Swaffer, Hannen (1879)

1963

Adams, Franklin R. (1883)
Baker, Phil D. (1898)
Barthelmess, Richard (1895)
Bell, Gaston (1877)
Blanche, Belle (1891)
Cocteau, Jean (1889)
Crane, Madge (1875)
De Mar, Carrie (1876?)
Drew, Margaret (1856?)
Gaxton, William (1893)
MacNamara, Brinsley (1890)
MacNeice, Louis (1907)
Maltby, Henry F. (1880)
Odets, Clifford (1906)
Pertwee, Roland (1886)
Quinlan, Gertrude (1875)
Shubert, Jacob J. (1880)
Tzara, Tristan (1896)
Vane, Sutton (1888)
Wheat, Lawrence (1876)
Young, Stark (1881)

1964

Allen, Gracie (1905)
Behan, Brendan (1923)
Caine, Georgia (1876)
Cantor, Eddie (1892)

Collins, Charles W. (1880)
Collins, Horace (1875)
Hardwicke, Cedric (1893)
Hare, Lumsden (1875)
Hecht, Ben (1893)
Marks, Jeannette A. (1875)
Marx, Harpo (1893)
Moore, Decima (1871)
O'Casey, Sean (1884)
Oliver, Vic (1898)
Porter, Cole (1891)
Rockwell, Florence (1880)
Schildkraut, Joseph (1896)
Watson, Henrietta (1873)
Wilson, Al H. (1888?)

1965

Bishop, George W. (1886)
Boland, Mary (1885)
Brice, Elizabeth
Britton, Hutin (1876)
Croy, Homer (1883)
Dane, Clemence (1888)
Dresser, Louise (1882)
Eliot, T. S. (1888)
Friede, Donald (1901)
Hansberry, Lorraine (1930)
Hengler, Flora (1897?)
Holliday, Judy (1923)
Marble, Mary (1876)
Maugham, W. Somerset (1874)
O'Neil, Nance (1874)
Purdom, Charles B. (1883)
Van Buren, A. H. (1879?)
West, Paul (1871)

1966

Berg, Gertrude (1899)
Breton, André (1896)
Clift, Montgomery (1920)
Crafton, Allen (1890)
Craig, Edward Gordon (1872)
Crouse, Russel (1893)
Devine, George (1910)
Dillon, William A. (1877)
Duhamel, Georges (1884)
Farquharson, Robert (1877)
Frawley, William (1887)
Harriman, Margaret C.
Hilliard, Harry S.
Hoffman, Emma
Hopper, Hedda (1890)
Keaton, Buster (1895)

Kreymborg, Alfred (1883)
Lawson, Wilfred (1900)
Leslie, Elsie (1881)
Morehouse, Ward (1898)
Reeve, Ada (1874)
Rose, Billy (1899)
Sorel, Cécile (1875)
Tucker, Sophie (1884)
Webb, Clifton (1893)
Wheatcroft, Stanhope (1888)
Wynn, Ed (1886)

1967

Bickford, Charles (1891)
Endrey, Eugene (1891)
Evelyn, Judith (1913)
Flavin, Martin (1883)
Gold, Michael (1893)
Holloway, Baliol (1883)
Hughes, Langston (1902)
Lahr, Bert (1895)
Leigh, Vivien (1913)
Masefield, John (1878)
McCullers, Carson (1917)
Middleton, George (1880)
Muni, Paul (1895)
Nesbit, Evelyn (1885)
Oklopkov, Nikolai P. (1900)
Quartermaine, Leon (1876)
Rains, Claude (1889)
Rathbone, Basil (1892)
Reed, Florence (1883)
Rice, Elmer (1892)
Rockwell, Kitty (1876)
Simonson, Lee (1888)
Williams, Marie (1921)

1968

Bainter, Fay (1892)
Bankhead, Tallulah (1903)
Brod, Max (1884)
Carroll, Paul Vincent (1900)
Eliscu, Fernanda (1880)
Everest, Barbara (1890)
Ferber, Edna (1887)
Gish, Dorothy (1898)
Hancock, Freddie (1924)
Lindsay, Howard (1889)
Maney, Richard (1891)
Post, Guy Bates (1875)
Rose, Clarkson (1890)
St. Denis, Ruth (1878)
Stallings, Laurence (1894)

Steinbeck, John (1902)
Wolfit, Donald (1902)
Zabelle, Flora (1880?)

1969

Brown, John Mason (1900)
Casson, Lewis T. (1875)
Castle, Irene (1893?)
Cowie, Laura (1892)
Dell, Floyd (1887)
Dovey, Alice (1885)
Garland, Judy (1922)
Hunt, Martita (1900)
Karloff, Boris (1887)
Malleson, Miles (1888)
Maschivitz, Eric (1901)

1970

Blakelock, Denys (1901)
Burke, Billie (1886)
Clunes, Alec (1912)
Dolly, Rosie (1892)
Genée, Adeline (1878)
Krutch, Joseph Wood (1893)
Lee, Gypsy Rose (1914)
Munshin, Jules (1915)
Price, Nancy (1880)
Rambeau, Marjorie (1889)
Treadwell, Sophie (1885)
Ulric, Lenore (1892)

1971

Boothe, Clare (1903)
Cohen, Nathan (1923)
Cooper, Gladys (1889)
Ervine, St. John (1883)
Fealy, Maude (1883)
Goodrich, Edna (1883)
Guthrie, Tyrone (1900)
Herbert, Alan P. (1890)
Holman, Libby (1906)
Hunter, N. C. (1908)
King, Dennis (1897)
Lewis, Joe E. (1902)
Marinoff, Fanny (1890)
Reicher, Hedwig (1884)
Santley, Joseph H. (1886)
Spewack, Samuel (1899)
Terriss, Ellaline (1871)
Unruh, Fritz von (1885)

Weigel, Helene (1900)
Young, Mary M. (1879?)

1972

Atkins, Robert (1886)
Beringer, Esmé (1875)
Carroll, Jean (1909)
Chevalier, Maurice (1889)
Deval, Jacques (1893)
Hannen, Nicholas (1881)
Herman, Selma (1876)
Howes, Bobby (1895)
Landis, Jessie Royce (1904)
Levant, Oscar (1906)
Montherlant, Henri de (1896)
Richman, Harry (1894)
Rutherford, Margaret (1892)
Shawn, Ted (1891)
Webster, Margaret (1905)
Winchell, Walter (1897)

1973

Auden, W. H. (1907)
Behrman, S. N. (1893)
Blackmer, Sidney (1895)
Brown, Joe E. (1892)
Coward, Noël (1899)
Field, Betty)1913)
Grable, Betty (1916)
Harrity, Richard (1907)
Harvey, Laurence (1928)
Hawkins, Jack (1910)
Inge, William (1913)
Lejeune, C. A. (1897)
Raeburn, Henzie (1900)
Reed, Joseph V. (1902)
Robinson, Edward G. (1893)
Starr, Frances (1886)

1974

Abbott, Bud (1895)
Ashton, Florence (1904)
Belfrage, Bruce (1901)
Benny, Jack (1894)
Brook, Clive (1891)
Brown, Ivor (1891)
Clarke, Austin (1896)
Collinge, Patricia (1884)
Compson, Betty (1897)
Cornell, Katharine (1898)

Greenwood, Walter (1903)
Hurok, Sol (1888)
Kelly, George E. (1887)
Morris, Lloyd (1891?)
Milton, Ernest (1890)
Moorehead, Agnes (1906)
Raymond, Ernest (1888)
Yurka, Blanche (1893)

1975

Armitage, Merle (1893)
Baker, Josephine (1906)
Brown, Pamela (1917)
Cardus, Neville (1889)
Dare, Phyllis (1890)
Daubeny, Peter (1921)
Green, Martyn (1899)
Kellermann, Annette (1888)
Kober, Arthur (1900)
Larrimore, Francine (1898)
Laver, James (1899)
March, Fredric (1897)
Sanderson, Julia (1887)
Sherriff, R. C. (1896)
Wilder, Thornton (1897)

1976

Baddeley, Angela (1904)
Cobb, Lee J. (1911)
Evans, Edith (1888)
Hughes, Richard A. W. (1900)
Hunter, Ruth (1902)
Leighton, Margaret (1922)
Mielziner, Jo (1901)
Miller, Ruby (1889)
Nash, Mary (1885)
Payne, Ben Iden (1881)
Redfield, William (1927)
Robeson, Paul (1898)
Sim, Alistair (1900)
Speaight, Robert (1904)
Thorndike, Sybil (1885)
Varconi, Victor (1891)

1977

Chaplin, Charles (1889)
Finch, Peter (1916)
Hull, Henry (1890)
Lawson, John Howard (1894)
Lunt, Alfred (1893)

Marx, Groucho (1890)
Marx, Gummo (1894)
Mostel, Zero (1915)
Oppenheimer, George (1900)
Petrova, Olga (1886)
Printemps, Yvonne (1895)
Taylor, Eva (1895)
Terry, Phyllis Neilson (1892)
Waters, Ethel (1900)
Zuckmayer, Carl (1896)

1978

Bergen, Edgar (1903)
Boyer, Charles (1899)
Chase, Ilka (1905)
Compton, Fay (1894)
Dean, Basil (1888)
Gordon, Max (1892)
Greenwood, Charlotte (1893)
MacLiammoir, Micheal (1899)
Pickles, Wilfred (1904)
Wood, Peggy (1894)

1979

Darlington, William A. (1890)
Geer, Will (1902)
Grenfell, Joyce (1910)
Hackett, Jeanette
Haley, Jack (1899)
Harris, Jed (1900)
Jones, Preston (1936)
Lacey, Catherine (1904)
Lehmann, Beatrix (1903)
Mitchell, Yvonne (1925)
Robson, Eleanor (1879)
Rodgers, Richard (1902)
Samuels, Rae
Skinner, Cornelia Otis (1901)
Taliaferro, Mabel (1887)

1980

Ardrey, Robert (1908)
Beaton, Cecil (1904)
Browne, E. Martin (1900)
Clurman, Harold (1901)
Courtneidge, Cicely (1893)
Douglas, Helen G. (1900)
Durante, Jimmy (1893)
Kaminska, Ida (1899)
Laurie, John (1897)